SPECIAL EDITION
USING
FileMaker® 8

Steve Lane

Scott Love

Bob Bowers

800 East 96th Street
Indianapolis, Indiana 46240

CONTENTS

SPECIAL EDITION USING FILEMAKER® 8

International Standard Book Number: 0-7897-3512-1

Library of Congress Catalog Card Number: 2006920311

Printed in the United States of America

First Printing: May 2006

09   08   07   06   4   3   2

Trademarks

Warning and Disclaimer

Bulk Sales

Que Publishing offers excellent discounts on this book when ordered in quantity for bulk purchases or special sales. For more information, please contact

U.S. Corporate and Government Sales
1-800-382-3419
corpsales@pearsontechgroup.com

For sales outside the United States, please contact

International Sales
international@pearsoned.com

Associate Publisher
Greg Wiegand

Acquisitions Editor
Stephanie J. McComb

Development Editor
Laura Norman

Managing Editor
Charlotte Clapp

Project Editor
Tonya Simpson

Copy Editor
Cheri Clark

Indexer
Ken Johnson

Proofreader
Mike Henry

Technical Editor
Jay Welshofer

Publishing Coordinator
Sharry Lee Gregory

Multimedia Developer
Dan Scherf

Book Designer
Anne Jones

Page Layout
Bronkella Publishing
Eric Miller

Contents

ABOUT THE AUTHORS

Steve Lane has worked with relational databases for 16 years. He has written for *FileMaker Advisor* magazine and co-authored two other books, *Advanced FileMaker Pro 6 Web Development* and *Special Edition Using FileMaker 7*, as well as this book's companion volume, *FileMaker 8 Functions and Scripts Desk Reference*. He is a founding partner with Soliant Consulting and has led training classes in FileMaker technologies all over the country, both in open sessions and in onsite client engagements. He regularly speaks at the annual FileMaker Developer's Conference, where in 2003 he was awarded the FileMaker Fellowship Award for "pushing the boundaries of FileMaker Pro."

Scott Love has been working with FileMaker for more than a decade. He is one of four founding partners at Soliant Consulting, a company dedicated to custom software development; is a speaker at the FileMaker Developer's Conference; and is an Authorized FileMaker Trainer. He served at *MacUser/MacWEEK* as an online managing editor, and at Apple Computer as its Web Publishing Technology Evangelist, followed by directing the Technical Marketing team at Macromedia. He has written dozens of feature and review articles on FileMaker and Internet/web topics and co-authored *Special Edition Using FileMaker Pro 7*, as well as this book's companion volume, *FileMaker 8 Functions and Scripts Desk Reference*.

Bob Bowers, CEO of Soliant Consulting, is a columnist and contributing editor for *FileMaker Advisor* magazine and has co-authored three other books: *Advanced FileMaker Pro 5.5 Techniques for Developers*, *Advanced FileMaker Pro 6 Web Development*, and *Special Edition Using FileMaker Pro 7*. At the 2002 FileMaker Developer's Conference, where he is a perennial speaker, he was awarded the FileMaker Fellowship Award for "developing outstanding technical and educational resources for FileMaker."

ACKNOWLEDGMENTS

This book could not exist were it not for the hard work and support of our colleagues and friends. Writing it would have been impossible otherwise, and we'd like to share our gratitude with those who have toiled with us.

First off, Stephanie McComb at Que Publishing gave us an impossible task some months ago: She asked that we update *Special Edition Using FileMaker* 7 for the upcoming release of FileMaker 8—and that we cut its length by 10%. Full of pluck, we suggested an alternative: Allow us to add 50% and create two books instead. The result was this (slimmer) book, along with the companion *FileMaker 8 Functions and Scripts Desk Reference*. We're deeply grateful to Stephanie for turning what started as a long shot into reality.

The rest of the team at Que Publishing is no less deserving of thanks. It's our deep pleasure to work with development editor Laura Norman again; her good humor and steady wisdom provide a strength of support that cannot be overstated. Tonya Simpson, our project editor, and Cheri Clark, our copy editor, have worked through our dense material diligently, and contributed countless improvements to our work. It's an immeasurable relief that they've been by our side through this whole process.

Taking a page from our own work in software development, Mickey Burns joined our team as a project manager who found a perfect blend between bullying and babying as he helped us through (and at times past) each deadline. Liz Kinsella, July Belber, and Will Danford put in tireless hours pulling together demo files, screenshots, facts, and figures. Jan Jung lent her tremendous design skills. Carlos Ramirez made vital technical contributions, especially to the Mobile chapter.

No acknowledgment would be complete without mentioning all the work our friends at FileMaker, Inc., do to make everything in our careers possible. FileMaker 8 is a fantastic suite of products and we're terrifically excited by the continued promise the FileMaker platform shows.

Finally, we'd like to thank some of the folks at FileMaker from whom we've learned a great deal, and whom it's our pleasure to know and work with: Jay Welshofer, our technical editor, along with Andy Lecates, Bill Heizer, and Tony Miller—all have contributed to this work and to our understanding of FileMaker, in ways large and small, and it's our pleasure to have their support and advice.

DEDICATION

To my crew out in the Wild West…without all of you, each of you (even the curmudgeons!), I'd be lost. You're an amazing group of colleagues and I'm grateful we're here building a company together.

—Scott Love

To Signe, Erlend, and Rona: I guess this doesn't quite count as "never again"?

—Steve Lane

To Eleanor, my new project management challenge.

—Bob Bowers

WE WANT TO HEAR FROM YOU!

As the reader of this book, you are our most important critic and commentator. We value your opinion and want to know what we're doing right, what we could do better, what areas you'd like to see us publish in, and any other words of wisdom you're willing to pass our way.

As an associate publisher for Que Publishing, I welcome your comments. You can email or write me directly to let me know what you did or didn't like about this book—as well as what we can do to make our books better.

Please note that I cannot help you with technical problems related to the topic of this book. We do have a User Services group, however, where I will forward specific technical questions related to the book.

When you write, please be sure to include this book's title and author as well as your name, email address, and phone number. I will carefully review your comments and share them with the author and editors who worked on the book.

Email: feedback@quepublishing.com

Mail: Greg Wiegand
          Associate Publisher
          Que Publishing
          800 East 96th Street
          Indianapolis, IN 46240 USA

READER SERVICES

Visit our website and register this book at www.quepublishing.com/register for convenient access to any updates, downloads, or errata that might be available for this book.

INTRODUCTION

In this introduction

BEST OF THREE WORLDS

Welcome to the world of FileMaker Pro. By simply browsing through this book, you're sure to have heard the word *database*. We'll cover what databases are ad nauseam in the rest of this book, but one of the first things you'll need to understand about FileMaker Pro is that it is far more than just a database application.

FileMaker Pro is nearly unique in the world of software. It is a powerful database system that can manage and store a wide range of information; it's an application for end users (like Microsoft Excel or Intuit's Quicken); and it's also a robust rapid application software development platform.

When you hear someone speak about FileMaker, keep in mind they may be viewing it from any one of these different perspectives. An IT professional likely sees FileMaker as a database engine that fits into a larger security and network infrastructure. An end user is probably thinking about a specific solution built in FileMaker Pro and how that solution helps (or doesn't help) make her work more efficient. A software developer may see FileMaker as one of many tools he employs in building a wide range of applications.

Our previous book, *Special Edition Using FileMaker 7*, was well received, but we did hear one consistent concern; namely, that the book was felt to be too advanced by some readers. So we'll try to be clear on our aims up front. This book was written with an eye toward the FileMaker developer community. If you're an IT professional who supports FileMaker applications, you'll probably find a few chapters (such as the one on FileMaker Server) to be of interest. If you're mostly interested in learning how to use the essential features of the FileMaker application, though, this book may not be for you. Although we've included some introductory chapters in order to be as comprehensive as possible, we've chosen to focus on an audience that we assume is largely familiar with the essential operations of FileMaker already, and is interested mostly in topics for the beginning to advanced developer.

We have also written a companion work, *FileMaker 8 Functions and Scripts Desk Reference*. As a reference, it is meant to be used daily as developers look up function syntax, refresh their memories on how specific script steps work, peruse useful custom functions, or uncover what a specific error code means. Each book is intended to complement the other, but the two are not interdependent. Some of the feedback we received for *Special Edition Using FileMaker 7* noted that it combined both reference material and deeper, conceptual topics and was perhaps serving two audiences. In this updated version of *Special Edition Using FileMaker 8*, we've focused on the exploration of various development topics, and left the reference material to our companion volume.

HOW THIS BOOK IS ORGANIZED

Special Edition Using FileMaker 8 is divided into five parts, organized into something like a tree. Part I, "Getting Started with FileMaker 8," and Part II, "Developing Solutions with FileMaker," constitute the "trunk" of the tree; they cover fundamental material that we recommend everyone read. If you're familiar with previous versions of FileMaker, you may need only to glance through Part I, but we still recommend you read Part II carefully.

Subsequent parts branch out from this base. Part III, "Developer Techniques," focuses on using FileMaker's features to develop complete, robust database applications. Part IV, "Data Integration and Publishing," covers getting data into and out of FileMaker. And Part V, "Deploying a FileMaker Solution," covers options for making a FileMaker solution accessible to others.

The five parts of *Special Edition Using FileMaker 8*, and the topics they cover, are described in the following sections.

PART I: "GETTING STARTED WITH FILEMAKER 8"

The chapters in Part I introduce you to FileMaker and its uses and features, and get you started with the basics of defining databases.

- Chapter 1, "FileMaker Overview," situates FileMaker Pro within the wider world of database and productivity software. It provides an overview of the new FileMaker 8 product line, and mentions the most important new features in FileMaker 8. This chapter is appropriate both for those who are new to FileMaker Pro and for those who have used previous versions and want a quick tour of the major innovations.

- Chapter 2, "Using FileMaker Pro," is intended as an introduction to the software from the perspective of a database user rather than a database developer. We introduce the major components and functions of the FileMaker interface, such as the Status Area, layouts, FileMaker's modes, and the basics of record creation, editing, and deletion. Note that FileMaker Pro 8 has added significant end-user functionality to the product line.

- Chapter 3, "Defining and Working with Fields," provides a thorough overview of all of FileMaker's field types and field options, including lookups, validation, storage types, and indexing. This chapter is intended to help lay the groundwork for talking about database development, and to serve as a thorough reference on FileMaker field types and options.

- Chapter 4, "Working with Layouts," covers all of FileMaker's layout-building options in detail. We cover all aspects of layout building, and offer guidelines for quicker and more efficient layout work.

PART II: "DEVELOPING SOLUTIONS WITH FILEMAKER"

Part II is intended to introduce you to the fundamental techniques of database application development using FileMaker Pro and FileMaker Pro Advanced. Chapters 5 through 7 cover the theory and practice of designing and building database systems with multiple data tables. Chapters 8 through 10 introduce you to foundational concepts in application and reporting logic.

- Chapter 5, "Relational Database Design," introduces you to relational database design concepts. We proceed by working "on paper," without specific reference to FileMaker, and introduce you to the fundamental vocabulary and techniques of relational database design (keys and relationships) through a series of modeling exercises based on fictional business and organizational problems.

■ Chapter 6, "Working with Multiple Tables," begins the task of translating the generic database design concepts of Chapter 5 into specific FileMaker techniques. We show how to translate a paper diagram into an actual FileMaker table structure. We show how to model different relationship types in FileMaker using multiple data tables, and how to create fields that function effectively as relational keys.

■ Chapter 7, "Working with Relationships," builds on the concepts of Chapter 6. Rather than focusing on FileMaker's relationships from the standpoint of database design, we focus on their practical implementation in FileMaker programming. We look in detail at the new capabilities of FileMaker 8, and discuss nonequality join conditions, file references, and some strategies for organizing a multitable system.

■ Chapter 8, "Getting Started with Calculations," introduces FileMaker's calculation engine. The chapter delves into the major types of FileMaker calculations. We cover a number of the most important functions, and discuss general strategies and techniques for writing calculations.

■ Chapter 9, "Getting Started with Scripting," introduces FileMaker's scripting engine. Like the preceding chapter, this one covers the fundamentals of an important skill for FileMaker developers. We cover some common scripting techniques and show how to use event-driven scripts to add interactivity to a user interface.

■ Chapter 10, "Getting Started with Reporting," illustrates the fundamental techniques of FileMaker Pro reporting, such as list views and subsummary reports, as well as some more advanced subsummary techniques, and some design techniques for improving the look and usability of your reporting layouts.

PART III: "DEVELOPER TECHNIQUES"

The chapters in Part III delve deeper into individual topics in advanced FileMaker application development. We build on earlier chapters by exploring more complex uses of portals, calculations, and scripts. We also offer chapters that help you ready your FileMaker solutions for multiuser deployment, and we examine the still-important issue of conversion from previous versions.

■ Chapter 11, "Developing for Multiuser Deployment," explores the issues and challenges of designing FileMaker systems that will be used by several or many people at once. We discuss how FileMaker handles concurrent access to data and discuss the concept of user sessions.

■ Chapter 12, "Implementing Security," is a thorough overview of the FileMaker 8 security model. We cover the role-based Accounts feature, Extended Privileges, and many of the complexities of server-based external authentication (against Windows or Mac OS user directories, for example).

■ Chapter 13, "Advanced Interface Techniques," provides detailed explanations of a number of more complex, applied techniques for working with layouts and data presentation in a FileMaker application. We look at different options for where and how to build interface layouts, explore an advanced, script-based navigation scheme, and discuss FileMaker's tools for building multiwindow interfaces.

- Chapter 14, "Advanced Calculation Techniques," looks closely at some of the more advanced or specialized types of FileMaker calculations, including the Let, Evaluate, and GetNthRecord functions, as well as the functions for text formatting and for list manipulation. The chapter finishes with an examination of custom functions, another important feature in the FileMaker 8 product line.

- Chapter 15, "Advanced Scripting Techniques," like the preceding chapter, is full of information specific to features of FileMaker 8 scripting. Here we cover programming with script parameters, the significant new FileMaker 8 feature of script variables, programming in a multiwindow system, and the complexities of scripted navigation among multiple tables and recordsets.

- Chapter 16, "Advanced Portal Techniques," looks at FileMaker's portal elements from two perspectives. First, we examine more advanced uses of portals for creating and viewing database records. Second, we examine the ways in which portals can be used to create new types of interface elements, such as filtered record browsers or pick lists.

- Chapter 17, "Troubleshooting," is a broad look at how to find, diagnose, and cure trouble in FileMaker systems—but also how to prevent it. We look at some software engineering principles that can help make systems more robust, and can reduce the incidence and severity of errors. The chapter also includes detailed discussions of how to troubleshoot difficulties in various areas, from multiuser record lock issues to performance difficulties over large networks.

- Chapter 18, "Converting Systems from Previous Versions of FileMaker Pro," explores the complex issues involved in moving to FileMaker 8 from versions prior to FileMaker 7. We begin by discussing migration scenarios that help you decide how much you stand to benefit from moving to 8. For certain systems the choice to move to 8 will be clear; for others it may be less so. We then discuss the mechanics of conversion in detail, and discuss some of the more significant pitfalls to be aware of.

Part IV: "Data Integration and Publishing"

Part IV covers technologies and capabilities that allow FileMaker to share data, either by exchanging data with other applications, or by exporting and publishing data, for example, via ODBC, JDBC, and the Web.

- Chapter 19, "Importing Data into FileMaker," looks at all the means by which you can import data into FileMaker. It covers how to import data from flat files, how to batch imports of images and text, how to import images from a digital camera, and how to import data from ODBC and XML data sources. (The full treatment of XML importing is reserved for Chapter 22.)

- Chapter 20, "Exporting Data from FileMaker," is in some respects the inverse of Chapter 19. It covers almost all the ways by which you can extract or publish data from

FileMaker, including simple export, XML export, and pushing data into SQL databases via ODBC, as well as means by which others can query FileMaker data over ODBC.

- Chapter 21, "Instant Web Publishing," looks at the features of the FileMaker 8 Instant Web Publishing model. Anyone interested in making FileMaker data available over the Web should begin with this chapter.

- Chapter 22, "FileMaker and Web Services," introduces you to FileMaker's XML capabilities. XML is the backbone of FileMaker's Custom Web Publishing technologies. This chapter introduces XML and its companion technology XSLT as they relate to FileMaker's XML import capability. Though no substitute for a book devoted to XML and XSLT, this chapter should teach enough for you to begin to get your footing with these technologies as they relate to FileMaker.

- Chapter 23, "Custom Web Publishing," covers FileMaker 8's Advanced Web Publishing technology. This chapter discusses how to configure the FileMaker Web Publishing Engine (WPE), and how to write XSLT stylesheets that exploit the WPE's capabilities to build FileMaker-backed web applications.

PART V: "DEPLOYING A FILEMAKER SOLUTION"

Part V delves into the choices you have for how to deploy a FileMaker database, including deployment via FileMaker Server and via kiosk or runtime mode using FileMaker Developer.

- Chapter 24, "Deploying and Extending FileMaker," provides an overview of the ways you can deploy a FileMaker database to one or more users, reviews plug-ins, and explores means of distributing standalone databases. Read this chapter for a quick orientation toward your different deployment choices.

- Chapter 25, "FileMaker Server and Server Advanced," explores in depth setting up and working with FileMaker Server and FileMaker Server Advanced. The chapter covers setup, configuration, and tuning of Server, as well as managing server-side plug-ins and authentication.

- Chapter 26, "FileMaker Mobile," reviews how to work with mobile computing devices and use FileMaker Mobile to both synchronize with and create databases on handheld organizers.

- Chapter 27, "Documenting Your FileMaker Solutions," covers how to put the final touches on a solution: It reviews some industrywide coding conventions, makes commenting recommendations, and explores how to extract information about a solution using the FileMaker Advanced feature Database Design Report.

SPECIAL FEATURES

This book includes the following special features:

- **Chapter roadmaps**—At the beginning of each chapter, you will find a list of the top-level topics addressed in that chapter. This list enables you to quickly see the type of information the chapter contains.

- **Troubleshooting**—Many chapters in the book have a section dedicated to troubleshooting specific problems related to the chapter's topic. Cross-references to the solutions to these problems are placed in the context of relevant text in the chapter as Troubleshooting Notes to make them easy to locate.

- **FileMaker Extra**—Many chapters end with a section containing extra information that will help you make the most of FileMaker Pro. In some cases we offer expanded, fully worked examples of tricky database design problems; in others we offer shortcuts and maintenance techniques gleaned from our collective experience with developing production FileMaker systems (creating custom function libraries, or getting the most out of team development); and in others we delve all the way to the bottom of tricky but vital FileMaker features such as the process of importing records.

- **Notes**—Notes provide additional commentary or explanation that doesn't fit neatly into the surrounding text. You will find detailed explanations of how something works, alternative ways of performing a task, and other tidbits to get you on your way.

- **Tips**—This element will identify some tips and tricks we've learned over the years.

- **Cautions**—Here we'll let you know when there are potential pitfalls to avoid.

 - **The new version icon**—This icon will identify things that are new in FileMaker 8.

- **Cross-references**—Many topics are connected to other topics in various ways. Cross-references help you link related information together, no matter where that information appears in the book. When another section is related to one you are reading, a cross-reference directs you to a specific page in the book on which you will find the related information.

TYPOGRAPHIC CONVENTIONS USED IN THIS BOOK

This book uses a few different typesetting styles, primarily to distinguish among explanatory text, code, and special terms.

KEY COMBINATIONS AND MENU CHOICES

Key (and possibly mouse) combinations that you use to perform FileMaker operations from the keyboard are indicated by presenting the Mac command first in parentheses followed by the Windows command in brackets: (⌘-click) for Mac and [Ctrl+click] for Windows, for example.

Submenu choices are separated from the main menu name by a comma: File, Define, Value Lists.

TYPOGRAPHIC CONVENTIONS USED FOR FILEMAKER SCRIPTS

Monospace type is used for all examples of FileMaker scripting. FileMaker scripts are not edited as text, but are instead edited through FileMaker's graphical script design tool, ScriptMaker. As a result, scripting options that are presented visually in ScriptMaker need to be turned into text when written out. We follow FileMaker's own conventions for printing scripts as text: The name of the script step comes first, and any options to the step are placed after the step name, in square brackets, with semicolons delimiting multiple script step options, as in the following example:

```
Show All Records
Go to Record/Request/Page [ First ]
Show Custom Dialog [Title: "Message window"; Message; "Hello, world!";
➡ Buttons: "OK"]
```

WHO SHOULD USE THIS BOOK

Like FileMaker itself, this book has several audiences. If you work with structured data a lot (Excel spreadsheets, for example) but are new to databases, this book will provide you with a solid foundation in the world of databases, in the basics of database theory, and in the practical skills you need to become a productive database user or developer. The book's more introductory chapters tell you what you need to know to get started building basic databases for your own use. Later chapters introduce you to the world of multiuser database design, and to some of FileMaker's more advanced application design features.

If you've worked with other database systems—either server-side relational database engines based on SQL, or desktop development environments such as Access—this book will help you see how FileMaker Pro fits into the universe of database software. Look over the section in this introduction titled "How This Book Is Organized" to get a sense of which chapters will get you started quickly with FileMaker.

If you're a web developer wondering how FileMaker might fit into your toolkit, note that we have extensive coverage of the new FileMaker web technologies in Chapters 21, 22, and 23.

And in case you're an old hand with FileMaker, we've provided a good bit of in-depth discussion of advanced techniques and have called out new FileMaker 8 features throughout the book.

GETTING STARTED WITH FILEMAKER 8

CHAPTER 1

FILEMAKER OVERVIEW

In this chapter

FILEMAKER AND ITS MARKETPLACE

However you approach FileMaker Pro, some core strengths of the platform are important for all types of users:

- **Flexibility**—Working with FileMaker Pro is inherently open-ended. It is simple to create ad hoc data queries, quickly manage data entry, add functionality to a live system, or deploy to the Web in minutes.

- **Ease of Use**—The folks at FileMaker, Inc. have labored hard to make FileMaker as approachable as humanly possible. Day-to-day users can easily learn how to add fields to a database, create reports, add form layouts, and more. With FileMaker Pro, organizations can be less dependent on specialized software engineers.

- **Interoperability**—FileMaker Pro supports many common, open standards for data exchange (SQL, ODBC, JDBC, XML) and allows users to connect their database solutions to the greater world of standards-based applications—both within their organizations and online on the Web.

- **Modern Data Architecture**—FileMaker Pro, despite being "just" a productivity application that lives on your computer along with Microsoft Word and Solitaire, allows users to create fully relational data structures and to properly build architectures that correctly manage real-world data.

Ultimately, FileMaker exists between the world of desktop applications and high-end, enterprise-level server systems. It is the third option: a flexible, robust workgroup application that can quickly come together, evolve over time, and be dramatically cost-effective.

RAPID APPLICATION DEVELOPMENT

In the world of software development, flexibility and speed are critical. We live in the world of Internet time, and usually businesses embark on a development project only when they need something yesterday.

The practices and experiences of the past two decades have proven software development to be a risky, unpredictable business. NASA's travails are painful reminders that this stuff is, in some ways, truly rocket science. New job functions have been developed in software quality assurance and project management. Certification programs exist to sift the wheat from the chaff.

FileMaker Pro exists in many respects to help organizations take on less risk and navigate the waters of software development without having to take on massive engineering efforts when they aren't warranted. Because this is a rapid application development platform, it is possible to build a system in FileMaker Pro in a fraction of the time it takes to build the same system in more classic, compiled software languages or by using enterprise-level systems.

LOW TOTAL COST OF OWNERSHIP

FileMaker Pro is focused around offering a low total cost of ownership for organizations. In October 2001, the Aberdeen Group, an independent research firm in Boston, found that "under conservative assumptions, FileMaker Pro was superior, with an average ratio of 5:1 in [cost of ownership] over the industry average database" (quote taken from the Aberdeen Group Executive White Paper "FileMaker Low-IT Database Cost-of-Ownership Study," October 2001).

Both the cost of the software itself and the rapidity with which systems can be built mean that IT organizations have a viable alternative to the massive enterprise-level systems of the past.

FILEMAKER IS A SEASONED PLATFORM

FileMaker Pro is now 20 years old. In the mid-1980s, Nashoba Systems created an initial version that was acquired and published by Forethought, Inc., in April of 1985. Nashoba then reacquired the rights to the software and published FileMaker Plus in 1986 and FileMaker 4 in 1988.

Claris Corp., which was then being formed by Apple Computer and was to become FileMaker's guiding parent, purchased Nashoba and published FileMaker II in 1988 and 1989. Finally in October 1990, FileMaker Pro 1.0 made its debut and set the product line on the course it has largely followed to this day. In December of 1995, Claris shipped FileMaker Pro 3.0, which saw the introduction of relational data modeling to the platform and, even more important, a completely seamless cross-platform application that's virtually identical between the Mac OS and Microsoft Windows. Today a majority of FileMaker's audience lives on the Windows side.

In 1998, at the time of version 4.1, Claris Corp. rechristened itself FileMaker, Inc. and focused all its energy around its flagship product.

FileMaker has been profitable every quarter since (an extraordinary feat considering the climate in Silicon Valley for the previous few years) and continues to enjoy the backing (as a subsidiary) of a cash-flush Apple Computer, Inc.

Other major innovations have occurred along the way, but nearly everyone in the community recognizes that it was the watershed version 3.0 that broke open the gates for FileMaker. Version 4.0 introduced web publishing to the platform, and version 6.0 offered significant support for XML-based data interchange.

In 2004, FileMaker Pro 7.0 was released. This major release featured a reengineered architecture from the ground up, a new model for working with relationships, modern security capabilities, and the capability to hold multiple data tables within a single file.

FileMaker Pro 8, launched in August of 2005, is the next release built on the new architecture of 7; it is a testament to that architecture that FileMaker 8 contains as many significant features as it does.

YOU'RE NOT ALONE

FileMaker, Inc. has sold more than 10 million units worldwide as of this writing. Users range from a single magician booking gigs in Denver, Colorado to Fortune 500 companies such as Citibank and Genentech. Just like any tool, FileMaker is noteworthy only when it has been employed to build something—and its builders come in all shapes and sizes. The only true common element seems to be that they own computers and have information to store.

There are some trends: FileMaker Pro is widely used in the world of both K–12 and higher education. All 50 of the top universities in the United States use FileMaker Pro. The non-profit industry is also a key focal point for FileMaker, as is the creative-professionals industry.

INTRODUCTION TO DATABASE SOFTWARE

At its heart, FileMaker Pro is database software; databases are useful for keeping track of contacts and their addresses and phone numbers, the students in a school, the sales and inventory in a store, or the results of experimental trials. Although this sort of information can be kept in spreadsheets and word processor documents, a database will make it much easier to take on these tasks:

- **Organize your data into reports**—Databases can organize information into reports sorted by city, last name, price, or any other criteria necessary.

- **Find one or several items in your collections**—Visually scrolling through a document with flat data displayed soon becomes unwieldy. Databases make it relatively simple to search for one record (or row) of data within potentially millions of others.

- **Create related associations among data**—Rather than duplicating the name of a company for multiple people (for example), or perhaps having to reenter an address in a dozen places, users can utilize databases to create associations between data elements (using a form of addressing) and preserve the integrity of their information.

- **Share data with other systems**—Databases are often built to exchange information with other systems; many become one component in multitiered technology solution for companies—even small businesses often exchange data between QuickBooks, for example, and FileMaker Pro.

There are other advantages to using database software, not the least of which is the capability in FileMaker Pro to construct a user interface that can map to an organization's workflow. Often the members of an organization will outgrow the documents of desktop applications when they need to support multiple authors, track data in structured, interrelated ways, or manipulate data sets based on differing criteria. Often the first herald of the need for a database is when users are frustrated with not being able to find a given piece of information.

The rest of this book gets into detail on how to do everything just mentioned and much more as well. You'll get a more detailed look at what a database is and how it works, how to build databases, and so on. But before we dive into the mechanics of databases, it's important to understand how they—and FileMaker—fit into the overall software computing world.

DATABASE SOFTWARE

A huge variety of software is on the market today. FileMaker generally falls into the category of business productivity software; however, it really is a hybrid application that marries

1

desktop application productivity to a server-based architecture and database. It is as accessible as programs like Microsoft Excel and Intuit's QuickBooks, yet it also allows developers to create complex workgroup databases that are deployed in the same manner as other IT server-based applications.

The idea of managing a collection of structured information is what database software is all about. Some database products on the market manage specialized collections such as business contacts. Products such as Act and Goldmine are good examples of those. Quicken, QuickBooks, and Microsoft Money manage collections of financial transactions.

FileMaker and other nonspecialized database products such as Microsoft Access are used to create database systems just as word processing software is used to create specific documents and Microsoft Excel is used to create spreadsheets. In fact, Microsoft Excel is often used as a database because it has several strong list-management features. It works well for managing simple databases, but it doesn't work well in managing multiple lists that are related to each other.

Often, simple grids of columns and rows of information (such as spreadsheets) are called *flat file* or *list* databases. Simple databases like these are generally self-contained; they usually don't relate to each other, so keeping information up-to-date across many such databases can become unwieldy or impossible. In such cases a *relational database* is called for. FileMaker is a fully relational database system and allows developers to associate a row (or record) in one area of the database (a customer list, for example) with records in another area of the database (a list of purchase orders, for example). To take another example, users of a relational database system can tie a single company entry to multiple contact people or even associate a single person with multiple company entries. Rather than entering this information in a dozen different places, relational databases, using a form of internal addressing, simply associate one item with another (customers with their orders, companies with their contacts). It is in this way that FileMaker gradates from a single-user productivity tool to a fully realized database development platform.

OFF-THE-SHELF SOFTWARE

There are many relational database products on the market: Specialized products such as Act and Quicken are also relational database products, but the difference is that those products are finished systems, offering a specific set of functionality, whereas products such as FileMaker are tools, used to create custom systems tailored to the individual needs of an organization or a person.

It is certainly possible to re-create the functionality of Act or Quicken by using FileMaker, and some organizations choose to do so when faced with the fact that such specialized products are relatively inflexible. If an organization has nonstandard ways of doing things, its members may find it difficult to work with specialized products. Although FileMaker Pro does come with several database templates that might be perfectly suitable for an organization to use right away, most users instead turn to FileMaker to create custom database systems that exactly match how their organization operates.

CUSTOM DEVELOPMENT SOFTWARE

With a database development tool such as FileMaker Pro, a person can build a system to be exactly what is needed. It's the difference between buying a house that is a pretty good match and building a custom home that has exactly the features one wants (or at least can afford).

Home construction is actually a great analogy for building a database because both follow similar trajectories. A home needs to be designed by an architect before it can be built. An owner needs to wait for the home to be built before he can move in, and questions or issues often arise during the construction process. After the home is built, the owner's needs may change and he may need to have an addition built onto the house to accommodate changed circumstances.

Building a custom home often follows a similar path: The foundation needs to be laid and the walls and plumbing need to be stubbed in before the final coat of paint can be applied to the drywall. Software development often is a complex layering of interdependent parts, and we in the software business don't have the good fortune to be able to run to Home Depot for standardized parts at a moment's notice! Often we need to build our own tools as well.

Finally, imagine that a home's construction is well under way and the owner decides to move the living room wall six feet. Although that is always possible, the impact of that change will vary a great deal depending on the stage at which the crew is working.

This last point is an important one, and it is also where we diverge from the home construction analogy because real-world environments always change. This is especially true for today's email-driven, connected-network world. One of the key advantages to developing database systems in FileMaker Pro is that these systems can be rapidly redesigned, even while the system is in use by other users. Any aspect of a FileMaker system can be changed while it's live if need be (although that may not always be advisable). FileMaker's greatest strength is its inherent flexibility.

WHAT DATABASE SOFTWARE DOES

FileMaker is database software. The thing that makes it unique in the market is the ease and means by which it allows developers to present information, but it's important to grasp the fundamentals of how all database software—including FileMaker—works.

The simplest kind of database is a list. It could be a list of employees or products or soccer teams. Consider an employee example. The information a Human Resources department might want to keep track of could look like the information shown in Table 1.1.

TABLE 1.1	EMPLOYEE TABLE		
First Name	**Last Name**	**Department**	**Extension**
Jane	Smith	Marketing	327
Calvin	Russell	Accounting	231
Renee	Frantz	Shipping	843

In database parlance, a list like this is called a *table*. Crudely put, a table is a collection of like things—in this case, people. After a table for people is established, one might extend it to include other attributes (or columns) for, say, phone numbers. The result is shown in Table 1.2.

→ For a thorough understanding of data modeling and the definition of tables, **see** Chapter 5, "Relational Database Design," **p. 129**.

TABLE 1.2   THE GROWING PHONE DIRECTORY

First	Last	Department	Ext.	Home	Cell
Jane	Smith	Marketing	327	555-1234	555-4453
Calvin	Russell	Accounting	231	555-8760	555-3321
Renee	Frantz	Shipping	843	555-9877	555-1122

As mentioned earlier, this type of database is called a *flat file* database because everything is in one table. Although it's nice to have everything in one place, this kind of structure has shortcomings. In this case, every time someone thinks up a new type of phone number to track, another column needs to be added to the table. This is likely fine for phone numbers—in the real world people usually have only a handful—but imagine what would happen if the example was tracking people's previous job titles? The spreadsheet or list would have a potentially unlimited number of columns, and there would be no logical correspondence between one person's "job #1" column and another's.

Furthermore, if someone doesn't have a particular type of phone number, that cell is left blank, resulting in a "Swiss cheese" look to the table. Unused cells take up space in the database and can slow things down for larger data sets.

In a relational structure only the first three columns would be in the employee table itself. The last three columns, which all represent phone numbers of some kind, would be moved to their own table. A label field could be added to identify each type of phone number, with the resulting two tables looking something like those shown in Tables 1.3 and 1.4.

TABLE 1.3   THE REVISED EMPLOYEE TABLE

Emp ID	First	Last	Department
1	Jane	Smith	Marketing
2	Calvin	Russell	Accounting
3	Renee	Frantz	Shipping

TABLE 1.4   THE NEW PHONE TABLE

Emp ID	Label	Number
1	Extension	327
1	Home	555-1234

continues

TABLE 1.4 CONTINUED

Emp ID	Label	Number
1	Cell	555-4453
2	Extension	231
2	Home	555-8760
2	Cell	555-3321
3	Extension	843
3	Home	555-9877
3	Cell	555-1122

Note that an additional field has been added: an Emp ID field. Think of this field as an internal address within a table. It is used to match employees with their phone numbers. In relational database terminology, this column is called a *key field*. The FileMaker Pro help system refers to it as a *match field*, but they are one and the same. Key fields are used to identify specific records.

Although FileMaker Pro can be used to build simple flat file database systems (see Figure 1.1), it shines at creating relational database systems (see Figure 1.2).

→ For a thorough introduction to database application development with FileMaker Pro, **see** Chapter 3, "Defining and Working with Fields," **p. 67**, and Chapter 4, "Working with Layouts," **p. 93**.

Figure 1.1
FileMaker can be used to construct simple flat file databases.

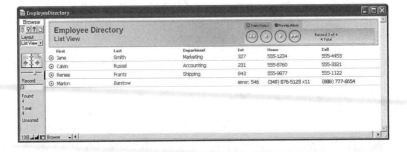

Figure 1.2
The two-table Employee/Phone example can look something like this when implemented in FileMaker.

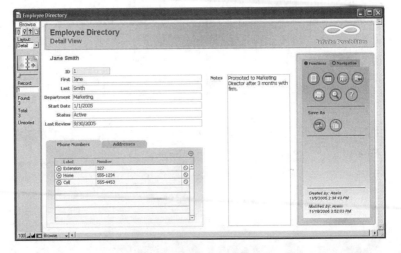

OVERVIEW OF THE FILEMAKER 8 PRODUCT LINE

FileMaker Pro is just one product in a broader product line. It's worth noting the differences between the products and how they work together:

- **FileMaker Pro 8**—This is the regular desktop client version of FileMaker. It can be used to author new database systems, to host systems for a limited number of guests, or to serve as a guest of a hosted system. It can also publish as many as 10 database files to up to five users with Instant Web Publishing (IWP).

- **FileMaker Pro 8 Advanced**—This version has all the capabilities of the regular version of FileMaker Pro; it also has additional functionality aimed at application developers. With FileMaker Pro 8 Advanced, developers can create custom functions, add custom menu sets to a database, and create tool tips for any layout object (all of these enhancements to the files are usable by both FileMaker Pro and FileMaker Advanced users). A Debug Scripts feature and the new Data Viewer allow developers to walk through scripts one step at a time and test calculations, watching the effect of each script step or process. The Database Design Report (DDR) enables developers to document and troubleshoot development issues from a systemwide perspective. The Advanced version also enables developers to create runtime versions of single-user solutions and enable kiosk mode.

  The authors of this book strongly recommend developing with FileMaker Pro 8 Advanced. The additional functionality in custom functions alone makes it well worthwhile, not to mention the added capability to control all menu selections in a solution and offer tool tips to end users. The debugging tools are invaluable and the DDR is a great source for documentation and troubleshooting alike.

  The prior version of this book devoted a chapter to FileMaker Developer, the precursor to FileMaker Pro Advanced; however, in this edition the authors have elected to interweave discussion of Advanced features in contextually appropriate sections throughout the book. Aside from having a new name, FileMaker Pro Advanced offers significant functionality beyond the Pro product, and a single chapter would have become unwieldy in attempting to cover all the material in an appropriate manner. It also would have been an arbitrary separation of topics throughout the book. The Script Debugger, for example, clearly belongs in the debugging and troubleshooting chapter.

- **FileMaker Server 8**—This software hosts FileMaker files on a hardware server and offers support routines, evaluates server-based calculations, and provides for a larger user load: FileMaker Server 8 can host a maximum of 125 database files and 250 FileMaker Pro 8 or FileMaker Pro 8 Advanced client connections. In addition, it can manage database backup schedules, log usage statistics, disconnect idle users, and manage FileMaker plug-in updates.

- **FileMaker Server 8 Advanced**—FileMaker Server 8 Advanced has all the features of FileMaker Server 8, and can also host ODBC/JDBC and web-based client session connections. It can serve up to 50 xDBC connections (which count against its limit of 250 client connections) and can serve up to an additional 100 web session connections through IWP or CWP (Custom Web Publishing). Put another way, Server Advanced can host a maximum of 250 FileMaker client connections and an additional 100 web session connections, or it can host 200 FileMaker connections, 50 xDBC connections, and 100 web session connections. The 100 web sessions include any Instant Web Publishing connections, as well as any Custom Web Publishing sessions configured to use database sessions. (It is possible to query a FileMaker database in CWP without using a database session. In such cases, the number of connections is limited by the server's operating system and hardware capabilities.)

→ For a complete discussion on Custom Web Publishing, including session handling and server capacity, **see** Chapter 23, "Custom Web Publishing," **p. 699**.

- **FileMaker Mobile**—FileMaker Mobile is a slimmed-down version of FileMaker designed to run on Palm and Pocket PC PDAs (personal digital assistants). FileMaker Mobile can synchronize with a hosted FileMaker solution so that data can be shared between a Palm or Pocket PC device and a hosted database. Changes made offline, on the handheld device, will be synchronized to the hosted database when the handheld device reconnects.

FILEMAKER DEPLOYMENT OPTIONS

After a database application has been developed in FileMaker Pro or FileMaker Pro Advanced, it can be deployed in various ways, and on various operating systems. FileMaker Pro 8 runs on Mac OS X 10.2 or later and on Microsoft Windows 2000 or later. The following sections describe different ways to deploy a FileMaker database system.

SINGLE USER

Many people get their start in FileMaker development by building a small application for their personal use. Although FileMaker Pro is inherently a networkable application, there's nothing wrong with a single user working with a system on his computer.

PEER-TO-PEER HOSTING

The next stage in a typical system evolution is that other members of an organization notice the system that a single person made and want to use it also. It's a simple matter to enable FileMaker Network Sharing on a file; after that's been done, other FileMaker users can become guests of one user's shared file. This kind of FileMaker hosting is called *peer-to-peer* because the database host and the database clients are all using the same application—desktop versions of FileMaker Pro or FileMaker Advanced.

You should keep some considerations in mind with this type of hosting. Only 10 files at a time can be hosted on a single machine this way. Up to five users can be guests of a file hosted in this fashion. Another consideration is that if you're the host of a file, you can't close the file while other users are working with it, and performance may suffer for other users as the hosting user puts her computer through its daily paces.

FILEMAKER SERVER HOSTING

FileMaker Server is optimized for sharing FileMaker databases, and it can host (share) more files (125) for more users (250) than FileMaker Pro peer-to-peer can. Administrators can remotely administer the server, create schedules for automated database backups, set the server to encrypt the network traffic between the server and the clients, and log server actions.

→ For more information about hosting database files with FileMaker Server, **see** Chapter 25, "FileMaker Server and Server Advanced," **p. 779**.

FILEMAKER SERVER ADVANCED HOSTING

FileMaker Server Advanced can host files for FileMaker users just as FileMaker Server can, but it can also allow ODBC/JDBC clients to access hosted files and provide service as a web host, allowing up to an additional 100 user connections for web clients.

→ For more information about hosting database files for ODBC/JDBC access, **see** Chapter 20, "Exporting Data from FileMaker," **p. 595**.

KIOSK MODE

Using FileMaker Pro Advanced, you can configure FileMaker databases to run without the menu bar or operating-system controls, effectively making a solution take over the entire computer screen. Developers will need to build whatever user interface controls users may need, given that menus are no longer available.

FILEMAKER SINGLE-USER RUNTIME

FileMaker Advanced also allows developers to bind files into a runtime application that will allow a single user to work with a FileMaker solution, without needing a copy of FileMaker. No authoring capabilities exist (a user cannot access layout mode or make schema changes via the runtime engine), nor can the application serve as a host (peer-to-peer or server-based); however, this is a great option for creating a commercial application without requiring that customers purchase copies of FileMaker Pro.

→ To learn more about Kiosk mode or the Runtime Engine, **see** Chapter 24, "Deploying and Extending FileMaker," **p. 755**.

EXTENDING THE FUNCTIONALITY OF FILEMAKER PRO

FileMaker solutions can be enhanced by incorporating plug-ins that extend the functionality of FileMaker Pro. The functionality that plug-ins offer varies widely and is determined by the third-party developers who write and market plug-ins. Some plug-ins provide advanced math capabilities, some generate charts from FileMaker data, some manipulate image files, and others provide security or user-interface enhancements. There are literally dozens if not hundreds of plug-ins actively supported by the FileMaker industry at large.

→ To get more information about plug-ins, **see** Chapter 24, "Deploying and Extending FileMaker," **p. 755**.

WHAT'S NEW IN FILEMAKER PRO 8

FileMaker, the database product, has been around since 1985, and has evolved a great deal since its inception. It is fully relational, offers both development- and user-level support in a single application, is completely cross-platform compatible, and takes advantage of a modern security architecture.

NEW FEATURES

The following is a brief list of the major changes and new features in FileMaker 8.

FEATURES FOR USERS

- **Calendar Picker**—Date fields can now feature a calendar picker (**p. 120**).
- **Auto Complete**—All fields (with the exception of container fields, summary fields, and calculation fields) can offer auto-complete ("type-ahead") options to users as they type (**p. 78**).
- **Send Mail**—Users can now email reports and information directly from the File menu (**p. 301**).
- **Save/Send As PDF**—FileMaker licensed the Adobe PDF technology and users now can create PDF documents and email them in one step (**p. 298**).
- **Save/Send As Excel**—Users can save data directly as Excel documents, rather than having to export data as comma-separated values, and, as with the Save/Send As PDF feature, email the results (**p. 300**).
- **Visual Spell Check**—FileMaker now highlights misspelled words within active fields as users type (**p. 42**).
- **Fast Match**—With one mouse click, Fast Match lets users find all matching records, even refine or broaden a search, all without typing (**p. 51**).
- **Field List Filtering**—Sort and Export dialog boxes can now be limited to showing only those fields that are on the current layout, making choosing fields much more straightforward (**p. 596**).

PROGRAMMING FEATURES

- **Script Variables and Script Results**—Powerful new programming features, script variables and script results, allow developers to build complex routines (**p. 444, p. 448**).
- **"Extended" Go to Related Record Script Step**—It is now possible to jump from an entire found set of records to a related set (**p. 462**).
- **Dynamic Repeating Values**—Repeating field and variable instances can now be dynamically controlled, giving FileMaker the equivalent of one-dimensional arrays (**p. 87**).
- **Value Lists Display Only Second Column**—It is now possible to use a two-column value list to populate a match field value in column one and to *only* display data from column two (**p. 175**).

- **Copy/Paste Schema Objects**—Fields, scripts,script steps, and tables can all be copied and pasted now (**p. 179**).

- **Import As New Table**—Developers can import just a table's definition or they can import both a definition and data (**p. 577**).

- **Relationships Graph Additions**—The Relationships Graph features new alignment tools, a comment/note object, and new selection capabilities (**p. 214**).

- **Layout Alignment Tools**—Layout tools now include the capability to align objects relative to each other's characteristics (**p. 114**).

- **Debugger, Data Viewer**—The Script Debugger has been enhanced in FileMaker 8 and a Data Viewer allows developers to see what values are populated into variables or as the result of an expression as needed (**p. 517**).

NEW USER INTERFACE CONTROLS

- **Tab Control**—The new Tab Control object allows developers to extend screen real estate on layouts (**p. 117**).

- **Custom Menus**—Developers can now control every aspect of FileMaker's menus, including contextual menus and toolbar controls, by using FileMaker Pro 8 Advanced (**p. 373**).

- **Tool Tips**—Users can get additional information via tool tips that a developer can attach to any layout object in a FileMaker solution (**p. 106**).

FILEMAKER 7/8 ARCHITECTURE

Version 7 was a major architectural shift for FileMaker, and many of the changes from prior releases of the platform represent critical issues that all current developers must know. To present a complete picture of FileMaker, the following section reviews, and compares to prior versions, the new architectural structure introduced in FileMaker 7 and extended in FileMaker 8.

FILE FORMAT

The file format for FileMaker 7 and 8 is radically different from that of earlier versions of FileMaker Pro. Earlier versions of the product were limited to one table per file, whereas FileMaker 7 and 8 allow one million tables per file. Not only is the file format different, but the network protocol that FileMaker uses to communicate between hosts and guests is different as well. That means that if you need to, you can run both FileMaker 6 and FileMaker 8 on the same network and the two versions won't "see" each other on the network, or conflict in any way. After you convert FileMaker 6 files into FileMaker 8 files, the FileMaker 8 versions will no longer be readable by FileMaker 6. *Conversion* in this sense is actually a misnomer because when FileMaker 8 converts a FileMaker 6 file, the original file is left untouched. Instead, FileMaker 8 uses the original to create a new version of the file.

Along with the FileMaker 7/8 file format come some dramatic benefits. One favorite is the significantly improved stability of files, leading to far less corruption when systems suffer crashes. Also, developers can now make changes to everything—field definitions, table definitions, access privileges—while the database is being hosted with guests logged on. This extends the flexibility of the platform even further.

RELATIONSHIPS GRAPH

The Relationships Graph is a visual representation of the relationships between table occurrences. The term *table occurrences* is used because there can be only a single relationship between two table occurrences. If a developer needs to create multiple relationships between two tables, those tables will be displayed multiple times on the Relationships Graph—hence the term *table occurrence* (see Figure 1.3).

Figure 1.3
This Relationships Graph shows two occurrences of the Person table, each with a different relationship.

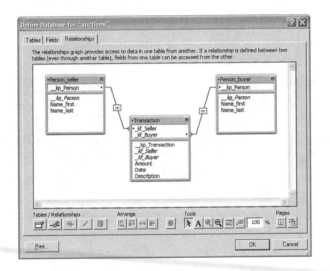

→ For more on the Relationships Graph, **see** Chapter 6, "Working with Multiple Tables," **p. 157**.

ENHANCED RELATIONSHIP FUNCTIONALITY

In versions of FileMaker Pro before version 7, relationships could be constructed only on the basis of a key field (match field) in one file being equal to a key field in another file. These relationships, or joins, are known as *equijoins* in relational database terminology. FileMaker Pro 8 supports multiple join types. Now relationships can be constructed in which one value is less than, greater than, or not equal to the other value.

In addition to the multiple join types, FileMaker 8 also supports complex, multiple-predicate joins, or joins with more than one criteria. In Figure 1.4, the Edit Relationship dialog clearly shows the different join types and the multiple join criteria.

Figure 1.4
This relationship shows all team members for the selected Team ID, excluding the current person's record.

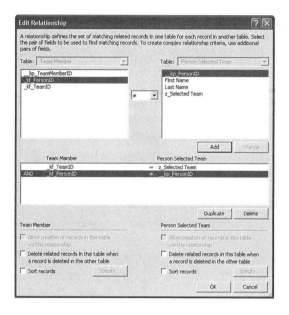

MULTIPLE WINDOWS PER FILE

In FileMaker 8, a user can have more than one window open per file and, more important, more than one window open per table (because it is possible to have multiple tables per file). It is possible to view two separate found sets of data at once, perform a search in one window while maintaining the state of another, or develop a multipaned application.

SECURITY

FileMaker 8 supports a centralized, modern security architecture in which accounts and privileges may be changed while a system is live. System behaviors are grouped into *privilege sets*; each account is associated with a single privilege set, ensuring that all users have their own accounts and passwords while sharing access levels with their peers.

Extended privileges serve as an additional feature that allows developers to define custom privilege settings. In scripts and calculations, a developer can test for the existence of an extended privilege and modify the behavior of a user's experience with a given solution accordingly.

Security capabilities also include the capability to integrate with an external authentication server (Open Directory or Active Directory) where an IT organization may maintain passwords on a central server for all the various applications in an organization, including FileMaker.

Although technically not really a security feature, it is possible to tie a FileMaker Server into an LDAP (Lightweight Directory Access Protocol) infrastructure so that users see only host servers that are applicable to their department/division, and so on.

→ For a complete overview of FileMaker's security features, **see** Chapter 12, "Implementing Security," **p. 325**.

CALCULATIONS

FileMaker 7 introduced support for commenting within calculations, included the Let() function for declaring variables, and shifted syntax from Status functions to the more broadly applied Get functions.

FileMaker 8 allows developers to extract data by related rows with the GetNthRecord() function, new functions have been added to remove text style attributes (font, text color, font size, style), and additional Get() functions have been added to determine the location of desktop and document folders on client machines.

FileMaker Developer 7 and FileMaker Pro 8 Advanced allow developers to create their own custom functions. Often underappreciated, custom functions give developers the capability of abstracting code into reusable, discrete units.

SCRIPTS

FileMaker 8 contains its own scripting tool, ScriptMaker, which allows developers to create logical routines that run at the press of a button or the selection of a menu choice.

Scripts in FileMaker 8 can be set to run with full access privileges on a script-by-script basis that then overrides a user's security privilege settings.

Scripts can also be set to be available for execution from the Web. A wide majority of script steps are supported via both Instant Web Publishing and Custom Web Publishing.

LAYOUTS

FileMaker 8 boasts new alignment tools, and, on a layout-by-layout basis, a developer can decide whether record changes will be automatically saved, as they were in previous versions of FileMaker Pro, or whether the user needs to deliberately commit the record to save changes.

Button objects can now be included in tab sequences, and when a user has tabbed to a button object, she may "click" the button by pressing the Enter key or spacebar.

The biggest change with layouts is the Tab Control object. Developers can now create a tabbed pane without any scripting whatsoever.

WEB

Instant Web Publishing was greatly enhanced in FileMaker Pro 7, and Custom Web Publishing was completely overhauled to utilize XML and XSLT. FileMaker 8 made no dramatic changes to web capabilities, but did refine both performance and stability.

TECHNICAL SPECIFICATIONS

FileMaker 7 represented a complete rearchitecting of FileMaker's file format and dramatically extended the platform's capabilities. The transition from the file format supported by FileMaker 3.0 through FileMaker 6.0 is still going on. A comparison between the two architectures demonstrates the dramatic growth the platform has undergone (see Table 1.5).

TABLE 1.5 FILEMAKER PRO 6 AND 8 CAPABILITY COMPARISON

Feature	FileMaker 6	FileMaker 8
Number of tables per file	1	1,000,000
Maximum file size	2GB	8TB
Maximum amount of data in a text field	64,000 characters	2GB of data, or 1GB of Unicode characters
Number of significant digits in a number field	14	FileMaker Pro indexes the first 400 significant digits (numbers, decimal points, or signs) of the field, ignoring letters and other symbols
Number of characters in a number field	120	800
Maximum number of files allowed open on the client	50	Limited only by memory
Maximum records per file (theoretical limit)	100 million	64 quadrillion over the lifetime of the file
Maximum amount of data allowed in a container field	2GB	4GB
Maximum number of fields in a table	N/A	256 million over the lifetime of the file
Number of script steps supported by Instant Web Publishing	10	74
Number of FileMaker clients hosted by FileMaker Server	250	250
Number of web clients hosted by FileMaker Server Advanced	N/A	100

CHAPTER 2

USING FILEMAKER PRO

In this chapter

GETTING STARTED

It's time to roll up your sleeves and actually put FileMaker Pro to use. Most of this book deals with being a FileMaker developer—someone who is focused on the programming side of creating and managing FileMaker solutions; however, ironically, development composes only a small percentage of the overall time a given database gets used. Much of the time a FileMaker solution will simply be in use, and its users will care nothing for scripting, calculations, or the vagaries of user interface design. They will simply be involved with working with a developer's creation and will not need to know anything of the programming side of FileMaker.

Becoming facile in working with FileMaker databases will prove quite helpful in allowing you to quickly access the information you want and to understand the underpinnings of any database, regardless of user interface.

This chapter introduces you to how to make the most of FileMaker databases that have already been built. All FileMaker databases—often called *solutions*, *systems*, or *applications*—have certain common elements, and becoming adept at using FileMaker Pro solutions will not only help you manipulate and analyze data better, but also assist you in extending what you can accomplish with that data. We'll cover some broad concepts at first, move into the nuts and bolts of working with databases, and finally wrap things up with some techniques to help you become a FileMaker Pro power user.

One quick note before we begin: This chapter assumes that you want to learn as much as you can about FileMaker Pro. Although the concepts and functions described can be fairly basic (how to open a database, for example), this chapter covers a fair number of advanced topics as well. This chapter is a good place to start if you're unfamiliar with FileMaker Pro, or if you still don't quite feel comfortable using a FileMaker Pro database.

Before going much further, we need to be clear on some basic FileMaker Pro vocabulary. *Databases* store collections of information, and one of their primary functions is to properly identify the information they store. It's not enough to simply save the text strings "Pink Floyd" and "Dark Side of the Moon" in a file. For a database to be useful, you need to know that Pink Floyd is a band and that *Dark Side of the Moon* is an album (one of the greatest of all time!).

For a database to fulfill its primary function, a developer needs to have properly identified all the appropriate elements of information you or your organization wants to store and use. It is in these identifications that information becomes meaningful.

RECORDS AND FIELDS

Databases store information about one or more kinds of entities. For example, a database might store information about music albums, or musicians, or guitar manufacturers. In FileMaker, each individual item is referred to as a *record*. So in a database of music CDs, each record represents an individual CD.

To track the attributes of items or specific information—for example, *Dark Side of the Moon*'s release date of March 24, 1973—*fields* are defined specific to each type of item. These fields hold and also identify the type of information found for each record. Examples of fields that might be found in the music CD database are release date, recording studio, and so on.

In FileMaker Pro you will be working with a specific individual record at a time and will be viewing (and storing) information from that record's fields.

> **N O T E**
>
> For those of you familiar with SQL, a *row* corresponds to a *record* in FileMaker Pro, and a *column* corresponds to a *field*.

➔ For more information on SQL and how it relates to FileMaker Pro, **see** Chapter 20, "Exporting Data from FileMaker," **p. 595**.

UNDERSTANDING TABLES

It's important to have a grasp of what a table is when you're working with FileMaker Pro.

Simply stated, a *table* is a collection of like records. You might have one table of automobile model records and another table of manufacturer records. Miata would belong in the automobile table, and Mazda in the manufacturer table. From the music example, music albums would belong to one table, musicians to another, and genres to another. An album isn't a genre, nor are musicians the same as the albums they create.

For the purposes of using FileMaker Pro, you need to remember one thing: Every layout (a view or form for data) in FileMaker Pro is associated with a specific table. If you're looking at a layout with a picture of a Mazda Miata, and fields that break out the attributes of that car, more than likely you're in an automobiles table. If you're seeing a layout with "Mazda" at the top and multiple car models listed, you're more than likely in the manufacturer table. This will come into play later in the chapter when you begin working with multiple records and found sets.

➔ To explore working with multiple recordsets, **see** "Working with a Found Set," **p. 51**.

> **N O T E**
>
> In FileMaker Pro, you can have as many tables in a single file (.fp7 document) as you need: FileMaker 8 is a relational database platform. Versions of FileMaker since version 3's introduction in 1995 were also relational, but earlier versions allowed only one table per file.
>
> Before FileMaker 7, database solutions would often be collections of files and require that you open all these multiple files at once to use a solution. In FileMaker 8, you can consolidate solutions into single files with multiple tables.

➔ To dig deeper into working with multiple tables and understanding relational data models, **see** Chapter 6, "Working with Multiple Tables," **p. 157**, and Chapter 5, "Relational Database Design," **p. 129**.

FILEMAKER PRO NAVIGATION

One of the first things you'll want to do when you open a database in FileMaker Pro is navigate the various screens, called *layouts*, that a developer designed as the interface for the database. Using these layouts, you can view records, enter data into fields, see reports, run scripts, and more.

In addition to the menus common to all software applications, there are two important work areas to distinguish from one another in a FileMaker Pro database: the Status Area on the left and the Layout area on the right (see Figure 2.1).

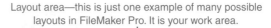
Layout area—this is just one example of many possible layouts in FileMaker Pro. It is your work area.

Figure 2.1
These are the primary areas of all FileMaker Pro databases; in some cases, however, a developer might have hidden the Status Area.

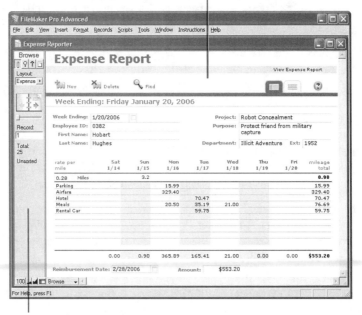

Status Area—this is where most of your controls lie.

 Note that the menus and menu items you see in your FileMaker database may well be quite different from those you see in the screenshots in this book or in other FileMaker solutions. FileMaker Pro 8 Advanced includes a feature to customize menus, and the developer who created the file you are working with may have changed its menu set from the standard.

LAYOUTS

Most FileMaker Pro databases open to a data-entry layout. Generally you have access to fields, commonly designated by a field border or embossing of some kind (depending on the aesthetic design or dementia of the database's developer), or you may come across a layout used for reporting purposes only. Figures 2.2, 2.3, and 2.4 illustrate just a few examples of layouts you might find with databases created in FileMaker Pro.

Figure 2.2
FileMaker's built-in starter solutions offer a simple, clean interface. Shown here are a *form layout* (one record per screen) and a *list layout* (multiple records per screen) .

Figure 2.3
FileMaker applications—commercially available database solutions from FileMaker, Inc.—demonstrate the possibilities of more feature-rich systems. (Screenshots provided by permission of FileMaker, Inc.)

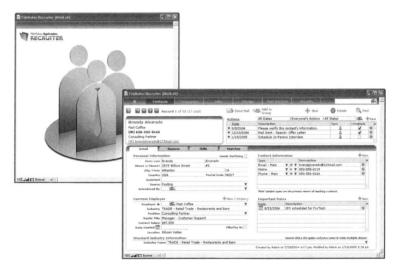

THE STATUS AREA   The Status Area serves as a primary control center for FileMaker Pro. In *Browse mode*—the state in which all data entry and general use occurs—the Status Area displays a book icon and other elements for navigating a database solution.

FileMaker Pro has four modes, which we'll explain later in this chapter. For now, note that the Status Area changes appearance and function depending on which mode you're using. In Find mode it allows access to search functions and special search wildcard characters. In Layout mode the Status Area contains most of the tools used for defining the look and feel of your database.

Figure 2.4
Here's a bit of a departure from the staid designs of typical productivity applications. FileMaker offers a wide range of layout possibilities.

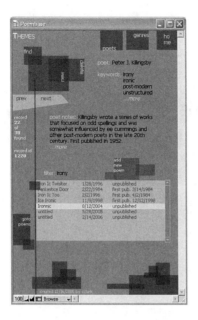

Figure 2.5 details the various elements of the Status Area, as it appears in Browse mode.

Figure 2.5
Note the various functions of the Status Area in Browse mode. To jump to a specific record, type a number into the record number field and press Enter.

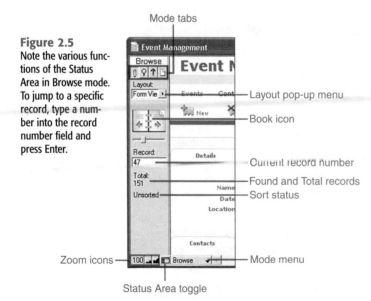

The elements of the Status Area include the following:

- **Layout pop-up menu**—Not to be confused with the Layout menu in Layout mode, this enables you to navigate from layout to layout in your database. Developers can control whether a layout appears in this list.

- **Book icon**—The book icon enables you to page through each record in your database. You stay on the same layout, but you see the information for each record in your database as you click through your records. The slider below enables you to jump ahead and back by multiple records.

- **Current record number**—Not to be confused with a record identifier, key, or ID, this number indicates which record in your current set you're viewing, relative to the others you're currently working with. FileMaker Pro allows you to establish *found sets*—groups of records with which you're currently working—and this number shows where your current record lies relative to the found set. In one situation a given record might be record number 1, in another (say after sorting your database differently) it might be number 20.

- **Found and Total records**—These numbers show how many records are in your found set compared to the total in your entire database. Found sets are covered in more detail later in the chapter.

- **Sort status**—FileMaker Pro allows you to sort your records based on some criterion. Depending on how your found set has been sorted, the Status Area shows Sorted, Semi-sorted, or Unsorted. A semi-sorted state would occur if you were to sort the records in your database and then create a new record.

- **Zoom icons**—These allow you to zoom in and out on a given layout.

- **Status Area toggle**—This allows you to show and hide the Status Area.

- **Mode menu**—This pop-up menu functions in the same way as the mode icons.

CAUTION

> You'll notice something missing from FileMaker Pro: back and forward buttons. It's important that you not confuse the book icon with such. The book icon enables you to page back and forward through your *data* as opposed to paging through your layouts in Browse mode.
>
> Some users familiar with the Web will wrongly expect the book icon to step forward and back through their navigation history within a database.

FILEMAKER PRO MODES

You'll interact with your FileMaker Pro databases via one of four modes. At times, developers choose to tailor a layout for use with a specific mode, but more often than not, layouts can be effectively used with all four. To switch between modes, use the View menu.

To familiarize you with the four modes, here's a simple description of each.

- **Browse mode**—Browse mode is FileMaker Pro's primary mode, where all data entry occurs, and generally is the principal mode you'll use in a given solution.

- **Find mode**—Here you create and then perform *find requests* to search for specific sets of records.

- **Preview mode**—When preparing to print from FileMaker Pro, you may opt to switch to Preview mode to see what a given layout will look like after it is printed. Developers may also build Preview mode steps into their reporting functions so that you can review a document before sending it to a printer. Preview mode is also necessary to view some summary-type reports.

■ **Layout mode**—It is in Layout mode that a great deal of development occurs. Here developers can manipulate all the elements of a given layout, including controlling all the things that appear on that layout.

NOTE

You can change modes in four other ways: You can use the menu at the lower left of your screen, you can use the mode tabs at the top of the Status Area, you can use various functions and/or buttons that a developer may have programmed to switch modes, and you can use keyboard shortcuts (listed under the View menu).

VIEWS

In addition to the modes of FileMaker Pro, there are three views as well. A *view* is a particular way of displaying record data on the screen. To change between them, use the View menu as well. These are the three views:

■ **Form view**—Allows you to see and manipulate only one record at a time (see Figure 2.6).

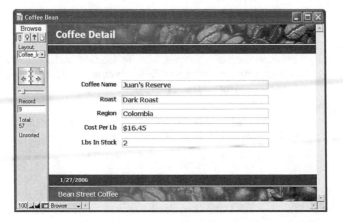

Figure 2.6
Form view is usually where most data entry is performed.

■ **List view**—Here you can display multiple records. At any given moment, you still are working with only one specific record while still being able to view the rest (see Figure 2.7).

■ **Table view**—Table view simply displays the raw data for a given record (depending on what fields have been placed on a layout). It looks quite similar to a spreadsheet application (see Figure 2.8). This is extremely handy for reviewing large groups of data quickly, but it offers few user interface controls.

Figure 2.7
Notice at the bottom of the screen that List views can also include summary data.

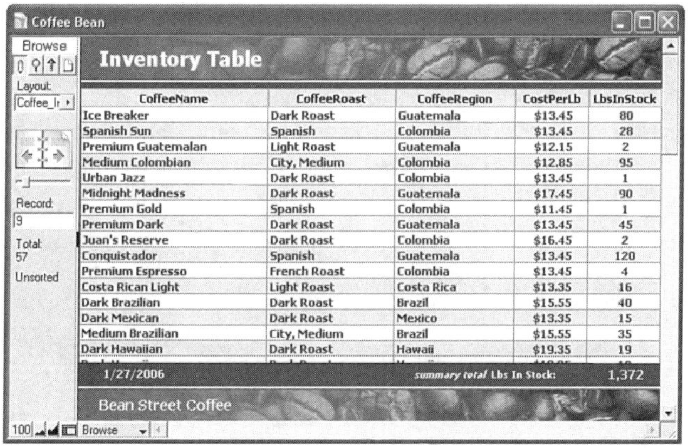

Figure 2.8
In Table view you can automatically resize, move, and sort with column headers.

BUTTONS

Notice that we've largely been talking about fields on layouts. Most FileMaker Pro solutions also include buttons. Figure 2.9 shows a few examples.

Buttons trigger actions—often by launching scripts that developers write—and are specific to a given FileMaker Pro database. Buttons can perform dozens of actions, such as creating a new record, deleting a record, navigating to another layout, performing a calculation, performing a find request, controlling windows, and even spell-checking and emitting a simple beep. The possibilities are nearly endless.

You'll need to become familiar with the specifics of a given FileMaker Pro solution to come to understand what its buttons do. The person who built the system should have those details, or should have provided some form of training or documentation.

Figure 2.9
Buttons can come in all shapes and sizes in FileMaker Pro. Text can be a button, a field can be a button, and even just a mysterious blank area in the middle of a layout can be a button.

TAB CONTROL OBJECTS

 Another element you'll work with on layouts is the new Tab Control object introduced in FileMaker 8. With it, developers can create multiple panes of information on a single layout, as shown in Figure 2.10, and users can flip from pane to pane as they need. Each tab pane displays information from the same record: Think of it as extending the amount of screen real estate you can view at any given time.

Figure 2.10
The Tab Control in FileMaker 8 allows you to organize and view data for a given record without having to scroll or move to other layouts. Note the three tabs shown here for Inventory, Picture, and Navigation.

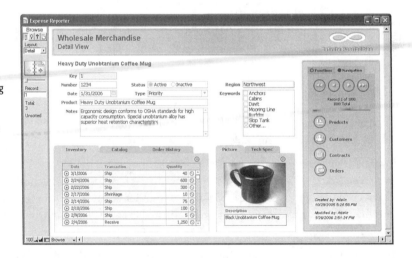

WORKING IN FILEMAKER PRO

This next section walks you through working in some typical FileMaker Pro situations and addresses many of the common tasks you need to be able to perform.

OPENING A DATABASE

The first step, obviously, is opening a database. FileMaker Pro databases can live in various places. They can sit on your own computer, just as any other document might; they can be hosted by another computer; or they can be served by FileMaker Server.

LOCAL FILES

Opening a local file is a simple matter of double-clicking its icon either in your Windows environment or in the Mac OS X Finder. You may also use FileMaker Pro's File, Open command.

REMOTE FILES

Working with remote files requires connecting to a server—which could be a database hosted on *FileMaker Server* (the software that allows you to host a FileMaker database for use across a LAN or WAN by up to 250 users)—or simply connecting to a file set to multi-user on another person's workstation. To a client computer, there's no distinction. FileMaker Pro treats both cases as a remote connection.

To open a remote database, click the Remote button in the Open File dialog, or choose Open Remote from the File menu.

As shown in Figure 2.11, you can choose from those hosts available to you locally (those on your network, within your domain in corporate environments, or accessible on the Internet), or you can navigate to a particular server via an LDAP server.

Figure 2.11
Use the Open Remote File dialog to open a database on a LAN, in a corporate domain, or (with a proper IP address) across the Internet.

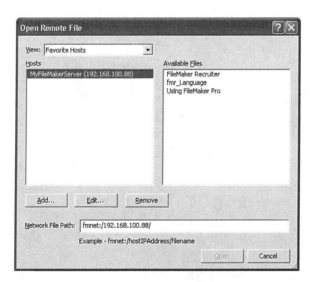

NOTE

> Note that some solutions contain multiple files. A developer can opt to hide some files from the remote hosts dialog and therefore present only a launch or menu file as needed.

TIP

> If you work in a large organization, your server list can become quite cluttered. Use the Favorite Hosts menu option for those you most frequently use. It enables you to add all the files from a server or just those you want.

CAUTION

> Opening a FileMaker database across an Internet connection is entirely possible, but you should be aware that connection speeds will vary, depending on your network, hardware, and the specific FileMaker Pro database. Don't plan on making this a deployment strategy until you've properly tested both your solution itself and your users' connections to it.

 If you've run into what might appear to be a corrupted file, refer to "File Corruption and File Recovery" in the "Troubleshooting" section at the end of this chapter.

CREATING A NEW DATABASE FROM A TEMPLATE

Because this could be your first foray into FileMaker Pro, you might not yet have a database to tinker with. FileMaker Pro's starter solutions are a great place to start. Ordinarily, you'd likely be working with a database either you or some other developer created; however, for our purposes, let's walk through how to open and use one of FileMaker Pro's existing starter solutions.

Navigate to File, New Database. Then select Create a New File Using a Template. The New Database dialog box shown in Figure 2.12 appears.

Figure 2.12
Dozens of starter solutions, or templates, ship with FileMaker Pro, ranging from an invoicing system to a tool to organize your personal DVD collection.

You are encouraged to explore FileMaker's starter solutions. They are fairly simple databases that show by example how FileMaker Pro can be used, and can also give you a jump-start on creating your own databases.

CREATING AND DELETING RECORDS

Creating and deleting records in FileMaker Pro is simple. Under the <u>R</u>ecords menu, choose <u>N</u>ew Record, <u>D</u>elete Record, or Duplic<u>a</u>te Record. Notice also that there's a Delete All Records option. For now, let's explore how to take care of simple data entry.

If you are in the midst of entering data in a record and want to undo the entry, use the Revert Record command under the <u>R</u>ecords menu. A record is saved—or *committed*—automatically when you click outside a field for the first time, change modes, change layouts, or press the Enter key. FileMaker Pro uses the term *commit* to indicate when a record is posted, or saved, to your database. Using the <u>R</u>evert Record command before committing a record will allow you to roll back all the changes you've made, returning that record to its last committed state.

CAUTION

> Keep in mind that even though there's an <u>U</u>ndo command in the <u>E</u>dit menu, it doesn't work at the record level. After a record is committed (saved to the database), it is a part of your database. After you delete a record, it's gone forever.

NOTE

> You never need to save a FileMaker Pro database. As users commit records, those records are automatically stored in the database file. If you want to save a copy of your database or create a duplicate for backup purposes, the Save <u>A</u>s option under the <u>F</u>ile menu will serve.

If Revert Record doesn't seem to do anything, refer to "Reverting Records" in the "Troubleshooting" section at the end of this chapter.

If you have trouble with data you believe to be lost, refer to "Data Loss" in the "Troubleshooting" section at the end of this chapter.

WORKING WITH FIELDS

If you are used to other productivity applications or have ever filled out a form on the Web, you should find data entry quite familiar in FileMaker.

Fields generally look like embossed or bordered areas with labels off to one side or the other. Keep in mind that developers control the look and feel of their systems, so it's entirely possible that someone could build a database with no labels, fields that are the same color as their background, and white text on a white background. Thankfully, when a field is being actively edited, the other fields on a given layout are highlighted by a dotted border, indicating that you're in the midst of editing a record (see Figure 2.13). That at least will help you see which fields allow entry and which don't.

Figure 2.13
FileMaker's field borders indicate the edit state of a record.

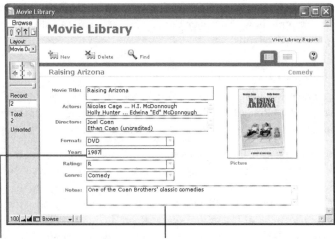

Solid line indicates that this specific field is being edited

Dotted line indicates that the record is currently being edited

Editing fields is as easy as clicking into them, typing some text, and clicking out again.

Although FileMaker has offered spell-checking capabilities for years, FileMaker 8 introduced a visual cue for misspelled words that appears while users are entering data. When a field is active—where the cursor is in the field itself—FileMaker underlines in red any words it concludes are misspelled. If you right-click (or Control-click on a Mac with a one-button mouse) on the word, you can choose from among possible other spellings or save a word to your local dictionary file.

Moving from field to field can be managed on your keyboard if you simply press the Tab key. Some solutions may also support the Return and Enter keys.

You can, depending on how the developer of a database has set things, also tab from button to button or tab panel to tab panel. To execute an action associated with an active button or tab, press the Enter key or spacebar on your keyboard.

→ For discussion on how to control object behavior from a development perspective, **see** "Working with Fields," **p. 118**.

You'll work with a few different formats of fields in FileMaker Pro:

- **Edit box**—This allows standard keyboard entry and sometimes includes a scrollbar.

- **Drop-down list**—When first clicking into a field, you are presented with a list of options from which you can select, or alternatively you can type directly into the field.

- **Pop-up menu**—A pop-up menu is similar to a pop-up list, except that a pop-up menu does not allow typing directly into the field and thus allows values from only the menu in question.

CAUTION

> Just as on the Web, it is possible to Shift-click multiple values in a pop-up list; however, only one value (the first selected) will be visible, and you may get unexpected results from using this technique.

- **Check box set**—Check boxes allow multiple values per field.
- **Radio button set**—These are similar to check boxes, with the exception that they are mutually exclusive. A user can select only one value at a time.
- **Pop-up calendar**—Some date fields may open to show a calendar that you can page through from month to month. To input a date into your date field, click on a specific day.

CAUTION

> Shift-clicking allows a user to select multiple values in certain input types, such as pop-up menus and radio buttons. Selecting multiple values in a pop-up menu or in radio button sets is generally a bad idea. Again, you will end up with unpredictable results because you're making an exception to a formatting choice meant to allow for only one value in a given field.

Figure 2.14 contains examples of these field formats.

Figure 2.14
Using field formatting can make data entry more intuitive. Notice that all types are present, although in a real database only one field would be active at a time.

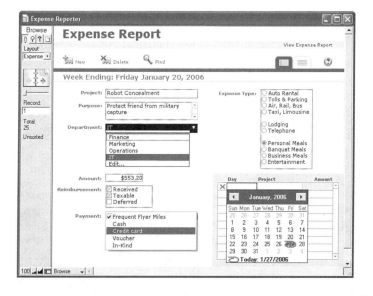

Note that a developer may have set a field to auto-complete (sometimes referred to as *type-ahead*) where FileMaker will suggest values based on what you've entered in previous records. This is a new feature in FileMaker 8.

DATA IN FORMATTED FIELDS

You might find it helpful to understand *how* multiple-value data is stored in fields: Remember that check boxes, radio buttons, drop-down lists, and pop-up menus are all nothing more than data-entry assistants. The actual data stored is a collection of values delimited by line returns. This means that you can accomplish the same result, from a data perspective, by simply entering a return-delimited list of values into your fields. This is an important thing for you to remember when performing find requests, which we'll cover later in this chapter.

→ To understand more about how multiple values in a field can lead to relational data structure problems, **see** Chapter 5, "Relational Database Design," **p. 129**.

MODIFYING VALUE LISTS

Often, you might need to add new values to a value list—the list that is used to create drop-down lists and pop-up menus, check boxes, and radio button items. Developers have the option of including an Edit option at the bottom of a drop-down list or pop-up menu. Selecting Edit then brings up a dialog that you can use to change or add to a list as needed (see Figure 2.15).

Figure 2.15
Editing value lists is a simple way to fine-tune a database to your specific needs without having to dig into programming.

To edit the items in a value list, simply type text into the Edit Value List dialog, followed by a carriage return. A hyphen adds a separator to the list.

NOTE

> Keep in mind that just because you replaced an old menu item with a new category—for example, "autos" became "cars"—doesn't mean that you've changed the actual values stored in your database's records. Remember that field formatting is nothing more than a data-entry assistant. By changing the assistant menu, you have *not* changed any data stored in your database.

USING THE "OTHER" VALUE IN VALUE LISTS

Radio button sets and check boxes work a bit differently than drop-down lists and pop-up menus. Developers do not have the choice to add an edit function to these formats; rather, they can include an Other option. This allows a user to enter virtually any custom text he wants, from a single value to hundreds of lines of text. Regardless of the value, the check box or radio button option that would be visibly displayed is Other; however, the data stored and included in the field's index includes whatever your other data is.

In contrast to adding values to a value list and changing the options available on all records, the Other function simply enables you to enter custom text into a specific record's field.

As you can guess, developers often disable this feature. Data can get buried behind another entry and can be difficult to account for. Just remember that all you're doing is using field formatting to help in entering consistent data. These fields are no different from standard fields that accept text data.

FIELD TYPES

In addition to enabling you to control how data gets entered into a field, FileMaker Pro databases use specific *field types* for different types of information.

Field types are independent from the field formatting we discussed in the preceding section. For example, it's entirely possible to format a calculation field as a check box (calculation fields are different from standard fields; they do not accept data entry and instead present the results of a formula). Although you as a user may expect to be able to click on a check box, if you do so FileMaker Pro will then prompt you and explain that calculation fields are not modifiable.

It's incumbent on the developer to sensibly identify, for a given system's users, which fields expect what sort of data. Often field labels make this clear. For example, you can often expect a Price field to be a number, and an Invoice Date field will no doubt be a date type.

The following list describes the field types available in FileMaker:

- **Text**—The most common data type, text allows a user to enter approximately 2GB of information, including carriage returns. Sorting by a text field is alphabetical.
- **Number**—Number fields store up to 800 digits, 400 on either side of the decimal, and sort as typical numbers.
- **Date**—Dates are managed in FileMaker by the Gregorian calendar, 1/1/0001 through 12/31/4000. It's a good practice, but not required, to use four-digit years when doing data entry. Sorting is by year, month, and day, as you would expect.
- **Time**—Time in FileMaker is stored in hours, minutes, and seconds, like so: HH:MM:SS. Sorting is based on a typical 24-hour clock.
- **Timestamp**—A timestamp is a tool generally used by database developers to identify exactly when a record has been created or modified. It combines a date with a time and looks like "6/28/1998 2:00 AM." For the user, occasionally you may want to use a timestamp for performing a find.
- **Container**—Container fields hold just about any binary information, be it an image, a movie, a PDF document, a Word document, or a file archive. These fields cannot be used for sorting purposes.

    Container fields are capable of holding files of up to 4GB in size, making it possible to use FileMaker Pro for managing all sorts of digital assets.

Data entry for container fields is slightly different from other types: You need to either paste a file or image into the field or use the Insert menu.

- **Calculation**—A calculation field stores the result of a formula, which may be based on other fields or related information in your system. The resultant data is assigned a type so that one can return a date, time, and so on. It's even possible for a calculation field to return container (binary) data.

NOTE

> The data in calculation fields is not modifiable by an end user; you can, however, access calculation fields for performing finds, sorts, and so on.

- **Summary**—Summary fields are similar to calculations, but they return information from your found set, or current group, of records. A summary field performing a `Total` operation, for example, totals a field across your current set of records. Other functions include averaging, totals, maximum, minimum, and so on.

SAVING AND RETRIEVING INFORMATION IN CONTAINER FIELDS

Container fields work differently than other fields. You cannot type data into them; rather, you will need to insert whatever file or media you want stored (or displayed) in them.

Note that a container field can do more than just store documents: For many image types it can display the image within FileMaker, for many sound types it can play the sound within FileMaker, and for a QuickTime movie it can allow users to play the movies. Whether you store something as a document or as a media type that FileMaker can play depends on how you save the information to the container field.

There are three general ways to store a file or media in a container field:

- **Paste**—You can place an image or a document on your clipboard and simply paste it into a container field. FileMaker will make its best guess as to what kind of information is on your clipboard and either store a document or display an image, a sound, or a QuickTime movie.
- **Insert**—Using the Insert menu, you can choose from among Picture, Quicktime (movie), Sound, and File. If you choose from the first three, FileMaker displays the media in question. If you choose File, you then load a document into FileMaker.
- **Import**—Under the File menu is the Import Records menu item from which you can further choose to import a file or a folder. If you choose to import from a folder, you will be able to point FileMaker to a directory of images or files and load them into a container field. You can also import container data directly from other FileMaker files.

NOTE

> On Windows you can also insert an object into a container field. If you choose this option, you will embed some OLE (object linking and embedding) file content in your FileMaker database. The end result is that you can provide interoperability between FileMaker and other applications: You can edit, say, a Word document directly from within FileMaker. Although this is convenient in some circumstances, we have found OLE support to be inconsistent and unstable. It is also not cross-platform compatible. We generally do not recommend using the Insert > Object command unless under special circumstances in which a developer can ensure that all users are able to consistently make use of the functionality.

In both the case of inserting a single media file and the case of importing many, you have the choice of inserting only a reference to the file, or of inserting the document itself. In the case that you insert a document itself, that document is then physically stored in FileMaker and is accessible by all users. They can select the container field in question and choose Export Field Contents from either the Edit menu or the contextual menu available from the field itself.

If you choose instead to store only a reference to the file, the file will be stored physically elsewhere (for example, on a shared hard disk). To have access to the file, your users will need to have access to the same shared directory on which the actual file sits. In this case you are performing the same sort of task as saving a shortcut or an alias to the file: It will remain on whatever storage device you found it.

The benefit of leaving documents on an external storage device and storing only references within FileMaker is that these documents require far less space within FileMaker for storage.

GLOBAL STORAGE

Field data in your database generally pertains to a specific, individual record. The baseball team field for your San Francisco record holds the data "The Giants," whereas for Chicago it's "The Cubs."

In some cases, however, a developer opts to define a field as globally stored. Developers will often use a shorthand, globals, to describe these sorts of fields. The value in that field is constant throughout the database, regardless of which record is currently being inspected. Some common examples might be fiscal year start and end dates, your company name, report headers, or a fixed commission rate.

As a user, you might not always be able to tell which fields in your database have been defined to store global values and which are record specific.

An important thing to keep in mind about global fields is that their behavior varies depending on how you're hosting a database. If you're using a database on your own local machine, with sharing set to single user, all global data is preserved from session to session. In other words, the next time you open the database, your global details remain from the last time you worked with the system.

If you're working with a database hosted on a server, all global information is session specific. It may contain default values, but if you change some data in a global field, other users of the system do not see that change, nor is it preserved for the next time you use the database.

If a developer has added global storage to a field in your system, it is quite likely that she has built routines to manage what information it holds when necessary.

DATA VALIDATION

Data integrity is one of the primary concerns of any database developer or of the team using a given system. If duplicate records appear, or misspellings and typos plague your database, or worse yet the wrong data is entered into the wrong fields, your system will soon become unreliable. For example, if you run a monthly income report, but in a few of your transaction records someone has entered a date value where in fact a transaction amount belongs, your monthly totals will be incorrect.

FileMaker Pro—or any application, for that matter—cannot read users' minds and fully safeguard against bad data, but developers do have a wide range of tools for validating information as it is entered. If your organization can come up with a business rule for validation, a developer can apply that rule to a given field or fields.

Consider the following examples:

- Transaction amounts can be only positive numbers, can have only two decimal places, and cannot exceed 100,000.
- Employee hire dates may be only equal to or later than 1/1/2001.
- Data in a given field must match established values in a status value list containing the values open, closed, and on hold. The field will not accept any other status descriptions.
- Company names in the database must be unique.

Understanding that these rules are in place will help you understand the underpinnings of your database application. When a validation check occurs, the system may prompt you with an appropriate message (see Figure 2.16).

Figure 2.16
This is an example of a default validation message. If you choose Revert Field, whatever data you've entered into the field reverts to the state it had before you started editing.

In addition to the default dialog shown in Figure 2.16, a developer can create his or her own custom text—for example, "This transaction amount must be a positive value greater than 99 cents."

If you choose Yes rather than Revert Field, your data is accepted as is and overrides the validation requirement. In some cases you may not have the option of posting an override.

 To explore additional thoughts on addressing data problems, refer to "Data Integrity" in the "Troubleshooting" section at the end of this chapter.

MANIPULATING RECORDS IN PORTALS

By now you've probably read the word "relational" a few times already in this book. Get used to it. One of FileMaker's core strengths is how it allows you to view and work with related information from a different but connected contextual set of records from other tables.

For example, in a table of car manufacturers you would likely have records for Audi, BMW, Chrysler, Mazda, and so on. Imagine that you also have a table for car models Mazda 6, MX-5 Miata, Protege5, and so on. FileMaker Pro allows you to view a car manufacturer, and on the same layout also see the models specific to that manufacturer (see Figure 2.17).

Figure 2.17
You are in the manufacturer table, looking at a record for Mazda, while also being able to see records from the car models table.

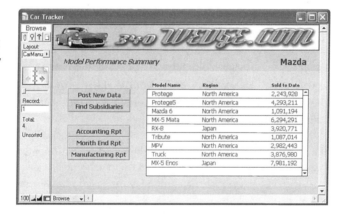

FileMaker Pro allows developers to build *portals* in which related information can be displayed.

UNDERSTANDING THE MECHANICS OF A PORTAL

A *portal* is simply a view into another table and includes rows of specific related records. Developers determine the rules by which records appear in portals, and at times the records displayed can dynamically change or a portal may display other records in the same table you're currently viewing.

→ To explore the depths of advanced portal development techniques, **see** Chapter 16, "Advanced Portal Techniques," **p. 471**.

Most portals have a scrollbar on the right. They feel a bit like List views, and act much the same way. To browse through your related records, simply scroll up and down through the list. Data entry works the same way it does in other areas of FileMaker: Simply click into a field and enter whatever data is appropriate.

At times developers include buttons in portals. In the case that they place a button within a portal, the button in question will appear on each portal row, and each row's button will act on that row's data or record.

CREATING AND DELETING PORTAL ROWS

To create a new portal row—which then creates a new child record—scroll to the first empty row of a portal and click into the blank fields there. *Child records* is a term often used to describe related, hierarchically dependent records—for example, Company and Employee. Employees would be considered children of a Company.

> **NOTE**
>
> Your developer might have turned off the capability to add or delete portal rows, in which case he has likely provided an alternative means of adding related records. Likewise, your developer might have disabled the capability to create new records using the first available row; again, he is likely to have provided an alternative mechanism.

If a developer has allowed for such, you can delete a portal row by following these steps:

1. Click outside the fields of a given portal on the row background. (You might have to mouse around a bit.) You should see the row become highlighted (see Figure 2.18).

2. Press the Backspace or Delete button on your keyboard. You can also use the Records menu. You are prompted as to whether you want to delete that one related record. Click Delete or Cancel to close the dialog box.

Note: It's important to remember that the developer of a given file needs to have turned on this portal behavior.

Figure 2.18
Notice that the sixth row in the displayed portal is highlighted. The delete dialog then pertains to it.

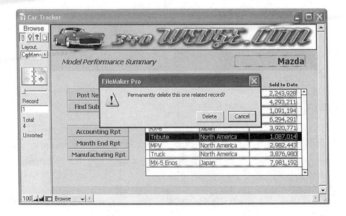

PORTAL SORTING

Sorting records is covered later in the chapter. For now, simply note that a developer determines by what means a portal is sorted and that there is no way for you as a user to change a portal's sort order unless the developer creates a specific mechanism allowing for that option. There are various ways a developer can build a dynamically sortable, command-driven portal, but this is not default behavior in FileMaker Pro.

→ To learn how to build sorting portals, **see** "Dynamic Portal Sorting," **p. 495**.

WORKING WITH A FOUND SET

Up to this point, we've discussed working with a single record and the fields on a given form layout, but at all times FileMaker holds a found set of usually multiple records. Refer to the Status Area on the left of your screen again. Notice the Found and Total numbers. It's also possible that your *found set* contains only one record, or even none; however, generally speaking, you are likely to have many records in your found set.

This is an important point to remember. Even though you may be able to see the contents of only one record's fields (more than likely in Form view), you can still work with either all the records in your table or a subset of such.

Think of it as working with a deck of cards. There are 52 total cards in your deck, some of which are in your hand, and one of which is frontmost—visible. Your current record would be akin to that front card and your found set like those cards in your hand.

In FileMaker many functions apply to a found set. A good example is sorting: You are ordering only those records in your found set.

Many FileMaker Pro databases offer layouts tailored to be viewed either in Form view, where one record encompasses the information on the screen, or in List view, where layouts resemble spreadsheets or tables and display multiple records at once. To grasp visually what we're discussing, see Figure 2.19.

Figure 2.19
List views pull data from multiple records. There is a small black bar in the left margin that indicates which record is current. The active field and the dotted lines indicate that you're currently editing this record.

Working with groups of records is important mainly for comprehension and processing of your information. Data entry usually occurs on one individual record at a time, unless you're importing or performing some other function that applies across multiple records. It's in the reporting and analyzing stage that working with multiple records becomes necessary.

One of the first ways to work with a group of records is to simply scan the list. Nothing beats the human brain for processing information.

Summary fields often lie at the bottom of a List view, as shown in Figure 2.19, and can total numeric data based on a current found set, or perform other summary operations such as counting or averaging.

For a quick example of how this might work, imagine a sales database. If you were to find (or search) for all records in January, your summary fields could then total January's sales. If you were to find again for the year 2003, your totals would be annual. The value of the summary field varies depending on your found set.

If you perform different find requests, the information on your screen can deliver different results, specific to a given group of records.

> **NOTE**
>
> Summary fields are quite powerful, but they do require processor time. If you have a large found set of thousands of records, waiting for a summary field to evaluate can take some time. You can press the Esc key to cancel the summary, or simply avoid scrolling or viewing that portion of a layout. Summary fields evaluate only when they are visible on the screen.

One last important note about found sets: They can be composed of records from only one table. You cannot, for example, display records from an automobile table and a manufacturer table in the same List view or Table view.

USING FIND MODE TO PERFORM A FIND REQUEST

To change your found set in FileMaker, you must perform a find request or search. This usually entails getting into Find mode, and then entering some set of search criteria into the field by which you want to search. FileMaker will then take you back into Browse mode after your search is complete.

To perform find requests in FileMaker, you need to use one of three options to change to Find mode: the tabs at the top of the Status Area, the menu on the bottom left of your application window, or the View menu. Developers may also opt to put various Find buttons into their systems.

After you're in Find mode, FileMaker waits for you to enter data for your find request. A *find request* is a single entry in Find mode that encapsulates the criteria by which you want to perform a search. It behaves and looks much like a record. You enter data into fields just as you would in Browse mode, but instead of saving records, these requests serve as instructions for finding your actual data. You can add a new request, create multiple requests, and delete requests. The requests disappear after the search is actually performed, although it's possible to use the Modify Last Find command (⌘-R) [Ctrl+R] to review (and if necessary modify) the most recently executed set of search requests.

A Find button appears in the Status Area in Find mode. FileMaker Pro enables you to search for any number of criteria throughout your database. Enter whatever fraction of characters or data you want on the same layouts you've used in Browse mode, and then click the Find button. Any records that match your request are then returned as your found set, replacing the set you had before performing the find.

Figure 2.20 shows the full data set in a database of coffee beans (an inventory database).

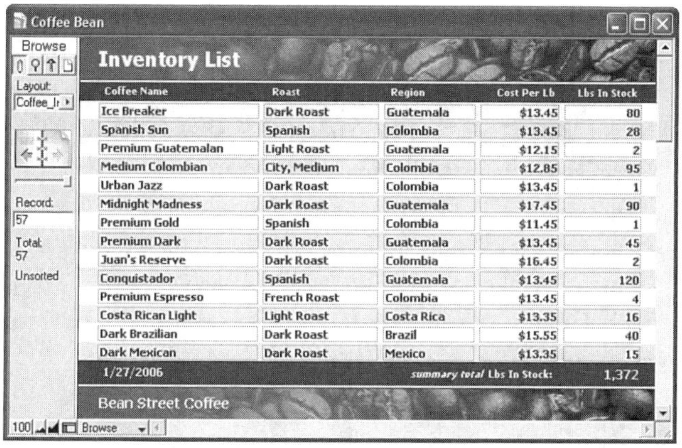

Figure 2.20
Notice that this is the full found set. There's no Found record count, just a total.

To find a specific set of records, you would enter Find mode (choose View, Find mode) and type a criterion by which to search. Refer to Figure 2.21. As an example, you might type Dark Roast in the Roast column and then click Find in the Status Area.

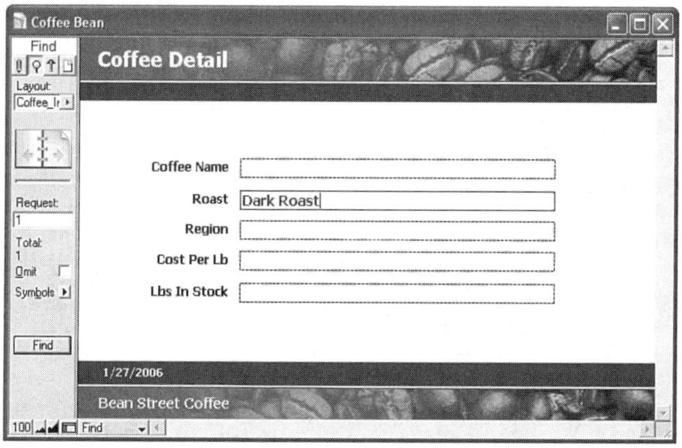

Figure 2.21
FileMaker matches the find criterion "Dark Roast" against the data in the database after you click Find.

Notice in Figure 2.22 that there are eight records in the resultant found set, all of which are dark roasts. Notice also that the summary total changed appropriately.

Figure 2.22
Note that the first record in the set is always the active, or current, record after a find is performed.

If you perform another find, your found set is replaced by the records matching your new requests (see Figure 2.23). In this example, the search criterion was all coffees with <3 in the Lbs in Stock field. The result is four coffees that are almost out of stock. (We'll cover special symbols such as < shortly.)

Figure 2.23
This figure shows a new find request and resultant found set: These four records are of different roasts, but all are low in inventory with less than three pounds in stock.

SEARCH SYMBOLS

To create the found set shown in Figure 2.23, a < (less than) symbol was used to act as an operator on the find request. Switch to Find mode again and notice the symbol menu on the left (see Figure 2.24).

Figure 2.24
Special symbols enable you to search for a wide range of match criteria.

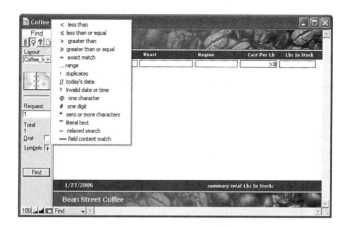

The less than, less than or equal, greater than, greater than or equal, and exact match symbols should be fairly obvious. An entry of >3 finds all records with a value 4 and above. An entry of <=100 finds all records with values of 100 or lower (including zero and negative numbers).

NOTE

> You need not use the symbol menu at all: A < and = typed from your keyboard work just as well as inserting the symbol from the pop-up menu in the Status Area.

The ellipsis (...) for ranges is a commonly used search symbol. The search criterion 1/1/2003...12/31/2006 returns all records for the span of 4 years. (Two or three periods from your keyboard work just as well.)

Use * and # for wildcards. The # symbol is for one digit exactly. An entry of 5# finds all whole numbers from 50 to 59. The # alone finds just numbers 1–9. A 1#1 criterion finds 101, 121, 131, and so on, but not 211 or 1211.

The ~ for relaxed search looks intriguing, doesn't it? Some fuzzy logic, perhaps? No such luck. It's used to search for common base characters in two-byte Asian phonetic alphabets. It doesn't do anything for any other languages.

SHORTCUTS FOR FAST FINDING

The right-click (Control-click for Macs using a one-button mouse) contextual menu for a field in FileMaker will show three "fast match" commands: Find Matching Records, Constrain Found Set, and Extend Found set. Here FileMaker will perform a find request on the data in the field in question. If, say, you right-click on a field containing the term dark roast and choose Find Matching Records, your found set will change to show all dark roast coffee records. Likewise, you can constrain and extend your found set based on the value in the field as well. (We'll cover these concepts in the next section.)

FileMaker 8 also introduced some shorthand date searching capabilities: You can type 2005 in a date field and FileMaker will correctly interpret that to be a "*/*/2005" search that will result in all the records for a given year.

Likewise, you can enter 1 through 12 and FileMaker will assume that you're searching for records within that month for a given year.

Finally, you can search for the names of the days to pull up records specific to days of the week.

MULTIPLE FIND REQUESTS

FileMaker Pro also enables you to perform complex searches involving multiple find requests. To find both the dark roast and the French roast coffees, a user would simply enter Find mode, type dark roast into the appropriate roast field, and then create a new record/request. Just as you can create new records in Browse mode, you can create and delete requests in Find mode. This process is identical to creating a new record in Browse mode. In the second record, a user would enter French roast in the roast field.

A user can flip between requests, using the book icon in the Status Area, and can delete requests as necessary. As soon as the user is satisfied with a series of requests, clicking Find on the left performs the find and returns the user to Browse mode with a new found set.

Multiple find requests can also include requests meant to be omitted. Say that a user wanted to find all the coffees from Colombia but exclude the premium coffees.

Take a look at Figure 2.25. Notice two requests appear in List view, the second of which is active. Notice too the checked Omit check box in the Status Area.

Figure 2.25
Notice which request is applying an Omit request. The prior request is a normal find request with the Omit function turned off. Your result will be all records from Columbia excluding those with "premium" in their names.

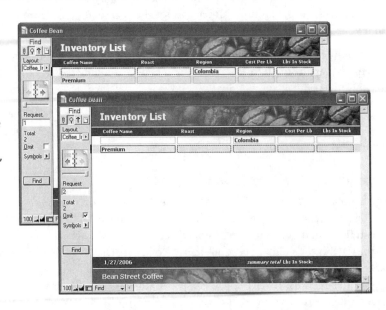

CONSTRAIN AND EXTEND REQUESTS

Performing find requests is all well and good, and as you can imagine, they can become quite complex. For example, you could search for all coffees with "roast" in their names, with 10–14 or more than 20 pounds in stock, excluding those of premium quality from Colombia. Now imagine if, after getting all that put together, you forgot you'd wanted to omit Brazilian coffees as well.

Rather than re-creating your find requests, enter Find mode again and create one request: omit Brazilian. Now instead of clicking the Find button in the Status Area, choose Requests, Constrain Found Set. This new find request will be performed only on the existing found set rather than on the entire database.

Using Requests, Extend Found Set works in a similar fashion by retaining the existing records and simply adding more to them.

For example, if you have a found set of all French roast coffees and decide you want to add Italian roast to this found set of records, you don't have to start the find process over. You simply switch back to Find mode, type Italian roast in the Coffee Roast column, and choose Requests, Extend Found Set. The resulting found set would include both French and Italian roasts: French from your original found set, and Italian from the results of your second find.

MODIFY LAST FIND

Modify Last Find is a great feature for find requests. In Browse mode, choose Records, Modify Last Find. You are placed in Find mode with the last set of Find requests you performed. This is handy if you want to continue to play with a particularly complex set of find requests, or simply are performing a series of similar requests.

FINDING ON MULTIPLE LAYOUTS

FileMaker's find functionality really is quite flexible. While you are in Find mode, it is entirely possible to change layouts. As long as the layouts on which you enter your requests are all associated with the same source table, your find performs just as though you had a layout with all the fields on it you needed. Finding is not layout specific.

Finding is, however, always table specific. Some more advanced FileMaker Pro solutions comprise multiple tables. Although it is possible to search across related information in FileMaker Pro, your find results will always display a found set of records from a single table.

→ To learn more about working with multiple tables, **see** Chapter 6, "Working with Multiple Tables," **p. 157**.

Each layout in your database is associated with a given table. When you perform a find, FileMaker returns your set of records on the layout, from which you may choose Requests, Perform Find, Constrain Found Set, or Extend Found Set.

OMITTING AND SHOWING ALL RECORDS

After performing a find, you can opt to omit individual records from the resultant found set. Choose Records, Omit Record (to omit a single record) or Omit Multiple (to omit a specified number of records).

To restore your found set to the full set of records in your current table, choose Records, Show All Records.

SORTING

When you're working with multiple records, an obvious requirement is the capability to sort. FileMaker doesn't store its records in a sorted order—it stores them in the order in which they were created. When you first open an unsorted table, the records follow that order. There aren't any real mysteries here; for a view of the Sort Records dialog, see Figure 2.26.

Figure 2.26
You can control how a field is sorted: ascending by type (alpha or numeric generally), descending, or in custom order by value list.

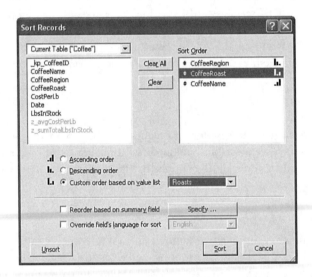

 By default, the Sort Records dialog will show only those fields that are available on your current layout, but you can use the menu in the upper left of the dialog to choose from among all the fields in your database (including those related to the records in your found set).

To sort the records from a table in your database, move fields from the right side of the dialog into the left. There you can choose to have a field sort ascending, descending, or based on the order in which values appear in a specific value list. (Choosing descending, for example, sorts a number field from largest to smallest.)

If you move multiple fields into the dialog, FileMaker sorts all records by the first field, and in cases in which records contain the same values in the first field, FileMaker then uses the second field as an additional criterion.

TIP

> Sorting by value list enables you to set up your own order in which things should appear. For example, if you have a workflow process that flows from Pending to Approved to Complete, you can have your records sort in that order rather than alphabetically.

By adding multiple fields to your sort criteria, you are specifying secondary sorts: First sort by last name, and then by first name, for example.

→ Sorting by summary field is a bit tricky. **See** "Summarized Reports," **p. 287**.

PRINTING

Printing is fairly straightforward in FileMaker. Choose File, Print. In the subsequent dialog that appears, you have the choice to print your found set, just the current record, or a blank record showing field names.

If you'd like to see what something will look like before wasting paper on something you don't want, use Preview mode (via the mode tabs at the top of the Status Area, or the View menu). Choose the layout from which you want to print, and change to Preview mode.

After you're there, you can see where page margins will fall, and the Book icon enables you to step through the pages you will send to the printer. Keep in mind that Preview mode shows you what will be sent to the printer if you choose to print current records.

PRESENTING DATA WITH SUBSUMMARY REPORTS

One prevalent type of report is a subsummary report. A subsummary report enables you to group records that share some bit of common data.

Let's start with a nonsummarized report. For example, a standard List view report might look like the one shown in Figure 2.27.

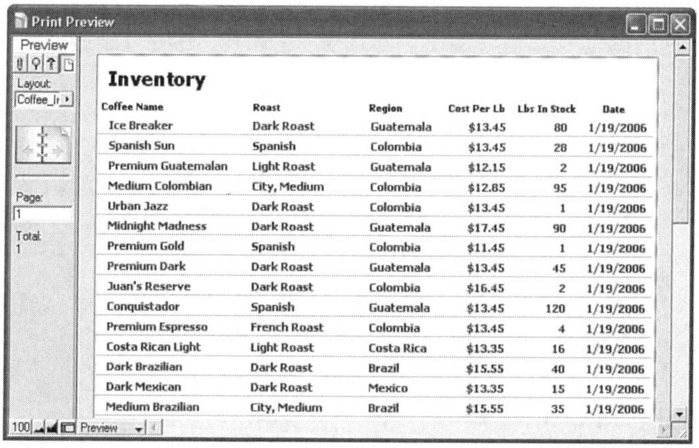

Coffee Name	Roast	Region	Cost Per Lb	Lbs In Stock	Date
Ice Breaker	Dark Roast	Guatemala	$13.45	80	1/19/2006
Spanish Sun	Spanish	Colombia	$13.45	28	1/19/2006
Premium Guatemalan	Light Roast	Guatemala	$12.15	2	1/19/2006
Medium Colombian	City, Medium	Colombia	$12.85	95	1/19/2006
Urban Jazz	Dark Roast	Colombia	$13.45	1	1/19/2006
Midnight Madness	Dark Roast	Guatemala	$17.45	90	1/19/2006
Premium Gold	Spanish	Colombia	$11.45	1	1/19/2006
Premium Dark	Dark Roast	Guatemala	$13.45	45	1/19/2006
Juan's Reserve	Dark Roast	Colombia	$16.45	2	1/19/2006
Conquistador	Spanish	Guatemala	$13.45	120	1/19/2006
Premium Espresso	French Roast	Colombia	$13.45	4	1/19/2006
Costa Rican Light	Light Roast	Costa Rica	$13.35	16	1/19/2006
Dark Brazilian	Dark Roast	Brazil	$15.55	40	1/19/2006
Dark Mexican	Dark Roast	Mexico	$13.35	15	1/19/2006
Medium Brazilian	City, Medium	Brazil	$15.55	35	1/19/2006

Figure 2.27
Notice that this report has been formatted for paper: It is black and white, vertically oriented, ready for printing.

The records are sorted by region. Instead of having a report like this, in which a column simply repeats for dozens of rows, a subsummarized view of this data enables you to collapse the information under a header that represents the group (see Figure 2.28).

Figure 2.28
Visually, this report is far more comprehensible. Your eye can see the delineation between regions instantly.

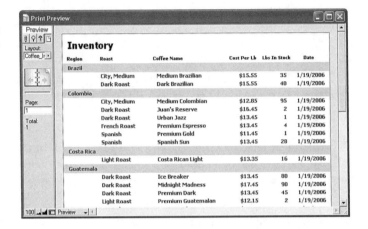

It's possible for a developer to create quite complex reports. More often than not, she will also provide scripts to drive those reports. As a user, you will find it valuable to understand that subsummary reports act on your found set, and, depending on sort criteria, some elements can collapse and be summarized (see Figure 2.29).

Figure 2.29
This somewhat more complex report, complete with formatting, should give you an idea of what's possible in FileMaker Pro.

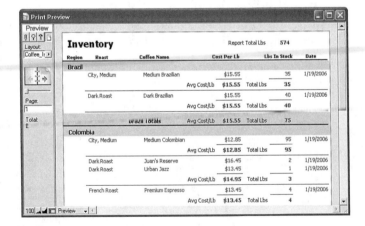

Notice in Figure 2.29 that the data fields with Brazil as a region have been collapsed into subheaders for individual rows.

IMPORTING AND EXPORTING DATA

Having to manually type every bit of data into a database can be an excruciating experience. Fortunately, FileMaker has excellent capabilities for importing data from a wide variety of sources.

Integration with other systems is covered in later chapters. For now, keep in mind that there are options other than spending all day at the keyboard.

Importing and exporting data isn't necessarily for the faint of heart. Depending on how complex your data structure is, you may be somewhat baffled as to how to match the fields of your incoming data with that of your FileMaker system. This is a primary problem all database developers face: getting the information from two different systems to integrate properly.

→ To explore how to bring data, including a directory of images, into your FileMaker Pro solution, **see** Chapter 19, "Importing Data into FileMaker Pro," **p. 567**.

→ To learn about ODBC connectivity and exporting, **see** Chapter 20, "Exporting Data from FileMaker," **p. 595**.

SAVING PDF AND EXCEL DOCUMENTS

It is often the case that you will want to prepare a report in FileMaker and create an electronic document you can then share with your colleagues. From the File menu you can now save directly to PDF or Excel without having to use any third-party software.

Notice also that you can automatically attach your documents to an email, or even use FileMaker to compose an email message from data within your database. This function depends on your having an email client installed on your computer.

→ For more information on saving PDF documents and sending email from FileMaker, refer to "Delivering Reports," **p. 298**.

TROUBLESHOOTING

Most of the trouble you'll run into as a user will be with the issues specific to your own database solutions. The best advice we can offer both developers and users is to work together!

When you run into problems, knowing your developer will be a great first step.

DATA LOSS

I've noticed that I'm suddenly missing some data. What happened? What can I do?

One of the most critical aspects of your database is its namesake: your data. There's a wide range of possible problems that can affect your data, but the most dangerous is accidentally deleting a record…or worse yet, discovering that you had the wrong found set when performing a Delete All Records command. FileMaker doesn't have an undo function, so if a record gets deleted, it's gone forever.

Be sure that you haven't simply altered your found set to exclude the records you're looking for. Go to Records, Show All Records to recall all the data in your table.

Back up your data. We can't stress this point enough. FileMaker Server 8 deployment best practices and backup routines are easy to learn. If you're not using FileMaker Server, just make timestamped copies of your files and store them on CD or on another computer.

DATA INTEGRITY

How do I ensure that the data I have in my database is "good" data?

Making sure that good data is entered into your database is vital. If you properly put people's names in the first name and last name fields of a contact database, but your office assistant decides to enter nicknames and other random tidbits, your data will be compromised.

Also, duplicate data is a problem that plagues all databases everywhere. If you've already created a record for, say, Uryas Forge, you won't want to create a second record for him. What happens if his phone number changes? You'll change one record, but not the other.

Dealing with bad data is a challenge and almost always requires the power of the human brain. Become adept at running find requests. Use the ! mark to find duplicates and use * characters for wildcard characters.

You can also work with your developer to put validation in place, or even build an approval process by which new data is added to your system.

REVERTING RECORDS

What does Revert Record do?

As you enter data into fields, that information is not saved—committed—until you exit the record in question. You do so by clicking outside any fields or by changing modes, changing layouts, and so on. Before the record is committed, you can choose Records, Revert Record. This undoes all the data you've entered while working with active fields. If you've tabbed from field to field, it reverts all those not yet saved. If you have created a new record, it even reverts the entire new record if you've not yet committed it.

FILE CORRUPTION AND FILE RECOVERY

What do I do if a file won't open or says it needs to be recovered?

In the rare case that a file is corrupted, you can attempt to recover it by using the File, Recover command. By recovering a file, FileMaker attempts to create a new copy of your database and rebuild its information, structure, and indices. Generally speaking, this is necessary only in drastic circumstances. It is extremely difficult to corrupt a FileMaker 8 file.

Be careful: If a file fails this consistency check but then is successfully recovered, a prudent user would still import her data into an empty copy of the database backed up before the corruption was evidenced. Then she should be sure to discard both the corrupted and the recovered files. Although FileMaker's technical notes say that a recovered file is good to use, we tend to be extremely conservative where damaged files are concerned.

FILEMAKER EXTRA: BECOMING A FILEMAKER PRO POWER USER

Manipulating data can illuminate a wide range of information and can allow business users to draw conclusions they may not have been able to perceive anecdotally. For example, in our consulting firm, we were able to analyze our time entry data and calculate the average amount of time we need for testing. This helped greatly for future estimating.

Becoming adept at using FileMaker Pro enables you to understand what information you can pull from the system, but, most important, it enables you to know what to ask for. In working with a developer, you can guide that person's priorities (or your own) based on a solid understanding of the platform.

Technique 1: Using Your Keyboard for More Speed

This one's obvious. Entering (⌘-F) [Ctrl+F] brings you into Find mode. Tabbing takes you from field to field. The (Return) [Enter] key executes default values in dialog boxes, performs finds, and so on. (⌘-up arrow) [Ctrl+up arrow] and (⌘-down arrow) [Ctrl+down arrow] page through your data. You'll become much faster with FileMaker Pro if you take the time to learn your key commands. FileMaker's online help details all the key commands available.

→ For a complete list of all keyboard shortcuts in FileMaker, refer to our companion book, *FileMaker 8 Functions and Scripts Desk Reference*.

Technique 2: Working with Table View

User interfaces have their purpose, and more often than not greatly assist data entry and working with a given solution, but if you just need to look at the raw data in your system, you can opt to change to Table view from any layout in FileMaker Pro (assuming that your developer hasn't disabled the option). This gives you a bird's-eye view of your information. Don't forget that clicking on a column header sorts for that column. A second click re-sorts descending.

Technique 3: Replacing Data

Fairly often you'll run across cases in which you need to globally replace some data with other data. For example, perhaps you've changed a value list of vehicle types to read "auto, bike, boat, plane," rather than "bike, boat, car, plane." If you leave things alone after changing the value list, you'll have both "car" and "auto" data in your system. Enforcing the consistent use of terms is important in maintaining your data integrity. To quickly take care of migrating from an old value to a new one, follow these steps:

1. Choose <u>R</u>ecords, Sho<u>w</u> All Records. (Otherwise your change is applied to only your current found set.)

2. Place your cursor into the field in question.

NOTE

In the case of a pop-up menu, you're out of luck. FileMaker Pro doesn't recognize a cursor in a pop-up menu. You need to do a little development (to be covered in Chapter 3, "Defining and Working with Fields"), copy the field to an open spot on your layout, and change its formatting to a pop-up list. Then don't forget to delete the layout field when you're finished.

3. Choose Edit, Find/Replace to open the Find/Replace dialog box (see Figure 2.30).

Figure 2.30
Find/Replace can step through your records, or can be applied across the entire database. Be careful: These functions cannot be undone!

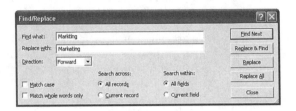

4. Type your old and new values.

5. Choose All from the Direction drop-down menu (so that your entire database will be covered).

6. Depending on your preferences, choose Current Field or apply your change to entire records. We recommend just the selected field because that's much safer than accidentally changing all instances of a text string.

7. Click Replace All.

CAUTION

It's important to note: This is a function that cannot be undone! Be sure that you know what you're doing with your data.

TECHNIQUE 4: INSERTING SPECIFIC INFORMATION

The Insert menu is an oft-ignored source of handy time-saving commands. From a single menu choice or keyboard command, you can insert the current time, the current date, or your username into an active field.

In addition to that, Insert, From Index allows you to select from all the values in a given field from all records in a database. If you can't quite remember the spelling of a given item, or simply want to be perfectly consistent, this is a great way to see the data in your system and make a compatible selection. (This works only if the field in question allows indexing.)

→ To learn about field indexing, **see** "Storage and Indexing," **p. 86**.

Finally, there's a handy way to pull data from another record in your database. If three or four fields need to contain identical data to another record in your database, visit the source record first, and then via a List view or Table view jump (by clicking on the appropriate row) to the destination record. Click into the specific fields you want and choose Insert, From Last Visited Record.

TECHNIQUE 5: GETTING TO KNOW YOUR ENTIRE DATABASE

This item isn't so much a technique as it is just common sense: One of the best ways to make the most of a FileMaker database is to learn how it works. Review all the layouts in your system, take a look at the fields you see, and explore other files (if there are others) in the solution. Be sure to discuss with your developer how the information fits together.

TECHNIQUE 6: USING MULTITIERED SORTS

Sorting can be a fairly powerful way to derive meaning and see patterns in data. To make the most of the Sort Records dialog, don't forget that you can provide multiple sort criteria. For example, in a contacts database you could sort by Last Name, First Name, City, descending by Age, and finally by Pet Name.

You can also sort by the custom order of a value list. If you have, say, a status field that is managed by a value list of "open, pending, closed," you can sort by that order.

TECHNIQUE 7: USING MULTIPLE WINDOWS

FileMaker provides you with a Window menu. If you'd like to work with multiple layouts at once, choose Window, New Window, and then navigate to the second layout in question (using either the Layout pop-up menu in the Status Area or the buttons a developer has provided).

Multiple windows are also useful when you open two windows looking at the same List view layout: It's possible for you to have two separate found sets. Imagine finding all the invitees of an event in one window and all the people who you've not yet invited in the other.

TECHNIQUE 8: APPLYING TEXT STYLING AND TABS

You can apply a wide range of formatting options to text within FileMaker Pro fields: bold, italic, font choice, color choice, and so on (see Figure 2.31). This information is preserved within FileMaker Pro, and you can copy and paste formatted text with other applications. For formats that support it, such as XML, you can export formatting as well.

Figure 2.31
You have a wide range of control over text appearance in FileMaker Pro.

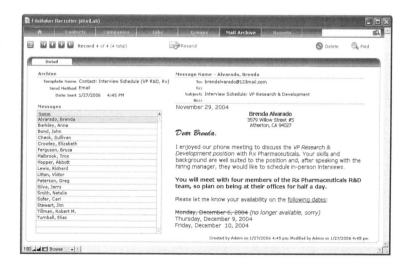

There is another neat trick in FileMaker Pro: In any field you can establish an internal tab placement and apply tabs by using (⌘-Tab) [Ctrl+Tab]. Choose View, Text Ruler. When you click into a field, a horizontal ruler appears above it, into which you can click to establish tabs. Double-click on a tab to set its properties: left, center, right, align to character, and whether to use a fill character.

2

CHAPTER **3**

DEFINING AND WORKING WITH FIELDS

In this chapter

WORKING UNDER THE HOOD

Fields are the heart of any database. By storing information in properly categorized fields, you impart both function and meaning to what would otherwise be an incomprehensible pile of raw data.

We'll spend much of this chapter describing what kinds of fields exist in FileMaker Pro, how they store information, and how to ensure proper data integrity in your database solutions.

If you're new to development in FileMaker Pro, this chapter is a good place to start. No doubt some of the topics we cover will lack a certain context, but establishing a solid foundation in field definition is a vital part of becoming a practiced developer.

If you have built a few FileMaker Pro databases, you may need only to skim this chapter. Of the topics we cover here, indexing is likely the most advanced; our discussion explores some subtle differences from prior versions of FileMaker Pro.

NEW DATABASES BEGIN WITH FIELD DEFINITIONS

To create a new database, simply launch FileMaker Pro and then choose File, New Database. You'll be presented with the option to start with a template or to create a new, empty file. To create a file of your own, select the Create a New Empty File option and click OK.

After you've stepped through these first tasks, you'll be taken to the Define Fields dialog.

Working with Templates

We recommend that you go back at some point and work with the templates that ship with FileMaker. They're a good learning tool, and you will be able to see how fields are defined in these finished solutions. There are dozens of templates, they're not all that complicated, and they'll give you some good ideas for designing your own solutions. From them you can learn about simple user interfaces and calculation functions and can see some basic scripts in action as well.

USING THE DEFINE DATABASE DIALOG

When you choose to start on a new, empty database, FileMaker Pro creates a file for you and automatically opens the Define Database dialog (shown in Figure 3.1). As a developer, you'll spend a good bit of time in the three tabs in this dialog. FileMaker Pro's Define Database dialog allows you to create the fields, tables, and relationships you need in order to form your database. It also enables you to modify a wide range of attributes associated with fields, such as auto-entry functions, validation, storage, and calculation formulas. It is these elements that compose a database's structure or *schema*. It is here that you form your database behind the scenes.

> **NOTE**
> Notice the active table in Figure 3.1. The fields you define are associated with this selected table.

Figure 3.1
The three tabs allow you to switch among defining tables, fields, and relationships.

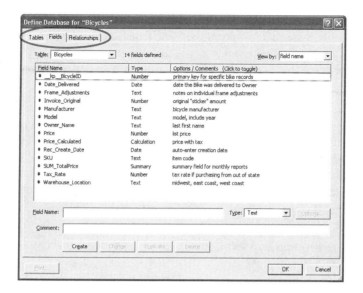

FileMaker Pro will have already created a default table for you, named the same as the file itself. Notice the Table menu selection on the Fields tab of the dialog in Figure 3.1. Any fields you create will be created in that table.

→ For some basic information on tables, **see** "Understanding Tables," **p. 31**.

→ For a detailed discussion of multiple-table solutions, **see** Chapter 6, "Working with Multiple Tables," **p. 157**.

Notice the third tab in the Define Database dialog: Relationships. We won't be covering multitable relational databases in this chapter, but it is on that tab that you'd create the relational associations among tables in your solution.

→ For information on relational data modeling, **see** Chapter 5, "Relational Database Design," **p. 129**.

> **TIP**
>
> Commenting is a vital discipline to develop. Spending a few moments to add information to the Comment text box, below the field name, as you create something will save time later in trying to figure out what you were thinking at the time.
>
> To view comments, toggle between options and comments at the top of your field list.

WORKING WITH FIELDS

Every table in any database—FileMaker Pro or otherwise—is a collection of information stored in fields (or columns, if you're familiar with that terminology). It is by storing information in appropriate fields that a database is given meaning.

For example, by entering "124 Main Street" in a field called Address, we've identified what "124 Main Street" is. In the case of a street address, it's fairly easy to identify without a field definition, but what about "912.5" all on its own? That could be a price, a number of units, a chapter heading, or a thousand other things. When you place that number into a named column or field, your data becomes meaningful. If "912.5" sat in a field named Temperature, you'd likely conclude that it is pretty darn hot. Conversely, if it sat in a Kilobytes Available field, you'd look to be buying a new hard drive. Keep this ultimate goal of imparting meaning in mind as you create and name fields, and assign appropriate data types to them.

FIELD NAMING CONVENTIONS

One of the nice things about FileMaker Pro development is the freedom developers have in naming fields. (FileMaker Pro is not unique in allowing developers field naming freedom, by the way.) That freedom also, unfortunately, gives rise to confusion and arbitrary naming conventions. Name_xTJm2 may mean something to someone, or Name might also, but both examples—the overly specific and the overly general—require a strong familiarity with a given system. If you ever return to a database months after building it, odds are you will have forgotten your clever abbreviations.

→ For a complete presentation of Soliant Consulting's coding standards, **see** Chapter 27, "Documenting Your FileMaker Solutions," **p. 841**.

We encourage you to take advantage of FileMaker's allowance for long field names of up to 100 characters. Use full text names (like Street Address line1), avoid abbreviations (or if you use them, be sure to provide an obvious key!), and try to group things logically. Note that although FileMaker allows for spaces and special characters, we recommend using underscores, letters, and numerals only.

Here's an example of what we'd consider a fairly reasonable approach to naming fields:

- Address_City
- Address_Postal_Code
- Address_State
- Address_Street_line1
- Address_Street_line2

- Person_Name_First
- Person_Name_Last
- Phone_Home
- Phone_Work

These fields are quite simple to identify and are neatly grouped together when sorted alphabetically. This isn't such a big deal for small databases, but if you ever work on a large database, with multiple developers, a well-established naming convention is vital. We encourage you to adopt good programming habits right from day one.

Another common approach many developers use includes abbreviations for data types. Often it's handy to know the data type of a given field when working with it without having to refer to the Define Database dialog. Here we've used "t" for text, "n" for number, and "c" for calculation:

- ProductName_t
- Price_n
- TaxRate_n
- Tax_c

We'll cover indexing later in the chapter, but some developers also note whether a field is indexed ("x" for indexed, "n" for unindexed):

- Location_Name_tx
- Location_Desc_tn
- Location_Size_nn

Some naming conventions also break out a division between data fields and what are commonly referred to as *developer fields*—those fields that you need only to make your FileMaker Pro solution work. If you ever went to import your database wholesale into another system, these fields would probably be left behind. Here we have two abbreviations: "k" for key (or match field), and "z" (so that it sorts to the bottom of the list) for developer utility fields. We also use underscores to ensure that keys sort to the top of our field list, with the primary key coming first.

→ To understand how keys are used to identify records in tables and form relationships, **see** Chapter 5, "Relational Database Design," **p. 129**.

- __kp_primary_AlbumID
- _kf_foreign_ArtistID
- AlbumName
- Date
- z_SelectedPortalRow
- z_UserColor_Preference
- z_UserGenre_Preference

Finally, here's a real example from a database we recently were hired to modify (used with permission and good humor!):

- Bike Type
- Wheel Dm
- Bike Name
- Model
- Type
- Temp
- Date
- Bike
- Bike2
- Sp.99 Meas
- Tire Dm
- Bikeid
- Sku
- 2002 Tire Diam
- 1999 Tire Diam
- BikeMODEL
- SUMMARY
- zTempzzz
- Phils field (no lie!)

We're sure that we've belabored the point, but this database was difficult to modify not because it was complex, but because it was hard to interpret. As in all things, a little planning goes a long way.

 If you're planning on using FileMaker Pro as a web back end, refer to "Problematic Field Names" in the "Troubleshooting" section at the end of this chapter.

→ For more information on using databases on the Web, **see** "Designing for IWP Deployment," **p. 648**, as well as Chapter 23, "Custom Web Publishing," **p. 699**.

→ For more thoughts on documenting and commenting in your database, **see** Chapter 27, "Documenting Your FileMaker Solutions," **p. 841**.

There are some restrictions on field naming in FileMaker Pro: A field name must be unique within its table, and must be less than 100 characters in length.

You can opt to use special characters, numbers, spaces, even the names of functions, but we recommend against using them. If you use , (comma), +, -, *, /, ^, &, =, ≠, >, <, (,), ", ; (semicolon), : (colon), or :: (double colon relationship indicator), you need to enclose such special characters within a $() in calculation formulas to have them interpreted as field names. For example, the calculation $(Tax,special) returns the value of a field named Tax,special.

We recommend strongly that you name fields without using special characters, names of functions, or operators (AND, OR, NOT, XOR, TRUE, FALSE).

The same is true for fields that begin with a space, a period, or a number: You'll have to contort your calculations to deal with them. Don't use them. Begin each field with a standard alphabetical letter or an underscore.

ADDING FIELD COMMENTS

Notice also that you can add comments to your field definitions. We don't mean to be pedantic, but we want to drive home that establishing good programming habits will serve you well for the rest of your life as a developer. Use the field comments feature. Explain to yourself a year from now why a field exists, any dependencies or assumptions you made, and possibly how you intend to use it.

CREATING NEW FIELDS

To create fields in FileMaker Pro, you need to enter some text in the Field Name area of the Define Database dialog and click Create.

One important aspect of databases to keep in mind is that it's important to establish a discrete field for each bit of information you want to store. If you create a field called Contact Information and cram an entire address and a set of phone numbers into it, technically it will work fine, but if it ever comes time to export that information, sort by area code, or run a report by city, you won't be able to cull the information you want from the field without suffering from a good headache.

→ To database wonks, the Contact Information example would be a violation of first normal form, or more colloquially, "one fact, one field." For information on relational data modeling and defining fields, **see** "Relationship Types," **p. 136**.

WORKING WITH FIELD TYPES

One of the most important aspects of understanding FileMaker Pro is understanding field types, how they're different from one another, and how to use them effectively.

Simply stated, field types identify what kind of information each field of your database is expected to hold. A person's name is text, the dollar amount for a transaction is a number, a birthday is a date, and so on. Generally it should be quite clear to you what each needs to be.

Field types determine what types of operations can be performed on a given field, what information a field can accept, and the rules by which a field is sorted. It's the combination of a proper identifying field name and a data type definition that gives a database its context and meaning.

Text

Text fields are the most free-form of the field types. Users can enter any range of information in them, including carriage returns, and there's no expectation of what form or sort of information a text field will hold. The only requirement is that it be character based—in other words, you can't place a picture in a text field. A text field can store up to 2GB of information, limited by RAM and hard drive space, of course, and indexes up to approximately 100 characters, depending on what language you're using. We'll cover indexing in more depth later in the chapter. For now, simply remember that each field type has different limits and approaches on indexing.

Number

Number fields can store values from 10^{-400} up to 10^{400}, and negative values in the same range. FileMaker Pro indexes the first 400 significant digits (numbers, decimal points, or signs) of a number field, ignoring letters and other symbols. Number fields can accept text (although not carriage returns), but any text in a numeric field is ignored. FileMaker interprets 12ax3 as 123 if you enter it into a numeric field, for example.

Something to keep in mind with FileMaker Pro: A number field can be expressed as a Boolean. A Boolean value is either true or false, and is often used to test the condition of something. A zero or null value in a number field is treated as false in the Boolean sense; any other data is treated as true. You will often run across number fields being used to store Boolean values.

The primary distinction between a number field and a text field lies in how they're sorted: A text field sorts 1, 10, 2, 20, 3, 4, 5, whereas a number field sorts 1, 2, 3, 4, 5, 10, 20.

Date

Date fields accept Gregorian calendar dates only. FileMaker Pro honors whatever date formatting your country follows by taking the standard your operating system uses at the time a new file is created. Date formats—the order of year, month, and day—are common for a given file. Although it's possible to change the way dates are displayed, it is this basic ordering that is fixed at the time of file creation.

Dates in FileMaker Pro are internally stored as the number of days since 01/01/0001. January 1, 2004, for instance, is 731581. If you need to compare dates or perform any functions on them, remember that behind the scenes they're really just numbers. This feature is actually quite handy. To switch a date to a week prior, all you need to do is subtract seven.

Date fields can store values from January 1, 0001, to December 31, 4000.

 If your fields are sorting or displaying oddly, refer to "Mismatched Data Types" in the "Troubleshooting" section at the end of this chapter.

Time

Time fields hold HH:MM:SS.ddd information. Notice that a decimal may be added to the end. Also useful: If a user enters 25:00, FileMaker Pro rightly interprets this as 1:00 a.m.

99:30 becomes 3:30 a.m. The clock simply keeps rolling over. This behavior is useful when you need to add, say, 30 hours to a time, and don't want to be bothered with calculating what hour that becomes. Likewise, if you are doing data entry in a time-tracking system and don't want to create two entries for a case in which you worked from 2:00 p.m. until 2:00 a.m. on Monday (really Tuesday), entering `26:00` for the ending time in your system rightly calculates to 12 hours.

As in dates, FileMaker Pro stores time internally as the number of seconds from 12:00:00 on the current day. 1 is 12:00:01, and 43200 is 12:00 p.m. As with date formats, your time format is established during the creation of the file, based on system operating system settings.

The maximum time value you can store in a FileMaker Pro time field is 2,147,483,647. That's a lot of time.

TIMESTAMP

The timestamp data type combines date and time information. It appears as a field with both date and time values, separated by a space: 1/1/2004 12:00:00. As in date and time formats, timestamps are also stored as numbers: the count of seconds from 1/1/0001 00:00:00. Be prepared to work with large numbers when using this field type. Timestamps are an important aid to interoperability with other databases (such as those powered by the SQL language), which often store date and time information in a single timestamp field.

The maximum value of a timestamp is 12/31/4000 11:59:59.999999 p.m. or 126,227,764,799.999999 seconds.

TIP

To extract just the date from timestamp data, simply use the `GetAsDate()` function. Likewise, use `GetAsTime()` to extract just the time.

CONTAINER

Container fields are different from the five already mentioned: They store binary information. Information is often inserted into container fields rather than being entered manually (you can copy and paste). You can place any sort of digital document in your database, limited again by the practical limits of your computer hardware, up to 4GB.

Container fields also support displaying/playing three native types of media: pictures, QuickTime movies, and sounds. Refer to the FileMaker help system for supported formats, but most common image formats are included...as well as some you won't expect. For example, by using QuickTime, it's possible to display and play a Macromedia Flash 5 `.swf` file.

Last, on Windows, a wide range of OLE objects are supported, including Microsoft Excel documents, PDF, and more.

There's one important thing to remember about using container fields: Either you can store the file or media in FileMaker itself—requiring disk space—or you can simply store a path reference to the file instead. If you choose to store just a reference to the file, FileMaker

Pro, somewhat like a web browser, displays the image or file icon as necessary, but does not hold the actual document itself. A nice feature of storing references is that you can then double-click documents in your container fields to launch them in your operating system.

CAUTION

> Keep in mind that if you move the source document, the FileMaker Pro reference remains but is no longer valid.

CALCULATION

Calculation fields evaluate formulas and display the requisite results. When you create a calculation field, the Specify Calculation dialog, shown in Figure 3.2, opens.

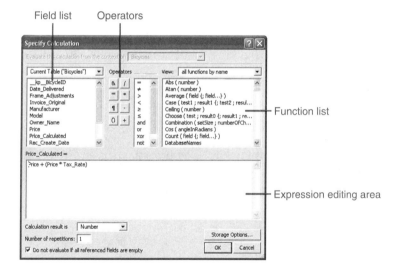

Figure 3.2
Calculations form an essential pillar of FileMaker Pro development.

→ Be sure to refer to FileMaker Pro's online help or our companion book, *FileMaker 8 Scripts and Functions Desk Reference*, for a complete list of functions. The book presents every function in FileMaker along with discussion and examples.

The features of the Specify Calculation dialog box include the following:

- **Field list**—Select fields to include in your calculation from the list below the table menu. Use the drop-down menu to change from table to table. Note that double-clicking inserts a field into your calculation where your cursor currently sits.

- **Operators**—Use these buttons to insert math and special operators.

- **Function list**—Just below the View drop-down menu is a list of functions. Here you're able to scroll through all of FileMaker Pro's various functions and then double-click to insert. It's a good idea to start here to get your syntax correct.

  The menu above enables you to filter your list by category to show the functions you need.

- **Expression text box**—This is where you assemble your actual formula or expression. This is a simple text entry area: If you want, work in a text editor and paste calculations here.

- **Calculation Result Is list**—Calculations return varying information, depending on what data/field type is required. If you want the field to be sortable by alphabet, set the return data type to Text. If you have a field returning, say, a price, set the type to Number.

Examples of calculations include the following:

- `3 + 4` always displays its result of 7.

- `Sale + Tax` displays the sum of two fields named Sale and Tax.

- `Position ( Notes; "a"; 1; 1 )` returns a numeric position, starting from the first character in the field Notes, for the first "a" found.

- `IsEmpty ( MyField )` returns a zero or one (Boolean) depending on whether MyField has a value in it, including zero. If a zero is entered, the field is technically not empty. Only a null value is considered empty.

- `If ( MyDate > 900; "yes" ; "no" )` displays a `yes` for dates entered in `MyDate` greater than 6/19/0003; otherwise, it displays `no`. (Remember that you've just tested for the number of days past 1/1/0001.)

Calculations are fundamental to FileMaker programming, and it's worth your while to master them fully.

→ For more detail on calculations, **see** Chapter 8, "Getting Started with Calculations," **p. 217**, and Chapter 14, "Advanced Calculation Techniques," **p. 391**.

 If your calculation formula looks correct, but FileMaker is returning an odd result or ?, refer to "Mismatched Calculation Results" in the "Troubleshooting" section at the end of this chapter.

SUMMARY

Summary fields allow you to evaluate information across a found set of records. Sum, Average, Max, Min, and Count are among the summaries you can establish. Don't forget that they apply to found sets: Change your found set, and the result changes.

For example, say you have a table called Transaction, which contains Transaction_Date and Transaction_Amount fields. You can then define and place on a layout a summary field to total the Transaction_Amount field. The summary field adds the values of the Transaction_Amount field for whatever set of records is currently active. If you perform a find, by date, on 10/1/2006–10/31/2006, your found set will be all the transactions for the month of October, and the summary field will show just the aggregate monthly transaction amount. Perform a different find request and your total changes, reflecting the aggregate of the new found set.

Table 3.1 contains a list of summary field functions.

TABLE 3.1 SUMMARY FIELD FUNCTIONS

Function	Summary Behavior
Total of	Adds values from the specified field in your found set. Think of it as a subtotal or grand total from a column of numbers. You may also enable the option to display a running total for your recordset. This then shows a running tally of your total if you place the summary field in the body area of a list.
Average of	Averages the values from the specified field in your found set. The weighted average option enables you to specify a second field to act as a weight factor for calculating the average. The field you choose must be a number or a calculation with a number result.
Count of	Counts the number of records in your found set that have valid data in the specified field. For example, if 18 of the 20 current found records have data, your summary field will display 18. A running count functions similarly to a running total: It displays the incremented count of each record in your found set.
Minimum	Returns the lowest number, date, time, or timestamp in a given found set from the referenced field.
Maximum	Returns the highest number, date, time, or timestamp in a given found set from the referenced field.
Standard Deviation of	Determines how widely the values in the referenced field differ. Returns the standard deviation from the mean of the values in your found set. The standard deviation formula is n–1 weighted, following the normal standard deviation. Standard deviation comes in two flavors; to perform a biased or n–0 evaluation, select the By Population option.
Fraction of Total of	Returns the ratio of a total for which a given record (or set of records, when the field is placed in a subsummary part) is responsible. For example, you can track what percentage of sales are attributable to a given person. The subtotaled option enables you to specify a second field by which to group your data.

When you create a summary field, the Options for Summary Field dialog opens, prompting you to choose the function you want to use and the field for which you want a summary (see Figure 3.3).

It's generally a good idea to place summary fields on their own layouts so that a user deliberately chooses to have them evaluate a found set.

Figure 3.3
Summary fields are useful for performing functions across sets of records, but use them with care. They can increase the time it takes to load any given layout.

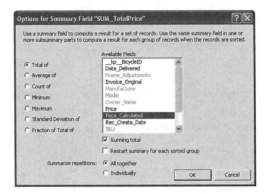

In Browse mode a summary field will evaluate your found set and display a result when it is actually visible on a layout. For example, if a summary field is below the visible portion of a layout, it will display information only when the user scrolls to that portion of the window.

Summary fields will evaluate a found set for a given layout whenever you enter Preview mode.

ASSIGNING FIELD OPTIONS

In addition to establishing fields and assigning data types, you may assign various options to your fields as well. These range in function from managing auto-entry of default data to validation checks and internal storage settings. They can vary for each field type.

After you have named a field and chosen its type on the Fields tab of the Define Database dialog box, click Create to save it to your database. You may then opt to apply further behaviors via the Options button on the right. The first set of options is the auto-entry behaviors.

AUTO-ENTRY FIELD OPTIONS

When defining noncalculation fields in FileMaker Pro, you can choose to have data automatically entered into a field as records are created and/or modified. The applications for this can range from assigning default values to fields, to automatically reformatting data, or inserting values from other fields based on certain trigger events.

In some cases you might also want to prevent users from modifying these auto-generated values, such as when tracking a serial ID or applying a date you don't want adjusted afterward (see Figure 3.4).

Auto-entry data is inserted into a field based on some trigger event. The most common event is record creation: When a user clicks New Record, data can be prepopulated into the record and then be accessible for changes to be made. Each Auto-entry function has its own particular rules for what trigger event applies.

In addition to new record creation, other trigger events include record modification and modification of a particular field. We will cover both cases in the sections that follow.

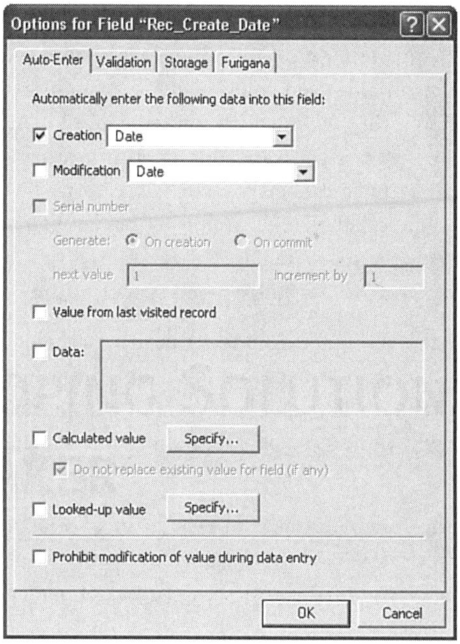

Figure 3.4
FileMaker's auto-entry options allow you to define rules for automatically populating data into fields in your database.

CREATION AND MODIFICATION

The first two options on the Auto-Enter tab deal with tracking and applying certain values as a record is committed to your database. They behave essentially the same way, with Creation values being applied the first time a record is committed, and Modification values applied thereafter as it is subsequently modified (committed again).

Values that can be automatically entered include the current date, current time, current timestamp, current username (from the General tab of the Preferences dialog under the Edit menu), or current account name (the one entered by the user when logging in to the database).

CAUTION

The name is something users can modify as they want via FileMaker's Preferences dialog, so you generally shouldn't depend on it for anything vital. If you want to depend on knowing who has created or modified a given record using auto-entry functions, always use the Account Name option.

NOTE

If you do not change any of the account settings of a new file, FileMaker will have established two default accounts for you: Guest and Admin. Both begin with full access to the database.

SERIAL NUMBER

Using this option allows you to auto-enter a number that increments every time a new record is added to the table. Often this is used to uniquely identify individual records in a table. The value can be generated either when the record is created or when it is committed. The difference is subtle: In the case of incrementing on creation, your number increments even if a user then reverts and effectively cancels a record's creation. The next record will then have skipped a number in your sequence. This doesn't have much of an effect on your database unless your business requires strict tracking of each serial number, even those voided. In those cases, choosing On Commit helps avoid spaces in the sequence.

It is possible to include text characters in addition to a number as the starting value if you want. This enables you to create serial numbers that look something like "a1, a2, a3, a4...." Only the rightmost numeric portion of the value is incremented; the text portion remains unchanged. If you do this, you will want to use a Text field to allow for the alphanumeric combination.

One of the common uses of auto-entry options is in establishing serialized key values, or IDs. This is a vital element of your database structure when you're working with more than one table, but regardless of how complex or simple your plans are, we encourage you to adopt some best practices.

For every table in your database, the first field you should create is a primary key or ID field. It is these IDs that uniquely identify each record in your database. There are several ways you could go about having the system establish unique IDs automatically; our recommendation in most cases is to use a serial number set to increment automatically.

We can't stress this practice strongly enough. If you ever want to tackle relational data structures, these serial IDs are a vital element in doing so. Further, if you ever export your data to another system or need to interact with other databases, having a key field that uniquely identifies each record in your database will guard against confusion or even possible loss of data integrity.

To create a serial key field, use the following steps:

1. Define a number field. (It is generally advisable to use number-based serial keys, but it is possible to use text as well; the important thing is to make certain your keys are unique and unmodifiable.)
2. Go into the Options for that field and select the Serial Number option.
3. Click the Prohibit Modification of Value During Data Entry option at the bottom of the dialog. This is an important step: If you establish unique identifiers that your users can then override, you're risking the chance that they'll introduce duplicate IDs.

If you need an ID field for a business purpose (SKUs, student IDs, employee IDs from your organization, and so on), we recommend that you create separate fields for such cases. Generally, users should never need to access this serialized ID field, but you can opt to put it on a layout and allow entry in Find mode so that they can search if they choose.

→ For a full discussion of the use of keys (or *match fields*), **see** the discussion in "Working with Keys and Match Fields," **p. 162**.

VALUE FROM LAST VISITED RECORD

Used most often as a way to speed data entry when information is often repeated for groups of records, this function copies the value from a prior record into a given new record. Bear in mind that "Visited" means the last record in which you entered data. If you enter data in a record, and then view a second record without clicking into a field and activating it, it is the data from the first, edited record from which a new record obtains its value.

DATA

Here you may specify literal text for auto-entry. This is frequently used to set default states for field entry. For instance, in an Invoice table, you might have a text field called Status where you want to enter Not Paid as a default. Being a regular text field, the value is still fully modifiable by a user.

CALCULATED VALUE

In addition to establishing a field as a calculation field, where its value will always be determined by its defined formula, it is possible to insert the results of a calculation into a field of another type—including a container field—by using an auto-entry option.

Furthermore, if you uncheck the Do Not Replace Existing Value for Field (If Any) option, the results of the calculation formula will be entered into the field, overriding any existing value, anytime a field referenced by the calculation changes.

Put differently, any field referenced in your calculation statement acts as a trigger—anytime that referenced field is updated, the calculation will be retriggered, and its result put back into the auto-entry field. In fact, the auto-entry field itself can act as such a trigger, if it's referenced in the auto-entry calculation. This enables you to dynamically reformat data as it is entered. One great example of this is a phone number field. You may always want phone numbers formatted as "(123) 456-7890" regardless of how a user entered the data. By using a calculated auto-entry function, you can reformat the phone number anytime it's modified.

For an example of this technique, refer to Figure 3.5.

The actual calculation for this auto-entry option looks like this (returned as text):

```
Let ( [
    //define variables:

rawNumber = Filter (Phone_Number; "0123456789") ;
length = Length (rawNumber);
red = RGB (160;0;0);

    //set error flag for a phone number that's too short
error = If ( length < 10 ; TextColor ("error: " & Phone_Number; red); "")

];
    // now apply the phone formatting and return results
```

```
If ( error ≠ ""; error;

    "(" & Left (rawNumber; 3) & ") " & Middle (rawNumber; 4; 3) &
    "-" & Middle (rawNumber; 7; 4) &

    // this condition tests for extra digits
    that we'll treat as an extension
    If ( length > 10; " x" & Middle (rawNumber; 11; length - 10); "")

)
)
```

Figure 3.5
By using a self-referencing calculation, FileMaker Pro is able to replace and correct data as it is entered by the user.

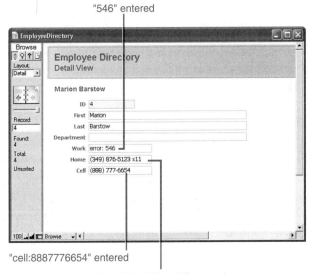

"546" entered

"cell:8887776654" entered

"349.876.5123 x-11" entered

Here the calculation is written as though it were being applied to a field called Phone_Number. To get the results shown in Figure 3.5, you would need to either redefine the calculation for each of the three fields shown, or (better) define a single custom function that contains the bulk of the logic in the preceding listing, and call that function from the auto-entry calculation for each field you want to filter in this way.

→ To learn more about advanced calculation functions, including custom functions, **see** Chapter 14, "Advanced Calculation Techniques," **p. 391**.

→ To see a version of this function that works more flexibly and for international formats, see our companion book, *FileMaker 8 Functions and Scripts Desk Reference*.

LOOKED-UP VALUE

This auto-entry option copies a value from a record in a related table into a field in the current table. Anytime the field controlling your association to the related record changes, FileMaker Pro updates the value in the lookup field.

For example, if a user enters a ZIP code into a given record, it's possible you could have another table and then auto-populate your city and state fields with the appropriate information.

When a user enters a ZIP code in the record in Figure 3.6, the City and State fields below are triggered to pull values from the ZipCodes table. An important fact to keep in mind is that FileMaker has *copied* the values from the ZipCodes table. If the source data changes or is deleted, this record remains unmodified until it is retriggered by someone editing the Zip Code field again.

Figure 3.6
Lookup functions work somewhat like relational data, but instead of displaying values from a related record, their information is copied and stored when a trigger event occurs.

Take special note that lookup auto-entry functions work just as all auto-entry functions do: They copy or insert information into a field. You are not displaying related information, nor are you controlling content by calculation. Thus, lookup values are not live links to related data. If you were to delete the records in the ZipCodes table in the preceding example, all your people records would remain untouched, preserving your city and state data.

This is an important distinction to understand, especially as we get into indexing later in this chapter. Consider an example for product prices: If you were to build an Orders database that tracked the prices of products, you'd want to store the price of each Order line item or product within the order itself. That way if your prices ever change, your historical orders will preserve their original prices.

To see how to create a lookup field, refer to Figure 3.7.

Remember that anytime your match field changes, your lookup refreshes. In this case, the auto-entry function does not act on record creation, but rather on committing/triggering.

When you're performing a lookup, it is possible to work with near matches, in addition to exact matches. In the case of the ZIP codes example, obviously you'd want only an exact match or you might end up with incorrect data. In a different case, however, you need not be so strict. Consider a scheduling system that automatically finds the closest available appointment: Enter a target date into a field, and the lookup function could return the closest match. Another application might be a parts database with units of measurement. You may not be able to find a .78" wrench, but a .75" might work. This sort of requirement is easy to meet by using the Copy Next Lower Value setting.

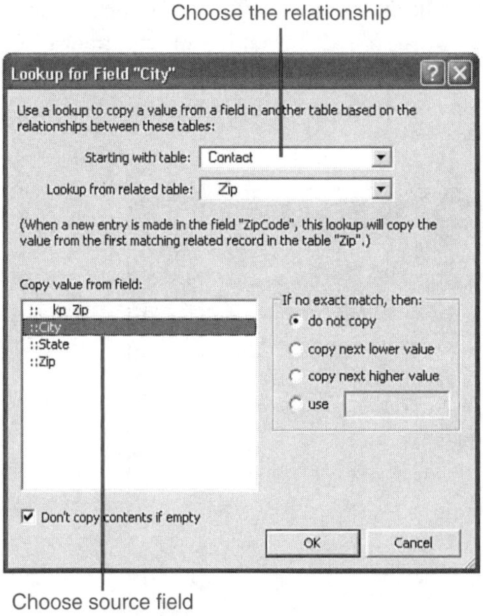

Choose the relationship

Figure 3.7
Often you'll want only exact matches, but in some cases you can use the closest value based on a compari-son of the trigger val-ues in your related table.

Choose source field

How you set up your trigger values is important here. It's easy to compare numbers and come up with the next closest value. If your trigger field is text, FileMaker Pro uses ASCII value rules to compare and determine order.

→ For further discussion of lookups, **see** Chapter 6, "Working with Multiple Tables," **p. 157**.

HOUSEKEEPING CREATION AND MODIFICATION FIELDS

As a best practice, we also recommend that you create another set of fields in all tables that help track changes. Create a timestamp field and in the Auto-Enter options, choose Creation Timestamp. Define another for Modification Timestamp, and text fields for Creation and Modification Account Names.

These four fields tell you exactly when a record was created or modified and by whom (assuming that you assign an account to each individual person using your database). If you ever need to identify problem records for a given day range, time, or account, these fields allow you to do this. We strongly recommend that you add them every time you create a new table.

The only downside to following this practice is that additional storage space is required for this data; in this version of FileMaker Pro, this is unlikely to be a concern.

TIP

Using FileMaker 8's capability to import tables allows you to create a boilerplate new table complete with a primary key serial ID, four housekeeping fields, and whatever other standard fields you want defined. Then whenever you need to add a table to your database, import from the boilerplate rather than having to re-create these standard fields.

FIELD VALIDATION

Storing correct and complete information is critical for generating accurate reports; establishing proper, expected conditions on which other functions and calculations are performed; and ensuring overall data integrity. Unfortunately, most data applications suffer from a chronic condition of having humans interacting with them; although some humans are worse than others, none is perfect. We all make mistakes.

As data is entered into FileMaker Pro, you may opt to apply one or more validation checks to test that certain conditions are met before allowing users to commit the record to your system. This can be as simple as ensuring that a field isn't empty, or as complex as making sure that an invoice doesn't contain multiple entries for the same product.

To review the various validation options available, see Figure 3.8.

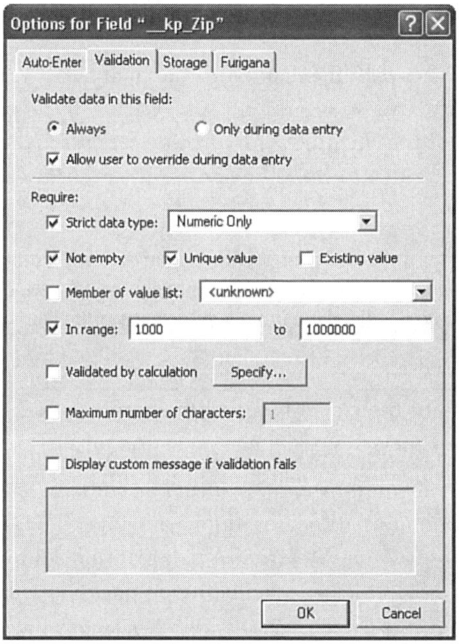

Figure 3.8
These are common validation settings for a numeric key value meant to always remain unique and unmodified by users. Even if your users can't access a given field on any layout, it's still a good policy to validate.

This example demonstrates a common approach to ensuring that your primary keys are properly maintained. This may be overkill if you've enabled the Prohibit Modification of Value During Data Entry option on the Auto-Enter tab, but on the chance that a developer turns that option off for some reason, or that users import records into your database, this is a handy bit of insurance.

→ Importing records can circumvent your carefully designed field validation rules. For a full discussion, **see** Chapter 19, "Importing Data into FileMaker Pro," **p. 567**.

VALIDATION CONDITIONS AND FAILURE

Field Validation simply tests whether one or more conditions, as defined in your Validation dialog, are false. If all validation tests are true, the user is not interrupted or prompted for action.

Figure 3.9 shows an example of what your users might see when validation fails.

Figure 3.9
The Yes option appears only if a user has the option to override the validation warning.

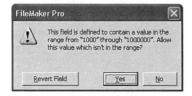

In this case, the check box allowing users to override has been left enabled, so they have the option to ignore the warning. When that function is disabled, the field does not allow bad data to be committed, and the system forces users to deal with the problem. They can choose either to revert the field to its previous state or to clear it.

WHEN VALIDATION OCCURS

Validation occurs when users enter data manually into the field being validated; some validation will happen the moment the user leaves the field, whereas other validations are deferred until the user commits the record. Remember, however, direct entry is not the only way to get information into a field. You can also import records or use various script steps, such as `Set Field()`.

Validation isn't triggered simply by clicking or tabbing into a field; a change needs to be attempted. And keep in mind that validation does not apply in cases in which users modify other, nonvalidated fields of a given record. A given field's validation check will be performed only when data in that specific field is changed.

At the top of the Validation tab of the Options dialog (refer to Figure 3.8), notice the Always and Only During Data Entry choices. The latter tests for validation conditions only when users modify the field in question. When the Always option is enabled, validation occurs during scripts and imports as well as during data entry.

If an import process attempts to write invalid data to a field, FileMaker Pro simply ignores the improper entry. The field remains unchanged and your data is not imported. You will see a note in the Import Records Summary dialog listing how many errors were encountered.

In the case in which the Only During Data Entry option is used, that improper data would be inserted into your database.

 If you get trapped in a series of validation dialogs, refer to "Validation Traps" in the "Troubleshooting" section at the end of this chapter.

STORAGE AND INDEXING

Field storage and indexing options are found on the Storage tab in your Field Options dialog; these options control how FileMaker Pro indexes each field in order to speed up searches and sorts and form relationships.

GLOBAL STORAGE

A developer can designate a field to have global storage on the Storage tab of the Field Options dialog. Commonly fields with this option are simply referred to as *global fields*, and collectively they're usually referred to as *globals*. Global fields exist independently from any specific record in the database and hold one value per user session.

Global fields are often used by developers to establish special relationships or to display unchanging information, such as interface graphics or field labels, across multiple records and layouts.

One vital element to learn is when data is committed and stored for globals: In a single-user environment, any change to a global field is permanent and is saved across sessions. In other words, the next time you open your database, whatever value you last entered into a global will have remained. In the case of a multiuser environment—where a FileMaker Pro solution is hosted on FileMaker Server or via multiuser hosting—global values for each guest default to the value from the last time the database was in single-user mode; any change made to these defaults will then be specific only to a given user's session. Other users continue to see the default values, and after the database session is closed it reverts to its original, default state.

Using globals is a great way to keep track of certain states of your database. For example, you could use a global field to store which row of a portal was last selected. This field could then be used in scripts or calculation formulas.

→ For an example of using a global to drive portal behaviors, **see** Chapter 16, "Advanced Portal Techniques," **p. 471**.

Another common use of globals is for storing system graphics. Establish a container field, set it for global storage, and paste a favorite company logo, a custom button graphic, or any number of elements that you can then control globally in a field rather than having to paste discrete elements on each and every layout.

Note that FileMaker 8 offers a new feature in the form of variables that are defined within scripts (and by using the Let() function, within calculations). These variables exist in memory only and are not permanent fields that you add to your database schema. In the past, developers had to content themselves with using a slew of global fields; in FileMaker 8, the need for global fields has dropped considerably.

→ To learn more about variables in FileMaker, **see** Chapter 15, "Advanced Scripting Techniques," **p. 435**.

REPEATING FIELDS

The second section of the Storage tab on the Field Options dialog lets developers allow a field to contain multiple values. Such fields are known as *repeating fields*. On a given layout the developer can array repetitions either horizontally or vertically, and in scripts can refer to specific repetitions within the field.

Repeating fields can be problematic. They behave just as individual fields might and are really just a shortcut for having to define multiple instances of a given field. It's possible, for example, to have no values in the first and second repetitions, but to have a value in the third. This sounds convenient and intuitively makes common sense, but imagine having to write a script that references that field. How do you know which repetition of the field to reference? Unlike an array in other programming languages, a repeating field cannot be manipulated as a whole. You can reference only one specific repetition at a time.

NEW FileMaker 8 extended the usefulness of repeating fields somewhat in allowing the script step Set Field to programmatically reference a repeating instance. You can now open a Specify Calculation dialog to point a script to a specific cell within a repeating field. (Note that the same is true for setting variables.)

Repeating fields do have their place, however. Imagine a spreadsheet. Even though an entire row may be blank, the cells are there, ready and waiting for input. If your users are familiar with Microsoft Excel or have been using a paper form for years, it may make sense for you to duplicate the look-and-feel in question, using repeating fields.

In addition to facilitating data entry, you could simulate a related child table with repeating fields.

→ For a detailed discussion of multiple-table solutions, **see** Chapter 6, "Working with Multiple Tables," **p. 157**.

Knowing when to use repeating fields can be somewhat tricky. If you ever have multiple bits of information that belong together—say, a product name and a price—it's always best to create a table and define fields for those items. They are attributes of the same item—a product. You might be able to grasp that Price[3] corresponded to Product[3], but only anecdotally. If another developer followed behind you in your work, that developer wouldn't necessarily make that same assumption.

The Excel spreadsheet example we gave previously could actually be exactly the wrong way to go: A spreadsheet assumes that a single row relates to all the information within that row. Repeating fields set next to each other on a layout do not share that programmatic logic.

We tend to use only repeating fields that genuinely need multiple instances of the same field: a graphics library, for example, or a simple place to store default values.

INDEXING

Databases store data by definition, of course, but they are also required to perform functions such as searches and sorts with that data. FileMaker Pro, like many databases, can index some of the data in a file to increase the speed at which it performs some of these functions and to enable it to relate data across tables.

An *index* is somewhat like a database within a database. FileMaker Pro can store, along with a specific value in a given field, a list of all the records in which that exact data is used. This then enables FileMaker to recall those records quickly without having to resort to a linear scan of your file. Aptly named, these indexes work just as a book index works: They facilitate finding all the locations in which a given item is used, without searching page by page through the entire book.

To familiarize yourself with the concept, take a look at a given field's index. Click into a field and select Insert, From Index. If the field is indexable, and has already been indexed, you are presented with a dialog box showing all the discrete values indexed for a given field. Just as with selecting from a value list, you may opt to choose from this list rather than type.

Allowing a user to select from an index is only one of the reasons indexes are used in FileMaker. Indexes enable FileMaker Pro to perform find requests, sort records, and establish relationships.

There are two kinds of indexes in FileMaker: value indexes and word indexes. *Value indexes* apply to all field types, with the exception of container or summary fields; *word indexes* apply only to text fields and are based on a given language or character set. The difference between the two, and when either is specifically enabled, lies in their applications.

FileMaker Pro's default indexing setting (found on the Storage tab of the Field Options dialog, displayed in Figure 3.10) is None, with the check box for Automatically Create Indexes As Needed enabled. Most developers, even the more advanced, should find that this setting serves most of their needs.

Figure 3.10
FileMaker creates either one type of index or both, depending on how a field is defined and used by users.

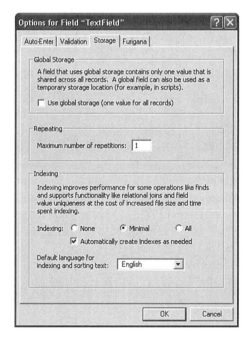

Value indexes are established by a database's schema definition—as a developer defines fields and builds relationships—and allow for relationship matches and value lists. If a developer creates a serial ID and joins a relationship via such a field, a value index is created for the serial ID field.

Unless a developer explicitly sets a field to generate an index, word indexes are created as users are interacting with and using a given database. They are utilized in text fields for find requests, or created when a user explicitly chooses Insert, From Index. If a user enters data in a find request for a field that lacks a word index, FileMaker Pro enables indexing for that field and builds one (unless it's explicitly unindexed, or an unindexable calculation).

At this point you may be wondering what all the fuss is about. Why not index every field in a database and be done with it? The downside to indexes is increased file size and the time it takes FileMaker to maintain the indexes. Creating new records, and deleting, importing, and modifying them, all take more time, in addition to the fact that the indexes themselves take up more file space.

Notice that FileMaker doesn't allow you to explicitly control word and value indices. Value indices are possible for all field types; word indices apply only to text fields. The Minimal setting will be an available option only for text fields, and when you see it marked, this indicates that at least one of the two indices exists for the field. There's no straightforward way of determining which. By explicitly setting the field to minimal, FileMaker will create, on demand, either of the two indices based on how the field is used: When a user creates a find request including that field, a word index will be created. If a developer uses the field in a relationship, a value index will be created.

Only a subset of the fields in your database will ever need to be indexed, and FileMaker's "on demand" approach makes things fairly simple for developers. Generally speaking, it's best if a field is indexed only when necessary.

→ To explore the vagaries of storage and indexing considerations for calculation fields, **see** "Other Options," **p. 224**.

An important point to remember is that some fields are not indexable. This means that they will be slow when used in sorts and find requests, but, most important, they cannot be used to establish relationships.

A field is unindexable if it is a calculation based on a related field, a summary field, or a global field, or if it references another unindexed, unstored calculation field.

You can also explicitly make a field unindexable by turning indexing options to None and unchecking the Automatically Create Indexes As Needed setting. In the case of a calculation field, an additional radio button option is available: Do Not Store Calculation Results Recalculate When Needed. These settings are important to remember; they allow you to force FileMaker to reevaluate and display dynamic information. The Get (CurrentDate) function, for example, displays the current date if you have indexing turned off, but displays whatever date was last stored with the record if you leave indexing (and storage) turned on.

FURIGANA

The fourth tab in the Field Options dialog is one that many English-speaking developers will have trouble properly pronouncing, let alone using. Because of the adoption of Unicode support in FileMaker Pro 7, it is now possible to offer Asian-language double-byte language support. As a result, you can now manage Japanese.

Japanese has four alphabets. One is based on glyphs from Chinese, known as Kanji, two are based on phonetic syllables known as Hiragana and Katakana, and the last is our own Roman alphabet, adopted in the nineteenth century for foreign words. When you're working in Japanese, it is possible to render the phonetic equivalents to a Kanji-based block of text. Quite useful when one doesn't know how to read one of the 20,000-plus characters in Kanji.

Suffice it to say that unless you're a student of Japanese (native or otherwise), this tab will likely not attract much of your attention.

TROUBLESHOOTING

MISMATCHED DATA TYPES

My data isn't sorting properly. Where should I look first to diagnose the problem?

One of the most common bugs you'll run into in FileMaker Pro is confusion stemming from mismatched data types. If your users are entering text data into a field you have defined as numeric, you're bound to get unexpected results, and sorting will be unpredictable. Check your field types when your data appears to be misbehaving.

MISMATCHED CALCULATION RESULTS

One of my date calculations looks like an integer. What's going on?

Some of the more subtle extensions of the data type problem are calculation fields. Note that their result is both the determination of their formula and a data type you set at the bottom of the Specify Calculation dialog. If you're working with dates and return a number, for example, you'll get an entirely valid calculation that will look nothing like "12/25/2003."

PROBLEMATIC FIELD NAMES

My web programmers are complaining about my field names in FileMaker Pro, and that I keep changing them. What should I consider when naming fields?

Some other systems are not as flexible as FileMaker Pro—this is especially true for URLs and the Web. Spend some time with Chapters 21 and 23 if you ever plan to publish your database to the Web. FileMaker Pro breeds a certain freedom when it comes to changing field names as the need arises, but you'll send your XSLT programmer into fits every time you do.

Also be sure to check the restrictions of various SQL databases in your organization. In the case that you need to interoperate with them, you might need to have your field names conform to stricter naming standards.

You'll be safe if you never use spaces or special characters and start each field with a letter of the alphabet or an underscore.

VALIDATION TRAPS

My field validation seems to have gone haywire. I defined a field that now simply throws up one error message after another. What's the problem?

At the end of the day, field validation is only a helpful bank of sandbags against the storm of human interaction your database will suffer. And as in all aspects of your database, the first and worst human in the mix is the developer. Just as with any programming logic, carefully test your validation conditions. FileMaker Pro can't totally prevent you from illogically conflicting restrictions. For example, if you set a field to be unique and nonempty, but also prohibit modification in the auto-entry options, the first record you create will trap your system in an irresolvable conflict.

It's a good idea to leave the Allow User to Override During Data Entry option enabled while you're building a solution and turn it off only when you have completely tested the field in question.

FILEMAKER EXTRA: INDEXING IN FILEMAKER

One of the more significant changes in FileMaker 7 and 8 revolves around indexing. In prior versions, indexing was restricted to 60 characters total, broken into blocks of up to 20-character words. Relationships had to be built around match fields, or keys, that were relatively short and generally nondescriptive. This is one of the reasons why we generally advocate using simple serial numbers for indexing purposes. It's rare that you'd need more than 20 digits to serialize the records in a data table.

In FileMaker 8, words can be indexed up to approximately 100 characters. Text fields can be indexed to a total of 800 characters, and numbers can be indexed up to 400 digits. The limits to indexing have been effectively removed.

What this means to developers is that we can now use far more complex concatenated key combinations (ironically there will be less of that in FileMaker 8, given that data can be related across multiple tables), use longer alphanumeric keys, or, as we suggested earlier, introduce a descriptive elements to keys.

In the past, FileMaker Pro would identify "Special_Edition_Using_FileMaker_8" (32 characters) as identical to "Special_Edition_Using_MS_Access"—clearly a terrible mistake to make. It's now possible to match against paragraphs of text or very large numbers. Determining matches will be more exact and finds and sorts more robust.

CHAPTER **4**

WORKING WITH LAYOUTS

In this chapter

WHAT'S A LAYOUT?

In the preceding chapter, we discussed how to define fields for holding the data you want to store in your database. In this chapter, we discuss the tools at your disposal for creating user interfaces to manage that data.

You use *layouts* to create user interfaces in FileMaker Pro. Layouts are similar in some ways to web pages, though they're structured quite differently. A layout is a collection of graphical objects that a user interacts with to view and modify data. These objects include things such as fields, buttons, static text blocks, graphic elements (such as lines or rectangles), and images. FileMaker Pro contains a rich set of tools for manipulating these objects, allowing you to create attractive and functional interfaces for your users easily.

You can create many kinds of layouts in FileMaker. Form layouts are useful for data entry; list layouts are generally used for reports and often contain summary parts. Some layouts may be designed for system administrators to clean up data quickly. Still others can serve as user navigation menus and contain no data at all.

One of the things that makes FileMaker unique among database products is that the layouts themselves are stored in a file, right along with data, scripts, access privileges, and other elements of application logic. Every FileMaker Pro file must have at least one layout; there is no practical limit to the number of layouts a file can contain. It's not unheard of, nor undesirable, to have anywhere from a dozen to a hundred or more layouts in a file.

Layouts are created and managed in what's known as *Layout mode*. To get to Layout mode, choose View, Layout Mode, or simply type (⌘-L) [Ctrl+L]. Almost all the material in this chapter deals with tools and functions that require you to be in Layout mode to access them, but for simplicity and brevity, we will not specifically mention that fact in conjunction with every tool and tip.

In this chapter, we take a top-down approach to learning about layouts. We begin by discussing layout creation and layout configuration options. We then move down to the level of the part, and finally down to the level of objects. Learning about layouts can entail "chicken and egg" problems: Most topics are intertwined to the extent that there's no convenient linear approach through the material. We therefore encourage you to skip around from topic to topic as necessary to fill out your knowledge.

Finally, this chapter does not comprehensively cover every layout tool or configuration option. Rather, our approach is to cover details that you might not otherwise discover on your own, and to present what we consider to be best practices for working with layouts.

CREATING AND MANAGING LAYOUTS

Creating and managing layouts is one of the most important tasks required of a FileMaker developer. It's also one of the most intuitive. There are, nonetheless, numerous subtle facts and details that you need to know. We encourage you to have a test file open as you go through the following sections so that you can try things firsthand.

CREATING A NEW LAYOUT

Every time you create a new table in a file, FileMaker automatically creates a new layout for you as well, based on the new table. The layout is given the same name as your table, and all the fields you defined at the time of table creation are placed on the layout for you. Figure 4.1 shows an example of what this default layout looks like.

Figure 4.1
The default layout created when you add a new table to a file.

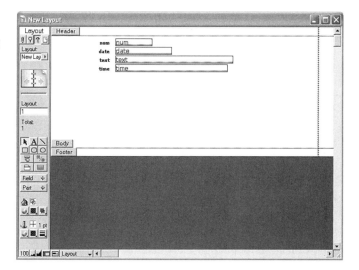

You can create new layouts anytime you want while in Layout mode simply by choosing Layouts, New Layout/Report, or by pressing (⌘-N) [Ctrl+N]. You are then taken to a setup wizard that can help you configure a layout according to one of a handful of types of common layout designs. Figure 4.2 shows the first screen of the Layout Wizard, on which you specify a name for the layout and choose a layout type. You also specify a layout's *context* here; that topic is covered in the next section.

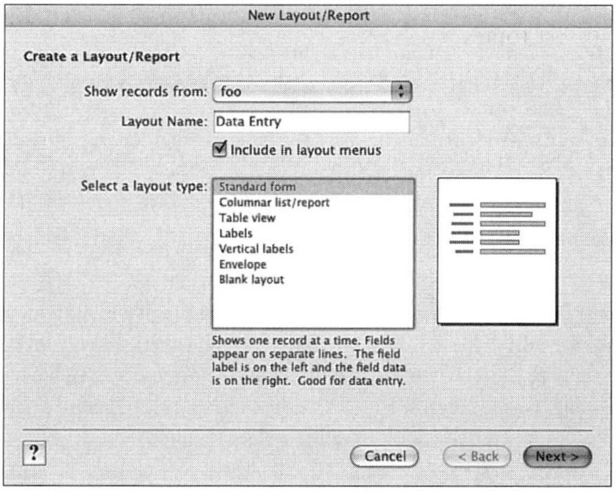

Figure 4.2
This is the first screen of the wizard for creating new layouts.

You can create the following six types of layouts:

- **Standard Form**—Useful for data-entry layouts, Standard Form generates a basic form view layout with a set of fields you specify. You can select a *theme* for the layout as well; themes specify the default background color and text styles that will be applied to the layout.

- **Columnar List/Report**—As the name implies, this type is used for creating basic list and subsummary reports. If you don't already have the necessary summary fields in your database, you can create them right from within the wizard.

- **Table View**—Table view gives you a spreadsheet-like view of your data. When you select Table View as your layout type, you can select the fields you want to appear on your new layout. They are then displayed according to your selected theme in Table view. Table view is quite useful for behind-the-scenes data manipulation, but it may not be suitable as an end-user interface.

- **Labels**—This type of layout is used for printing sheets of labels in standard or custom sizes. The Layout Wizard prompts you to specify the type of labels you will be using—Avery 5160/5260 are the labels used most commonly. If you don't see your label type listed, you can specify custom measurements. See the "Multicolumn Layouts" section later in this chapter for some tips that will come in handy for working with label layouts.

- **Envelope**—You are prompted to select fields you want to use for the address portion of the envelope. The default layout is sized for standard business envelopes. You may need to do some testing and tweaking of the layout to get things just right for your envelopes and printer.

- **Blank Layout**—Choosing Blank Layout gives you just that: a completely blank layout, which you can then manipulate any way you want, free of wizards.

We do not discuss all the screens of the New Layout/Report Assistant here; they're quite intuitive, even for new developers. Besides, if you are new to FileMaker, nothing beats spending an hour just playing around with the assistant to see firsthand what the various configuration options do for you. You won't cause harm to any existing layouts by doing so, nor can you hurt the database even if you mess up the creation of a new layout.

After a layout has been created, it can be completely modified and turned into whatever you need it to be. Much of the remainder of this chapter is devoted to the tools at your disposal to do just that.

TIP

No tool is available for importing layouts from one file to another. If you ever need to do this, the best method is to set up a new, blank layout with layout parts sized the same as the source layout. Then, copy all the objects from the source file and paste them into the new file. Fields, buttons, and portals need to be respecified to point to their correct referents, but at least all your formatting will be retained.

- In a multitable file, consider having the base table name as part of the layout name. For instance, Customer:Data Entry or Data Entry (Customer) may be good names if you need to differentiate among multiple data-entry layouts.

- Finally, if you use a single hyphen (-) as a layout name, this appears in the layout pop-up list as a divider. Users can't select divider layouts, which merely serve to help organize what might otherwise be an unwieldy list. Typically, such layouts would be left completely blank, but this isn't a requirement.

> **TIP**
>
> The single-hyphen naming trick works in other areas of FileMaker as well, such as within value lists and as a script name.

VIEW OPTIONS

Every layout you develop can potentially be viewed in three ways: as a form, as a list, or as a table. A user with access to standard menu commands can use the View menu in Browse mode to switch between them. When you navigate to a layout, you will see it in whatever state it was last saved in, so bear in mind that switching from layout to layout may change the view setting as well.

The differences between the three view types are quite straightforward:

- **View as Form**—This view type always shows one record at a time. Any header and footer parts are not fixed on the layout; if the layout has a long body, a user might need to scroll to see the footer. If the body part is short, the last part on the layout expands to fill the empty space. Subsummary parts are visible in Browse mode, but any summary fields in them represent summaries of all the records in the found set. The maximum height and width of a layout is just over 111 inches. For some long forms, such as legal contracts, you may need to split the form into two separate layouts.

- **View as List**—With View as List, the number of records displayed is determined by the height of the layout body part and the height of the window. If more records are present in the found set than can be displayed onscreen, the vertical scrollbar enables users to see additional records. Any header and footer parts are fixed onscreen at all times, even when a user scrolls to see additional records. Subsummary parts are never visible in Browse mode with View as List. If fields are placed in the header or footer parts, they take their values from the currently active record. Any modification to a field in the header or footer part likewise affects the currently active record.

- **View as Table**—In Table view, all the fields placed in the layout's body are presented in a spreadsheet-like grid. The initial order of the fields is determined by their top-to-bottom position on the layout. That is, the first column is the topmost field on the layout. No nonfield elements (for example, buttons, text, graphics) from the body of the layout are rendered in Table view. Field formatting (for example, color, font, font size) is honored, however. The column headers conform to the format of the first field. Other properties of the Table view can be specified under the Views tab of the Layout Setup dialog. As shown in Figure 4.4, you can specify whether header and footer parts should be visible and whether columns can be sorted, reordered, and resized.

Figure 4.4
You can alter the look and functionality of the table view by using the Table View Properties dialog.

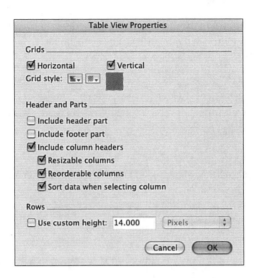

Using the Views tab of the Layout Setup dialog, you can disable user access to certain view types. Although usually not necessary, this can be a good precaution to take to keep adventurous users on the right track. Accessing an inappropriate view type is likely not going to cause much harm, but it certainly can confuse users.

MULTICOLUMN LAYOUTS

When printing labels and certain types of reports, you might want to present your data in multiple columns. You can specify the number of columns to display on the Printing tab of the Layout Setup dialog; this is shown in Figure 4.5.

Figure 4.5
You can customize the print settings for a particular layout on the Printing tab of the Layout Setup dialog.

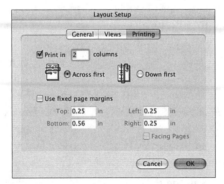

In Layout mode, dashed vertical lines represent the boundaries between columns. Columns other than the first are grayed out; the idea is that you need to place any objects you want displayed in the first column, and these objects are replicated to the other columns as necessary. Figure 4.6 shows an example of a three-column layout used to display a phone directory. Notice that the header and footer part are not divided into columns. This means that if you want headers to appear above the second and third columns, you need to add those explicitly, as we've done in Figure 4.6.

Figure 4.6
This example shows how a layout for a three-column phone directory might appear in Layout mode.

It's not possible to have columns of differing widths; every column is the same width as the first one. You can manually adjust the column width by clicking on the dashed divider between the first and second columns and dragging left or right as appropriate.

Subsummary parts and leading and trailing grand summaries can be used on multicolumn layouts, but they behave slightly differently depending on whether you've chosen to display data Across First or Down First. If you chose Down First, any summary parts are also columnar. On the other hand, if the data is displayed Across First, summary parts span the full width of the layout, just as the header and footer parts do.

→ Subsummary parts are covered in depth in "Working with Parts," **p. 103**.

The effects of a multicolumn layout can be viewed only in Preview mode. In Browse mode, a user sees only a single column of data.

HIDING AND REORDERING LAYOUTS

In Browse mode, layouts can be designated to be either accessible or inaccessible via the layout pull-down menu in the Status Area. If a layout is accessible, users can see it and navigate to it at will (assuming that the Status Area is visible and/or accessible). If the layout is inaccessible, users can navigate to it only by running a script that takes them there. (In Layout mode, all layouts are accessible.)

Typically, layouts are set to be inaccessible when you need to prevent users from manually navigating to a layout. For instance, you might have report layouts or find screens that require certain preparation before they become useful. There may be unanticipated and/or undesired results if a user is able to bypass the scripts you've created and navigate directly to a layout.

The option to have a layout be accessible or not is on the first screen of the New Layout/Report Assistant; it can also be set through the Layout Setup dialog. The Set Layout Order dialog, shown in Figure 4.7, also has a check box on each line that can be toggled to change a layout from visible to hidden and vice versa. Using this method is the quickest way to hide (or show) a number of layouts at once.

The Set Layout Order dialog, as you might guess from its name, also enables you to change the order in which layouts appear in the layout pop-up list. You can use the double-arrowed selection tool to move a layout up or down in the order. You can accomplish the same thing by selecting a line and pressing (⌘) [Ctrl] and the up or down arrow.

Figure 4.7
Use the Set Layout Order dialog to set the accessibility and order of layouts.

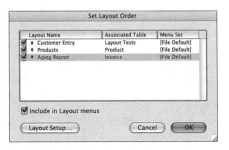

RESTRICTING ACCESS TO LAYOUTS

Using the methods discussed in the preceding section to hide layouts is a good way of keeping users from going places they shouldn't, but it's not adequate security if you truly need to restrict access to layouts. Moreover, making layouts inaccessible affects all users; you can't set up rules determining which layouts are accessible for which users.

Added protection for layouts can be achieved by restricting access via security privilege sets. A privilege set can be defined to provide All No Access, All View Only, or All Modifiable control over all layouts at once; alternatively, you can specify custom layout privileges for each individual layout, as shown in Figure 4.8. You can protect editing of the layouts themselves, as well as the data displayed on them. Any user who has no access to a layout doesn't see that the layout exists, even in Layout mode.

Figure 4.8
Custom layout privileges enable you to restrict certain users from modifying or viewing certain layouts.

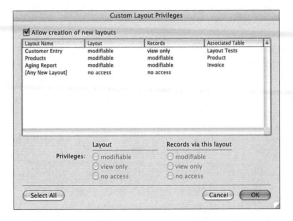

→ For more information about setting up privilege sets, **see** "Working with Privilege Sets," **p. 334**.

If you want to prevent certain users from creating new layouts, leave the Allow Creation of New Layouts option at the top of the Custom Layout Privileges dialog unchecked. Additionally, you can set default privileges that users will have for new layouts by editing the options for the [Any New Layout] line.

Note that the preceding security settings allow developers to give users the ability to edit some layouts and not others, and also to create their own layouts (or not). It is possible in FileMaker to establish "junior developer users" who can exercise a degree of freedom within certain areas of a given system without jeopardizing critical or more complex areas.

WORKING WITH PARTS

Layouts are made up of parts. Depending on your objectives, your layout may contain header and footer parts, a body part, one or more subsummary parts, and maybe even a leading or trailing grand summary. Every layout must contain at least one part.

Briefly, the purpose and some characteristics of each type of part are as listed here:

- **Title Header**—Title headers are used when you need a header on the first page of a multipage report that differs from the header on subsequent pages. In Form view, a user can view a title header (while in Browse mode), but not in List or Table view.

- **Header**—Objects in the header part appear at the top of each page of a multipage report (except the first page when a title header is present). A header part remains fixed onscreen in List and Table views, even when a user scrolls to see additional records. Data in fields placed in a header part can be edited; fields in a header part always display data from the currently active record.

- **Leading Grand Summary**—Typically used on report layouts, a leading grand summary appears between the header and any subsummary or body parts. Summary fields placed in this part aggregate across the entire found set.

→ For more information about using summary fields and summary parts to create reports, **see** "Summarized Reports," **p. 287**.

- **Body**—The body part is used to display data from a single record. A data-entry layout often consists of nothing other than a body part. Almost every layout you create will have a body part.

- **Subsummary**—Subsummary parts are used primarily for displaying subtotals on reports. For a subsummary to display properly, the found set must be sorted by the same field as that on which the subsummary is based, and you must be in Preview mode. Subsummaries can be placed either above or below the body part, depending on whether you want the subtotals displayed before or after the data they summarize.

- **Trailing Grand Summary**—Similar to a leading grand summary, a trailing grand summary is typically found on report layouts and is used to display aggregate summaries. When printed, the trailing grand summary report appears directly following the body part and any trailing subsummaries.

- **Footer**—Objects in the footer appear on every page of a multipage printout (except on the first page when a title footer is present). In List view, the footer remains fixed on the layout when a user scrolls through records.

- **Title Footer**—A title footer part is used when you want to display a different footer on the first page of a multipage printout.

4

ADDING AND ORDERING PARTS

There are two ways of adding parts to a layout. The first is by clicking and dragging the Part button in the Status Area to the point where you want the new part to appear. You are prompted to select a part type when you let up the mouse. Although it is convenient, we discourage this method of adding new parts. New parts, except when added to the very bottom of the layout, always come at the expense of existing parts. That is, if you have a 50-pixel header followed by a 200-pixel body, and you attempt to add a subsummary between these parts, the body part shrinks by the size of the subsummary part. Moreover, fields that were in the body part may now be part of the subsummary part.

The other option for adding new parts, which we prefer in almost every circumstance, is to use the Part Setup dialog (shown in Figure 4.9), which can be found under the <u>L</u>ayouts menu. When parts are added with this tool, it's not at the expense of any existing part; the total height of the layout increases.

Figure 4.9
You can add, edit, delete, and reorder the parts on a layout from the Part Setup dialog.

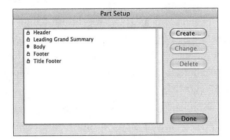

The Part Setup dialog can also be used to reorder, edit, and delete parts. The only types of parts that can be reordered are the body and subsummary parts. To reorder these, click the arrow in front of the part name and drag it to the desired position. Other part types appear with a lock in front of them, indicating that they are fixed in a certain order by definition.

You can delete a part from a layout either by selecting it from the Part Setup dialog and clicking Delete, or by clicking the part label while in Layout mode and pressing the Backspace or Delete key on your keyboard. Either way, when you delete a part, any objects contained in that part are also deleted.

FORMATTING A PART

You can configure a few attributes of parts directly from Layout mode itself. First, you can set a background color and/or fill pattern for a part by clicking on the part label, and then selecting a color and/or fill pattern. (Control-clicking) [right+clicking] on the part label similarly pulls up a contextual menu with access to these attributes.

You can achieve much the same effect simply by drawing a large rectangle on the layout, sending it to the back, and locking it. Setting a background color for the part is preferred, though, because the color extends to the right and downward if the user expands the window beyond the boundaries of your rectangle.

TIP

For users with monitors set to higher resolutions than your database was designed for, consider adding a footer with a background color different from your body part so that users can visually see where the layout "ends" and size their windows appropriately.

You can also change a part's size. To do this, simply click on the dividing line between two parts and drag either up or down. When making a part smaller, you can remove whitespace from the part, but you are prevented from dragging through any objects in the part. Any expansion of a part increases the overall size of the part.

Holding down (Option) [Alt] as you resize a part changes the rules slightly. First, any expansion or contraction comes at the benefit or expense of the neighboring part; the overall height of the layout remains the same (except, of course, when enlarging the last part on the layout). Also, you can "run over" objects this way; an object that was in one part may end up belonging to another part after you've resized things. An object that ends up straddling two (or more) parts belongs to the part that contains its upper-left corner.

The Size palette can also be used to see and set a part's length. This is the best way to precisely set part lengths, especially when trying to duplicate complex layouts from one file to another. Click the part label to display that part's data in the Size palette.

→ For more information about the Size palette, **see** "Positioning Objects on a Layout," **p. 109**.

PART DEFINITION

Beyond the size and background color of a part, some part attributes can be set only in the Part Definition dialog, shown in Figure 4.10. You can get to this dialog either from the Part Setup dialog (by clicking Create or Change), or by double-clicking on the part label itself.

Figure 4.10
The Part Definition dialog is used to specify a part's type and attributes.

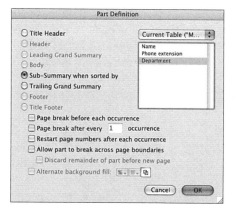

The type of part is indicated by the radio buttons on the left side of this dialog. You can change the type of a part simply by selecting a different radio button. If a type is grayed out, that means you already have a part of that type. The only part type for which you can have multiples is subsummary.

The fields on the right side of the dialog apply only to subsummary parts. When you make a subsummary part, you must specify which field will act as the break field for the summary. The break field doesn't need to actually appear in that part, but the found set must be sorted by the break field for the subsummary part to appear on a report.

→ For more information on break fields and subsummary reports, **see** "Summarized Reports," **p. 287**.

At the bottom of the dialog are some options for configuring page breaks and page numbers. Often in subsummary reports, you'll want each new subsection to start on a new page. To do this, you would edit the part definition of the subsummary part to include the Page Break Before Each Occurrence option. As you would expect, it's actually only each occurrence *after the first one* that's preceded by a page break.

You can also opt to use the Alternate Background Fill feature. This option is available only on body parts. Any color and/or fill that you specify is used as the background for every other record. It alternates with any background color that has been specified for the part itself. Often, a slight shading of alternate rows on a report makes it easier to read.

WORKING WITH OBJECTS ON A LAYOUT

As stated previously, a layout is essentially a collection of objects that is manifested as a "screen" that allows users to see and/or modify data. We'll refer abstractly to anything that can be placed on a layout as a *layout object*. There are many tools and techniques for configuring and manipulating layout objects. Some of these apply only to specific types of objects, whereas others are more general in nature. The better you know how to work with the tools for crafting layouts, the better your user interface will be. (Although there are of course no guarantees.)

ADDING OBJECTS TO A LAYOUT

The Status Area in Layout mode provides a set of design tools for adding and manipulating layout objects. These tools are shown in Figure 4.11.

Figure 4.11
The Status Area contains most of the tools you need for designing layouts.

TIP

> In Layout mode, the book icon can be used to move from layout to layout. The keyboard shortcut for this, (⌘-up arrow) [Ctrl+up arrow], is the same one used in Browse mode to move from record to record, and in Preview mode to move from page to page.

The layout tools in the middle of the Status Area are used to add new objects to a layout. There are tools for adding text blocks, lines, rectangles, rounded rectangles, ovals, buttons, fields with value list controls, Tab Control objects, and portals. With each, you can simply click on the tool to activate it, and then click and drag on your layout where you want the object to appear.

Normally, when you are finished creating an object, the pointer tool is reselected automatically. At times, however, you'll want to create multiple objects of the same type at once. In these cases, it's useful to lock in the selection of a particular tool. You can do this by double-clicking on the tool in the Status Area. There's also a preference on the Layout tab of the application preferences screen to Always Lock Layout Tools, though we generally advise against enabling it.

The Insert menu provides another means for adding objects to a layout. At the top of this menu, you'll find selections for adding all the object types found in the Status Area.

CAUTION

> Unless your Status Area is closed and locked for some reason, we prefer not to use the Insert menu because it doesn't give you an opportunity to specify location or size during object creation. Either duplicate existing objects or use the tools from the Status Area when at all possible.

To insert a picture or another graphic element developed externally, you can use the Insert, Graphic menu command. Or you can simply cut and paste objects from many other applications directly into your FileMaker layouts.

SPECIFYING OBJECT ATTRIBUTES

You have a great deal of control over the attributes of any object you place on a layout. Different object types may have different attribute options. You can always tell what attributes of an object can be configured by (Control-clicking) [right-clicking] the object. A contextual menu appears, listing any formatting options that are appropriate to that particular object type. There are menu commands and Status Area tools that provide access to the same attribute settings, but the most efficient way to set an object's attributes is to use the contextual menus.

THE FORMAT PAINTER TOOL

You can copy the formatting attributes from one object to other objects on your layout by using the Format Painter tool. The Format Painter can be found under the Format menu and in the Standard toolbar, which you can enable from the View, Toolbars menu.

To use the Format Painter, you simply select an object that has the formatting attributes you want to propagate, and then turn on the Format Painter, using either of the two methods just mentioned. A small paintbrush appears next to your mouse pointer, indicating that the Format Painter tool is active. Then simply select an object (or a set of objects) to which you want to apply the formats. You can lock in the Format Painter tool by double-clicking its icon from the Standard toolbar. This enables you to click on several objects, applying formats as you go.

SETTING DEFAULT OBJECT ATTRIBUTES

The default format attributes include such things as the font, font size, font color, text style (for example, bold, italics), pen width, alignment, shading, paragraph settings, and object effects. In short, any configurable attribute of a layout object has a default setting. Not all objects, of course, have all the potential attributes. Rectangles, for instance, have shading and pen width attributes but don't have any font attributes. When a new object of any sort is added to a layout with the layout tools, the applicable attributes of that object inherit the current default settings. You can, of course, change the attributes of an object after it has been placed on a layout.

The default format attributes are stored at the file level. This means that as you move from layout to layout within a file, the defaults stay the same, but if you're working with multiple files, each may have its own defaults.

When you first create a file, the default text format is fairly vanilla: 12-point black Helvetica (Mac), 12-point Arial (Windows), no object effects, no text styles, no field borders, and no shading. You can change the default settings in one of two ways:

- In Layout mode, if you have no objects selected, any formatting options you change are applied to the default text attributes. Only the attributes you change are affected.
- If you (⌘-click) [Ctrl+click] on an object, that object's characteristics become the default. This is the easiest way to set the default; you can simply format one object with the settings you want and then (⌘-click) [Ctrl+click] it. All that object's attributes together become the new default; any attributes that the object doesn't possess are not affected.

> **TIP**
>
> If multiple layout objects are selected and you (⌘-click) [Ctrl+click] on any one of them, the frontmost object's characteristics become the default.

If you have opened a file as a guest (either of FileMaker Pro or of FileMaker Server), any changes you make to the default attributes persist only until you close the file; those defaults aren't stored in the file and don't affect other developers in the system. When you're the host of a file, any changes you make to the default attributes are stored and persist until you change them again, even if you close and reopen the file.

DUPLICATING LAYOUT OBJECTS

Any object on a layout can be duplicated in one of two ways. When you duplicate an object (or a set of objects), the new objects have all the same attributes of the source objects. It therefore is often faster and more efficient to create a new object by duplicating an existing one and modifying it rather than adding a new one using the layout tools.

The first way is simply to select some set of objects and choose Edit, Duplicate or press (⌘-D) [Ctrl+D]. The entire set of objects is duplicated, with the new objects appearing 6 pixels to the right and 6 pixels lower than the original set. The new objects are selected (as opposed to the original set), so you can easily move them to wherever you want.

There's a useful technique for creating multiple copies of an object, spaced out at consistent intervals. Begin by selecting a set of objects, which we'll call set A, and duplicate it as described, creating set B. Without deselecting any of the objects in set B, move them to some desired place on a layout. Choose Edit, Duplicate again; and the new copy, set C, instead of having the "6 pixels to the right, 6 pixels down" relationship to its source, is spaced an equal distance from set B as B is from A. Continued selection of Edit, Duplicate results in additional new sets, each positioned a consistent distance from its source. This technique is very useful for creating columnar lists and grids of equally spaced lines.

The second way to duplicate layout objects is to (Option-drag) [Ctrl+drag] them. Simply select a set of objects, and then start to drag them as if you intended to move them to a new location on the layout. As you're moving the objects, however, hold down the (Option) [Ctrl] key. Continue to hold this key down until after you have released the mouse click; the objects are not moved, but a copy of them is placed at the new location.

TIP

> You can also hold down the Shift key as you're dragging the objects to constrain movement to a vertical or horizontal axis. This is generally our preferred method for duplicating layout objects.

POSITIONING OBJECTS ON A LAYOUT

Much of layout design is simply moving things around until they look just right. This is also one of the most intuitive things for new developers to learn. So much so, in fact, that many never learn some of the fine points of working with objects on a layout. We will attempt to remedy that problem here.

SELECTING OBJECTS ON A LAYOUT

Most all formatting and positioning of objects on a layout begins with the selection of a set of objects to work with. You can go about selecting objects in several ways; knowing these methods can greatly increase your efficiency at designing layouts. Here are your options:

- **Click on an object**—You can select any object simply by clicking on it. When you do so, small squares, called *handles*, appear at the four corners of the object, indicating that the object is indeed selected.

- **Shift+click**—When you have one or more objects selected, you can Shift+click on an additional object to add it to the selected set. Similarly, Shift+clicking on an object that is already selected removes it from the selected set.

- **Selection box**—If you click on the background of the layout (that is, any place there's not an object), and drag a rectangle across the screen, when you release the mouse, any objects that were completely contained within your selection box are selected. This is typically the easiest and quickest way to select multiple objects.

> **NOTE**
>
> If you hold down the (⌘) [Ctrl] key while dragging a selection box on the screen, any objects *touched* by (instead of contained by) the box are selected. This technique works well for selecting objects that might partially overlap other objects, when using the enclosing method would result in too many selected objects.

- **Select all objects**—To select all the objects on a layout, choose Edit, Select All, or use the (⌘-A) [Ctrl+A]) keyboard shortcut.

- **Select all instances of a type of object**—It's also possible to select all instances of a particular type of object, such as all the text objects, or all the fields, or all the rectangles. There are several ways to do this. If the Arrange toolbar is visible, you can select an object, and then click the Select Objects by Type button in that toolbar to select all similar objects. Or you can select an object, and then press (⌘-Option-A) [Ctrl+Alt+A] to accomplish the same thing. Finally, if you have a tool (other than the Button or Portal tool) selected from the layout tools, you can select all the objects of that type by choosing Edit, Select All.

MOVING OBJECTS

After you have selected a set of objects, you can move those objects around on the layout—provided that they are not locked—in a few ways. First, you can click on the interior of any object in the selected set and drag the set to a new location. You can also use the arrow keys on your keyboard to move a selected set of objects pixel by pixel.

Using the click-and-drag method, hold down the Shift key after you start dragging the objects, and the movement will be constrained to either the vertical or the horizontal plane. That is, there would be no way of moving the objects other than up and down or from side to side. This is very useful for keeping objects properly aligned as you reposition them.

RESIZING OBJECTS

When you select an object, four small black or gray squares appear at the corners of the object. These define the object's boundaries; they are called the object's *handles*. All objects, even circular ones, have a rectangular "footprint" defined by the four handles. Gray handles indicate that the object is locked; it can't be moved or resized in this state. (Refer to the "Locking Objects" section later in this chapter.)

You can resize an object by clicking on one of the four handles and dragging in the desired direction. Unlike some other graphic applications, FileMaker does not enable you to click on the sides of the object to change just the height or width of the object. You must always use the object's corners. Just as when moving objects, you can, however, constrain movement to the vertical or horizontal plane by holding down the Shift key as you drag to resize the object.

If you have selected multiple objects, resizing any one of them causes all the objects to resize by a similar amount. This is very useful in cases in which you want to select, for instance, five fields and make them all slightly longer or shorter. Resizing them as a set ensures that they will all be changed by the same relative amount.

FileMaker 8 introduced the new Resize To alignment tools. Available in the Arrange menu in Layout mode, these tools allow developers to make a group of objects consistent by resizing all objects in the group to the largest or smallest width or height of the objects selected.

THE OBJECT GRID

You have the option, when working with layouts, of enabling or disabling an *object grid*. You can change the status of the object grid by toggling the Object Grids command, found at the bottom of the Arrange menu. You can also toggle the status of the object grid by pressing (⌘-Y) [Ctrl+Y].

When object grids are enabled, all movement and resizing of objects takes place against a virtual grid. Each square of the grid measures 6 pixels by 6 pixels. The effect of this is that when you are moving or resizing objects, movement happens in 6-pixel chunks. When the object grids are disabled, movement happens in 1-pixel units, resulting in fluid motion.

> **TIP**
>
> You can change the default grid spacing to something other than 6 pixels by using the Layouts, Set Rulers menu.

The object grids are defined relative to each object. That is, there's not a static grid to which everything snaps. If object A and object B are 2 pixels apart, with object grids enabled, you could move each object one "chunk" in any direction and they'd still be 2 pixels apart, each having moved 6 pixels from its original location.

Whether or not you choose to have object grids enabled as you design layouts is purely a personal preference. Some developers love object grids; others loath them. Even the authors of this book are passionately divided on this subject. The benefit of using the object grids is that they make it easy to keep things arranged and sized nicely. It's much easier to notice visually when an object is 6 pixels off-line rather than 1 pixel. Plus, if you ever need to move things in finer increments, you can simply use the arrow keys to "nudge" the objects into line. Also, you can temporarily suspend the object grids by holding down the (⌘) [Alt] key as you are moving or resizing an object. On the con side of things, for developers used to positioning things exactly to the pixel, the object grid can get in the way and prove simply cumbersome to work around.

The object grid's status is a file-level setting. That is, as you work on different layouts within a file, the grid status carries through to them all, but if you have multiple files in a solution, you can conceivably have the object grid enabled in some files and not in others.

THE SIZE PALETTE

The Size palette is a floating toolbox that can be used to see and set very precise object positions. It's shown in Figure 4.12. To make the palette appear, choose View, Object Size.

It's an application-level setting, so after you have the palette onscreen, it is available no matter which layout you are working with. You can move the palette around on your screen so that it's positioned optimally for whatever task you need it for.

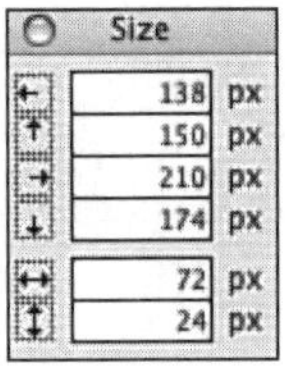

Figure 4.12
The Size palette is quite useful for positioning and sizing objects on a layout.

The Size palette provides six pieces of data about the position and size of a selected object (or set of objects). From top to bottom, these data points represent the following:

- The distance from the left edge of the object to the left edge of the layout
- The distance from the top edge of the object to the top edge of the layout
- The distance from the right edge of the object to the left edge of the layout
- The distance from the bottom edge of the object to the top edge of the layout
- The object's width
- The object's height

In these definitions, the left edge and top edge of the layout may be outside the area you can actively work with. Most layouts have a default page margin, usually .25 inches on each side. You can make your layout's page margins visible by choosing View, Page Margins. Fixed page margins can be set under the Printing tab of the Layout Setup dialog.

CAUTION

It's important to know that page margins are factored into the distances displayed in the Size palette. You can't move or position an object in the page margin. If you are trying to use absolute positioning to align objects on different layouts, any differences in page margins need to be taken into consideration.

The Size palette can measure distance as inches, centimeters, or pixels. You'll see the unit displayed on the right edge of the palette itself. You can toggle among the three available units simply by clicking on any of the unit labels.

TIP

We find that setting the Size palette to display pixels is much more intuitive and useful than using inches or centimeters.

The Size palette doesn't merely report on the position and size of a selected object; it can also be used to set these attributes. With an object selected, you can click into and edit any of the six data points. Pressing the Tab or Return key moves you through the palette's fields.

Pressing the Enter key exits the palette (for users with both keys on their keyboard; if you're working on a laptop, there's usually just an Enter key). As you change the numbers in the palette, the selected object moves or resizes as you have specified. This makes it very easy to precisely align, position, and size objects on a layout.

TIP

> If you're working on a laptop that lacks a Return key, (⌘-Enter) [Ctrl+Enter] will exit the Size palette and return focus to your prior window with your objects still selected.

ARRANGING OBJECTS

FileMaker provides many tools to help you organize and arrange objects on a layout. This section discusses some of these tools.

GROUPING OBJECTS

Objects can be grouped together to form a new object. You do so by selecting the desired objects and choosing Arrange, Group or pressing (⌘-R) [Ctrl+R]. The resulting object behaves just like any other object. It has a single set of selection handles, and it can be moved and resized as described in the previous sections. Any formatting applied to the grouped object is applied to each of the elements of the group, as if you had simply selected all the elements individually. Grouped objects can be further grouped with other objects to form yet new objects.

To ungroup an object, select the object, and then choose Arrange, Ungroup or press (⌘-Shift-R) [Ctrl+Shift+R]. If an object was formatted as a button, ungrouping it deletes the button definition.

TIP

> Ungrouping an object is the easiest way to remove a button definition from an object. This works even if the object in question isn't a grouped object.

LOCKING OBJECTS

To prevent an object from being moved, resized, reformatted, or deleted, you can lock it by selecting it and choosing Arrange, Lock or pressing (⌘-Option-L) [Ctrl+Alt+L]. When you select a locked object, its handles appear grayed out rather than black.

When you select a combination of locked and unlocked objects, if you attempt to move or resize them as a set, only the unlocked objects are affected. If you attempt to change the formatting of the selected set, you see an error that the formatting can't be applied to some objects in the set because they are locked.

Locking objects is very useful when you have objects stacked on top of or overlapping one another. It's as if the locked objects become a backdrop against which you do your work. Whether you leave the objects permanently or temporarily locked, it becomes much easier to select and work with certain objects when the objects behind them are locked.

To unlock an object, choose <u>A</u>rrange, Unloc<u>k</u>, or press (⌘-Option-Shift-L) [Ctrl+Alt+Shift+L].

ALIGNING OBJECTS

It's often desirable to align objects on a layout relative to one another, and FileMaker has some built-in tools to make this easy to do. For instance, you might have 10 fields on a layout that you want to be aligned along their left edges.

You can use the Align, <u>D</u>istribute, and Re<u>s</u>ize To menu options, under the <u>A</u>rrange menu, to manipulate objects relative to each other.

You can specify a Top to Bottom alignment, or a Left to Right alignment, or both. You can also distribute objects or resize to the largest or smallest dimensions of the selected objects.

When you align a set of objects relative to one another, one of the objects usually serves as the reference point. For instance, when you left-align a set of objects, the leftmost object is the reference point. The other objects move left while the leftmost object remains in place. Similar results are obtained for aligning to the right, top, and bottom. The exception to this is when one or more of the selected objects is locked. If this is the case, and you want to, say, left-align a set of objects, the leftmost *locked* object becomes the reference point.

The rules for centering are slightly different. When centering left to right, the objects are centered on the midpoint between the leftmost and rightmost selection points. For top-to-bottom centering, they are aligned on the midpoint between the topmost and bottommost selection points.

The option to distribute space is useful when you want to be sure that objects in a set are equidistant from one another. The two outermost objects, whether left-to-right or top-to-bottom, act as anchors for the distribution: The selected objects in between them are spaced apart evenly.

> TIP
>
> Even the sloppiest of developers can benefit from this simple process: Select a group of fields, irregularly placed and irregularly sized. Then choose <u>A</u>rrange, Align, <u>L</u>eft Edges, followed by <u>A</u>rrange, <u>D</u>istribute, <u>V</u>ertically. Last, select Re<u>s</u>ize To, Largest <u>W</u>idth and Height. Voilá—your layout objects are now nicely sized and positioned.

 Although not a new feature, it's necessary to mention that FileMaker 8 did away with the old layout alignment dialog and keyboard shortcuts in favor of adding capabilities to the <u>A</u>rrange menu. We won't weigh in on the debate that ensued; we're just glad we don't have to be the ones making those sorts of decisions.

LAYERING OBJECTS

FileMaker maintains a *stacking order* for objects on a layout. When a new object is added to a layout, it becomes the frontmost item in the stacking order. The stacking order becomes important when objects overlap one another. If two objects overlap, object A appears in front of object B if it is forward in the stacking order. Also, if object B is completely behind object A, it is impossible to select object B simply by clicking on it. When you click on a spot on a layout where multiple objects overlap, you select the frontmost of the objects.

There is no way to visually review the stacking order of the objects on a layout, but you can manipulate the stacking order by using the Bring to Front, Bring Forward, Send to Back, and Send Backward functions, all of which can be found under the Arrange menu.

→ The stacking order also determines the tab order of layouts published to the Web with Instant Web Publishing. For more on IWP, **see** "Layout Design," **p. 653**.

NOTE

> The stacking order also determines the order in which objects draw on the screen. With a local file or on a fast network, it's probably imperceptible, but on slow networks, you will sometimes see the objects draw one by one, from back to front.

SLIDING OBJECTS

If you are developing layouts that are intended to be printed, and you have variable amounts of text in certain fields, you may want to configure some objects on your layout to slide. Sliding eliminates excess whitespace from an object, allowing it to appear closer to its neighboring objects. You can configure an object to slide either up or to the left, using the dialog shown in Figure 4.13, which you open by selecting a set of objects and choosing Format, Sliding/Printing.

Figure 4.13
You can configure an object to slide either up or to the left by using the Set Sliding/ Printing dialog.

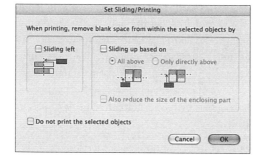

The effects of sliding can't be seen unless you are in Preview mode (or you actually print). If you set a field to slide, any whitespace in the field is removed in Preview mode. One caveat to know is that the contents of a field must be top-aligned to slide up and left-aligned to slide left.

Sliding does not reduce the amount of space between objects. Say you have a large text field, as in Figure 4.14, with a horizontal line located 10 pixels below the bottom of the field. If you set both objects to slide up, empty space in the field will be removed, and the line will slide up until it is 10 pixels away from the bottom of the field. Figure 4.15 shows how the record in Figure 4.14 looks in Preview mode. All objects on the layout have been set to slide up.

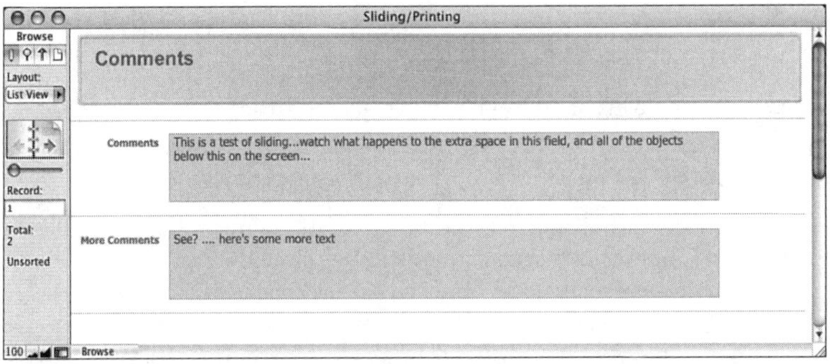

Figure 4.14
You can't see any effects of sliding while in Browse mode.

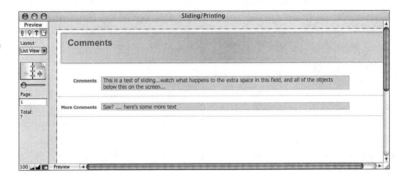

Figure 4.15
In Preview mode, objects slide either up or to the left, removing whitespace within fields.

The option to Also Reduce the Size of the Enclosing Part is useful when you have a list of variable-length records. Set the layout to accommodate the longest possible amount of data, and then turn on sliding for all the fields in the body and reduce the size of the enclosing part. The rows of the list will then have a variable length when they are previewed and printed. You must be sure to set all the objects in the list to slide; a single nonsliding object may cause the part to not reduce properly. Objects such as vertical lines do not shrink in size to accommodate variable record widths, so if you need this effect, use left or right field borders, which do shrink appropriately.

Sliding can be applied to portals as well, but objects in a portal can't slide. If a portal is set to slide up, any blank rows of the portal are suppressed, but there's no way to make the height of the individual rows of the portal variable. Portal sliding is useful and necessary in reports that must pull in data from related files. Typically, if there's a portal on a printable report, you should set the portal to display a large number of records and not to have a vertical scroll. If you enable sliding as well, any unneeded portal rows simply disappear.

The Set Sliding/Printing dialog also has an option to make a layout object nonprinting. As with sliding, this setting is apparent only in Preview mode. Typically, you use this option to allow buttons, background images, and data entry instructions—items you typically wouldn't want to have on a printout—to be visible only in Browse and Find modes.

WORKING WITH THE TAB CONTROL OBJECT

NEW FileMaker 8 introduced the Tab Control object. It is a fantastic development time-saver and can dramatically reduce the number of layouts you're used to working with in FileMaker solutions.

The Tab Control does one thing: It extends the amount of screen real estate you can provide users by allowing them to flip from one pane to another while remaining on the same layout and same record. For an example, refer to Figure 4.16.

Figure 4.16
These tab objects allow users an intuitive means of working with multiple panes of information and controls.

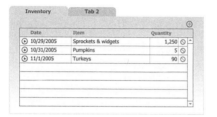

ADDING A TAB CONTROL OBJECT TO A LAYOUT

To add a Tab Control object to a layout, click the Tab Control button in the Status Area and drag a rectangular area on your layout. You are then presented with the Tab Control Setup dialog, as shown in Figure 4.17.

Figure 4.17
The Tab Control Setup dialog enables you to create however many panes you require.

In the Tab Control Setup dialog, you can add as many tab panes as necessary and then choose alignment and tab styles. Although the options aren't exhaustive, the simplicity of working with the Tab Control object will no doubt quickly win you over.

Notice that the width of the tabs on the Tab Control will conform to their text labels if you've chosen anything other than Full justification. If you'd like a little more whitespace for your tabs, or want to tweak their look, you can use our low-tech approach of adding spaces before and after the tab pane labels.

NOTE

> Note that in version 8, you cannot programmatically control the names of tabs, unless you lay a text object over the location of the tab in question. This can be a time-consuming workaround: You'd need to do it for each tab pane.

After you close the dialog, you'll remain in Layout mode and will be able to add layout objects—including additional Tab Control objects—to the tab pane currently selected.

The Tab Control is operational in Layout mode. If you click once on a tab, you'll flip to the pane it represents. If you want to return to editing in the Tab Control Setup dialog, double-click the Tab Control object. If you'd like to edit the properties of the tab pane (color, line weight, and line color), click a second time on the tab itself. You will see an active rectangle appear.

Be aware that you cannot control what color a non-active tab will display. FileMaker automatically determines that color based on the color of the active pane. An obvious workaround is to lay a rectangular object over the top of the tabs in question.

When you leave Layout mode, the default pane for that Tab Control object will be the last active pane in which you were working in Layout mode.

When you select the Tab Control object, notice that its rectangular area includes its tab space. The negative space next to your tabs when they're not set to Full justification is still space that is considered part of the selected pane. One handy technique we've learned is to place a button or text or even field objects in that space: They appear and disappear just as all objects members for a pane do.

One last feature of the Tab Control object is the capability to add objects to a pane by moving the Tab Control behind them in the stacking order. If you move the Tab Control object to the back and then drag it to a location where it encloses a layout object, that object will then automatically become associated with the Tab Control. This is a nice way to save time when you've got to add a new Tab Control to an existing layout. Simply drag a selection rectangle for the Tab Control object onto a layout, select Move to Back from the Arrange menu, and your object will "slurp up" all the objects higher in the stacking order that it encloses. (The FileMaker team affectionately refers to this feature as "hoovering" objects.)

WORKING WITH FIELDS

The primary purpose of a layout is to allow users to interact with data. By *interact*, we mean everything from viewing, editing, and formatting to finding and sorting. Although a field is at some level just another type of layout object and can be manipulated using the same tools as other layout objects, a number of tools are designed specifically for working with fields. These provide you with a great deal of freedom and flexibility for creating the interfaces that work best for your users and your solution. We don't cover every option of every tool here, but rather try to give you a sense of what the tools are and some of the situations in which to use them.

ADDING FIELDS TO LAYOUTS

There are essentially two ways you can add fields to a layout: by using the Field button in the Status Area and by duplicating an existing field.

The first of these—which is generally also the first method that people learn—involves clicking and dragging the Field button in the Status Area out to the section of the layout where you want to place the field. The attributes of a field added this way are governed by the current default format attributes. However, the field's width is always 79 pixels. Its height is determined by a combination of the default font, font size, pen width, and object effects (for example, embossing, engraving, drop shadow).

As with other layout objects, when you duplicate an existing field, the new field has all the attributes of the previously existing field (including its width). Remember, to duplicate any layout object, either you can select it and choose Edit, Duplicate or press (⌘-D) [Ctrl+D], or you can select it and then (Option-drag) [Ctrl-drag] to a new location. In either case, if you have selected a single field, when you duplicate it, you see the Specify Field dialog and can select the new field. On the other hand, if you have selected multiple objects, when you duplicate them, you get just the duplicated objects.

Keep in mind that you will be duplicating *all* the attributes of a field—including any button behaviors you've attached to it, tool tips you may have assigned, and so on.

 There are some issues to be aware of when copying and pasting fields from a layout in one file to a layout in another file. See "Copying and Pasting Fields Between Files" in the "Troubleshooting" section at the end of this chapter.

Each field object on a layout is defined to display data from a particular field. Unless you have selected Sample Data in the View, Show menu, you see the field's name on the object when you're in Layout mode. If the field name begins with ::, that's an indication that the object is linked to a related field. To know which relationship is used, you need to go into the Field/Control Setup dialog. That's also where you can redefine a field object to display the contents of a different field. You can get to the Field/Control Setup dialog by double-clicking the object.

TIP

> If a field has been defined as a button, double-clicking it takes you to the Button Definition dialog, not the Field/Control Setup dialog. Similarly, if multiple fields are grouped together, right-clicking will only give you the control elements of the dialog.

FIELD CONTROL STYLE

You can apply several field control options to the fields on a layout. To get to the Field/Control Setup dialog, which is shown in Figure 4.18, either double-click or right-click the object and choose Field/Control Setup from the contextual menu.

For standard fields where a user will be manually entering and editing data, the Edit Box format is appropriate. The option to include a vertical scrollbar is normally used only when a user is able and/or expected to type multiple lines of text.

→ For more information on creating value lists, **see** "Working with Fields," **p. 41**.

The options to format a field as a Drop-Down List, Pop-Up Menu, Checkbox Set, or Radio Button Set require that you specify a value list that will provide the content for the selection values.

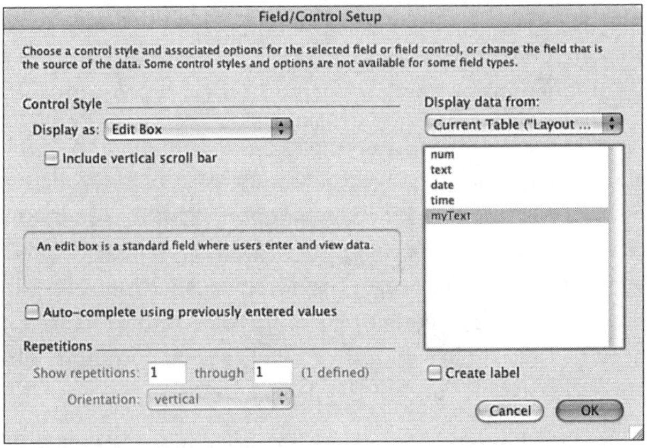

Figure 4.18
The Field/Control Setup dialog enables you to format a field with a range of control choices, set auto-complete behaviors, or set repeating values to display.

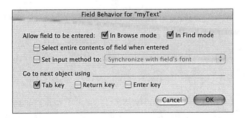

NEW Note that in FileMaker 8 you can apply a Drop-Down Calendar to a field, to help with entering dates, and you can also toggle either a drop-down indicator icon or a calendar picker icon for the fields you're working with. The two icons—drop-down indicator and calendar icon—will appear only if a field has its right border turned on.

The lower left of the Field/Control Setup dialog is relevant only for fields that have been defined to allow multiple repetitions. You can hard-code the starting and ending repetitions and specify whether a vertical or horizontal orientation should be used.

On the right of the dialog you can opt to change the field associated with the selected object.

FIELD BEHAVIOR

The Field Behavior dialog contains controls for setting when a field is enterable and how a user can exit it. To access this dialog, select one or more fields on a layout, and then choose Format, Field Control, Behavior. You can also (Control-click) [right-click] a field and choose Field Control, Behavior from the contextual menu. The Field Behavior dialog is shown in Figure 4.19.

Figure 4.19
Using the Field Behavior dialog, you can specify which modes a field can be entered in, as well as the keystrokes that can be used to exit a field.

In this dialog, you can control whether a user is able to enter a particular field while in Browse or Find mode. Before version 7 of FileMaker, there was no distinction between modes; a field was either enterable or not. Typically, a user should be able to enter a field in both Browse and Find mode. Sometimes, though, you'll want a field to be enterable in only one of these modes. For instance, you might have a field that you don't want users to manually edit, but that they may need to use as part of a query. On the other hand, there may be unindexed fields on your layout that, for performance reasons, you don't want users to search on.

The other setting in this dialog is the Go to Next Object Using option. By default in FileMaker Pro, pressing the Tab key lets users move to the next field on the layout. Developers may also specify the option to allow the Return and/or Enter keys to perform this function. This is desirable in some cases to allow rapid data entry and to prevent data-entry mistakes. For instance, by setting a text field to use the Return key to go to the next field, you prevent users from accidentally adding stray returns at the ends of fields. Obviously, if a user needs to be able to enter carriage returns in a text field—say in a Comments field—you wouldn't set the Return key to go to the next field.

CAUTION

> Normally, the Enter key serves to commit a record and exit all fields. If you change all your field behavior to have Enter go to the next field, be aware that users need to explicitly click on the background of a layout or perform some script or navigation routine to commit record changes.

SETTING THE TAB ORDER

When moving from field to field on a layout with the Tab key—or (Return) and/or [Enter], as described in the previous section—the order in which the fields are activated is known as the *tab order*. The default tab order is the order in which the fields appear on the layout from top to bottom. Rearranging fields changes the tab order.

Tab order is stored with the layout, so there's no opportunity to customize the tab order for different users. The Set Tab Order dialog is shown in Figure 4.20. After the tab order has been edited manually, rearranging fields doesn't change the tab order. New fields are added to the end of the tab order automatically, regardless of position.

Figure 4.20
You can change the tab order of a layout to make data entry flow in a logical progression for end users.

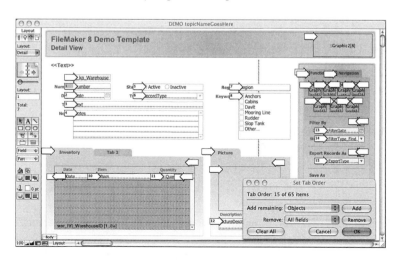

Anyone with the ability to modify a layout can change its tab order; do so by selecting Layouts, Set Tab Order. The Set Tab Order dialog has changed in FileMaker 8. It is no longer modal and allows developers to click on both fields (the arrows to the left of objects) and objects themselves (the arrows to the right of objects) to manually edit the tab order for a given layout. You can also opt to remove items by pressing the Delete or Backspace key.

The dialog operates on like objects. If you want to add all fields to the tab order or remove all objects, choose from the two menu options in the dialog and click the button for the appropriate command.

Note that it is entirely possible to attach a button behavior to a field and for that field to then appear twice in the tab order. One instance will tab into the field for editing, and another will select the field to perform the button action.

 The Set Tab Order dialog allows developers to add and remove both fields and objects (including Tab Control object tabs) from the tab order of a given layout. Note that new in FileMaker 8 is the capability to tab from object to object on the screen and, with a press of either the spacebar or the Enter key, to perform whatever action is associated with an object, including scripted button actions. Any object that has been made active by tab order will display a highlight rectangle to the user (regardless of its actual shape). This is a great new feature for users who prefer to drive their computers from their keyboards.

→ To further enable users to work from keyboard commands, and review adding keyboard shortcuts via Custom Menus, **see** "Working with Custom Menus," **p. 373**.

MERGE FIELDS

If you've ever done a mail merge, the concept of merge fields should be familiar to you. Merge fields give you a way of incorporating field data within text blocks on a layout. This is useful for creating form letters, labels, and reports.

Merge fields display field data, but they don't behave like or have all the properties of normal fields. A user can't click into a merge field to do data entry, for instance.

To add a merge field to a layout, choose Insert, Merge Field, or press (⌘-Option-M) [Ctrl+Alt+M]. You are then prompted to specify a field. After you make your selection, the field name shows up on your layout surrounded by angle brackets, as shown in Figure 4.21. Note that you can add a merge field alone to a layout, or you can incorporate it (and potentially others) into a block of text within a text object.

The primary benefit of merge fields is that field data can be flexibly placed within a text block; text before and after the merge field is repositioned to close up any extra space. Thus, within a text block, you could have "Hi, <<First Name>>, how are you?" On one record, that would come out as "Hi, Joe, how are you?" whereas on another it might be "Hi, Frederick, how are you?"

Text, number, date, and time formatting applied to a text block are applied to any appropriate merge field within the text block. It is not possible to have a single text block that contains multiple merge fields that have different number formats applied to them.

Figure 4.21
Merge fields allow field data to be displayed inline with text and avoid the need for sliding fields.

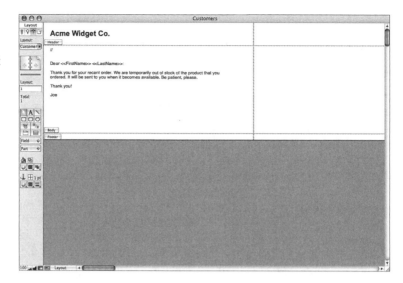

PORTALS

Portals are the last remaining tool you will find in the Status Area. Portals, as mentioned in Chapter 2, "Using FileMaker Pro," display information from related records that are associated with not only the layout but also the record a user is currently viewing on a layout.

Portals are a deep topic and cannot be separated from an in-depth discussion on data modeling. Furthermore, they can involve some advanced techniques to put them to good use. We've opted to cover portals in two chapters: Chapter 6, "Working with Multiple Tables," and Chapter 16, "Advanced Portal Techniques."

TROUBLESHOOTING

COPYING AND PASTING FIELDS BETWEEN FILES

When I copy and paste fields from a layout in one file into another file, sometimes the fields retain their proper identity, sometimes they have no identity, and sometimes they have the wrong identity. Why is that?

When you copy fields from a layout in one file and paste them into another file, they may or may not retain their identity, as you've discovered. A field retains its identity when there exists a field in the destination file that has the same source table and field name as the source field. Additionally, the layouts must be based on identically named table occurrences. (It's not enough for the source tables to be named the same.) If the table occurrences match, but no similarly named field is found in that table, the field displays <field missing> when it's pasted into the destination file. If the table occurrence names don't match, the field shows up without any identity in the destination file.

Given the ease with which you can copy and paste tables using FileMaker Pro 8 Advanced, we recommend first creating a compatible schema in the destination file, and then copying your layout objects.

DETERMINING WHICH RECORDS WILL BE DISPLAYED ON A LAYOUT

I created a table occurrence that's supposed to display only invoices that are more than 60 days over-due. However, when I build a layout based on this table occurrence, I still see all the invoice records. What did I do wrong?

The problem here isn't anything you've done or haven't done, but rather your expectations. The table occurrence to which a layout is tied never determines which records from the source table are displayed on that layout. It merely determines the starting point on the Relationships Graph from which any action or object involving a relationship is evaluated. To view a set of related records, you will need to establish a perspective through which those records are viewed; in other words, you'll need a portal.

If you have a layout that's tied to an occurrence—*any* occurrence—of an Invoice source table, all the records from the Invoice table can be viewed from the context of that table occurrence. Think of it this way: A layout's table occurrence doesn't determine what records *you* can view from that layout, but rather, it determines what records the *records* of that table can view. So in the case of your table occurrence, which is supposed to show only invoices that are more than 60 days overdue, you'd need to view those via a portal from a layout tied, say, to a Customer table.

FILEMAKER EXTRA: DESIGNING CROSS-PLATFORM–FRIENDLY LAYOUTS

One of the things that sets FileMaker apart from other database applications is that it runs on both Windows and Macintosh operating systems. You can even have a mixed platform of client machines. If you are developing a system that needs to run on both platforms, there are a few design considerations you'll need to keep in mind.

First, text blocks may be rendered slightly differently between platforms because of differences in the dots per inch (dpi) that each supports. Macintosh operating systems use 72 dpi, whereas Windows is built at 96 dpi. Font sizes are always described as 72nds of an inch regardless of platform, which means that a 12-point font takes up 12 pixels (12/72nds of 72) on a Macintosh monitor, but 16 pixels on a Windows monitor (12/72nds of 96). In either case, this represents 1/6th of an inch.

The problem is that graphics and other layout objects are set to be a precise number of pixels tall and wide. If, for instance, you have a text block or field on a layout that's set to be 72 pixels wide, you'd be able to see fewer characters in that space on Windows. To account for this situation, you should make text blocks and buttons slightly oversized so that you don't truncate characters on Windows.

Not all fonts available on one platform are supported on the other; platform-specific fonts should be avoided. Some fonts display different baselines on Mac and PC. Trebuchet, for example, is a particularly bad culprit. The text baseline determines where the bottom of a font appears within a text block. Different baselines may mean that letters that hang below the baseline (such as g, y, j, p) have their tails cut off. Verdana tends not to be so bad, but it's a wide font and may consume too much horizontal space in a database. Lucinda is often a fairly safe font, if it is available to all your users. Tahoma also is fairly consistent between platforms. The combination of font and field box size is tricky, and you'll just have to experiment. Note that 10-point Verdana with a 16-pixel field height tends to work well on both platforms, but it's a very wide font. Use Arial/Helvetica if you're pressed for space.

The other big cross-platform layout problem is the viewable size of your layouts. It's generally desirable to create layouts on which users won't need to scroll to see important information. Different operating systems, even within a platform, may have different viewable layout areas, even at the same monitor resolutions. The problem is compounded by users who position their Dock or Start menu bar in different places. Windows XP tends to be the "piggiest" consumer of screen real estate and represents your lowest common denominator for a given resolution.

In the end, of course, the best advice when developing cross-platform applications is simply to test everything *early in your development process* on all operating systems you plan to support.

We also strongly urge you to create a template layout in which all your fonts have been selected, your field sizes established, and layout size and window size set. Then rather than having to carefully duplicate these standards across your solution, simply start all new layouts by duplicating this template.

4

DEVELOPING SOLUTIONS WITH FILEMAKER

CHAPTER

RELATIONAL DATABASE DESIGN

In this chapter

UNDERSTANDING DATABASE DESIGN

By now you've designed a simple FileMaker database, and built some nice data-entry screens and some reports. Your friends and co-workers are clamoring for you to add features. Can your system do invoicing? Inventory tracking? Bar-coding?

Well, it can probably do all those things. But it's going to take some planning. If this is your first time out with FileMaker, you're like the home carpenter who's just built her first bird-house. It's a nice birdhouse, but your kids want a tree fort. That's not just going to take more work; it's going to take more thought as well.

FileMaker is a tool for building *database applications*. Both parts of that term are important. By *applications* we mean coherent pieces of software with which users can interact in defined and predictable ways. And by *databases*, of course, we mean databases, pointing to the fact that FileMaker applications are, in the end, designed to help generate, store, and retrieve data.

Much of the rest of this book concentrates on either the application angle or the database angle. In this chapter, we're going to lay out for you the fundamentals of database design. When you're designing a simple contact manager or recipe book, the database structure is pretty clear. You know what fields you need to track and what kinds of fields they are. But when you get into tracking additional categories of data in the same database, things get trick-ier. If you want to build bigger and better databases, you'll need a firm grounding in database analysis and database design. Don't worry if that sounds ominous. It's easier than it appears.

DATABASE ANALYSIS

One of the great beauties of FileMaker is that it's very easy to just jump right in and start build-ing things that work. And this is fine, as long as you can keep the whole plan in your head.

Earlier chapters have looked at some practical techniques for separating and organizing data in a FileMaker database system. This chapter takes that work another step. Here you'll learn some tools for analyzing database problems and translating them into buildable designs.

This chapter approaches things and their relationships somewhat abstractly. Your goal here won't be a finished FileMaker system, but rather a more general design document. You'll learn a simple but powerful design process to help you take a real-world problem description and translate it into a blueprint that a database designer could use to build the database in a real-world database development system. This design document is known as an *entity-relationship diagram* (ERD). The process for creating an entity-relationship diagram, some-what simplified, looks like this:

1. Identify all the types of things involved in the problem that's being modeled (customers and sales, for example, or trucks, drivers, and routes).

2. For each type of thing, identify its attributes (customers have first and last names, truck routes have a beginning and an end).

3. Looking across all the types of things, determine the fundamental relationships between them (truck drivers have routes, trucks have drivers).

4. Draw up your findings into an entity-relationship diagram.

The ERD, again, is an abstract document that you can implement (build) with FileMaker or some other database tool. The sections that follow examine each of the steps of this process in much more detail.

Working with Entities and Attributes

When you set out to design a database system, there are two concepts you simply must be familiar with before you can say you have a solid planning foundation. You need to know the types of things your system will track, and you need to know the characteristics of each of those things. In a recipe list, for example, you track one kind of thing: recipes. A recipe's characteristics are, for example, recipe name, recipe type, calories, ingredients, and cooking time. You could draw it out like this:

Recipe

- Name
- Type
- Ingredients
- Cooking Time
- Calories
- Directions

Here is one thing followed by a collection of its characteristics. A bigger database system may store information about several kinds of things, each with its own set of characteristics. For example, if I want to write a database system for a motorcycle company, I might want to track information about motorcycles, customers, and sales. Now I have three kinds of things, each with its own set of characteristics.

In database design terminology, the things in your database system are called *entities*. Each entity is a specific, distinct kind of thing, about which you need to track information. This system tracks data about three distinct kinds of things. And each kind of thing has certain characteristics, which in the technical jargon are called *attributes*. The motorcycle example includes three entities, and each has some specific number of attributes (see Table 5.1).

5

TABLE 5.1   SIMPLE ANALYSIS OF A DATABASE STRUCTURE

Motorcycle	Customer	Sale
Model Number	First Name	Customer Name
Model Year	Last Name	Date
Vehicle ID Number	Birth Date	Amount
Factory Serial Number	Street Address	
Accessories	City	
Manufacturer	State	
Model Name	ZIP	

The first indispensable step in solid database design is to determine what entities (things) your proposed system needs to track, and what the attributes (characteristics) of each entity are. It's not just the first step, though—it's also the third, fifth, seventh, and so forth. Your list of things and their characteristics will inevitably change during your analysis, sometimes quite frequently. This is not a bad thing. It's a natural part of database design. You'll inevitably revisit and refine your list of entities and their attributes several times in the course of designing the system.

Roughly speaking, an entity is a class of things that all look more or less alike. In other words, from a database standpoint, you track many instances of an entity, and you track the same kind of information about each one. In a banking system, you'd probably have an entity called Customer because a banking database wants to keep track of many different customers, and wants to record roughly the same kinds of data about each one. (You'll always want to know a customer's birth date, Social Security number, home address, and the like.)

Attributes, on the other hand, refer to the kinds of information you track about each entity. If Customer is an entity in our banking database, birth date, home address, and Social Security number are among the attributes of a customer.

It won't surprise you to learn that entities often correspond to actual database tables, and attributes often correspond to database fields. More likely than not, a banking database will have a Customer table with fields for date of birth, address, and Social Security number.

NOTE

> The entities in these diagrams are purely abstract things. They may or may not translate directly into database tables. Your FileMaker solution may (and almost certainly will) end up with tables that aren't represented on your design diagram.

It's fairly easy to represent entities and attributes in the graphical notation of an ERD. Sometimes it's more convenient to draw an entity without showing any of its attributes, in which case you can draw it in a simple box, as shown in Figure 5.1.

Figure 5.1
A simple preliminary ERD showing entities for customers and accounts, with no attributes shown.

Customer		Account

Sometimes it's appropriate to show entities with some or all of their attributes, in which case you can add the attributes as shown in Figure 5.2.

Figure 5.2
An ERD showing entities for customers and accounts, with attributes shown.

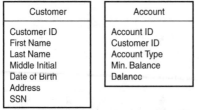

Customer	Account
Customer ID	Account ID
First Name	Customer ID
Last Name	Account Type
Middle Initial	Min. Balance
Date of Birth	Balance
Address	
SSN	

ENTITIES VERSUS ATTRIBUTES: A CASE STUDY

The focus of this chapter is in taking descriptions of real-world problems and turning them into usable ERDs. As was noted earlier, your first step in trying to model a problem into an ERD is sorting out the entities from the attributes. To see how to tackle this, let's begin with an example of a simple process description:

Maurizio's Fish Shack is ready to go digital. Maurizio sells fish out of his storefront but he's not worried about electronically recording his sales to consumers just yet. He just wants to keep track of all the fish he buys wholesale. Every time he buys a load of fish, he wants to know the kind, the quantity, the cost of the purchase, and the vendor he bought it from. This will give him a better handle on how much he's buying and from whom, and may help him negotiate some volume discounts.

Now you know the basics of Maurizio's business. Next you need to develop a list of potential entities. Here are some possibilities:

Fish	Load of fish	Purchase
Storefront	Variety	Vendor
Sale	Quantity	Volume discount
Consumer	Cost	

> **TIP**
>
> Usually the rule of thumb to apply when coming up with a list of possible entities is to pull out every word that's a noun; in other words, every word that represents a specific thing.

These are typically referred to as *candidate entities*, in that they all represent possible entities in the system. But *are* they all entities? You can immediately cross "storefront," "sale," and "consumer" off the list, for the simple reason that the process description already says that these are parts of his business that Maurizio *doesn't* want to automate at this time. That leaves us with the following potential entities:

Fish	Cost
Load of fish	Purchase
Variety	Vendor
Quantity	Volume discount

Well, "fish" and "load of fish" look like they refer to the same thing. According to the process description, a load of fish is actually a quantity of fish that Maurizio bought to resell. Put in those terms, it's clearly the same thing as a purchase. Now the list looks like this:

Purchase (of fish)	Quantity	Vendor
Variety	Cost	Volume discount

These all seem like reasonable things to track in a database system. But are they all entities? Remember that an entity is a *kind of thing*. The thing will probably appear many times in a database, and the system will always track a coherent set of information about the thing. Put that way, a purchase of fish sounds like an entity. You'll record information about many fish purchases in Maurizio's database.

What about something like "cost"? The "cost" in the process description refers to the price Maurizio paid for a load of fish, so cost isn't really an entity. It's the price paid for one load of fish. It's actually a piece of information *about* a fish purchase because each fish purchase has an associated cost. The same is also true for "variety" and "quantity." These are all attributes of the "purchase" entity.

Then you get to "vendor." A vendor is clearly a category of thing; you'll probably want to store information about many vendors in this database, so you can consider a vendor to be an entity. This leaves "volume discount." Well, that one's a bit tricky. It probably applies to a vendor, and might reasonably be called an attribute of a vendor. If you assume that each vendor may offer a discount of some kind, it makes sense for it to be an attribute of a vendor.

Figure 5.3 shows what the fledgling ERD for this system might look like, with the two entities from the process description and their various attributes.

Figure 5.3
An ERD showing entities for fish purchases and vendors, with attributes shown.

Purchase	Vendor
Purchase	Vendor Name
Date	Address
Fish Type	Volume
Weight	Discount
Unit Price	
Total Price	
Vendor	

A few things are noteworthy about this diagram. Notice that the entities are called Purchase and Vendor, instead of Purchases and Vendors. When naming entities, it's preferable to name them in the singular, rather than the plural. (You're trying to answer the question "each instance of this thing is a....") In FileMaker, we usually extend that convention to the database table that ends up being built for each entity.

DESIGN AS AN ITERATIVE PROCESS

Your general task when designing a database (or indeed any piece of software) is to take a set of things in a real-world *problem domain* and translate them into corresponding things in the *software domain*. In your software, you create a simplified model of reality. Concepts like "fish purchase" and "fish vendor" in the problem domain turn into concepts like "purchase entity" and "vendor entity" in a design, and may ultimately turn into things like "purchase table" and "vendor table" in the finished database.

But this translation (from problem domain to software) is not a one-way street. It's rare that there's a single, unambiguous software model that corresponds perfectly to a real-world problem. Usually, your software constructs are approximations of the real world, and how you arrive at those approximations depends a lot on the goal toward which you're working.

In general, software design follows an *iterative* path, meaning you perform a similar set of steps over and over again until you end up with something that's "close enough." For example, in your initial reading of the design problem, you might miss an entity or two. Or you might create entities you don't really need on later examination. Later, as you do more work on the project and learn more about the problem domain, you may revise your understanding of the model. Some entities might disappear and become attributes of other entities. Or some attributes might turn out to be entities in their own right. You might find it's possible to combine two similar entities into one. Or you might find out that one entity really needs to be split in two. We're not trying to make you feel uncertain or hesitant about your design decisions. Just recognize that it's not imperative, or necessarily even possible, to get the design exactly right the first time. You'll revisit your design assumptions frequently over the course of the design process, and this is a natural part of the process.

UNDERSTANDING RELATIONSHIPS

We've dealt with the first two steps of the design process now: the sorting out of entities and attributes. After you have what you think is a decent draft of a set of entities and attributes, the next thing to do is to start considering how these entities relate to one another. You need to become familiar with the fundamental types of entity relationships, and also with a simple notation for representing relationships graphically in a diagram.

REPRESENTING RELATIONSHIPS IN A DIAGRAM

Consider a system that stores information about farmers and pigs, among other things. Farmers and pigs are each entities, and these two entities have a direct relationship, in that each pig ties back to a single farmer.

There's a name for the farmer-pig relationship. It's called a *one-to-many* relationship, meaning that for each farmer there may be any number of pigs. "One farmer," as we usually put it, "can have many pigs."

Now you can expand on the entity-relationship notation. You already have a graphical shorthand for depicting the entities and attributes in a database system. Next you should add some conventions for showing the relationships among them. Each entity can be represented by a box, as before, and each relationship can be represented by a line that indicates the relationship type. In this simple notation, you'd depict the relationship between farmers and pigs along the lines of what's shown in Figure 5.4.

Figure 5.4
Entity-relationship notation for a database that stores information about farmers and pigs.

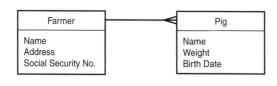

Notice that the line between the two entities that depicts their relationship branches out where it touches the Pig entity. In a one-to-many relationship, this fork or branch indicates the "many" end of the relationship. So this notation tells us that one farmer may be linked to many pigs. If the fork were on the other end, this would imply that one pig could be associated with many farmers, which would be a very different assertion about the data we're trying to model.

RELATIONSHIP TYPES

Those simple graphical conventions are the foundation of what you need in order to draw your entity-relationship diagrams. Another important concept is an understanding of the different relationship types you could encounter. You need to reckon with four types: the one-to-one relationship, which is a rare case you probably won't encounter much; the one-to-many and many-to-one relationships (the latter is simply a one-to-many relationship looked at from the other direction); and the many-to-many relationship, a common but more complicated relationship to which we'll need to devote special attention.

We'll consider each of these relationship types in turn, and show how to represent them in the ERD notation.

ONE-TO-ONE RELATIONSHIPS

The one-to-one relationship type is rather rare in practice. For example, consider a dataset concerning children and their birth records. Let's say that for now, you've decided that children and birth records should represent separate entities.

In a standard analysis sequence, after you've decided on entities and attributes, you'll start to ask questions about relationships. What's the relationship between children and birth records? Can one child have many birth records? No, each child is born only once. And can one birth record pertain to more than one child? Again, probably not. So the relationship between a child and a birth record appears to be one-to-one. You can depict that as shown in Figure 5.5.

Figure 5.5
This ERD shows the one-to-one relationship between children and birth records. A single line with no "crow's-foot" is used.

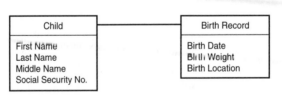

It's rare to let the two sides of a one-to-one relationship stand as separate entities. Instead, you'll often fold one of the entities into the other. In this case, you might decide to move all the attributes of a birth record into the Child entity and get rid of Birth Record as a separate entity.

When Is One-to-One the Right Choice?

There are some circumstances that would justify keeping two separate entities, even when the relationship between them is one-to-one. Probably the clearest case occurs when one of the entities represents data that's filled out only in infrequent cases. Such could be the case in a database that stores information about spacecraft. For simplicity, assume that all the relevant information on a spacecraft can be represented by a single entity, called Craft.

Now further suppose that when a spacecraft reaches the end of its useful life, it's formally decommissioned, and at that point a huge amount of data is gathered—once and only once—as part of the decommissioning process. For this example, assume that there are an additional 300 attributes you need to track when a craft is decommissioned. You could add all those attributes to the Craft entity. But in actual use, those columns are almost always going to be empty. They won't be filled until a craft is taken out of service. This leads to the potential for large "holes" in the actual, physical database. In other words, at the implementation level, it could be very wasteful to have those 300 data slots ready and waiting when they're used very infrequently. They might not take up much, if any, extra space, but it would be unwieldy to scroll through them all during ordinary development and use.

One solution here would be to have Craft and Decommission as two separate entities in a one-to-one relationship. You would create a Decommission entry for a Craft only when you actually needed it, and your view of the data would be a little cleaner as well. For example, to find all ships that had been decommissioned, you'd just run a search in the Decommission table. On the other hand, if the system contained only a Craft entity, you might end up needing some special additional attribute to signify that a ship had been decommissioned, or else you'd have to rely on certain specific attributes, such as "decommission date" being empty if the ship hadn't been decommissioned yet.

ONE-TO-MANY RELATIONSHIPS

We've already devoted some attention to the one-to-many relationship. The relationships of a customer to sales, of a farmer to pigs, and of a worker to timesheets are all examples of one-to-many relationships. And you've seen the crow's-foot notation for indicating these relationships, in which the fork notation indicates the "many" side of the relationship.

There's another piece of terminology for one-to-many relationships that's helpful to know. You'll frequently see the entity that represents the "one" side of the relationship referred to as the *parent* entity, whereas the "many" side is often referred to as the *child* entity. If you hear a database architect blurt out a reference to a "child" table, odds are she's referring to the entity on the "many" side of a one-to-many relationship.

MANY-TO-ONE RELATIONSHIPS

There's no difference at all between the concepts of a one-to-many and a many-to-one relationship. They're the same idea, just seen from different points of view. If the relationship between customers and sales is one-to-many, then it's equally true that the relationship between sales and customers is many-to-one. Customer is the parent of Sale, Sale is the child of Customer. These statements are equivalent. Figure 5.6 shows the Customer-Sale relationship. Whether you choose to describe this as a one-to-many or a many-to-one depends on which side you start from in your description. The relationship of a customer to a sale is one-to-many; the relationship of a sale to a customer is many-to-one. One-to-many and many-to-one are two sides of the same coin; a relationship can't be one without being the other.

Figure 5.6
The Customer-Sale relationship drawn as both a one-to-many and a many-to-one relationship.

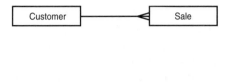

MANY-TO-MANY RELATIONSHIPS

Consider the relationship between actors and movies. One actor may play roles in many movies, and one movie involves roles played by many actors. So each actor can relate to many movies, and each movie may be associated with many actors. This is a classic many-to-many relationship. You can depict it as shown in Figure 5.7.

Figure 5.7
Entity-relationship notation for a many-to-many relationship.

Many-to-many relationships are extremely common in relational database systems. Here are examples of some other many-to-many relationships:

- **Attorney-Case**—One attorney may serve on many cases, and one case may involve many attorneys.
- **Player-Game**—One player may play in many games, and one game involves many players.
- **Product-Invoice**—One invoice may contain orders for many products, and one product may be ordered on many different invoices.
- **Student-Class**—One student may participate in many classes, and one class may have many students enrolled.

You can probably think of your own examples pretty easily as well.

Many-to-many relationships are a bit trickier than the others to actually implement in real life. When we get to the details of how to build a FileMaker database based on an ERD, you'll see the specific techniques you need to bring a many-to-many relationship to life in FileMaker. For now, though, we'll just use the ERD as an analysis tool, and not worry about implementation.

RELATIONSHIP CARDINALITY

You've seen how to filter a process description into a list of entities and their attributes, and you've seen a useful language for describing the relationships between those entities. So far, in describing these relationships, we've been mainly concerned with the question "How many?" How many purchases can relate to a customer? One, or many? And how many customers can participate in a purchase?

The answers to these questions tell you into which of the three (or four) relationship types a given relationship falls. This information is sometimes referred to as the *cardinality* of the relationship. Cardinality specifies whether a relationship is one-to-one, one-to-many, many-to-one, or many-to-many.

RELATIONSHIP OPTIONALITY

Relationship cardinality answers a fairly simple question: Given an entity A, how many instances, at most, of another entity B might potentially be linked to a given instance of A? The answer could be "zero" (in which case there's no relationship between the entities), but in general the answer is either "one" or "many" (in other words, more than one).

It can be useful to know one additional piece of information about a relationship. This is what's called the relationship's *optionality*. This information is not strictly necessary for a complete ERD, but it can be very useful information to gather.

Cardinality allows you to answer the question "How many?" What is the maximum number of orders with which a customer may be linked? One, or many? Optionality, by contrast, answers the question "How few?" What is the *minimum* number of orders with which a customer may be linked and still be considered a valid customer? Is it permissible to have a customer with no recorded orders? Answering these questions often reveals important information about business rules and workflow in the intended system. The answers probably won't mean designing your data structures any differently, but could be quite important when it comes to data validation and workflow in the finished system.

OPTIONALITY IN MANY-TO-MANY RELATIONSHIPS

Suppose that you have a database system designed to track information about college students (including their high school transcripts and grades from other schools, sports, student organizations, and classes). Two of the entities in this system are a Student entity (of course) and a Class entity. The relationship between these two entities is many-to-many. So you know that one student record can potentially be linked to many class records, if a student is enrolled in many classes. But is there a *minimum* number of classes that a student must be associated with at any time? Put differently, should it be permissible to have a student record in the system that's not associated with *any* class records?

Your first instinct might be to say no. After all, students have to take at least one class, don't they? But that's not quite the question that's being asked. The question is not whether all student records *eventually* have to be associated with at least one class record. Presumably they do. The question is, must a student record, always and at all times in its existence, be associated with at least one class record? And the answer to this question is clearly no. New students, or transfers, are not associated with class records until they first enroll for classes. But their records might be entered into the system weeks or even months prior to enrollment. So the answer here is that it's acceptable for student records to have no associated classes.

Here's how to show this rule in the ERD notation. Take a look at Figure 5.8 and notice that we've added some adornment to the Class end of the Student-Class relationship. In addition to the crow's-foot, which shows the fact that, potentially, multiple class records can be associated with a single student, we now also have an open circle to indicate that it's all right for a student to have *no* associated class records.

Figure 5.8
Entity-relationship
notation for the
Student-Class rela-
tionship, with option-
ality shown at the
Class side.

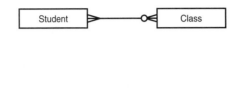

In an ERD in which you fully diagram all the optionalities, each end of a relationship line has two notations: one to show the smallest number of records that *have* to exist in the related entity (the optionality) and the other to show the largest number that *can* exist (the cardinality). The graphical notation closest to the entity specifies the cardinality, and the one farther away specifies the optionality. So the way to read the notations at the Class end of the diagram in Figure 5.8 is something like this: "One student record may be associated with as few as zero class records or with many class records."

Now consider the other end of the relationship, the Student side. What's the fewest number of students with which a class may be associated? Well, before anyone enrolls for the class, the answer is zero. And what's the largest number of students with which the class may be associated? It doesn't matter whether the answer is 10 or 100. As long as the answer is more than 1, you can just use the generic term "many" again. The Student end of this relationship is drawn as shown in Figure 5.9.

Figure 5.9
Entity-relationship
notation for the
Student-Class rela-
tionship, with option-
ality shown at both
sides.

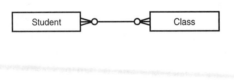

This diagram now provides a bit more information than a plain, unadorned ERD would have. Now you've specified not only that the relationship of Class to Student is many-to-many, but also that it's permissible to have classes with no associated students, and students with no associated classes.

This set of questions about optionality applies equally to all relationship types. But each relationship type has some optionality scenarios that are, for lack of a better term, more typical of that relationship type. In the sections that follow we'll examine some of these typical scenarios. Nothing in the sections that follow, though, should suggest that a given relationship type will never exhibit other types of optionality.

OPTIONALITY IN ONE-TO-MANY RELATIONSHIPS

In dealing with one-to-many (and, by extension, with many-to-one) relationships, there are two broad scenarios, which can be called "loose binding" and "tight binding."

OPTIONALITY IN ONE-TO-MANY RELATIONSHIPS: LOOSE BINDING

Consider the relationship between the entities Customer and Sale. It seems to be one-to-many: One customer may have many sales. That's the cardinality. What about the optionality? Take it one side at a time. Is it permissible to have a customer with no associated sale records? This is a business rules question; in many business scenarios, it seems likely that this would be all right. Until people actually buy something, they're better described as prospects than customers, but we probably still want to allow them in the database without a sale. So a customer can have anywhere from zero to "many" sale records.

Now look from the other side. Is it permissible for a sale record not to be associated with any customer records? This, again, is a business rules question, and will need to be determined based on the system's intended use. If the answer is no, a sale must be associated with at least one customer. Zero customers on a sale would not be permitted.

Figure 5.10 shows this relationship with all the optionalities drawn in on both sides. This optionality pattern is very typical of one-to-many or many-to-one relationships: The "many" side may range from zero to many associated items, whereas on the "one" side each child record must have exactly one parent, no more, no less. The double lines on the Customer side indicate the cardinality and optionality of a Customer seen from the perspective of a Sale: Each Sale must have a minimum of one Customer, and a maximum of one Customer. Put more succinctly, a sale is associated with one and only one customer.

Figure 5.10
Entity-relationship notation for the Customer-Sale relationship. This is a very typical optionality pattern for one-to-many and many-to-one relationships.

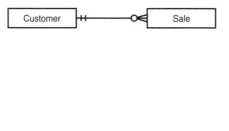

We call this optionality configuration a "loose binding" because it's permissible to have Customer records with no associated Sales. A given customer may have one or more sale records—or then again, she may not.

OPTIONALITY IN ONE-TO-MANY RELATIONSHIPS: TIGHT BINDING

Consider another common business model: the model for an order of some kind. Each order can contain requests for multiple kinds of goods. You would put each request on its own order line: five kumquats on the first line, three bass lures on the second, and so on. Each order can have as many order lines as it needs in order to list everything that was ordered.

So, clearly, you have a one-to-many relationship from order to order line. If you look at the "one" side first, you'll see that, as with other one-to-many relationships you've seen, the "one" side is pretty hard and fast: Each order line must be tied to one and only one order. On the other side, we know that an order can possibly contain many order items. But what's the fewest items an order may contain and still be considered a valid order? Should it be permissible to leave an order sitting there with no items on it?

This, as is generally the case with optionality questions, may end up being a question about business rules that a database designer may not be able to decide on his own without conferring with someone involved on the business side of the process being modeled. Let's assume that you learn that it should not be permissible to create an order with no associated order items. Every order has to be an order *for* something. You can't leave it blank. So an order needs a minimum of one associated order line, and the ERD with optionalities will look as shown in Figure 5.11.

Figure 5.11
Entity-relationship
notation for the
Order–Order Line
relationship. This
shows a parent entity
that must always have
at least one child.

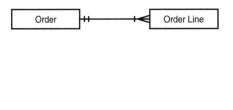

NOTE

> This kind of tight binding between a parent and a child entity is not as common as the looser type of one-to-many relationship, in which it's permissible for the parent to be childless, so to speak. But it does happen, so you should be familiar with it.

OPTIONALITY IN ONE-TO-ONE RELATIONSHIPS

Optionality is a concept that's easily learned by example, so let's look at a few more examples. Look again at the earlier example of a legitimate one-to-one relationship. The scenario that was previously discussed included spacecraft that would have an associated Decommission record created at the end of their lives. So a Craft spends most of its time without an associated Decommission record. As a result, the minimum number of Decommission records associated with a craft is zero: It's fine to have a Craft with no associated Decommission record. That's just an active Craft!

From the other side, it's not logical to have a Decommission record that doesn't relate back to some Craft record. Having a Decommission record that stood alone would be meaningless. So your optionalities for this relationship appear as shown in Figure 5.12. The optionalities tell a lot in this case. With the optionalities added to the ERD, you can easily tell which of these two is the "strong" entity, and which is the "weak" or optional one. This diagram reveals clearly that there will *always* be a Craft record, and there will *sometimes* be an associated Decommission record.

It's worth noting that this specific optionality pattern is the one that's most likely to lead to preserving two separate entities in a one-to-one relationship. When one of the two entities is optional, and loosely coupled to the other, it is often the most compelling argument for keeping the loosely coupled entity distinct.

Figure 5.12
Entity-relationship notation for the Craft-Decommission relationship. This is a typical optionality pattern for one-to-one relationships.

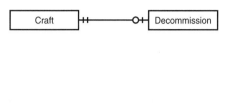

Optionality Recap

Not everyone uses optionality in ER diagrams, but we think it's a good habit to cultivate. After you do it for a while, you might start to omit it except in cases in which the optionality is a little different from what you might expect. Most one-to-many relationships, for example, are of the "loose binding" type, in which the children are optional. With sufficient practice, you may find you want to write in the optionality of a one-to-many relationship only when the binding is tight (that is, when at least one child record must always be present). Likewise, it's rather rare to find a many-to-many relationship that isn't "loose" on both sides. So you may eventually decide to annotate only the exceptional cases.

UNDERSTANDING THE ROLE OF KEYS IN DATABASE DESIGN

So far, this chapter has presented quite a few ERDs. Many of them depict relationships, but so far there's been no discussion of exactly *how* a relationship between two entities is created and maintained. The answer is simple: We create fields in each entity called *keys*, which allow instances of one entity to be associated with instances of another. You might relate orders to customers, for example, by using a customer's Social Security number as a key. Each order would then contain the Social Security number of the related customer as one of its attributes. The following sections explore the concept of keys in more detail.

KEYS THAT DETERMINE UNIQUENESS

One of the crucial tenets of relational database theory is that it has to be possible to identify any database row, anywhere, without ambiguity. Put differently, every row in every table should have a unique identifier. If I have a record in a table of orders, I want to be able to ask it "What customer do you tie to?" and get an unambiguous answer. I need a simple answer: "Customer 400." End of story. The number 400, as it appears in the customer table, is a unique identifier.

A piece of data that is capable of uniquely identifying a database row is known as a *primary key*. A primary key is an attribute the values of which are (and always will be) unique for every single row in the database. It's a unique identifier, like a Social Security number, an ISBN number for a book, or a library card catalog number.

We recommend that *every database table you design* have a primary key, without exception. Some database systems force you to create a primary key for each new table. FileMaker Pro doesn't, but we strongly recommend that you do so anyway. There's very little to lose and a great deal to gain by following this practice.

5

The discussions in this chapter assume that every table you design, without exception, has a primary key.

What Makes a Good Primary Key?

So far, we've mentioned that every database table should have a primary key, and that those keys have to be unique, to distinguish one row from another absolutely. There's one other important rule: Primary keys are best (in our opinion) if they're *meaningless*.

The important idea here is that data chosen to act as a primary key should be free of real-world meaning or significance. When data has meaning in the real world, such meaning is subject to change. In simple terms, data that is supposedly unique may turn out not to be.

Here's an example. You're designing a database that holds information about the different offices of a company. Offices are stored in their own table. You decide that, because there's no more than one office in a city, the City field in the Office table will make a great primary key. It's unique, after all, and every Office record has a City value.

Just to be sure, you check with someone highly placed in the firm, and they assure you that, no, the company will never need to open more than one office in any one city. So you go ahead and build a database structure around the assertion that the City field in the Office table is unique.

Seven months later the company announces plans to open its second office in New Delhi, and you're left to explain why an important part of the database structure needs to be rewritten.

Imagine instead that you'd decided that the database system itself should generate a primary key. Offices will be numbered sequentially starting from 1. The important thing about this data is that it has meaning only to the database system itself. No one else cares, or even knows, that the New Delhi office is office number 14. The number 14 has no business significance.

The critical difference here is that when you used the City field as a primary key, you were relying on the stability of an assertion about the real world (a place notoriously subject to change). By contrast, when you create your own key, you're working in an environment that no one but the database programmers care about, so you're at liberty to design uniqueness rules that won't be affected by decisions beyond your control.

KEYS THAT REFER TO OTHER TABLES

Keys are essential to specifying relationships between tables. Going back to the example of customers and orders, the relationship between these entities is one-to-many: One customer may have many orders.

If you've followed the rule about always having a primary key, your Customer entity has a primary key, which you might call Customer ID. Now, each unique customer may have many related orders. To forge that relationship, each record in the Order table needs to store the Customer ID (the primary key) of the related customer. This value, when it's stored in the Order table, is known as a *foreign key*. The reason for the term is simple: The value in the Order table refers to a primary key value from a different ("foreign") table.

Figure 5.13 demonstrates how primary and foreign keys work together to create relationships between database tables. In a one-to-many relationship, the "many" side of the relationship always needs to contain a foreign key that points back to the "one" side. The child record thus "knows" who its parent is.

Figure 5.13
A one-to-many relationship between customers and orders, showing primary and foreign keys.

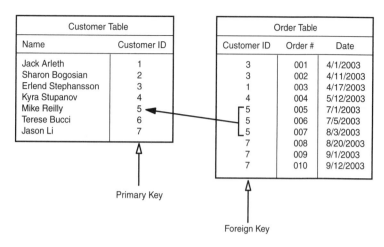

Primary Key

Foreign Key

→ FileMaker Pro has several built-in capabilities that help you add strong key structures to your FileMaker databases. For some ideas on how best to define key fields in FileMaker Pro, **see** "Working with Keys and Match Fields," **p. 162**.

MANY-TO-MANY RELATIONSHIPS: SOLVING THE PUZZLE

It was mentioned earlier that many-to-many relationships are slightly tricky. After you have an understanding of keys and have seen how they work in a simple ERD, the solution to the many-to-many problem becomes clearer. But first you should understand why it's a problem.

Assume that you're building a class registration database. It's intended to show which students are enrolled in which classes. It sounds as if you just need to deal with two entities: students and classes.

Students and classes have a many-to-many relationship. One student may participate in many classes, and one class may contain many students. That sounds fine, but how would you actually construct the relationship?

Based on the fundamental rule mentioned earlier, you need a primary key for each entity. Student needs a Student ID, and Class needs a Class ID. If you look at things from the student side for a moment, you know that one student can have many classes. Accordingly, from that viewpoint, Student and Class have a one-to-many relationship. If that's the case, from what you now know about foreign keys, you might conclude that each Class record should store a Student ID to indicate the student record to which it relates.

This won't work, though, for the simple reason that one class can contain many students. This means that the Student ID attribute in Class would have to contain not just one student ID, but a list of student IDs—one for each enrolled student. The same would be true in the other direction: Each student record needs a Class ID attribute that stores a list of all classes in which the student is enrolled.

One rule of relational database design that has already been touched on is that it's almost always a bad idea to store *lists* of things in database fields. As a general rule, when you find

5

you're using a field to store a list of some kind, that's a sign that you need to add another entity to your system where you can then store the list items as single records. This should suggest to you that the many-to-many problem can't be solved without some kind of additional entity. This is true, and it leads to a simple rule:

> Resolve a many-to-many relationship by adding an additional entity between the two in question.

Figure 5.14 shows an ERD for students and classes with an additional entity to solve the many-to-many problem.

Figure 5.14
An ERD for students and classes.

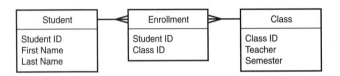

This middle entity is often called a *join table*. Each of the "outer" entities now has a one-to-many relationship with this middle entity. Not surprisingly, then, the middle entity has *two* foreign keys, because it's on the "many" side of two different relationships. It needs to hold both a Student ID *and* a Class ID.

What, if anything, does this entity represent in the real world, and what should it be called? One useful exercise, after you've resolved a many-to-many relationship, is to say to yourself, "This join entity represents the association of one A with one B." In the example of students and classes, the middle entity represents the association of a specific student with a specific class. If you think of the entity as a database table (which it will almost certainly become), each row of the table holds one student ID and one class ID. If such a row holds the student ID for student number 1009023 (Sam Tanaka) and the class ID for class H440 (History of the Sub-Sahara), this record tells us that Sam is (or was at some point) enrolled in History 440. This also suggests a good name for the entity: Enrollment. Each record in this table records the enrollment of one student in one class.

ATTRIBUTES IN A JOIN ENTITY

You've seen that this join entity needs, at the very least, two foreign keys: one pointing to each side of a many-to-many relationship. What other attributes does it need?

We emphasized earlier that "every entity, without exception, should have a primary key." Does this mean you should be adding an Enrollment ID to the Enrollment entity? Well, maybe, but not necessarily. Often the two foreign keys, taken together, constitute a unique key in themselves. In the enrollment example, it wouldn't make sense to have a student enrolled twice in the same class. So student ID 1009023 and class ID H440 should never both occur in the same record more than once. This is an example of something we haven't discussed yet: a *multicolumn key*. Often, the two foreign keys in a join entity constitute a primary key when taken together.

You'll need to assess this situation for yourself. If the two foreign keys together constitute a primary key, you're off the hook. But if the combination of those two keys isn't necessarily unique, you need an additional primary key in the join entity. As an example, suppose that you have a many-to-many relationship between People and Projects. A join table between the two contains Project Assignments. But in this system, a person may play several roles on a project, and thus be assigned to the project several times, in different capacities. In this case the combination of ProjectID and PersonID in the join table would not be considered unique, and you'd be well advised to add an additional unique AssignmentID.

Besides primary and foreign keys, are there other attributes that are appropriate in a join entity? Well, looking at the example of students and classes, you might wonder where you'd store an important piece of information such as a student's GPA. A student has only one GPA at one time, so you should store that as an attribute of the student. But what about course grades? Where do you record the fact that Sam earned a B+ in H440? Well, Sam can be enrolled in many courses, and so can receive many grades. So it's not appropriate to try to store the grade somewhere on Sam's student record. It belongs instead on the enrollment record for that specific course. And, if attendance was being taken, Sam's attendance would logically go on his enrollment record as well.

Sometimes join entities have attributes of their own, and sometimes they don't. You'll have to ask yourself whether you're merely trying to record the fact that the entities are associated or whether there are additional attributes of their association.

ADDITIONAL MANY-TO-MANY EXAMPLES

Resolving many-to-many relationships correctly is something that becomes easier with practice. We'll present a few more examples here, just to make the concepts clearer.

ACTORS AND MOVIES

One actor may be in many movies, and one movie generally involves several actors. To resolve this, you need a join entity containing an Actor ID and a Movie ID. This entity records the participation of one actor in one movie: An appropriate name might be Role or Casting. Do Actor ID and Movie ID together form a primary key? Put differently, can a single actor appear more than once in the same movie? Well, yes—some virtuoso actors occasionally take several roles in a movie. So you'd want a Role ID in addition to the other two keys. Attributes of the join table might include the name of the character played by the actor and the salary received for the role.

BOOKS AND LIBRARIES

One library obviously holds many books. But can one book be in many libraries? It depends. If you mean a physical copy of a book, the answer is no. If by "book" you mean something more like a "title," the answer is yes. Only one library can hold a given physical copy of Ole Rolvaag's *Giants in the Earth*. But as a book title, it can be held by many libraries.

Let's concentrate on the idea of the book as a title. In this case, the relationship of Titles to Libraries is many-to-many. The join entity contains a Title ID and a Library ID. Is this combination of keys unique? No, it isn't. One library may hold several physical copies of *Giants in the Earth*. So if you call your join entity a Holding, you can either add a special

Holding ID or add something else, such as a copy number, as an additional attribute. In the latter case, the combination of Title ID, Library ID, and Copy Number would be unique, and would constitute a compound primary key.

TIP

> Good names for join entities can greatly increase the clarity of your designs. If you can find a descriptive name like Role, Enrollment, or Holding, you should use it. If no clearer name presents itself, we recommend naming the join entity by a combination of the names of the entities it's joining: AttorneyClient, for example.

THE BASICS OF PROCESS ANALYSIS

So far this chapter has illustrated the principles of relational database design, and provided examples of a notation (the ERD notation) that can be used to produce a compact visual representation of a database structure. But this activity needs to fit into a broader type of activity that we refer to as *process analysis*.

Process analysis (in this book, anyway) refers to the act of deriving a database design from a real-world problem. In a sense, almost all database design needs to be preceded by some form of analysis to determine the scope of the problem being solved and focus on what needs to be built and why. Process analysis begins with a process description and ends with an ERD. That ERD will be the basis for implementing a real solution in FileMaker, a process covered in more detail in Chapter 6, "Working with Multiple Tables." To perform such analysis, you need a firm grip on entities, attributes, and relationships. Understanding relationship optionality is also a helpful tool.

Here again is the strategy for going from a problem to an ERD:

1. Capture the problem in a process description of some kind. (You might already have one, or might need to interview one or more people and write one up yourself.)
2. Boil the process description down into a list of candidate entities.
3. Figure out which of the candidate entities are "real" entities.
4. Figure out the attributes of each entity.
5. Determine the important relationships that link the entities together. Include cardinality information.
6. For greater clarity, determine the optionalities of the relationships from step 5.

PROCESS ANALYSIS: LEGAL DOCUMENTS

Karen Schulenberg's law office handles a great many estate issues. In particular, it handles a lot of wills. It needs a software system to track individual wills. For each will, the staff members need to know the identities of the testator, the executor, the beneficiaries, and any witnesses. They also need to know the date of the will itself and, if applicable, the testator's date of death. This information constitutes your process description.

DETERMINING ENTITIES

Next, you need a list of candidate entities. One rule of thumb, you might remember, is to pull out anything that looks like a noun.

Doing so, you'd get a list like the following:

Law office

Estate issue

Will

Testator

Executor

Beneficiary

Witness

Date of will

Date of death

The challenge here is to decide which of these are *types of things* (entities), and which are *characteristics of things* (attributes). For example, "date of will" and "date of death" both seem like characteristics of things (characteristics of a will and a testator, respectively). Witnesses and beneficiaries, by contrast, look like types of things—you could store additional information about witnesses and beneficiaries (name, address, height, and so on).

As far as the rest of the entity list, you can discard "law office" and "estate issue" because these pertain to the running of the law office, which is not what the desired database is about. "Will" is clearly an entity; in fact, it's the central entity of the proposed system.

What about "testator" and "executor"? By the logic we applied to witnesses and beneficiaries, these could both be entities: You could track plenty of additional information about them. So for now, leave them as entities.

The current universe of entities is shown in Figure 5.15.

Figure 5.15
An initial diagram showing entities for will, testator, executor, beneficiary, witness.

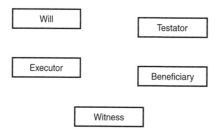

With this entity list in place, you need to fill in the attributes. Some of these may arise from the process description, whereas you may need to fill in others based on common sense or further investigation. Take a look at the entities one by one.

For the will, you know that the date is one important attribute. Witnesses and beneficiaries are important too, but you've decided that these are entities in their own right. So for now leave the Will entity with just a date.

The Testator is a person, so even though nothing lengthy was specified in the process description, you can reasonably assume that you'd want to capture information such as name and address. The process description states that you need to capture the death date, and you might as well ask for birth date also.

Similar logic applies to the Executor, Witness, and Beneficiary entities. All are people, so you'd presumably want their names and probably addresses as well. For witnesses, you'd also like to know the date on which they witnessed the will.

Figure 5.16 shows the developing diagram with these attributes added.

Figure 5.16
Developing ERD for a database of wills, with attributes added.

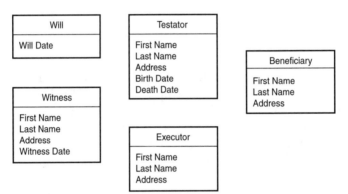

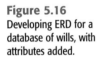

With this done, you need to consider the relationships that apply among these entities. Because Will is the critical entity, your instinct should be to look first at the way wills relate to the things around them. For each entity pair you examine, you should determine the relationship type: one-to-one, one-to-many, or many-to-many.

Consider first the relationship between a will and its witnesses. This is clearly a one-to-many relationship: A will might have only one witness, but it could certainly have several as well. The same is true of the relationship of a will to its beneficiaries. What about the relationship of a will to an executor? Well, there is generally only one executor, but in extraordinary cases there might be more than one. Again you have a one-to-many relationship.

And finally, what about the relationship between a will and a testator? Well, a will can apply to only one testator, so you might first be tempted to call this a one-to-one relationship. But one person (testator) could in theory have several wills, one superseding the other over time. To retain that flexibility, you might be better off thinking of this as a one-to-many relationship (one testator, many wills).

What about other relationships? Is it meaningful to talk about a relationship between witnesses and beneficiaries, for example? Probably not. In any case, you now have an ERD that connects all the entities together: Each entity is now related to every other entity through the main entity, which is Will. The resulting ERD is shown in Figure 5.17.

Figure 5.17
The wills ERD with all relationships drawn.

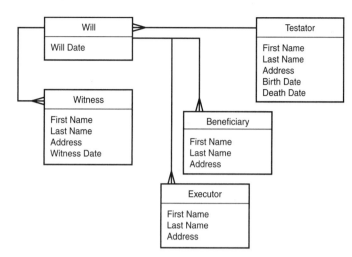

The last step in the process, though not a mandatory one, is to add the optionalities to the existing relationships. There won't be too many surprises with this system. The couplings here are generally loose. It might well be permissible to have a testator with no wills in the system, for example. It's not likely that a will would have no beneficiaries, but it is possible. And a will need not have associated witnesses, at least not until it's signed. A will might even sit in limbo for a while with no executor assigned. So these relationships are all fairly loose. The ERD with optionalities might appear as in Figure 5.18.

We've made a slight simplification here, for the purpose of clarity. The diagram indicates that one witness can only ever witness one will. In truth, one person could witness quite a number of wills, which would entail a many-to-many relationship between witnesses and wills. Here, we're effectively presuming that we'll make a new Witness record every time someone witnesses a will, whether or not that person has already done so.

Figure 5.18
The wills ERD with optionalities added.

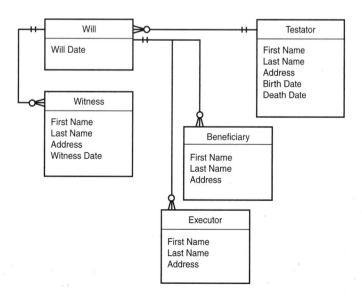

ADDING ATTRIBUTES

Now you have a pretty good list of entities, but they still need attributes. (These, again, are likely to turn into database fields when you actually build the system.)

ADD THE PRIMARY KEYS   You might remember that earlier it was recommended that every entity, without exception, have a primary key. So the first thing to do is add a primary key to each entity in the diagram. Figure 5.19 shows the result.

Figure 5.19
The wills ERD with primary keys added.

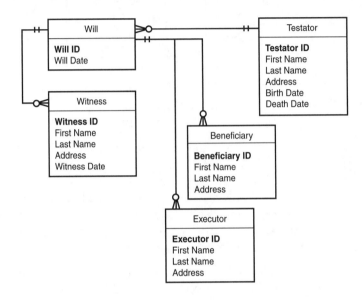

ADD THE FOREIGN KEYS   Foreign keys, you'll remember, tie the rows of one table to the primary key of another table. Anywhere you have a one-to-many relationship indicated on your ERD, you need two things: a primary key on the "one" side, and a foreign key on the "many" side. In the current example, beneficiaries and witnesses both have a many-to-one relationship with wills. So, in addition to their own primary keys (Beneficiary ID and Witness ID, which you've already added), they each need to store a foreign key called Will ID that ties each beneficiary or witness record back to a unique record in the Will table. Figure 5.20 shows the ERD with foreign keys added.

ADD THE "OTHER" ATTRIBUTES   The keys you've just added represent the ERD's structural attributes. These are the minimal attributes needed to create the relationships you identified in earlier steps. What's left, of course, is all the "actual" data—the information a user of the system expects to work with.

You will have identified some of these attributes during the initial design process, and may have wrestled with the question of whether they should appear as attributes or entities (as with testator and executor in this example, both of which we're calling entities in this design). You'll find out about others as you dig deeper into the requirements for the particular system you're building. In the current example, there may be many other pieces of data about a will that these lawyers want to track. All that information would appear as additional attributes of the Will entity.

Figure 5.20
The wills ERD with
foreign keys added.

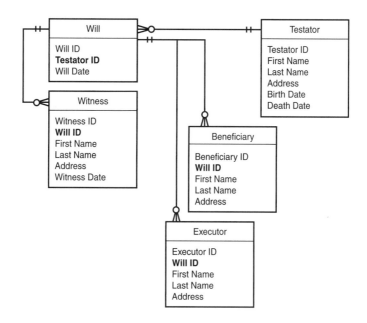

Strictly speaking, attributes don't need to appear in an ERD. An ERD, after all, is mostly about entities and relationships. In a system with complex entities, showing all the attributes on the ERD would be unwieldy and would obscure the main structure of the ERD. Just make sure that an attribute list for each entity appears *somewhere* in your design documents.

> **TIP**
>
> When you first start sketching your ERD, you might just be scribbling on the back of an envelope. But sooner or later, especially for large projects, you'll want to turn your ERD into an electronic document of some kind. We recommend that you find a suitable tool for doing this. If you want to go with a dedicated diagramming tool, Visio is popular for the PC platform, and on the Mac, OmniGraffle is an excellent tool.
>
> But if you don't want to spring for (or worse, spend time learning) a new tool, well, FileMaker's Layout mode also makes a great ERD tool! It's easy to whip up a small set of ERD adornments and cut and paste them where needed. That way, each of your FileMaker solutions can contain its own ERD, squirreled away in a hidden layout somewhere.

FILEMAKER EXTRA: COMPLEX MANY-TO-MANY RELATIONSHIPS

Most of the examples in this chapter involved fairly simple, commonly found data modeling problems. But in the real world, matters can get quite complex. Some problems are hard to model in the language of relational databases. Others involve concepts you've already seen, but in more complex forms.

Let's say you've been asked to sketch out a database system for a trucking company. The company needs to track which drivers are driving which trucks, and where they're driving them. After some thought, you decide you're dealing with three entities: Driver, Truck, and Route. A route consists of a start location, a destination, and a number of miles driven.

With the entities fixed, you start to think about relationships. Driver and Truck seem to have a many-to-many relationship: One driver can (over time) drive many different trucks for the company, and one truck will be driven by many drivers (again, over time). Driver and Route also seem to have a many-to-many relationship. Route and Truck also are many-to-many, for similar reasons.

A first sketch of the system might look as shown in Figure 5.21.

Figure 5.21
The initial ERD for a trucking system.

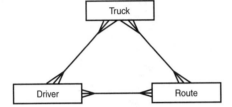

Earlier you learned how to resolve a many-to-many relationship. For any two entities that have a many-to-many relationship, you add a join entity between them that holds a primary key from each side of the relationship. You relate each side to the new join entity in a one-to-many relationship. If you fix the diagram of Figure 5.21 using those rules, you end up with something that looks as shown in Figure 5.22.

Figure 5.22
The trucking-system ERD with the many-to-many relationships resolved.

5

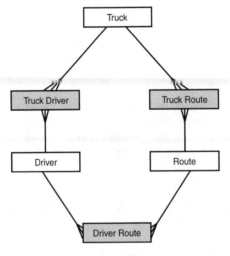

This diagram seems to be following the rules, but it's hard to know what it means or how it would work. What happens when trucker Samson drives truck T14302-B from Lubbock to Odessa? You need to record this fact by making entries in three places—once in each of the join entities. You note the association of the truck and driver in one place, the association of the driver and the route in a second place, and the association of the truck and the route in a third place. What's more, it's possible to make an incomplete entry. What if you make additions to only two of the three join tables? It seems very confusing.

Let's say that the trip starts on Monday and ends on Wednesday and you want to record that fact. With three join entities, where do you put that data? In theory, you'd need to put it into each of the three join records. That amounts to repetitive data entry, and in relational database modeling, a design that promotes redundant data entry is usually a sign that something's not quite right.

One clue is that these three associations (truck-driver, truck-route, driver-route) are not independent of each other. They all happen at the same time. When a trucker drives a truck from point A to point B, all three associations happen at once. Why not put them all into just one record? That's the right answer, as it turns out, and it implies the structure shown in Figure 5.23.

Figure 5.23
The trucking system ERD with a single central join entity.

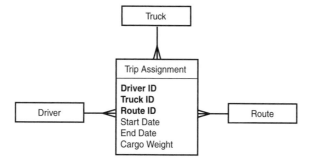

What you're dealing with here is not three many-to-many relationships, but a single "many-to-many-to-many" relationship. This kind of structure is sometimes referred to as a *star join*. The central entity in a star join (which in the example stores information about the associations between a truck, a driver, and a route) is sometimes called a *fact table*. If you see a number of join entities in your diagram that are "symmetrical," as they are here, and seem to capture different pieces of the same data, you might want to think about whether you have a star join of some kind on your hands.

5

WORKING WITH MULTIPLE TABLES

MULTITABLE SYSTEMS IN FILEMAKER PRO

Chapter 5, "Relational Database Design," laid a heavy dose of abstract database theory on you. This chapter shows you how to take those ideas and use them to build FileMaker database systems. You'll learn how to use FileMaker to create database systems that model the types of relationships covered in Chapter 5. In general, we don't like to prescribe a linear path through this book, but for this chapter (and really the one following, as well), we're going to assume that you either have read Chapter 5 or have a reasonable familiarity with the terms and concepts of relational database design. If terms such as *entity-relationship diagram*, *primary key*, *foreign key*, and *one-to-many relationship* are unfamiliar to you, we recommend that you review Chapter 5 before proceeding here.

Chapter 5 laid out a set of design concepts that centered around the ideas of *entities*, their *attributes*, and the *relationships* between entities. In FileMaker Pro, you'll generally represent a database entity ("student," for example) as a *table*. You'll generally represent an entity's attributes ("first name," "year of graduation," for example) by the *fields* of that table. And you'll create relationships among tables with FileMaker's Relationships Graph, a tool we'll be showing you in this chapter.

Before you get into the meat of this chapter, it's a good idea to review FileMaker's default behavior when you create a new database. When you create a new database, FileMaker creates a database with just one table in it, and that table initially has the same name as the name you gave the database as a whole. This is a sensible default behavior if you only ever intend to work with one table in the given database.

But FileMaker also has facilities for adding more tables to a system, adding different fields to each table, and creating many kinds of relationships between tables. We explore these tools in the context of some of the fundamental relationship types discussed in Chapter 5.

CREATING A ONE-TO-MANY RELATIONSHIP IN FILEMAKER

Let's consider a simple case. We're doing a database for a municipal government. The database is intended to store information on all the towns in an area, as well as a list of government officials such as mayors, commissioners, and the like. If we follow the principles mentioned in Chapter 5 and try to think of this in entity-relationship terms, it should be clear that we have two different entities here: "town" and "town official." The two have a one-to-many relationship: One town may have many officials. (We'll assume for the sake of simplicity that a single person can't hold more than one official post at once.)

Each entity in an entity-relationship diagram (ERD) generally translates into one table in a FileMaker system. To make this happen for our example, begin by creating a database that initially contains just the Town table, and then add a TownOfficial table and join the two in a relationship. The following sections describe how.

CREATING THE FIRST TABLE IN A MULTITABLE SYSTEM

Again, when you create a FileMaker database for the first time, you get a single table with the same name as the database. If you create a new database called Town, you'll get within it a single table, also called Town, and the option to add fields to that table. The initial field definition might look as shown in Figure 6.1.

Figure 6.1
Field definitions for an initial table in a database of town information.

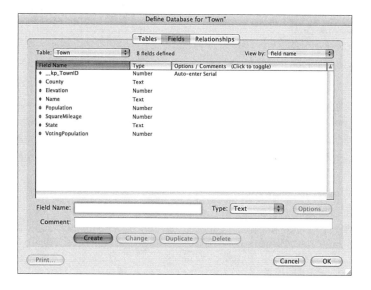

We've defined a number of basic fields containing town information. You should notice two things here. First, there is a field called __kp_TownID. That field will be the *primary key* field, which will be essential when it's time to build a relationship to another table. Notice also the small menu at the upper left of the Define Database dialog called Table. In a multitable system, this menu names the table you're currently working with, and lets you switch easily among field definitions for different tables.

→ For a refresher on the details of creating fields within a single table in FileMaker, **see** Chapter 3, "Working with Fields," **p. 69**.

ADDING A TABLE TO A MULTITABLE SYSTEM

That takes care of the Town table. To add a table for TownOfficer, stay in the Define Database dialog, but switch to the Tables tab. You'll see just one table, which in this example is called Town. To add a new table, type the name in the Table Name box and click Create, and the new table will be added to the list, as shown in Figure 6.2.

You're now free to add fields to the new table. Figure 6.3 shows a suggested field list for the TownOfficer table.

Pay attention to two fields here. The first is __kp_TownOfficerID. Like __kp_TownID in the Town table, this is the primary key for TownOfficer. Notice also the field called _kf_TownID. This is the *foreign key* that makes it possible to specify in *which* town this particular town officer serves. The foreign key will be crucial to making the relationship back to the Town table. Later in this chapter we discuss the principles of making effective key fields in FileMaker.

6

Figure 6.2
FileMaker's Tables view, showing a database with multiple tables.

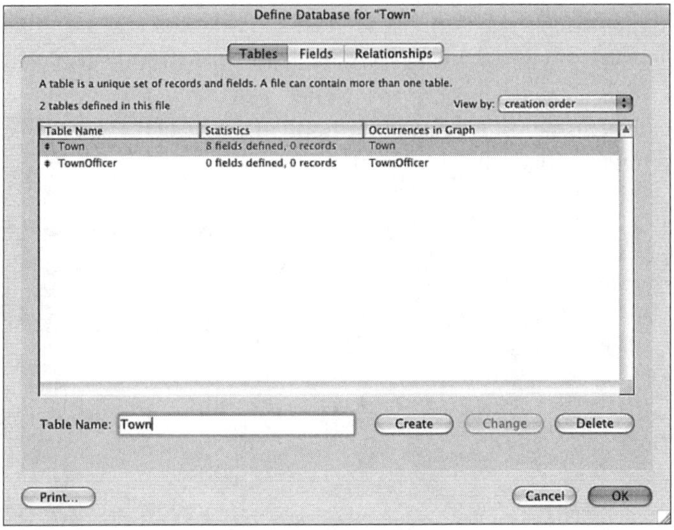

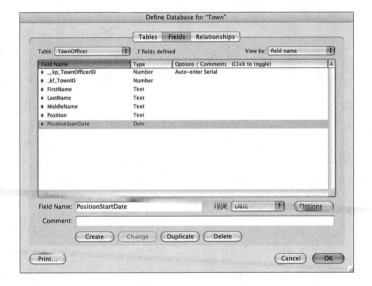

Figure 6.3
Field structure for a table of town officers.

NOTE

You might find the naming convention used here for key fields a bit puzzling. For primary keys, we precede the field name with a double underscore (__), and then "kp" to signify a primary key. For foreign keys, we precede the field name with a single underscore and the designation "kf". The effect of this convention is to cause all the key fields to sort to the top of an alphabetized field list in FileMaker, and further for the primary key to sort to the very top, above all foreign keys. This makes it very easy to access the keys when you're building relationships in the Relationships Graph.

→ For a refresher on primary and foreign keys, **see** "Understanding the Role of Keys in Database Design," **p. 143**.

ADDING A RELATIONSHIP

There are now two tables, as well as the primary and foreign keys that good database design demands. To create a relationship between these two tables, move to the Relationships tab of the Define Database dialog. This window, known as the *Relationships Graph*, should have a couple of graphical elements already displayed. Each one represents one of the database tables that exist in this database. These elements are known as *table occurrences*. Each shows the name of the table it represents, along with that table's fields. Figure 6.4 shows the Graph with the two tables presented there.

Figure 6.4
FileMaker's Relationships Graph, with table occurrences for two tables.

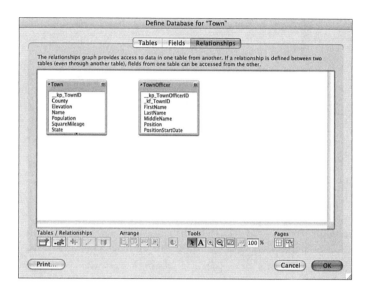

Adding a relationship between these two table occurrences is simple: Position the mouse over the __kp_TownID field in the Town table occurrence, and drag until the mouse is over the corresponding _kf_TownID field in the TownOfficer table occurrence. You should see a line extend from one table to the other. When you release the mouse, FileMaker creates the relationship and displays it as a link between one or more match fields at the top of the table occurrence pair. Figure 6.5 shows how the Graph will look as a result.

You might have noticed the "crow's-foot" at the end of the relationship line, where it touches the TownOfficer table occurrence. This is none other than the indicator that you're accustomed to seeing on the ERDs from the preceding chapter. It's intended to indicate the "many" side of a one-to-many relationship. Be warned, though! FileMaker provides this graphical adornment as a kind of a hint or guess about the relationship—it may not always be accurate, though in this case it is. We explain that point fully in the next section, where we discuss the creation of key fields in FileMaker.

At this point you've seen how to add a new table to FileMaker's default one-table database configuration and how to define a one-to-many relationship between two FileMaker tables. The next sections clarify some important points about multitable systems.

6

Figure 6.5
FileMaker's
Relationships Graph,
with a relationship
between two table
occurrences.

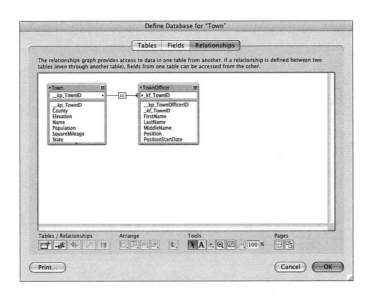

WORKING WITH KEYS AND MATCH FIELDS

You should remember from Chapter 5 that keys are *table* fields—fields that are essential elements in forming the relational structure of a multitable system. FileMaker takes a somewhat broader view of keys, as you'll see, and for that reason these fields are referred to as *match fields* when you're working in a FileMaker context. A match field in FileMaker is any field that participates in a relationship between two FileMaker tables. Primary keys and foreign keys fit this definition, of course, but so do a number of other types of fields that are explored more in the next chapter.

→ For more on the broader uses of match fields in FileMaker Pro, **see** "Relationships as Queries," **p. 184**, as well as other sections of Chapter 7, "Working with Relationships."

Key fields (which form the structural backbone of the system) need to play by some special rules—especially primary keys. Consider the current example, the Town database system, and consider the __kp_TownID field in the Town table. This field has been identified as the primary key for the Town table. To play the role of primary key, there are a few rules the field has to follow. In the first place, the value in it has to be *unique* within the given table. In the example, this means that no two towns should share the same __kp_TownID (though it's fine if there's a town *official* with an ID of 27, as well as a town with an ID of 27—they're in two different tables, so you won't get them mixed up). The reasons for this are fairly obvious: A town ID isn't much use if two towns can share a single town ID; we'd have no way to identify one single town uniquely. And by the same token, we never want the __kp_TownID field to be empty. FileMaker helps us work within these constraints.

To make a field suitable for use as a primary key, use FileMaker's field options to add some important restrictions to the field definition. You do this in the Options dialog that's available when you have a field selected in the Define Database dialog.

On the Auto-Enter tab of the Options dialog, click the Serial Number check box (see Figure 6.6). (Leave the specific serial number options alone for now.) This instructs FileMaker to enter a new, unique number into the field every time a record is created, starting at whatever number you specify and going as high as necessary.

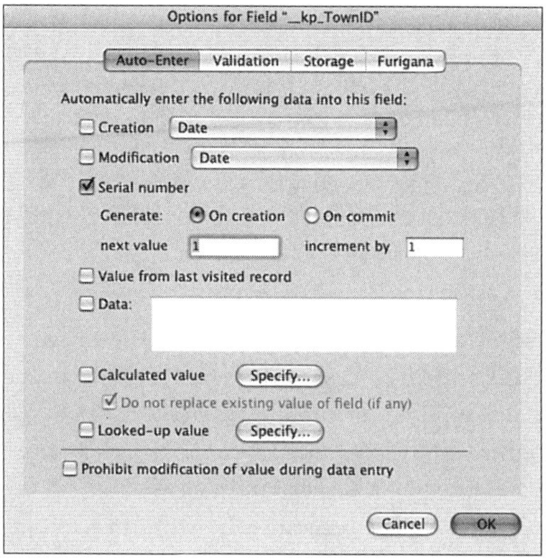

Figure 6.6
Use a serial numbering auto-entry option to populate a primary key field.

Click the Validation tab, and then click to check the Not Empty and Unique Value check boxes, found in the Require section. This ensures that the field follows the earlier criteria for a good primary key field: never empty, always unique. Lastly, in the upper portion of the box, uncheck the choice that says Allow User to Override During Data Entry. With that box checked, the user could enter his own data values in the field, possibly breaking the established uniqueness rules, or creating incorrect associations between records. You certainly don't want this to be possible. Figure 6.7 shows the Validation tab in use.

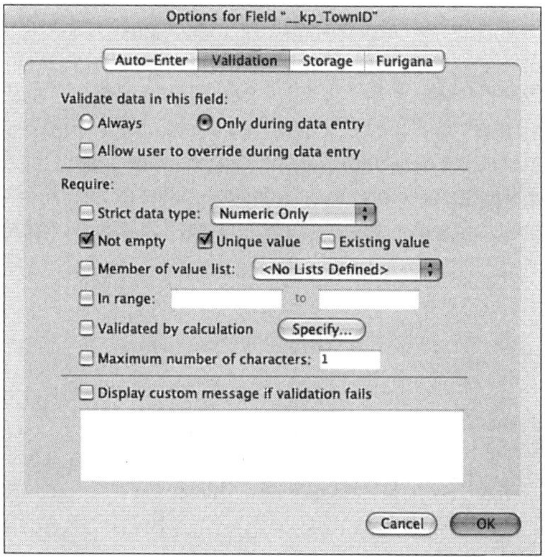

Figure 6.7
These validation options are appropriate for a primary key field.

Primary Key Options

Using an automatically entered serial number is one of the simplest ways to create a primary key, but there are other schools of thought. These serial numbers are not globally unique (in other words, unique across multiple tables), or even unique in the context of a single database. As we mentioned earlier, two records in different tables can share the same primary key when this kind of record numbering is used. The odds of any kind of mix-up are slight, but you may want to avoid the concern entirely. Some developers create a key based on complex random criteria, such as the current timestamp or current user ID, for example. A simpler scheme we've seen used involves still using FileMaker's serial numbers but adding a prefix to them so that invoices are numbered INV1, INV2, and so on. FileMaker's serial numbering option accepts text prefixes and suffixes of this sort, and such a scheme can add a useful descriptive dimension to your keys while also better ensuring uniqueness (assuming that you never use duplicate prefixes within one database).

We consider these settings to be essential for any field used as a primary key. For a *foreign key*, the constraints are less severe. Consider the _kf_TownID field in the TownOfficer table. First, there doesn't need to be a uniqueness constraint. For example, many town officers should be permitted to have the same _kf_TownID. And the _kf_TownID in the TownOfficer table shouldn't be a sequential serial number, either. That's a characteristic of a primary key. The main thing is that it not be empty. So you can simply apply the "not empty" validation rule to a foreign key field and leave it at that.

NOTE

There's another important constraint you may want to place on a foreign key field. It's called a *referential integrity rule*, and it's discussed later in this chapter in the section "Relational Integrity."

Cardinality in the Relationships Graph

This discussion provides an opportune moment to look again at that crow's-foot that FileMaker so cleverly applied to the Town-TownOfficer relationship created earlier. FileMaker looks at the field definition options to try to determine the cardinality of a relationship. Any field that is either defined to be unique or has an auto-enter serial number is assumed by FileMaker to be the "one" side of a relationship. Lacking either of those characteristics, it's assumed to represent the "many" side. That, in brief, is how FileMaker determines how to draw the cardinality indicators (that is, the crow's-foot) in the Relationships Graph. It's a useful indicator, to be sure, but not bulletproof, and is really just advisory. The cardinality indicator neither creates nor enforces any rules, and it can't be changed from FileMaker's default "guess" value. It simply tells you what FileMaker thinks is going on.

→ For a discussion of cardinality, **see** "Relationship Cardinality," **p. 138**.

UNDERSTANDING TABLE CONTEXT

FileMaker 7 and 8 differ greatly from previous versions in their capability to work with many database tables in a single physical file. But there's a bit of a price to be paid for this power. Many, if not most, actions in FileMaker assume that some particular table is somehow the "active" table. Say you reach up to the Records menu and select Delete Record. Which table does that command affect? It affects the current table—but how does

FileMaker decide which table is current? The answer is that FileMaker determines this from what's called the *table context*.

Table context, it turns out, is determined by the currently active layout. Let's continue to refer to the Town-TownOfficer example. The steps to add the new table were simple, but there's some complexity underneath. After you're back in the Town database, you're still probably looking at the town entry layout, the one where you can view basic town information. But FileMaker has silently added another layout to the database.

In Layout mode, make sure that the status area is showing, and click on the layout pop-up list near the top of the status bar. There are now two layouts: one called Town, the other called TownOfficer. The new layout is named for the second table you added. You've already learned how the displays in the Status Area work. Add a few records while you're on the Town layout, and you'll see the total number of records, as listed in the Status Area, grow. More towns, more records—no big surprise there.

But if you use the layout pop-up list to switch to the TownOfficer layout, a surprise *is* in store: The record total drops back to zero. Why?

The answer is that each layout is showing something different. The Town layout shows records from the Town table, and the TownOfficer layout shows records from the TownOfficer table. These tables can, and probably will, have different numbers of records. To make the concept still clearer, go ahead and add a bunch of records while you're on the TownOfficer layout. For TownID, pick some of the IDs of towns you've already created— they'll probably be low numbers such as 1–5. You may want to choose View, View as Table to see the list in its entirety as it grows. Now switch back and forth between the two layouts to see the record totals shift.

In FileMaker 8, each layout represents a view into a particular database table. If you think back to the analogy of a database table as a card file, you can think of each table as a file containing a different kind of card. In the Town card file, each card holds information about one particular town. In the TownOfficer card file, each card holds information about a town officer in one of those towns. When you move from one layout to another in FileMaker, it's as though you're closing one card file and opening up another. Each new card file you open may have a different number of cards, with different information on each card.

FileMaker keeps track of all this by storing a *table context* with each layout. To see this, drop into Layout mode on the Town layout and choose Layouts, Layout Setup. Notice the menu that says Show Records From (you can see it in Figure 6.8). If you click on that menu, it lists all the tables for this database and shows that the layout is currently linked to the Town table.

In practice, you're unlikely to need to change the table context of a layout after it's been established. When you create a new table in a database, FileMaker adds the new table to the Relationships Graph, and also adds a new layout based on the table. You may, though, want to create additional layouts that refer to the same underlying table. In that case, you need to set the table context for the layout in the course of creating the layout. Again, you're unlikely to need to change this after it's been set. If you have a working layout that's displaying data from a particular table, you're likely to discover odd consequences if you change the table context.

6

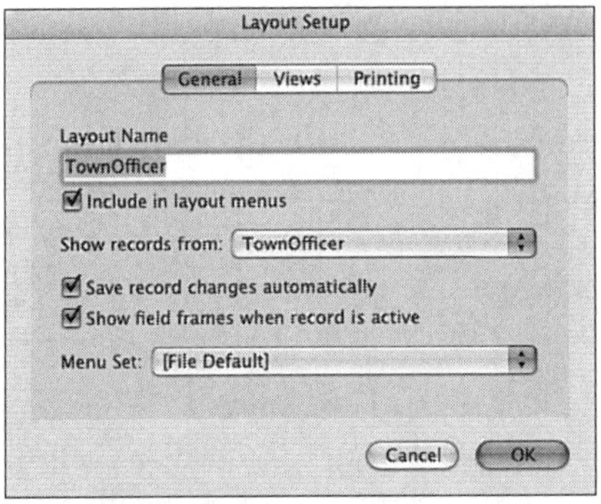

Figure 6.8
This is the Layout Setup dialog, showing the table context for the TownOfficer layout.

NOTE

There's some simplification in that last paragraph. Here's a more accurate rendition of the second sentence: "When you create a new table in a database, FileMaker adds a *table occurrence* for the new table to the Relationships Graph, and also adds a layout based on that table occurrence." The full importance of the distinction is made clear in the next chapter.

→ For a discussion of table occurrences, **see** "Adding a Table Occurrence to the Relationships Graph," **p. 187**.

WORKING WITH RELATED DATA

So far in this chapter you've learned how to create additional tables in a FileMaker system and how to build relationships between those tables based on well-constructed match fields. This section shows you how to begin to *use* your relationships to work with and create data in multiple tables at once.

USING A PORTAL TO VIEW RELATED CHILD DATA

The town records database system has two tables in it now. But how do we use them? Say there's a record for a town called Gorre, with a TownID of 1, and you want to enter information about the mayor and town councilors of Gorre. One way would be to navigate to the TownOfficer layout and create a record for each official, assigning a TownID of 1 to each. That seems like a tedious way to create data, and it's potentially error-prone because a user must know and correctly enter the TownID of every town. Additionally, there's no way to see a list of town officials when looking at the master town record in the Town table.

FileMaker solves both these problems with a tool called a *portal*. A portal is a special FileMaker layout element that lets you work with data across two (or sometimes more) tables at once. In the case of the Towns database, a portal lets you look at records in the TownOfficer table while you're sitting on the "parent" Town record.

→ For addition discussion of the "parent/child" naming convention, **see** "One-to-Many Relationships," **p. 137**.

To see a portal in action, navigate to a layout that has the parent table (Town, in this case) as its *table context*. After you're on this layout, drop into Layout mode and you'll see the portal tool among the available tools in the status bar (see Figure 6.9).

NOTE

You should be able to tell the table context by the fields on the layout, but you'll recall that the Layout Setup dialog, accessible from the Layouts menu while in Layout mode, gives the definitive answer.

Figure 6.9
This is a layout in Layout mode, showing the FileMaker portal tool.

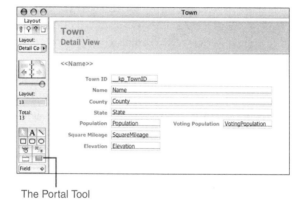

The Portal Tool

Click once on the tool, and then, on the layout, drag out a box wide enough to show an entire town officer's name and release the mouse. You'll get a dialog box asking for details about the portal's contents, behavior, and display. The dialog is shown in Figure 6.10.

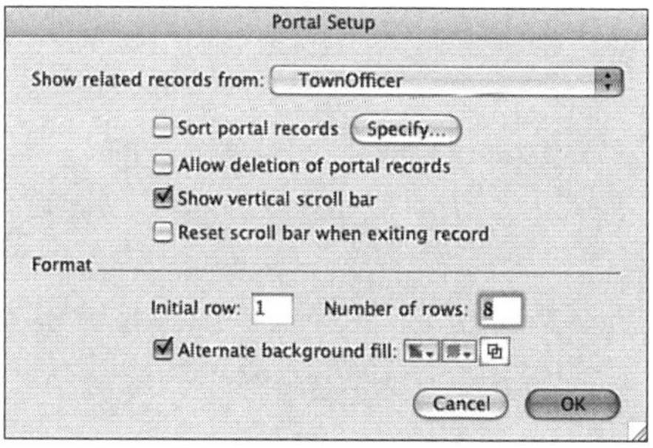

Figure 6.10
FileMaker's Portal Setup dialog.

In general, when you set up a portal for the first time, you'll need to do the following:

- Choose a table occurrence from which to display data
- Choose additional portal options
- Choose data fields for display in the portal

More details on each of these steps follow.

First, you need to specify where the portal gets its data. In the Portal Setup dialog, the Show Related Records From list enables you to choose which table to draw data from. The list is divided into sections: one for related tables and one for unrelated tables. (The question of whether a table is "related" or "unrelated" is determined by the Relationships Graph.) In the current example, for a portal on a layout in which the table context is the Town table, there should be only one available choice in the menu: the TownOfficer table, which is the only other table related to Town in the Relationships Graph. By choosing TownOfficer from this menu, you're instructing FileMaker to show you all town officer records that are related to the currently visible town record (in other words, all that share the same town ID).

The Portal Setup dialog contains a number of other choices as well. For now, you can opt to display just 12 portal rows, and put a vertical scrollbar on the portal so that you can scroll down if a town has more than 12 officers. You can also apply coloring or striping to the portal if you choose.

FileMaker also displays a dialog at the end of the portal creation process, asking which fields from the related table you want to show in the portal. For this example, we chose to show FirstName, LastName, Position, and PositionStartDate from the TownOfficer table. You can always change or add to these selections later as well.

Back in Browse mode, you should see a list of town officers in the portal (assuming that you created some and they're still around), as shown in Figure 6.11. It would be ideal if you could type right into the rows of the portal and enter your data that way. By default, this isn't possible (try it and see), but it's easy to add this capability to the portal.

Figure 6.11
A portal can display multiple records from a related table.

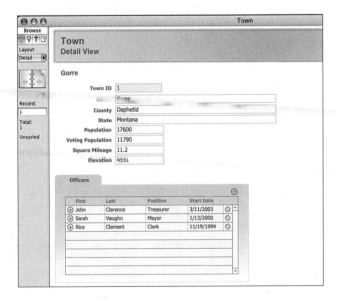

If you don't see the records you expect to see in the portal, you might need to check your portal settings. See "Repeating Portals" in the "Troubleshooting" section at the end of this chapter.

USING A PORTAL TO ADD RELATED RECORDS

Portals can be used for data entry, as well as data viewing. It's possible to configure the portal and its underlying relationship so that a user can add officers to a town record by typing directly into the portal rows.

To accomplish this task, you need to edit the relationship between Town and TownOfficer. On the Relationships Graph, double-clicking on the relationship line between the two tables brings up the Edit Relationship dialog, shown in Figure 6.12.

Figure 6.12
The Edit Relationship dialog is where you can edit individual relationships in the Relationships Graph.

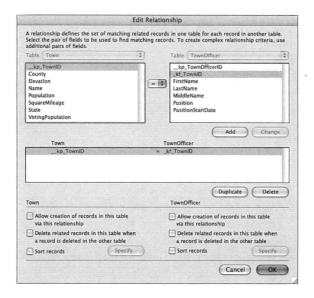

For each of the tables participating in the relationship, there's a check box under it called Allow Creation of Records in This Table via This Relationship. If you check this box on the TownOfficer side of the dialog, it becomes possible to create TownOfficer records via this relationship.

If you check this option, and return to the Town layout in the parent table, you'll discover that you can now click on an empty row of the portal and type in an officer for this town.

This is all good in its own right, but another payoff comes if you flip over to the TownOfficer layout to get a direct look at the records in the TownOfficer table. You'll notice that there are new records in TownOfficer, corresponding to those you entered in the portal. Notice in particular that the _kf_TownID has been set automatically to the ID of the town record from which you were performing the data entry. FileMaker has created the foreign keys in TownOfficer for you automatically. Figure 6.13 shows a possible view of the TownOfficer table after portal-based record creation.

With portals, it's easy to view, create, and manipulate records on the "many" side of a one-to-many relationship.

6

Figure 6.13
Adding records to the portal on the Town layout creates linked records in the TownOfficer table.

WORKING WITH RELATED PARENT DATA IN A CHILD FILE

You've seen how to use a portal to add related (child) records to a master (parent) record. Suppose that you want to turn the problem around, and see information about the *town*, on the *officer's* data record. Figure 6.14 shows a somewhat bare-bones rendition of the TownOfficer layout. In addition to information about the town officer, you can see the TownID, but you can't tell what the name of that town is, much less any other information about it. Given a record for John Samuel, who's the Sheriff of the town of Gorre, you'd like to be able to view the town's name, county, and population on John's data record. So far, this database doesn't do that. But it's not hard to configure.

Figure 6.14
A simple view of a town officer record. No information about the associated town is shown, other than the TownID.

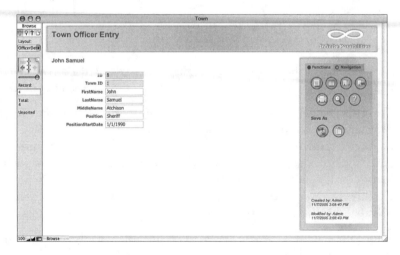

6

To make this happen, you need to edit the TownOfficer layout a bit. Enter Layout mode and shrink the _kf_TownID field so that there's some room to the right of it. Drag another field to the right of _kf_TownID. You'll see the Field/Control Setup dialog, as shown in Figure 6.15. If you inspect the menu at the upper right of the box, you can see that it indicates that the box is currently allowing you to choose fields from the TownOfficer table (the current table). But you can change the menu to show fields from a related table; in this case, Town is your only choice (TownOfficer is not related to any other tables in the Relationships Graph). Figure 6.15 shows the dialog after the user has chosen to show fields from the related Town table.

Figure 6.15
It's possible to display individual fields from related records on a FileMaker layout.

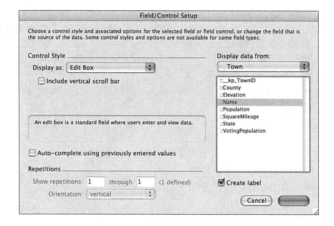

Change the menu to read Town, and select the Name field you find there. Back in Layout mode, you'll see a subtle change in the display. The field name now has two colons preceding it, as Figure 6.16 shows. This is FileMaker's cue that the field doesn't come from the current table, but from a related table. At this time, you can use the same technique to bring in the County and Population fields from the Town table.

Figure 6.16
Fields from related tables are displayed with a preceding double colon in Layout mode.

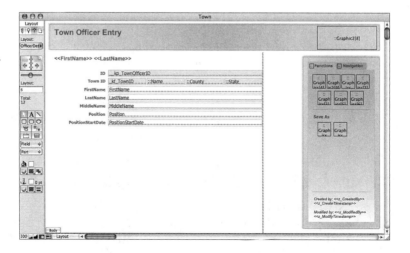

Drop back into Browse mode and you'll see that the Name field now shows the name of the town of Gorre, along with its county and population. Just to understand the point, clear out the _kf_TownID field. Notice that the town name and other information disappear. Reset the _kf_TownID field to 1 again, and back comes the town data.

Editing Related Fields

One thing to be aware of is that the data you see in these related fields is not in any sense a copy of the related data. Displaying related fields can give a user direct access to the data on the master record (the town record in this case). To see this, edit the data in a related field, say by changing the town name. Now shift to a layout that shows you the master town record. You'll see that the town record itself has a new name!

In some situations, you probably don't want to let this happen. Those fields are intended to *show* information from the master record, not necessarily to allow it to be edited. To prevent the data in a layout field from being edited, you can drop into Layout mode, select the field in question and choose Format, Field Behavior. At the top of this box, uncheck the box that says Allow Field to be Entered in Browse Mode. That way, on this layout, users cannot enter the field in Browse mode.

This restriction applies only to the current field (though you can apply it to as many layout fields as you like) and *applies only on the current layout*.

To repeat: Related data is the real data, not a copy, and unexpected things can happen if you allow users to edit related fields.

PORTALS VERSUS RELATED FIELDS: WHICH IS WHICH?

You might be puzzled that previously we used a portal to access and view related data, and here we're using this seemingly quite different technique. Which is which, and how do you know when to use each one?

The answer is actually quite simple:

> Use a portal to view multiple related child records from the perspective of a parent record. Use related fields to see a single parent record's information from the perspective of a child record.

In the town example, we used a portal on the parent record (the town) to view multiple related child records (the town's officers). Looking from the other side, we used individual related fields on a child record (the town officer) to view information from the single parent record (the town).

To put this in terms of the "one-to-many" language we've been using, a portal is used to look at the "many" from the perspective of the "one," and single related fields are used to look at the "one" from the perspective of the "many."

CREATING A MANY-TO-MANY RELATIONSHIP

The preceding sections introduced you to most of FileMaker's fundamental tools for working with multiple related tables. Now it's time to extend those concepts and see how to use them to create a many-to-many relationship structure.

BUILDING THE STRUCTURE

Let's say that you've been asked to create a database for a town militia (assuming that databases were prevalent in Colonial America). You need to keep track of militia members in their own right, and you also need to be able to assign them to different guard shifts. An ERD for the proposed system is shown in Figure 6.17. On the one hand there are guard shifts, each of which can be staffed by several militia members. On the other hand, there are militia members, each of whom can work many shifts. This is a classic many-to-many relationship. You'll recall from Chapter 5 that such relationships are resolved with an intermediate *join entity*. In this case, we'll call the join entity a "shift assignment." Each shift assignment records the posting of a single person to a single shift.

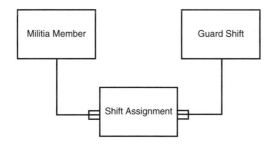

Figure 6.17
An ERD for a system that tracks guard shifts and shift assignments.

As before, we map the abstract entities directly onto FileMaker tables. This produces a three-table system. The appropriate key structure is essential: primary keys in the Shift and MilitiaMember tables, and *two* foreign keys (_kf_ShiftID and _kf_MilitiaMemberID) in the middle ShiftAssignment table.

→ For additional discussion of the key structure of join tables, **see** "Many-to-Many Relationships: Solving the Puzzle," **p. 145**.

We're going to assume that you're familiar enough with the field and table definition process by now that we can skip over the details. We'll take you straight to the Relationships Graph. Figure 6.18 shows the Graph after we've created all three tables and established the two relationships into the ShiftAssignment table.

CREATING A DATA ENTRY INTERFACE

As before, the structural part is not so hard. But it takes some work to make data entry easy. Creating and editing militia members or guard shifts is pretty straightforward: The user navigates to either the Shift layout or the MilitiaMember layout and adds, edits, and deletes records there.

But what about shift assignments? As with the earlier example of town officers, shift assignments are a type of child record you want to create in association with a parent record of some kind. In the town/officer example, the data-entry interface we discussed enables users to add officers to a particular selected town. In the guard system under discussion, the intent is to be able to choose a shift, view that shift record, and assign militia members to that specific shift. In a similar vein, users should also be able to choose a militia member, view his record, and see on the same screen a list of all of his current shift assignments.

Figure 6.18
The FileMaker Relationships Graph with three related table occurrences representing a many-to-many relationship.

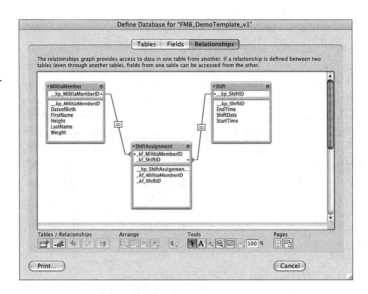

Let's assume that you've created records for a few militia members and a few shifts already. You'd like to edit the Shift layout so as to be able to view and create shift assignments from the Shift layout itself. You can add a portal to the layout. It will be a portal showing records—*not* from the MilitiaMember table, but from the ShiftAssignment table. We want users to be able to add multiple assignments to this shift and specify a militia member for each assignment.

Recall the data structure from Figure 6.17. There's no way to record a member's *name* in the shift assignment table—only his primary key. That's not a very friendly data-entry mechanism. The watch commander is more likely to know his staff by name, not by database ID. We can fall back on a familiar FileMaker tool for this data entry task: the value list.

Before doing this, by the way, you're going to want to make sure that the relationship between Shift and ShiftAssignment is configured to allow creation of related ShiftAssignment records. This is necessary if the portal is to be used as a data-entry tool.

USING A VALUE LIST FOR DATA ENTRY

Even though users know militia members by name, the key structure of the data is rigid (as it should be). What the user needs to enter into each shift assignment record is a member's primary key, not his name. But it's not realistic to memorize member IDs. You need some kind of data-entry mechanism that will give a hint as to which member ID goes with which member.

FileMaker's value lists are the right tool for this. Chapter 4, "Working with Layouts," discussed creating value lists from a hand-entered list of custom values. In the current example, to speed the assignment of members to shifts, what you need is a way to build a value list dynamically, based on the contents of the MilitiaMember table, so that the value list has one entry for each member in the database. And each entry should show two pieces of data: not only the member ID, but also the member's name.

DEFINING A VALUE LIST TO DRAW DATA FROM A TABLE

Choose File, Define, Value Lists, and click New to create a new value list. In the Edit Value List dialog, rather than choosing the third radio button (Use Custom Values), choose the first one, Use Values from Field, as shown in Figure 6.19.

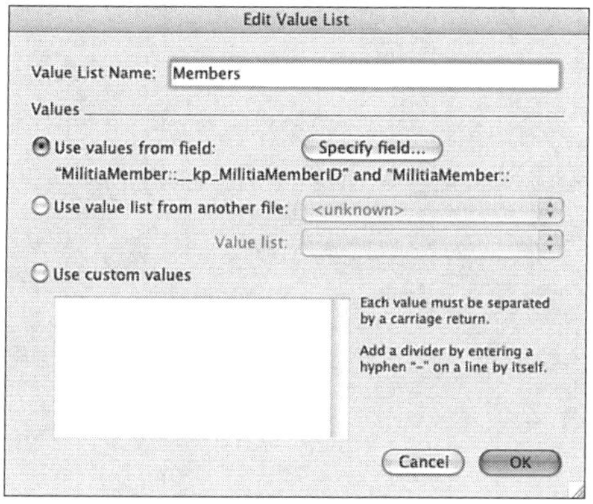

Figure 6.19
This is the first of two dialogs you use to create a new value list.

When you do this you'll get a second dialog box. Go to the menu that says Use Values from First Field. This lets you pick first a table, and then a field from that table. Choose __kp_MilitiaMemberID from the field list in the first column. In the second column, select the check box that says Also Display Values from Second Field, and then choose LastName from the list of fields in that table. At the lower left, select the Include All Values radio button. You can also select the radio button at the lower right that instructs FileMaker to sort the value list by the second field. This ensures that the list will be sorted in order of last name, rather than in order of the member ID.

Finally, you'll probably also want to check the box that says Show Values Only from Second Field. The first field is quite important: This is the data value that actually gets entered and stored when the user makes a selection from the value list. But it's the second field that's likely to make more sense to the user. Again, we're more likely to know people by name than by number. In previous versions of FileMaker it was necessary to display both the cryptic key field and the more descriptive name. In FileMaker 8, it's possible to hide the key field so that the user sees only a menu of names. Regardless of whether the first (key) field is hidden, though, data from the key field is what will be entered and stored when the user make a choice.

This second dialog box is shown in Figure 6.20.

With the value list created, it's time to return to the ShiftAssignment layout and build the data-entry portal. The first step is, of course, to use the Portal tool to draw the portal. Choose whatever features you like, such as vertical scrollbar or row striping. When you're finished, FileMaker prompts you to choose fields to put into the portal.

Figure 6.21 shows the Add Fields to Portal dialog. Notice that the table selection menu at the left lets you choose fields from either of two tables: You can choose fields from the intermediate ShiftAssignment table or from the more "distant" MilitiaMember table itself.

6

Figure 6.20
The second value list dialog allows you to specify an additional field to display in the value list.

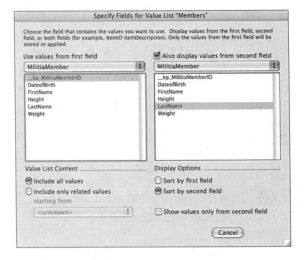

Figure 6.21
In FileMaker 8, a portal can display records from tables that are more than one "hop" distant from the current table.

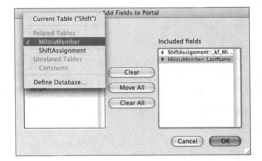

In this case, you need to do both. Choose the _kf_MilitiaMemberID field from ShiftAssignment. You need to fill that field in with a member ID, so it needs to be in the portal. But when you're viewing the portal, you're really more interested in the member's name. Well, that field isn't in the join table, so you just need to reach farther down to get to it. Switch the Available Fields menu to show fields from the MilitiaMember table and select LastName.

NOTE
If you're used to older versions of FileMaker, you'll recognize that this capability to reach more than one relationship deep was a huge advance in FileMaker 7. Making this happen was possible in earlier versions, but did require setting up additional calculations in the join table to pipeline data through to the portal. In FileMaker 7 and 8, it's possible to look several levels deep, if necessary, to bring back related information.

With the portal created on the layout, you're almost finished. You still need to apply the value list to aid in record creation. In Layout mode, select the _kf_MilitiaMemberID field in the portal. Choose Format, Field Format. In the Field Format dialog box, choose Format Field as Pop-Up List and choose Display Values from Members because Members is the name of the member value list you created.

Back in Browse mode, if you click into the ID field, you should see a neatly formatted list of possible members to add to the shift. Figure 6.22 illustrates the behavior.

Figure 6.22
Using value lists built on table data is a powerful way to aid data entry in related tables.

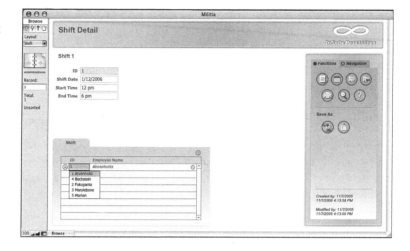

CAUTION

As before, you should use the Field Behavior dialog box to prevent users from entering into that LastName field while in Browse mode. If they edit the name there, the name on the original MilitiaMember table is changed.

RELATIONAL INTEGRITY

No doubt the topic of this section sounds suspiciously like some form of couples therapy. Not to fear—it's a good deal less interesting than that, unless you're a database designer, in which case it's endlessly fascinating.

Relational integrity, also known as *referential integrity*, speaks to the notion that a database structure, as expressed in an ERD, also implies certain rules about what can and cannot happen in a database. If you read Chapter 5, you encountered the concept of *optionality rules*. An optionality rule may, for example, assert that an order must have at least one order line item. Or it may assert the more obvious truth that an order line item that doesn't relate to an existing order is an error.

Consider the example of shift assignments again. Suppose that there's a record in the ShiftAssignment table that references a militia member with an ID of 1002, when in fact there is no member with that ID. This could have happened because of data entry error (again, a great reason to use a value list in the way we demonstrated in the preceding section). It could also happen if that member had existed once upon a time and has since been deleted. In that case, without integrity rules to protect against this, the member's assignment records would be left dangling in the ShiftAssignment table. Database analysts usually refer to such records as *orphans*, and their existence is a violation of referential integrity.

This state of affairs clearly looks like an error you should avoid. There are a couple of things you can do to prevent this problem. To prevent erroneous entry of a nonexistent member ID, you can use field validation. To prevent the creation of orphaned records as a result of deletion, you can use an *integrity rule*.

USING A VALUE LIST TO ENSURE RELATIONAL INTEGRITY

We'd like to add a validation rule to the ShiftAssignment table that says it's not valid to create a record with a nonexistent militia member ID. The best way to do this in FileMaker is to create a value list containing all the extant militia member ID numbers, and apply validation that allows only IDs from that list to be used. You'd do that as explained here:

1. Define a new value list, called MemberID. You can make it by duplicating the Members list you already created. This differs from the earlier list only in that it does not use values from a second field, so that box should remain unchecked. (Because the earlier value list sorts based on the Name field, it cannot be used to validate based on the contents of the ID field.)

2. Go to Define Database, edit the ShiftAssignment table, and edit the field options for the _kf_MilitiaMemberID field. Choose the Validation tab, and on that screen check the Member of Value List box. For the value list, choose the MemberID value list you created earlier to help with data entry. While you're here, you might as well also stipulate that the field can't be empty and that the user may not override these restrictions. You can also provide a custom message if the validation should fail. These options are shown in Figure 6.23.

Figure 6.23
Use FileMaker's validation options to enforce a referential integrity rule between two tables.

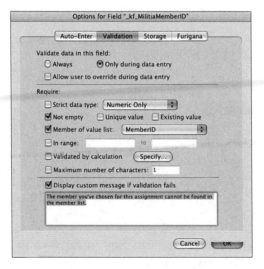

Now, if you were to try to enter a member ID that didn't already exist in the MilitiaMember table, you'd get a warning that the action was disallowed.

PRESERVING REFERENTIAL INTEGRITY DURING DELETION

Deletion is another pitfall if you're picky about keeping your database consistent. What happens if you want to delete a member, and he already has shift assignments? Well, you have two choices: either forbid the deletion on the grounds that related assignments exist, *or* delete all the shift assignments along with the member himself.

These two options are known in database parlance as *restricted delete* and *cascading delete*, respectively. A restricted delete ensures that parent records with related children can't be deleted—an attempt to do so produces an error. A cascading delete, on the other hand, deletes all the associated child records along with the parent record. FileMaker doesn't at this point support restricted delete directly, although the effect can be achieved in other ways.

FileMaker does, though, support cascading delete directly. To add a cascading delete rule to a relationship, simply edit the MilitiaMember-ShiftAssignment relationship in the Relationships Graph. On the ShiftAssignment side of the dialog box, look for a check box that says Delete Related Records in This Table When a Record Is Deleted in the Other Table.

CAUTION

> Be sure not to check the corresponding box under MilitiaMember. This would have the effect of deleting a member record anytime a corresponding shift assignment was deleted. This is the wrong direction in which to cascade! Also be aware that cascade effects are cumulative. If you define multiple cascade-deletion rules in a system, a single deletion can sweep across multiple tables. Pay careful attention to the details of this feature until you're comfortable working with it. As with other mass-update operations in FileMaker, such as Replace Field Contents, or a data import, there is no way to undo such deletions.

 It's possible to configure FileMaker's security privileges in a way that interferes with the enforcement of integrity rules. See "Accidental Delete Restrictions" in the "Troubleshooting" section at the end of this chapter.

RAPID MULTITABLE DEVELOPMENT

 Working with the complex database schemas of a multitable file, or a solution composed of several such files, can sometimes be daunting. FileMaker Pro 8 Advanced adds some powerful features for working rapidly with complex systems. Using FileMaker Pro Advanced, it's now possible to import the definitions for multiple tables from one file to another. This schema import does not import any data, only the table and field definitions for selected tables. If you have a standard set of tables that you like to add to most of your solutions (utility tables, logging tables, resource tables), it's now as simple as importing the table schemas from one file to another. It's also possible to copy and paste table definitions, between or within files.

Additionally, the same is now also true of field definitions. They can be copied and pasted, either between files or within files, allowing you to quickly reuse blocks of "standard" fields.

The enhancements extend to ScriptMaker as well, where scripts and script steps can now be copied and pasted with ease.

6

All these new features are particularly useful in certain scenarios involving conversion from FileMaker 6 or earlier to FileMaker 8. If you're attempting to consolidate many converted files into a single file, the capability to copy or import tables is a huge timesaver.

→ For an additional discussion of conversion issues, **see** "Converting Systems from Previous Versions of FileMaker Pro," **p. 537**.

TROUBLESHOOTING

REPEATING PORTALS

I've created a portal, but instead of seeing a set of different records, I see that every row of the portal shows exactly the same data.

This indicates a mismatch of table occurrences. Specifically, it suggests that although the portal is set to look at records from table occurrence A, the fields you've chosen to display in the portal are actually from table occurrence B. Because it's possible to have several different table occurrences that are based on the same underlying table, it's possible to see the same field list for several different table occurrences. Nevertheless, if the portal and the fields displayed in it draw from different table occurrences, you probably won't get a meaningful display, even if the different table occurrences are all based on the same underlying table.

ACCIDENTAL DELETE RESTRICTIONS

I set up a cascade-delete relationship between my Customer table and my Invoice table so that when I delete a customer, all related invoices are deleted as well. But when I try to delete a customer, it tells me I don't have sufficient privileges. I checked my privileges and I do have delete privileges in the Customer table.

Check to make sure that you have delete privileges on the Invoice table as well. To perform a delete operation successfully in FileMaker, a user needs delete access to any and all records that are to be deleted. If you have delete privileges for customers but not for invoices, the entire deletion operation is forbidden.

FILEMAKER EXTRA: BUILDING A THREE-WAY JOIN

In the "FileMaker Extra" section at the end of Chapter 5, we sketched out the ERD for a many-to-many-to-many relationship among truckers, trucks, and truck routes. We follow up on that discussion here and show you how you might build such a thing in FileMaker.

Structurally, it's not too complex—we already worked out the relationships at the end of Chapter 5. You need a four-entity system: Trucker, Truck, Route, and the central three-way join entity, called in this case RouteAssignment. The Relationships Graph for such a structure might look as shown in Figure 6.24.

Figure 6.24
The FileMaker Relationships Graph showing table occurrences and relationships for a three-way join.

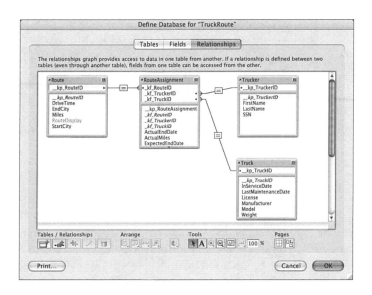

What about data entry? This is a bit more challenging. In theory, you could have a portal in any of the parent tables that would enable you to create RouteAssignment records. If the portal were in the Trucker table, you'd be entering a Truck and a Route on each portal row to make the assignment. If the portal were in the Truck Table, you'd enter a Trucker and a Route on each row. If the portal were in the Route table, you'd enter a Truck and a Trucker on each row.

Well, these portals are probably useful for data viewing. Certainly, if I'm on a trucker record, I'd like to see a portal with all that trucker's route assignments. Same for a truck: I'd like to see a list of all the routes over which the truck has been driven in its service lifetime. But none of these is obviously the right place from which to do data entry.

In a case like this, it may be best to set aside the portal-based method for entering data in a related field and allow the user to create the assignment records directly. You still want to use value lists to assist data entry; if it's hard to remember one set of keys, it's surely impossible to remember three sets! So you'd define three value lists, one based on each table, with the first field in the value list being the primary key for the table, and the second field being some nice identifying field from the rest of the table. Such a set of value lists is shown in Figure 6.25.

TIP

This last point raises a difficulty with two-field value lists. You're limited to a total of two fields, so if the first field is a key field of some kind, that leaves you a total of one field of identifying data. Sometimes that's not enough. For the truckers, last name may be enough for the second field. For trucks, the license plate number might suffice. But for routes, we'd really like to see both the start and the end city of the route. The only way to do this is to create a calculation field to display the start and end nicely—such as Poughkeepsie-Hopalong. You can then use this calculation as the second field in the value list.

6

Figure 6.25
These value lists
speed data entry into
the join table in the
midst of the three-
way join.

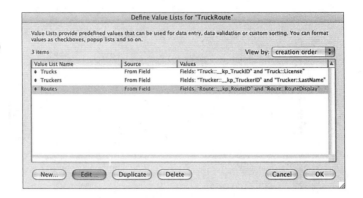

After you have the three value lists, you can create a layout, based on the RouteAssignment
table, where users can easily create a new route by using the value lists to populate the three
key fields. You could set things up so that the data entry would take place in Table view, as
shown in Figure 6.26.

Notice that related fields have been added from each of the three main tables to make the
display more intelligible.

Although FileMaker excels at modeling and implementing the standard one-to-many and
many-to-many relationships, it's equally capable of working with more esoteric structures
as well. In such cases you're likely to find that modeling and building the relationships is relatively straightforward, whereas designing the data-entry interface takes some more thought.
The techniques described in this section may be instructive, or you may find you need a different solution, depending on the nature of the problem and the needs of your users.

Figure 6.26
You can use value
lists, as well as the
display of appropriate
related fields, to cre-
ate a usable data
entry interface for
this complex three-
way join setup.

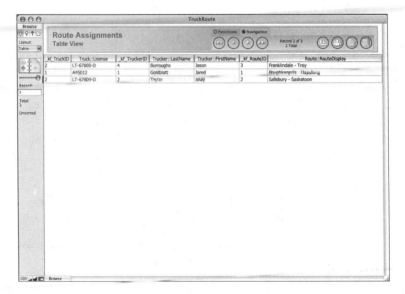

## CHAPTER 7

WORKING WITH RELATIONSHIPS

In this chapter

RELATIONSHIPS GRAPHS AND ERDS

Chapter 5, "Relational Database Design," outlined some database theory that helps produce an ERD—an *entity-relationship diagram* that shows the fundamental building blocks of a database system and the ways in which they relate. In Chapter 6, "Working with Multiple Tables," we showed how to use FileMaker's relationship tools to turn an ERD into a working FileMaker database. This might mislead you into thinking that the Relationships Graph is really the same thing as an ERD, and that the relationships you build there match one-to-one with the relationships you sketch out on your ERD.

In fact, there's a lot more to relationships in FileMaker. The Relationships Graph certainly handles all the structural relationships present on an ERD. But there are many other ways to use relationships in FileMaker. The ERD-based relationships are the structural core of any FileMaker database (or *any* relational database), but this chapter takes you beyond the core and shows you some other ways you can use relationships in FileMaker. It also delves further into the features of the Relationships Graph, and discusses different ways of organizing files, tables, and table occurrences in a FileMaker system.

Bottom line: The Relationships Graph is actually a *superset* of your ERD. It certainly has the ERD wrapped up in it, but it may well contain other important structures and relationships as well. Those techniques are the subject of this chapter.

RELATIONSHIPS AS QUERIES

We want to introduce you to the idea of a relationship as a kind of query. Consider a database that stores information about customers and their invoices. On a layout specific to the Customer entity, you can add a portal of invoice information. Figure 7.1 shows that layout.

Figure 7.1
Using a portal to display a particular customer's invoices.

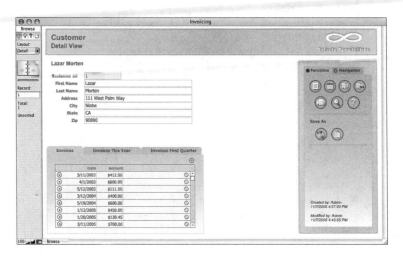

The portal looks into a table of invoices, and is based on the fundamental one-to-many relationship between a customer and an invoice, based on a shared key called CustomerID (the name varies slightly depending on whether it's a primary or foreign key; see Figure 7.2). But the portal also represents a kind of query, which says, "Show me all invoices that have the same customer ID as this customer."

Figure 7.2
A Relationships Graph for a simple customer-invoice system.

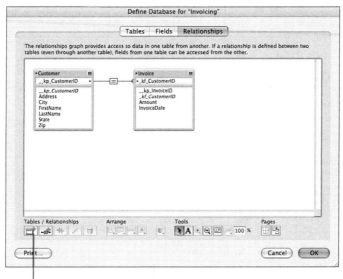

Add Table Occurrence button

That's all well and good, but suppose that a user comes to you and asks for a portal that shows only this year's invoices for that customer. That's a different query than before, and therefore requires a different relationship. Well, FileMaker can do that. Creating this new query requires delving into three new concepts in FileMaker relationships: the concept of *non-equijoins*, the concept of a *table occurrence*, and the concept of a *multiple match*.

Non-Equijoins

Don't let the scary terminology throw you. The concept is simple. Refer again to Figure 7.2, which illustrated the relationship between Customer and Invoice. Notice that the line representing the relationship has an equals sign right in the middle. To explore what that means, you would double-click on the relationship line to edit the relationship. The Edit Relationship dialog is shown in Figure 7.3.

The middlemost box shows the match field or fields defined for this relationship. This current relationship is built between a __kp_CustomerID in Customer and a _kf_CustomerID in Invoice. The match criterion is based on equality, meaning that invoices match (and hence are displayed in a portal that shows records from this relationship) if and only if the _kf_CustomerID in Invoice is exactly equal to the __kp_CustomerID in Customer. This is the correct behavior for the structural relationship represented on the ERD. Such a relationship, based on equality, is often called an *equijoin*.

The upper part of the Edit Relationship dialog is where the match actually gets defined. And you'll notice, in Figure 7.3, that equality is not the only operator available for defining a match. In fact, you can build relationships based on combinations of any of the seven comparison operators.

7

Figure 7.3
FileMaker can use any of seven different operators to compare match fields.

How does this help you with that user who wants to see a portal of invoices for this customer for the current year only? Well, it implies that you need to extend the match criteria somewhat. In addition to matching on the customer ID, you also need to restrict the match to just those invoices on which the date is *greater than* the start of the current year.

The Edit Relationship dialog enables you to build matches between fields in different tables. You know you want to build a match that incorporates the invoice date, but you need to somehow compare that to the start of the current year, and the database doesn't have a field for that at present.

You can solve that problem by defining a *calculation* field that gives you the start of the current year. The definition for such a calculation is shown in Figure 7.4. It's a simple formula that returns the first day of the current year, expressed as a date.

NOTE

The figure doesn't show the storage options, but we've chosen to make the calculation unstored so that it updates properly as the current date changes.

→ For more on calculations and storage options, **see** "Storage Options," **p. 227**.

With the calculation in hand, you can proceed to build the "this-year-only relationship." You could certainly just edit the relationship you originally created between the two tables, but it's more likely that you'll want to keep that structural relationship intact and add a new one to represent this new query.

7

Figure 7.4
You'll be able to incorporate this calculation (which we've chosen to call CurrentYearStart) into a relational match for invoices within a certain date range.

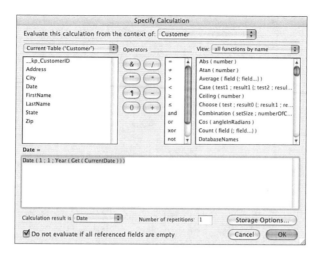

ADDING A TABLE OCCURRENCE TO THE RELATIONSHIPS GRAPH

We used the term *table occurrence* sporadically throughout Chapter 6 when referring to the graphical table representations in the Relationships Graph. Why not just call them tables and be done with it? Well, they're not the same thing. An underlying table (or *source table*, meaning those tables that appear in the Tables tab of the Define Database screen) can appear multiple times in the Relationships Graph. In fact, anytime you want to have more than one relationship between two source tables, you need to add an additional *occurrence* of at least one of the source tables to the Graph. You cannot create multiple relationships between two table occurrences in the Graph. If you want to relate table A to table B in two different ways, you need two occurrences of at least one of the tables.

In the current example, you want a new view of invoices from the perspective of a customer. Therefore, you need to add a new occurrence of the Invoice table to the Graph. So far, FileMaker has created all table occurrences for you automatically. Anytime you add a new table to a database, FileMaker adds a corresponding table occurrence to the Graph, and gives it a name identical to that of the underlying table. Now you need to add a new occurrence of Invoice to the Graph by hand. To do this, open the Relationships Graph in the Define Database dialog box and click the Add Table Occurrence icon in the lower-left corner. Figure 7.5 shows the resulting Specify Table dialog box.

In the Specify Table dialog, choose a source table to include in the Graph. In this case, you want to add another occurrence of Invoice. Notice that FileMaker instructs you to "give this table a unique name in the graph." At the bottom of the box is a place for you to name the table occurrence. Because the original occurrence of the Invoice table is already named Invoice, you need a new name. We recommend a name that says something about the way the new relationship will be used. In this case, something like InvoiceByYear should fit the bill. Figure 7.6 shows the Relationships Graph with the new table occurrence, as well as the CurrentYearStart field you added to Customer.

7

Figure 7.5
You can add a new table occurrence to the Relationships Graph.

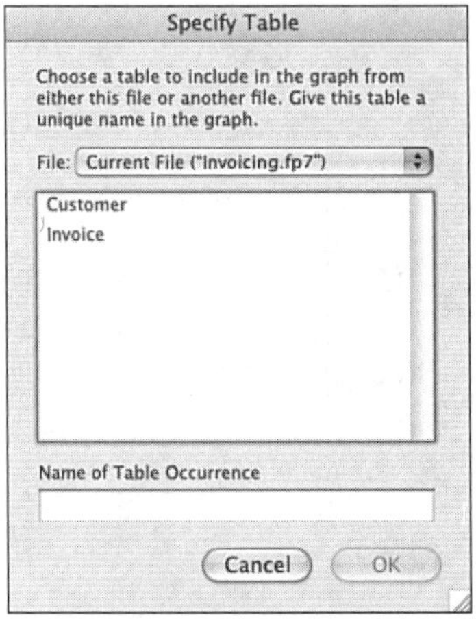

Figure 7.6
A second occurrence of the Invoice table has been added to the Graph.

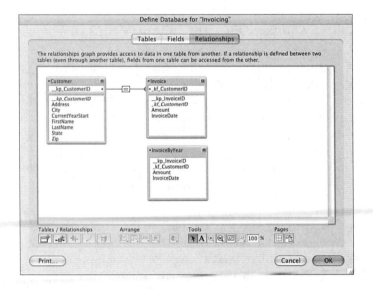

All that's left is to create a relationship from Customer to this new table occurrence, which will incorporate the CurrentYearStart field into the match criteria.

DEFINING A RELATIONSHIP WITH MULTIPLE MATCH CRITERIA

Chapter 6 showed you how to define new relationships in the Relationships Graph with a graphical technique consisting of dragging from one match field to another. Also, a new relationship can be added simply by clicking the small Add Relationship icon (the second icon in the Tables/Relationships icon group at the lower left of the Relationships Graph). Clicking that icon brings you the familiar Edit Relationship dialog, but it's initially completely empty.

Begin by selecting the two tables that are to participate in the relationship. Choose Customer on the left, and InvoiceByYear on the right. Then define the first match criterion.

Select the correct customer ID field under each table name, make sure that the menu of operators in the middle shows an equal sign, and click the Add button. So far it looks exactly like the Edit Relationship screen for the original Customer-Invoice relationship, as shown in Figure 7.3, except that the table occurrence on the right is now InvoiceByYear instead.

But you still need to tell FileMaker to consider only those invoices on which the invoice date is greater than the start of the current year. To make this happen, you can add another criterion. Select CurrentYearStart on the left, InvoiceDate on the right, and from the operator menu in the middle, select the "less than or equal to" sign. (This signifies that January 1 of the current year must be less than or equal to the invoice date.) Click Add, and the new match criterion is added in the middlemost box, as shown in Figure 7.7.

Figure 7.7
Using a non-equality condition to build a relationship.

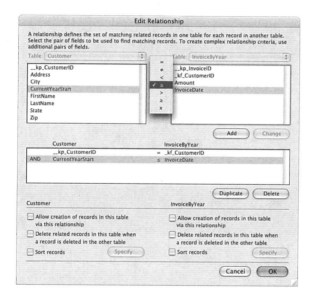

Notice what that middle box is saying now. There's a large "AND" in the left margin, which says that this relationship pulls back only those invoices for which the customer ID matches *and* the invoice date is sometime this year.

 You might be wondering how to create a multiple-match relationship that works if any of the criteria is true, as opposed to those that work only if all the criteria are true. This isn't possible, unfortunately. To learn more, see "No OR Conditions with Multiple Match Criteria" in the "Troubleshooting" section at the end of this chapter.

Notice also how FileMaker represents this new relationship in the Relationships Graph. Each end of the relationship line forks, to indicate the multiple match criteria—and the operator symbol in the middle of the line is a curious kind of X, indicating a complex match with multiple operators at work. Figure 7.8 shows the Graph with the new relationship.

To use the new relationship, you could draw another portal on the Customer layout. Base it on InvoiceThisYear instead of plain Invoice, and use the same data fields from the source table. The result should be similar to what you see in Figure 7.9.

7

Figure 7.8
The Graph indicates when a relationship is based on multiple match fields. The [X] comparison operator shows that multiple operators are in use as well.

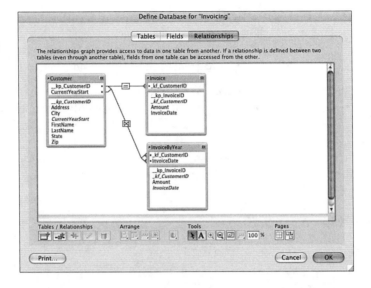

Figure 7.9
More complex relationships can produce sophisticated views, such as the Invoices This Year view shown here.

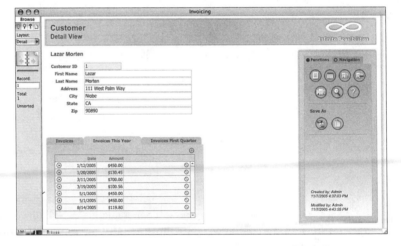

These three concepts—non-equijoins, multiple table occurrences, and multiple match criteria—afford you extraordinary flexibility as a database developer. The sections ahead explore examples that show how to use these tools to solve particular problems of database design.

CREATING SELF-RELATIONSHIPS

A self-relationship sounds like another dubious (if not illegal) concept. We assure you that it's just one more tool in the database developer's arsenal. Self-relationships are an important tool even at the ERD level, though we didn't explore them in Chapter 5. We'll go into some detail here on how to create and use them.

MANAGERS AND EMPLOYEES: A "STRUCTURAL" SELF-RELATIONSHIP

Suppose that you want to create a database system that models a company's organizational chart. Your process description tells you that the system should show, for each employee, who that employee's manager is, and for each manager, a list of all that manager's direct reports. On the strength of this, you draw an ERD like that in Figure 7.10, with two separate entities, Manager and Employee, in a one-to-many relationship.

Figure 7.10
An ERD for a system that models an organizational chart.

This diagram seems fine until you come to list attributes for each entity. Besides the difference in "type" (manager versus employee), it appears that managers and employees look pretty much alike. They each have a first and last name, a department, an employee ID, and so on. Worse, as you think about it, many people in the chart are *both* a manager and an employee—they manage several others as managers, but also report to their own superiors.

It turns out that the correct way to solve such a problem is to collapse the two entities into one. The trick here is that the relationship of managers to employees doesn't quite fit the regular one-to-many or many-to-many criteria. The relationship is *hierarchical*, in the sense that one person can have many levels below her, and many above, similar to a family tree in some ways. A more accurate ERD for the system looks as shown in Figure 7.11.

Figure 7.11
An ERD for an organizational chart system, with attributes shown.

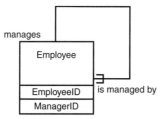

Each instance of the Employee entity has a __kp_EmployeeID, but also a _kf_ManagerID, which points to the particular employee who is this employee's manager.

> **NOTE**
>
> This does beg the question of what to enter into the _kf_ManagerID field when you get to the CEO's record. This can be solved by adopting some convention: either leaving the field empty or (probably better) setting it equal to the CEO's own __kp_EmployeeID.

USING VALUE LISTS TO SPEED UP SELF-JOIN DATA ENTRY

How would you implement such a system in FileMaker? You'd begin with a one-table system matching the ERD. The structure is shown in Figure 7.12. You'll also find it useful to create a couple of value lists, based on field data from the Employee table. The first should

7

be a two-field value list, in which the first field is the __kp_EmployeeID, and the second field is either the employee's last name or a calculation that shows both the last and first names together. You'll use that value list for data entry. The other list should be just alike, but contain only the __kp_EmployeeID—you can use this value list to validate the contents of the _kf_ManagerID field. Figure 7.13 shows the value list definitions.

NEW As you saw in the preceding chapter, you may want to use FileMaker 8's new Show Values Only from Second Field check box to hide the employeeID in the value list designed for data entry.

→ For a discussion on using value lists to speed data entry in related files, **see** "Using a Value List for Data Entry," **p. 174**.

Figure 7.12
The FileMaker field structure for an organizational chart system.

Figure 7.13
Two value lists are defined in the system to aid with data entry.

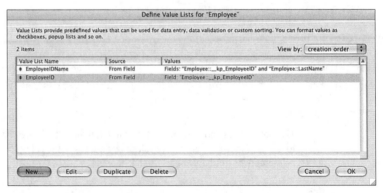

At this point, without even touching the Relationships Graph, you've done enough work to begin data entry. If you apply the EmployeeIDNames value list to the _kf_ManagerID field on the Employee layout, you can begin entering data. Of course, the list is initially empty, so you need to either begin with the CEO and work your way down, or enter a bunch of other employees and come back and fill in their managers later. Figure 7.14 shows how the system might look during data entry.

Figure 7.14
Using a value list to select an employee's manager.

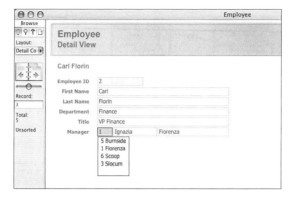

CREATING ADDITIONAL TABLE OCCURRENCES TO DISPLAY RELATED DATA

The setup shown in Figure 7.14 works fine, but soon you'll find a few things missing. When you enter a manager ID, you probably want the manager's name to somehow appear as well. Likewise, on the layout for an employee who manages others, you'd probably like to see a list of those who report to the current employee.

These problems sound quite similar to the ones we covered in the preceding chapter (see the section "Working with Related Data" in Chapter 6). Whether you want to see a manager name when you choose a manager ID, or see a list of managed employees in a portal, some kind of relationship appears to be needed.

To make this work, you need to relate your single Employee table to *itself*. To do this, you need to add it to the Relationships Graph—*twice* more, in the form of two separate table occurrences. To do this, open the Relationships Graph and click the Add Table Occurrence button at the lower left. Add another table occurrence for Employee and name it Manager.

Now relate the two table occurrences by dragging a relationship line from the __kp_EmployeeID field in the Manager table occurrence to the _kf_ManagerID field in the Employee table occurrence. If the significance of that isn't obvious right away, think about it for a bit. If I'm an employee, my manager is the person with an employee ID equal to my manager ID.

That handles the employee-manager relationship. What about the relationship between an employee and those she manages? (Let's call them, clumsily, "managees.") To capture that relationship, you need to add another table occurrence. Once again, the table occurrence is based on the Employee table. Name it Managee and add it to the Graph. Then define an employee-managee relationship between Employee::__kp_EmployeeID and Managee::_kf_ManagerID. Looking again from the context of the employee, the "managees" are all those employees whose _kf_ManagerID is the same as a given __kp_EmployeeID. Figure 7.15 shows the resulting Relationships Graph.

7

you *know* she lives in Montana, and you're really just interested in pairing her up with her fellow Montanans for a few evenings of tracklaying and dispatching.

Let's say the basic data of your Railfan database looks like what's depicted in Figure 7.18.

Figure 7.18
This database needs to perform some sophisticated filtering of this list of railfans.

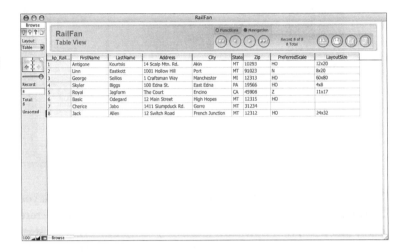

If you want to view other Montanans in a portal from Antigone's record, you need to create a relationship that somehow looks for others in the same state. If you think about that more precisely, from the viewpoint of Antigone's record, you want to see all other railfans who live in the same state as she does, but who do *not* have the same RailfanID—all Montanans except Antigone. This, again, is a kind of query, and you can implement it with a relationship.

To make this happen, go to the Relationships Graph and add a new table occurrence. Base it on Railfan and call it OthersInState. You need to create a relationship from Railfan to OthersInState based on multiple match criteria. Select `State=State` in the upper boxes and then click Add. Then select `__kp_Railfan ID ≠ __kp_RailfanID`, and then click Add again. Figure 7.19 shows the Edit Relationship dialog as it will appear after this step.

You can now create a portal on your main Railfan layout that uses this new relationship. The resulting display might look as shown in Figure 7.20.

If you work with non-equijoins, you might notice that the option Allow Creation of Records in This Table via This Relationship has disappeared from the Edit Relationship dialog. To learn more about why, see "Trouble Creating Related Records with Non-Equijoins" in the "Troubleshooting" section at the end of this chapter.

Figure 7.19
This relational match finds all other railfans in the same state as the current record.

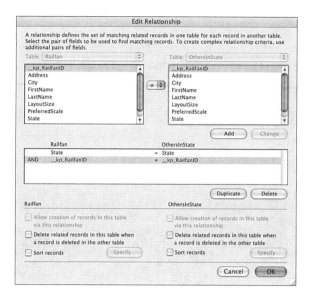

Figure 7.20
The portal on this layout shows all other records that share the current record's State. The current record will always be excluded from the list.

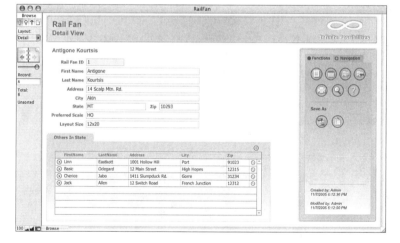

CREATING RANGED RELATIONSHIPS

FileMaker Pro's new non-equijoin feature has a great number of uses—too many to cover exhaustively. We'll touch on a couple more before moving on. In an earlier example, we looked at a relationship that let you see a customer's invoices for the current year only. What if you wanted to refine those criteria further, and look at invoices for just the first fiscal quarter (January through March)?

Let's return to the Invoicing example (shown in Figures 7.4 through 7.9). The first "date filtering" relationship was created when a calculation field was added in the Customer table to produce the start of the current year. For this new query, you need to add one more calculation field—one that will give you the end of the first quarter. This one is also quite simple; the new calculation is shown in the field list in Figure 7.21.

Figure 7.21
This table of customer data also contains two calculation fields for performing ranged relational comparisons.

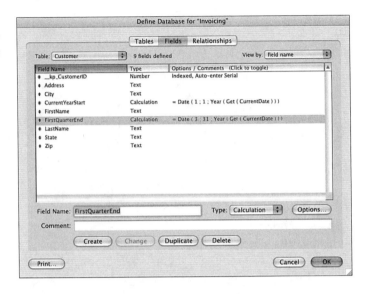

To factor this new calculation into the query logic, you need a new relationship. That in turn means a new table occurrence in the Relationships Graph. Open the Relationships Graph and add a new table occurrence called InvoiceFirstQuarter. Then add a new relationship. Define it to have Customer on the left and InvoiceFirstQuarter on the right. You need three match criteria in this case: __kp_CustomerID = _kf_CustomerID, CurrentYearStart ≤ InvoiceDate, FirstQuarterEnd ≥ InvoiceDate. All three have to be true for a match to exist. Figure 7.22 shows the Edit Relationship dialog for this new relationship, and Figure 7.23 shows the Customer layout with a third portal added to show just the first-quarter invoices.

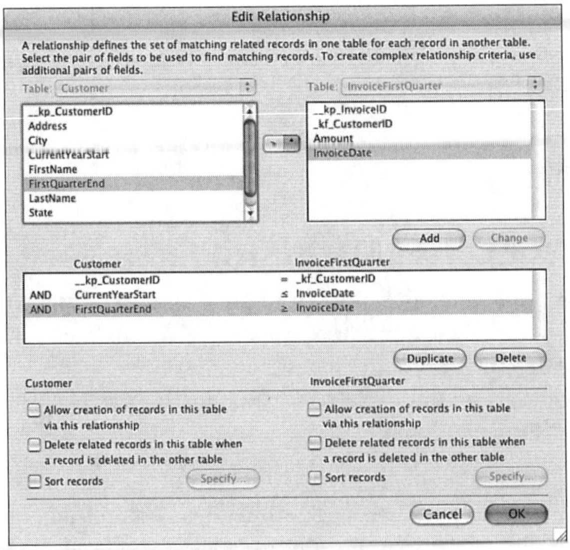

Figure 7.22
This complex relationship is intended to find all of a customer's invoices between two dates.

Figure 7.23
FileMaker's multiple match criteria can easily be used to create relationships that pick out ranges of related records.

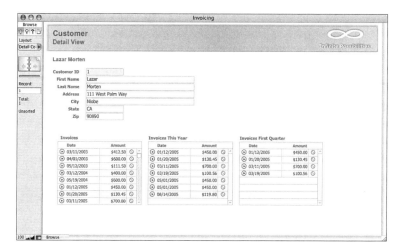

→ For a range of additional techniques for doing interesting things with portals and nonstructural relation-ships, **see** Chapter 16, "Advanced Portal Techniques," **p. 471**.

CREATING CROSS-PRODUCT RELATIONSHIPS

In working with non-equijoin relationship matches, you may have noticed one oddball operator in the little menu of match criteria. Most of them are familiar comparison operators—but what about the last one, the one that looks like an [x]?

That operator is known as a *cross product* (or *Cartesian product* if you really want to show off). The cross product does one and only one thing: It provides a "universal match" between the records in two tables. What this means is that it does no limiting of any kind. If you think of a relationship again as a kind of query, a cross-product relationship is a "find all" query. If you define a cross-product relationship from Customer to Invoice, a portal based on that relationship would always show all invoices, no matter which customer record was being viewed. The choice of fields on the left and right sides is more or less unimportant; this "all to all" relationship is fulfilled regardless of the choice of match fields.

Cross products really make sense only by themselves, in single-match relationships. They have no effect at all if they're added into multimatch criteria sets. A cross-product match condition is always true, so it can never further limit the potential matches of other criteria. Of course, if that makes your head spin, you can just take our word for it.

NOTE

Savvy users of older versions of FileMaker may recognize that the cross-product operator replaces the technique that used to be known as a "constant" or "always-true" relationship. In that technique, you had to define specific fields on either side that explicitly matched each other (generally a pair of calculations that each evaluated to 1) and build a relationship between the two fields. FileMaker 7 and 8's cross products provide the same feature in a more integrated fashion.

7

Well, that explains what a cross-product relationship is, but not how you might want to use one. The cross product is the ultimate nonstructural relationship. After all, its purpose is to show *all* of something. These are generally used for various user-interface purposes. Sometimes you might want users to pick from a list of things, for example, and it's more pleasing to allow them to pick from a scrolling list in a portal than from a drop-down list or menu. Generally such techniques need to be coupled with some scripting to react to users' choices.

→ For further examples of the uses of cross-product relationships, **see** Chapter 16, "Advanced Portal Techniques," **p. 471**.

WORKING WITH DATA FROM DISTANT TABLES

The relational model of FileMaker 8 has significant power in its capability to handle a relational tree. As an example, suppose that you have a classic Customer-Product-Invoice system with a Relationships Graph like the one shown in Figure 7.24.

Figure 7.24
Relationships Graph for a system that tracks customers, products, and invoices.

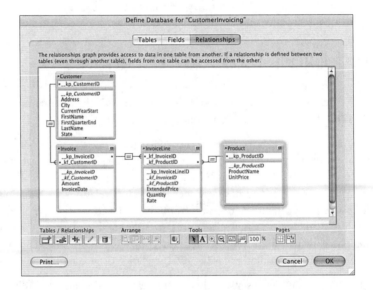

You might want to do a number of things in this system that would have been slightly cumbersome in versions of FileMaker prior to FileMaker 7. Suppose, for example, that you'd like a portal on a customer layout showing all the products that customer had ever purchased. Previously, you might have used a somewhat complicated technique involving global fields and the Copy All Records script step to "hop" from a customer record to the customer's related invoices, and then again from the invoices to their related line items, and finally from the line items over to products. Scripting this process was relatively slow, and the technique was not guaranteed to work for large data sets.

By contrast, in FileMaker 7 and 8 it's as simple as creating a portal on the Customer layout and choosing the Product table occurrence as your data source. FileMaker correctly navigates the Relationships Graph from Customer to Product and brings you back a listing of all products ever purchased by a given customer. Although this is somewhat difficult to illustrate concisely (we'd need to show the intervening invoices), Figure 7.25 shows what the result might look like. Even though some of the products have been entered on several invoices for this customer already, each one appears only once, as you would expect.

Figure 7.25
FileMaker 8 lets you perform a deep relational view, allowing you to display, for example, all products a customer has purchased in a given year.

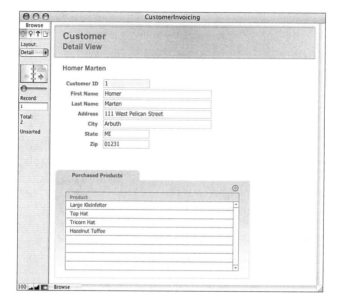

The technique could be reversed. For example, from the viewpoint of a Product record, you could just as easily see a portal of all customers who had ever purchased that product.

This capability to perform multistep relational navigation in a single swoop is a powerful feature of FileMaker. Combined with some of the multimatch and non-equijoin relationships you saw earlier, this technique can produce quite sophisticated queries. Think back to the example that used a relationship to isolate a customer's invoices in the first quarter. Well, if those invoice records eventually contained a link back to a products table, you could use a *deep* relationship (as we sometimes call them) to produce a portal of just those *products* purchased by a given customer in the first quarter.

WORKING WITH MULTIPLE FILES

In all the discussions of multitable systems in Chapters 5 and 6 and so far in this chapter, we've assumed that all the tables you want to work with live within a single FileMaker file. The capability to have many tables in a single physical file is, after all, one of the more convenient features of FileMaker. But there are still many reasons to build systems that are multi*file*, in addition to being multitable. This section reviews the mechanics of working with several files at once, and then discusses different design strategies that use a multifile structure.

So far we've looked just at relationships between tables within the same file. But it's also possible to build relationships between tables in different files. As an example, suppose that you're (again!) being called on to build an invoicing system of some kind. Naturally you'll want to start with some set of customer data and a place to hold it. Well, it may happen that a FileMaker file already exists with a bunch of tables of customer information: a table of companies, a table of individual contacts at each company, and a table of company addresses, to name a few. There's no need to redo all that work—all you need is the data. But let's assume that the designer of the Customer file is not eager to have you in there adding things to her file. She'd rather you kept the invoicing tables separate, in their own file.

Well, you might find her lack of faith disturbing, but it won't create any actual technical hurdles for you. To reference her customer file from your new invoicing file, you only need to create a *file reference* to her file. You can then use that file reference to create new table occurrences for her customer tables, inside your invoicing file.

CREATING A FILE REFERENCE

File references are an extremely important topic in FileMaker. In a number of places in FileMaker, you might want to refer to or work with another file. Here are some of the things you can do with other files in FileMaker:

- Call a script in the other file
- Use a value list that's defined in the other file
- Refer to one or more tables from the other file in your Relationships Graph

To do any of these things, you first need to create a reference to the other file. A file reference simply tells FileMaker where and how to find another file. FileMaker is capable of working with external files that are present on a local hard drive, that are present on a shared network volume, or that are present on an available FileMaker Server. You can also specify multiple search locations for a file, and the priority in which they should be searched. You can, for instance, create a file reference that says, "First search for the invoicing file on the FileMaker server at 192.168.100.2. If you don't find it there, look on the FileMaker server at 10.11.1.5. If you don't find it there, give up."

Previous versions of FileMaker used file references as well. But these earlier versions kept track of these references behind the scenes, and didn't let you alter the order in which FileMaker searched for a given file. Problems with file references were harder to spot in previous versions, and could occasionally give rise to a problem called *crosstalk*, in which the wrong copies of files could be accessed by mistake.

→ For more on the concept of crosstalk and its relationship to file references, **see** "Crosstalk," **p. 526**.

In FileMaker 8, each physical file maintains its own list of file references. You can work with these references centrally, and also create them on the fly as needed. Let's see how this works in practice.

Going back to the invoicing example, say you have your own invoicing file, called InvoicingSeparate. The aforementioned untrusting colleague has a file called CustomerSeparate, with a Customer table. You want to use that Customer table from the CustomerSeparate file in InvoicingSeparate.

Your first step is to define a file reference to the external file. To do this, choose File, Define, File References. Click the New button on the next screen, and you'll see the Edit File Reference dialog, shown in Figure 7.26.

Figure 7.26
You can add search paths to a file reference by typing them manually, or by using the Add File button to choose a specific file.

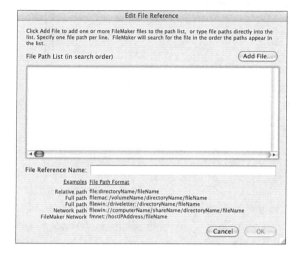

A file reference is a more complex object than it sounds at first. A file reference is really a name given to a series of file paths. (See Figure 7.28 for an example of a file path with multiple entries.) FileMaker resolves the file reference by searching through the path list in the specified order. In general, the point is to use a file reference to tell FileMaker the best (or perhaps the only) place for FileMaker to look for a file.

NOTE

> In general, all the different file paths in the path list point to the same file; that is, a file with the same name and contents. In theory, you could also use a single path list to point to a number of different files, indicating that the later ones should be used if the earlier ones can't be found. You could perhaps use this feature to fall back to other versions of a file or system if necessary.

In the case of the external Customer file to which you want to relate, say that file is being hosted under FileMaker Server. One way to build the file reference is simply to click the Add File button in the Edit File Reference dialog. This brings you to a standard Open File dialog, from which you can click the Remote button to look for servers on your network. When you find the server hosting the Customer file, you can select and open the Customer file. After you do this, FileMaker adds an element to the file path list that looks something like `fmnet:/192.168.101.66/Customer`, as shown in Figure 7.27.

There's nothing magical about the text FileMaker added to create this file path. The file path list is a free text area, so you're free to add entries to the list yourself by hand, separating each one with a carriage return. Again, the list order is the order in which FileMaker looks for the file.

7

Figure 7.27
File references tell FileMaker where to look to find externally referenced files.

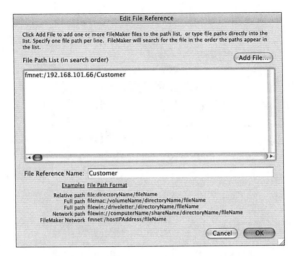

Suppose that your colleague had also given you a copy of the file to use "offline" while you were doing your development work. You'd want the file reference to resolve to a copy on your local disk instead. But after the file was hosted on FileMaker Server, you'd want to avoid that local copy being found by accident. One way to do this is to add another element to the file path list, possibly by using the Add File button again and navigating to the copy of CustomerSeparate that's on your local hard drive. This places the new path element second in the list, but you can cut and paste it in front of the first path (see Figure 7.28).

Figure 7.28
A search path can contain multiple search locations. FileMaker scans them in the specified order.

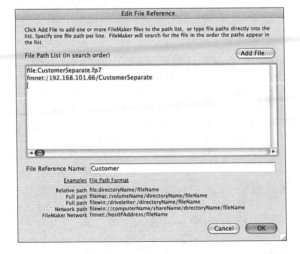

CAUTION

If you've inserted a local reference to the file to aid offline development, you need to remember to remove that reference later, or perhaps move it lower on the list. Otherwise, FileMaker continues to search your local drive first, which is probably not desirable.

The file reference displayed in Figure 7.28 instructs FileMaker first to look for the file locally and then, if it can't be found locally, to look for it on the server at 192.168.101.66. If FileMaker searches the entire file path and can't find a file at any of the specified points, it presents a dialog telling you that it's failed to find the file, and then throws up an Open File dialog inviting you to find the file by hand. If you find and specify a file by hand, that file is used for the current external file operation. Figure 7.29 shows the warning you see when a file reference can't be resolved.

Figure 7.29
If FileMaker cannot find a referenced file after searching the specified search path, it displays an error dialog.

"Customers.fp7" could not be opened. Either the host is not available, or the file is not available on that host.

OK

 In previous versions of FileMaker, when an external file reference failed, FileMaker would also prompt the user to find the referenced file by hand. But in previous versions, FileMaker would remember this choice and add it into the internally stored file path list. This was not always the right thing to do; the path could easily be altered or reset by a flustered user just trying to close the ominous dialogs on her screen. When FileMaker 8 fails to resolve a file reference, and prompts the user to find the file, any selected file choice is valid for the current action, but FileMaker doesn't alter the stored file reference in any way based on this choice.

ADDING AN EXTERNAL TABLE TO THE RELATIONSHIPS GRAPH

If you've followed along with the example to this point, you've now built a file reference pointing to the CustomerSeparate file that looks for it first on your local hard drive, and next on a networked FileMaker Server. You can now use this reference to add tables from the external file to the Relationships Graph in your InvoicingSeparate file. If you open the Relationships Graph and click the Add Table Occurrence icon, you'll notice something we didn't highlight before. In the resulting Specify Table dialog, there's a menu that lets you choose which file you want to browse for table choices. This menu always includes the current file, and also includes any file references you have defined using the techniques covered in the previous sections of this chapter. Figure 7.30 illustrates this point.

With the file reference in place, you can choose the Customer file reference (remember that the name of the file reference can be different from the name of the file to which it resolves, much as the name of a table occurrence can differ from the name of the underlying source table), and from the resulting table list you can choose the Customer table. The table is then added to the Relationships Graph, much as all the other tables we've seen, and you can create the usual relationship between the Customer table and the Invoice table based on CustomerID. The result is shown in Figure 7.31. There's one subtle visual indication that the Customer table occurrence is based on a table from another file: The table occurrence name for Customer is italicized. Otherwise it's just as though you were working with a table in the same file.

7

Figure 7.30
When adding a table occurrence to the Relationships Graph, you can base the new occurrence on a table in another file.

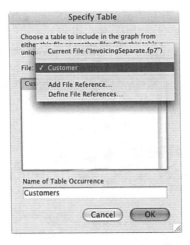

Figure 7.31
In this Relationships Graph, the italicized title of the Customer table occurrence shows that the source table exists in an external file.

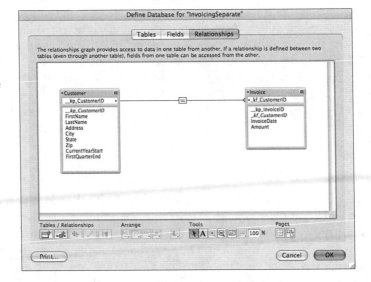

So that's all there is to using external tables in your Relationships Graph. Add a file reference that points to the appropriate file, and use that reference to pull in tables from the external file.

TIP

File references—like tables, table occurrences, fields, layouts, and scripts—can benefit from a consistent naming scheme. Here, as elsewhere, the naming scheme you choose is less important than the consistency with which you apply it. By default, FileMaker names a file reference after the actual file to which it points. You may feel, though, that you want some added information in the name—an "Ext" prefix or the like, for example, to show that the file is external. This may be even more helpful when naming table occurrences from external files. In the Relationships Graph, the only clue that a table occurrence is external is the fact that the name is italicized. If an occurrence of an Employee table from an external file is named ExtEmployee, this may be a helpful clarification.

HOW AND WHEN TO USE MULTIPLE FILES

The preceding section showed the mechanics of creating a FileMaker system that uses tables from different files. It didn't say much about the reasons why, in general, you might want to do such a thing. We offered the example of needing to work with a preexisting file owned by someone else. This is certainly a relevant case, but there are also reasons why you might choose to build your own systems with multiple files from the start. This section looks over some of the major reasons for using multiple files in a single database solution.

WORKING WITH CONVERTED FILES

FileMaker 7 and 8 represent a very new way of building FileMaker databases. The differences between FileMaker 7/8 and previous versions are significant enough that converting a system from a version older than 7 is not quite the easy, nearly transparent process that conversions between different versions of the product have been in the past.

→ For greater detail on the conversion process, **see** Chapter 18, "Converting Systems from Previous Versions of FileMaker Pro," **p. 537**.

In versions of FileMaker prior to version 7, each database table was represented by a single physical disk file. A 10-table system would use 10 different FileMaker files. In FileMaker 7 or 8, if you build that 10-table system from scratch, you could choose to put all 10 tables into a single physical file. But if you're converting that system from, say, FileMaker 6 to FileMaker 8, you won't have that option. The conversion process cannot roll separate files together into a single new FileMaker 8 file. Your 10-file (that is, 10-table) FileMaker 6 system becomes a 10-file FileMaker 8 system as well. The conversion process brings forward all the appropriate file references into each of the new FileMaker 8 files, and populates the Relationships Graphs of each file appropriately, but structurally you'll still have a set of 10 interlocking files, just as you did before. From that point, of course, you might be able to start rolling the tables together, but the process is largely a manual one.

Any system converted from previous versions of FileMaker is sure to have a large number of external file references. Many of these may be to the same file, but in different forms (with different directory paths, for example). The new system will probably work perfectly well like this. And if it's working, you're likely to leave it alone. At most you may consider adding any new tables into existing files, when and if new tables become necessary.

NOTE

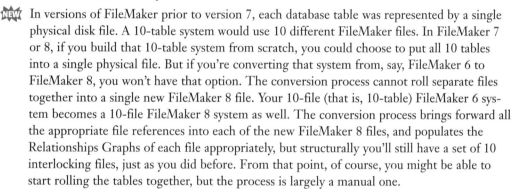

The presence of multiple redundant file paths in a single file reference is characteristic of files converted from FileMaker 6 and earlier to FileMaker 8. In previous versions, if you worked with a file in multiple places over time, many or all of those places might end up in the file path list. Because FileMaker needs to search the entire file reference, item by item, all the unused file paths can cause significant slowdown in opening files.

→ For more information on this problem, and on approaches to solving it, **see** "Fix File References," **p. 548**.

7

SEPARATION OF A SYSTEM INTO MODULES

FileMaker 8 makes it possible, even tempting, to put all the tables for a database system into a single file and be done with it. But is that always the best choice? Not necessarily. There are still several reasons to suggest that breaking things into multiple files may sometimes be a more suitable choice. The sections that follow examine a number of potential benefits to using multiple tables. We're not presuming anything about *how*, exactly, you might choose to split up your tables. There are a few possibilities. If your system falls cleanly into several different modules, for example (let's say Accounting, Orders, and Inventory), it may make sense to take the tables contained in each module and group each set in its own file. You may also want to split your system into a file of data tables and another file dedicated to interface layouts and application logic such as scripts; this possibility is discussed later in this chapter in "Separation of Data and Application Logic."

EASE OF SHARED DEVELOPMENT

FileMaker has always been a great Rapid Application Development (RAD) tool, but the product has tended to retain an emphasis on the single developer. It's often been challenging for multiple people to work on the same FileMaker system simultaneously without getting in each other's way.

In FileMaker 8, anyone with sufficient privileges can open the ScriptMaker. If others have ScriptMaker open as well, you'll be inhibited from editing only any scripts they have open, and any subscripts called by those scripts. But in other ways FileMaker 8 exacerbates the earlier problem, in that scripts in FileMaker 8 can span multiple tables within a single file, aggregating together scripts that would be separated into different files in a multifile system. The more tables you group into a single file, the more likely it may be that multiple developers will interfere with each other when editing scripts.

Things are a bit tougher with the database definition tools. Multiple developers can open the Define Database dialog at once. But only one at a time can be in control of the database definition. The others can view any aspect of the structure, but cannot change it.

So if you expect you'll often have more than one person making script or database definition changes inside your system, it may make sense to try to separate your tables into groups and put each group in its own file to minimize the chances of developers getting in each other's way.

EASE OF MAINTENANCE

Every database system needs maintenance. Files become fragmented, which makes access to them slower. Lost space needs to be reclaimed; indexes need to be optimized. FileMaker is no different. It's a good idea to perform periodic file maintenance on your FileMaker files.

→ For a discussion of file maintenance, **see** "File Maintenance and Recovery," **p. 533**.

One thing to consider is that the larger your file, the longer it takes to perform this periodic maintenance. The same is true for other maintenance tasks, such as backing up. If your system is particularly large, say in the hundreds of megabytes or into the gigabyte range, your backups will take a long time to run. This may not be a problem if you run your backups at night, but in many mission-critical systems the data is backed up periodically during the day, sometimes as often as hourly. If all your tables are in a single file, your choices are to back up all, or nothing. There's no way to back up only a few tables from a single file. Suppose that the system had one massive table of fairly static data, which changes on the order of only once a week, as well as many smaller tables of critical, highly changeable data. In the best of all worlds, you'd back up the huge table daily or weekly, the smaller ones perhaps as often as hourly. If all the tables are in one file, you're out of luck. Each backup has to copy the single massive table again, even though it's unlikely to have changed.

In the worst case, consider the problem of file recovery. In rare circumstances, a FileMaker file can become damaged or unusable due to a crash. If all your tables and data are in that one file, the consequences of a crash are potentially catastrophic. One bad event can in theory compromise your entire system.

Even if the worst doesn't happen, you may still need to run a recovery on such a file. As with maintenance and backups, the time it takes to recover the file is in proportion to its size. And you need to recover everything—all the tables—even if the massive ones were undamaged and only the little ones were damaged in some way. Had the tables been separated into additional files, the consequences of a crash could have been mitigated.

None of this is to suggest that you should go back to the one-file-per-table model of previous versions, necessarily. It does mean that you should think carefully about how your database is going to be used, and whether there will be wide variation in size or usage pattern among tables. If such differences exist and can be predicted, it may be worthwhile to isolate certain tables in their own file or files.

SEPARATION OF DATA AND APPLICATION LOGIC

In FileMaker 8, as in previous versions, data and application logic are mixed together in a single file. A physical file contains not only a system's data (the "database" portion of things), but also all the scripts, layouts, value lists, and the like that make up the "user application" portion of things. After a system has been rolled out and is in use, if you want to continue to make changes to it, you have a limited range of choices.

One possibility is to work directly on the running copy. FileMaker permits this; you can edit scripts, add layouts, even add entire tables to a running system. Still, just because you *can* doesn't mean you should. What if you make a mistake? (Mistakes do happen from time to time—in fact we devote an entire chapter to avoiding and repairing them.) That mistake will affect users who are probably trying to get work done. It may be merely annoying, or it may be catastrophic. If the changes are small and you know what you're doing, you may be fine making the changes online, so to speak. For more extensive changes, it's not a great idea.

Another possibility is to work on a copy of the system. Make all your changes, test them every which way, and, when they're all ready, integrate them into the current live system. But here's where the data-and-logic problem rears its head. You can't just replace the existing production files with your development copy—the production files almost certainly contain a different data set. And there's no convenient way to merge your structural changes with the data in the live copy. To do this, you'll need to shut down the live file and import

7

its data into your development copy, and then bring the development copy online as the new production copy. Depending on the size of the data, this is often a long process, and there are several small potential pitfalls along the way, such as accidental generation of overlapping serial numbers, or forgetting to reset global fields to default values.

Things are not really better on this front with FileMaker 8. Because a file can contain multiple tables, performing an update on a file may mean importing data into a great many tables, even if only a small area of the system has really changed. Separating the tables into several modules, as discussed previously, can help, but the problem remains.

Ideally, we'd be able to take a given data set and just swap a new interface in on top of it without all this talk of mass imports. Using a multifile architecture, this is a reasonable possibility if you separate your data and your interface into two or more separate files.

Let's consider a library book tracking system. It has two main entities, called Item and Patron. An Item is anything the library holds, such as a book, movie, DVD, or CD. There is a many-to-many relationship between Item and Patron, so you also need a join entity, which we'll call Checkout.

This is a thriving public library, and the tables are very large: hundreds of thousands of Items, tens of thousands of Patrons, and literally millions of Checkout records. If you have to reload that data when we make programming changes to the system, you're in for some misery.

Figure 7.32 shows the Relationships Graph for a file called Library. Here you can see the entities, related in the way you'd expect.

Figure 7.32
A Relationships Graph for a system that models a many-to-many relationship between library patrons and library items, via a join file that records each checkout of an individual item.

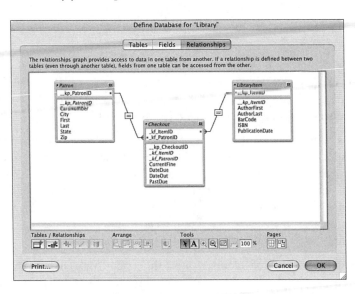

There's one slight difference here. As you can tell from the italicized table occurrence names, *all* these table occurrences are from externally related files. The three data tables now have a single separate physical file of their own.

In theory, you can now do all your interface work in the Library file. You can create all your scripts and user screens in the Library file, leaving the file containing the three data tables alone. If you update a screen or change a script's logic, rather than tinkering with the massive data file, you can just swap in a new Library file (the "viewer" file, if you will) and you'll be all set. And if Library 2.1 has a problem, it's easy enough to roll back to Library 2.0 until you can get 2.1 fixed up.

This is all true and good so far. In all fairness, though, we have to point out that there are some limitations to this technique:

- **Security**—Accounts and privileges are maintained separately in each file. It's not possible to instruct one FileMaker file to draw its accounts and privileges from another FileMaker file. It's possible to use external authentication methods to offload a lot of the work to an external authentication server, but it's still necessary to create group-to-privilege mapping information in each separate FileMaker file. (For more information on security matters, see Chapter 12, "Implementing Security.") So in this example, privileges would have to be created and maintained in parallel in both the interface and the data files.

- **Multiple Relationships Graphs**—Even in this kind of scenario, the data file is going to need to be aware of most or all of the structural relationships between data tables. If, for example, you want to create a calculation field that tells you how many items a given patron currently has checked out, that calculation field, which lives in a data table, needs to use a relationship between Patron and Checkout to compute that number. So it isn't possible to build a Relationships Graph in just the "interface" file—substantial portions of it may need to be replicated in the "data" file as well.

- **"Stickiness" of the data tables**—In theory, changes to scripts or layouts can be accomplished just by swapping out the interface file. But in our experience, many if not most significant updates end up touching the data side as well, even if only to add certain new calculations. The separation methodology described here still doesn't give you a means to avoid making these additions to the data file. However, data file changes are quite a bit easier to write down and replicate than wide-ranging script and layout changes. Manual work may still be necessary in many updates, but it is still much less onerous than doing a massive import of one or more tables.

FileMaker's multitable architecture is new enough—and different enough from its predecessors—that best practices in these design areas are still emerging. The idea of separation of data and interface certainly shows promise. It won't cure all woes, and it won't always be the right thing to do; but it clearly has the potential to address some vexing problems and open some new doors.

WORKING TOWARD REUSE

As a final reason to consider a multifile structure, consider the idea of reuse. This is in some ways an extension of the earlier discussion of the idea of separating a system into modules. Suppose that there's a module you want to use in several or many different FileMaker systems. You may want to consider isolating the functionality of the module in a single file and including that file in solutions that need the functionality.

As an example, suppose you have a custom-built user management system that keeps track of users, passwords, and privileges. FileMaker 8's new account management features are great, but you still might want to roll your own sometimes.

NOTE

> This is especially true in multifile situations. FileMaker's access privilege system is still slightly hampered because each separate file stores its own account and privilege information, as we discussed previously.

You could create a User file that would include a table for user information, as well as tables for user groups—or even subgroups, if applicable. If records of user activity, such as logon and logoff times, were required, that information could be stored here as well.

To promote a module's reusability, you could take advantage of some FileMaker features that promote abstraction, such as custom functions, script parameters, and script results. Suppose that you wanted to create a somewhat generic logging facility (that is, the capability to log user actions to a database table). You could create a Log table with fields for user ID, timestamp, and a textual description of the event. You could then create a logging script that takes a script parameter containing the text to be written to the log, and writes out a log record with this text, the current user ID (presumably stored in a global), and the current timestamp. With planning and forethought, it's possible to create a module in FileMaker 8 with a high degree of reusability.

Let's think about how you might use such a module. First suppose that you're pursuing a strategy of data/interface separation such as the one described earlier in this chapter. Your main system consists of two files, MainData (containing all the data tables, but no scripts or interface) and MainViewer (the interface file that contains scripts, layouts, and interface logic). You also have your user module, which is split into two files, UserData and UserAdmin.

You need to create a file reference from MainViewer to UserAdmin. You probably should *not* need to create a file reference from MainView to UserData. All the main system's interactions with the UserData file should ideally be calls to scripts in UserAdmin; adding log records or checking a user's privileges should not be done by checking the UserData tables directly, but by asking UserAdmin to do this and report on the success or failure of the request.

You would especially want to avoid any logic that would force you to create a table reference *from* UserAdmin to MainViewer or MainData. UserAdmin shouldn't care about the nature or internals of any files or system that wants to use its services.

Not every group of related tables is likely to be suitable for this kind of modularization. But you might want to consider splitting out any subsystems that provide somewhat nonspecific functions, such as logging or user management, and making them into their own, semi-connected modules. Careful planning and exploitation of new features such as script parameters can help you create modules that can be smoothly integrated with various FileMaker systems.

TROUBLESHOOTING

TROUBLE CREATING RELATED RECORDS WITH NON-EQUIJOINS

I want to create a relationship that allows creation of related records on one side of the relationship, but the box that enables that capability is grayed out.

You might have noticed (for example, in Figure 7.19) that the option Allow Creation of Records in This Table via This Relationship has mysteriously been disabled. This suggests that you have one or more non-equality conditions in your relationship match criteria. The rule is this: FileMaker can allow creation of related records only if the relationship in question consists only of conditions involving an equality comparison. This limits such relationships to using only the equal (=), less than or equal (≤), or greater than or equal (≥) operators.

Multiple match criteria are fine, as long as they're all based on one of those three operators. (This can actually be rather useful: A multimatch relationship that allows creation of related records automatically fills in *all* the key fields of the related record.) But as soon as any non-equality condition becomes involved in the match, the capability to create related records goes away.

This makes sense if you think about it. FileMaker can create a record via an equijoin because there's only one condition that satisfies the match criteria for the current record. Suppose that you're on a Customer Layout, looking at customer number 17, and you have a portal into Invoices, in which the relationship to Invoices is an equijoin on CustomerID. FileMaker can create a new record in the portal by creating a new invoice record and setting the CustomerID to 17. But suppose that the relationship instead were based on a "not equal to" relationship? To create a record on the other side, FileMaker would need to create an Invoice record with a customer ID *other than* 17. Fine, but what customer ID should it use? There's really no way to say. Similar reasoning holds for other non-equijoin types: There's no sensible way for FileMaker to decide what match data should go into the related record.

If the capability to create related records is enabled, the key fields in the related record will always be populated with values equal to the key field in the parent record, regardless of which of the three allowable relational operators is chosen.

NO OR CONDITIONS WITH MULTIPLE MATCH CRITERIA

Whenever I add multiple match criteria to a relationship, FileMaker always tells me the match will work if condition 1 AND condition 2 AND condition 3 are true. But I have a match that needs to work if 1 OR 2 OR 3 is true. Where do I set that up?

You don't, unfortunately. Using the native FileMaker relationship features, relational matches are always AND matches whenever multiple match criteria are specified. If you want to mimic the effect of an OR search in another table, you need to find another means of doing that. Say, for example, that you have a database with tables for teachers, classes, enrollments, and students. From the viewpoint of a teacher, you want to be able to view all students who are outside the norm—they have either a very low GPA or a very high GPA.

You could try to do this with two match criteria, but that would necessarily be an AND match, which would never be fulfilled (no student would have both a low and a high GPA at once).

The solution here would be to create a stored calculation in the student table called something like ExceptionalGPA, defined as

```
If ( GPA < 2 or GPA > 3.75; 1; 0)
```

The calculation will have the value 1 when the student's GPA is exceptionally high or low, and a value of 0 otherwise.

You could now create a field in the teacher table called Constant, and define it as a calculation that evaluates to 1. Then specify a relationship between the teacher table and the student table, with multiple match criteria: TeacherID=TeacherID, and Constant=ExceptionalGPA, meaning, "Find me all students with the same teacher ID and an exceptional GPA."

FILEMAKER EXTRA: MANAGING THE RELATIONSHIPS GRAPH

The Relationships Graph in FileMaker is a nice answer to developers who clamored for years for a visual representation of relationships in FileMaker systems. But for large or complex systems, with many table occurrences, the Graph has the potential to be a bit unwieldy. Table occurrences in the Graph take up a fair amount of space, and it can be difficult to organize the occurrences without creating a web of overlapping relationship lines.

You can use a number of tools for Graph management. For one thing, the small "window-shade" icon at the upper right of a table occurrence can be used to hide the fields in the table occurrence, leaving only the match fields used in relationships. This can save valuable space. If you like to work from the keyboard, (⌘-T) [Ctrl+T] will cycle through the various table occurrence display states (fully open, key fields only, fully closed). If you use (⌘-A) [Ctrl+A] to select all objects in the Graph, you can windowshade your entire Graph with a few keystrokes. Figure 7.33 shows a Relationships Graph in windowshade mode.

You can also resize an individual table occurrence manually to save space. This, again, needs to be done one table occurrence at a time. It's also possible to zoom out from the Graph as a whole and view it at 75% or 50% of regular size, or smaller.

It might also be useful to you to organize your table occurrences into logical groups of some kind within the Relationships Graph. Let's say you're working on a trucking module with four table occurrences, and you also have a file reference to an external user-management module and you've used that to bring a number of user-oriented table occurrences into the Graph. FileMaker enables you to color-code table occurrences in the Graph, so it's possible to give each group of table occurrences its own color.

In FileMaker 7 there was no way to add notes or comments directly to the Graph. The previous version of this book suggested using "dummy" table occurrences to add headers and labels to object groups. In FileMaker 8, you can add notes directly to the Graph. If you drag a rectangle in the Graph while holding (⌘-N) [Ctrl+N], you'll create something like a sticky note. You can choose the color and typeface, and adjust the size and position. Notes appear behind other objects in the Graph.

Figure 7.33
Individual table occurrences can be made into "windowshades" that display only the match fields that participate in relationships.

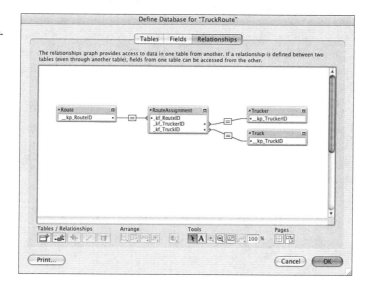

Figure 7.34 shows a Relationships Graph with table occurrences from both the trucking module and the user module. The trucker tables are colored red here, the user tables are blue, and each group has a "wrapper" of a sort, formed by a note. In addition, in the figure the Graph has been reduced to 75% of its normal size.

Figure 7.34
Use color coding and group naming to help organize the Relationships Graph.

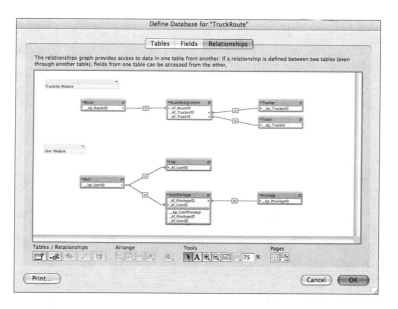

→ For some more discussion of annotating and documenting your systems, **see** Chapter 27, "Documenting Your FileMaker Solutions," **p. 841**.

NEW In addition to notes, FileMaker 8 adds a few other nice enhancements that let you better manage the Graph. Pressing (⌘-Y) [Ctrl+Y] will select all related table occurrences that are one step away from the current table occurrence. Pressing (⌘-U) [Ctrl+U] will select all table occurrences with the same source table as the current table. Finally, you can now use (⌘-D) [Ctrl+D] to duplicate one or more selected table objects, as well as any relationships between them. This last point is a big convenience: You can select a complex group of related table occurrences and duplicate the entire cluster, and its relationships, at once. All of these functions can be performed with the mouse as well, by new buttons that appear in the FileMaker 8 Relationships Graph.

All these techniques can help make your Graph more manageable. Still, if you have a system with a hundred table occurrences, your Graph will be crowded, without question. It's been suggested that offering a list view of relationships as well, in a manner similar to previous versions of FileMaker, would be helpful, and it's possible we may see such a list view in future versions of the product.

CHAPTER **8**

GETTING STARTED
WITH CALCULATIONS

In this chapter

8

UNDERSTANDING HOW AND WHERE CALCULATIONS ARE USED

Calculation functions are among the most important and powerful tools at your disposal in the development of FileMaker Pro solutions. Some people find learning calculations to be an easy task, whereas others can find writing complex calculations to be daunting. Whichever camp you fall into, calculations will enable you to unlock much of the advanced power within FileMaker—we encourage you to stick with it. Our hope is that this chapter and its companion, Chapter 14, "Advanced Calculation Techniques," will provide you a solid grounding.

This chapter focuses on basic calculation functions and techniques for using them well. Chapter 14 looks at more advanced calculation formulas and specific techniques. If you're new to FileMaker, you should start here. Those who have been using FileMaker for years may want to just skim this chapter. (There are probably a few nuggets of information that will make it worth your while.) We've also included a complete function reference in our companion book, *FileMaker 8 Functions and Scripts Desk Reference*. That book is intended to serve as a reference when you need to look up specific information. Here, we take more of a tutorial approach and explore how and why one employs calculations.

From the outset, it's important to understand the difference between calculation fields and calculation formulas. The term *calculation* is often used ambiguously to denote both concepts ("That table has more than 100 calculations!" or "What's the calculation used to determine access to this record?"). *Calculation fields* are a particular type of field whose value is determined through the evaluation of a calculation formula. *Calculation formula* is a broader concept that refers to any use of a formula to determine an output. When you learn "calculations," you're really learning calculation formulas. It so happens that you'll use calculation formulas to construct calculation fields, but the formulas are applied widely throughout FileMaker solutions.

WRITING CALCULATION FORMULAS

Essentially, the purpose of a calculation formula is to evaluate an expression and return a value. In Figure 8.1, for example, you can see the field definition for a calculation field called Mileage Calc. The value of this field is defined to be the result of multiplying the contents of the Mileage field by .37, which is a typical mileage reimbursement rate.

Most of the expressions you use in calculation formulas are intended to return a value, and that value might be a number, a text string, a date or time, or even a reference to a file to place in a container field. Another class of formulas, however, is intended to evaluate the veracity of an equation or statement. The value returned by these formulas is either a 1, indicating that the equation or statement is true, or 0, indicating that the equation or statement is false. Typically, calculations are used in this manner in If script steps, in calculated validations, and for defining field access restrictions.

→ To learn more about field validation, **see** Chapter 3, "Defining and Working with Fields," **p. 67**.

Figure 8.1
When defining calculation fields, you specify an expression to evaluate in the Specify Calculation dialog.

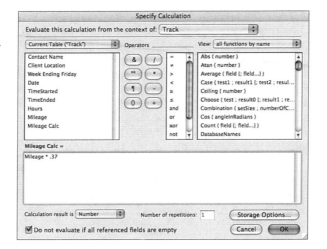

In Figure 8.2, for instance, you can see a calculation dialog that specifies the condition for an `If` script step. When the script executes, FileMaker evaluates whether the number of hours is in fact greater than 8 (based on the current record's data). Depending on the value of the Hours field for any particular record, the statement may be either true or false and the script will presumably react accordingly.

Figure 8.2
Calculation formulas are often used to determine the truthfulness of an equation or a statement.

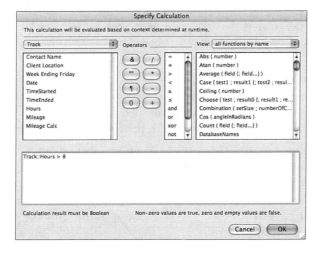

For certain uses, then, the purpose of a calculation formula is to return a value; for other uses it's simply to evaluate the veracity of an equation or statement. In situations in which FileMaker is expecting a formula that returns a true/false result, you see the words `Calculation result must be Boolean` near the bottom of the calculation dialog. The `If` script step shown earlier is a typical example of this situation. *Boolean* is a software programming term for a value with one of two states: true or false. Any value returned other than `0` or a null value (for example, an empty string) is considered true.

8

NOTE

Note that Boolean rules apply for text values, dates, negative numbers, and so on. `"Hello"` is true (not zero and not null), a single space character (`" "`) is true, and `-1` is true. Note also that the results of a formula are evaluated in the same way: (`0 * 100`) is false. (`0 + 100`) is true. Last, also note that you can use comparative operators: `1` and `1` is true (where each clause on both sides of the `and` operator evaluate to true), `1` or `1` is true, `1` `xor` `1` is false, and so on. You'll learn about operators later in the chapter.

CAUTION

The `GetAsBoolean()` function treats all data as numeric, such that, for example, `"hello"` evaluates as false and `"hello999"` evaluates as true. This is an inconsistency with the way in which other Boolean logic operates, so be sure to take note of it.

USES FOR CALCULATION FORMULAS

This chapter focuses on the use of calculation formulas in field definitions, but it's important that you understand that there are other places where calculation formulas are used as well. Briefly, these include the following:

- **Script steps**—Calculation formulas come into play in many script steps. The `If`, `Set Field`, and `Set Variable` script steps are notable examples. Many other script steps allow you to use a calculation formula to act as a parameter. A sampling includes `Go to Layout`, `Go to Field`, `Go to Record`, `Pause/Resume Script`, and `Omit Multiple`. Additionally, calculation formulas can be used to define script parameters and script results.

- **Field validation**—One of the options available to you for validating data entry is validating by calculation. This, in effect, lets you define your own rules for validation. For example, you might want to test that a due date falls on a weekday, or perhaps that a status field not allow a value of "complete" if there is data missing elsewhere in a record.

  The equation you provide is evaluated every time a user modifies the field. If it evaluates as true, the user's entry is committed. If it doesn't, the user is presented with an error message. For instance, if a user is supposed to enter a callback date on a contact record, you might want to validate that the entry is a future date. To do this, you might use the formula `Call_Back_Date > Get ( CurrentDate )` as the validation for the Call_Back_Date field.

- **Record-level security**—When you define privilege sets, you have the option of limiting a user's access to view, edit, and delete records based on a calculation formula you provide. If the equation you provide evaluates as true, the user can perform the action; if not, the action is prohibited. For instance, you might want to prevent users from inadvertently modifying an invoice that has already been posted. So you'd set up limited access for editing records based on the formula `Invoice_Status ≠ "Posted"`. Only records for which that is a true statement would be editable.

- **Auto-entry options**—When you're defining text, number, date, time, and timestamp fields, several auto-entry options are available for specifying default field values. One of these options is to auto-enter the result of a calculation formula. For instance, in a contact management database, you might want a default callback date set for all new contact records. The formula you'd use for this might be something like `Get ( CurrentDate ) + 14`, if you wanted a callback date two weeks in the future.

- **Calculated replace**—A calculated replace is a way of changing the contents of a field in all the records in the current found set. It's particularly useful for cleaning up messy data. Say, for example, that your users had sometimes entered spaces at the end of a name field as they were doing data entry. You could clean up this data by performing a calculated replace with the formula `Trim ( First Name )`.

EXPLORING THE CALCULATION DIALOG BOX

Now that you know something about how and where calculation formulas are used, it's time to turn next to the layout of the calculation dialog box itself. There are some small differences among the calculation dialogs you find in particular areas within FileMaker Pro. We'll focus our attention on the dialog used for defining calculation fields because it's the most complex. Figure 8.3 shows the calculation dialog for a field called FullName, which serves as the model for this anatomy lesson.

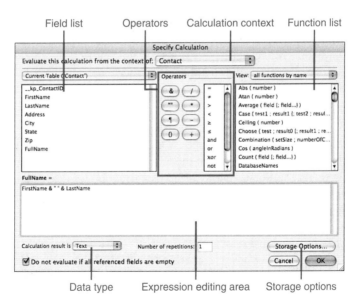

Figure 8.3
When you're creating calculation fields, it helps to know your way around the Specify Calculation dialog box.

SPECIFYING CONTEXT

Across the top of the dialog, you're asked to specify the context from which to evaluate this calculation. This choice is necessary only when the source table you are working with appears in your Relationships Graph more than once. And even in those cases, it really matters only when your calculation formula involves related fields. In such cases, the calculation may return different results, depending on the context from which it's evaluated.

To make this point clear, consider the example in Figure 8.4.

Figure 8.4
Notice that the Transaction table occurrence has two related parent table occurrences derived from the same source table of Person.

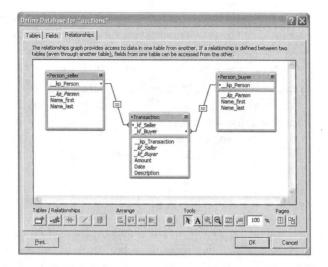

In this example, a person can act as either a buyer or a seller for a given transaction. This means then that a person record will have potentially two sets of related transactions: those for which that person is a seller, and those for which he or she is a buyer. If you were to create a calculation field in the Person table that produced a total of transactions, you'd get very different results depending on from which context you calculate. Both versions of the calculation would use a SUM (Transaction::Amount) formula, but the originating context will determine whether you're viewing records from the buyer perspective or the seller perspective. In this example, it's critical that the originating context be set deliberately in order to determine *which* transactions get totaled.

WRITING THE FORMULA

The large box in the middle of the Specify Calculation dialog is where you define the formula itself. If you know the syntax of the functions you need and the names of the fields, you can simply go ahead and type in the formula by hand. In most cases, though, you'll want to use the lists of fields and functions above the text box. Double-clicking on an item in those lists inserts that item into your formula at the current insertion point.

> **NOTE**
>
> On a Macintosh, after an item is highlighted, you can also press the spacebar to insert it into your formula. On Windows, the Insert key functions similarly.

Every calculation formula is made up of some combination of fields, constants, operators, and functions. All the following are examples of formulas you might write:

```
2 + 2
FirstName & " " & LastName
Get(CurrentDate) + 14
Left( FirstName; 1 ) & Left ( LastName; 1 )
"Dear " & FirstName & ":"
$loopCounter = $loopCounter + 1
LastName = "Jones"
```

In these examples, FirstName and LastName are fields. $loopCounter is a variable by virtue of being prefixed with a dollar-sign character. Get (CurrentDate) and Left are functions. The only operators used here are the addition operator (+) and the concatenation operator (&). (*Concatenation* means combining two text strings to form a new text string.) There are also numbers and text strings used as constants (meaning that they don't change), such as 14, "Dear", and "Jones". Text strings are the only things that need to be placed within quotes. FileMaker assumes that any unquoted text in a formula is a number, a function name, or a field name. If it's none of these, you get an error message when you attempt to exit the dialog.

→ To learn about variables, **see** Chapter 15, "Advanced Scripting Techniques," **p. 435**.

SELECTING FIELDS

In the calculation dialog, above the formula box to the left is a list of fields. By default, the fields in the current table are listed. You can see the fields in a related (or unrelated) table by making a selection in the pop-up above the field list. Double-click a field name to insert it into your formula. You can also type field names directly.

CAUTION

> Be aware that the only fields you can use from an unrelated table are those with global storage. There's no way FileMaker could determine which record(s) to reference for non-globally stored fields. You get an error message if you attempt to use a nonglobal field from an unrelated table in a formula.

 If you're having difficulty with field name syntax in formulas within ScriptMaker, see "Formulas in Scripts Require Explicit Table Context" in the "Troubleshooting" section at the end of this chapter.

CHOOSING OPERATORS

In between the field and function areas in the Specify Calculation dialog is a list of operators you can use in your formulas. *Operators* are symbols that define functions, including the math functions addition, subtraction, raising to a power, and so on.

NOTE

> Strictly speaking, not all the symbols listed here are operators. The ¶ paragraph symbol (or pilcrow), for instance, is used to represent a literal return character in strings.

There is often some confusion about the use of &, +, and the and operator. The ampersand symbol (&) is used to concatenate strings of text together, as in the previous example in which we derive the FullName by stringing together the FirstName, a space, and the LastName. The + symbol is a mathematical operator, used, as you might expect, to add numbers together. The and operator is a logical operator used when you need to test for multiple Boolean conditions. For instance, you might use the formula Case (Amount Due > 0 and Days Overdue > 30, "Overdue"). Here, the and indicates that both conditions must be satisfied for the test to return true.

8

The other operators are quite intuitive, with the exception of xor. xor, which stands for *exclusive or*, is used to test whether either of two statements is true, but not both of them. That is, (A xor B) is the same thing as "(A or B) and not (A and B)." The need for such logic doesn't come up often, but it's still handy to know.

SELECTING FUNCTIONS

The upper-right portion of the Specify Calculation dialog contains a list of the functions you can use in your formulas. By default, they are listed alphabetically, but you can use the View pop-up menu above the list to view only formulas of a certain type. The Get functions and External functions, in fact, will display only if you change to View by Type.

Double-clicking a function inserts the function into your formula at the current insertion point. Pressing the spacebar (Macintosh) or the Insert key (Windows) while the function is highlighted also adds the function to your formula. The "guts" of the function—the portion in between the parentheses—is highlighted so that you can begin typing parameters immediately.

➔ To learn more about how to read and use functions, **see** "The Parts of a Function," **p. 229**.

WRITING LEGIBLE FORMULAS

Whether you're typing in a formula by hand or are using the selection lists to insert fields and functions, we have a few general comments about how to make your functions easy to read.

First of all, when you're writing functions, spacing, tabs, and line returns don't matter at all. You can put spaces, tabs, and returns just about anyplace you want without changing how the formula evaluates. For legibility, it's therefore often helpful to put the parameters of a function on separate lines, especially when you have nested functions.

You can also add comments to calculation formulas. You can prefix a comment with two forward slashes (//) and anything following on that line will not be evaluated. To comment a block of multiple-lined text, begin with /* and close with */.

Compare, for example, the legibility of a complex function written two different ways. In Figure 8.5, you can see a mildly complex function with no commenting or spacing. In Figure 8.6, that same formula has been rewritten with comments and extra spacing to make it more legible. Legibility isn't merely an idle concern; it has real value. If you, or someone else, ever need to debug or alter one of your formulas, it will take much less time and effort if you've formatted your formula well in the first place.

OTHER OPTIONS

Before ending this calculation dialog anatomy lesson, we must cover the miscellaneous options you can see at the bottom of the Specify Calculation dialog. These options pertain only to defining calculation fields; you don't see them in any of the other calculation dialogs.

Figure 8.5
A complex formula written without adequate spacing can be very difficult to understand and troubleshoot.

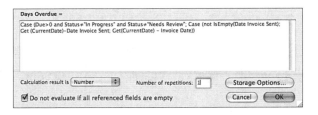

Figure 8.6
Adding spaces, returns, and comments to a formula can make it much more legible, and hence easier to maintain in the future.

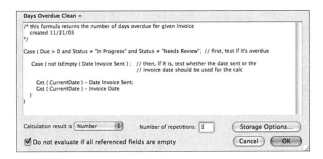

DATA TYPE

The first of these miscellaneous options is to specify the type of data the calculation will return. Usually, it's quite obvious. If you're concatenating the FirstName and LastName fields to form the FullName field, your calculation result will need to be a text string. If you're adding the SalesTax to an InvoiceSubTotal to generate the InvoiceTotal, the expected result will obviously be a number. Adding 14 days to the current date to generate a callback date should result in a date. Simply ask yourself what type of data the formula should produce and select the appropriate result.

 If you do choose the wrong data type for a calculation field, you may experience some unexpected results. See "Errors Due to Improper Data Type Selection" in the "Troubleshooting" section at the end of this chapter.

NUMBER OF REPETITIONS

The only time you'll ever have to worry about the number of repetitions in a calculation field is when your formula references one or more repeating fields. If it does, you'll typically define your calculation to have the same number of repetitions as the fields it references. The formula you define is applied to each repetition of the source fields, resulting in different values for each repetition of your calculation field.

If you reference nonrepeating fields in your calculation, they affect only the first repetition of output. You can, however, use the Extend() function to allow a nonrepeating field to be applied to each repetition of output.

For instance, in Figure 8.7, Quantity and Line Cost are both number fields defined to allow 10 repetitions. Tax Rate is a regular number field. The formula used to determine the LineTotal is as follows:

```
Quantity * LineCost * (Extend(TaxRate) + 1)
```

LineTotal itself is defined to allow 10 repetitions.

Figure 8.7
Calculation fields can be defined to allow multiple repetitions.

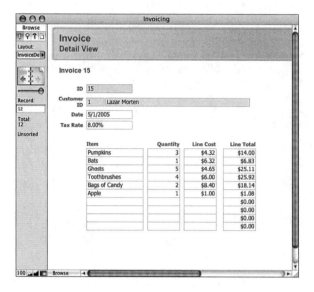

DO NOT EVALUATE

By default for new calculation fields, the Do Not Evaluate If All Referenced Fields Are Empty box on the Specify Calculation dialog is checked. This means that the calculation will return a null (empty) value as long as all the fields it refers to are empty. If this box is unchecked, the formula will be evaluated using the empty values in the referenced fields. For instance, say you had a StatusCode field in an invoice database and wanted to use it to generate a status message, the formula of which was If (StatusCode = "P"; "Paid"; "Not Paid"). If you left the Do Not Evaluate… box checked, invoices with no status code would have no status message. If it were unchecked, their status message would be Not Paid.

Another example draws from this feature's most common use: financial calculations. If you have a field that calculates, say, a price total based on quantity and sales tax fields, it's often helpful to return an explicit zero rather than leaving the calculation field null or blank.

Consider a calculation field that calculates a discount based on a transactionAmount field:

```
If ( transactionAmount >= 1000; 50; 0 )
```

If the check box is unchecked, this evaluation will return a zero if either transactionAmount is less than 1000 or the field is empty. In this way, the zero is explicit and demonstrates for the user that the calculation was performed. If the check box is left checked and transactionAmount is empty, this discount field will be empty as well, leading to possible ambiguity on the part of users.

There's no simple rule we can provide as to when you want to check or uncheck this option. You need to look at your formula and determine whether the inputs to the formula (those fields referenced in the formula) could all ever be blank, and if so, whether you would still want the formula to evaluate. Typically, if your formulas have default results (as in the

StatusCode example) rather than using explicit logic for determining results, you probably want to uncheck the box.

STORAGE OPTIONS

The last things we'll touch on in this anatomy lesson are the storage options available when you're defining calculation fields. Be aware that the output of your calculation formula may differ depending on the storage method selected. The Storage Options dialog box is shown in Figure 8.8.

Figure 8.8
The Storage Options dialog enables you to set calculation fields so that they have global results and to specify indexing options.

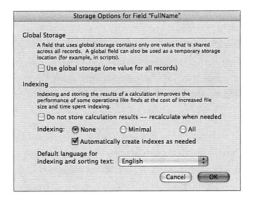

In the top portion of the dialog, you may specify global storage as an option. This is a concept introduced in FileMaker Pro 7, and one perhaps not immediately intuitive even for longtime FileMaker developers. Global storage for regular fields (that is, text, number, date, time, timestamp, or container) is typically used when you need a temporary storage location for a value or for infrequently changing, solutionwide values such as your company's name and address. For instance, globally stored text fields are often used in scripts as a place to hold users' preferences or selections as they navigate through your interface.

→ For more information on global storage of field data, **see** "Storage and Indexing," **p. 86**.

If you set a calculation field to be stored globally, the results of the calculation formula will be available to you from any record, and indeed, any table, in your system without having to establish a relationship to a table occurrence tied to its source table. The formula isn't evaluated for each record in the system; it is evaluated only when one of the inputs of the formula changes or when you modify the formula.

Consider a scenario involving a sales commission calculation. You might create a utility table containing the fields necessary to calculate a daily sales commission (based on market values or whatever variable data affected the business in question) in which a manager could modify the data in the formula on demand. A global calculation then would provide the system with its current sales commission without requiring a series of relationships.

Note that this example assumes there to be one record in the utility table in question. If there were multiple records, it would be possible to include the concept of an active/inactive status into the calculation or simply rely on the fact that the last edited record will be that from which the calculation will draw its source information.

The bottom half of the Storage Options dialog enables you to specify indexing options. Indexing a field speeds up searches based on that field, but it results in larger files. FileMaker also uses field indexes for joining related tables.

→ For more detailed information on indexing, **see** "Storage and Indexing," **p. 86**.

In most cases, the default indexing option for a calculation field will be set to None, and the Automatically Create Indexes as Needed box will be checked. For most calculations you write, this configuration is perfect. FileMaker determines whether an index is needed and creates one if it is. Performing a find in the field or using the field in a relationship are both actions that trigger the automatic indexing of a field.

For some calculation formulas, the default storage option is to have the Do Not Store Calculation Results option checked and for everything else to be grayed out. This is an indication that the field is unindexable. Calculation fields that return text, number, date, time, or timestamp results can be indexed as long as they are stored. Calculations can be stored as long as they don't reference any unstored calculations, globally stored fields, related fields, or summary fields.

There are a few circumstances in which you'll want to explicitly turn off storage. For instance, when you use any of the Get functions in a calculation, you should make sure that the calculation result is unstored. (Get functions typically return information relating to the state of one's user session. By definition, that information changes on a second-by-second basis, and formulas based on it should not be stored so that they continue to reflect present reality.) If you do so, the calculation is forced to evaluate based on the current environment each time it's evaluated (as opposed to always "remembering" the environment at the time the record was created or modified). Imagine you defined a calculation to return the number of records in the current found set by using the Get (FoundCount) formula. If you don't explicitly set the results to be unstored, then for a given record, the formula evaluates once and keeps that value, regardless of changes to the size of the found set. The count of found records the first time the calculation is triggered is the value that will be stored. As their name implies, unstored calculations do not make your files larger, but because they must evaluate each time you view them, they can slow down a system if they're based on complex formulas.

As a rule of thumb, you should stick with the default storage options unless you know for sure that you need the result to be unstored. You'll almost never need to explicitly turn indexing on; let FileMaker turn it on as necessary. Very seldom should you uncheck the option to have FileMaker turn on indexing as needed. Be aware that indexing increases the size of your files, sometimes by a great deal. By unchecking the option to have FileMaker turn on indexing as needed, you can ensure that certain fields won't be indexed accidentally just because a user performs a find on them.

ESSENTIAL FUNCTIONS

Now that you know your way around the Specify Calculation dialog itself, it's time to start learning more about particular calculation functions. Here we'll present an in-depth tutorial on what we feel are the most essential functions and techniques. These will form a solid base for your own work and for assembling complex formulas. As a reminder, Chapter 14 covers advanced calculation formulas and techniques, and there's a complete function reference in our companion book, *FileMaker 8 Functions and Scripts Desk Reference*.

THE PARTS OF A FUNCTION

Let's begin with a general discussion about what functions do and how to learn about them. Their sole mission in life is to act on some set of inputs and produce an output. The inputs are usually referred to as *parameters*; the function's syntax specifies the number of parameters it expects to be fed, and provides a clue about what the nature of each of those parameters is.

An example will help clarify this point. Look at the syntax of the `Position` function as it's taken directly from the function list in the calculation dialog:

```
Position ( text ; searchString ; start ; occurrence )
```

A function's parameters are always placed in parentheses directly after the name of the function itself. They are separated from one another by semicolons.

> **NOTE**
>
> In English versions prior to FileMaker 7, the parameter separator was a comma. In fact, if you use commas now, they are transformed into semicolons for you.

You can see that the `Position` function has four parameters. Any function reference will tell you that the first parameter should be a text string in which you want to search, and the second should be a text string you want to find within it. The third parameter is a number that specifies the character number at which to begin searching. The final parameter is also a number; it specifies which occurrence of the search string to find.

Besides knowing what to feed a function (here, two text strings and two numbers), you also need to know what type of output the function produces. Again, you first learn this by consulting some reference source or the help system. There, you'd learn that the `Position` function returns a number—not just any number, of course, but the character number where the search string was found within the initial text string. If the string was not found at all, it returns a 0. So, for example, if you had the function

```
Position ( "Mary had a little lamb"; "a"; 1; 1 )
```

the function would return 2 because the first occurrence of the letter *a* is at character 2 of the input string. If you change the function slightly, to

```
Position ( "Mary had a little lamb"; "a"; 1; 2 )
```

you'd now expect a value of 7 because that's the position of the second occurrence of the letter *a*.

In these examples, all the parameters were hard-coded with constant values. More typically, the parameters that you feed a function will be either fields or the outputs of other functions. For instance, if you have a field called PoemText and another called SearchCharacter, you might end up using the `Position` function as shown here:

```
Position ( PoemText; SearchCharacter; 1; 1 )
```

8

Now, each record in your database will contain a different result, dependent on the contents of those two fields.

Using functions as parameters of other functions is called *nesting*. In those cases, the inner functions evaluate first, and their results are used as the inputs for the outer functions. For instance, you might have the following function:

```
Position ( PoemText; SearchCharacter; Length( PoemText ) - 5; 1 )
```

Notice that the third parameter of the `Position` function here is the expression `Length( PoemText ) - 5`. The `Length` function (which we'll discuss in more detail shortly) takes a single parameter, a text string, and returns the number of characters in the string. So in the preceding function, the length of the `PoemText` field will be determined, and that value less 5 will be used as the third parameter of the `Position` function. There is no practical limit on the number of layers you can use to nest functions within one another. Just remember that readability becomes very important as your calculations become more complex.

At this point, you know quite a bit about the `Position` function. You know about its inputs and outputs; you've worked with a few examples. Eventually, you'll likely want to memorize the inputs and outputs of a core set of functions. For lesser-used functions, you can look up the parameters and usage on an as-needed basis. There's still a difference between proficiency with a function and a complete understanding of it. For instance, to truly master the `Position` function, you'd need to know such things as whether it's case sensitive (it's not), and what happens if you supply a negative number for the occurrence (it searches backward from the specified start character). Over time and with use, you'll learn about the subtle and esoteric usage of various functions, thereby moving from mere proficiency to mastery.

Let's turn now to a close look at those functions and techniques that should form the core of your calculation knowledge.

TEXT OPERATIONS

Text functions enable you to interrogate and manipulate text strings. If you haven't done much programming before, the concept of a string may need some explanation. Essentially, a *string* is a series of characters. Think about threading characters on a string like you do popcorn to make holiday decorations, and you'll have a good mental image of a text string. The characters can be anything from letters and numbers to spaces and punctuation marks.

NOTE

> In versions of FileMaker prior to 7, the size limit for text strings was 64,000 characters. In FileMaker 7 and 8, it's been expanded to a whopping 2GB. This fact alone has driven many organizations to upgrade.

Typically in FileMaker, text strings are found in text fields, but be aware that you can treat any numeric, date, and time data as a text string as well. When you do that, it's called *coercing* the data. FileMaker automatically coerces data into the type expected for a given operation. If you ever need to override the automatic coercion for any reason, you can use the `GetAs` functions. These include `GetAsDate()`, `GetAsNumber()`, `GetAsTime()`, and `GetAsText()`.

The simplest text operation you can perform is concatenation. *Concatenation* means taking two or more text strings and placing them beside each other to form a new, longer text string. As an example, consider the following formula:

FirstName & " " & LastName

Here, we're taking three strings, two of which happen to be field data, and we're concatenating them into a full name format.

Let's look next at several functions that can be used to interrogate text strings. By *interrogate*, we mean that we're interested in answering a specific question about the contents of a text string. For the examples in this section, assume that you have a field called fullName with the string "Fred Flintstone" and the field someString which contains "The quick brown fox jumped over the lazy dog". The following is a list of some of the core calculation functions with examples that apply to the fullName and someString fields:

- Length (*text*)—The Length function takes a single argument and simply returns the number of characters in the string. Remember that spaces and return characters are considered characters. So Length (fullName) would return 15.

- PatternCount (*text*; *searchString*)—The PatternCount function tells you the number of times a search string occurs within some string. As an example, PatternCount (someString; "the") would return 2. Note that this function is *not* case sensitive. If the search string is not found, the function returns 0. Although the function returns an integer, it's often used as a true/false test when you just want to know whether something is contained in a string. That is, you don't care where or how many times the string is found—you just care that it's there somewhere. Recall that any nonzero value represents "true" when being used as a Boolean value.

- Position (*text*; *searchString*; *start*; *occurrence*)—You've already looked in depth at the Position function. To recap, it returns an integer that specifies the place where one string is found in another. The *start* argument specifies where to begin the search; the *occurrence* argument specifies whether you want the first occurrence, the second, and so on. Much of the time, you'll simply use 1 for both the *start* and the *occurrence* parameters.

- WordCount (*string*)—WordCount is similar to the Length function, except that instead of counting every character, it counts every word. So WordCount (someString) would return 9, because there are 9 words in the phrase. Be careful if you use WordCount that you have a good understanding of what characters FileMaker considers as being word delimiters.

What's in a Word?

Several FileMaker functions, such as WordCount(), LeftWords(), RightWords(), and MiddleWords(), treat text strings as collections of words rather than as collections of characters. But how does FileMaker determine what constitutes a word? It's actually quite simple. There are a handful of characters that FileMaker recognizes as word separators. Spaces and carriage returns are both word separators, as you'd probably expect. Additionally, just about every punctuation symbol or other special character is considered a word separator. The two exceptions are worth knowing: Neither a period (.) nor an apostrophe (') is a word separator. Also, in versions of FileMaker prior to 7, hyphens (-) were *not* considered word separators, but they are in FileMaker Pro 7 and 8. If you have multiple word separators right next to each other, they're considered together as a single delimiter. For instance, the string " hello ,-, world " is considered to have two words, even though there are a total of nine word separators in the string.

8

- Exact (*originalText*, *comparisonText*)—The Exact function takes two strings as its inputs, and it compares them to see whether they are exactly the same string. It returns a 1 if they are, a 0 if not. By "exactly," we mean *exactly*; this function is case sensitive. The order of the two input arguments is irrelevant.

The other broad category of text operators consists of those functions that enable you to manipulate a string. Whereas the interrogatory functions returned a number, these functions all return a string. You feed them a string; they do something with it and spit back another string. The text operators that fall into this category are explained in the following sections.

Trim()

The simplest of these functions is the Trim (*text*) function. Trim() takes a string and removes any leading or trailing spaces from it. Spaces between words are not affected; no other leading or trailing characters other than a space (that is, return characters at the end of a field) are removed.

There are two common uses of Trim(). The first is to identify data entry problems. Imagine you have a field called FirstName, and that some users have been accidentally typing spaces after the first name. You might want to display a message on such records, alerting users to that error. You'd define a new calculation field, called something like SpaceCheck. Its formula could be one of the following:

```
Case ( FirstName ≠ Trim ( FirstName ), "Extra Space!" )
Case ( not Exact( FirstName, Trim ( FirstName )), "Extra Space!" )
Case ( Length( FirstName ) > Length( Trim( FirstName )), "Extra Space!" )
```

→ To review the use and syntax of the Case() function, **see** "Using Conditional Functions," **p. 238**.

The other common usage of Trim() is in a calculated replace to clean up fixed-length data that's been imported from another application. *Fixed-length* means that the contents of a field are padded with leading or trailing spaces so that the entries are all the same length. After importing such data, you'd simply replace the contents of each field with a trimmed version of itself.

Substitute()

The next text manipulation function we'll explore is the Substitute() function. Substitute (*string*; *searchString*; *replacementString*) is used to replace every occurrence of some substring with some other substring. So Substitute(fullName; "Fred"; "Wilma") would return the string "Wilma Flintstone". If the initial substring were not found, the Substitute function would simply return the original string. You should be aware that the Substitute() function is case sensitive.

One common use of Substitute() is to remove all occurrences of some character from a string. You just substitute in an empty string for that character. For instance, to remove all occurrences of a carriage return from a field, you could use Substitute (myString; "¶"; ""). If there are multiple substitutions you want to make to a string, you simply list them all as bracketed pairs in the order in which they should be performed. Let's say you have a

PhoneNumber field from which you want to strip out any parentheses, dashes, or spaces that users might have entered. One way to do this would be to use the following formula:

```
Substitute (PhoneNumber; ["("; ""] ; [")"; ""] ; ["-"; ""] ; [" ", ""])
```

Be aware when performing multiple substitutions like this that the substitutions happen in the order in which they are listed, and that each subsequent substitution happens on an altered version of the string rather than on the original string. Say you had the string "xxyz" and you wanted to put *z*'s where there are *x*'s, and *x*'s where there are *z*'s. The formula Substitute ("xxyz"; ["x"; "z"]; ["z"; "x"]) incorrectly returns "xxyx". First, the two leading *x*'s are turned to *z*'s, yielding "zzyz"; then all three *z*'s are turned into *x*'s. If you ever want to swap two characters like this, you need to temporarily turn the first character into something you know won't be found in your string. So to fix this example, we could use the formula Substitute("xxyz"; ["x"; "**TEMP**"]; ["z"; "x"]; ["**TEMP**", "z"]). That would correctly yield "zzyx".

CASE-ALTERING FUNCTIONS

There are a few text functions you can use to alter a string's case. These are Lower (*text*), Upper (*text*), and Proper (*text*). It's quite intuitive how these act. Lower ("Fred") returns "fred"; Upper ("Fred") returns "FRED". Using Proper() returns a string in which the first letter of each word is capitalized. For instance, Proper ("my NAME is fred") returns "My Name Is Fred".

TEXT-PARSING FUNCTIONS

The final category of text operators we'll look at here is text-parsing functions. Text-parsing functions enable you to extract a substring from a string. The six text-parsing functions are Left(), Middle(), Right(), LeftWords(), MiddleWords(), and RightWords(). The first three operate at the character level; the other three operate at the word level.

The Left() function extracts a substring of length *N* from the beginning of some string. For example, Left ("Hello"; 2) returns the string "He"; it simply grabs the first two characters of the string. If the number of characters you ask for is greater than the length of the string, the function simply returns the entire string. A negative or zero number of characters results in an empty string being returned.

The Right() function is similar, except that it grabs characters from the end of the specified string. Right ("Hello"; 2) would return "lo". Middle(), as you might expect, is used to extract a substring from the middle of a string. Unlike the Left() and Right() functions, which require only a string and a length as parameters, the Middle function requires a starting position. The syntax is Middle (*text*; *startCharacter*; *numberOfCharacters*). For example, Middle ("Hello"; 2; 3) yields "ell".

The LeftWords(), MiddleWords(), and RightWords() functions all operate exactly as Left(), Middle(), and Right() functions, except that they operate at the word level. One typical use of these functions is to extract names or addresses you've imported as a lump of data from some other application. Say that your import resulted in contact names coming in as full names. You might want to create a LastName calculation field so that you could sort the records. If you knew that the last name was always the last word of the `FullName` field, you could use the formula `RightWords ( FullName; 1 )`.

NESTED FUNCTIONS

The text operators we have discussed often appear nested within each other in formulas. Writing nested formulas can be tricky sometimes. One thing that helps is to think of a particular example rather than trying to deal with it abstractly. For instance, let's say that you have a big text field, and you need a formula that extracts just its first line—that is, everything up until the first carriage return. So imagine that you had the following text:

```
The quick
brown fox
jumped over the
lazy dog
```

Think first: What text-parsing formulas would potentially yield `"The quick"` from this text? Well, there are several of them:

```
Left (myText; 9)
LeftWords (myText; 2)
Middle (myText; 1; 9)
```

Of course, at this point these formulas apply only to this particular example. Think next: Could one of these be extended easily to *any* multiline text field? If there were a constant number of words per line, the `LeftWords()` formula would work. And if not? What do the text interrogation formulas tell us about this field? `Length ( myText )` is 44. Not particularly helpful. `PatternCount ( myText; "¶" )` is 3. This indicates that there are four lines total. Interesting, but not obviously helpful for extracting the first line. `WordCount ( myText )` is 9. It's just coincidence that this is the number of characters in the first line; be careful not to be misled. `Position ( myText; "¶"; 1; 1 )` is 10. Finally, something interesting. In this example, the length of the first line is one less than the position of the first carriage return. Is that true in all cases? At this point, if you write out a few more examples, you'll see that indeed it is. Therefore, a general formula for extracting the first line of text is

```
Left ( myText, Position( myText, "¶"; 1; 1 ) - 1 )
```

How about extracting the *last* line from any multiline text field? You should approach this problem the same way, working from a specific example. Counting characters by hand, assemble a list of options:

```
Middle ( myText; 36, 8 )
Right ( myText; 8 )
RightWords ( myText; 2 )
```

What clues do the interrogatory functions yield? If you spend a few minutes thinking about it, you'll realize that 36 is the position of the last return character. You can derive that by using the number of returns as the occurrence parameter in a `Position()` function, like this:

```
Position ( myText; "¶"; 1; PatternCount( myText; "¶" ))
```

After you have the 36 figured out, recall that the length of the string is 44 characters, and notice that 44 – 36 = 8. Given these discoveries, you'll soon see that a simple and elegant generalized formula for grabbing the last line of a text field is

```
Right (myText; Length ( myText ) - Position( myText; "¶"; 1;
➥ PatternCount( myText; "¶" )))
```

Number Functions

In general, most people find working with math functions simpler and more intuitive than working with string functions. Perhaps this is because they remind us of various high-school math courses. Or it could be they typically have fewer parameters. Regardless, you'll find yourself using number functions on a regular basis. This chapter focuses not so much on what these functions do, but rather on some interesting applications for them.

The first set of functions we'll look at includes `Int()`, `Floor()`, `Ceiling()`, `Round()`, and `Truncate()`. Each of these can be thought of as performing some sort of rounding, making it sometimes difficult to know which one you should use. You can look up these functions in the help system for complete syntax and examples, but it's helpful to consider the similarities and differences of these functions as a set. Here's a rundown:

- `Int ( number )`—The `Int()` function returns the integer portion of the number that it's fed—that is, anything before the decimal point. `Int ( 4.5 )` returns 4. `Int ( -2.1 )` returns -2.

- `Floor ( number )`—`Floor()` is similar to `Int()`, except that it returns the next lower integer of the number it's fed (unless that number is an integer itself, of course, in which case `Floor()` just returns that integer). For any positive number, `Floor ( number )` and `Int ( number )` return the same value. For negative numbers, though, `Floor ( number )` and `Int ( number )` don't return the same value unless *number* is an integer. `Floor ( -2.1 )` returns -3, whereas `Int ( -2.1 )` returns -2.

- `Ceiling ( number )`—The `Ceiling()` function is complimentary to the `Floor()` function: It returns the next higher integer from the number it's fed (unless, again, that number is already an integer). For example, `Ceiling ( 5.3 )` returns 6 and `Ceiling ( -8.2 )` returns -8.

- `Round ( number; precision )`—`Round()` takes a number and rounds it to the number of decimal points specified by the precision parameter. At the significant digit, numbers up to 4 are rounded down; numbers 5 and above are rounded up. So `Round ( 3.6234; 3 )` returns 3.623, whereas `Round ( 3.6238; 3 )` returns 3.624. Using a precision of 0 rounds to the nearest whole number. Interestingly, you can use a negative precision. A precision of -1 rounds a number to the nearest 10; -2 rounds to the nearest 100, and so on.

- `Truncate ( number, precision )`—`Truncate()` is similar to `Round()`, but `Truncate()` simply takes the first *n* digits after the decimal point, leaving the last one unaffected regardless of whether the subsequent number is 5 or higher. `Truncate ( 3.6238; 3 )` returns 3.623. For any number, `Truncate ( number; 0 )` and `Int ( number )` return the same value. Just as `Round()` can take a negative precision, so can `Truncate()`. For example, `Truncate ( 258; -2 )` returns 200.

Which function you use for any given circumstance depends on your needs. If you're working with currency and want to add an 8.25% shipping charge to an order, you'd probably end up with a formula like `Round ( OrderTotal * 1.0825 ; 2 )`. Using `Truncate()` might cheat you out of a penny here or there.

8

Floor(), Ceiling(), and Int() have some interesting uses in situations in which you want to group numeric data into sets. For instance, imagine you have a list report that prints 10 records per page, and that you have a found set of 57 records to print. If you wanted, for whatever reason, to know how many pages your printed report would be, you could use Ceiling (Get(FoundCount)/10). Similarly, if you wanted to know what page any given record would print on, you would use the formula Floor ((Get(RecordNumber)-1)/10) + 1. The Int() function would yield the same result in this case.

Another common use of these functions is to round a number up or down to the multiple of some number. As an example, say you had the number 18, and you wanted to know the multiples of 7 that bounded it (...14 and 21). To get the lower bound, you can use the formula Floor (18/7)* 7; the upper bound is Ceiling (18/7)* 7. These generalize as

```
Lower bound:  Floor ( myNum / span ) * span
Upper bound:  Ceiling ( myNum / span ) * span
```

The span can be any number, including a decimal number, which comes in handy for rounding currency amounts, say, to the next higher or lower quarter.

You should know a few other number functions as well:

- Abs (number)—The Abs() function returns the absolute value of the number it's fed. There's nothing tricky to understanding the function itself, but there are a few handy uses you might not think of. One is to toggle a flag field between 0 and 1. The formula Abs (Flag-1) always "flips" the flag. If Flag is 0, Flag-1 is -1, and Abs (-1) is 1. If Flag is 1, then Flag-1 is 0, and Abs (0) is 0.

- Mod (number; divisor)—The Mod() function returns the remainder when a number is divided by a divisor. For instance, Mod (13; 5) returns 3 because 13 divided by 5 is 2, remainder 3.

- Div (number; divisor)—The Div() function is complimentary to the Mod() function. It returns the whole-number result of dividing a number by a divisor. For instance, Div (13; 5) would return 2. In all cases, Div (number; divisor) and Floor (number/divisor) return exactly the same value; it's a matter of personal preference or context which you should use.

- Random()—The Random() function returns a random decimal number between 0 and 1. Usually, you'll use the Random() function when you want to return a random number in some other range, so you'll need to multiply the result of the function by the span of the desired range. For instance, to simulate the roll of a six-sided die, you'd use the formula Ceiling (Random * 6). To return a random integer between, say, 21 and 50 (inclusive), the method would be similar: First you'd generate a random number between 1 and 30, and then you'd add 20 the result to translate it into the desired range. The formula would end up as Ceiling (Random * 30) + 20.

WORKING WITH DATES AND TIMES

Just as there are functions for working with text and numbers, FileMaker Pro provides functions that enable you to manipulate date and time fields. This section introduces you to the most common and discusses some real-world applications you'll be likely to need in your solutions.

The most important thing to understand at the outset is how FileMaker itself stores dates, times, and timestamps. Each is actually stored as an integer number. For dates, this integer represents a serialized number beginning with January 1, 0001. January 1, 0001, is 1; January 2, 0001, is 2; and so on. As an example, October 19, 2003, would be stored by FileMaker as 731507. FileMaker understands dates from January 1, 0001, until December 31, 4000.

Times are stored as the number of seconds since midnight. Midnight itself is 0. Therefore, times are typically in the range of 0 to 83999. It's worth knowing that time fields can contain not only absolute times, but also elapsed times. That is, you can type 46:18:19 into a time field, and it will be stored as 166699 seconds. Negative values can be placed in time fields as well. FileMaker doesn't have the capability to deal with microseconds; however, it can manage fractional elements: 10:15:45.99 is a valid time within FileMaker and 10:15:45.99 - 10:15:44 = 00:00:01.99. Note that this is not hundredths of a second, but rather simply a case of using a decimal instead of an integer.

Timestamps contain both a date and time. For example, "10/19/2003 8:55:03 AM" is a timestamp. Internally, timestamps are converted to the number of seconds since midnight on January 1, 0001. You could derive this number from date and time fields with the formula ((myDate - 1) * 86400) + myTime.

The easiest way to begin learning date, time, and timestamp functions is to split them into two categories: those that you feed a date or time and that return a "bit" of information back, and those that are *constructors*, in which you feed the function bits and you get back a date, time, or timestamp. These aren't formal terms that you'll find used elsewhere, but they're nonetheless useful for learning date and time functions.

The "bit" functions are fed dates and times, and they return numbers or text. For instance, say that you have a field myDate that contains the value 10/19/2003. Here's a list of the most common "bit" functions and what they'd return:

```
Month ( myDate ) = 10
MonthName ( myDate ) = October
Day ( myDate ) = 19
DayName ( myDate ) = Sunday
DayOfWeek ( myDate ) = 1
Year ( myDate ) = 2003
```

Similarly, a field called myTime with a value of 9:23:10 AM could be split into its bits with the following functions:

```
Hour ( myTime ) = 9
Minute ( myTime ) = 23
Seconds ( myTime ) = 10
```

You need to know only three constructor functions. Each is fed bits of data and returns, respectively, a date, time, or timestamp:

```
Date ( month; day; year )
Time ( hours; minutes; seconds )
TimeStamp ( date; time )
```

For example, `Date ( 10; 20; 2003 )` returns `10/20/2003`. `TimeStamp ( myDate; myTime )` might return `10/19/2003 9:23:10 AM`. When using these formulas in calculation fields, be sure to check that you've set the calculation result to the proper data type.

One very interesting and useful thing to know about these constructor functions is that you can "overfeed" them. For example, if you ask for `Date ( 13; 5; 2003 )`, the result will be `1/5/2004`. If the bits you provide are out of range, FileMaker automatically adjusts accordingly. Even zero and negative values are interpreted correctly. `Date ( 10; 0; 2003 )` returns `9/30/2003` because that's one day before 10/1/2003.

There are many practical uses of the date and time functions. For instance, the "bit" functions are often used to generate a break field that can be used in subsummary reports. Say that you have a table of invoice data, and you want a report that shows totals by month and year. You would define a field called `InvoiceMonth` with the formula `Month ( InvoiceDate )` and another called `InvoiceYear` with a formula of `Year ( InvoiceDate )`.

A common use of the constructor functions is to derive a date from the bits of a user-entered date. Say, for example, that a user entered `10/19/2003` into a field called `myDate`, and you wanted a calculation formula that would return the first of the next month, or `11/1/2003`. Your formula would be `Date ( Month( myDate ) +1; 1; Year( myDate ))`.

If you're importing dates from other systems, you may need to use text manipulation functions in conjunction with the constructor functions to turn the dates into something FileMaker can understand. Student information systems, for example, often store students' birth dates in an eight-digit format of MMDDYYYY. To import and clean this data, you'd first bring the raw data into a text field. Then, using either a calculated replace or a looping script, you would set the contents of a date field to the result of the formula:

```
Date (
    Left ( ImportedDate; 2 );
    Middle( ImportedDate; 3; 2 );
    Right( ImportedDate; 4 )
)
```

Timestamps are quite useful for logging activities, but sometimes you'll find that you want to extract either just the date or just the time portion of the timestamp. The easiest way to do this is via the `GetAsDate()` and `GetAsTime()` functions. When you feed either of these a timestamp, it returns just the date or time portion of that timestamp. Similarly, if you have a formula that generates a timestamp, you can set the return data type of the calculation result to date or time to return just the date or just the time.

Using Conditional Functions

Conditional functions are used when you want to return a different result based on certain conditions. The most basic and essential conditional function is the `If()` function. If takes three parameters: a test, a true result, and a false result. The test needs to be a full equation or expression that can be evaluated as true or false.

Let's look at an example. Suppose that you have a set of records containing data about invoices. You'd like to display the status of the invoice—"Paid" or "Not Paid"—based on whether the AmountDue field has a value greater than zero. To do this, you'd define a new field, called InvoiceStatus, with the following formula:

```
If ( AmountDue > 0, "Not Paid", "Paid")
```

For each record in the database, the contents of the InvoiceStatus field will be derived based on the contents of that record's AmountDue field.

The test can be a simple equation, as in the preceding example, or it can be a complex test that uses several equations tied together with and and or logic. For the test

```
If ( A and B; "something"; "something else")
```

both A and B have to be true to return the true result. However, for the test

```
If ( A or B; "something"; "something else" )
```

if either A or B is true, it will return the true result.

The true or false result arguments can themselves be If() statements, resulting in what's known as a *nested* If() statement. This allows you to test multiple conditions and return more than two results. For instance, let's revise the logic of the InvoiceStatus field. Say that we wanted invoices with a negative AmountDue to evaluate as Credit Due. We could then use the following field definition:

```
If ( Amount Due > 0; "Not Paid"; If (Amount Due < 0; "Credit Due"; "Paid" ))
```

The other commonly used conditional function is the Case() statement. The Case() statement differs from the If() statement in that you can test for multiple conditions without resorting to nesting. For instance, say that you have a field called GenderCode in a table that contains either M or F for a given record. If you wanted to define a field that would display the full gender, you could use the following formula:

```
Case ( GenderCode = "M"; "Male"; GenderCode="F"; "Female" )
```

A Case() statement consists of a series of tests and results. The tests are conducted in the order in which they appear. If a test is true, the following result is returned; if not, the next test is evaluated. FileMaker stops evaluating tests after the first true one is discovered. You can include a final optional result that is returned if none of the tests comes back as true. The gender display formula could be altered to include a default response as shown here:

```
Case ( GenderCode = "M"; "Male"; GenderCode="F"; "Female"; "Gender Unknown" )
```

Without the default response, if none of the tests is true then the Case() statement returns a null value.

AGGREGATE FUNCTIONS

Another important category of functions includes those known as *aggregate* functions. These include Sum(), Count(), Min(), Max(), and Avg(). These all work in similar, quite intuitive ways. Each operates on a set of inputs (numeric, except for the Count() function) and

8

produce a numeric output. The name of the function implies the operation each performs. `Sum()` adds a set of numbers, `Min()` and `Max()` return the smallest and largest items of a set, `Avg()` returns the arithmetic mean of the numbers, and `Count()` returns the number of non-null values in the set.

The inputs for an aggregate function can come from any one of three sources:

- **A series of delimited values**—For example, `Sum ( 6; 4; 7; 2 )` yields `19`. `Average ( 6; 4; 7; 2 )` yields `4.75`. An interesting use of the `Count()` function is to determine the number of fields in a record into which a user has entered values. For instance, `Count ( FirstName; LastName; Phone; Address; City; State; Zip )` would return `2` if the user had entered values into only those two fields.

- **A repeating field**—Repeating fields enable you to store multiple values within a single field within the same record. For instance, you might have repeating fields within a music collection database for listing the tracks and times of the contents of a given disc. The functions `Count ( Tracks )` and `Sum ( Times )` would produce the number of tracks and the total playing time for a given disc.

- **A related field**—By far, this is the most common application for aggregate functions. Imagine that you have a Customer table and an Invoice table and you want to create a field in Customer that totals up all the invoices for a particular customer. That field would be defined as `Sum ( Invoices::InvoiceTotal )`. Similarly, to tell how many related invoices a customer had, you could use the formula `Count ( Invoices::CustomerID )`.

NOTE

> When using the `Count()` function to count related records, it usually doesn't matter what field you count, as long as it's not empty. The count will not include records in which the specified field is blank. Typically, you should count either the related primary key or the related foreign key because these by definition should contain data.

LEARNING ABOUT THE ENVIRONMENT

FileMaker has two categories of functions whose job it is to tell you information about the environment—the computing and application environment, that is. These are the `Get()` functions and the `Design()` functions. There are more than 70 `Get()` functions, and 20 `Design()` functions. Here, our goal is to give you an overview of the types of things these functions do and some of the most common uses for them.

Get FUNCTIONS

`Get()` functions provide a broad array of information about a user's computing environment and the current state of a database. None of the `Get()` functions takes parameters; each simply gives you some tidbit of information you can use however you want.

As an example, the `Get ( TotalRecordCount )` function returns the total number of records in some table. One typical use for this is as the formula for a calculation field. If you have hidden the Status Area from users, this field could be used as part of constructing your own

"Record X of Y" display. If you're using this function in a script—or any Get() function, for that matter—be sure that you're aware that the active layout determines the context in which this function is evaluated.

Whenever you use a Get() function as part of a field definition, you need to be acutely aware of the storage options that have been set for that field. For Get() functions to evaluate properly, you must explicitly set the calculation to be unstored. If it is not set this way, the function evaluates only once when the record is created; it reflects the state of the environment at the time of record creation, but not at the current moment. Setting the calculation field to be unstored forces it to evaluate every time the field is displayed or used in another calculation, based on the current state of the environment.

Although you don't need to memorize all the Get() functions, a handful of them are used frequently and should form part of your core knowledge of functions. To remember them, it's helpful to group them into subcategories based on their function.

The first subcategory includes functions that reveal information about the current user:

```
Get ( AccountName )
Get ( ExtendedPrivileges )
Get ( PrivilegeSetName )
Get ( UserName )
Get ( UserCount )
```

Another subcategory includes functions that are frequently used in conditional tests within scripts to determine what actions should be taken:

```
Get ( ActiveModifierKeys )
Get ( LastMessageChoice )
Get ( LastError )
Get ( ScriptParameter )
```

There are four functions for returning the current date and time:

```
Get ( CurrentDate )
Get ( CurrentHostTimeStamp )
Get ( CurrentTime )
Get ( CurrentTimeStamp )
```

Many Get functions tell you where the user is within the application and what the user is doing:

```
Get ( FoundCount )
Get ( LayoutNumber )
Get ( LayoutName )
Get ( LayoutTableName )
Get ( PageNumber )
Get ( PortalRowNumber )
Get ( RecordNumber )
```

And finally, another group of functions reveal information about the position, size, and name of the current window:

```
Get ( WindowName )
Get ( WindowTop )
Get ( WindowHeight )
Get ( WindowWidth )
```

8

Finally, to see the list of Get functions in the Specify Calculation dialog, you need to toggle the view to either All Functions by Type or to just the Get functions. They don't show up when the view is All Functions by Name. Be aware that there are a number of functions with "Get" in their name that aren't Get() functions. These include things like GetRepetition(), GetField(), GetAsText(), and GetSummary(). These are not functionally related in any way to the Get functions that have just been discussed.

Design FUNCTIONS

The Design functions are used to get information about the structure of a database file itself. With just two exceptions (specifically, DatabaseNames() and WindowNames()), none of the Design functions is session-dependent. That is, the results returned by these functions won't differ at all based on who is logged in or what they're doing. Unlike the Get functions, Design functions often take parameters.

Fully half of the Design functions simply return lists of names or IDs of the major structural components of a file. These include the following:

```
FieldIDs ( fileName; layoutName )
FieldNames ( fileName; layout/tableName )
LayoutIDs ( fileName )
LayoutNames ( fileName )
ScriptIDs ( fileName )
ScriptNames ( fileName )
TableIDs ( fileName )
TableNames ( fileName )
ValueListIDs ( fileName )
ValueListNames ( fileName )
```

Six other Design functions return information about a specified field:

```
FieldBounds ( fileName ; layoutName ; fieldName )
FieldComment ( fileName ; fieldName )
FieldRepetitions ( fileName ; layoutName ; fieldName )
FieldStyle ( fileName ; layoutName ; fieldName )
FieldType ( fileName ; fieldName )
GetNextSerialValue ( fileName ; fieldName )
```

The DatabaseNames() function returns a list of the databases that the current user has open. The list doesn't include file extensions, and it doesn't distinguish between files that are open as a host versus those that are open as a guest.

Similarly, the WindowNames() function returns a list of the window names that the current user has open. The list is ordered by the stacking order of the windows; it includes both visible and hidden windows across all the open database files.

Typically, the DatabaseNames() and WindowsNames() functions are used to check whether a user has a certain database file or window open already. For instance, if you have a navigation window that you always want to be open, you can have a subscript check for its presence and open it if it has been closed by the user. To do this, you would use the formula PatternCount (WindowNames; "Nav Window"). This would return a 0 if there was no window open whose name included the string "Nav Window".

The final `Design` function is `ValueListItems ( fileName ; valueList )`. This function returns a list of the items in the specified value list. As with most of the `Design` functions, the primary purpose of this function is to help you catalog or investigate the structure of a file. There's another common usage of `ValueListItems()` that is handy to know. Imagine that you have a one-to-many relationship between a table called Salespeople and a table called Contacts, which contains demographic information about all of a salesperson's contacts. For whatever reason, you might want to assemble a list of all the cities where a salesperson has contacts. You can do this by defining a value list based on the relationship that shows the City field, and then creating an unstored calculation field in Contacts with the formula `ValueListItems ("Contacts"; "CityList")`. For any given salesperson record, this field will contain the "sum" of all the cities where the salesperson has contacts.

TROUBLESHOOTING

FORMULAS IN SCRIPTS REQUIRE EXPLICIT TABLE CONTEXT

I'm used to being able to type field names into calculation formulas rather than selecting them from the field list. Sometimes, even if I've typed the field name correctly, I get a `Field` not found *message when trying to leave the calculation dialog. It seems that sometimes calculations need the table occurrence name before the field name, and sometimes they don't. What are the rules for this?*

When you define calculation fields, any fields within the current table can be entered into the formula without the table context being defined. For instance, you might have a `FullName` field defined to be `FirstName & " " & LastName`.

All formulas you write anywhere within ScriptMaker require that the table context be explicitly defined for every field, even when there's only a single table in the file. For instance, if you wanted to use a Set Field script step to place a contact's full name into a field, you wouldn't be able to use the preceding formula as written. Instead, it would need to be something like `Contact::FirstName & " " & Contact::LastName`.

If you're used to being able to manually type field names into formulas, be aware that the table context must be included for every field referenced in the formula.

The reason for this is that the table context for a script is determined by the active layout when the script is executed. `Contact::FirstName` may have a very different meaning when evaluated on a layout tied to the Contact table than it would, say, on one tied to an Invoice table.

ERRORS DUE TO IMPROPER DATA TYPE SELECTION

I've heard that the data type selection for calculation fields is important. What kind of problems will I have if I select the wrong data type, and how do I know what type to choose?

Every time you define a calculation field, no matter how simple, be sure to check the data type that the formula is defined to return. The default data type is number, unless you're defining multiple calculations in a row, in which case the default for subsequent fields will be the data type defined for the previous calculation.

A number of errors can result from selecting the improper data type. For instance, if your formula returns a text string but you leave the return data type as number, any finds or sorts you perform using that field will not return expected results.

Be especially aware that formulas that return dates, times, and timestamps are defined to have date, time, and timestamp results. If you leave the data type as number, your field displays the internal serial number that represents that date and/or time. For instance, the formula Date (4 ; 26 ; 2004) returns 731697 if the date type is set to number.

FILEMAKER EXTRA: TIPS FOR BECOMING A CALCULATION MASTER

As we mentioned at the outset of this chapter, it takes time to master the use of calculation formulas. We thought it would be helpful to compile a list of tips to help you get started on the path:

- **Begin with a core**—Don't try to memorize everything at once; chances are you'll end up frustrated. Instead, concentrate on building a small core of functions that you know inside and out and can use without having to look up the syntax or copy from examples. Then, gradually expand the core over time. As you have a need to use a new function, spend a few minutes reading about it or testing how it behaves in various conditions.

- **Work it out on paper first**—Before writing a complex formula, work through the logic with pencil and paper. This way you can separate the logic from the syntax. You'll also know what to test against and what to expect as output.

- **Search for alternative methods of doing the same thing**—It's uncommon to have only one way to approach a problem or only one formula that will suit a given need. As you write a formula, ask yourself how else you might be able to approach the problem, and what the pros and cons of each method would be. Try to avoid the "if your only tool is a hammer, all your problems look like nails" situation. For instance, if you always use If() statements for conditional tests, be adventurous and see whether you could use a Case() statement instead.

- **Strive for simplicity, elegance, and extensibility**—As you expand your skills, you'll find that it becomes easy to come up with multiple approaches to a given problem. So how do you choose which to use? We suggest that simplicity, elegance, and extensibility are the criteria to judge by. All other things being equal, choose the formula that uses the fewest functions, has tightly reasoned logic, or can be extended to handle other scenarios or future needs most easily. This doesn't mean that the shortest formula is the best. The opposite of simplicity and elegance is what's often referred to as the *brute force* approach. There are certainly situations in which that's the best approach, and you shouldn't hesitate to use such an approach when necessary. But if you want to become a calculation master, you'll need to have the ability to go beyond brute-force approaches as well.

- **Use comments and spacing**—Part of what makes a formula elegant is that it's written in a way that's logical and transparent to other developers. There may come a time when someone else needs to take over development of one of your projects, or when you'll need to review a complex formula that you wrote years before. By commenting your formulas and adding whitespace within your formulas, you make it easier to expand on and troubleshoot problems in the future.

- **Be inquisitive and know where to get the answer**—As you write formulas, take time to digress and test hunches and learn new things. Whip up little sample files to see how something behaves in various conditions. Also, know what resources are available to you to get more information when you get stuck or need help. The Help system; our companion book, *FileMaker 8 Functions and Scripts Desk Reference*; and online discussion groups are all examples of resources you should take advantage of.

- **Use your keyboard**—Entering a less-than character followed by a greater-than character (<>) equates to the "not equal to" operator (≠) within an expression. The following expressions are functionally identical:

  1 <> 2

  1 ≠ 2

  This is also true for >= and <= for ≥ and ≤, respectively.

- **Use tabs to improve clarity**—To enter a tab character into an expression (either as literal text or simply to help with formatting), use (Option-Tab) [Ctrl+Tab].

- **Learn the exceptions**—FileMaker allows for a shorthand approach to entering conditional Boolean tests for non-null, nonzero field contents. The following two expressions are functionally identical:

  ```
  Case ( fieldOne; "true"; "false" )

  Case ( (IsEmpty (text) or text = 0); "false"; "true" )
  ```

  Note that the authors do not recommend this shortcut as a best practice. We tend to believe you should write explicit (and, yes, more verbose) code, leaving no room for ambiguity, but if you ever inherit a system from another developer who has used this approach, you'll need to be able to grasp it.

- **Use defaults with conditionals**—FileMaker allows for optional negative or default values in both the Case() and If() conditional functions. The following expressions are both syntactically valid:

  ```
  Case (
      fieldOne = 1; "one";
      fieldOne = 2; "two"
  )

  Case (
      fieldOne = 1; "one";
      fieldOne = 2; "two";
      "default"
  )
  ```

  We strongly recommend you always provide a default condition at the end of your Case statements, even if that condition should "never" occur. The next time your field shows a value of "never happens," you'll be glad you did.

- **Remember that `Case` short-circuiting can simplify logic**—The `Case()` function features a "short-circuiting" functionality whereby it evaluates conditional tests only until it reaches the first true test. In the following example, the third test will never be evaluated, thus improving system performance:

```
Case (
    1 = 2; "one is false";
    1 = 1; "one is true";
    2 = 2; "two is true"
)
```

 - **Repeating Value Syntax**—Note that fields with repeating values can be accessed either using the `GetRepetition()` function or via a shorthand of placing an integer value between two brackets. The following are functionally identical:

```
Quantity[2]
```

```
GetRepetition ( Quantity; 2 )
```

CHAPTER **9**

GETTING STARTED WITH SCRIPTING

In this chapter

SCRIPTS IN FILEMAKER PRO

Scripts are sets of stored instructions that specify a series of actions FileMaker should perform when they're initiated; they're programs that run within FileMaker Pro solutions. They can be just one command attached to a button, or they can be hundreds of commands long.

Scripts do two important things in FileMaker Pro: They automate internal processes, and they add interactivity to custom user interfaces. Internal processes might consist of such things as creating a batch of monthly invoices, setting the status of sales leads, or exporting data for an aggregated report. And by "adding interactivity" we refer to the capability to create interface elements (such as buttons or icons) that will *do something* in response to user actions. Scripts help with both of these needs.

Scripts are written in FileMaker Pro's ScriptMaker, a point-and-click interface. Scripts can perform tasks ranging from simple things (such as simply entering Find mode) to complex automated import/export processes, multitable reporting, data reconciliation, and really anything that can be expressed as a programmed series of FileMaker steps.

It's a bit of an oversimplification, but you can think of scripts as automating a process that a human using your database solution might perform by hand.

After a script is initiated through some user action or external trigger (we'll cover how scripts get initiated later in the chapter), it runs in sequence from its first step to the last, exiting or ending after it is complete. Here's a simple example:

```
Show All Records
Go to Record/Request/Page [ First ]
Beep
Show Custom Dialog [ Title: "First Record";
➥Message: "This is your first record."; Buttons: "OK" ]
```

As you can see from this short example, FileMaker Pro scripts are easy to read and comprehend. This script resets the found set of the current layout/window to consist of all the records in a given table, then takes the user to the first record in that set, beeps, and shows a dialog box with an OK button. Each step of the script is executed in order: Show All Records is completed, and then Go to Record/Request/Page is dealt with.

It's possible to create branching scripts by using logical If statements, and it's also possible to construct scripts that execute other scripts (hereafter referred to as *subscripts*). We'll get into both such techniques later in the chapter.

We have found over the years that the best way to learn scripts is to be presented with examples. We will endeavor in this chapter to review what we consider important and widely applicable topics for scripts and to provide as many examples as these pages allow.

CREATING SCRIPTS

Creating and editing scripts in FileMaker is fairly straightforward. Simply choose Scripts, ScriptMaker and the Define Scripts dialog opens. You can also use the keyboard shortcut (one of our favorite features added in FileMaker 7) of (⌘-S) [Ctrl+S]. Keep in mind you'll need to have signed in with an account that allows script access.

After you're in ScriptMaker, you'll see a list of existing scripts and can manage all the scripts in your file (you can delete, reorder, and so on). From there you can delve into a single script and edit its individual script steps.

Writing an actual script requires first that you have a goal in mind—what purpose is the script intended to accomplish? A script will step through a series of instructions, one at a time, until the script either reaches its last instruction or reaches some exit condition. Exit conditions can vary, and many of their implementations are covered in this chapter.

Here's an example of the logical outline of a script you might use to take users to a Main Menu layout after they log in. Presumably this script would be set to run when a file is first opened by an individual user. Assume that someone named Kim has just logged in.

After valid login, carry out these steps:

1. In a table of users, set the LastLoginDate field in Kim's record to today's date.
2. Set the gUserNameDisplay field to `"Kim"`.
3. Set the gUserMessage field to `"Welcome back, Kim"`.
4. Perform Go to Layout: `Main_Menu`.

This simple four-step process takes care of some background tasks first, and then from a user's standpoint navigates to the main menu on which, presumably, a welcome message sits. All the user would see is that the system landed him on the Main Menu layout.

To implement a script like this, a developer would open ScriptMaker, create a new script, give it a name, and then use the Edit Script dialog to insert various steps into the script. The actual script that would manage the preceding logic could look like this:

```
Go to Layout [ "zdev_GlobalAdmin" (Globals) ]
Set Field [ Globals::gAccountName; Get (AccountName) ]
Set Field [ Current_User::LastLoginDate; Get (CurrentDate) ]
Set Field [ Globals::gUserNameDisplay; Current_User::Name_First ]
Set Field [ Globals::gUserMessage; "Welcome Back, " & Globals::gUserNameDisplay &
"." ]
Go to Layout [ "Main Menu" (Globals) ]
```

There are a number of ideas contained in the preceding example that we'll detail in the forthcoming pages. The important thing in this case is to become more familiar with reading a script and following its logic.

This script first goes to a layout called `zdev_GlobalAdmin`. It then posts information into four fields. One of these steps draws data from a related field in a `Current_User` table occurrence, and another sets information in that related record. The script then last navigates again to a Main Menu layout. This conforms to the flow we mapped out previously; you might think of the original four pseudocode steps as an outline for the finished script.

THE SCRIPTMAKER INTERFACE

The Define Scripts dialog (see Figure 9.1) allows you to manage all the scripts in your current file. To reorder scripts, simply drag individual scripts up or down along the list. Unfortunately, there's no means of sorting scripts, so you need to do your best to stay organized. We generally advocate keeping scripts either grouped by function (for example, all your Invoicing scripts in a group) or organized alphabetically.

Figure 9.1
The Define Scripts dialog box allows you to create, edit, and organize your scripts, and decide which ones to display in FileMaker's Script menu.

TIP

Use (⌘-up/down arrow) [Ctrl+up/down arrow] to move scripts via your keyboard.

You can perform various actions in the Define Scripts dialog box as outlined in the following list:

■ You can create new scripts, edit existing scripts, or delete those you no longer need.

■ By selecting a given script and clicking Perform, you can execute scripts directly from this dialog. Using this button to initiate scripts saves you the extra step of having to close the dialog and launch them from within your database.

■ You can now copy and paste scripts and script steps, using FileMaker Pro 8 Advanced; note that this works perfectly well across different files. You are likely to find yourself writing scripts that are similar to those you've written before, or needing to migrate from an older file into a newer. Luckily, you need not reassemble all your scripts by hand. In this latest version of FileMaker, copied scripts match field, relationship, layout, and other references by name. It's a good idea to look at any script steps that refer to fields, layouts, subscripts, related records, or anything that is layout-driven and assumes that the object in question is on a given layout to be sure that they function correctly after they are copied into a new file.

TIP

> If you use FileMaker Pro 8 Advanced, one of the easiest ways to confirm that a script has imported or copied well is to run it the first time with the Script Debugger turned on.

■ You can use the <u>P</u>rint button to print a script. Printing a script is a good way to create documentation—especially in combination with Adobe Acrobat's capability to create PDFs—or spot problems more easily.

■ You can import scripts in batches from one file to another. This feature works similarly to copying scripts. For FileMaker Pro 8 users (not Advanced), this is your only option for moving scripts from file to file.

■ The Edit button opens the Edit Script dialog for any selected script. A much faster way to work is to simply double-click the script you want to edit.

■ The D<u>u</u>plicate button can be used to duplicate a script so that you need not start from scratch when writing a new script. We recommend creating a script template and duplicating it to begin new scripts.

→ For an example of the script template that the authors use in their consulting practice, **see** Chapter 27, "Documenting your FileMaker Solutions," **p. 841**.

■ The check-box column along the left of the dialog controls whether a given script appears in FileMaker's standard Script menu. If you hide a script by unchecking its check box, you need to provide the user with another means of performing, or executing, the script. Typically this entails either associating the script with one or more button objects that appear on various layouts or tying the script to a custom menu item.

Note also that just as in other areas of FileMaker, a single hyphen becomes a menu divider. If you create a script named -, you insert a divider in your list. This is useful in organizing your scripts visually. Plan to have a good many scripts; it is a good idea to keep them well organized.

TIP

> Notice that by using (⌘-click) [Ctrl+click] you can select multiple, noncontiguous scripts and then delete, duplicate, or print as you need. Shift-click selects multiple contiguous scripts.

SCRIPT NAMING PRACTICES

Keeping your scripts well organized and following good script naming practices is even more important in FileMaker 7 and 8. Versions of FileMaker Pro prior to 7 generally involved more individual files than today, and hence scripts tended to be naturally distributed throughout a given system. In a system in which one file can contain many tables, all your scripts may very well live in a single file.

NOTE

> FileMaker 8's capability to store many tables in one file has many implications, but in particular with scripts, you won't be constantly closing and reopening ScriptMaker in different files as you would have with FileMaker 6 or earlier. Fewer scripts are also required in many cases: Many operations that would have required executing a series of external subscripts across several files can now be accomplished by a single script in FileMaker 8.

Script naming practices vary quite widely from developer to developer; even the authors of this book find it difficult to agree to a common standard. It's less important that you follow any particular naming convention than that you use a logical and consistent system. We do, nonetheless, recommend you consider some of the following ideas:

- Use hyphens, underscores, and so on to divide your scripts into logical groupings. As in other areas of FileMaker Pro, a single hyphen displays as a menu separator in the Scripts menu.

- Don't show all your scripts to your users. Choose deliberately which scripts you want to make available to users in the Scripts menu. Note that FileMaker Pro 8 Advanced allows developers to create custom menu sets. Quite often you may want to have a menu item run a certain script. You may want to use custom menus to hide the regular Scripts menu altogether, and attach your scripts to other menu items throughout other menus.

→ To learn about how to implement custom menus in a solution, **see** Chapter 13, "Advanced Interface Techniques," **p. 353**.

- Think of adding headers as shown previously in Figure 9.1. Organize your scripts into groups and then label them accordingly.

- When using subscripts that are exclusively subordinate to another "main" script, you might consider indenting the names of the subscripts with underscores or using a prefix naming style to indicate that a set of scripts is to be used as a unit.

- Scripts are often intended to operate on a specific table occurrence (for example, if you're using a script to control the creation of a new customer record, you want to make sure that a new record gets created in the Customer table, not the Product table). It's a good idea to use short table prefixes or suffixes when a script applies to only a given table, and "all" when it doesn't—for example, New_Record_contact_to, Report_invoices_to, or Resize_Window_all.

- If you plan to use Custom Web Publishing, we encourage you to avoid spaces and special characters in your script names. They're a pain to parse if you plan to call these scripts from the Web. (Clearly those scripts you allow to be displayed in the Scripts menu need to follow user-friendly naming conventions.)

SCRIPT EDITING

After you create a new script in ScriptMaker, or edit an existing script, the Edit Script dialog opens (see Figure 9.2). Here you construct the actual script by inserting script commands from the list on the left into the window on the right. Nearly every script step has additional options you need to specify, such as the name of a layout to go to, or the name of a file from which to import. These options appear under your script when you highlight a given step in it.

Figure 9.2
The Edit Script dialog presents you with additional dialogs as needed to configure settings for specific steps in your script.

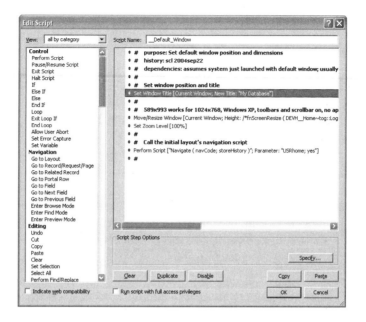

TIP

You can (⌘-click) [Ctrl+click] multiple script steps at once and insert the batch into a script in one move.

To reorder script steps, simply drag them by the two-headed arrow icon located to the left of the step.

In FileMaker Pro 8 Advanced you can copy and paste script steps (and the same Shift-click and Ctrl-click behaviors apply as elsewhere). This works perfectly well from script to script and from file to file. This is also an alternative way to reorder script steps in a large script.

If Indicate Web Compatibility is enabled, script steps that are incompatible with web publishing display in gray.

As an example, `Go to Layout` is a common step you'll use quite often. Notice that when you insert it into a script, a menu appears in the Script Step Options area at the lower right, from which you can choose an existing layout, the layout on which the script began, or one determined by calculation.

FULL ACCESS PRIVILEGES

Notice the Run Script with Full Access Privileges check box at the bottom of the Edit Script dialog. Designating that a script run with full access privileges means simply that for the duration of that script, FileMaker will override all security restrictions. When this option is *not* enabled, scripts run subordinate to whatever privilege set the currently signed-in user has. For instance, if a script makes a call to delete a record and the user who is running that script cannot do so based on his current security privileges, the script usually presents an alert message to the user and ignores that step of the script. The rest of the script is still performed.

Note that when this option is checked, the security privilege set for the current user actually does change for the duration of the script: If you use the calculation function Get (PrivilegeSetName), it will return [Full Access] as long as the script is running. If your script contains logic in which you need to check a user's assigned privilege set, you'll need to capture the user's privilege set information elsewhere before running the script and refer to it however you've stored or captured the information.

→ Error management in scripts is an important element in all scripting. For more detail, **see** "Set Error Capture," **p. 257**.

→ To understand FileMaker security and privilege sets, **see** Chapter 12, "Implementing Security," **p. 325**.

COMMENTING SCRIPTS

Keeping track of what scripts do is a difficult task. What seemed perfectly intuitive at the time you wrote a given script may become hopelessly obscure a few weeks—or sometimes even hours—later. Although developers vary in how they use comments, nearly all developers recognize the value of commenting their work.

Remember that you're not coding in a vacuum. We can virtually guarantee that although you may never intend that a given database be seen by someone else's eyes, if it stands the tests of time and proves useful, at some point you'll crack it open with the infamous words, "Let me show you how I did this...." Likewise, professional-grade systems are nearly all collaborative efforts. Comments exist to help your peers understand what your caffeine-sodden brain was thinking at the time you wrote a particular routine.

A simple example of a commented script is seen in Listing 9.1. Notice that in FileMaker Pro comments are prefixed by the # symbol.

LISTING 9.1 SCRIPT WITH COMMENTS

```
#    Purpose: initiate the running of a report while allowing users
#      to choose what sort order they want
#    History: sl 2004 02 04; bb 2004 02 05
#    Dependencies: Invoices: Monthly Report layout
#
#          prompt user for sort order
Show Custom Dialog [ Title: "Sort Order"; Message: "Do you want to sort by
➥amount or date?"; Buttons: "Date", "Amount", "Cancel" ]
#
#          check for cancel first
If [ Get (LastMessageChoice) = 3 ]
Go to Layout [ original layout ]
Halt Script
#
#          sort by Amount
Else If [ Get (LastMessageChoice) = 2 ]
Go to Layout [ "Monthly Report" ]
Perform Script [ "Sort by Amount" ]
#
#          sort by Date
Else If [ Get (LastMessageChoice) = 1 ]
Go to Layout [ "Monthly Report" ]
Perform Script [ "Sort by Date" ]
#
End If
```

USING A SCRIPT TEMPLATE

It is often helpful to create a template script that you can duplicate when you need to create a new script. In our templates, we include several comment lines at the top where we record information about the purpose and revision history of the script. A template script looks something like this:

```
# purpose: TYPEHERE
# dependencies: TYPEHERE
# history: XXX DATE
#
#    set error handling
Allow User Abort [ Off ]
Set Error Capture [ On ]
#
#    establish context
Go to Layout [ Original Layout ]
#
#
```

Although it is simple, this template does save time and promote good code. If you don't need a particular piece of it, it's easy enough to delete.

Adding the Go to Layout step to your template can help ensure that the script begins on the correct layout and thus is associated with the proper base table attached to that layout. Including this step in the template prompts developers to make a conscious decision and reminds you that context needs to be managed.

USING SUBSCRIPTS

One of the most useful things in ScriptMaker is the Perform Script step itself. One FileMaker script can call another script, which is then commonly known as a *subscript*. This then allows you to divide scripts into smaller logical blocks and also break out discrete scripts for anything you are likely to want to use again. This degree of abstraction in your system is one that we very much recommend. Abstraction makes scripts easier to read, easier to debug, and modular—in that a subscript may be generic and used in a variety of scripts. Here's an example:

```
Sales_Report
# purpose: to run the Sales Report, weekly or monthly
# history: scl 2-5-2004
#
Perform Script [ "CheckPermission_forSales" ]
Perform Script [ "Find_CurrentSales" ]
#
Show Custom Dialog [ Title: "Run Report"; Message: "Would you like this
➥report broken out by Weekly or Monthly subtotals?"; Buttons:
"Monthly", "Weekly", "Cancel" ]
#
If [ Get (LastMessageChoice) = 1 ]
Perform Script [ "Monthly_Report" ]
#
Else If [ Get (LastMessageChoice) = 2 ]
Perform Script [ "Weekly_Report" ]
#
End If
```

Notice that the script actually doesn't do much on its own. It will first run a permission check script, and then run another script to establish a found set. It then prompts the user to make a choice and runs one of two report subscripts based on what choice the user makes. This approach is quite common and demonstrates a flexible approach to programming. The Find_CurrentSales subscript could well be used elsewhere in the database. Creating separate routines for weekly and monthly reports makes the script more readable; imagine seeing all the logic for those two reports embedded here as well.

As another example of script abstraction, imagine sorting a contacts database by last_name then first_name for a given report. If you've written a script to produce that report, sorting is a step in the process; however, odds are that you'll want to be able to sort by last_name, first_name again—perhaps for a different report, perhaps as a function that lives on a list view or in a menu, or perhaps before running an export script (or perhaps all the above). Whenever reasonable, we recommend looking for ways to abstract your code and foster reuse. It saves time and complexity if suddenly your client (or boss) comes to you and says you need to now present everything by first name. If that logic lives in one place, it's a one-minute change. If you have to hunt for it, the change could take days and require extensive debugging.

Even if you're not planning to reuse blocks of code, it's still a good idea to break scripts into subscripts. They're easier to read, they're easier to enable and disable during testing, and they allow you to name them in logical ways that are comprehensible even at the Define Scripts dialog level.

Some other good candidates for subscripts are sort and find routines; these are often reusable by a wide range of scripts or by users as standalone functions. Other uses of subscripts might be for the contents of a loop or If function. Sometimes it's easier to separate logic into separate paths by dividing logical groups into separate scripts, as in the example we gave a little earlier. When you have a branching script (covered later in the chapter), it's helpful to encapsulate a single branch in a subscript. This allows you to see the flow of logic in the parent script and cover each branch in its own respective subscript.

COMMON SCRIPTING TOPICS

We will now delve into some useful and common scripting techniques and discuss topics that are germane to a wide range of scripts. This is not meant to be a comprehensive list—the function of the Beep script step should be fairly obvious to you—but rather these are the important areas to understand. They will help you establish a solid foundation in scripting.

→ For a complete reference to all the script steps in FileMaker 8, refer to our companion book, *FileMaker 8 Functions and Scripts Desk Reference.*

ERROR MANAGEMENT

Error management is an important part of the scripting process. Frequently scripts make assumptions about the presence of certain data or the existence of certain objects, or depend on a layout to establish context. If any of a given script's assumptions are not met, it either might not work or might produce unintended results. Error management involves identifying these assumptions and creating ways of dealing with them. You can bank on users finding odd, unpredictable ways to break your system. Applying some thought to how to manage such situations will serve you well in the long run.

 Notice that FileMaker Pro 8 Advanced has the capability to enable and disable individual script steps. This facilitates testing significantly: You can turn off sections of your script that aren't finished and run discrete sections of your logic.

→ For further discussion of error handling, **see** "Handling Errors in Scripts," **p. 512**.

→ For more ideas on error management, **see** Chapter 17, "Debugging and Troubleshooting," **p. 501**.

Allow User Abort

`Allow User Abort` enables and disables a user's ability to press (⌘-period) [Esc] to cancel a script in midstream. Generally speaking, it's the rare script that's designed to be cancelled gracefully at any time in its process. There's really no reason to ever turn `Allow User Abort` on, unless you're testing a loop script or some other long-running process. Any script that doesn't have `Allow User Abort` disabled allows users to cancel a script in progress, with consequences you may not intend.

Note that this is true for scripts that users are running, but the opposite is true for developers: If you're in the midst of writing a script and need to test a loop, for example, you should leave this setting turned on in order to halt your script if need be.

The other thing `Allow User Abort` does is take away the Cancel button when a script pauses, giving users only the option to continue. There are many cases in which canceling a script would leave the user stuck on a report layout or stranded midstream in some extended process.

To learn more about how to deal with incomplete script completion (atomicity in database lingo), refer to "Unfinished Scripts" in the "Troubleshooting" section at the end of this chapter.

Set Error Capture

The `Set Error Capture` script step either prevents or allows FileMaker's default error messages to be displayed to the user. When error capturing is off, FileMaker displays its own alert dialogs to the user if, for example, a record fails validation or a user runs a search without any find criteria. When error capture is turned on, the script in question captures errors and doesn't present them to the user. This allows you, the developer, to present your own, customized error messages, but imposes a greater burden in terms of checking for and managing errors yourself.

→ Handling errors well in scripts is a black art: It's difficult to always anticipate what errors will crop up. For more information on using the `Set Error Capture` script step, **see** Chapter 17, "Debugging and Troubleshooting," **p. 501**.

When doing your own error checking and managing, you'll want to use the `Get ( LastError )` calculation function to programmatically deal with errors within your script. Use the `If` function to test `Get ( LastError )` and present dialogs to the user as appropriate. Refer to FileMaker Pro's online help system for a list of error codes.

Be careful with the `Set Error Capture` script step. It certainly doesn't prevent errors from happening—it simply doesn't show the user a message about one that did. An error may happen, but the user's experience won't be interrupted to deal with it. This allows you to control how errors are managed within your script itself. You should not turn error capture on unless you have also added steps to identify and handle any errors that may arise.

 To explore problems with error messages you think are being wrongly suppressed in scripts, refer to "Lost Error Messages in Scripts" in the "Troubleshooting" section at the end of this chapter.

Here's an example of a script segment that tests for an error—in this case a find request that results in zero found records:

```
Find_BirthdaysThisMonth
Enter Find Mode [ ]
Set Field [ Person::birthMonth[Month ( Get (CurrentDate) )] ]
If [ Get( LastError ) ≠ 0 ]
Show Custom Dialog [ Title: "No Birthdays Found";
        Message: "There are no birthdays listed for this month.";
        Buttons: "OK" ]
End If
```

SETTING AND CONTROLLING DATA

Some of the primary uses of scripts lie in manipulating, moving, and creating data. Most of the script steps for manipulating field data are found in the Fields category.

Essentially, these Fields steps allow you to insert data into a given field programmatically, just as a user otherwise would. This can mean setting the field contents to the result of a calculation, copying the contents of one field into another, or simply inserting into a field whatever is on the user's clipboard.

As an example, imagine that you wanted to give users a button that would insert their name, the current date, and the current time into a comments field, and then place the cursor in the proper place for completing their comment:

```
# purpose: To insert user and date/time data into a comment field, preserving
#       the existing information, and place the cursor in the correct position
#       for the user to begin typing.
# dependencies: Need to be on the Main_Info layout, with the Comment field
#       available. The script takes the user there.
# history: sl 2004 jan 25
#
#
Allow User Abort [ Off ]
Set Error Capture [ On ]
#
#
Go to Layout [ "Main_Info" (Movie) ]
#
#    this next step applies the comment info in italics.
Set Field [ Movie::Comment; TextStyleAdd (
Movie::Comment & "¶¶" & Get ( AccountName ) & " " &
Get ( CurrentDate) & " " & Get ( CurrentTime);
Italic)
& "¶" ]
#
Go to Field [ Movie::Comment ]
Commit Records/Requests [ No dialog ]
```

NOTE

> This script includes the full commenting approach described in this chapter and the two `Allow User Abort` and `Set Error Capture` steps. From here on out, we'll forego those details in the interest of brevity.

When using a `Go to Field` step, FileMaker Pro places the cursor at the end of whatever content already exists in the field, unless the Select/Perform option is enabled, in which case the entire field will be selected. If you wanted, you could use the `Set Selection` script step to place the cursor somewhere within the body of text.

Notice that the comment info is nested within a `TextStyleAdd()` function so that it will be displayed in italics.

→ For more information on calculation functions, including text formatting, **see** Chapters 8 and 14.

`Set Field` is by far the most used of the field category steps. The other functions in this category nearly all depend on the field in question being on the layout from which the script is being performed. You should get into the habit of using the `Set Field` command whenever possible, in preference to the others. It doesn't depend on a field being on a specific layout—or any layout, for that matter—and it usually can accomplish what you're trying to do with one of the other steps.

You'll generally need the `Insert` script steps only when you expect user input. For example, you might place a button next to a field on a given layout called "index" that then calls up the index for a given field and waits until the user selects from its contents.

That script could often be a one-step script: `Insert from Index (table::fieldname)`. As always, you'd use your template for clarity, but this script would open the index for a given field and wait for the user to select a value. Again, you should tend to think of scripts as evolutionary. Consider writing a script even for a one-step process because you might want to attach that script to multiple buttons or extend its operation in the future.

 To manage cases in which your script seems to be affecting the wrong portal row or related record, refer to "Editing the Correct Related Records" in the "Troubleshooting" section at the end of this chapter.

→ For more discussion on indexes, **see** "Storage and Indexing," **p. 86**.

CAUTION

> You might also discover the `Copy`, `Cut`, and `Paste` script steps. These work as you would expect. `Copy` and `Cut` place data onto the user's clipboard and `Paste` inserts from it. `Cut` and `Copy` overwrite anything already on the user's clipboard. Furthermore, `Copy`, `Cut`, and `Paste` depend on having access to the specified fields, and are therefore layout dependent. If, for some reason, you remove those fields from the specific layout in the future, your script will stop working. You should almost never use `Copy` and `Paste` for these reasons, and should defer instead to `Set Field`.

→ For further discussion of layout dependencies, as well as other types of dependencies that can get your scripts into trouble, **see** "Context Dependencies," **p. 528**.

Another example of using the Set Field script step concerns totaling child record data calculations and saving the results in a new record (presumably to track the growth of some quantity over time). Often a simple calculation field with a Sum (*related field*) function works, but consider that with a large related data set, the performance of such calculations can become a problem. Furthermore, you cannot index that sort of a calculation field—which might prove problematic for users performing find requests or for your needs as a developer. Consider instead creating a script to calculate and store your totals and calling that script only on demand:

```
StoreCurrentCustomerTotal
Go to Layout [ "Customer" (Customer) ]
Set Field [ Customer::storedTotal; Sum ( OrderbyCustomer::Amount ) ]
Set Field [ Customer::storedDate; Max ( OrderbyCustomer::Date ) ]
Commit Records/Requests
[ No dialog ]
Go to Layout [ original layout ]
```

The preceding script is a fairly typical example of drawing data from related records, of moving from layout to layout to establish proper context, and finally of using SetField to populate data.

PROVIDING USER NAVIGATION

You might have noticed in FileMaker's Edit Script dialog a section of the script steps list devoted to navigation. One of the most common uses of scripts is to provide a navigation scheme to users whereby they can navigate from layout to layout, record to record, or window to window by using buttons or some other intuitive means.

There's not too much magic here: By using the Go to Layout script step, you'll get the fundamentals. Consider placing buttons along the top of each layout to offer a means of navigating to all user-facing layouts in your solution with a Go to Layout script attached.

By building complete navigation scripts, you can control the entire user experience of your solutions and can opt to close the Status Area if you want. Armed with find routines, sort buttons, reporting scripts, and a navigation interface, it is possible to build a complete application with a look and feel all its own.

SCRIPT CONTEXT AND INTERNAL NAVIGATION

Consider that FileMaker uses layouts to determine script context: For any script step that depends on a specific table, you need to use Go to Layout steps to provide that context. Review the script we introduced at the beginning of the chapter:

```
Go to Layout [ "zdev_GlobalAdmin" (Globals) ]
Set Field [ Globals::gAccountName; Get (AccountName) ]
Set Field [ Current_User::LastLoginDate; Get (CurrentDate) ]
Set Field [ Globals::gUserNameDisplay; Current_User::Name_First ]
Set Field [ Globals::gUserMessage; "Welcome Back, "
       & Globals::gUserNameDisplay & "." ]
Go to Layout [ "Main Menu" (Globals) ]
```

This script takes itself to a zdev_GlobalAdmin layout, executes some steps (in this case sets data into fields), and then brings the user to a Main Menu layout. All the users see (presumably when they log in) is that they've landed on a Main Menu layout. They'll never see, or interact with, the zdev_GlobalAdmin layout, but the system will have done so. Had we written the script without the initial Go to Layout step, the routine would have had quite unexpected results.

Notice that the script makes use of a Current_User table occurrence. As related data, that information would likely be very different depending on the perspective from which a user viewed it. The purpose of navigating internally to a specific layout is to precisely control this context.

The point here is that you'll need to bring a script to a specific layout to establish a different context. Context is determined by the table occurrence associated with a given layout. The user might never see this internal navigation going on, but if you were to walk through the script step by step (for example, using the Script Debugger, covered in Chapter 17), you'd see the system go to the zdev_GlobalAdmin layout and then to the Main Menu layout.

SAVED SCRIPT OPTIONS

Scripts tend to mirror the actions a user could perform manually but, obviously, do so without human intervention. It is possible in FileMaker to save find, sort, export, and other actions in a script (hard-coding them, if you will), or to prompt the user for some input to help perform these steps.

The advantages of hard-coding requests should be fairly obvious. If, for example, you need to prepare a report on active real estate listings, it makes sense to have one of your script steps be a Perform Find that returns all the records with a status of "active." The requirements of your report will rarely change, so you'll save users time (and possible errors) if you hard-code the find request.

On the other hand, allowing the user to provide input is a great way to make scripts more flexible. Continuing the example, you might create a real estate listings report and then in your script prompt the user for some search criteria. This can be done by either using a dialog that gives the user one or two choices (we'll cover that later in the chapter, in the "Working with Custom Dialogs" section), or simply allowing the report to act on the current found set and sort.

You will often find it helpful to build hard-coded find and sort routines. For example, you might want a script for finding overdue invoices, or easy-access buttons for sorting by first name, last name, or company.

FileMaker allows you to save complex find, sort, export, and import requests as necessary, and allows you to edit these requests within ScriptMaker.

FIND SCRIPT STEPS

FileMaker allows you to assemble and store complex find requests within scripts. In Figure 9.3, the script finds all overdue invoices over $500 and, in the same Perform Find step, omits invoice number 2004.1.1; the result replaces the found set.

Figure 9.3
Assemble as many find requests as necessary.

Notice that multiple requests have been added; this enables you to perform Or finds where you will be left with records that match either the first condition *or* the second.

A single find request is assembled via the Edit Find Request dialog (see Figure 9.4).

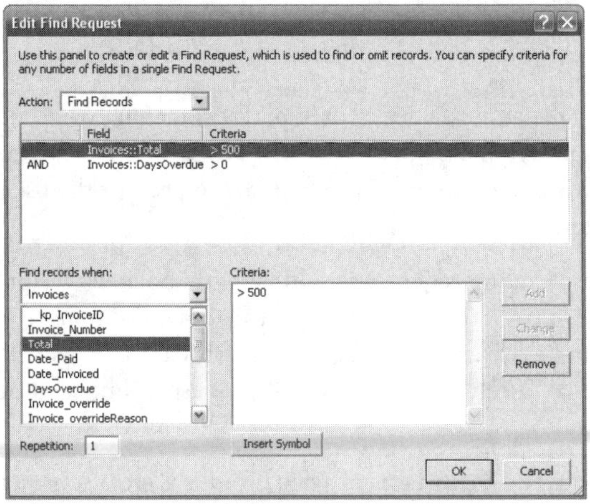

Figure 9.4
By adding multiple criteria to a single find request, you will be performing an And search.

Note in Figure 9.3, however, that we have opted to omit records that match the second request. Setting a request to omit records simply means that FileMaker will find those records that match the overall request and then take out or ignore those that meet the omit criteria. If you create a find request that does nothing but omit records, it replaces your existing found set with all records that don't match your request. (How's that for a double negative?) The following example shows a script that combines a find request with an omit request:

```
Find_Overdue_Invoices
Perform Find [ Specified Find Requests: Find Records;
      Criteria: Invoices::Total:"> 500"

      AND Invoices::DaysOverdue: "> 0"
Omit Records; Criteria: Invoices::Invoice_Number: "= '2004.1.1'" ]
      [ Restore ]
```

Other search-related script steps include Constrain Found Set and Extend Found Set. Just as though a user had chosen each command from FileMaker's menu-driven interface,

`Constrain` reduces the current found set, eliminating any records that don't match the search criteria, and `Extend` adds those records from outside the set that match its criteria to the current found set.

SORT SCRIPT STEP

Establishing saved sort orders in the Sort dialog works, happily, just as it does for users performing a manual sort (see Figure 9.5).

Figure 9.5
It's generally quite helpful to create sorting scripts for users. Sorting needs are usually fairly predictable and are always needed more than once.

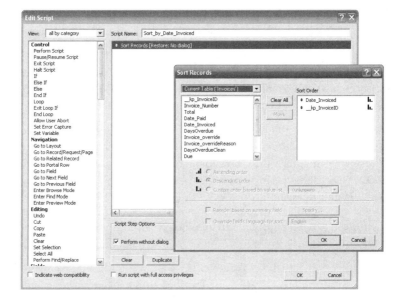

One of the most common applications of sort scripts is in building column header buttons. Simply create a series of sort scripts and apply them to the buttons along the top of a list view (see Figure 9.6).

Figure 9.6
Scripting is often employed in creating more intuitive user interfaces for users.

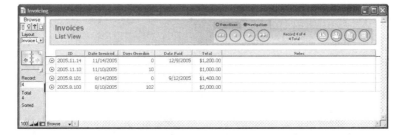

Keep in mind that many of your reports depend on sorting, especially as you get into reporting by summary data. It's a good idea to create sort scripts for your reports and call them as subscripts, rather than hard-coding sort criteria into your report scripts themselves.

You may well create reports that behave differently depending on different sort orders—by setting up different, multiple subsummary parts on one report layout, for example—so you'll want to factor the sorting logic into its own script or subscripts. A report with both a week-of-year subsummary part and a month subsummary part will display by week, by month, or by week and month depending on the sort options your script establishes. This is a handy technique for reducing the number of layouts you need in a system—with a little bit of scripting you can use a single layout for three different reports.

→ For more on summary reporting, **see** Chapter 10, "Getting Started with Reporting," **p. 273**.

USING CONDITIONAL LOGIC

Another important element of scripting is the capability to branch scripts based on various conditions. To manage logically branching scripts, you use the If, Else, Else If, and End If script steps.

These conditional script steps work by performing a logical test, expressed as a calculation. If that calculation formula resolves to a true statement, FileMaker then executes all the script steps subordinate to (that is, nested within) an If or Else If statement.

One of the most common applications of conditional logic in FileMaker revolves around Perform Find script steps. Because we as developers can never guarantee the state of a given table's data—in other words, how many records it contains—we have to test for their existence in scripts that perform find requests and then branch accordingly if no records are found. Here's an example:

```
Find Overdue Orders
Set Error Capture [ On ]
Allow User Abort [ Off ]
#
Go to Layout [ "Order" (Order) ]
#
Perform Find [ Specified Find Requests:
        Find Records; Criteria: Order::Status: ""Overdue"" ]
[ Restore ]
If [ Get ( LastError ) = 401 ]
Show Custom Dialog [ Title: "Overdue Orders";
        Message: "There are no overdue orders in the system.";
        Buttons: "OK" ]
Show All Records
End If
```

In this simple script two outcomes are possible: Users will either be presented with a set of order records where their statuses have been set to Overdue or they will be presented with a dialog informing them that there are no overdue orders and will end with a full set of all orders.

The entire idea behind conditional logic is to allow the computer to determine which of multiple possible paths to take. Computers aren't terribly smart, so they make these decisions based entirely on Boolean (true/false) tests. At the end of every script step, FileMaker records an internal error that can be retrieved using the Get (Last Error) function. In the preceding script, if that function is storing a value of 401 then the nested steps within the If clause will be performed; otherwise, they won't be.

Figure 9.7 elaborates on the idea with a real-world example in which multiple branches are possible. At the conclusion of its script, one of three possible outcomes will have happened: A standard invoice will have (presumably) been printed, an overdue invoice will have been printed, or, if a stop work limit has been reached, a letter and review process will be initiated. The exact specifics here aren't important, but notice that the script results in one certain outcome (a standard invoice or an overdue invoice being printed) and then a second possible outcome (a letter and review occurring if a stop work condition also exists).

Figure 9.7
Notice that scripts within FileMaker's Script Editor are automatically indented. Liberal use of comments will help make scripts readable.

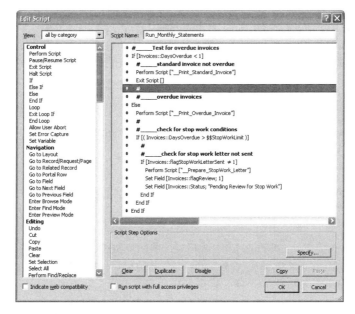

 To learn how to bake error checking into your conditional tests, refer to "Conditional Error Defaults" in the "Troubleshooting" section at the end of this chapter.

There's no practical limit to the number of branches a script might take. For scripts of particular complexity, we recommend breaking them into subscripts (as the script in Figure 9.7 was) and, when necessary, creating a flowchart of the process before writing the script.

USING LOOPS

Another key scripting technique is looping. Looping allows you to execute a series of script steps over and over until some exit condition is met. This is very much the same as an If/Else If construct, but this time instead of performing a new branch of logic, you're simply telling the script to perform the same actions over again until a controlling conditional test returns a true value (for example, if the end of a found set is reached, or the results of a calculation come to some specific number).

A simple example of this might be stepping through each record in an invoice table's found set and generating a new invoice for any invoice that remains unpaid or that needs to be sent out again for some reason. The logic, without worrying about syntax, might look like this:

```
Go to first record in found set.
Begin Loop.
    Check whether the invoice is closed. (We'll assume
    unclosed invoices are those that need to be resent.)
    If CLOSED
        Go to next record.
        If there is no next record (you're at the end of
        your found set), then exit the loop.
        Else begin loop again (go to the "Begin Loop" step).
    If NOT CLOSED
        Close current invoice.
        Create/duplicate new invoice. (In a real system,
        there would likely be more steps involved here.)
        Go to next record.
        If there is no next record (you're at the end of
        your found set), then exit the loop.
        Else begin loop again (go to the "Begin Loop" step).
End Loop
Exit Script
```

Notice that an exit condition is established. The system tests in both If branches whether you're at the end of a found set and exits the script regardless of whether the last record in the set was closed.

Imagine you're a user doing this manually. You'd start at the top of a found set, use the book icon to page through each record one at a time, and then stop the process after you reach the end of your recordset.

Here's another example, this time in FileMaker's scripting syntax. It creates a series of new order records based on a request from the user (posted in a global field):

```
Set Field [ Globals::gCurrentCustomer ]
Show Custom Dialog [ Title: "New Order Items";
        Message: "How many Order Item rows do you want to create?";
        Buttons: "OK"; Input
#1: Globals::gNumNewOrderItems, "New Order Items to Create:" ]
Go to Layout [ "OrderbyCustomer" (OrderbyCustomer) ]
Loop
Exit Loop If [ Get (FoundCount) > Globals::gNumNewOrderItems ]
# note: new records in the OrderbyCustomer table auto-enter
#       customer foreign key from the gCurrentCustomer field
New Record/Request
End Loop
Go to Layout [ original layout ]
```

This simple example demonstrates all the essential logic for working with loops. First, some condition by which the script exits the loop must be established. In this case a number provided by the user is used to exit the script. (Note that if this were a real-world script, we'd recommend some error-checking to make sure that the user input a positive integer.)

A loop exit condition is almost always useful if something changes during the course of a script. (It's possible you might be sitting in a loop, waiting for something elsewhere to change and checking periodically, but this kind of polling activity is not commonly needed in FileMaker Pro.)

Notice too where the commands are placed. The exit condition tests for a greater-than con-dition. This ensures that the script does, in fact, run the number of times a user requests. If the New Record/Request script step were placed above the Exit Loop If step, this script would still be perfectly valid, but it would generate one fewer new orders than the user requested.

Note too that if you're a perfectionist, it's possible to write the script like so:

```
Set Field [ Globals::gCurrentCustomer ]
Show Custom Dialog [ Title: "New Order Items";
       Message: "How many Order Item rows do you want to create?";
   Buttons: "OK"; Input
#1: Globals::gNumNewOrderItems, "New Order Items to Create:" ]
Go to Layout [ "OrderbyCustomer" (OrderbyCustomer) ]
Loop
New Record/Request
Exit Loop If [ Get (FoundCount) ≥ Globals::gNumNewOrderItems ]
# note: new records in the OrderbyCustomer table auto-enter
#       customer foreign key from the gCurrentCustomer field
End Loop
Go to Layout [ original layout ]
```

In this scenario you're saving one iteration through the loop by testing conditions immediately after the creation of a new record. It's unlikely that this makes much of a difference in this par-ticular example, but when you write particularly large scripts, especially those that involve looping, we recommend you look for ways to make them perform as efficiently as possible. Speed and system performance should always be considerations when writing scripts.

Loops get more interesting when combined with conditional logic more complex than checking for an incremented counter. The first example for closed invoices did just this. It is possible to build a loop that tests for certain conditions within your system and exits only when those conditions are met—for example, a loop that processes all unclosed invoices, checking at the end of each cycle whether it has reached the end of a found set.

Loops can be exited in various ways. The simple conditional in the script example shown earlier is quite common. Another common technique is to use the Go to Record/Request/Page [Next, Exit After Last] script step. It enables you to step through a found set and exit a loop after the last record is reached.

Another way to exit a loop is to exit or halt the script altogether. You have two processes running: the script itself, which can be terminated, and the internal loop.

 To cope with endless loop problems, refer to "Testing Loops" in the "Troubleshooting" section at the end of this chapter.

WORKING WITH CUSTOM DIALOGS

One of the most common user interactions necessary for a system is to capture a response to a question. "Are you sure you want to delete all records?" "Do you want to report on all records, or just your found set?" "Would you like fries with that?"

The Show Custom Dialog script step is a great, built-in way to capture this sort of interac-tion. (There are ways to create layouts that act and behave like dialog boxes, but they're a good bit more work.) Custom dialogs allow you to present some descriptive text or a question to a user and capture a response (see Figure 9.8).

Figure 9.8
Here's an example of a custom dialog. Notice that it has an appropriate title and specific, data-derived text.

→ To learn how to create pop-up layouts that behave as modal dialogs, **see** "Multiwindow Interfaces," **p. 368**.

Naturally, after you've created a custom dialog, you need to deal with the results. FileMaker Pro stores the user's button choice until the end of the current script or until you present another custom dialog. Think of these dialogs as existing solely within the space of a given script.

To identify which response the user chose to your dialog, use the Get (LastMessageChoice) function. This function returns a 1, 2, or 3 based on which button was clicked, from right to left. The rightmost button is identified as 1. The label you assigned to the button is inconsequential.

Conditional scripting similar to what was covered previously also allows you to test the choices a user made and respond accordingly. Here's an example:

```
Report_Revenue_Start
Show Custom Dialog [ Title: "Revenue Report"; Message:
"Do you want to view a Revenue
➥Report by month, year, or a date range?";
Buttons: "Range", "Year", "Month"; Input #1:
➥Invoices::Date_Range, "Date Range (e.g., 1/1/2004...2/15/2004)" ]
If [ Get ( LastMessageChoice ) = 1 ]
    Perform Script [ "__Report_DateRange" ]
Else If [ Get ( LastMessageChoice ) = 2 ]
    Perform Script [ "__Report_YearSummary" ]
Else If [ Get ( LastMessageChoice ) = 3 ]
    Perform Script [ "__Report_MonthSummary" ]
End If
```

Custom dialogs are fairly flexible, but they do have limitations. The most obvious limitation is that their appearance cannot be altered. In a FileMaker layout you're able to apply images, background color fills, and other graphical attributes of the screen. Not so in a custom dialog. You are limited to a system-style dialog.

Second, and more important, if you provide input fields (as was shown in Figure 9.7), data entered is posted to your database only if the user clicks the first, rightmost button in the dialog. You do not have programmatic control of the input field behaviors. This then means that your users will have "post to database" as their default. Not optimal, but there you have it.

The third limitation of the dialog lies in scope: You're limited to three input fields and three buttons. If you need anything more complex, you have to use a standard FileMaker layout to build a custom pop-up layout.

TIP

One alternative to keep in mind is a range of plug-ins available that also offer dialogs. Visit FileMaker's website to explore those options.

TRIGGERING SCRIPTS

There are six ways to initiate—or perform—scripts:

- By selecting a script via the Scripts menu
- By establishing a custom menu item tied to a script
- By opening the Scripts dialog, selecting a script, and clicking Perform
- By calling a script from another FileMaker script (within the same file or externally)
- By calling a script from an external web source
- By attaching a script to a layout element, which a user then clicks (and thus it becomes a button)
- By attaching a script to the startup or shutdown routines in the file options dialog

FileMaker lacks most procedural *triggers*—functions that fire automatically when certain events occur, such as creating or editing a record. (An exception is that you may configure a file to run a specific script when the file is opened or closed.) For a script to be performed, the user generally needs to actively click something. Scripts can be attached to layout objects so that they are triggered by a user clicking on the object, or they can be activated directly from the Scripts menu, if you've chosen to make particular scripts visible there. You can also use FileMaker Pro 8 Advanced to create custom menus that run scripts. There are other ways to call scripts externally through web publishing as well.

→ To tie a script to a custom menu item, **see** Chapter 13, **p. 373**.

→ To call scripts externally through Instant Web Publishing, **see** Chapter 21, "Instant Web Publishing," **p. 633**.

Finally there are some plug-ins on the market that offer event trigger functionality. Events from Waves in Motion is one such plug-in. We encourage you to visit FileMaker's website to see the latest offerings.

WORKING WITH BUTTONS ON LAYOUTS

More often than not, clickable layout objects are graphical buttons, but it is possible to attach a script to anything you can place on a layout: a field, a graphic, even a portal. These layout objects then become button-like so that when a user clicks such an object, the object's associated script runs.

Creating buttons on FileMaker layouts is fairly straightforward. You can opt to use the Button tool to draw a 3D-esque button, or you can attach a button behavior to any object on a layout (including fields, merge fields, text, images, and even binary files pasted onto layouts).

Apply button behaviors to an object either by right-clicking and choosing Specify <u>B</u>utton, or, with a layout object selected, by navigating to the format menu and choosing <u>B</u>utton.

We've talked about buttons as a tool for triggering scripts. This is actually a little inaccurate. A button, when clicked, can perform any single script step: `Go To Layout`, for example, or `Hide Window`. Of course, one of the available script steps you can attach to a button is `Perform Script`. Choose that option, and your button can perform a script of any length or complexity.

Given that fact, when adding interactivity to a button, why use any of the other single script steps other than `Perform Script` itself? Well, we're going to argue that you shouldn't. If you use single script steps, you're out of luck if you ever want a button to do two things, and you're out of luck if you create a bunch of buttons that perform the same step (such as `Go to Layout`) and you need to change them all—it's insufficient abstraction to not allow the same button behavior to be reused elsewhere. Because it's likely that you will want to add steps, or duplicate a button and edit its behavior globally, you should ignore every button behavior other than `Perform Script`. Even if a script is one step long and is likely never to be reused, still take the few extra seconds to create a script. If the button performs a script, you can easily add steps whenever you need them, and all the buttons that need to go to, say, the Invoice layout can be changed at once. After you've selected the script in question, you can opt to modify the behavior of the script that may or may not be currently running.

→ For more details on controlling script flow via button attributes, **see** "Script Parameters," **p. 437**.

TROUBLESHOOTING

LOST ERROR MESSAGES IN SCRIPTS

My script is not working properly, but I'm not getting any error messages. Where do I start?

Be sure that you properly account for potential errors if you turn error capture on. What if a find request returns zero records? What if a user doesn't have access to a given layout that is needed for a script? To manage debugging, turn error capture off while you're testing. Some developers write scripts that toggle error capture for all scripts in a system. This is a convenient way to turn on and off a debugging mode.

UNFINISHED SCRIPTS

I need a script to run to completion without fail. I set `Allow User Abort [off]`, *but it appears that the script was aborted at some point by a user. How can I make sure that users can't muck with my scripts?*

Remember that turning `Allow User Abort` off doesn't always save you from errors in the script itself, power outages, the user closing FileMaker Pro, or other random acts of unpredicted computer wonkiness. You can never absolutely depend on a script completing in FileMaker Pro. If need be, write a "check conditions" script in your system and run it when appropriate. Another way to deal with this problem is to write a script log that saves a record when a script starts and another when it ends. You can check for incomplete pairs.

Editing the Correct Related Records

My Set Field *script step is just continually changing the first record in a portal instead of the one I want. How do I get the script to act on the proper row?*

Be careful when setting fields through relationships. It's possible to think that you're pointing to a single record when you're really pointing to the first of many. In that case, FileMaker blithely applies your script steps to the first related record it finds. Either put a button directly in a portal—in which case the script will apply to that row—or use a Go To Related Record script step to explicitly control both the context and the record against which a script operates.

Conditional Error Defaults

My If/Else *statement isn't returning the proper result. How can I test what's going on?*

Be sure to account for all variations of logic in your conditional scripts. It is strongly recommended that you build If routines that end with an option that you think will never occur. Here's a quick example:

```
If [Invoices::Total > 0]
    Do something
Else If [Invoices::Total = 0]
    Do something
Else If [Invoices::Total < 0]
    Do something
Else
    Handle error conditions here
End
```

This function should *never* return the default error, but you cannot perfectly predict all such behaviors. For example, what if a calculation for Total is wrong and returns a null or empty value? Or if a calculation you expect to be numeric returns text in some cases?

Testing Loops

My loop seems to be stuck endlessly looping. How do I debug the problem?

It's the rare developer who gets everything right the first time, and if you don't, you might find yourself in the middle of an endless loop. A handy trick is to always create an exit condition that tests whether the Shift key is held down by using the Get(CurrentModifierKey) function. It's a backdoor out of your loop that's quite handy if you have an error in logic. A much easier way to go if you own FileMaker Pro 8 Advanced is to simply turn on the script debugger the first time you test a new loop.

FileMaker Extra: Creating a Script Library

You might consider having a utility file sitting around your hard drive with all the basic scripts each of your solutions will need. You can then import these scripts into your own solution files as needed. We always have the following in our databases:

9

- `Relogin`—This script should be the first you have in every file. Press (⌘-1) [Ctrl+1] (if it's turned on in the menu) and you'll be able to log in again and test how things work for your end users. This is a critically useful script to have access to during development and testing.

- `StartUp`—Here's a script we use to open all the files of a given solution at once, to set default values for globals, to set a login history record if need be, and so on.

- `ShutDown`—The partner for `StartUp`, the `ShutDown` script can close out your user session by setting any tracking info and can close all the files in a solution so that FileMaker Pro need not be quit.

- `ToggleAllStatusAreas`—This is another critical script for developers working in multiple files or windows. Very often we'll close and lock the Status Area to maintain control and keep users from accessing records or layouts we have carefully scripted around. This handy script reopens the Status Area for development.

- `ToggleMultiUser`—A script that simply turns on or off peer-to-peer sharing. It is useful to use the `Set Multi-User [on/off]` script step when you need to isolate your system during testing.

- `InitializeGlobals`—Often a subscript of `StartUp`, but best abstracted as it is here, this script sets all the initial values of globals and global variables in your system, ensuring that they all start out user sessions in a predictable state. You need to add explicit steps for each global you add to your system as you work, but you'll find it invaluable to have a "global" global initializer.

- `ScriptTEMPLATE`—This is the template we duplicate for new scripts. It has initial comment headers and default script steps as needed.

- ·—Okay, maybe it only saves you a single keystroke, but having an already-ready hyphen handy just means a quick click on the duplicate button. (And a nice touch from the engineers at FileMaker: Since FileMaker Pro 7, hyphens simply duplicate and don't get suffixed with a "copy"!)

- `PrintSetUp_landscape` and `PrintSetUp_portrait`—Every printer-bound output of your system needs page properties established. Write them once.

- `___ScriptHEADER_____`—Here's an empty script for dividing your script menu into logical subsections. Again, clicking the Duplicate button means you don't need to count how many underscores to use.

If you find yourself writing certain scripts time and time again, add them to your library. Using the capability in FileMaker Pro 8 Advanced to copy and paste scripts enables you to more easily leverage prior work.

## CHAPTER 10

GETTING STARTED WITH REPORTING

In this chapter

DERIVING MEANING FROM DATA

Reporting is an important component in almost every database project. Indeed, the need to create reports that summarize or synthesize data is often the reason many databases exist in the first place. No matter what your database does, it's a fair bet that you have many reporting needs.

Reports come in many shapes and sizes: There are simple list reports, summarized reports, workflow reports, cross-tabulated reports, variance reports, and graphic reports (to name but a few). There are standard reports that need to be generated periodically; there are ad hoc reports for which the report criteria need to be defined on the fly. Some reports need to be printed and distributed, whereas others are meant to be viewed onscreen.

Despite the wide range of things that can be classified as reports, most reports tend to have a few characteristics in common:

- Reports are generally used for viewing data rather than creating or editing data.
- Reports generally display (or draw on data contained in) multiple records from a table. They are usually designed to provide an overview or higher-level understanding of a data set than you would obtain by looking strictly at data-entry screens.
- Reports capture a snapshot in time and reflect the database's current state. Running the same report at different times may yield different results if the data in the system has changed.
- Often, but not always, reports are distributed by some means other than FileMaker: on paper, via email, or as an electronic document.

To generate meaningful reports, you should learn several standard reporting techniques. From there, it's just a matter of coming up with variations that suit your particular needs. This chapter covers working with lists of data and reporting with grouped data (also known as *subsummary reports*).

BEGIN WITH THE END IN MIND

In our experience, one of the keys to creating successful reports is beginning with the end in mind. By this, we mean that you should begin thinking about the reports that a system will need to generate right at the beginning of a project. A system's intended outputs can have a profound impact on its design and implementation.

A few simple illustrations will help clarify this point. Say that you've been asked to design a contact management system, and the client mentions that he wants the system to be able to track a history of conversations and interactions with each of his clients. From a data-entry standpoint, you could create this sort of functionality either by having a single long Notes field in the Contact table, or by setting up a related Contact History table and using a portal to capture information about each interaction separately.

All other considerations aside (for example, time/cost to implement, rules of normalization), the reporting needs of the client will likely influence your decision about how to implement this feature. If you don't ask the right questions up front, you may find out in two months that the client expects to be able to generate a report of call activity summarized by account representative, or sorted by date. This report would be relatively simple to generate if you had chosen the route of the related Contact History table; it would be virtually impossible to generate from a single undifferentiated Notes field.

Another typical example of reporting needs driving feature implementation is the decision to use check boxes to capture data. Check boxes are fantastic from a data-entry standpoint, but they may limit your reporting capabilities because they store multiple pieces of data in the same field. For instance, imagine that in the contact management system you're building, the client asks you to put a check box field on the layout so that users can select one or more sources for the contact (such as Referral, Conference Attendee, Website).

If you know that one of the reports the client wants is a Contact Source Summary that lists the various sources and the total number of contacts each has generated, one would hope that you wouldn't implement the feature as a check box field. With potentially multiple sources selected for a given contact, it's not straightforward to split the selections apart. Instead, if you set up a Source table and a ContactSource table (as a join table between Contact and Source), you could display and maintain the contact's sources via a portal from Contact into ContactSource. The desired report could easily be generated from the ContactSource table. The point here is simply that the reporting requirement informs both the table structure and the user interface.

In both of the preceding examples, choosing a more fully normalized data structure happened to provide the more robust reporting capabilities, but there are certainly just as many occasions when you'll find that opting for a denormalized data structure makes for better, faster reporting. For example, imagine you're a teacher creating a system that will track the scores on eight quizzes you plan to give to your class. You could set up a Student table and a related Quiz table (which would eventually contain eight related records for each student record), or you could just create a Student table with eight QuizScore fields. If one of your goals was to get a spreadsheet-like report that listed students down the side and quizzes going across, you'd have a significantly easier time using a flat file than you would if quiz scores were broken out into their own table. Of course, the flat file approach is not without its own problems and limitations. By hard-coding the number of quizzes, you restrict possible future expansion. Similarly, a seemingly simple ad hoc question like "Which students scored a perfect 100 on at least one of the quizzes?" would be difficult to answer with the scores spread across eight fields.

The point of both of these examples is simply to demonstrate what we mean by "begin with the end in mind." Over the course of this chapter, you'll learn more about these types of reports. For now, what's important is that as you define the requirements for any database system, you think carefully about the reporting needs. If you don't, you may end up having to rewrite sections of your system and/or create more complex reporting routines later.

10

DETERMINE REPORT REQUIREMENTS

Just as a system's reporting requirements influence its design, an organization's business needs influence the design of the reports themselves. When thinking about how you'll go about generating any given report, ask yourself (or your client/users) the following types of questions:

- What questions is this report trying to answer? Focus first on the purpose the report will serve, not on its design. Is it trying to monitor progress toward a goal? To be an early warning of potential problems? To help spot business trends? The more you know about how a report will be used, the more effective you can make it.

- Who will read this report? Is it going to be used strictly for internal purposes, or might it be presented to customers or vendors? Should the report be accessible to everyone, or should certain users be prohibited from viewing it?

- How will be it read? Will it be distributed in hard copy, emailed to a group of people, or read onscreen 18 times a day? If the report is distributed, should the document be secured with a password or encrypted?

- Is this a one-time report, or will it be used on a regular basis? For one-time or special-occasion reports, you probably won't go to the trouble of setting up scripts and/or find screens, but you should do so for reports that are intended to be run regularly.

- What level of granularity is appropriate? Will the consumers of the report be interested in seeing details, or just the big picture?

After you've collected answers to questions like these, we strongly recommend writing out a sample report (using whatever tools you choose—pencil and paper and whiteboards are our favorites) and showing it to its appropriate consumers for feedback.

GENERIC VERSUS SPECIFIC REPORT STRUCTURES

Another part of report planning is determining whether the report is to meet a specific or a generic need. That is, should users be able to select a data set to feed into a report shell, or should the search criteria for the report be hard-coded?

For example, say you have a List view layout that displays customer data. If you feed it a found set of customers obtained since a certain date, it becomes a New Customers report. If you feed it a set of inactive customers, the same shell is transformed into an Inactive Customers report.

In instances like this, it's often helpful to think of a report as consisting of two distinct components: its format and its content. If you can create a generic multipurpose format, then simply by sending in different content, you create different reports. The point is that in planning reports, you should have the distinction between format and content in mind. You can sometimes save yourself a lot of work if you recognize when a report can be created by simply feeding new data into an existing format.

As a classic example of this separation between format and content, we had a client who wanted a 10 a.m. activity report and a 2 p.m. activity report. The reports showed the same columns or fields of information; they just contained different sets of data—different found sets of records. We simply created two scripted report routines that used the same layout to present their information; however, during discussion of these reports, it was clear that to the client these were two very different reports. Anytime we made a change to the 10 a.m. report, he would always remind us to be sure to change the 2 p.m. report also. Happily, as you can imagine, we never once failed to do so....

WORKING WITH LISTS OF DATA

Many reports are nothing more than simple lists of data. Examples include such things as task lists, customer lists, overdue invoice reports, student test scores, and phone directories. Besides being the most frequently encountered type of report, lists of data are also the easiest type to create. As such, they provide us with a good starting place to begin delving into report creation.

List view layouts can be created with the Layout Wizard or by hand. Figure 10.1 shows an example of a basic List view layout that displays student names and quiz scores. Depending on your needs and aesthetics, this alone might serve as a report.

➔ For more on creating layouts and working with layout tools, **see** "Working with Objects on a Layout," **p. 106**.

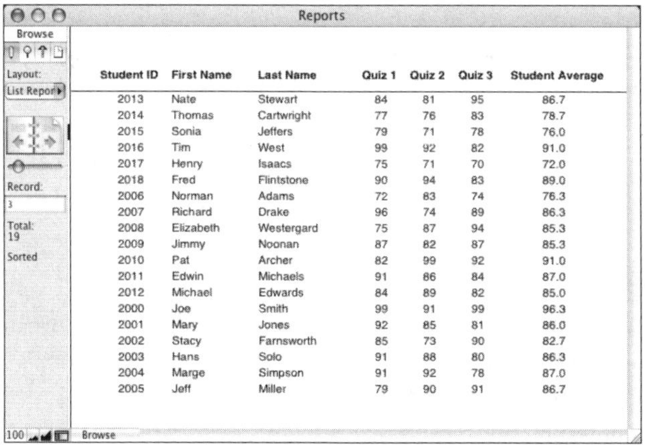

Student ID	First Name	Last Name	Quiz 1	Quiz 2	Quiz 3	Student Average
2013	Nate	Stewart	84	81	95	86.7
2014	Thomas	Cartwright	77	76	83	78.7
2015	Sonia	Jeffers	79	71	78	76.0
2016	Tim	West	99	92	82	91.0
2017	Henry	Isaacs	75	71	70	72.0
2018	Fred	Flintstone	90	94	83	89.0
2006	Norman	Adams	72	83	74	76.3
2007	Richard	Drake	96	74	89	86.3
2008	Elizabeth	Westergard	75	87	94	85.3
2009	Jimmy	Noonan	87	82	87	85.3
2010	Pat	Archer	82	99	92	91.0
2011	Edwin	Michaels	91	86	84	87.0
2012	Michael	Edwards	84	89	82	85.0
2000	Joe	Smith	99	91	99	96.3
2001	Mary	Jones	92	85	81	86.0
2002	Stacy	Farnsworth	85	73	90	82.7
2003	Hans	Solo	91	88	80	86.3
2004	Marge	Simpson	91	92	78	87.0
2005	Jeff	Miller	79	90	91	86.7

Figure 10.1
Basic List view layouts are the simplest types of reports you can create.

Beyond being simple to create, List views make nice reports for several other reasons. The first is that they're very flexible. You can allow users to perform ad hoc finds, or you can write scripts with canned searches, and then simply display the results using your List view.

Users can also view list reports while in Browse mode. We recommend that you consider the final delivery of a report as a separate issue from generating the report for users to view onscreen. We often design systems in which a report displays for a user (in Browse mode) and then the user can, as a second step, send it to a printer, attach it to an email, and so on.

The key benefit of being able to work with a report in Browse mode is that you can place buttons on your report that give the user additional functionality, such as drilling down to additional levels of detail, re-sorting the data without having to regenerate the report, or providing buttons for printing, emailing, and so on.

This isn't the case with subsummary reports, however: They can only be viewed in Preview mode. Subsummary reports depend on being sorted in order to group data together. Display of summary fields is a special operation that FileMaker performs in Preview mode. In these cases we still recommend thinking of final output as a second step in the process, but in the case of subsummary reports you'll need to build routines that take the user into Preview mode and then back again into Browse mode at the conclusion of the process.

There might be buttons (or other objects) on your layout that you wouldn't want to appear when the report is printed (such as navigation buttons). While building the report in Layout mode, select those objects and then choose Format, Set Sliding/Printing to open the Sliding/Printing dialog, and then select Do Not Print the Selected Objects.

NOTE

If your users are likely to print from a List view, be sure that you constrain your report to the width of the printed page rather than the monitor screen width. You'll also find that although 10- to 12-point fonts generally work well for reports that will be viewed onscreen, 8- to 10-point fonts are more appropriate for printed reports. Be sure to actually print your reports to proof them rather than simply relying on what you see onscreen.

If you have problems printing your reports, see "Printed Reports Show Only a Single Record" in the "Troubleshooting" section at the end of this chapter.

Of course, you can make your List view layout as crafted and attractive as you desire. You might consider employing some common techniques, however, for enhancing List view reports.

TRAILING SUMMARIES

A list report in and of itself does little synthesizing of data; it just organizes data for easy review. The main tools at your disposal for synthesizing a set of data are summary fields. Summary fields enable you to perform aggregations across a set of records, including counting, totaling, and averaging.

→ For more information about creating summary fields, **see** "Working with Field Types," **p. 72**.

Adding a trailing grand summary part to a basic list report gives you a place to put summary information about the set of records in your report. For example, in a list report that displays invoice data, you might choose to put the total amount invoiced in the trailing grand summary part.

→ For more information about working with layout parts, **see** "Working with Parts," **p. 103**.

Summary fields placed in a leading or trailing grand summary part summarize the entire found set of data, so as you view different found sets of records on a report layout, your totals change accordingly. Figure 10.2 shows the same report as Figure 10.1, except that here four summary fields (Average_Quiz1, Average_Quiz2, Average_Quiz3, Average_Overall) have been added to the database and placed in a trailing grand summary.

Figure 10.2
Summary fields placed in a trailing grand summary part act on the entire current found set.

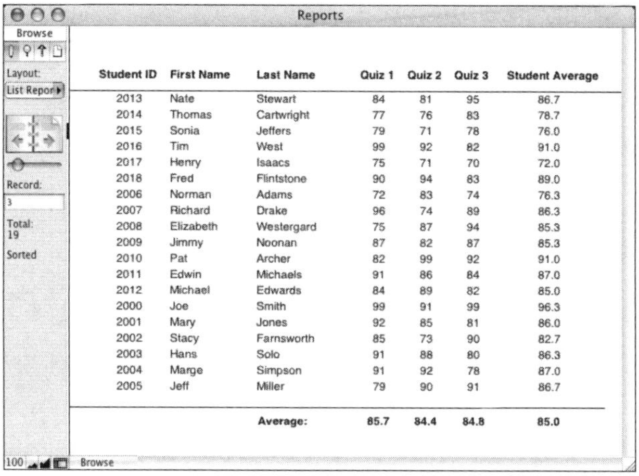

Student ID	First Name	Last Name	Quiz 1	Quiz 2	Quiz 3	Student Average
2013	Nate	Stewart	84	81	95	86.7
2014	Thomas	Cartwright	77	76	83	78.7
2015	Sonia	Jeffers	79	71	78	76.0
2016	Tim	West	99	92	82	91.0
2017	Henry	Isaacs	75	71	70	72.0
2018	Fred	Flintstone	90	94	83	89.0
2006	Norman	Adams	72	83	74	76.3
2007	Richard	Drake	96	74	89	86.3
2008	Elizabeth	Westergard	75	87	94	85.3
2009	Jimmy	Noonan	87	82	87	85.3
2010	Pat	Archer	82	99	92	91.0
2011	Edwin	Michaels	91	86	84	87.0
2012	Michael	Edwards	84	89	82	85.0
2000	Joe	Smith	99	91	99	96.3
2001	Mary	Jones	92	85	81	86.0
2002	Stacy	Farnsworth	85	73	90	82.7
2003	Hans	Solo	91	88	80	86.3
2004	Marge	Simpson	91	92	78	87.0
2005	Jeff	Miller	79	90	91	86.7
		Average:	85.7	84.4	84.8	85.0

ALTERNATING ROW COLOR

Another enhancement you may want to make to a list report is to alternate the row color. The option to alternate row color is found in the Part Definition dialog, which is shown in Figure 10.3; the quickest way to get there is by double-clicking on the body part label while in Layout mode. Figure 10.4 shows the effect this feature can have on a list report.

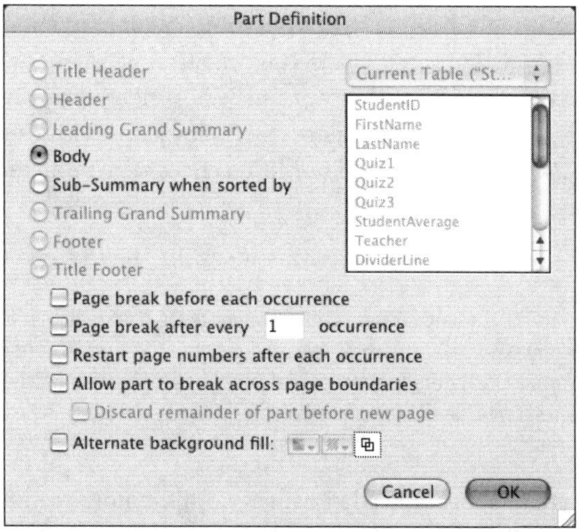

Figure 10.3
The option to alternate row colors can be applied only to body parts; it is grayed out as an option for any other type of part.

Figure 10.4
Adding a subtle alternate row color can make a list report easier to read.

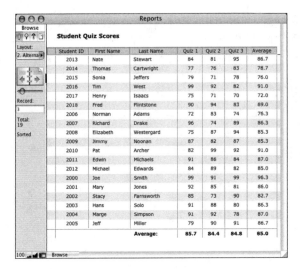

Alternating the row color is more appropriate for use in reports that are to be viewed onscreen rather than printed, but if you use a light enough color, it may still print well. If you have a need for both print and onscreen versions of the same report, you may end up creating two different layouts, each optimized for a particular usage.

HORIZONTAL AND VERTICAL DIVIDERS

Another method of increasing the readability of a list report is to add horizontal and/or vertical lines between the columns and rows. When both are used, the resulting report may resemble a spreadsheet; your perception of whether this is good or bad should guide your use of dividers.

We find that using thin gray lines as dividers is more effective than using solid black lines. That way it's easier to differentiate the data on the report from the grid. There's a risk, though, that too many grid lines, especially in a complex list report, can actually obscure the data. Try to use as many lines and/or field borders as necessary to increase the readability of your report, but no more.

Report Aesthetics
In one way of thinking, the use of dividing lines is certainly an aesthetic choice. But an argument could be made that the decision is not entirely subjective. The well-respected design expert Dr. Edward Tufte wrote in *The Visual Display of Quantitative Information* about the concept of data-ink ratio. Eliminating "chart junk," such as most borders, frames, and gridlines, gives the data room to breathe without sacrificing any readability or meaning.

Placing dividers into your report typically involves nothing more than drawing some lines on the layout. When adding a horizontal line between rows of data, we generally put it below the data as a baseline rather than above it. You can then add whatever effect you need under your column headers to set them apart from the first row of data.

Adding vertical dividers to a list report can be a bit tricky until you get the hang of it. The key is that your vertical lines need to be the same height as the height of the body part itself. If they're too small, you'll get a dotted-line effect. Use the Object Size palette to ensure an exact fit. The top of your vertical line should begin one pixel below the top of the body part. It usually looks better if there's some horizontal space between vertical lines and your data cells. If users are allowed to click into fields on the report, however, the field frames that appear may not look aesthetically pleasing. If your List view is truly acting as a report, you should turn off entry into all fields (using the Field Behavior dialog). That also means that your field frames will never be visible, which is a good thing. Your vertical lines can define the space between fields without interference from field frames. If users need to be able to click into fields, consider turning off the option Show Field Frames When a Record Is Active, in the Layout Setup dialog.

→ For more on the Layout Setup dialog, **see** "Creating and Managing Layouts," **p. 94**.

If you find that having horizontal lines between every row of your report makes the report look too cluttered, it's possible also to add horizontal lines that appear just, say, every fifth row. This effect is illustrated in Figure 10.5.

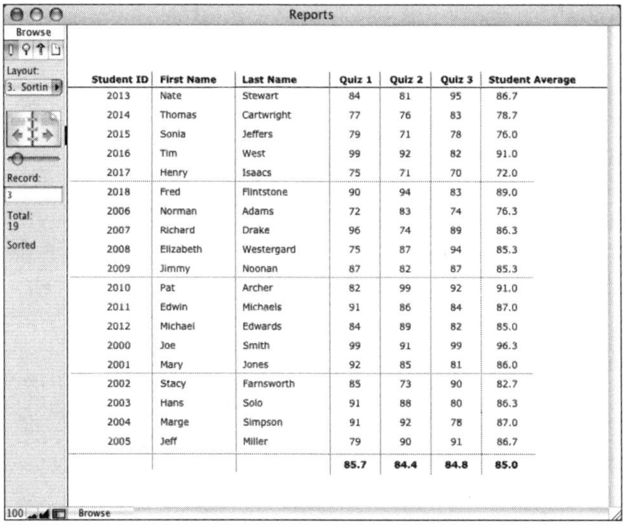

Figure 10.5
Having lines appear less often provides the visual guide necessary to follow a row across but doesn't overpower the data itself.

You need to add two new fields to your table to achieve this effect. The first is a global container field, which we'll call gLine. Place this field on a layout that you can use as a resource area (we generally refer to these as *developer* or *utility layouts*), and then draw a horizontal line on your layout. Copy the line to your Clipboard, switch back to Browse mode, and paste the line into the gLine field.

The other field you need is a calculation field (set to return a container result) with the following formula:

```
Case ( Mod ( Get (RecordNumber) ; 5 ) = 0 ; gLine )
```

In effect, this formula says that for any record that's a multiple of 5, be the contents of gLine, or else be nothing.

On your list layout, finally, place the calculation field as a long, thin object along the bottom of your body part. You need to reduce the field's font size to make the object thin. Also, go into the Graphic Format options for the field (by right-clicking it in Windows, Control-clicking it on Mac), and select the Reduce or Enlarge Image to Fit Frame option, uncheck the Maintain Original Proportions option, and set the alignment to be Left, Bottom.

NOTE

> You might be wondering whether you can just use Table view for your list reports; it provides a lot of the functionality discussed here (gridlines, sortable headers) for free. In general, though, Table view isn't suitable for reports, especially those that need any degree of polish to them. For one thing, the column labels must be the names of your fields; if you use any naming conventions, your field names may not be terribly user friendly. Another issue in some reports is that you can't have multiple lines of data per row or any objects that overlap one another.

SORTING BY COLUMNS

One of the easiest methods to use for sorting reports is to teach users how to make use of the built-in Sort dialog in FileMaker; however, an interface convention that's been widely adopted by software applications is that of clicking on the various column headers of a list report to sort the set of records by that column. It's relatively easy to add this functionality to your list reports in FileMaker Pro, but it does take some additional development work. There are several ways you can go about this task; they're all essentially variations on the same basic theme, so we present a relatively vanilla method that can be elaborated on as a solution warrants or a developer prefers.

NOTE

> Another easy way to sort a set of records is to (Control-click) [right-click] on any field and choose one of the three sort options. You don't need to know the name of the field or fret about finding it in a long list of available fields.

NOTE

> The Sort dialog in FileMaker 8 has been enhanced to present to users only those fields that are present on a given layout. Although the interface convention we're describing is still important and commonly preferred, FileMaker 8's field list filtering has significantly improved the ease with which users can sort.

The two components of a sortable column header routine are a script (which does the actual sorting) and a graphic indicator to let the user know by which column the list is sorted. You can use whatever graphic indicator you want for this purpose. One of the simplest is a special background color, but you can also use iconic indicators if you prefer.

Figure 10.6 shows an example of what a list layout might look like after sortable column headers have been implemented. In the example, the set of records has been sorted by the values in the Quiz1 field, and the fourth column header is highlighted with a darker color.

TIP

> An alternative to indicating the sort column graphically is to use text formatting functions to change the appearance of the column labels. It's quite similar to the approach discussed here, except that you would use calculated text fields rather than calculated container fields.

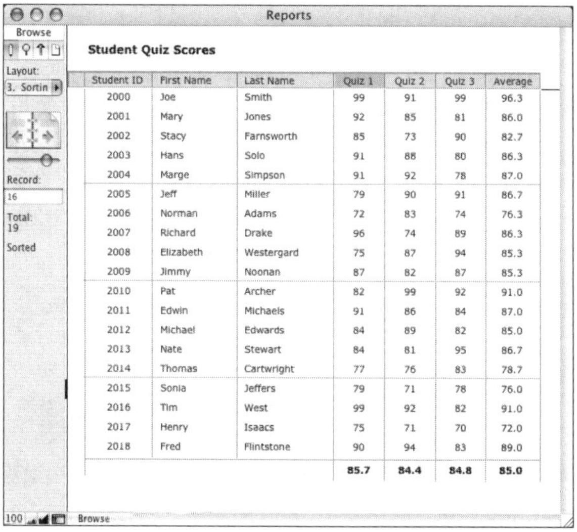

Student ID	First Name	Last Name	Quiz 1	Quiz 2	Quiz 3	Average
2000	Joe	Smith	99	91	99	96.3
2001	Mary	Jones	92	85	81	86.0
2002	Stacy	Farnsworth	85	73	90	82.7
2003	Hans	Solo	91	88	80	86.3
2004	Marge	Simpson	91	92	78	87.0
2005	Jeff	Miller	79	90	91	86.7
2006	Norman	Adams	72	83	74	76.3
2007	Richard	Drake	96	74	89	86.3
2008	Elizabeth	Westergard	75	87	94	85.3
2009	Jimmy	Noonan	87	82	87	85.3
2010	Pat	Archer	82	99	92	91.0
2011	Edwin	Michaels	91	86	84	87.0
2012	Michael	Edwards	84	89	82	85.0
2013	Nate	Stewart	84	81	95	86.7
2014	Thomas	Cartwright	77	76	83	78.7
2015	Sonia	Jeffers	79	71	78	76.0
2016	Tim	West	99	92	82	91.0
2017	Henry	Isaacs	75	71	70	72.0
2018	Fred	Flintstone	90	94	83	89.0
			85.7	**84.4**	**84.8**	**85.0**

Figure 10.6
Users can re-sort this list report any way they want by clicking on the column headers.

Several fields need to be added to your database to make the graphic indicators for this routine. These fields can be added to whatever table you're working with (here, Student), but it's arguably better to place these new fields into a separate resources table. This allows them to be reused in other places, and it also helps keep your data tables free of clutter. In this example, the utility table is called globals.

The following fields need to be created in the globals table:

```
gHighlight - Container - Global

Highlight_Quiz1 - Global Calculation - Case ($$columnSort = "Quiz1" ; gHighlight)

Highlight_Quiz2 - Global Calculation - Case ($$columnSort = "Quiz2" ; gHighlight)

Highlight_Quiz3 - Global Calculation - Case ($$columnSort = "Quiz3" ; gHighlight)

Highlight_Average - Global Calculation - Case ($$columnSort = "Average" ;
➥gHighlight)
```

```
Highlight_FirstName - Global Calculation - Case ($$columnSort = "FirstName" ;
➥gHighlight)

Highlight_LastName - Global Calculation - Case ($$columnSort = "LastName" ;
➥gHighlight)

Highlight_StudentID - Global Calculation - Case ($$columnSort = "StudentID" ;
➥gHighlight)
```

Notice that all the calculation fields have been set to use global storage. This is so that they can be used on any layout, even those attached to unrelated tables. They should also be set to return a container result. After the variable $$columnSort has been set to the name of a field from the quiz score report (this happens in the script shown in Listing 10.1), one of the seven calculations will resolve to the contents of gHighlight; the other six will be empty.

Note also that we've opted in this example to use separate fields for our various functions. You can make this approach a bit more elegant by using repeating fields (and thus reducing the elements you'd be using); for an example of this, see the following discussion.

After these fields have been defined, you need to put a swatch of color into the gHighlight field. Switch to Layout mode and draw a colored rectangle. Copy it to your Clipboard, return to Browse mode, and paste it into the gHighlight field.

There's still a little layout work to be done on the report itself:

1. Position a single gray rectangle behind all the column labels.
2. Place horizontal lines on top of the gray bar as necessary to segment the header row.
3. On top of the gray bar (but under the column labels), place the seven Highlight calculation fields from the globals table. Each should be sized to fit its particular label.
4. Define each to be a button that calls a script called List Report-Sort (which is shown in Listing 10.1; you need to create the script before defining the headers as buttons).

Although all seven buttons call the same script, each passes that script a unique parameter. In this example, the parameters are simply the names of the fields themselves. That is, clicking on the Quiz 1 header sends the parameter Quiz1, and clicking on the First Name field sends the parameter FirstName. You can also choose to pass a numeric code instead of the field name. This type of abstraction makes the buttons more reusable and means that you don't have to edit the parameter if your field names change or if you choose to use the same routine for multiple reports, but we think it's more intuitive when learning this routine to use the actual field names.

→ For more information about using script parameters, **see** "Script Parameters," **p. 437**.

LISTING 10.1   LIST REPORT-SORT SCRIPT

```
Set Variable [$$columnSort; Get(ScriptParameter)]
If [$$columnSort = "Quiz1"]
    Sort Records [Restore; No dialog]
Else If [$$columnSort = "Quiz2"]
    Sort Records [Restore; No dialog]
```

```
Else If [$$columnSort = "Quiz2"]
    Sort Records [Restore; No dialog]
Else If [$$columnSort = "Average"]
    Sort Records [Restore; No dialog]
Else If [$$columnSort = "FirstName"]
    Sort Records [Restore; No dialog]
Else If [$$columnSort = "LastName"]
    Sort Records [Restore; No dialog]
Else If [$$columnSort = "StudentID"]
    Sort Records [Restore; No dialog]
End If
```

Each of the Sort Records steps is defined to sort by the appropriate field. Also, because $$columnSort is set in the first step, the correct Highlight field will be turned on in the globals table; after the sort is performed, the column heading will therefore accurately reflect the sort order.

CAUTION

> If you have your list report displayed simultaneously in multiple windows, each report can be sorted differently, but the graphic sort indicator highlights the same field in all the windows. That is, if you were to click on the Last Name header in the active window, that window's found set would be sorted appropriately, but all open windows would have Last Name highlighted as the sort order, even when they may in fact be sorted differently.

USING REPEATING FIELDS FOR COLUMN HIGHLIGHTS

It is arguably inelegant to add a field to your database for each column by which you intend to sort. This approach adds clutter and incremental complexity and time to the development of your solution.

If you are comfortable working with repeating fields, you can collapse the logic we've presented into just four fields for your entire database. The overall technique is the same, but instead of creating a separate calculation field for each column highlight, we use the extend function to compare the name of the column label to the text in the gSort field:

```
gHighlight - Container - Global
gColumnLabels_r - Text, Repeating - Global
gSortPref - Text - Global
gColumnHighlight_r - Calculation, Container, Repeating - Global:
    Case ( Extend ( gSortPref ) = gColumnLabels_r ; Extend ( gHighlight ); "" )
```

Set the field gColumnHighlight_r to be a calculation field that returns a container result and has an equal number of repetitions to the gColumnLabels_r field.

You should then enter the names of your columns into the gColumnLabels_r field and use those same names as script parameters attached to your sort script.

FileMaker will then compare the repeating field labels to the gSortPref contents and apply a highlight to the repeating highlight field as appropriate. If the third repetition of the gColumnLabels_r field contains Last Name and $$gSortPref contains Last Name, the third repetition of gColumnHighlight_r will resolve to hold the contents of the gHighlight container field.

You then should place copies of your gColumnHighlight_r field in the header of your report and use the Field/Control Setup dialog to show only the appropriate repetition. For example, the third column of the report shown in Figure 10.6 (Last Name) would be set to show repetition 3 through 3. The fourth column (Quiz 1) would use repetition 4 through 4.

Notice that we opted to use a global field instead of a variable to store the user's sort preference. The Extend function works only with fields. If we were to use a variable, this process would work fine for the first value in the repetition, but not for any of the others.

ADDING ASCENDING/DESCENDING LOGIC FOR COLUMN SORTING

You can easily extend this example on your own to allow for both ascending and descending sorts. To do so, you need another variable (or field in the globals table) to indicate the direction of the sort. Then add more conditional statements to the script so that a combination of field name and direction determines how to sort the records. Finally, alter the Highlight calculations in the globals table so that they display different images for ascending and descending sorts (perhaps triangles pointing up or down). You can either create a separate global container field to house the descending image, or simply turn gHighlight into a repeating field and have a conditional statement in the calculation resolve to the appropriate repetition. As an example, the definition for Highlight might end up as the following:

```
Case (gSortField = "Quiz1" Case ( $$sortDirection = "Ascending" ; gHighLight[1] ;
➡ gHighlight[2] )
```

Alternatively, if you prefer to use the repeating field technique described previously, your gColumnHighlight_r field might look like this:

```
Case ( Extend ( gSortField ) = gColumnLabels_r ; Extend ( gHighlight ); "" )
```

Finally, because the sort order and the column images are all based on global values, this routine is multiuser friendly. Two different users can be viewing the same report but have it sorted differently.

GO TO DETAIL

No matter whether the set of records displayed in your list report is the result of an ad hoc find by a user or a canned report routine, you'll probably want to enable users to see additional details for a particular record. Typically, if you allow users to enter into fields in the list report, you have a discrete button at the beginning or end of the row that a user can click on to get to a detail view. If you don't allow data entry, it's common to let a user click anywhere on the row to be taken to a detail screen, or perhaps to format the primary bit of information to look like a blue underlined hyperlink. To make the entire row a clickable button, place a long transparent rectangle (to which you attach a navigation script) on top of the row. It should be the same height as the body itself so that there aren't any dead spaces between rows.

You have a few choices about how to display the detail record. The easiest thing to do is have the script navigate to a form view data-entry layout. Another option to consider is to have the detail record pop up in its own window. This enables users to go back and forth more easily between detail and list layouts.

→ For more on scripting techniques like this, **see** "Window Management Techniques," **p. 455**.

SUMMARIZED REPORTS

Subsummary reports are perhaps the most useful of all the reporting techniques in FileMaker Pro. It takes but little effort to extend a list report into a summary report, but the additional amount of information subsummary reports can convey is significant. After you become comfortable with the basic techniques for creating subsummary reports, you'll find that they form an important part of your reporting repertoire.

As a good place to start thinking about subsummary reports, consider the sample data set in Table 10.1.

TABLE 10.1   STUDENT DEMOGRAPHIC DATA

Gender	Name
Male	Erlend
Female	Eleanor
Male	Kai
Male	Nate
Female	Rowena

If this data set were to be presented in FileMaker Pro as a subsummary report, it might be structured something like the following:

> Female
> > Eleanor
> >
> > Rowena
>
> Male
> > Erlend
> >
> > Kai
> >
> > Nate

You can easily see that the difference in the subsummary version is that the data has been grouped by gender. The heading for each particular group of data appears only once instead of redundantly on each record of the list.

USING A BREAK FIELD

In this example, the Gender field is acting as the break field. Understanding break fields is crucial for understanding subsummary reports. The *break field* is the column of data that determines what records appear with what grouping of information. The number of unique entries in the break field for the current found set of data (here, two: Male and Female) determines the number of groupings, or subsummaries, that will be present on the report.

The purpose of a break field is to segment your data into useful subdivisions. As such, break fields are almost always categorical (rather than continuous) data elements. As an example, in a billing system you probably wouldn't choose to use an invoice total or invoice date field as a break field, but you might use an invoice type, invoice status, or invoice month field. The main purpose of subsummary reports is to enable you to roll up data to a less granular level so that you see larger trends in your data that may be obfuscated when looking at simple lists. The break field defines how those larger trends will be manifested on your report. Thus, it makes no sense to use a field with unique values (that is, a primary key) as a break field because no grouping of records by common values could possibly take place in such a situation.

→ For more detail about when you might choose to use a unique field as a break field, **see** "Subsummary Reports with No Body Part," **p. 296**.

NOTE

> Break fields can be text, number, time, date, or timestamp fields, or a calculation that returns one of these data types. Fields with global storage should not be used as break fields because they provide no categorization of the data.

CREATING A SUBSUMMARY REPORT

The physical creation of a subsummary report is quite similar to the creation of a simple list report. The Layout Wizard, in fact, has an option within the Columnar List/Report type to make your list a report with grouped data. For our purposes here, we discuss how to turn a list report into a subsummary report. You can explore the wizard's capabilities on your own.

→ For more on the Layout Wizard, **see** "Creating a New Layout," **p. 95**.

Earlier in the chapter, we developed a Student Quiz Scores list report. Now that example will be extended into a subsummary report. Assume that each of the students has been assigned to a teacher (Donovan, Ferris, or Young); the present goal is to produce a subsummary report of the scores by teacher. Figure 10.7 shows the data from which the report will be generated (as a simple list).

The first step in turning this into a subsummary report is to add a new part to the layout. It's possible to do this simply by clicking on the Part tool in the Status Area (in Layout mode, of course) and dragging a new part into existence. We prefer, however, to use the Part Setup dialog (select Layouts, Part Setup) to create new parts.

→ For a discussion of why it's better to use the Part Setup dialog than to drag from the Status Area, **see** "Working with Parts," **p. 103**.

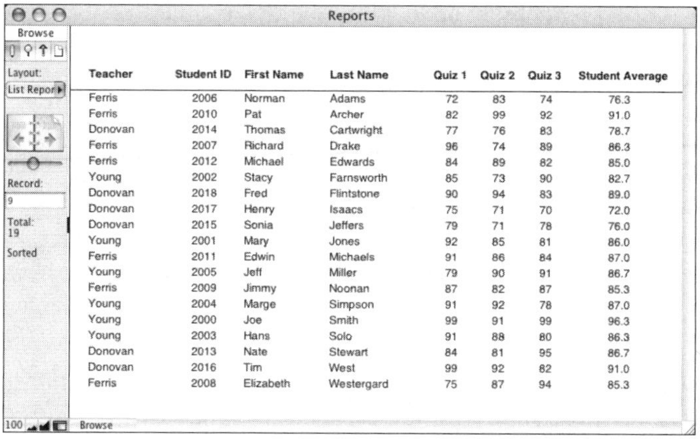

Figure 10.7
Anytime data can be grouped according to a common element, you have the potential for a subsummary report.

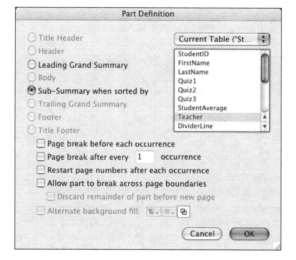

Teacher	Student ID	First Name	Last Name	Quiz 1	Quiz 2	Quiz 3	Student Average
Ferris	2006	Norman	Adams	72	83	74	76.3
Ferris	2010	Pat	Archer	82	99	92	91.0
Donovan	2014	Thomas	Cartwright	77	76	83	78.7
Ferris	2007	Richard	Drake	96	74	89	86.3
Ferris	2012	Michael	Edwards	84	89	82	85.0
Young	2002	Stacy	Farnsworth	85	73	90	82.7
Donovan	2018	Fred	Flintstone	90	94	83	89.0
Donovan	2017	Henry	Isaacs	75	71	70	72.0
Donovan	2015	Sonia	Jeffers	79	71	78	76.0
Young	2001	Mary	Jones	92	85	81	86.0
Ferris	2011	Edwin	Michaels	91	86	84	87.0
Young	2005	Jeff	Miller	79	90	91	86.7
Ferris	2009	Jimmy	Noonan	87	82	87	85.3
Young	2004	Marge	Simpson	91	92	78	87.0
Young	2000	Joe	Smith	99	91	99	96.3
Young	2003	Hans	Solo	91	88	80	86.3
Donovan	2013	Nate	Stewart	84	81	95	86.7
Donovan	2016	Tim	West	99	92	82	91.0
Ferris	2008	Elizabeth	Westergard	75	87	94	85.3

When you add a subsummary part to a layout, you must specify what break field should be represented by that part. In this example, shown in Figure 10.8, the Teacher field has been selected as the break field.

Figure 10.8
The only time you'll be able to select from the field list in the right side of this dialog is when you choose the Sub-Summary When Sorted By option.

Subsummary parts can be placed either above or below the body part. The body part presents the most granular individual rows in your report and contains data from each record in your found set. You can change the order of parts from the Part Setup dialog. Place a summary part above the body if you want it to act as a header for the data set; place it below if you want summary information about a subset of records to appear below the data set. You can (and indeed often will) place both a leading and a trailing subsummary part on a layout.

After you've added a subsummary part to the layout, you next place fields, texts, and/or graphic elements in the part. Any objects you place in the subsummary part appear on your report once for each group of data.

As discussed in Chapter 2, "Using FileMaker Pro," subsummary parts appear only if the user has sorted by the part's break field, and only if the user is in Preview mode. This is an important point: Each subsummary part will appear in Preview mode only if the user's database sort order includes the controlling break field in question. (It doesn't matter how it's sorted—ascending, descending, or by the contents of a value list.) By controlling the sort order of your found set, you can make subsummary elements appear and disappear as needed.

One of the implications of needing to be in Preview mode is that the user can't directly interact with the report in any way; buttons aren't functional in Preview mode. Users can, however, still run scripts from the Script menu (or a custom menu).

You will typically place the break field itself in the subsummary part, but this isn't required. Any other fields you place in the subsummary part are generally summary fields; if they are not, they will display data from the first record in the applicable set. Figure 10.9 shows what the new Quiz Scores by Teacher report looks like in Layout mode; the Teacher field and a horizontal line have been placed in the subsummary part. Notice also that the Teacher field has been removed from the body part because it would be redundant.

Figure 10.9
A subsummary part is used to display data relating to a set of records.

In Layout mode, the part labels can appear either as they do in Figure 10.9—as horizontal blurbs at the lower-left corner of the part—or as rotated text alongside the part. Labels are easier to read as horizontal text, but they tend to get in the way; we usually leave them alongside the parts. You can toggle between the two settings either by clicking on the part label orientation button (the fifth button in from the left at the bottom of your window) or by (⌘-clicking) [Ctrl+clicking] on any of the part labels themselves.

If you ever have problems with getting a subsummary report to work correctly, the first thing you should check is that you have the data sorted by the same field(s) you're summarizing by and that you're in Preview mode.

Figure 10.10 shows the completed (for now) subsummary report. Comparing this to Figure 10.7, you can see how simply grouping data together according to a common data element makes it much easier to read.

Figure 10.10
This subsummary report groups records together based on the contents of the Teacher field.

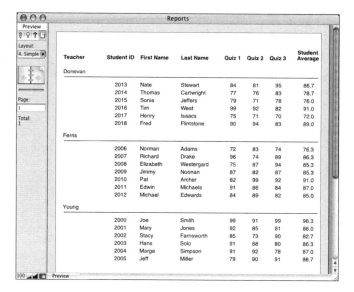

After you have a good grasp of the concepts at work in a basic subsummary report (like the one presented in this section), you can extend them in various ways to produce even more interesting and/or meaningful reports.

 If you are experiencing performance issues when generating subsummary reports, see "Slow Generation of Subsummary Reports" in the "Troubleshooting" section at the end of this chapter.

USING SUMMARY FIELDS IN SUBSUMMARY REPORTS

Earlier in this chapter, we discussed how you could add summary fields to a leading or trailing grand summary part to enhance a basic list report. Summary fields, not surprisingly, are also quite appropriate for use in subsummary reports.

A summary field placed in a subsummary part generates aggregate results for each group of data presented in the report. You need to do nothing in terms of field definitions to make it work this way. After you've defined a summary field, you can place it in any subsummary part and it will be intelligent enough to act on the correct group of records.

In the sample file we've been discussing, for instance, the summary field Average_Quiz1 is defined to be the average of the Quiz1 field across some set of records. When this field is placed in a trailing grand summary, it displays the average of that field across the entire current found set. When it's placed in a subsummary (by teacher) part, it displays the average across each teacher's set of students. In Figure 10.11, a trailing subsummary by teacher and a trailing grand summary part have been added to the layout shown previously in Figure

10.9. The same four summary fields appear in both parts. The report generated by this layout is shown in Figure 10.12.

Figure 10.11
Summary fields placed in a subsummary part calculate aggregate results for each group of data presented in the report.

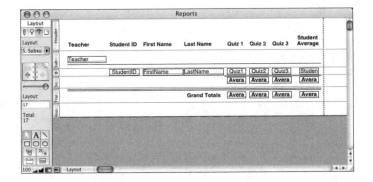

Figure 10.12
The leading and trailing subsummary parts can be thought of as providing a header and footer for each group of data presented in the report.

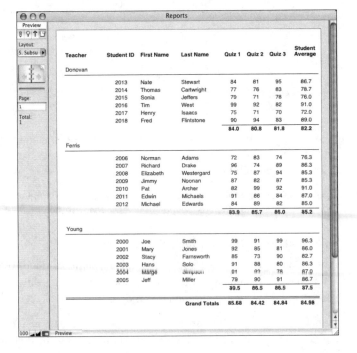

If another subsummary report were built that summarized on, say, students' genders or favorite pizza toppings, the same summary fields could be used in that report. Summary fields are thus quite versatile and powerful. You'll find that after you've developed one subsummary report it's quite easy to duplicate the layout and change the break field specified for the summary part(s), thereby creating an entirely new and different report. For example, the layouts needed to generate Quiz Scores by Teacher, Quiz Scores by Gender, and Quiz Scores by Favorite Pizza Topping would be nearly identical to each other; you wouldn't need to modify the definitions of the summary fields in any way.

Note that if you wanted, you could add all three subsummary parts to a single report and, depending on how your sort order was set, use one layout to present multiple views of your data. This is often an economical way to extend the reporting capabilities of your databases.

CAUTION

> If you ever put a summary field into the body part on a layout, it displays, for every record, the aggregated result for the entire found set.

CALCULATIONS INVOLVING SUMMARY FIELDS

After you begin using summary fields on reports, you're likely to come across situations in which you need to perform some sort of calculation involving a summary field. For instance, in the Student Quiz database, imagine that Quiz 1 was a pretest for a unit and that Quiz 3 was a post-test for the same unit. You might want to find out the change in scores from the pretest to the post-test.

For an individual student, you could generate this by simply adding a calculation field called something like ScoreIncrease, defined as `Quiz3 - Quiz1`. But what if you wanted to find out the average increase for each class? Can you do math with summary fields?

The answer to the last question is both yes and no. Summary fields can be, but should not be, used directly in calculation formulas. There's nothing to prevent you from doing so, but it's usually nonsensical to do so. Inside a calculation formula, a summary field is evaluated as the aggregate result of the entire found set. Thus, if you were to define a field called Average_ScoreIncrease as `Average_Quiz3 - Average_Quiz1`, the result would be `-0.84` no matter what record you were viewing or in what layout part you placed the field. This formula doesn't properly generate subsummary values.

The solution to the problem is to use the `GetSummary` function. `GetSummary` takes two parameters: a summary field and a break field. When the current found set is sorted by the break field, this function returns the same value that would appear if the summary field were used in a subsummary layout part (based on the same break field, of course). If the found set is *not* sorted by the break field, the function returns the value of the summary field over the entire found set, which the astute reader may recall is the same value returned by simply putting a summary field in a calculation without the `GetSummary` function.

In the current situation, to produce a summary ScoreIncrease at the teacher level, the following calculation (called Average_ScoreIncrease_Teacher) would be necessary:

```
GetSummary (Average_Quiz3 ; Teacher) - GetSummary (Average_Quiz1 ; Teacher)
```

This field could then be placed in the trailing subsummary part to display the results for each teacher.

The fact that you must name a break field explicitly means that calculations involving summary fields aren't as reusable as summary fields themselves. If you were making another report showing quiz scores by gender, you would need a new calculation field called Average_ScoreIncrease_Gender that specified Gender as the break field instead of Teacher.

Similarly, for use in a trailing grand summary, you'd need yet another version of the formula that didn't use GetSummary at all.

If this lack of reusability is a problem for you, there actually is a way around the break field problem. The solution is to make a new field—a global text field—that you set (either manually or via script) to be the name of the break field that you need. Then you can dynamically assemble an appropriate GetSummary function and use the Evaluate function to return the proper value. Using this technique in the present example, you would just define a single Average_ScoreIncrease field with the following formula:

```
Evaluate ( "GetSummary(Average_Quiz3; " & gSortValue & ")") -
➥Evaluate ( "GetSummary(Average_Quiz1; " & gSortValue & ")")
```

Although the purpose of using a GetSummary function is to produce a value appropriate for display in a subsummary part, the values also display properly when placed in a body part. That is, each of the records of the subgroup knows the aggregate value for its particular set. This is distinctly different from the result of simply placing a summary field into a body part, in which case the value displayed represents an aggregation of the entire found set.

SUMMARIZING ON MULTIPLE CRITERIA

All the examples thus far in this chapter have had a single summary criterion. It's but a small additional effort to produce a report that summarizes on multiple criteria. In fact, there's no practical limit to the number of subsummary parts you can add to a layout, except perhaps your ability to make sense of the results.

Summarizing based on multiple criteria is simply another way of categorizing a set of data. In the examples you've seen here, the student quiz scores have been grouped by teacher—a single criterion. What if within each teacher's group of students, you wanted to subcategorize by gender?

To accomplish this task, you would add another summary part to your report layout. The subsummary part by gender would be positioned between the subsummary by teacher and the body. If you wanted trailing summary information as well, a second subsummary by gender would be placed between the body and the trailing summary by teacher. Figure 10.13 shows what such a layout would look like.

Figure 10.13
To summarize on multiple criteria, create additional subsummary parts on your layout.

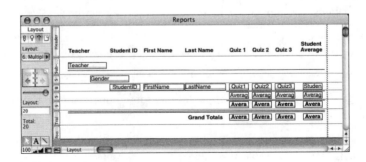

To properly generate this report, you would need to make sure that your found set was sorted first by teacher and then by gender. The finished report is shown in Figure 10.14. If it were sorted by only one of those fields, you would end up with a single-criterion subsummary report; the other part would not be displayed on the report. This means that a single layout can generate several different reports, if just the sort criterion is changed.

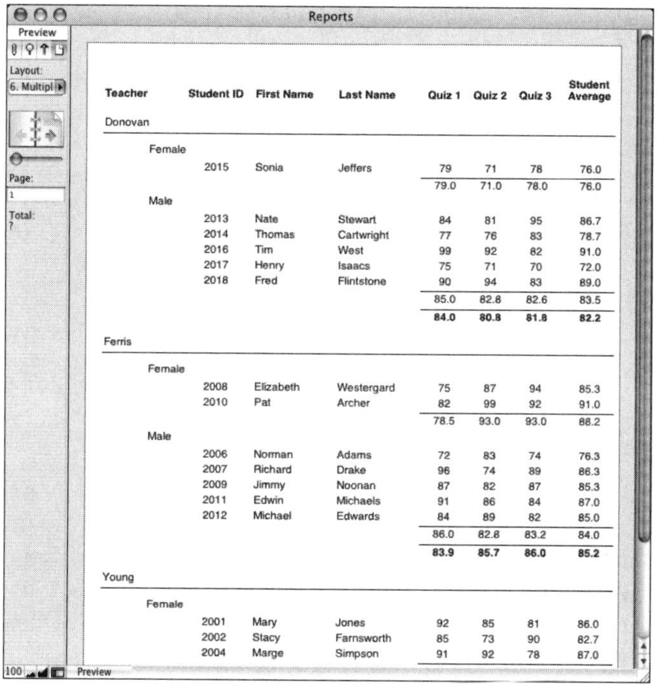

Teacher		Student ID	First Name	Last Name	Quiz 1	Quiz 2	Quiz 3	Student Average
Donovan								
	Female							
		2015	Sonia	Jeffers	79	71	78	76.0
					79.0	71.0	78.0	76.0
	Male							
		2013	Nate	Stewart	84	81	95	86.7
		2014	Thomas	Cartwright	77	76	83	78.7
		2016	Tim	West	99	92	82	91.0
		2017	Henry	Isaacs	75	71	70	72.0
		2018	Fred	Flintstone	90	94	83	89.0
					85.0	82.8	82.6	83.5
					84.0	**80.8**	**81.8**	**82.2**
Ferris								
	Female							
		2008	Elizabeth	Westergard	75	87	94	85.3
		2010	Pat	Archer	82	99	92	91.0
					78.5	93.0	93.0	88.2
	Male							
		2006	Norman	Adams	72	83	74	76.3
		2007	Richard	Drake	96	74	89	86.3
		2009	Jimmy	Noonan	87	82	87	85.3
		2011	Edwin	Michaels	91	86	84	87.0
		2012	Michael	Edwards	84	89	82	85.0
					86.0	82.8	83.2	84.0
					83.9	**85.7**	**86.0**	**85.2**
Young								
	Female							
		2001	Mary	Jones	92	85	81	86.0
		2002	Stacy	Farnsworth	85	73	90	82.7
		2004	Marge	Simpson	91	92	78	87.0

Figure 10.14
Typically, when you develop a subsummary report based on multiple criteria, you should use dividing lines and/or indentation to clarify the report structure.

TIP

If you were to sort the found set first by gender and then by teacher, your report might look a bit strange. That would have the effect of reversing the placement of the two subsummary parts; the data set would be separated first by gender, and then within each gender by teacher. If you've built your report with any sort of indentation (as in these examples), reversing the summary hierarchy would mean that the wrong headings would be indented.

REORDERING A REPORT BASED ON SUMMARY DATA

When you create a subsummary report, the groups are ordered according to how you have sorted the break field. For example, in the Quiz Scores by Teacher reports, the groups are ordered as Donovan, Ferris, Young. A descending sort would have resulted in the groups being ordered as Young, Ferris, Donovan.

It's possible also to reorder the groups based on a summary field. To do this, when you sort the found set, click one of the sort criteria and then select the Reorder Based on Summary Field option. Figure 10.15 shows the Sort Records dialog with this option specified.

Figure 10.15
An option in the Sort Records dialog in FileMaker 8 is the capability to reorder the set based on a summary field. This enables you to generate ranking reports at a group level.

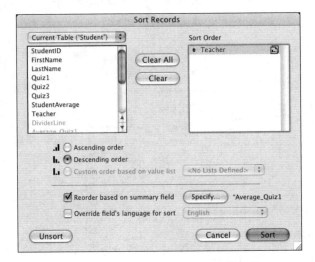

The typical reason you would want to reorder your report based on a summary value is to produce group-level ranking reports. As an example, if the Quiz Scores by Teacher report used the sort shown in Figure 10.15, in which the Teacher sort criteria is reordered by the value of Average_Quiz1, the results would be the report shown in Figure 10.16. Notice that Young is the first group; her student average on Quiz 1 was 89.5. Donovan is next with a student average of 84.0, followed by Ferris at 83.9.

If you have a subsummary report with multiple summary levels, you can reorder the subgroups at any level of the report. When you do this, keep in mind that you can (and probably will) end up with a situation in which the subgroups are ordered differently within the groups. That is, if you did a secondary sort by gender (reordered by one of the summary fields) on the data in Figure 10.16, you would find that sometimes Male appeared before Female and that other times Female appeared first; each group's subgroups are ordered independently.

SUBSUMMARY REPORTS WITH NO BODY PART

In a typical subsummary report, a subsummary part serves to organize and/or present summary data about a subgroup of data that is detailed on the report. All the subsummary reports presented so far in this chapter, in fact, fit this structure.

But there's no reason why you can't remove the body part from your report, thereby just presenting some sort of listing of the groups themselves. Especially if your groups consist of large recordsets, simply presenting the aggregated groups may result in a report that's much more meaningful. If a more detailed view of things is required, you can either provide it in a different report or simply allow users to perform ad hoc searches.

Figure 10.16
Reordering the set by a summary field produces a group-level ranking report.

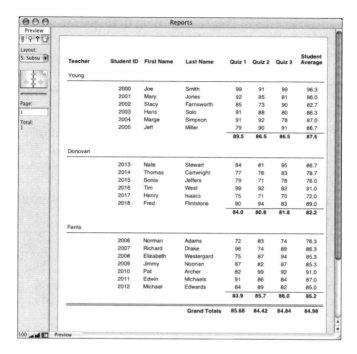

TIP

> You can also allow users to toggle the body part on and off by redefining it as a subsummary using the (unique) primary key as a break field. That way, when the found set is sorted by the primary key, the faux body part is visible. When the found set is sorted by just the break field, it disappears. Given that the break field contains unique values, no summary function will be performed (the data won't collapse into groups), but you can control whether the part appears or disappears as you want.

Figure 10.17 shows a quiz scores report in which the body part has been removed. The absence of a body part means that it's not necessary to have both a leading a and trailing subsummary part; nothing would appear in between them, so it's not necessary. Similarly, the only columns of the report are the break field (Teacher) and four summary fields. It doesn't make any sense to have fields like FirstName or StudentID because those aren't representative of an entire group of records.

The subsummary techniques presented in this chapter represent just about everything you can do with a subsummary report. After you fully learn these techniques, you can pick and choose which ones you need to use to produce a given report. You'll also find that simply knowing the tools at your disposal will influence the way you design reports. The more you can design reports that work within the constraints of the tools, the easier it will be to generate those reports.

Figure 10.17
Without a body part, a subsummary report becomes a group-level list report.

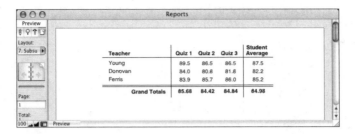

CHARTING IN FILEMAKER

FileMaker does not include any native charting capabilities; however, there are some excellent plug-ins on the market that very capably fill the void. We tend to use xmChart from X2max Software in our consulting practice, but Cleveland Consulting's CC Gantt Chart tool is a specialized application for scheduling, and oAzium Charts from Waves in Motion is an aging but well-regarded plug-in in the industry as well. Brian Dunning has created a tutorial file, Chart Maker Pro, which presents a series of techniques within FileMaker that don't make use of a plug-in to produce charts. We encourage you to visit FileMaker's website to look for the latest tools to extend your reporting capabilities.

In addition to xmChart, you can merge FileMaker data with an Excel workbook and drive charting in that manner using ODBC queries.

DELIVERING REPORTS

Reports are typically one of the most important things a database solution will produce. Workflows will often include using a database for data entry and then running a routine of some sort to have that data synthesized and presented as output in the form of a report. After a report has been generated (usually onscreen in Preview mode), users almost always want to take an additional step and deliver that report to some other medium.

Often, delivering a report is as simple as clicking a Print menu option; however, FileMaker 8 provides additional capabilities for distributing reports to various users.

SAVE/SEND AS PDF

 Available from the File menu is the option to Save/Send Records as PDF. For the FileMaker 8 family of products, FileMaker, Inc. offers the complete PDF API; the new creation features provide comprehensive control over PDFs generated from FileMaker (see Figure 10.18).

Just as with printing, users can opt to save to PDF a single record, a set of records, or a blank view of their current layout. The end result is a PDF file that can be viewed by anyone with the capability of opening PDF files—virtually everyone with a modern Windows or Mac computer.

Figure 10.18
From any layout in FileMaker, users can save PDF reports directly from the File menu.

Mac OS X includes the capability of saving print requests to PDF as well, but FileMaker's capabilities extend beyond those of the Mac OS, in addition to being fully cross-platform compatible and available on Windows as well. (Windows users would otherwise need to purchase and install a copy of Adobe Acrobat.) FileMaker offers complete access to all file options, as shown in Figure 10.19, and also provides access to the full range of PDF security features, as shown in Figure 10.20.

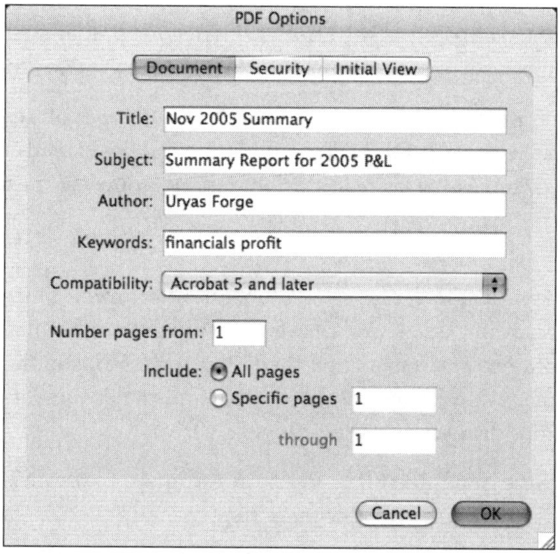

Figure 10.19
Document metadata for PDF files is useful for archival purposes; FileMaker offers access to the full range of PDF features in this regard.

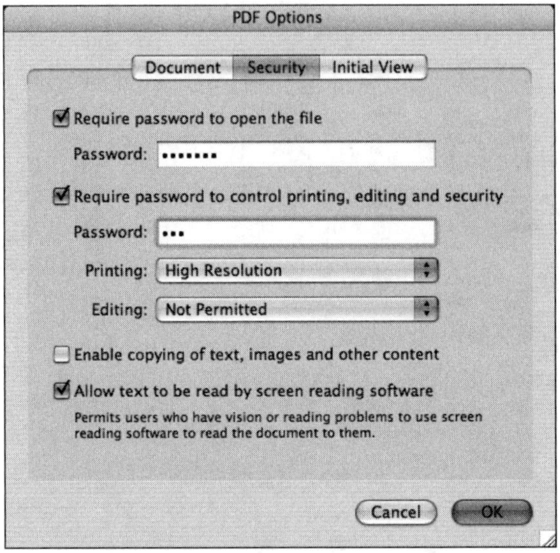

Figure 10.20
FileMaker 8 offers access to a wide range of PDF security features: Users can protect an entire document or choose from various more-specific options.

One of the most important things to note about this new functionality in FileMaker 8 is that PDF output is fully scriptable, via the script step `Save Records as PDF`. With this script step, a developer can automate the generation of PDF reports complete with metadata options, security, and other PDF features. Each document option, from its title to its password, can be programmatically controlled from a script.

Last but certainly not least, notice the Create Email with File as Attachment option at the bottom of Figure 10.18. When this choice is selected, FileMaker will create a PDF and automatically open a new email message with the PDF document as an attachment. This one-step process makes it simple to send documents directly from FileMaker.

Saving to PDF is a straightforward act and doesn't warrant pages of explanation; however, it is one of the key new features in FileMaker 8 and dramatically extends the ease with which developers can deliver reports to users in this ubiquitous, convenient package.

SAVE/SEND AS EXCEL

Just as FileMaker allows you to export data, users can now save and email Excel documents directly from the File menu. Users won't have to manipulate export dialogs; they will simply get whatever data columns are available on their current layout, and the resultant file will be a native Excel document. No formatting is available, but the document properties can be set from the Excel Options dialog, as shown in Figure 10.21.

Notice that as with Save/Send Record as PDF, users can opt to create a new email message with the resultant file attached in a single, easy step.

Likewise, as with the `Save as PDF` script step, developers can automate the creation of Excel documents by the `Save As Excel` script step.

Figure 10.21
Saving documents to Excel directly can save multiple steps and delivers information in a form that is often more familiar to other constituents in an organization.

SEND MAIL

FileMaker has had the capability to send email via the Send Mail script step for many years. New to FileMaker 8 is the capability for users to do so directly from the File menu without having to do any scripting or development work.

Although it's perhaps tangential to the topic of reporting in the traditional sense of getting a printed synthesis of information on an 8 1/2 × 11 sheet of paper, consider that email is simply another means of output.

→ For a discussion of how to work with the Send Mail dialog, **see** Chapter 2, "Using FileMaker Pro," **p. 29**.

Note that the Send Mail dialog allows users to pull calculated values from a database and can send multiple emails—one per record in the found set—in a batch process.

The Send Mail script step has been extended in an identical manner. It allows developers to automate batch email processes and can dynamically generate recipient addresses, subject lines, email body text, and more from the records in a given database.

→ To learn more about scripting routines, **see** "Getting Started with Scripting," **p. 247** and "Advanced Scripting Techniques," **p. 435**.

TROUBLESHOOTING

PRINTED REPORTS SHOW ONLY A SINGLE RECORD

Sometimes, my printed reports contain only the first record of data. Why is that?

Chances are that your print settings are configured to print the current record rather than the current found count. When printing from a List view, be sure to select the Records Being Browsed option. This configuration can be specified within a script, so be sure to set your print scripts to use this configuration as well.

SLOW GENERATION OF SUBSUMMARY REPORTS

I have built several subsummary reports, but many of them take quite a while to generate. Is there anything I can do to speed them up?

This is a common source of performance issues many developers face. Various factors can influence the time it takes to generate a subsummary report. The most important of these is the size of the found set. A subsummary report over a found set of 50,000 records takes considerably longer to generate than one with 100 records. Another factor is the amount of summarization the report performs: A report with one summary field will generate faster than one with a dozen.

Consider what a subsummary report is doing in combination with summary fields: It is synthesizing data across multiple records dynamically. In other words, it is calculating up-to-date information based on your found set, sort criteria, and so on. This information is difficult to "pre-bake" (by having it be already calculated or indexed), so FileMaker (and other database technologies) has to generate this information on demand.

Another potential bottleneck is the complexity of the summarization. Summary fields that operate on plain number fields generally perform better than summary fields that operate on calculations that return number results. This is especially true if the calculations contain complex logic or aggregate functions that operate on large recordsets. It's even more true if any of the calculations is unstored—a performance drain you should strive to avoid if at all possible.

Unfortunately there's no magic fix here. Subsummary report performance depends entirely on how a given database is structured, on the needs of the organization it serves, and on the hardware and network on which it is deployed. General rules of thumb are to avoid using unindexed fields for sorting and finding, and to keep the number of summary type fields to a required minimum.

Beyond that, there are a few things you might try to improve the performance of subsummary reports by building routines that rely less on dynamic, on-demand information. The first is to automate the reports to run during the middle of the night; you can view the results as a PDF in the morning. Another option is to pre-summarize some of the data. This might involve running a script to set plain number fields to the result of complex calculations. Or you might create utility tables where you can store summarized data. For instance, every month you might run a month-end closing routine that posts monthly totals for each product or salesperson to a utility table. Then, rather than having summary reports based on granular data, you can run reports against the pre-summarized data.

FILEMAKER EXTRA: INCORPORATING REPORTS INTO THE WORKFLOW

The focus of this chapter has been on the creation of list and subsummary report layouts. There's a bit more to creating useful reports, however, than merely setting up nice-looking layouts: You have to incorporate reports into the user workflow, controlling how a user both accesses and exits a report. The methods you choose may vary from solution to solution, and your choice is a function of both what the system does and the particular audience. If the users are proficient with FileMaker, they may be comfortable manually finding and sorting a set of records and navigating to the appropriate layout. More often, however, users benefit from your taking some time to set up some infrastructure to help them access the reports properly.

There are many ways you can go about building reports into the workflow of a solution. Following are some of the most common we've seen over the years:

- **Place buttons to run reports on relevant data-entry layouts**. For instance, on an Invoice Entry screen you might have buttons for creating an Invoice Aging report, and on a Contact entry layout there might be a Callback Report and a Contact Activity Report. Users typically are expected to find whatever data they want included in the report; the script simply goes to the correct layout, sorts, and previews, and then potentially returns the user to the original layout.

- **In your report scripts, use custom dialogs to give users certain choices about how the report will be generated**. For instance, a dialog may prompt users as to whether they want to produce a report for the current month's data or the previous month's.

- **You can create a centralized Report Menu layout that can be accessed from anyplace in your solution**. By centralizing your reports, you can avoid having to clutter data-entry layouts with report buttons. Also, you give your users one place to go anytime they want a report, rather than requiring that they memorize which reports can be generated from where. A centralized report menu works well when the report scripts run predetermined finds.

- **As a variation on the Report Menu concept, you can give users control over finding and sorting the data**. You can, for example, place global fields on a layout so that the user can enter a date range on which to search. The find criteria is usually specific to a certain report or group of reports, so you need to branch to the appropriate "finder" layout when a user makes a selection from the report menu.

- **A third variation on the Report Menu idea would be to literally create a Reports custom menu**. A custom menu of reports could offer contextual listings of available reports from a given area of your database, or it might simply offer all the reports available within your solution.

- **You can enable users to modify the title of a report or to add a secondary header of their own choice**. This typically is done with custom dialogs, but you can also incorporate this element into a report menu or layout dedicated to preparing records sets for reports.

After the report has been generated, you'll probably want to return users to wherever they were before running the report. Try to avoid a situation in which a user gets stranded on a report layout without any tools to get back to familiar territory.

You should also strive to have some consistency in how reports look and function in your system; this will make using them easier and more intuitive for your users. For instance, you might set up as a convention that reports are always (or never) previewed onscreen, and then users are prompted as to whether they want to print a report. Similarly, place layout elements such as the title, page number, and report date and time in consistent locations on your reports so that users don't have to hunt for them.

10

DEVELOPER TECHNIQUES

## CHAPTER 11

DEVELOPING FOR MULTIUSER DEPLOYMENT

In this chapter

DEVELOPING FOR MULTIPLE USERS

Some of the best, most lovingly developed FileMaker Pro systems are only ever used by a single person. A certain author's mother is a prime example: Her entire insurance sales practice is driven by a FileMaker Pro database. It is a mature system, built so that "someone's mom" can use it, and lives without any expectation of being extended to include other users.

Then there are the rest of the databases out there. FileMaker Pro enjoys a graceful growth curve from single-user applications to systems that support enterprise-level workgroups and operations of hundreds of users.

This graceful transition from single-user to multiuser thankfully means that issues to take into consideration when building multiuser systems are reasonably modest. Much of what you already know about building FileMaker Pro systems—regardless of your planned deployment—also applies directly to building a multiuser application.

We'll cover two primary topics: how the FileMaker engine handles multiple users, and development techniques you need to consider when building multiuser applications. As a third discussion, we also go into some depth about audit trails, given that they often are used to help ensure data integrity in systems used by larger organizations and are used specifically to track multiple-user scenarios.

We recommend that anyone intending to deploy a system to multiple users read this chapter. Some of the issues we discuss become necessary considerations only in systems that are getting heavy use from multiple users, but they're good to have in mind nonetheless.

→ This chapter is a good companion to Chapter 24, "Deploying and Extending FileMaker," **p. 755**.

→ To grasp the IT infrastructural logistics of hosting a FileMaker Pro solution, read Chapter 25, "FileMaker Server and Server Advanced," **p. 779**.

"SESSIONS" IN FILEMAKER PRO

FileMaker Pro is a client/server application (at least when files are being hosted by an individual user or by FileMaker Server). Each time someone using FileMaker Pro (a client) connects to FileMaker Server and opens an instance of the files hosted there, he creates a *session*.

In practical terms, this means that one of your users can be on layout #10 while you yourself are working with layout #2. You can run a script and nothing will necessarily happen on another user's computer; likewise, someone else can export data on her machine, while you're performing a find request in the very same database table on yours. You each have a separate connection to the database, with its own unique environment. While working with the same data, all your users can be performing separate, distinct tasks in your system. Each user can have a separate view of the database, with different active windows, active tables, or active found sets, among other things.

Generally, these individual user sessions don't interfere with each other at all; however, there are cases in which they can conflict—for example, when two users try to edit the same record at the same time. We will cover throughout this chapter various techniques for identifying and coping with such issues.

The one thing that *is* consistent across all user sessions is the actual data in the database. Changes you make to records you are editing are immediately visible to other users in the system, and vice versa. Our discussion of sessions pertains only to global fields and variables, window states, and layouts. Actual data is stored and displayed consistently for everyone.

Before approaching how to manage sessions and potential conflicts, it is important to understand what a session is and how FileMaker Pro manages multiple users. In FileMaker Pro, sessions are implicit and enjoy a stateful, persistent, always-on connection to the server. The system preserves and isolates each user experience in the FileMaker Pro client. Keep in mind that after the session is over (an individual user closes the database), all information about that session—what layout was in use, where windows were positioned, what the found set was—is discarded. The next time that user opens the database in question, it opens in its default state, with no preservation of how the user last left the system.

You might have heard the term *session* as applied to the Web. FileMaker Pro is quite different. On the Web, connections are stateless by default—they have no memory. The web server does not maintain a connection to a user; the effect of a persistent session is approximated by the explicit creation of an identifier for a given user when she logs in to a system. That identifier is then passed (and often stored/retrieved via a cookie) through all the page requests a person may make in a given time period. Web developers need to explicitly create the mechanics of a session to preserve a user's experience from page to page. Whenever you buy a book from Amazon, the developers there have no doubt labored to make sure that each page you visit tracks sensibly your use of the site—especially when it comes to the multipage shopping cart experience. FileMaker, by contrast, provides persistent database sessions with no additional effort by you, the developer.

SESSION-SPECIFIC ELEMENTS

FileMaker Pro's sessions maintain a consistent user experience until the application itself is closed. This experience includes your login account (unless you specifically log out and log back in), the position and number of windows you have open, which layouts you're on, your current found set, your current sort order, and portal scroll positions. On the development side of things, custom colors you've stored in the layout tools are, unfortunately, lost at the end of a session as well.

GLOBAL BEHAVIOR

Globals (fields specified as having global storage, as well as global script variables) are session-specific and require additional discussion. In a multiuser client session, they utilize and hold values unique to one specific user's session. This enables you as a developer to depend on globals storing different information for each user. A simple example is a displayed account name at the top of each layout set at the time of login.

→ For more details on global field storage, **see** "Storage and Indexing," **p. 86**.

At the start of a session, each global field is initialized to the last value it had in single-user mode. If you run in single-user mode only, this makes the global field value appear to persist across sessions, but it's misleading to infer that there are multiuser and single-user types of sessions. Storing information in global fields for single users is a handy way to leave things the way they were, but it also allows developers to create a default state for global fields.

Global fields are used for a range of functions in multiuser databases: They often hold images for navigation and user interface purposes and they sometimes hold session information such as the current date or the active, logged-in user. It makes sense, then, that they'd be specific to a given user's experience.

 If your global fields suddenly seem to be holding wrong data, refer to "Unpredictable Global Default Values" in the "Troubleshooting" section at the end of this chapter.

Global variables, on the other hand, do not have stored values from session to session in single or multiuser mode. As a developer you will need to explicitly initialize the variables you intend to have the system utilize, ideally at the beginning of each session.

→ For a complete discussion of script variables, **see** "Script Variables," **p. 448**.

USER ACCOUNTS AND SESSION DATA

One common use of global behavior in a multiuser environment is to set a global field with your currently logged-in account. This enables you to always have a central stored value that's easy to use in calculation formulas and scripts. One could argue that simply using the Get (AccountName) function wherever necessary would accomplish the same end, but there's an additional use for storing the current account name in a global: You can drive a relationship with it into a User table by using the account name as a unique match field.

NOTE

> Note that a global variable, as opposed to a global field, cannot drive a relationship. This difference can play a significant role in determining whether to store particular session data in a global field or a global variable.

This enables you to tie account information to data. You might want to do this if, for example, you need to store someone's real name, her preference to always start on a specific layout when the system opens, or (in a particularly abstract example) in what language she wants to use your database.

All these examples depend on your having done something with the information you store in a user table. It's useful to store someone's preference for a starting layout only if you then write the requisite script that uses this as a reference.

Another possibility lies with tracking database use. Although you might debate whether a database (or database administrator) should be looking over someone's shoulder, you could write routines that post records to a user log table whenever users log in, log out, or even when they perform certain scripted actions (delete records, create records, run an invoice report, and so on).

One more user-friendly option is to accommodate users simply by enabling them to specify where they prefer a window to be positioned and sized. All these various options can be enabled by storing information specific to a single person's session in global fields.

CONCURRENCY

You might have heard the term *concurrency* as it relates to databases. It refers to the logic and behavior of database systems when two (or more) users attempt to interact with the same information. A simple metaphor might be two people trying to use a phone book or dictionary at once—they're likely to trip over each other a bit. Every multiuser database platform has to address this issue.

Certainly it'd be easiest to simply restrict using the database to one user or function at a time, but clearly that's an unrealistic solution.

THE ACID TEST

To address issues of concurrency and transaction integrity, database engineers have developed what has come to be known as the *ACID test*. Database software needs to pass this test to completely manage concurrency issues. ACID stands for *atomicity*, *consistency*, *isolation*, and *durability*; these four terms describe the features and requirements for processing transactions in a database system. If a system does not meet these requirements, the integrity of the database—and its data—cannot be perfectly guaranteed.

In the context of databases, the term *transaction* relates to a single logical operation comprising one or more steps that results in data being posted to the system. Examples might include committing a new record to the database, performing a script that calculates summary information, or in real-world terms, completing the multiple steps of debiting one financial account and crediting another. The ACID test exists to ensure such transactions are reliable.

FileMaker Pro databases, unfortunately, do not fully meet ACID compliance, nor is it realistic to develop a solution in FileMaker that perfectly does. FileMaker Pro scripts can be interrupted (a machine crash or a force-quit of the application) and as such it is possible to leave a transaction half completed.

We're including this section not to point out a shortcoming of FileMaker, but rather to illustrate some important guidelines on how you should consider building solutions for critical business systems or large workgroups. It is possible to go a long way toward ACID compliance in a FileMaker Pro database—if it's properly engineered. It's also quite possible to build a FileMaker Pro database that leaves wide opportunity for data integrity problems to crop up (as with any other database tool).

As consultants, we're pragmatists. Often the craftsman in all of us yearns to build the world's most perfect system, but in reality there are trade-offs in complexity, time, and flexibility to consider. We use the guidelines that follow as just that—guidelines. By identifying the criticality of certain data and using sensible safeguards to ensure its integrity to the degree possible, we are able to cover all but the most extreme cases of database failures.

- **Atomicity**—Atomicity requires that transactions be completed either in their entirety or not at all. In other words, a logical routine (say, crediting one account and debiting another) cannot be left half done. In FileMaker Pro terms, data is either committed or not committed to your database, a script needs to reach its logical conclusion, and a

11

calculation function stores and indexes its results properly. Although a script can be interrupted, it is important to approach atomicity by writing scripts that conclude whatever routines they're designed for.

- **Consistency**—Consistency ensures that your database is left in a legal state at the beginning and end of any given transaction. This means that the transaction won't break any of the rules, or integrity constraints, of the system. This often can encompass business logic: An example might be that all financial credit transactions be positive numbers.

- **Isolation**—Transactions in mid-process are never exposed to other processes or users. In the credit/debit example, a user should never see a credit appear on one account before the debit has been posted. Likewise, an account balance report should not be allowed to run when a credit or debit is in the midst of being added.

- **Durability**—After a transaction has been performed and completed, the information resulting from that process needs to be persistent. It should be saved with the database, and if someone pulls that computer's plug, the information is then still present in the file.

ACID compliance is a goal of development to ensure data integrity. We encourage you, especially when writing scripts, to focus on delivering on these guidelines to an appropriate degree, especially in a multiuser environment.

Script Log

One technique we use for verifying processes and debugging is a *script log*. By building one, you better approach atomicity and are able to identify cases where it fails.

In large, complex solutions where transaction integrity is vital, it may be warranted to create a process that causes all scripts to write log records to a separate table (often in a separate file as well) when they start and again when they are successfully completed. It's possible to track other data as well: who initiated the script, on what layout the user was, which instance of a window was in use, timestamp data for start and end (for performance and troubleshooting purposes), and potentially any data the script manipulates. This is not to be confused with an audit trail, covered later in the chapter. Audit trails enable you to record all data transactions in a database. A script log is a means of confirming that your functional routines are completed properly.

By adding a script log to your system and periodically checking it for incomplete conclusions, you can identify cases where scripts fail and manually address such issues when necessary. By definition, if a script log start entry doesn't have a corresponding close entry, it failed ACID's atomicity test and possibly the consistency test as well.

TIP

> One final note on script logs: We encourage you to create a single flag in your database that, when turned off, disables all script logging in your system.

COMMIT VERSUS CREATE AND SERIAL IDS

In FileMaker 8, data is committed (saved) after a user exits the record, either by clicking outside a field or by performing a range of other actions such as running a script, changing modes, changing layouts, or pressing a "record-entry" key. (The default is the Enter key, but field behaviors can be changed to allow the Return or Tab keys as well.)

→ For more details on field behaviors, **see** "Field Behavior," **p. 120**.

It is possible to use the Records, Revert Records option to undo the creation of a record. Until a record has been committed, it exists in a temporary state, not yet visible to other users of the system. Relying on a transaction remaining unsaved until expressly committed helps ensure better ACID compliance. This is important to remember in a multiuser environment where you may be operating on assumptions established with prior versions of FileMaker. For example, if you're attempting to serially number certain records and two users create two records at the same time, it is possible that one will commit the record in an order different from that in which the records were initially created. It is also possible that a user will undo his or her changes with a Revert Record command and leave you with a gap in your serialization.

In the case of auto-entry serial values, FileMaker enables you to specify when the serial number is incremented—on creation or on commit. This enables you to control auto-enter serialization; however, it does not protect you from other assumptions. For example, if you're relying on GetSummary() calculation fields to keep track of an incremented total, remember that the calculations that control this are evaluated and displayed only after a record is committed.

RECORD LOCKING

Just as a record is not saved to your database until it is committed—maintaining an isolated state while you create new records—FileMaker does not allow editing of a record by more than one person at a time. In this way, FileMaker Pro meets the isolation test of ACID for posting data. Record locking exists to ensure that no two edits collide with each other (such as when multiple users attempt to edit the same record simultaneously).

After a user begins editing a record, FileMaker locks that record from other users and script processes, and (when not captured and suppressed by a script) presents users with an error message if they attempt to enter or change any data in that record.

It's possible to place your cursor in a field and still leave the record unlocked (safe for other users to enter data into the same record), but at the point at which you actively begin typing, that record essentially becomes yours until you either commit or revert it.

NOTE

> For those of you familiar with prior versions of FileMaker Pro, remember that those versions locked records as soon as a user clicked in a field. That behavior changed in FileMaker Pro 7.

Locking applies to related records in portals as well. If you are modifying a record in a portal row, that record's parent is also locked. This behavior occurs only when the related child record is edited via a portal or related field from the context of a parent record. If you are simply editing the child record on its own table-specific layout (within its own context), just that single child record is locked.

Also keep in mind that record locking applies only to editing. You can still find locked records, view reports with them included, change sort orders with locked records in your found set, and even export data. Only editing is protected.

If another user has a record locked and you get an error message, you can ask that user to release the record to you. The error dialog appears in Figure 11.1, along with a resultant message that user might see if you send one.

Figure 11.1
You see this message if you try to edit a record someone else is modifying. If need be, use the Send Message command to ask for control.

The one downside to record locking is that you cannot force a user out of a record remotely through FileMaker Pro. If someone begins editing a record and then decides to fly to Tahiti, you need to kick him off by using the Server Administration Tool, shut down the file, restart the server, or address the issue at the user's local computer.

 To help with multiuser account testing, refer to "Use Re-Login for Testing Access and Sessions" in the "Troubleshooting" section at the end of this chapter.

TRAPPING FOR RECORD LOCKING IN SCRIPTS

A subtle way your database might prove error prone is in always making the assumption in scripts that the routine in question has access to all the records in the current found set. Some of the records your script needs to work with may, in fact, be locked.

A script can explicitly open a record for editing with the Open Record/Request script step. After it has issued that script command, the record is reserved for that routine, and other users who try to edit the record get a record lock error until the script (or the user running the script) releases the record. Because any attempt to modify a record results in the same condition, explicitly using an Open Record/Request script step might not be technically necessary, but we find it helpful to turn to for clarity within scripts. The more important step is deliberately checking to see whether a given record is open for editing or if some other user (or routine) has it locked.

To capture the error that results in cases where either one's current privileges don't allow editing of the record in question or the record is locked by another user, we recommend testing first to see whether a record can be opened. If that doesn't work, deal with the result prior to attempting an edit. Use the `Open Record/Request` script step followed by a `Get(LastError)` check. Here's how it might look:

```
Set Error Capture [On]
Open Record/Request
Set Variable [$$error; Get (LastError)]
If[$$error <> 0]
    Show Custom Dialog ["Error"; fnErrorMessage ( "recordLock" )]
    // or write an error handler process here...
End If
//Execute your "real" script here...
//and don't forget to commit your record at the end.
```

Use a `Commit Record/Request` script step at the end of your script to release the record back into nonedit mode and unlock it for other users.

> **NOTE**
>
> Consider building error utility tables, or perhaps using custom functions, for error handling. This enables you to easily tailor error messages in a central, easy-to-edit location based on whatever value is held in `$$error`. The `Custom Dialog` step in the preceding code snippet references a custom function that presumably returns error handling text to the user.

Instead of checking simply for a nonzero error, you could also write a series of `If -> Else If` script steps checking for errors such as 301 (Record is in use by another user), 303 (Database schema is in use by another user), and so on. There is a wide range of possible errors.

→ For a reference on error codes in FileMaker Pro, refer to FileMaker Pro's online help, or turn to our companion book, *FileMaker 8 Functions and Scripts Desk Reference*.

MULTIWINDOW LOCKING

Multiwindow locking is closely related to multiuser record locking. It is possible to open a new window, via the <u>W</u>indow, <u>N</u>ew Window menu command, begin editing a record there, and in so doing, lock yourself out of editing the same record in your original window. If you are actively editing a record that has yet to be committed and you try to edit the same record in another window, you'll see an error message that says, This record cannot be modified in this window because it is already being modified in a different window. FileMaker tries to ensure that you're not losing data or edits you're in the midst of creating.

The point here is that a user can lock himself out of a record. Someone might not realize he's left a record in an edit state before moving on to a new window. The simple answer is simply not to try to edit a record in two places at once. A user would have to go a bit out of his way to encounter this problem. If you've scripted routines for creating new windows with a script, you may want to include a `Commit Record/Request` step before opening the new window.

Given the fact that window locking so closely resembles multiuser record locking, testing a solution with multiple windows is an effective and efficient way to ensure that your scripts manage record-locking checks properly, without having to resort to using two computers.

MULTICONTEXT LOCKING WITHIN SCRIPTS

This problem is related to the problem of multiwindow locking. We've seen it most often in systems converted from previous versions of FileMaker Pro to FileMaker 7 or later. Suppose that you have a script that's working with a series of related tables, each in its own file (as is typical of converted systems). Your script makes some edits to an invoice record, via the `Set Field` script step, and then calls a script in the Invoice Line Item table to do some more work at the line item level. When that script finishes, it needs to write a little more data back to the invoice record. When it attempts to do so, you see the message that `This record cannot be modified in this window because it is already being modified in a different window`. Because the script on the invoice side never explicitly committed the invoice record before calling the subscript, you are indeed still editing the record in another window. Again, this error is common in converted FileMaker solutions that use cross-file scripting.

The solution is simple, if tedious: If you have made edits to a record within a script, be sure to commit those changes before the flow of control leaves your script. This means you should perform an explicit `Commit Records/Requests` before calling a `Perform Script` step to invoke a subscript, or at the end of the script.

Again, this is an issue only where scripting across multiple windows is involved, and this again is most typical of systems converted from FileMaker 6 and before.

AUDIT TRAILS IN FILEMAKER PRO

Data integrity is vital in a multiuser database. A well designed database, properly structured, will go a long way toward ensuring proper data integrity, but no database will ever be perfect. Pesky humans have a habit of introducing a certain unpredictability into the mix. Although $.02 may very well be a perfectly valid number as an invoice total, the truth that the invoice in question was actually $200.00 isn't something a database will ever be able to discern. Then there are cases where a client accidentally makes alterations across a number of records using an import or replace function.

For cases like these, you may choose to build a mechanism to first identify and then undo changes. Possible problem records might be identifiable by date, by user, or by some other criteria. In some cases, maybe only a field needs addressing. The process of undoing changes is referred to as a *rollback*, and for it to be possible, you first need an audit trail of logged transactions in your database to provide the breadcrumbs necessary for a series of undo steps.

Audit trails track the edits made to a database at the granular field level. Changes tracked usually include the field name, a timestamp, and the user account for the person (or function) that made the change. Although FileMaker Pro doesn't have audit trail capabilities built in by default, it is entirely possible to build them. The following sections illustrate three increasingly complete techniques.

RECORD CREATE/MODIFY META DATA

The simplest way to track the evolution of your data is to create fields for creation and modification events. This alone doesn't allow for rollbacks, but it certainly gives you visibility into the events of your database and provides a layer of accountability.

This sort of data is not related to a given business or organization, but helps describe when and by whom data is entered into a database. It is often referred to as *meta data*: data about data.

When building a system for multiuser deployment, we recommend establishing timestamps for creation and modification of records, along with account names. (We don't recommend recording the machine username because this can easily be modified by the user.) This enables you to track who's responsible and when edits have been made to your database so that you can, at a minimum, identify problems. For example, if one of your users consistently makes a data entry error, or if a bug in development leads to wrong lookup values, you can isolate such records by timestamp and account name.

CAUTION

> You might have noticed that we specified *account name* rather than *username* for these meta fields. Individual users can modify their names in the preferences dialogs of FileMaker Pro clients, and there's no corresponding authentication for such. Because this data isn't reliable, we always opt to use the account name.

 To explore error trapping practices, refer to "Trapping for Errors" in the "Troubleshooting" section at the end of this chapter.

SCRIPT-CONTROLLED EDITING

A second technique for controlling edits to your database solutions is scripting-intensive, but allows for the most control. It's conceptually straightforward: Lock down the actual fields of your database in Browse mode and have your users make edits in global fields with a Submit or Cancel button. The script attached would then move the data from temporary fields into actual fields. This allows you to control, via script, any checks you might want to make on the data, and also allows you to write records to an audit trail database to record changes.

One of the more difficult aspects of this approach is what to do with portals and related records. A technique that works well (but again will have you working in ScriptMaker quite a bit) is to use a temporary scratch table. Users place edits in its temporary child records and if they click Cancel, those records are simply discarded. Your audit trail would then need to track to which table a given row of data belonged.

This scripted approach isn't for the faint-of-heart. You'll need to be quite adept with scripting, and this sort of approach will dramatically add to the time it takes for you to deliver a solution. You can also run into significant performance issues when forcing users through a script-intensive process for every record edit they want to make. The upside, of course, is a solid system that does everything it can to protect against honest mistakes—both in terms of trapping data changes and providing a complete, deliberately designed user experience.

AUTO-ENTRY TECHNIQUE FOR AUDIT TRAILS

The third technique in building audit trails relies on the auto-entry options of FileMaker Pro and the capability for fields to modify their own contents (see Figure 11.2). An audit trail should track when and by whom a change was made, and also the change itself. For situations that require an audit trail, more often than not the auto-entry approach is the one we choose. It is practical, it doesn't require scripting, and it doesn't impede typical use of the system.

Figure 11.2
Notice that the AuditLog field on the bottom has a chronological (time stamped) history.

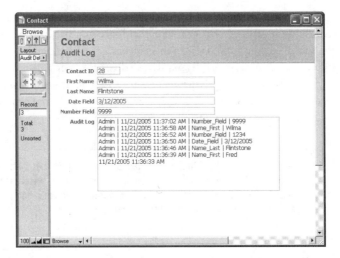

This technique might seem somewhat advanced, but it's actually quite simple. The system stores a text string for each edit made to a given field or record; you may see some performance issues arise as your database grows, so we recommend moving this data into an archive when (if) you need.

The AuditLog field displayed in Figure 11.2 is nothing more than a text field with auto-entry options enabled. Specify that you want to have a calculation result auto-populate the AuditLog field, be certain to turn off the Do Not Replace Existing Value for Field (If Any) option, and add some seed data to the field as well via the another Auto Entry option (see Figure 11.3).

Define your calculation as shown in Figure 11.4.

You need to combine a few different functions and elements to assemble this auto-entry calculation:

- **Evaluate**—Evaluate returns the results from an expression passed to it. You might wonder why we're bothering with it; after all, this is a calculation entry—by definition it will be evaluated. However, any fields added to the optional properties of an Evaluate function serve as triggers (much as a Lookup function works). When they are changed, so too will be the Audit_Trail field. Be sure to add however many trigger fields as you'd like tracked in your audit trail.

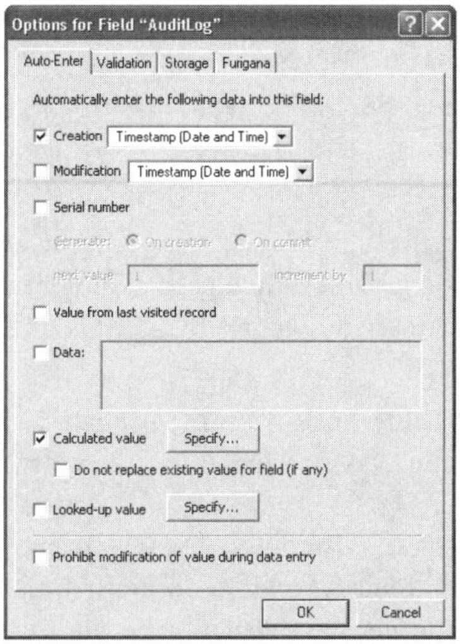

Figure 11.3
Notice that you need two auto-entry options enabled where the timestamp seeds the field.

Figure 11.4
Use the Evaluate function's optional trigger field parameters to cause the AuditLog field to be reevaluated.

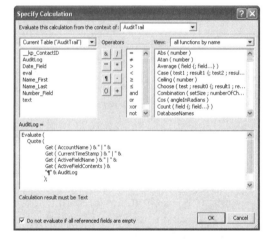

- **Quote**—Quote in this approach will allow you to treat text as data and prevent it from being evaluated within the Evaluate function. With it you can properly concatenate the label and text values in the function. Without the Quote function, your evaluated result would be a "?".

- **Get (CurrentAccount)**—Returns the account currently signed in from the database's security settings.

- **Get (CurrentTimeStamp)**—This simply returns the time and date at which the user changed one of the trigger fields. An exceedingly minor point: The timestamp occurs when the audit log field is written/committed, not when the actual edit occurred.

- **Get (ActiveFieldName)**—This Get function returns the active field name of the field being edited. Because the field in question (say, for example Name First) is also listed as a trigger in the Evaluate function, there's a brief moment as the record is being committed that FileMaker Pro resolves the `Evaluate` function while still recognizing the trigger field as active. It is this behavior that enables the audit trail to work.

- **`Get (ActiveFieldContents)`**—Just as `Get (ActiveFieldName)` works at the moment of a trigger to capture the edited field name, `Get (ActiveFieldContents)` captures the actual contents of the field in question.

- **`& "¶" & AuditLog`**—If you append the `AuditLog` field itself to the end of your calculation, you'll be able to save prior entries and simply keep adding to the top of the log. If you prefer to have your entries sorted chronologically, begin your formula with `AuditLog & "¶" &`.

- **`[Name_First; Name_Last; Date_Field; Number_Field]`**—These last elements of the formula are the optional criteria for the `Evaluate` function. They serve as your triggers.

The seed data you added on the Auto-Entry Options dialog (creation timestamp) allows you to leave the Do Not Evaluate If All Referenced Fields Are Empty option turned on; otherwise you'd need to turn this option off to get the calculation to work the first time (when the AuditLog field was empty). Despite the triggers, it is the only actual field referenced in the calculation.

CAUTION

> If you turn off the Do Not Evaluate If All Referenced Fields Are Empty option, you'll end up with a blank row in your audit log. Somehow that didn't feel proper to us, and theoretically it's possible for someone to create a record and leave it unedited for a period of time. Adding at least the initial timestamp to initialize the `Audit_Log` at least offers more information.

You'll want to consider some additional issues before using this technique in your database solutions. First, FileMaker cannot recognize the current field name or field contents while a replace function is being performed. The audit trail will record that a change was made, but it will lack both the data itself and the field name in question. This same issue applies in the case of imports, and all script steps that don't actively mimic user actions. `Set Field`, for example, does not actively enter a field. In the case of using `Set Field`, the symptoms are identical to the case of a `Replace` or `Import`; however, presumably because `Set Field` exists in a script, you could opt to record whatever audit information your system required.

Second, keep in mind that your data still lives with the record in question. If you were to delete a record, you would presumably lose your audit trail. To preserve all audit trails and to ensure the capability to perform a rollback, we suggest writing a script routine that controls delete processes and properly records all data in an audit table before erasing it from your system.

Related records work in the same manner: Their audit trail routines would live in their respective records, just as in a parent record. If you delete a related record, you will need to store that state in an audit table of some kind.

 For help with controlling auto-entry behaviors, refer to "Making Sure That Your Auto-Entry Always Edits" in the "Troubleshooting" section at the end of this chapter.

CREATING ROLLBACK FUNCTIONALITY

Regardless of whether you choose to move your audit information into its own table or leave it in each record to which it pertains, a rollback follows the same basic principles.

A rollback, true to its name, allows a database administrator, in backward fashion, to re-create the state of a database as it existed at any point in time. She can do so without having to resort to deploying a backup (which may not include the latest functionality of the system).

This involves writing a script to walk through each record's audit trail (from top to bottom as an audit trail writes its data), using Set Field script steps, and re-creating a record at a given date and time. The logic relies on a loop that tests to see whether each iterative row in your audit trail data is older than (or equal to) the point in time you've selected for rollback. If the result of the test is true, your script would be set to parse the data at the end of the line (using the Middle function), and by referencing the stored field name in that row, it would populate your data.

CAUTION

> If your database relies on Set Field script steps (for possibly tracking various status flags or data you've scripted), don't forget that you need to re-create that information via other means. It is not just the data a user sees that needs to be rolled back.

LAUNCH FILES

One of the challenges users on a network have is actually finding the specific FileMaker files they need to use. This is a no-brainer if you have only one FileMaker Pro solution with a single file, but over time your Hosts dialog can become quite crowded in multiuser situations. This is less problematic in FileMaker 7 and 8 than in previous versions, given that FileMaker now allows multiple tables per file and thus requires fewer files, but in large organizations or companies with many different FileMaker files, a server's file list can be a bit daunting.

To offer a solution to this simple problem, we often build *launch files*. These are utility files that are distributed as single-user files and sit on each individual person's computer. They have generally one layout and one script that calls an open routine in a network file.

NOTE

> We generally put a solution logo and system loading...please wait... message on the single layout.

Although it's tempting to put other niceties in these launch files—the capability to load clusters of files, or perhaps some sense of acknowledging the individual user logging in—we encourage you to leave things as simple as possible. You'll have dozens of these files distributed on your network with no easy means of replacing them with upgrades. The simpler you keep them, the easier they will be to maintain.

A final nice touch on launch files is that they close themselves after launching the system in question. They're no longer needed and shouldn't have to clutter the <u>W</u>indow menu.

TROUBLESHOOTING

UNPREDICTABLE GLOBAL DEFAULT VALUES

I have global fields, used for holding system settings, that have been working perfectly for weeks, but today suddenly they have different data in them. What happened?

It's likely they got reset by some script modification you've recently made, or when you had files in an offline, single-user state. In our practice, we find it difficult to remember to set globals for default states in single-user mode through the course of developing and maintaining a system. This is a common source of bugs and we've found over the years not to make any assumptions about global values; it's better to simply set them explicitly within a startup script. It's also important to either explicitly set or test for values at the beginning of a script that depends on them.

USE RE-LOGIN FOR TESTING ACCESS AND SESSIONS

One of my users is reporting a problem that I don't see when I'm logged in. I'm getting sick of having to re-login time and again to test this. Is there an easier way to test this?

If you're having trouble testing how other users, with different access levels, might be interacting with your system, write a re-login script that enables you to hop into another account at the click of your mouse. It's even possible to store passwords when using the Re-Login step. Connect it to a convenient button or place it in the Scripts menu and you have one-click account switching.

Another approach might be to create a "debugging" custom menu (with the various login scripts available) and disable the menu before deploying the system.

MAKING SURE THAT YOUR AUTO-ENTRY ALWAYS EDITS

My auto-entry function worked the first time I edited a field, but then it remains stuck and won't update again. What setting is the likely culprit?

If your auto-entry field for your audit log isn't updating—it does it once, but then never again—make sure that you uncheck the Do Not Replace Existing Value for Field (If Any) option. It is always checked by default and is easy to miss.

Likewise, the Audit Log routine we described depends on there being data in the field to begin with. Either seed it with something (we use Creation TimeStamp) or turn off the Do Not Evaluate If All Referenced Fields Are Empty option. It too is enabled by default.

TRAPPING FOR ERRORS

I need to tighten my scripts, and don't want to have to code for every exception under the sun. What's the best approach for trapping for errors?

Trapping for errors is always a smart development practice. Get into the habit and you'll save yourself years of your life debugging. A simple approach is to simply use the `Get(LastError)` function and use a `Case` or `If / If Else` routine to display meaningful messages and logic branches to your users. You can trap for either explicit errors or just a nonzero number.

A better way to abstract your code and provide yourself with a central place to reuse error handling is to simply write an error routine once and be done with it.

There are two ways to manage error messaging. You can either set up your own errorCodes table or build a custom function. Setting up a table is simple and allows you to add your own custom error conditions and messages. You can do this as well with a custom function. The idea is simple: Establish a global `gError` field in your main system and relate that to an `errorID` in your error table. You can also use a `$$error` global variable and have a custom function reference it.

FILEMAKER EXTRA: DEVELOPMENT WITH A TEAM

Sometimes systems are big enough that they warrant multiple developers in addition to multiple users. Developing as a team can be a bit complex with FileMaker Pro, but one of the best (and often unsung) features of FileMaker is that database schema changes can be made while the database is live, on a server, as other users are in the system. This is an extraordinary boon for FileMaker developers and will make a real difference in all of our lives.

The idea is simple: Set up a server (far better than multiuser peer-to-peer hosting) and have as many developers as a given system needs work together.

It's important to keep a few things in mind: Only one person can adjust the schema in a given file at a time. This is true for editing scripts as well. If another developer is working in ScriptMaker, you can view scripts there, but you will be unable to make changes or add new scripts until your teammate is finished. This means you can have one person focused on scripting, one defining a new calculation field, and a handful of others working on different layouts all at once. One way to avoid conflicts in this regard is to split your solution into multiple files and have those files reference external table occurrences as needed.

Over the years we've assembled some best practices for working on a team. Here's a list of techniques we draw on:

- **Use FileMaker Server**—Server (as opposed to simply working peer-to-peer) allows you to run frequent backups, and if any one machine crashes, the files are still protected from the crash.
- **Use FileMaker Pro Advanced**—The Script Debugger is handy to use in the multideveloper environment, and the Data Viewer is an invaluable tool as well. When another developer is editing scripts, and you can't open a script in ScriptMaker, turn on the debugging tool and you'll at least be able to see the script in question.
- **Use custom functions**—Custom functions can be written while other programming activities are underway, and they provide a deep layer of possible abstraction. It's

possible to have multiple developers building custom functions while others work in the core system, and it's also a great way to reuse code across a team.

- **Set up a bug-tracking database**—If you're working on a multiuser system, testing, requests, random ideas, and other communication is vital. You've got some of the world's best database software at your fingertips; put it to use and build a bug-tracking system for your development team and your users.

- **Build re-login scripts, toggle status area scripts, and developer layouts**—Giving developers access to the back stage area of a system is vital. Build scripts to get them there.

- **Assign a chief architect**—With creating a meal, too many cooks in the kitchen spoils the broth. Similarly, one person should ultimately be responsible for the overall technical directions the system requires.

- **Comment**—Comment. Comment. Comment. Your team will either thank or kill you, depending on how well you take this to heart.

11

CHAPTER 12

IMPLEMENTING SECURITY

In this chapter

APPROACHING SECURITY

Security is a primary concern for all database developers and a significant factor in an organization's requirements for both the internal workings of a database system and the technology used to build it. IT departments in particular pay close attention to security issues and often have specific needs that go beyond those of the users of your database solution.

FileMaker's security architecture was completely overhauled in the FileMaker 7 product line, and it offers a robust set of features for managing security. Although security models in versions before 7 were (at best) cumbersome, we're pleased to say that FileMaker 8 offers a complete set of security capabilities and serves as a "good citizen" for IT organizations: It meets the common standards for security and account administration most IT organizations require of modern server-based technologies.

Regardless of how you plan to deploy a solution (you may not even have an IT department), we strongly urge all developers to learn about security and choose appropriate levels of safeguards for their FileMaker solutions. This may be as simple as locking down the capability to modify the database schema or as complex as deploying your solution on a network with ties to an external authentication server.

Whatever your specific needs for security are, there are three primary concerns that bear consideration:

- **Physical File Access**—The first issue for security is making sure that you protect the database file itself. No matter how robust a security architecture is (for any kind of software or server application), you will face risks if a malevolent person gets direct access to your database file or server.

- **Network Access**—The second area for security is the network traffic between a FileMaker hosting computer and the client computers connected to it. If you are working on an open network, you might want to consider encrypting the data stream between FileMaker Server and its clients.

- **Internal Data-Level Security**—The third area for security has to do with the internal logic of your specific database solution when someone is legitimately logged in. Who has rights to delete records, who can make programming changes to the database, and who can view various layouts in the system? These details are internal to the workings of a FileMaker solution and deal with ensuring that your data remains both secure and reliable.

Every database solution should address these three areas. They may be addressed by the fact that your database will never leave your personal hard drive nor be available to the network at large, but if the data in your solution is particularly sensitive, what might happen if your computer was stolen or if a colleague sat down at it while you were away from your desk? We encourage all developers to consider security issues and make deliberate choices that are appropriate to the sensitivity of their information and the consequences they might face if it were compromised.

IDENTIFYING RISKS

Security concerns are not all targeted at the clichéd image of a sophisticated hacker sitting in a dark room somewhere surrounded by Mountain Dew cans and pizza boxes. Most FileMaker systems will never be exposed to that level of threat. If you have a reasonably secure network and keep access to your server (or hosting computer) controlled, you will have addressed many of the concerns an extreme case like hacking represents.

The biggest security threat a database system faces is actually from the legitimate users of the system itself, and often has most to do with data integrity. We'll use an example to illustrate: Consider a system for managing invoices that a company depends on for reporting monthly revenue. If every user of the system (including perhaps a temporary employee there to answer phones for a few days) has the capability to delete records, the chances that someone would inadvertently delete invoice records are quite high. Or take a less clear-cut example: What if someone duplicated a record, intending to use the new record to create a similar invoice, but mis-keyed the command and duplicated it twice? In these situations, the database could not be reliably depended on to deliver accurate revenue totals. Although these sorts of issues are not the result of intended harm to a database, they are a risk to the system and need to be addressed by its security architecture and data validation mechanisms.

The second general threat developers face is data sensitivity: In the examples given previously, would it be appropriate for everyone in the system to be able to run the monthly invoice summary report and see the financial performance of the organization? Or in the case of a database that tracks, say, human resources information, which users should have the ability to view the layouts on which people's salary history appears? Security plans need to include an assessment of what data users can access (see and manipulate) in a given solution in addition to what they can do to that data.

We find it useful to work with two general categories of risks to data within a database:

- **Data Sensitivity**—Define the degree to which information should be visible and accessible after a user has legitimately logged in to a system. Risks include inappropriate access to private and proprietary information.

- **Data Integrity**—Define the actions various users can perform on the data in your solution. Often revolving around the creation and deletion of records, risks can also include the capability to edit certain fields or run specific scripted routines.

When you're approaching security for a given solution, it is important to identify the risks the organization faces in terms of both of these areas. We advocate the creation of a risks document in project planning that identifies these issues and the planned means of addressing them.

PLANNING SECURITY

When you're approaching a new system, it's important to identify the security issues you face and include early in your development process a plan for your security architecture. For example, you will need to plan ahead if some users of your system should not be allowed to view or work with some set of fields, records, or layouts. Security, like reporting, is often left until last when building a system, and as with reporting, this tends to be a mistake. You will need to interweave access issues throughout your database solution (taking security into account when placing objects on layouts, writing scripts, and so on), and it is best to have this mapped out before building a solution.

Using a Security Matrix

To make sense of the myriad security issues many systems face, we recommend the use of a security matrix. A simple example is shown in Table 12.1.

Table 12.1   Security Matrix Example

	Developer	IT Admin	Manager	Sales	Finance	Admin
Server Administration						
Access to server	Limited[1]	Full	None	None	None	None
Access to backup directory	Limited[1]	Full	None	None	None	None
Access to server admin tool	Limited[1]	Full	None	None	None	None
User Accounts						
New account	Full	Full	None	None	None	None
Delete account	Full	Full	None	None	None	None
Change password	Full	Full	None	None	None	None
Data Tables						
Customer view	Full	None	Full	Limited[2]	Full	Full
Customer new	Full	None	Full	Limited[2]	Full	None
Customer delete	Full	None	Full	None	None	None
Customer edit	Full	None	Full	Limited[2]	Full	Full
Invoice view	Full	None	Full	Limited[2]	Full	Full
Invoice new	Full	None	Full	Limited[2]	Full	None
Invoice delete	Full	None	Full	None	Full	None
Invoice edit	Full	None	Full	Limited[2]	Full	None
Product view	Full	None	Full	Full	Full	Full
Product new	Full	None	Full	Full	None	Full
Product delete	Full	None	Full	None	None	None
Product edit	Full	None	Full	Full	None	Full

	Developer	IT Admin	Manager	Sales	Finance	Admin
Script Routines						
Monthly Revenue Report	Full	None	Full	None	None	None
Regional Revenue Report	Full	None	Full	Limited[3]	None	None
Layouts						
Customer List	Full	None	Full	Full	Full	Full
Customer Detail	Full	None	Full	Full	Full	Full
Invoice List	Full	None	Full	Full	Full	None
Invoice Detail	Full	None	Full	Full	Full	None
Product List	Full	None	Full	Full	Full	Full
Product Detail	Full	None	Full	Full	Full	Full

[1] *Database developer will have full access to server during testing, but after deploymen,t passwords will be changed.*

[2] *Salespeople will be able only to create, view, and edit customer and invoice records for customers and invoices in their region only.*

[3] *Salespeople will be able to run the regional revenue report, but it will report only on the region to which a salesperson belongs.*

Note in Table 12.1 that Managers have full access to create and delete data records, that Salespeople have limited access to do so for customer records, and that people in the Admin role cannot make any changes to invoices (however, they can view invoice information).

An additional distinction to note is that although people in the Admin role can view invoice information, they do not have access to the Invoice List or Invoice Detail layouts. This suggests that invoice information may be displayed on other layouts, perhaps as related fields or within a portal. It is important to consider both the capability to view data globally throughout a system and the capability to make use of specific layouts. In most cases, it is not enough to simply limit access to specific layouts; you need to also limit access to the data itself.

Security grids such as the example in Table 12.1 need to be as detailed as they need to be: In other words, they depend on the circumstances you face. If you don't have six different roles in your organization, clearly you won't need the distinctions made in the example. If you want to grant some development privileges to people other than developers (say, the capability to modify certain layouts), you'd need to add a subsection for that. This table should be taken as an instructional example and is not a comprehensive representation of a real-world system.

Finally, be sure to grasp the use of the phrase "to view" (both in this book and within FileMaker itself). In this context we mean the ability to consume the data in various ways; a user can see the data onscreen, can choose to print (if printing is enabled for the user's account), can export that data (if exporting is enabled for the user's account), and can email data.

12

PLANNING IMPLEMENTATION

Implementing security is done largely in the Define Accounts & Privileges dialog, but before walking through the mechanics of setting up security, you will need to plan where and how to implement it from an overall perspective.

A significant part of your planning will need to include user interface considerations. If a user shouldn't have access to run a script, for example, she should be presented with a graceful message to that effect if she inadvertently attempts to do so (as opposed to the script simply not doing anything). Likewise, if someone doesn't have access to a layout, your navigation system should reliably prevent him from ever being left on that layout, or at least you should provide a way to get back to the part of the system to which he does have access.

Another consideration is the aesthetics of seeing <no access> displayed in various places throughout the system. FileMaker will display <no access> when a user isn't allowed to view field data, record data, or a layout. If you do not want to remind your users of their own limited privileges, you may choose to hide away restricted areas by controlling navigation or window access.

FileMaker 8 introduced the Custom Menus feature, allowing you to deal with many security considerations by simply disabling access to certain menu items. For example, if you want to restrict users from being able to delete all records, you can choose to disable that menu item. It is critical to note, however, that this is simply a user interface mechanism. If users have some other means of deleting records (say, through a custom script you've written or some other aspect of FileMaker's interface), the only way to ensure that they cannot perform the restricted action is to control their ability to perform the fundamental action in their security settings. User interface issues should really be considered only for aesthetic and usability reasons.

→ For more detail on custom menus, **see** "Working with Custom Menus," **p. 373**.

Here's another example of how security plays a role in your planning: If you want to prevent people from having to see fields to which they have no access, you can choose to place them on their own layout. In FileMaker 8, you can control access to specific layouts; however, you cannot prevent users from accessing a tab pane if they have access to the layout on which it sits. Given this, you may choose to create separate layouts where a Tab Control object might have served had you not considered security issues.

Your solution's scripts are another area where you will want to plan for different levels of access. If a user has a means of running a restricted script (say, by clicking a button that is omnipresent on all layouts), you will need to present him with a message that he is not permitted to use that function. A more subtle issue is what to do with scripts that are internal to the database operations; for example, you might write a script that allows users to choose different printer settings. If you restrict access to this script for some users, but then reference the script from all your reporting and printing routines, you will need to address that conflicting dependency. Likewise, if a script takes the system to a layout tied to a data table in order to establish context but the current user doesn't have access to that layout, your script may deliver unexpected results.

However you choose to approach security in your system, thinking through the user experience will be an important part of the overall plan. You should note in your layout designs and scripting where security considerations need to be taken into account.

USER-LEVEL INTERNAL SECURITY

The mechanics of implementing security begin with the database file (or files) within your solution itself. Generally, security is first a development task (first planning and then implementation), and is then followed by issues of deployment. This chapter follows that same approach by first discussing how to grant individual users access to your database.

USER ACCOUNTS

If you select File, Define, Accounts & Privileges, you will be taken to the Define Accounts & Privileges dialog. This dialog has a good deal of depth, and it is through this dialog that you will implement much of your security architecture.

On the first tab of the dialog, Accounts, you create individual user accounts and assign a privilege set to each. It's important to grasp that various security settings in FileMaker are not controlled at the user account level but rather are assigned with privilege sets. Accounts are associated with a privilege set, and it is that association that determines the functionality a given user has access to, as shown in Figure 12.1. This allows you to define a privilege set for each role in your system and assign individual users to the corresponding set that matches their role for the database.

Figure 12.1
The Accounts tab of the Define Accounts & Privileges dialog allows you to see which accounts are active and what their respective privilege sets are.

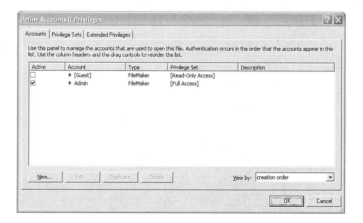

NOTE

If you are used to working with FileMaker Pro 6 or prior, one of the first things you should notice is that accounts in FileMaker 8 (and FileMaker 7, the version in which the new security features were introduced) contain both a username and a password as opposed to the password-only approach of FileMaker 6 and before. We strongly recommend that you adopt single accounts for each user in your FileMaker 8 files and no longer share passwords among teams of individuals.

If you've converted your files from FileMaker Pro 6 or prior and are having difficulty with your old passwords, refer to "Converted Passwords" in the "Troubleshooting" section at the end of this chapter.

DEFAULT ACCOUNTS AND AUTOMATIC LOGIN

By default, any new FileMaker file will be created with an account named Admin with a blank password, and it will be set to log in to that account. The Admin account will be assigned to full access privileges, so in effect the file will be created with no restrictions whatsoever, but will have an account and privilege set in place. If you choose to lock down your database, either give the Admin account a password or delete it. You should also disable the File Options setting that first tries the Admin account and password on login.

In addition to the Admin account, FileMaker provides a [Guest] account with each new database. The [Guest] account cannot be deleted and is set to be inactive by default. You can choose to enable this [Guest] account in cases in which you want to restrict the development functions of a database but want to open the rest of the system to any user.

To set a file to a default state in which users are not prompted to log in, create an account with the appropriate access level you prefer, and then turn on the Log In Using option in the File Options dialog shown in Figure 12.2.

Figure 12.2
A system can automatically log users in with a default account via the File Options dialog.

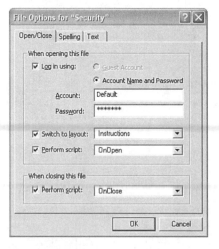

ACCOUNT MANAGEMENT

The settings in Figure 12.3 are more typical for a small workgroup application: The Admin account has been deleted and there are three individual users with full access. Note the full list of accounts (some of which are disabled) and the assignment of privilege sets.

The Type column shows the means by which authentication is set to occur. It will show either FileMaker, in which case a user's password is stored within FileMaker (in a fully encrypted, reliably secure form), or External Server, in which case authentication is managed by a separate authentication server. (We will cover external authentication later in the chapter.)

Figure 12.3
Note that in the Accounts tab of the Define Accounts & Privileges dialog, you can review which accounts are active and to what privilege sets they belong.

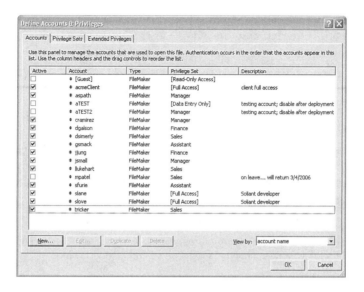

When editing an individual account via the Edit Account dialog shown in Figure 12.4, you can control settings specific to that user. The setting to prompt users to change their password on their next login allows developers and database administrators to reset passwords without having to know the private passwords of their users. To administer a FileMaker database, we recommend creating temporary passwords for people and requiring them to change passwords on their next login. (Note that this practice is not recommended for Instant Web Publishing or for external authentication, both of which are covered later in this chapter.)

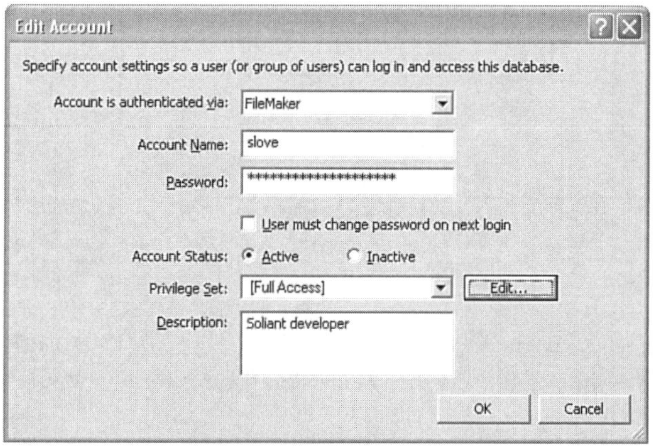

Figure 12.4
The Edit Account dialog allows you to control the authentication and active status for each user.

Note also that you can disable an account from the Edit Account dialog. This allows a database administrator to turn off an account without having to delete it. Having the ability to turn off an account is useful if some users are gone for extended periods or if you want to preserve the fact that an account exists with that specific name. You can also simply toggle the check box on the leftmost side of the Accounts tab (unchecking it to disable an account).

Last, you can assign a user's privilege set. An account can have only one privilege set assigned, and that privilege set determines the specific rights and privileges the user will have.

PRIVILEGE SETS

Privilege sets compose the bulk of security control in FileMaker. With a privilege set you can set various access levels, restrict functions and areas within a database, and control who can do development work within a given file. Privilege sets are associated (one to many) with accounts, and they can be thought of as analogous to groups. It is common to see privilege sets established for developers, managers, and so on.

 If you need help with the testing process for privilege sets, see "Closing and Reopening File for Testing" in the "Troubleshooting" section at the end of this chapter.

The Privilege Sets tab of the Define Accounts & Privileges, shown in Figure 12.5, allows you to see at a glance which accounts are assigned to which privilege set.

Figure 12.5
The three sets in brackets are defaults created for each new FileMaker file; those below are custom sets created for a specific database solution.

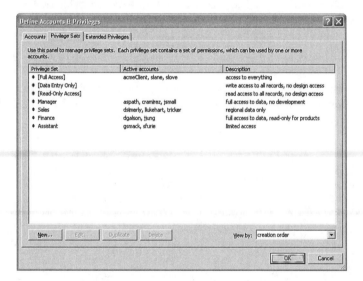

Notice the three sets at the top of the dialog: [Full Access], [Data Entry Only], and [Read-Only Access] are the default sets that FileMaker creates for a new FileMaker file. These cannot be deleted.

The [Full Access] privilege set is a unique set: It is the single set that has complete access to the file including all development functionality. It cannot be duplicated and your file must have at least one FileMaker-authenticated account associated with the [Full Access] privilege set. Without [Full Access] you wouldn't be able to get in and modify your database.

NOTE

Note that by using the Remove Admin Access feature of the Developer Utilities features in FileMaker Pro 8 Advanced, you can remove the administrative/full access accounts associated with a file and prevent any future development.

→ To learn more about Developer Utilities, **see** "Removing Admin Access," **p. 768**.

If you select a privilege set from those listed and double-click (or click the Edit button), you will be taken to the Edit Privilege Set dialog, shown in Figure 12.6. It enables you to control both the features within FileMaker that assigned users can access and to what degree members of a privilege set can do additional development work on your database file.

Figure 12.6
The Edit Privilege Set dialog allows you to define the security access for all accounts associated with a given privilege set.

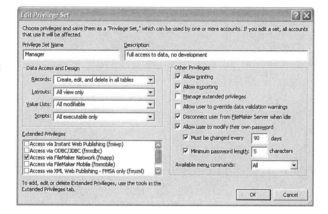

The Edit Privilege Set dialog is divided into three areas: Data Access and Design, Other Privileges, and Extended Privileges. We'll look more closely at each area in the sections that follow.

CONTROLLING DATA ACCESS

The actual data of your file is protected by the Records drop-down list in the Edit Privilege Set dialog. It is important to remember that although there are various ways in which you can hide fields from users (for example, by not placing any field layout objects on layouts), the only way to fully protect your data is through the Records drop-down list.

The menu allows you to apply global permissions where a privilege set can have full access to all tables, no access at all, only the capability to create and edit records, or view-only access. View-only access means that users with this privilege set can see data but cannot make changes or create new records.

If you choose the fifth option, Custom Privileges, you will open the Custom Record Privileges dialog, shown in Figure 12.7. Within this dialog, you can control on a table-by-table basis, or even a field-by-field basis, what data a given set of users can view, edit, create, and delete. Each table in your file is listed. You can select multiple tables by Shift-clicking for contiguous selections or Control-clicking for noncontiguous selections. Any changes made to the settings below will then be applied to each table selected.

Figure 12.7
These settings show that access to this database has been restricted to a significant degree. The hyphen indicates no access.

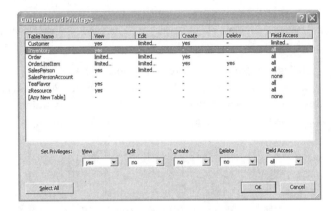

Notice that there are settings for [Any New Table] at the bottom of your table listings. This privilege controls tables added to the file after your security settings have been defined. In other words, if you were to add a TeaPackage table to the database shown, this privilege set would initially have no access to the records in that table.

The settings at the bottom of the dialog are listed here:

- **View**—Controls whether or not a set of users can consume the information stored in a selected table. By "consume," we mean see in Browse mode, search for in Find mode, export, print, email, and so on. Users with View access can perform such actions as clicking into a given field and copying data to their clipboard.

- **Edit**—Allows users to make changes to data within a given table. Note that if you set View to no, Edit will automatically show as no as well.

- **Create**—Controls whether users can create new records in a selected table.

- **Delete**—Determines whether users can delete records from a given table.

- **Field Access**—Allows developers to apply view or edit privileges to individual fields rather than to an entire record. In cases in which you have applied settings to the View, Edit, and Field Access settings, the most restrictive setting will take precedence. In other words, if you set a table's View privileges to yes but Field Access to none, users will not be able to see or edit any of the fields within that table. Likewise, if you set Field Access to all and View privileges to no, users will not be able to view any records in the given table.

The first four privileges listed offer yes, no, and limited options (with the exception of Create, which offers only yes and no). We will cover limited privileges shortly. Field Access controls have more granularity than the other record privileges. The all and none options should be self-explanatory, but the limited option presents a list of all the fields in a given table, as shown in Figure 12.8.

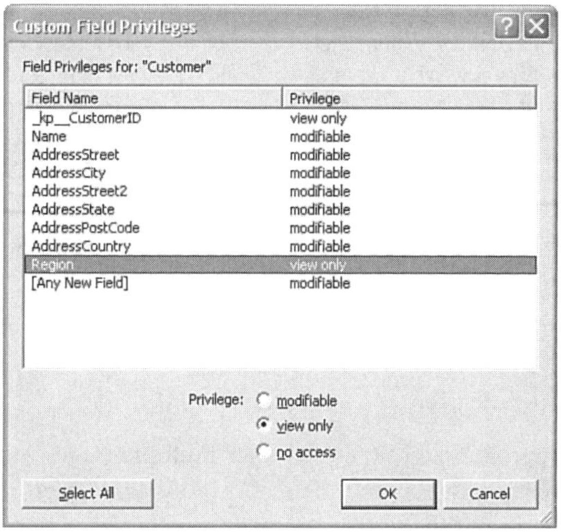

Figure 12.8
Field-level access allows you to control individual fields for a given privilege set.

In the example shown, by setting a field to view only, you are ensuring that users logged in with this privilege set will be able to see (in this case) what region a customer belongs to, but not be able to make changes to the region field.

CONDITIONAL PRIVILEGES

For record privileges except Create, you also have the option to choose limited privileges. When doing so for <u>V</u>iew, <u>E</u>dit, and <u>D</u>elete, you will open a calculation dialog and can create conditional circumstances by which access can be controlled on a record-by-record basis.

→ For a review of the calculation dialog and working with formulas, **see** Chapter 8, "Getting Started with Calculations," **p. 217**.

For example, you might have a business in which sales teams are divided by region and you want to prevent one region's team members from seeing the orders from another region. A simple way to enable this is to compare the name of a region assigned to a salesperson to the name of a region assigned to each order. Assume that your SalesPerson table contains a Region field and likewise your Order table contains a Region field. To control the capability to view Order records, take the following steps:

1. First create a startup script, set in the File Options to run when your file is opened, that finds a given person's SalesPerson record based on login account, and sets a global variable to the region to which that person is assigned. Your script might look like this:

```
SetRegion
# purpose: to set a global variable to the region
#   for the person who has just logged in
# dependencies: access to the SalesPerson table and Region field
Go to Layout [ "SalesPerson" (SalesPerson) ]
Enter Find Mode [ ]
Set Field [ SalesPerson::Account; Get (AccountName) ]
Perform Find [ ]
Set Variable [ $$userRegion; Value:SalesPerson::Region ]
Go to Layout [ original layout ]
```

→ To learn more about working with variables, **see** "Script Variables," **p. 448**.

TIP

> We recommend, if you implement this script, that you create some error-trapping conditions in cases in which no records are found during the find request, a user doesn't have access to the SalesPerson layout, and so on. For instructional purposes, we've kept it brief.

2. Make sure that you have a Region field in both the Order table and the SalesPerson table and that they both have data populated.

3. Change the View privileges for the Order table to limited and set the calculation to be this:

```
$$userRegion = Order::Region
```

You could modify this approach slightly to check for multiple values within the variable as well. This would allow you to assign multiple regions to a single person:

```
PatternCount ( $$userRegion; Order::Region & ¶ ) > 0
```

There is a wide array of functionality you can deliver via the capability to conditionally set access levels within record privilege sets. You could, for example, lock records from being edited by setting a flag field, or you could prevent records older than a day from being deleted.

Note that you will want to close any backdoor opportunities for users to get around your security settings. In the example given previously, make sure that users cannot change their own region, nor those of the Order records. Furthermore, make certain that they cannot write scripts or calculation functions (in which they might be able to change the value of the $$userRegion variable).

CONTROLLING LAYOUT USE AND DEVELOPMENT

In the Edit Privilege Set dialog, the next setting after Records is the Layouts drop-down list for controlling layout privileges. With it you can set the following:

- **All No Access**—This setting ensures that people associated with the privilege set you're defining will have no access to any layouts within the current file.

- **All View Only**—The term "view," again, really means "consume" or "use." Users assigned this privilege will not be able to make changes to a layout (in Layout mode), but they will be able to use the layout and (assuming that the developer hasn't omitted the layout from that menu) see it in the menu of layouts offered via the Status Area.

- **All Modifiable**—This option enables the capability to change to Layout mode and to then edit all the layouts within a file.

- **Custom Privileges**—Choosing this option takes you to the dialog shown in Figure 2.9.

Figure 12.9
This dialog allows you to control who can modify which layouts.

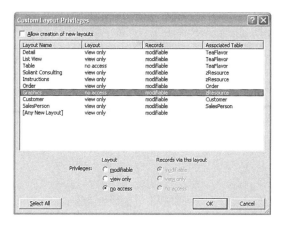

The Custom Layout Privileges dialog enables you to set only specific layouts as modifiable, or to turn off access to selected layouts. Furthermore, you can control how users interact with records via the layout in question. You can choose to lock down record access on a layout-by-layout basis. Be aware of the Allow Creation of New Layouts option. With it you can enable someone to add layouts to a file without giving them access to the layouts you as a developer created. Imagine the possibility of allowing users to, say, add columns to report layouts without having to give them unfettered access to the entire system.

One important note about layout access: Just because you lock down access to a certain layout does not mean that your users cannot get access to the data in your file. They may be able to pull information via export, might be able to create another FileMaker file and create their own layouts, and so on. The best way to control your data is to lock down both record access and layout access as appropriate.

CONTROLLING ACCESS TO VALUE LISTS

The drop-down list for controlling value list privileges in the Edit Privilege Set dialog is quite similar in function to that of layouts. You can enable all value lists to be modifiable, view (or use) only, and all no access. Likewise, you can choose Custom Privileges and will be presented with the Custom Value List Privileges dialog shown in Figure 12.10.

The dialog shown in Figure 12.10 can be used to prevent value lists from being edited or, indeed, from being used at all. In the case that a field has a value list associated but a given user doesn't have access to use it, that user will be presented with <No Access> messages for radio buttons or check boxes. In the case of a pop-up menu, the user will be able to see an already selected value but will not be able to select a new one. And, last, for a drop-down list, the list will simply not appear (nor will the down arrow, if present, do anything), and the field will behave as though no value list were associated with it.

Note that, as with layouts, you can control the capability to create new value lists. If you've given some users limited abilities to create layouts, it's somewhat likely that they will need to create value lists as well. The two settings often go hand in hand.

Figure 12.10
The Custom Value List Privileges dialog allows you to, among other things, enable others to edit value lists.

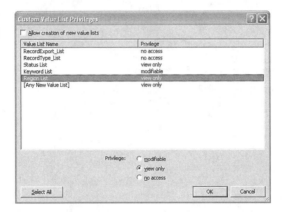

CONTROLLING THE CAPABILITY TO RUN SCRIPTS

Often developers can control access to scripts by controlling where in a database's interface scripts are executed (by button, via the Scripts menu, or as associated with a custom menu); however, in cases in which you simply do not want a class of users to run scripts, the fourth drop-down list in the Data Access and Design area of the Edit Privilege Set dialog controls the capability to execute scripts. As with the other menus, you can quickly set permissions so that all scripts are executable, all modifiable, or all disabled (no access) for a given privilege set. In addition to the global menu choices, you can choose Custom Privileges, which presents the dialog shown in Figure 12.11.

Figure 12.11
The Custom Script Privileges dialog allows script-by-script control over access.

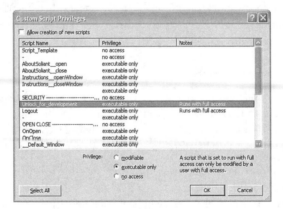

The dialog shown in Figure 12.11 lets you to set scripts to be modifiable, executable only, or to allow no access for the current privilege set.

Note that in the third column of the dialog, FileMaker displays the fact that a script has been set to run with full access. It also reminds you that only people logged in with the [Full Access] privilege set can modify scripts set to run in full access. This is also true for the capability to enable running scripts with full access: If someone is not logged in with

[Full Access] privileges, she will not be presented with the Run Script with Full Access check box in ScriptMaker.

→ For more discussion of running scripts with full access, **see** "Full Access Privileges," **p. 253**.

It is important to understand that a script set to run with full access will do exactly that: A user's security privileges will be overridden and the script will execute as though it were run by a user with [Full Access] privileges. This dialog, then, is useful in making sure that you can prevent users from executing a script, even if it is set to run with full access privileges.

SETTING OTHER FEATURE PRIVILEGES

The area on the right of the Edit Privilege Set dialog controls access to a few of FileMaker's interface commands and offers some specific settings related to security.

The Allow Printing and Allow Exporting options should be somewhat obvious, but be sure to note that they also control the functions to Save as PDF (tied to the capability to print) and Save as Excel (tied to the capability to export). If you want to prevent your users from taking data elsewhere, you will need to turn off printing and exporting. Note too that the only way to prevent users from making use of the Email command is to use a custom menu to remove that menu item. There is no security setting that controls whether someone can use the Email command in the File menu.

Allowing users to override data validation warnings should be obvious as well. When a validation error occurs, users with this privilege will not be presented with the capability to accept an invalid entry into a validated field, regardless of whether Allow User to Override Data Validation Warnings is turned on for the field. This provides you with a means of taking away the capability to override validation warnings from some users.

→ For more detail on validation, **see** "Field Validation," **p. 85**.

The option Disconnect User from FileMaker Server When Idle (the time interval is defined in FileMaker Server's settings) should almost always be enabled. When it's disabled, the server will never disconnect idle users who have this privilege set. One occasion to disable this setting is if for some reason you need a client computer set up to perform automated tasks.

We recommend using the Allow User to Modify Their Own Password feature and requiring that users change their password, but remember that Instant Web Publishing and external authentication do not support this. Recommended best practices suggest that passwords should be changed regularly and they should be of a certain minimum length. (There is no capacity in FileMaker to set rules about the content of a password, only its length.) Note, though, that these settings can get you in trouble: If you disallow someone from changing his own password, but then on the Edit Account dialog require that he do so on the next login, the user can get trapped and unable to log in to the database.

CAUTION

> Note that the feature to change passwords is not supported by Instant Web Publishing. Do not enable it for users who will exclusively access your database via IWP.

The last setting, Available Menu Commands, allows you to disable FileMaker's menu items, leaving just those to open and close a file, run scripts, and so on, or additionally the clipboard and spelling items in the Edit menu. This option is often used to completely lock down a FileMaker solution. When you disable all menu items here, it's an all-or-nothing proposition that will then require that you re-create all the functionality you want users to be able to have. We often recommend instead using a custom menu set that doesn't contain the items you're trying to hide from users.

Note that if you do choose Minimum or Edit Only, those settings will disable custom menus just as they will standard FileMaker menu items.

→ To learn about custom menus, **see** "Working with Custom Menus," **p. 373**.

EXTENDED PRIVILEGES

The third area of security within FileMaker files comprises extended privileges. Think of extended privileges as nothing more than on/off switches. A privilege set has a specific extended privilege either enabled or disabled. There are no other settings or logic to extended privileges.

DEFAULT EXTENDED PRIVILEGES

FileMaker Pro 8 and FileMaker Pro 8 Advanced ship with some extended privileges already in place, as shown in Figure 12.12. These are used to enable access into FileMaker by various means; the behaviors of these privileges are controlled by FileMaker itself.

Figure 12.12
FileMaker ships with a set of preexisting extended privileges.

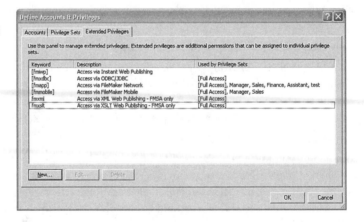

The default, precreated extended privileges are listed here:

- **Access via Instant Web Publishing**—This privilege allows users to access the file via a web browser using Instant Web Publishing.

→ To learn about Instant Web Publishing, **see** Chapter 21, "Instant Web Publishing," **p. 633**.

- **Access via ODBC/JDBC**—Access via ODBC/JDBC needs to be enabled if you want an ODBC or JDBC client to use SQL to converse with FileMaker.

→ To learn more about xDBC connectivity, **see** Chapter 19, "Importing Data into FileMaker Pro," **p. 567**, and Chapter 20, "Exporting Data from FileMaker," **p. 595**.

- **Access via FileMaker Network**—This privilege allows users to access the file remotely, across a network, using FileMaker Pro (or Advanced) client connections. This is true for both peer-to-peer sharing and hosting files on FileMaker Server.

→ To learn about hosting FileMaker via FileMaker Server, **see** Chapter 25, "FileMaker Server and Server Advanced," **p. 779**.

- **Access via FileMaker Mobile**—This privilege enables synchronization with FileMaker Mobile. In addition to enabling this extended privilege, you will also need to use FileMaker Mobile's configuration functions to prepare a file for synchronization.

→ To learn about FileMaker Mobile, **see** Chapter 26, "FileMaker Mobile," **p. 821**.

- **Access via XML Web Publishing**—As noted in the dialog, this extended privilege works with files hosted by FileMaker Server Advanced. It allows users (or other systems) access to your data via XML.

- **Access via XSLT Web Publishing**—As with XML, this extended privilege works with files hosted by FileMaker Server Advanced. It allows the file to serve as a data back end for XSLT Custom Web Publishing.

→ To learn about Custom Web Publishing and XML/XSLT, **see** Chapter 23, "Custom Web Publishing," **p. 699**.

 If you are having trouble getting your database files to appear on FileMaker Server and are sure that your authentication is correct, see "Database Doesn't Appear on FileMaker Server" in the "Troubleshooting" section at the end of this chapter.

CUSTOM EXTENDED PRIVILEGES

Beyond the six extended privileges included with FileMaker, you can add your own. After the extended privileges are created, you can use the Get (ExtendedPrivileges) function to see what extended privileges have been granted to the current user. This then gives you the capability of modifying your solution's logic to take these extended privileges into account; script branching, calculation results, field validation, and even custom menu loading could all take the current extended privileges into account. The options are nearly endless.

One of the advantages of extended privileges is that you can grant users the ability to manage them. On the right of the Edit Extended Privilege dialog, as shown in Figure 12.13, you can give users access to a security dialog devoted only to extended privileges. You might choose to do this if you want to expose some security control in your system without granting someone [Full Access].

Another advantage to extended privileges is that they are not session specific: If you enable an extended privilege for a privilege set, it is immediately available to all users logged in with that privilege set. If, for example, you want to disable access to a file via the Web while you complete some development, you can simply turn off the extended privilege for all the associated privilege sets.

12

Figure 12.13
Users can assign which privilege sets are associated with an extended privilege when the Manage Extended Privileges security setting is enabled.

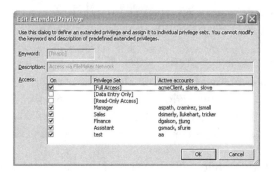

As an example of putting extended privileges to use, consider a database with a series of reports that many, but not all, users will need to have access to. You could certainly control whether users could execute the individual scripts and navigate to the layouts in question, but creating an extended privilege for these reports will allow you to enable them across your various privilege sets in one central place. You can also disable them when perhaps it would be inappropriate to run them before some full set of data is input.

A portion of the script you might use to begin the reporting procedure could look like this:

```
If [PatternCount (Get (ExtendedPrivileges); "yearendReports")]
  Perform Script ["Goto Report Menu"]
Else
  Show Custom Dialog ["Reports Offline"; "The Year End Reports
  ➥ have not yet been compiled and are offline."]
End If
```

Extended privileges are a useful way extend to FileMaker's security model into the logic of your solutions.

FILE-LEVEL ACCESS SECURITY

After you have a FileMaker database properly secured from a development standpoint, you need to consider how people will gain access to the file itself and log in. If you are hosting the file peer-to-peer, FileMaker's internal file security is your only option. FileMaker Server, on the other hand, has additional security settings and capabilities that can better safeguard your solutions.

 If you've forgotten your Admin-level password to a database (and mostly just need sympathy), see "Forgotten Admin Password" in the "Troubleshooting" section at the end of this chapter.

SERVER ADMINISTRATION SECURITY

To protect the files and access to your databases properly, you will need to consider the physical makeup of your server and its environment. Is it in a locked room? Is it properly situated behind a firewall? The actual hardware configuration for FileMaker Server from a security standpoint requires that you follow the best practices of IT organizations in general. Although this is not an exhaustive list, here are some guidelines:

- Place your physical server in a controlled, locked room.
- Make certain that the server is situated behind a firewall and that as few ports as possible allow traffic, especially incoming, to it.
- Do not turn on file sharing for the server. Putting files on the server should be something you do *from* the server.
- Do not allow file sharing on your backup directory, or at least secure it from your organization's general network.
- Make certain to secure the server with OS-level accounts and passwords, and set it to lock automatically after a short period of idle time.

As stated previously, this is hardly a comprehensive list. The intent here is that you consider the environment in which you place FileMaker files as carefully as you've considered the development of your files internally. If you spend effort to lock away data from certain accounts, but then leave backup files within easy reach of everyone on your network, your exposure to risk will increase.

The first step in securing your server is to establish a password for administering the server itself. You will need to use the Server Administration Tool to configure these settings.

→ To understand how to configure FileMaker Server using the Server Administration Tool, **see** "Server Administration Settings," **p. 788.**

You also have the option of enabling remote administration and setting an additional password for such. This will allow you to open the Server Administration Tool from any computer and, using a network address, connect to your server to perform tasks such as opening and closing databases, and running backup routines.

> **NOTE**
>
> We have found that it is more convenient to use remote desktop control software such as Terminal Services, Citrix, GoToMyPC, or Timbuktu to remotely control a FileMaker Server. It is rare that you will need to use only the Server Administration Tool when performing admin tasks on the server, so we tend not to use the remote access feature.

Even in cases in which your server is perfectly secure, we recommend setting a password for administering FileMaker Server. Good security is a case of rainy-day thinking, and the more precaution you take, the better you'll avoid unanticipated problems.

SECURITY OVER THE NETWORK

In addition to the administration of the server, you will need to consider securing the data stream that passes from FileMaker clients and FileMaker Server. FileMaker uses TCP/IP as its network protocol, and when you either host a file via FileMaker Server or share it via peer-to-peer connections, information passes from host to client in a near-constant exchange. To secure this stream of data from possible threats like network packet sniffing software, you should minimally use firewall and VPN technologies to prevent outsiders from gaining access to your internal network. To provide the most secure environment possible, you can also choose to encrypt the data passing from FileMaker Server to FileMaker Pro 8 and FileMaker Pro 8 Advanced, the setting for which is shown in Figure 12.14.

Figure 12.14
You can protect your data stream using Secure Sockets Layer encryption.

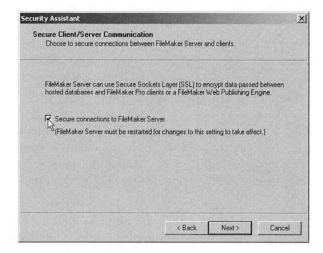

FileMaker client computers will decrypt encrypted information before displaying it, and as such you may have some performance considerations to test for. A rule of thumb is that encryption will slow down the overall performance of your solution, but the specific impact to it will be driven by your network architecture, the hardware involved, the programming decisions you've made within FileMaker, and so on. We recommend simply testing it and determining the pros and cons for encryption in your specific circumstances.

USER AUTHENTICATION

After your server is secure and you have protected your network traffic by either isolating your network itself or encrypting your data (or both), you need to establish a means for each individual user to authenticate to your databases.

An account can be authenticated either internally or externally. In the Edit Account dialog, if you set the authentication method to FileMaker, the account names will be stored within the file. Passwords are not actually stored in the file; they are encrypted every time they are used or changed with a one-way hash algorithm (based on respected industry-standard security methods). Each time your password is used, its encrypted hash changes. If someone were to gain access to your FileMaker file and crack the file somehow, he would be able to decipher only the last used hash algorithm. If you take the added precaution of securing your FileMaker files on FileMaker Server, you will remove even the opportunity to manipulate the physical database file.

EXTERNAL AUTHENTICATION

External authentication is the other means by which users' credentials can be tested before they gain access to a database file. When you designate an account as externally authenticated, the Edit Account dialog changes to be slightly different in that no password or individual user account is specified. Instead, a group name is associated with a privilege set (just as accounts are), as shown in Figure 12.15.

Figure 12.15
External authentication passes credentials to an external server and expects a list of valid groups in return.

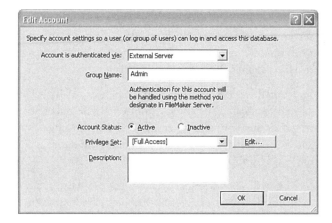

Instead of creating an account name and password, with external authentication you designate just the account name. Most often this name will correspond to a group that has been created on the external authentication server. For example, consider a user of your system, Merzal Gold, with an Active Directory account of mgold and a password of c0pp3r. He's been assigned to the companywide groups Sales and Marketing by his active directory administrator. When he logs in with mgold/c0pp3r, FileMaker Server passes these credentials to the active directory server. That external server then verifies that he's logged in correctly according to his credentials and returns a list of groups—Sales and Marketing—to FileMaker. FileMaker scans its accounts list for externally authenticated accounts with either of those names, and logs Merzal into the first match it finds.

It is important to understand that, for an externally authenticated account, individual user accounts and their passwords are managed and stored not by FileMaker itself, but by your server's operating system (hence, external to FileMaker). If your FileMaker Server is part of an Active Directory (on Windows) or Open Directory (on Mac OS) domain, your users will be authenticated by the server that controls access to your domain. This authentication server could be the same computer on which FileMaker Server is hosted, or a different computer. If your server instead makes use of local users and groups, those accounts will be used by FileMaker Server for authentication.

This external authentication is used solely to determine whether someone should have access to a FileMaker file and to what groups they belong. The only thing FileMaker relies on in external authentication is to have the operating system verify a person's password and return the group names to which they belong. Those names will then be compared to the externally authenticated accounts within FileMaker and a user's privileges determined by the first valid match.

12

Note that within FileMaker an account can be associated with only one privilege set; however, in an externally authenticated scenario, a single user might belong to multiple groups. It is the first group, from top to bottom (when sorted by authentication order), to which a user will be associated when externally authenticated.

This then means that you will need to coordinate the naming of groups between your authentication server and accounts within FileMaker. We recommend adopting a naming convention that will remind your server administrator that the groups established are there to serve your FileMaker databases.

Keep in mind that authentication is determined on an account-by-account basis. You can combine externally authenticated accounts with internal FileMaker accounts as needed. In fact, FileMaker requires that you keep at least one internally authenticated account associated with the [Full Access] privilege set to ensure that if the external authentication server is unavailable you will still be able to access the file.

Note that you can opt to have an internal account name and externally authenticated account name be identical. You as a developer may have credentials on the external server but may also want internal authentication. The first account listed by authentication order in the Define Accounts & Privileges dialog will be that which is used if duplicates are present.

By default, FileMaker Server 8 is set to allow only internal authentication. To enable both external and internal authentication, you will need to use the Server Administration Tool and configure it as shown in Figure 12.16.

Figure 12.16
Enabling FileMaker Server to manage both internal and external authentication is controlled by the security assistant in the Server Administration Tool.

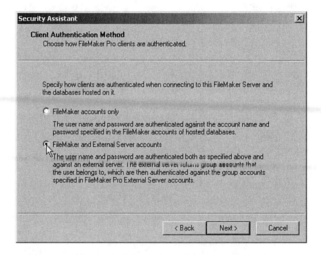

One word of caution regarding external authentication: It is theoretically possible for someone to gain access to the physical file of your database, host it on his own FileMaker Server, and then manage to rightly determine what group names were used in its security scheme in order to grant himself access. This multistep process is fairly unlikely, and you can protect against it by securing your server and keeping your [Full Access] accounts tightly controlled.

Note too that external authentication requires FileMaker Server. It is not supported in peer-to-peer hosting.

FILE LIST FILTERING

The last element in security is a final bit of protection and convenience: Users can't break into databases they don't know are there. Using FileMaker Server, you can limit the list of databases a user sees to only those to which they have access. In the Server Administration Tool, enable the Display Only the Databases Each User Is Authorized to Access setting.

When a user uses the Open Remote File dialog and chooses a server, FileMaker will first try the credentials the person used to log in on her computer (based on operating system). If that fails, the user will be asked for a username and password. (You can go directly to the username and password prompt by holding down the Shift key when selecting a server.)

On the Mac OS the process is similar, but the credentials used are stored in the keychain. To override the keychain, hold down the Option key when selecting a server.

After users are authenticated, they will be shown a list of databases within which they have valid accounts or group memberships. In the case of external authentication, this is a seamless process. In the case of internally authenticated databases, users will have to enter their login information twice: once to get a list of databases and a second time when logging in to the specific database they then choose.

TROUBLESHOOTING

FORGOTTEN ADMIN PASSWORD

What can I do if I forget my Admin password and no longer have [Full Access] privileges?

Unfortunately, you're out of luck. In the past, FileMaker was able to open its own databases and provide access again, but this is no longer technically possible given the encryption used.

We recommend that you create two accounts with [Full Access] privileges and make sure that you (or a single person in your organization) aren't the only one who can gain full access into a database file.

CONVERTED PASSWORDS

I have converted my files from FileMaker Pro 6 to FileMaker Pro 8, and it appears my passwords no longer work. Why might this be the case?

Passwords in FileMaker 8 (and FileMaker 7 before it) are case sensitive. In versions prior to 7, passwords were not case sensitive. For instance, "fish" might open your database when "Fish" is the actual stored password. To remedy this problem, simply return to your database in FileMaker Pro 6 (or earlier) and change the offending password, and then reconvert the files.

DATABASE DOESN'T APPEAR ON FILEMAKER SERVER

I am hosting a file on FileMaker Server. It's open and I know my [Full Access] admin account information, but the file doesn't show up in the list of databases available on that server.

Remember that to access a FileMaker file remotely through the network, you will need to turn on the extended privilege for FileMaker Network Access. Even though you have a [Full Access] account, by default no extended privileges are enabled for any accounts within FileMaker.

CLOSING AND REOPENING FILE FOR TESTING

I'm trying to enable security settings, and I keep having to close and reopen the file to do proper testing. Is there some better way to test other accounts?

We strongly recommend that you create a logout script and button for your users to use. Then, after that's available via whatever interface you choose, we recommend folding some conditional logic in for you as a developer. If, for example, you hold down the Shift key in the following script, it will perform a relogin step without forcing the user to close and reopen the file:

```
Logout
# purpose: Logout with relogin for testing
# Shift key performs relogin
If [ Get ( ActiveModifierKeys ) = 1 ]
    Re-Login [ ]
Else
    Close File [ Current File ]
End If
#
```

FILEMAKER EXTRA: WORKING WITH MULTIPLE FILES

Throughout this chapter we have been careful to note that security settings are specific to a single file within FileMaker. If you have a solution that spans multiple files, you will need to duplicate your account and privilege settings across those multiple files. This can become onerous when you have more than a handful of accounts or groups.

Privilege sets within FileMaker cannot be programmatically controlled. In other words, you cannot use a script to define a privilege set. You will need to create the appropriate privilege sets in each file of your solution. This is as expected: By definition each privilege set should be specific to the file in which it sits.

Accounts, on the other hand, can be managed by script, and there are some techniques you can use to simplify the management of accounts within your suite of files.

These are the Accounts script steps available to you:

- **Add Account**—Using this script step, you can add an account to your file. Note that the script step dialog shown in Figure 12.17 requires that it be associated with a specific privilege set. You will need to create as many Add Account scripts as you have privilege sets. Note that this script step works only for internally authenticated accounts.

Figure 12.17
The Add Account script step allows you to add internally authenticated users to a file.

- **Delete Account**—This allows you to permanently remove an account (by name) from your file.

- **Reset Account Password**—Resetting the account password allows you to change it to a default of some sort without knowing the prior password.

- **Change Password**—Change Password requires the current password followed by the new password.

- **Enable Account**—This allows you to activate and deactivate an account. This is a non-permanent way to deny someone access.

- **Re-login**—FileMaker will prompt the user to log in again, or you can store credentials in this script step to do so without a dialog.

To use these script steps to support work in multiple files, you will need to create a user interface that allows users to create accounts and change passwords. Note that in the dialog shown in Figure 12.17, there is a Specify button next to both the Account Name and the Password boxes.

First, create a layout (or dialog) that will ask a user for a new account name and password she wants to add to your multifile solution. You should have the user enter that information into two fields set with global storage. You will also need a pop-up menu of privilege sets available within your solution (and certainly you should feel free to omit those that are sensitive, such as [Full Access]).

Second, write a script that calls subscripts in each of your solution files. The subscript should use the Add Account script step to create the new user account. Where you need to provide an account name and password, simply reference the two global fields you had set up previously. Note that with global fields, you can add an external table occurrence from a different file and gain access to the fields as you need.

You can follow similar techniques for changing passwords, deleting accounts, and enabling them.

12

CHAPTER **13**

ADVANCED INTERFACE TECHNIQUES

In this chapter

USER INTERFACES IN FILEMAKER PRO

Every new FileMaker Pro database essentially begins with a single, blank layout. User interface designers—and, yes, you're now one by definition—often have to approach each solution they design somewhat differently, to tailor it for the specific use in question, for the users for whom the system is ultimately intended, and in keeping with the time/budget/scope variables we all struggle with in some form or another. This chapter is not intended to present a complete user interface discourse. How to approach a user interface is a widely debated topic in both the FileMaker and the computer science worlds. On the Web, as you no doubt know, what works for one site doesn't often work for another—nor should it. We won't presume to know what the world's most perfect user interface might be.

Rather than trying to present the "what" or "why" of user interface and layout design, we're going to focus on the "how." There *are* some constants in FileMaker interface design: Almost every database solution ever built has some form of navigation, meaning a button-and-script–driven means of moving from layout to layout. Data presentation—how you view and access information in your system—varies, and we explore some of the options there as well. We also examine how to approach working with multiple windows, and delve into FileMaker 8's new Custom Menus feature as well.

This chapter presents several topics. Each section could comfortably stand on its own; the idea here is to present you with some ideas you can apply to your solutions as you see fit. The chapter assumes a moderately advanced familiarity with FileMaker Pro, but beginners should be able to grasp the concepts quite easily, if they don't immediately understand the implementation.

User interfaces are central to most FileMaker databases. It is rare (although entirely possible) that a FileMaker database would serve only as a back-end data repository, with some other system providing a visual front end. Custom web-published databases are an obvious exception, but many FileMaker-based web systems also have administrative or data-entry functions built into native FileMaker Pro layouts and accessed with FileMaker Pro, not to mention IWP (Instant Web Publishing) that depends on layouts being created in FileMaker. Some FileMaker systems also serve as front-end extensions of larger systems through ODBC or XML connections; one of the core reasons organizations choose to use FileMaker in such cases is the rapidity and flexibility with which interfaces can be built. It's safe to say that not only is storing data fundamental to FileMaker Pro, but the presentation of data is fundamental as well.

→ For more detail on Instant Web Publishing, **see** Chapter 21, "Instant Web Publishing," **p. 633**.

Figures 13.1, 13.2, and 13.3 present some interface examples we've come across in our travels.

Figure 13.1
This is a fairly typical example of a tabbed interface in FileMaker Pro; the tabs in this example have been created as graphic objects.

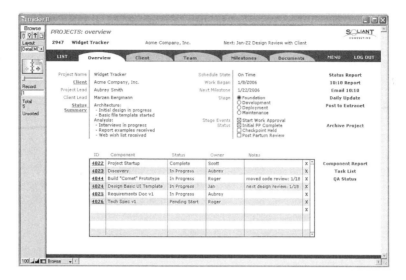

Figure 13.2
FileMaker Recruiter 2.0, produced by FileMaker, Inc., itself, is a solid example of a classic design. Notice the two tiers of navigation with the section headers at the top of the window.

Primary considerations when you approach designing a user interface include how to trigger functions specific to your database solution (for example, a series of scripts that create monthly invoices), how to manage creating and deleting records, whether to build some form of interface to help with Find requests, and how a user might run a report.

Other issues will also need to be worked out: What color scheme do you want your user interface to follow? How much screen real estate do you have? What fonts will work for all the users in your system?

13

Figure 13.3
Here's a different twist on user interface—lean, with lots of whitespace and navigation in more of a web-style approach.

New in FileMaker Pro 8 Advanced is the capability to customize menus. How you approach menus significantly extends the planning you'll need to do when approaching a new application. What often were interface elements that developers would have to build into custom layouts can now be managed with sensible use of menu sets.

→ To learn how to create custom menus, **see** "Working with Custom Menus," later in this chapter, **p. 373**.

TIP

> We recommend two things when defining an interface for a new solution. First, define one. Rather than having things just evolve at random, you'll be well served by spending a few minutes up front coming up with a standard interface approach.
>
> Second, create a prototypical layout and menu set for your system and then test it with users before building the rest of your system. Establish a common standard for where things go, how large the screen is, how portals look, where field labels sit, and how you'll use menus, and then get buy-in from the people who will ultimately live with the database day in and day out. It's far easier to spend a little time in the beginning discovering that your boss deeply loathes the color green than to go back and rework your database.
>
> When moving forward in your system, it will be easier to duplicate your template layout than to start from scratch each time. This also saves time: After the problem of look and feel is solved, you won't need to spend more time thinking about it as you create new layouts.

FILEMAKER'S NATIVE USER INTERFACE

Another critical consideration for your user interface (UI) is to what degree to use FileMaker's own native elements—the Status Area, menu commands, and Scripts menu—or how to go about replacing them with your own buttons, scripts, or custom menus.

It is entirely possible to build a perfectly usable FileMaker database without adding a single button to any of your layouts. Users can rely on the Layout pop-up menu in the Status Area and, for those reports and functions that require scripts, turn to the Scripts menu, or to any special menus you may have added as custom menus. Relying heavily on FileMaker's native UI delivers some significant benefits in the time it takes you to build a database. Your users are likely already to understand at least some of the basics of working with a FileMaker database as well. This bare-bones approach can "just get it working" quite quickly. The downside, aside from simple aesthetics, is that your database may not be particularly intuitive for nondevelopers to manipulate in cases in which your data structure becomes complex.

We strongly recommend embracing FileMaker's *raison d'être*: flexibility. Although it's possible to pull off some quite advanced custom-crafted user interface designs, make sure that you take on added complexity deliberately, by choice, and recognize the cost.

> **TIP**
>
> Be sure if you use a native approach in FileMaker to do so fully and make use of its security. You can still leave FileMaker's menu commands available to your users if you carefully think through your security setup.
>
> You can also disable the native menu choices you don't want used, or override them with your own custom scripts, by creating custom menu sets. Refer to the section "Working with Custom Menus," later in this chapter.

→ For complete details on FileMaker security, **see** Chapter 12, "Implementing Security," **p. 325**.

BUILDING YOUR OWN INTERFACE

The alternative to a native FileMaker approach is to replace the Status Area and menu functions with your own buttons, scripts, and custom menus. The approach here gives you the most control, but also signs you up for the most work. (Notice that the Status Area seen Figure 13.2 is closed. The designers of this system replaced the functions of the Status Area with their own buttons elsewhere on the layout.)

When following such an approach, you will need to replace all the functions of the Status Area in three of the four modes (it is not possible to replicate its functions in Layout mode), and you'll likely opt to close and lock the Status Area after you've done so.

This process is identical in nature to building other interface elements: You will need to create objects to serve as buttons (images, text, or some other FileMaker layout object) and then create scripts to replicate the functions of the Status Area, such as "go to next record" or "go to previous record." One of the more challenging elements of re-creating all the functions of the Status Area can be the Omit check box control while in Find mode.

 To understand how to replicate the functionality of the Omit check box in Find mode, refer to "Omit Re-created" in the "Troubleshooting" section at the end of this chapter.

NEW Note also that with the capability to modify menus via FileMaker Pro 8 Advanced's Custom Menus features, FileMaker systems no longer have to be either/or propositions with regard to using all native FileMaker controls or locking them down completely. In past versions, if there was one element of the native FileMaker controls you wanted to prevent users from accessing—the Delete All Records menu item, for example—you had only one choice: Lock down all menus. This then meant you faced replicating a good deal of functionality to control just those items you wanted to customize.

By using FileMaker Pro 8 Advanced, you can leave elements of native FileMaker functionality available while locking down just those you need to restrict. This mix-and-match approach is one of the best reasons to upgrade to FileMaker 8.

INTERFACE LOOK AND FEEL

Remember that container fields, as well as graphical objects pasted onto a layout, can be turned into buttons and thus associated with a script action. This enables you to design quite complete user interface elements in the image-editing software of your choice. Buttons can be far more than simply gray rectangles, and it's quite possible to create a user experience that feels nothing like FileMaker in its native state.

We recommend that you insert all such graphical UI elements into container fields set for global storage, rather than pasting them directly on layouts. If you ever need to make a change, you need only do so in one place, rather than having to paste a modified element back onto all the layouts on which it was used and reapply its script or button behavior.

To use this container method, simply create a single repeating container field, set to global storage. Then when placing buttons on your layouts, instead of placing the graphic element itself, simply place a field with the proper dimensions and set it to show repetition X through X (say 3 through 3) to display the applicable graphic. Then attach a button behavior to that field. From this point forward in the chapter, when we speak of placing button objects on a layout, this is the method we prefer, but we will not reference it continually throughout the chapter.

> **TIP**
>
> Remember, when you are placing a button object on multiple layouts, first apply the script behavior to the object, and then copy and paste on all layouts with the button behavior intact.

For maximum control, it's even possible to create a kiosk experience in FileMaker Pro that takes complete control of the screen. FileMaker's menus will not appear in kiosk mode, and you can choose to close and hide the Status Area as well. For all intents and purposes, the entire look and feel of the screen will be in your hands. A kiosk typically isn't something you'd want to deploy for use on desktops: It takes over the entire screen and isn't well suited for working with other applications.

→ To learn more about creating kiosks in FileMaker Pro Advanced, **see** "Developing Kiosk Solutions," **p. 769**.

SINGLE FILE INTERFACE VERSUS DISTRIBUTED INTERFACE

Aside from the approach of building an interface, its architecture should be considered as well. One of the most frequent questions we receive is whether it is better to build a solution as a single file or to create a distributed architecture across multiple files. There are a wide variety of opinions on this topic in the FileMaker community, and some experts strongly advocate one approach over the other. Our answer is less definitive: It depends.

A single file system, with all your interface layouts in one place, is generally easier to build and requires less architectural overhead. FileMaker 8's capability to reference external table occurrences makes the overhead arguably minimal in some cases, but you will need to replicate security settings, value lists, and custom functions in each file separately, and you will need to work out window management and navigation schemes to support multiple files. (Although, again, it's possible to build all of your interface in a single window that then references a separate or multiple data files, so…it depends.)

A multiple file system (possibly with interface layouts in multiple files) has the benefit of allowing multiple developers to work on each file in parallel (whereas working in Script Maker or making database schema changes can be done by only one person at a time), as well as keeping FileMaker elements organized in discrete, separate packages. A single file system tends to balloon with scripts, value lists, and layouts. In a multiple file system it's possible to isolate those elements to just the functionality or operational group necessary. As an example, you might put all your customer-related interfaces in a Customers file, and all of your finance-related interfaces in a Finance file.

→ To review working with multiple files from an architectural perspective (beyond just interface considerations), **see** "How and When to Use Multiple Files," **p. 207**.

In our consulting practice, we implement systems with both types of architectures. Generally, smaller systems end up as single file systems, and larger systems (ones with more than 40 or so data tables) have to some degree tended to be distributed. This is a somewhat specialized observation, though: We tend to create distributed file systems to support multiple developers, which generally is not an overriding concern for many organizations.

Obviously, there might be times when you have no choice: Your database might have been converted from a version before FileMaker 7, in which case you'd need to do substantial rewriting to bring the interface elements into one file. It is often best to live with the separate files created by the conversion process, given that security settings, and so forth, have already been replicated for you during conversion.

→ To explore table architecture options, **see** Chapter 6, "Working with Multiple Tables," **p. 157**.
→ For more information on converted files, **see** Chapter 18, "Converting Systems from Previous Versions of FileMaker Pro," **p. 537**.

13

NAVIGATION

In addition to the look and feel of a system and its architecture, nearly every FileMaker solution we've ever seen contains some degree of navigation—buttons and scripts designed to help users move from layout to layout. The considerations for navigation are fairly involved and warrant in-depth exploration. From this point forward in the chapter, we will discuss the nuts and bolts of various interface mechanics; assembling all these elements into one solution will then define your user interface.

Navigation implementations can come in many forms, and depending on how you define navigation, your navigation system can include various other functional elements as well. You might work with multiple windows, you may want to build a portal-only view into your data, you may want to separate your data files from your interface files, and so on. Internally, your system might need to perform validation checks in the course of navigation, run security routines, manage audit trails, and more. In FileMaker 8, scripts depend on layout context to establish table context. This then means that your users won't be the only ones needing to navigate around the system: Scripts will need to switch to different layouts to establish context, and return to the original to maintain the user experience. Although this issue is not strictly related to your user interface, you will likely still need to consider the needs of your internal system (routines that run without user control) when approaching navigation. Likewise, users won't want to *only* navigate. For example, at times they'll be interested in also manipulating found sets or perhaps seeing record selections made, automatically changing modes, or having navigation include a sort command. Before building a navigation system, consider what functional aspects it needs to include.

In addition to the wide variety of functions navigation performs, its presentation can vary as well. Tabbed interfaces are common, which boil down to simply a series of buttons that have Go To Layout scripts attached on a layout. Other options are different visually, but ultimately you'll be attaching navigation scripts (or a script) to various buttons. Navigation has two inseparable elements: its visual presentation and its functionality.

This chapter explores the behind-the-scenes techniques you'll find necessary to build navigation systems; these techniques are intended to be relatively independent from any particular graphical scheme, so you can adapt them to whatever particular visual scheme you choose for your system.

TABBED NAVIGATION

Tabbed navigation is one of the classic ways to get around a FileMaker database. Regardless of whether you make your buttons actually look like tabs, the basic idea is that you have a series of buttons on each layout, one of which is in a "current" selected state, and that users can see this omnipresent navigation element as they use the system (see Figure 13.4). Again, we're not advocating one visual approach over another; this technique can be applied to a wide range of styles.

NOTE

NEW

FileMaker 8 introduced the Tab Control object that allows developers to add tab panes to a layout in order to show more information on that layout. Using a Tab Control is a great way to extend screen real estate and make interface refinements, but they exist on only one layout. When we speak of navigation, we're talking about moving from one layout to another. The Tab Control is a fantastic addition to FileMaker that has dramatically reduced the number of layouts necessary in most solutions, but it isn't a navigation control.

→ To learn more about the Tab Control object, **see** "Working with the Tab Control Object," **p. 117**.

Figure 13.4
The tab look was created by simply laying a one-pixel line along the bottom of the Products button that needed to appear as a front or current tab.

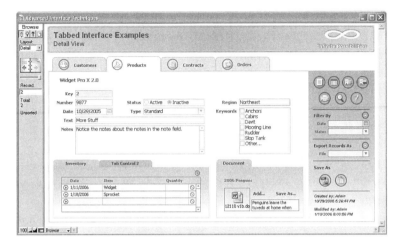

To create the layout shown in Figure 13.4, first place three gray curved-corner rectangles above a white square rectangle. These will become your gray "inactive" tab buttons. A fourth curved rectangle in white serves as the "currently selected" tab. Then it's a matter of overlaying objects, using the Arrange menu's Send Forward and Send Backward commands, to put the gray buttons behind the white rectangle, and the white button in front. Then finally create a white line (that isn't visible against white objects) to hide the bottom edge of the button.

After you have your layout visually set up as you'd like, simply set the tabs as buttons with the appropriate actions or scripts attached. Implementation methods vary widely. At the simplest level, you need only create a button for each layout in your system and attach a Go To Layout button behavior to it. This basic approach isn't the best way to manage buttons in a database solution, but it's a perfectly serviceable method.

You should try to abstract things a bit more. First off, never attach anything other than scripts to buttons to avoid having to rework a great many layout objects down the road in case something changes. It's better to attach a single script to what then becomes multiple buttons on various layouts within your system. Second, because navigation routines are almost always the same regardless of destination (ultimately it's *only* the destination layout that is different) and will very likely evolve over time with a given solution, we tend to recommend that you manage navigation in a single script and centralize your logic to a reasonable degree. If you can rely on one central place for your navigation routine, it is relatively easy to add functionality to your database or to, say, change one layout from an old version to a new updated version.

Finally, although we've presented here one approach to building a navigation scheme that looks like a series of tabs, we are presenting only one simple example. We'd hardly suggest that this is the only visual approach you can or should take.

→ For discussion on scripting best practices, **see** Chapter 9, "Getting Started with Scripting," **p. 247**.

NAVIGATION MEDIATOR AND THE GLOBAL Nav SCRIPT

We touched on using a single script for navigation in the preceding section. By using script parameters you can drive most, if not all, of your navigation through a single script. The layers of abstraction here could potentially become fairly complex, so we recommend keeping an eye on your goal: creating a simple, single routine for handling navigation. This routine might be called from a button on a layout or from another script. It needs to work both for situations in which a user wants to shift to another layout (and stay there) and for situations in which the system itself needs to move to a layout to establish context.

The basic technique makes use of script parameters: Attach a single Nav script to all your navigation buttons and set a parameter for each button that corresponds to its destination layout.

→ For more information on script parameters, **see** Chapter 15, "Advanced Scripting Techniques," **p. 435**.

You could certainly pass a layout name as a parameter and, within the Nav script called, use the Go To Layout script step combined with a Get(ScriptParameter) calculation, but that still means you have hard-coded layout names attached to buttons. We recommend against that practice because it would break if you ever had to change the name of any of your layouts.

To create a single navigation script, plan on never changing the script parameters you attach to buttons after your layouts have been created. Use a navigation code scheme—in which, for example, cust_detail might correspond with the Customer Detail layout. You could just as easily use nav1 as your code that corresponds with the Customer Detail layout, or even button1.

The point here is that you use codes of your own choosing to identify which button has been clicked by a user and then match each code to a destination layout. That way if you ever need to change the destination, you need only do so in one place; all navigation steps that used that code will now point to the new layout.

There are three general ways you can create this matching between navigation codes and their respective layout names. The most straightforward is to simply create a branching If/Else script. Another way is to use a Case statement to set a script variable, and then use that variable's value in a single Go To Layout step. This method is used here in an example of a central navigation system using multiple navigation codes:

```
Navigate ( navCode )
# purpose: Move the focus of the current window to a new layout
# dependencies: requires a navCode (text script parameter) that
#       is recognized within this script
#
Set Variable [ $navCode; Get (ScriptParameter) ]
Set Variable [ $layoutName;
    Case (
        $navCode = "cust_list"; "Customer List";
        $navCode = "cust_detail"; "Customer Detail";
        $navCode = "prod_list"; "Product List";
        $navCode = "prod_detail"; "Product Detail";
        $navCode = "cont_list"; "Contract List";
        $navCode = "cont_detail"; "Contract Detail";
```

```
            $navCode = "ord_list"; "Order List";
            $navCode = "ord_detail"; "Order Detail";
            $navCode = "menu"; "Main Menu";
            $navCode = "about"; "About this Database";
            "unrecognized navCode parameter"
        ) ]
Go to Layout [ $layoutName ]
Exit Script [ ]
#
```

This approach has several benefits, not the least of which is the fact that controlling your navigation occurs within this single place and doesn't require that you work with multiple fields, multiple scripts, and so on.

The goal of each of these methods is to centralize the mapping of navigation codes to layout names. In one example, this association took place within a script. Another possibility would be performing the matching within a custom function. With either choice, the mapping is stored in a single place. Yet another approach would be to move your layout and navCode information into its own data table. Each row of the table would store, at a minimum, a navigation code and the name of the associated target layout. You can add additional fields to each navigation record, of course, and this would allow you to track other attributes about your layouts and would enable further customization.

There are downsides to putting control information in a data table, however. First, if ever someone saved a clone of your database, that vital information would be missing. Second, you'd likely have to relate your navigation table occurrence (or occurrences) to a number of other table occurrences within your system, potentially cluttering your Relationships Graph significantly. The goal of code abstraction is to compartmentalize the logic of your system; if by building an abstracted navigation routine you burden your work with a good deal of overhead, it may defeat the purpose.

BRANCHED LAYOUT NAVIGATION

One interesting possibility this approach also offers is the potential to branch your navigation routines based on differing states within your system. Imagine building two layouts and driving users to them by either preference or privilege: You could offer two different List views, for example, and your navigation system could direct users as appropriate. Here's an example of what the Case statement from the preceding Navigate script could become:

```
Case (
    $navCode = "prod_list"; "Product List";
    $navCode = "prod_detail"; "Product Detail";
    $navCode = "cont_list"; "Contract List";
    $navCode = "cont_detail" and $$contractPref = "Full";
        "Contract Full Detail";
    $navCode = "cont_detail" and $$contractPref = "Lite";
        "Contract Lite Detail";
    "unrecognized navCode parameter"
) ]
```

This example drives home the point of the exercise. Imagine building this navigation scheme and having your users request exactly that which we've described: Some users want to see

13

the full version of a contract, and other users need to access a "lite" version. If you had built your navigation with separate, multiple scripts or attached Go to Layout script steps to buttons without the benefit of scripts, the alterations your database would require would undoubtedly be fairly numerous. In this abstracted navigation approach, you need only modify and test this one Navigate script, and need not modify your layouts or buttons at all.

Note that you could also add security privilege checks to your navigation system and gracefully let your users know when they cannot access a given area of your system, rather than having FileMaker dutifully take them to a screen with <No Access> showing and no means of getting back to the layout from which they came.

A script that more gracefully manages cases in which a user tries to navigate to a restricted layout might look like this:

```
Navigate ( navCode )
# purpose: Move the focus of the current window to a new layout
# dependencies: requires a navCode (text script parameter) that
#       is recognized within this script
#
Set Variable [ $navCode; Get (ScriptParameter) ]
Set Variable [ $layoutName;
    Case (
        $navCode = "cust_list"; "Customer List";
        $navCode = "cust_detail"; "Customer Detail";
        $navCode = "prod_list"; "Product List";
        $navCode = "prod_detail"; "Product Detail";
        $navCode = "menu"; "Main Menu";
        $navCode = "about"; "About this Database";
        "unrecognized navCode parameter"
    ) ]
#
# Check for access
If [
        Let ([
            layoutValues = LayoutNames ( Get(FileName));
            filteredLayout = FilterValues ( layoutValues; $layoutName )
            ];
            Case ( IsEmpty (filteredLayout); 1; 0 )
        ) ]
    Show Custom Dialog ["No Access";
        "Sorry, you do not have access to that area."; Button: "OK" ]
    Exit Script [ ]
End If
#
Go to Layout [ $layoutName ]
Exit Script [ ]
```

The test for access depends on the fact that the LayoutNames function will return a list of only those layouts to which a person has access. By filtering the list and testing to see whether the result is empty, your script can check for access and, if the user does not have access, exit the script before getting to the Go to Layout step.

BACK BUTTONS

One of the most dreaded questions we used to hear while working with FileMaker Pro 6 and earlier was "Where's the Back button?" It's not that Back buttons were technologically that big a deal...it's just that they used to be a lot of work, and they added unwelcome overhead to database solutions. In FileMaker 8 they're a snap, and the ceiling on storage limits introduced in FileMaker Pro 7 makes overhead a complete nonissue. This is a great example of how FileMaker Pro 7 dramatically extended the horizon forward for all of us.

FileMaker has two layers of navigation (a subtlety many novice users don't immediately grasp): navigation from record to record and navigation from one layout to another. Web browsers aren't troubled by such things, nor in their stateless world is there a distinction between data and page. The metaphor of a Back button isn't a perfect fit in FileMaker, but users will immediately understand what it does. A Back button can help users distinguish more easily between navigating from record to record using the book icon (or your replacement for it) and navigating from layout to layout.

The approach given here leverages the abstracted navigation routine described in the preceding section. Our goal is to track each instance of navigation that a user makes—by saving them to a navigation history variable—and then be able to trace backward along those historical entries. The navigation script with a Back button capability looks like this:

```
Navigate ( navCode )
# purpose: Move the focus of the current window to a new layout
# dependencies: requires a navCode (text script parameter) that
#       is recognized within this script
#
Set Variable [ $navCode; Get (ScriptParameter) ]
Set Variable [ $layoutName;
    Case (
        $navCode = "back"; GetValue( $$navHistory; 2);
        $navCode = "cust_list"; "Customer List";
        $navCode = "cust_detail"; "Customer Detail";
        $navCode = "prod_list"; "Product List";
        $navCode = "prod_detail"; "Product Detail";
        $navCode = "menu"; "Main Menu";
        $navCode = "about"; "About this Database";
        "unrecognized navCode parameter"
    ) ]
#
# Manage history variable
If [ $navCode = "back" ]
    # If navCode is "back", remove first value in stack
    Set Variable [ $$navHistory;
        RightValues ( $$navHistory; ValueCount ( $$navHistory ) - 1 ) ]
Else
    # If navCode is not "back", add the layout name to the history stack
    Set Variable [ $$navHistory;
        $layoutName & "¶" &
        $$navHistory ]
End If
#
Go to Layout [ $layoutName ]
Exit Script [ ]
```

13

To get the back functionality to work, you'd need to create a "back" button on all the applicable layouts and pass the navCode "back" into the Navigate script.

The script assumes that the $$navHistory variable has a list of layout names in it, with the most recently visited in the first position. As you navigate to different layouts, you build a stack of layout names in the $$navHistory value list. When the Back button is used, the $layoutName variable is set to the second value in the $$navHistory list (the one just before the current layout), and then later in the script that value is removed so that the second value becomes the first.

Note that the script throws away old layout names as the user moves backward down the value stack. You could modify the script further still to offer a "forward" button. Instead of removing layout names from the history values, create an additional variable, an integer, to keep track of the position within the stack on which the user is currently.

Last, we'd recommend building some more error-checking into your script. The example given here doesn't check whether the $$navHistory variable is empty.

CAUTION

Remember the distinction between navigating through layouts and navigating through records. The example we've provided here does not preserve and restore found sets. Although users will be familiar with how Back buttons work on the Web, you're not actually reloading previously viewed pages; the found set a user is working with will not change to match any prior state without significant scripting on the part of the developer.

CONTROLLING THE TAB CONTROL OBJECT USING A SCRIPT

In addition to controlling how users navigate from layout to layout, there are some cases in which you may want FileMaker to take a user automatically to one of the specific panes on a Tab Control object (which may be different from its default pane). For example, if you had a Tab Control in a contacts database that included, say, people's phone number information on its second tab, you might want to link directly to that pane from elsewhere in your system. Imagine elsewhere a portal of company employees on a company layout that perhaps shows a column of their office extensions and a button next to it used as a hyperlink. Your users could click the hyperlink and arrive at that person's contact record and, as an added nicety, have the second pane of the Tab Control showing that person's phone information as well.

FileMaker 8 doesn't include any programmatic access to a Tab Control, but there's a simple technique that works perfectly well.

→ To review the Tab Control, **see** "Working with the Tab Control Object," **p. 117**.

First, create a Tab Control object with as many panes as are necessary for your layout. Second, define a global repeating field in your database and name it something like "tab controller." Place this field on each pane of the Tab Control, but in doing so, select repetition 1 through 1, 2 through 2, and so on such that each pane shows only one unique repetition.

You can now write a script that makes use of the `Go to Field` script step. Add the following to the scripts that navigate to these tab panes:

```
Go to Field [resourcesTable::tabController[1]]
```

You can change the repetition number (referenced in the brackets) to dictate to which of the tabs the user will go.

Finally, we recommend that you turn off the capability for users to click into these fields; users have no need to alter data in them. We also recommend that you format the fields so that they're not visible on the layout. They need to be there, but the users don't need to have entry access for this technique to work. (They do, however, need to have security privileges that permit them access to the field, or you can write your navigation scripts to run with full access.)

OTHER NAVIGATION USER INTERFACES

There are many other approaches you could use for navigation, but in general they are variations on the themes we've mapped out so far in this chapter. Scripts—however they're controlled—call `Go to Layout` script steps and send the user to a new layout. From there it becomes a question of how to visually present navigation to the user.

There are a wide variety of user interfaces for navigation as well. The sample file we've used in this book places navigation on a Tab Control pane. In an extreme case, we once ran into a database that used the four corners and edges of the screen for navigation. A degree of luck was involved because the system lacked any labels or indication that there were any buttons at all. The person who designed it said that the people in their organization had just learned where to click. Some navigation schemes are better than others, no doubt. The following are a few approaches other than the one described here.

One approach FileMaker Pro 8 Advanced makes possible is to offer an entirely menu-driven user interface. You could create a menu of layouts, or perhaps subdivide your solution into areas using submenus.

Another approach some developers choose is to create *navigation portals*. Each portal row contains a button and some attribute (the equivalent of the navCodes from the previous example) that then determines what script or layout should be the result of a button click. This could work with script parameters passing a layout name, or it would fold in nicely with the navCode approach as well. The advantage to this approach is that you can control your navigation interface through a relationship, dynamically showing various related records as you'd like.

In other cases, perhaps a simple pop-up menu and Go button can be used. In this instance, a user would make a navigation choice from a menu directly on a layout, and then click a Go button, initiating a script that would use the navigation choice to determine which script to perform or destination layout to target. It could make this determination using a series of If/Else statements, or the system could be set up for some kind of data-driven navigation, as in the navigation example earlier in the chapter. In this case the user's choice would be a key that would point to a data record fully describing the chosen navigation option and its logic.

Yet another idea is to establish a separate layout as a kind of navigation palette, and populate that layout with buttons that give access to system features and areas; scripts could handle the opening and maintaining of that window. The downside of this approach is that your users need to click twice to use it: once for the window to come forward, and once again to activate a navigation button/script; however, this is a great approach for people with different monitor resolutions (allowing those users with large monitors to place their navigation window wherever they choose), and it makes navigation a distinct process, separate from other functions.

Regardless of which visual and presentation approach you prefer, we encourage you to think ahead and try to bake in some flexibility and room to grow when dealing with navigation scripts. They are more often than not some of the most interwoven and omnipresent script routines in your solutions.

MULTIWINDOW INTERFACES

Opening a new window for your navigation or other button elements is only the tip of the iceberg when it comes to working with multiple windows. It is possible in FileMaker 8 to strictly control multiple windows—their positions, sizes, and titles.

The simple nuts and bolts of these features can be found in the New Window script step options. With them you can create new windows, close windows, select (bring to front) a specific window by name, adjust and resize windows, tile and cascade multiple windows at once, and control the availability of the Status Area as well.

Figure 13.5 shows a simple example of the script options for the New Window script step.

Figure 13.5
This 400-pixel by 300-pixel window opens with a title of My Window and is positioned in the upper left of the screen.

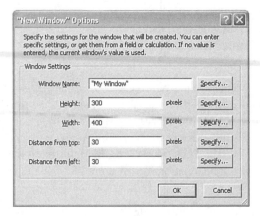

The possible uses for multiple windows are quite varied:

- To view as many layouts at once as your screen real estate allows
- To create multiple List view windows of the same table, with different found sets, at once.

- To use a form for editing a single record while still viewing multiple records via either List or Table view

- To create a pop-up window, similar to a dialog box

- To keep navigation, function, and other palettes off to the side of your workspace

- To view reports while not having to leave the windows/layouts in which you're working

The possible list is virtually endless. What we will present in the following sections are some common examples that should serve to demonstrate the mechanics of working with multiple windows.

TOOL AND FUNCTION PALETTES

As discussed previously, it's possible to build a palette for navigation, functions, or any number of options for buttons in your solution. For example, you might want to present your users with a new window containing a portal of all the possible reports in their database solutions—that also open in their own individual windows. Another idea might be to have a central control panel that allows you as a developer to unlock certain layouts, run test scripts, re-log in, view internal field data, and so on.

The only drawback to this approach is that users need to click twice to perform button actions: once to bring the window forward, into an active state, and a second time to click the chosen button.

From an implementation standpoint, this functionality is simple to deliver: Create a layout with all of your various button or control objects on it and write a script to open this window and tie it to your startup routine.

RICH DIALOG WINDOWS

Modal dialogs—windows that stay open in the foreground while waiting for some action to be performed by the user—are a common user interface standard that users will find familiar. Certainly the `Show Custom Dialog` script step will take care of some of your basic needs, but in cases in which you'd like to control the look and feel of a dialog or need more than three simple text-entry fields, you will need to turn to crafting your own window dialogs.

This technique is entirely driven by scripts. You are free to build whatever type of layout and window you'd like. The only stipulation here is that you give users a means of continuing with the process after you've brought them to a modal dialog (a Close button, for example). Your database will be in a paused state, waiting for user input. More often than not, resuming from this state is accomplished with a Continue button or, with a bit more scripting, Submit and Cancel buttons.

Cancel buttons imply that whatever action the user has taken in the modal dialog window can be undone. That can be problematic (especially if you've allowed the user to add and remove records from a portal), so be careful with the use of that term. One technique for managing the undo process is to use global fields for data entry and to populate true fields only when the user clicks Submit. Other techniques involve record-level rollbacks. (A *rollback* essentially undoes a transaction in a database, returning it to a previous state.)

→ To learn more about rollbacks and undo operations, **see** Chapter 11, "Developing for Multiuser Deployment," **p. 307**.

To build a modal dialog, follow these steps:

1. Build a layout intended to act as your pop-up dialog, called Pop Up. Size it in such a way that it is smaller than a main layout that is to remain behind it. You can add whatever functions and layout objects to it that you want. The layout can be as simple as a single field, or it can be as complex as one that displays a subsummary report in preview mode.

2. Add a Done button to your Pop Up layout. For now, attach it to its own placeholder script with just a comment. You will deal with writing the script itself later.

3. Now place a button on your main layout. For now, create a label for it: Open. Attach it to the following script:

```
Allow User Abort [ Off ]
New Window [ Name: "Pop Up"; Height: 300; Width: 500; Top: 100; Left: 100 ]
Go to Layout [ "Pop Up" (MyTable) ]
Show/Hide Status Area [ Hide, Lock ]
Pause/Resume Script [ Indefinitely ]
```

It's important to disallow user abort; otherwise, users can close your window without performing the action you're attempting to require. It's also a good idea to lock the Status Area. Finally, you need to hold FileMaker in a paused state so that users can't perform any other action while attending to the dialog. Generally it's a bad idea to leave a script paused—users can get stuck in limbo—but in this case it is exactly the behavior you want. The script ends, leaving the user in a paused state. You need to remember that a pause state is active when performing any additional scripts or when providing other functions in your Pop Up window.

 For details on the caveats and pitfalls of using this technique, refer to "Modal Dialog Dangers," in the "Troubleshooting" section at the end of this chapter.

Keep in mind that your users will still be able to run scripts that are visible in the Scripts menu or elsewhere. In solutions that use this technique, developers often opt to *not* set scripts to display in the Scripts menu (and to control or change any custom menu sets in use), or write their scripts such that all scripts that are visible in the Scripts menu take into account this paused state (by either refusing to run or ending gracefully so that the user's state in the modal dialog window is not disrupted).

Now return to ScriptMaker and create the Done script. You need to write whatever application logic your solution requires (for example, committing data to fields from globals, performing an evaluate function, or running a report) and end your script with this:

```
Close Window [ Name: "Pop Up" ]
```

One final element is critical. You'll notice we haven't yet dealt with the pause state. If you add a Pause/Resume script step to the Done script, FileMaker won't know that you want it to resume a currently paused script. The behavior it respects is to overlay a new pause state on top of the earlier pause state. This is entirely as it should be because this allows you to build routines with multitiered pause states.

Multitiered Pause State

A *multitiered pause state* can occur when you have one routine running, paused, while another runs and then hits a pause state of its own. For example, you might be running a report that pauses for a user to enter some find criteria. In performing the find subscript, your process might turn up zero records and pause again to have the user respond to some options on what do to about the situation. These multilayered pause routines fold into each other like Russian dolls: Each pause needs its respective resume script step performed before the outer pause state can itself be resumed.

The solution to dealing with your pause state lies with the button options attached to each button object. Select your Done button object and either right-click or navigate to the Format menu (in Layout mode) and choose the Button option. Another technique is to simply double-click the button object in Layout mode. Refer to the Current Script options shown in Figure 13.6.

Figure 13.6
Notice the rarely used Current Script option in the Button Setup dialog.

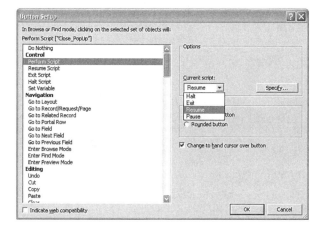

The Current Script option for the Perform Script button behavior is almost never changed. Most often its default state of pausing a currently running script while performing whatever new script is necessary will meet your needs. In this case, however, you need it to resume the current script (which will simply continue from the pause state, effectively ending it) before proceeding through the Done script and closing the pop-up window.

This then closes the pause state without creating a nested second one and allows the user back into the state of using the database solution normally. This, combined with the Close Window script step, gives the user the experience of clicking Done and seeing the window close. Clicking the Open button sends users back to the layout from which they began.

➔ For another example of working with modal dialogs using script results, **see** "Script Results," **p. 444**.

13

SPECIAL EFFECTS

Other window techniques don't seem to add much more functionality to your solution, but they can certainly be fun to include for more polish (or to just show off). Calling these techniques "special effects" is probably a stretch—we hope those of you who are Flash developers will just let this section roll by for what it's worth—but many developers in the community have had some fun coming up with a few tricks you can pull off with window script steps.

MARQUEE TITLES

Using a simple loop, you can rename the title of a window with progressively scrolling text. Use a `Set Window Title` script step inside a loop. Use a number increment (stored in a variable) and apply it to a `Right` or `Left` function with the text you want to display. The script looks like this:

```
New Window [ Height: 500; Width: 500; Top: 20; Left: 20 ]
Set Variable [ $loopCounter; 1 ]
Loop
    Exit Loop If [ $loopCounter = Length (myTable::windowTitleText) ]
    Set Window Title [ Of Window: Current Window; New Title: Middle
    ➡( myTable::windowTitleText; $loopCounter; $loopCounter) ]
    Set Variable [ $loopCounter; $loopCounter + 1 ]
    Commit Records/Requests [ No dialog ]
    Pause/Resume Script [ Duration (seconds): .1 ]
End Loop
```

Not the greatest use of computer technology ever made, but you can certainly draw attention to a warning message or alert of some kind by using it.

EXPANDING WINDOWS

By using a similar looping technique, you can alter the horizontal and vertical dimensions of a window so that it appears to grow or expand onto the screen:

```
New Window [ Height: 500; Width: 500; Top: 20; Left: 20 ]
Set Variable [ $loopCounter; 1 ]
Loop
    Exit Loop If [ $loopCounter = 500 ]
    Move/Resize Window [ Current Window; Height: $loopCounter;
    ➡Width: 500; Top: 40; Left: 40 ]
    Set Variable [$loopCounter; $loopCounter + 1 ]
    Commit Records/Requests [ No dialog ]
End Loop
```

This particular example is somewhat slow because it needs to loop 500 times to draw the window in question. Play with the increments in your `Set Variable [$loopCounter; $loopCounter + 1 ]` script step to make your window draw more quickly. You could just as easily set the width in a similar manner.

HIDING WINDOWS

The `Adjust Window` script step includes an option to hide a window that does more than just minimize it: Users can access the window only from the Window menu within FileMaker. If you use a custom menu (discussed later in this chapter) to disable that menu item, you truly have the capability of hiding a window completely from a user.

WORKING WITH CUSTOM MENUS

NEW The capability to customize menus in FileMaker files is arguably the single most powerful new feature in FileMaker 8. To modify the menu sets in FileMaker, you will need to develop using FileMaker Pro 8 Advanced; however, anyone working with FileMaker Pro (or a bound runtime solution) will be able to utilize the custom menus you create. The custom menus feature dramatically alters the user interface landscape for FileMaker: Developers can now control menus beyond simply turning them off and can drive a great deal of application logic.

An example will serve to illustrate the usefulness of custom menus. Suppose that you have built a solution with a section for customers and another for orders. Assume that the system is somewhat complex and that for some specific reason you as a developer do not want users creating new order records or new customer records by selecting Ｎew Record from the Ｒecords menu in FileMaker (perhaps new record creation needs also to create child records in parallel or do some other bookkeeping within your system). Instead you want scripts that you've written to manage the creation of these important records.

In past versions of FileMaker, you would have had to either train your users not to use the New Record menu item—an impractical solution at best—or disable user access to most of the menu system. This in turn would have forced you to re-create much of FileMaker's functionality, beyond the new order and new customer scripts, for all the other commands users would need and ordinarily access from the menus. Disabling menu commands was an all-or-nothing proposition.

NOTE

> Note that some third-party developers created plug-ins for FileMaker that would allow you to control menus in earlier versions. One such plug-in, CNS Menu from Comm-Unity Networking Systems, allows you to create additional hierarchical menus beyond those offered in FileMaker. We encourage you to visit FileMaker's website and review the plug-ins available; many allow you to further modify its interface.

In FileMaker Pro 8 Advanced, you can create your own menu set and control at the most granular level when menu items appear, how they work, and even what keyboard shortcuts they use. Such customizations, if made, will apply throughout the FileMaker interface, affecting contextual menus, the close box on Windows systems, and potentially every menu item in FileMaker.

Using custom menus allows you to do the following:

- Change the names of menus or menu items
- Override or extend the functionality of native FileMaker menu items with your own scripts

13

- Change or add keyboard shortcuts to existing or new menu items
- Disable or remove individual menu items or entire menus
- Load custom menu sets on demand, or tie menu sets to particular layouts, modes, or operating systems

Before delving further into custom menus, you will need to be clear on the nomenclature used. There are four separate elements to consider when working with custom menus:

- **Menu Item**—This is a single item on a menu that a user can select. For example, New Record and Save As menu items can also be separators or submenus.
- **Command**—Commands refer to the native controls "baked into" FileMaker: They perform an action in FileMaker. In FileMaker's standard menu set, all the actions are predefined by the application—for example, entering Find mode or opening the Help system. You can also create custom commands that initiate a script you as a developer will have written. It is possible to tie a menu item to a command in FileMaker and thus offer the native functionality that the command controls.
- **Menu**—A *menu* is a collection of menu items and comprises the full set of menu items available, regardless of whether they are all active or visible in any given mode or situation. Examples of menus are File and Edit. The File menu starts with the New Database, Open, and Open Remote menu items.
- **Menu Set**—A *menu set* is the set of all menus currently active or potentially available in FileMaker. It is a collection of menus and is the element you will load or associate with layouts. The FileMaker Standard menu set includes all the menus we've worked with for years: File, Edit, View, Insert, and so on.

Note that any specific menu or menu item may be present or not, grayed out or not, depending on certain conditions. For example, in Browse mode the standard FileMaker Pro 8 Advanced menu set includes the Records menu, but in Layout mode, the Records menu is not available and instead the Layouts menu becomes available. These conditional states can be tied to FileMaker modes, layouts, or user platform.

One important concept you will need to grasp is that FileMaker controls all custom menu elements at the menu set level. That means that if you want your Records menu to show New Customer on a Customers layout and New Order on an Orders layout, you will need to create two additional custom menu sets, one to contain each new variant of the Records menu.

This does not mean, however, that you need to create duplicate menus or menu items. Menus and menu items can be used by multiple menu sets. You need only create menu items that are unique and require customization. In the preceding example, you'd need to create two menu sets (a Customers set and an Orders set), two versions of the Records menu, and also two new menu items (New Customer and New Order).

When you change from one set to the other, all the user will see is that one menu item has changed; however, in the mechanics of working with custom menus, you will in fact have loaded a new menu set altogether.

MENU SETS INTERFACE

The interface for managing custom menus is somewhat complex, but just as with the security controls in FileMaker 8, there's a lot of power under the hood. When you choose Tools, Custom Menus, Define Custom Menus, you'll see a dialog box with two tabs, shown in Figure 13.7.

Figure 13.7
The initial view of the Define Custom Menus dialog shows each menu available in the file, both those that are standard and those you've created.

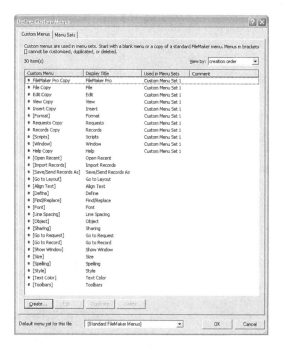

The first tab, Custom Menus, shows all the individual menus in your file. Remember that you can mix and match menus and menu sets; a single menu might appear in multiple menu sets. This list then is the superset of all menus defined within a given file.

Each FileMaker file contains duplicates of the standard FileMaker 8 menus, grouped into a single custom menu set called Custom Menu Set 1. This provides developers with an easy starting point from which you can further customize these duplicates without fear of breaking your system. If you turn to the second tab, Menu Sets, in Figure 13.8, you will see that two menu sets are already defined: the standard FileMaker menu set and Custom Menu Set 1, ready for modification.

One aspect of custom menus that can prove a little confusing is the interplay between FileMaker's standard menu set and its menus and your own additional custom menus. The term *custom menus* really refers to *additional* menus within your file. It is not possible to delete or change FileMaker's standard menu set or its menus. As a developer, you will need to load a custom menu set and work with copies of the standard menus in FileMaker to change your interface.

13

Figure 13.8
The Menu Sets tab allows you to view all the menu sets defined in a given file.

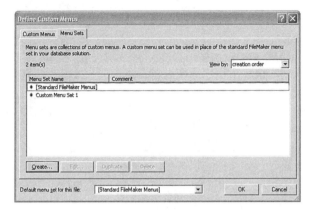

If you refer to Figure 13.7, you'll notice that some menus have a value in the third column denoting to which menu sets they belong, but in other cases no information is given. These menus might not be used anywhere or they often are submenus, available as hierarchical children to other menus. You can opt to add additional hierarchical submenus to menus as needed.

Some menus have square brackets around their names. These are the standard menus in FileMaker used by FileMaker's standard menu set. They are included in this list so that they can be used in other custom menu sets, but they cannot be edited or deleted.

In Figure 13.9 notice that Custom Menu Set 1 includes the [Format], [Scripts], and [Window] menus, which are not editable.

Figure 13.9
The Edit Menu Set dialog is where you can add and remove individual menus to and from a menu set, picking and choosing from among standard and custom menus.

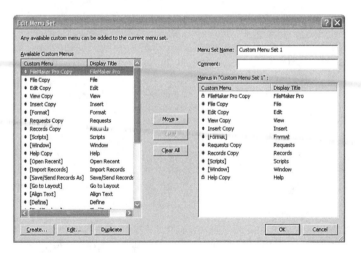

It is here in the Edit Menu Set dialog that menu sets can be created, deleted, and assembled from various menus available. If you select a menu in the left column, you can then click Edit to edit a single menu and create menu items.

CUSTOMIZING A MENU

Recall from the previous sections that to present users with a custom menu item, you will need to load an entire custom menu set, and that the standard menu set for FileMaker is not modifiable. To change any behavior in FileMaker's menus, you will need to work with either the pregenerated Custom Menu Set 1 or a menu set you've created. (We will cover how to create your own menu set later in the chapter.)

To illustrate this process, we will begin with the default state of Custom Menu Set 1, as shown in Figure 13.9. You reach this by selecting Custom Menu Set 1 from the Menu Sets tab and clicking the Edit button.

We will use the example presented previously: Assume that you want to change the Records menu to become Customers. To do so, you will need to edit the Records Copy menu. Select it and click Edit to be presented with the Edit Custom Menu dialog shown in Figure 13.10.

Figure 13.10
The Edit Custom Menu dialog allows you to change the appearance and behavior of a menu, which is composed of menu items.

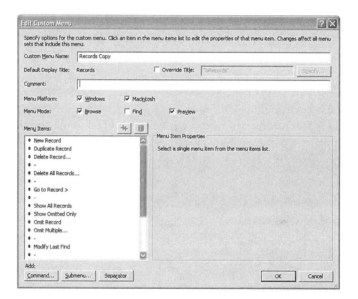

This dialog offers a range of options for controlling a menu. Notice that the name of the menu and its title are different. The name is an internal identifier you can use in whatever ways you need. The title is that which users see and select in their FileMaker interface. Here you can override the Records Copy menu name to read Customers. We recommend you keep the custom menu name and its title somewhat in line with each other to avoid confusion.

It's important to note that the title of a menu can be not only changed with a fixed value but also controlled programmatically via the Calculation dialog. This would allow you to create dynamic labels in which (for example) your FileMaker database could be localized in different languages based on a global preference setting.

13

Also note that each menu can be set to appear only within certain FileMaker modes (Browse, Find, and Preview) and can be tied to an operating system platform as well. It's important to remember that this behavior will remain true for *all* the menu sets with which this menu is associated.

Consider the scenario you're exploring here: You want to change the Records menu to be Customers, and New Record to become New Customer. It is likely that you'd want this change to be applied only in Browse mode; in Find mode, New Request would likely be more appropriate than New Customer. For this you'd need to create two separate menus and set the modes in which they appear appropriately.

Below the settings for mode and platform, you can manipulate individual menu items. Menu items belong to a specific menu and are not shareable across multiple menus in the way that menus may be shared across multiple menu sets. The New Record menu item in Figure 13.10 belongs to the Records Copy menu.

You can add separators, create submenu items, and insert new commands—menu items—to the list as you need. Note too that you can reorder the list of menu items using the up/down icon in the leftmost portion of the Menu Items list.

CUSTOMIZING A MENU ITEM

To make a change to an individual menu item (like, for example, modifying New Record to instead read New Customer and attaching a script to the action), first select the menu item in the Edit Custom Menu dialog. Various settings will appear to the right of your menu item list. Refer to Figure 13.11 for an example.

Figure 13.11
Select a menu item on the left in order to change settings that control how it appears or to attach a script.

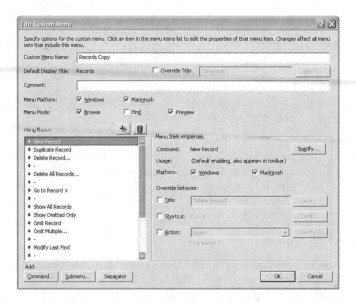

In its default state, the New Record menu item is set to execute the standard FileMaker command New Record and has no script attached. You can opt to turn off the preestablished behavior and instead substitute your own script or choose from among the range of conventional FileMaker commands within the application.

You can opt to leave a FileMaker command attached to a menu item and *add* your own script to it, rather than disabling the command. This approach will ensure that anywhere the command appears in FileMaker (for example, as an icon on a toolbar, in a contextual menu, or as the close-window button), those interface controls will remain in place. Your script will still override the behavior of the FileMaker command, but by leaving it attached to the menu item, you ensure that it replaces all controls within FileMaker.

This is an important distinction to make: If you create a menu item with no FileMaker command attached, it will appear only in the appropriate menu. If you attach a command, your menu item may appear in a contextual menu or may override behavior controlled from a toolbar or window control. If you want to completely override a FileMaker behavior, we recommend that you leave the command attached to the menu item. (Among many other useful effects, this would allow you to have your own script run anytime a user clicked the Close box on a window.)

In addition to changing the application-level behavior of a menu item, you can enable or disable its appearance for a given operating system platform, change its title (*nomenclature* within FileMaker's interface), and finally control whether it has a keyboard shortcut. Note that it is entirely possible to create keyboard shortcut conflicts. As with menu names, you can programmatically control the titles of menu items via the Calculation dialog.

To change the appearance of the New Record menu item to read New Customer and to subsequently control the creation of new records within your customer table by script, make the changes that appear in Figure 13.12.

Figure 13.12
This menu item replaces the default New Record menu item in your database. Instead of relying on FileMaker's default New Record command, this item overwrites its behavior with a New Customer Record script.

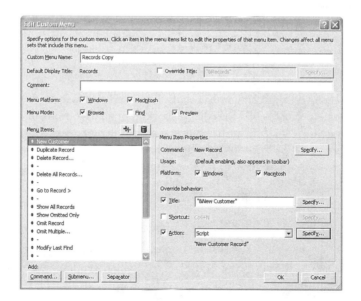

13

To test how your custom menu works, go to Tools, Custom Menus, and select Custom Menu Set 1 to make it active. You can then see the visual changes to the FileMaker interface and test to see that your scripts are controlling your database properly. (Control-click) [right-click] on a customer layout (using the preceding example) to see that your New Customer menu item appears in the contextual menu FileMaker uses in Browse mode.

LOADING AND ACTIVATING MENU SETS

As we've described in previous sections, the way to make a new menu item or custom menu available to your users is by including it in a menu set and then making that set active. There are several ways in which you can load a menu set:

- Assign a custom menu set as the default menu set for an entire file.
- Assign a specific custom menu set to a layout.
- Load a menu set on demand by using a script.
- Load custom menu sets on demand, or tie menu sets to particular layouts, particular modes, or a particular operating system.
- Choose from among the available custom menus in the Tools, Custom Menus menu choices. This last option assumes that you're working with FileMaker Pro 8 Advanced and that you have [Full Access] privileges in the file.

You can assign a custom menu set to work across an entire file at the bottom of the Define Custom Menus dialog shown earlier in Figure 13.7. The menu set you choose will load with the file and be overridden only if you employ one of the means of loading another custom menu set in its place.

Custom menu sets can also be applied on a layout-by-layout basis. On the General tab of the Layout Setup dialog, shown in Figure 13.13, you can specify which menu set a given layout should present to users.

Figure 13.13
You can assign a custom menu set to each layout within your system.

Last you can exert the most control over your database solution by using the Install Menu Set script step. When you use this script step, you can override a file's default menu set or you can simply load a menu set that will remain active until some other condition prompts it to change, such as encountering another `Install Menu Set` script step or navigating to a layout that calls for a different menu set.

Note that running this script will change the menu set only for the current session (for the user running the script) and will not affect either the permanent default menu set assigned in the Define Custom Menus dialog or other users in the system. When a user closes and reopens a FileMaker file, the default menu set will load again.

CREATING A NEW MENU FROM SCRATCH

So far we've worked with the Custom Menu Set 1 provided within FileMaker; however, it is entirely possible to create new custom menu sets and display entirely new menus as needed.

Consider the scenario of giving your users a menu of report scripts to run. Developers have been able to give users access to scripts for many years, under the Scripts menu, but they weren't able to assign different keyboard shortcuts, could list *only* custom scripts in the Scripts menu, and could customize neither the name of the Scripts menu nor the name of each individual script. With custom menus you can create your own menus and submenus as needed, making your solutions easier to use and your interfaces more informative.

To create a new menu, once again you will also need to create a menu set with which to control when and how the new menu loads. We recommend never modifying Custom Menu Set 1 and instead simply duplicating it whenever you have a new menu set to create. Custom Menu Set 1 in its default state replicates the entire set of FileMaker controls so that it is possible to make one or two changes without having to re-create every menu item within FileMaker.

After you've duplicated Custom Menu Set 1 and named it something appropriate, remove the [Scripts] menu from the set. (Remember, this only removes it from being accessible in this set. You've not modified the menu itself.) Then, by clicking the Create button, add a new menu to your menu set. When you do you, you'll be presented with the dialog shown in Figure 13.14.

Figure 13.14
You can choose to associate a new menu with an established FileMaker menu or make it an entirely additional menu.

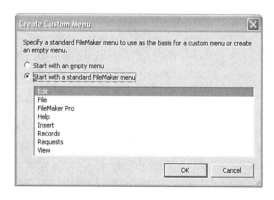

Here you can associate a new menu with an established FileMaker menu (thus making use of its accessibility in toolbars and contextual menus) or create a new, empty menu. In the scenario we're describing here, an empty menu is the way to go. You are adding to the interface, not replacing it.

NOTE

> Note that when you add a menu to those available within a menu set, you won't be able to remove or reorder the FileMaker Pro menu that displays in Mac OS X, nor will you be able to remove or reorder the Help menu from either the Mac or the Windows versions of the software. Furthermore, the Tools menu will always appear in FileMaker Pro 8 Advanced.

After you've created a new menu, simply click the Edit button and you will be able to add new menu items as you need. If you have other custom menus prepared, you can choose to add them to a menu as a submenu, or you can choose to add commands to your menu. In this scenario, you'd likely want to create a single command for each report you want listed, and then attach the script that drives that report to each new menu item. The complete settings for a Reports menu are shown in Figure 13.15.

Figure 13.15
A custom Reports menu is often a welcome addition to many FileMaker databases. (Notice the inclusion of a submenu and the use of separators.)

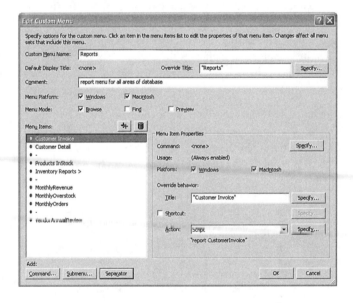

Custom menus are an extremely powerful new addition to FileMaker; in the past many developers would opt to shut down access to the standard menus in FileMaker to maintain control and ensure data integrity within their database solutions. With this new feature, it's possible to drive much more of the application from its native controls provided out of the box and to tweak only those elements necessary as a given solution requires.

SHOWING/HIDING LAYOUT ELEMENTS

In addition to presenting various windows for your users, you may at times want interface objects and other layout objects to appear and disappear (or change) depending on various conditions. A simple example might be a Delete button: Not everyone who uses your database should be given delete privileges. If you have placed a button on your layouts for deleting records, you'll need to either trap for an unauthorized attempt to use it (and likely present a graceful "you're not permitted to do that" message with FileMaker's security settings), or craft separate layouts that offer both the full and the limited functionalities you need.

That's the first low-tech approach: Create different layouts that look nearly identical but offer one without a Delete button to users without that privilege.

The downside to this multiple-layout approach is that you will need to build and maintain multiple layouts so that the time you spend making changes will be multiplied by however many layout versions you have. This approach also requires a fairly sophisticated navigation scheme in which you control which version of a given layout a user is presented. In many regards, maintaining multiple versions of a layout is an impractical solution.

To deliver the functionality of having layout objects appear and disappear, remember that portals can contain not only fields, but buttons as well. You can place layout objects on a portal row, set the portal to display only one row, and control the availability of the layout objects within that portal by controlling that portal's respective child record's relationship to the parent record from which it is being viewed.

You can implement this sort of functionality in your database solution in various ways. The simplest approach is to create an on/off resource table with one record in it (simply a table you'll use as a developer to store internal logic). When necessary, simply relate to that record by populating a global field in the current table with a constant that matches the same in the resource table. You could control the global match field by script, toggling it on and off as part of your navigation or as part of a user's other actions. You could also create a global calculation based on checking certain privilege sets (including an extended privilege). Refer to Figure 13.16 for an example of a Delete button being controlled by a relationship and disappearing when appropriate.

To implement one example of this technique, follow these steps:

1. First create an extended privilege meant to control the appearance of a Delete button (as shown in the example in Figure 13.16). In this case, name it `portalDelete`.

2. You will be controlling the appearance of your button objects by controlling whether a related record is available within a portal. To tie this to an extended privilege, first create a match field (called _ka_PortalControl) and set it to be a calculation field with the following formula:

```
Case ( PatternCount( Get(ExtendedPrivileges); "portalDelete" ) = 1; 1; 0 )
```

Set the field to be unstored and to be evaluated on demand. Make sure that it is in the table from which you intend to view this portal.

Figure 13.16
By placing a button within a one-row portal (set to appear transparent), you can create a place where layout objects appear based on a relationship.

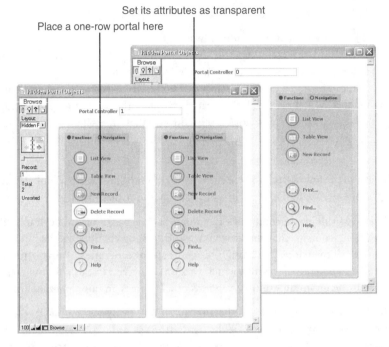

Set its attributes as transparent

Place a one-row portal here

3. You now need a record to which to relate. Create a match field, _ka_PortalControlconstant, to a resources table. Make sure that there's at least one record in the table.

4. Create a relationship from the table occurrence that is showing data to your resources table occurrence.

5. You can now place a portal, showing one row, on the layout in question, tie it to the resources table occurrence you've created, and then place buttons as you need within the one-row portal.

When you assign the portalDelete privilege to users, they will see the Delete Record button shown in Figure 13.16. If you have not enabled the extended privilege for the currently logged-in user, the user will see only a blank area on the screen. If the user clicks in that area, nothing will happen.

Place whatever layout objects you need in the single portal row. Because you likely won't be drawing from any data in the resources table, you need only one related record. Note that because these are layout objects, they will appear on every related row in a portal. It actually doesn't matter how many related records are in the resources table as long as there's at least one.

DEDICATED FIND LAYOUTS

Entering Find mode and performing Find requests is a crucial part of FileMaker Pro, but it's also one of the more difficult things to manage at the user interface level. As your solutions become more complex, Find mode will not be as intuitive for users: They might not have all the fields by which they want to search on one layout, or they may want to perform find requests on related data. Although FileMaker Pro can manage this task quite easily, users may be disoriented or confused by the results.

For example, say you've created a utility relationship that displays related data based on selected criteria or some temporary condition in the database. The fields sitting on your layout are not a structural one-to-many representation of your primary data architecture. Nonetheless, human users will intuitively want to hop into Find mode and have the process act on the primary relationship rather than your utility relationship.

Here's another example: Imagine looking at an author table with a related book-title field showing the most recent book written by that author. By definition, only one book can be the most current. Now imagine that someone is searching for an author who wrote a given book a long time ago. She is likely to click into the related book-title field in Find mode and be baffled as to why her search returned zero results—or worse yet, she might not realize her mistake and might conclude wrongly that the data doesn't exist. (The book she's looking for is not the most recent, so the search fails.) Given that the fields on the right relate to only the most current book for an author, the search would be accurate but yield undesirable results.

Furthermore, there may be dozens of fields in your database, related and otherwise, but users will want to search on only a small handful of these 90% of the time.

To make the Find process as intuitive as possible, you can create a separate find layout. An additional nicety is setting it up to open in a pop-up window. Your users will remain in context—in other words, they'll see where they were in the window behind the current one—and will intuitively understand the process going on.

You can build Find processes generally in two ways, each of which is covered in the following sections.

Dedicated Find Mode Layouts

The first process is perhaps the most simple. Create a separate layout and populate it with all the appropriate fields specific to the table in which a find is to be performed. Take care to place primary related fields on these layouts: Using the book example again, you'd place a book title from a primary-key-to-foreign-key relationship between the Book and the Author tables. The find result would then properly return authors who wrote books—any books, not just the most current—that matched the find criteria.

You can rely on users navigating to these find layouts themselves, along with entering Find mode and performing finds, or you can script the process. The scripted process would involve a button on your standard layouts to take the user to the special Find layout and enter Find mode. A second button on the Find layout itself would perform the request and return the user to the original layout and Browse mode.

This is a great way to give your users an intuitive process and shield them from unpredictable results. It's also a nice way to reduce the sheer volume of fields from which they have to choose in Find mode.

13

SCRIPT-DRIVEN FINDS

A more complex Find routine replaces the fields in the preceding example with global fields. Providing a dedicated Find layout will likely be something you may want to deliver in Browse mode. Instead of having users work with the related fields themselves (which in Browse mode would display actual data and pose, potentially, a problem if users didn't realize they had access to actual data), you can control access and the entire process using a script, and offer users empty global fields for entering find criteria.

This is a labor-intensive approach, and it relies on heavy scripting. As in the example in the preceding section, you need to bring users to the Find layout. This time, leave them in Browse mode. After their find criteria are entered, they need to click a Find button that then takes the system into Find mode, populates and performs the find request (by using Set Field script steps), and then returns the user to some proper results layout.

The difficulty here lies in replicating all the Find functionalities: inserting omit requests, extending found sets, constraining found sets, and working with multiple requests. We'd recommend using this technique only in rare cases when you want to fully control the user experience.

DATA PRESENTATION

Just as the functional side of your solutions has to be intuitive—navigating from layout to layout or window to window, gaining access to various functional buttons, and interacting with FileMaker's Find processes—viewing data needs to be so as well.

We don't need to cover some of the basics, such as differentiating between fields and field labels, or logically grouping information together (as in a company's street address, city, state, and zip fields), but you should take note of FileMaker's capabilities to auto-format data and manipulate text style formatting.

TEXT FORMATTING

By using the text formatting functions—RGB, TextColor, TextFont, TextSize, TextStyleAdd, TextColorRemove, TextFontRemove, TextSizeRemove, and TextStyleRemove—you can precisely control how information is displayed in your database solutions. Consider that a field showing payment status (current or overdue, for example) could convey additional information through different color and text style applications. You could use FileMaker's layout-based formatting options (Format, Text in the menus) to cause numbers to change color when negative; by using the text formatting functions, they could also take on shades based on how close to, say, a quota they are. You might color-code the names of regions in a geographical area or want to highlight certain keywords within a body of text.

→ To learn about the basics of calculation functions, **see** Chapter 8, "Getting Started with Calculations," **p. 217**.

→ For detailed examples of text formatting functions, **see** Chapter 14, "Advanced Calculation Techniques," **p. 391**, and Chapter 17, "Debugging and Troubleshooting," **p. 501**.

→ For a complete reference to all calculation functions, refer to Chapter 6 of our companion volume, *FileMaker 8 Functions and Scripts Desk Reference*.

AUTO-FORMATTING DATA TO PROVIDE VISUAL CUES

Just as you can apply text formatting functions by using a script or through calculation fields, your database can automatically change text formatting on entry. Both Chapter 3, "Defining and Working with Fields," and Chapter 8, "Getting Started with Calculations," have covered this functionality. This auto-entry capability to reformat data on entry enables you to capture information on the way in and impart additional meaning through making it bold, red, and so on. Note that you will be changing the data in question; more than simply a display technique, this modifies the data itself. One application of this technique could be changing your text to red if some validation condition fails. Another example is to color-code or to apply bold and italic styles to a status field. For example, note in the example shown in Figure 13.17 that the status of various to-do items is immediately apparent.

Figure 13.17
The text is formatted as users enter it using the Auto Enter By Calculation field options.

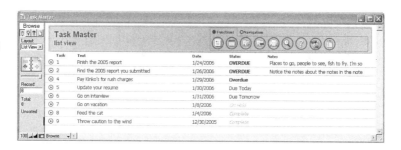

Although this is hardly an advanced technique from a technical perspective, it's important to learn how FileMaker's capabilities can be used to make data and information more accessible.

WORKING WITH TABLE VIEW

There's a lot to be said for something that's free and "just works." If you're in an environment where a simple user interface is an option for your users, consider turning to Table views. They deliver a fair amount of functionality with zero development effort. Regardless of your end users' needs, as a developer you'll find Table views invaluable for working with simple views of raw data.

→ To learn more about Table view, **see** Chapter 2, "Using FileMaker Pro," **p. 29**.

One technique we use to make Table views even more useful can be found in the Table View Properties dialog under the Layout Setup dialog: You can opt to include header and footer parts on your layout, as well as control other aspects of your layout.

Header and footer parts can hold any FileMaker layout object you need. This includes your navigation or function buttons and whatever header might be common to the rest of your system, but most important, it can hold fields. Your users can see a combined list-and-detail view that displays the currently selected row's data in either the header or the footer.

There are a few drawbacks to using this technique. For one, you cannot overlay buttons on top of the rows—which is otherwise a handy way to allow users to navigate to detail layouts or perform other functions directly from List view. You also cannot turn off or alter the column headers. Your column headers are based directly on your field names, which, depending on your naming conventions, may be aesthetically imperfect or downright abstruse.

Nonetheless, this is a cheap, easy way to deliver a good bit of advanced functionality for virtually no effort.

TROUBLESHOOTING

OMIT RE-CREATED

I am trying to create a scripted find process so that I can keep the Status Area hidden, but the Omit check box is found only in the Status Area. What's a technique for offering the same functionality from a script?

Most of the Status Area functions are fairly straightforward to reproduce in a script: next record, previous record, switch mode, displays for record X of Y, sorting state, and so on. There's one that's not so obvious, though: the Omit check box in Find mode.

A scripted Find mode often takes users into Find mode and pauses the script in question (disallowing abort). The system then waits in a paused state for the user to click a button (often labeled something like Find, Continue, or Search). After the button is clicked, the script continues by utilizing the `Perform Find` script step. (An alternative to this is to have users enter find criteria into global fields and to manage populating find requests programmatically.)

It would be a no-brainer to add a check box to a layout, call it `omit_flag`, and test for a value in it when you've scripted a find routine. But here's the rub: If you're actually in Find mode, in a paused state as just described, what happens to that flag if you perform a find?

That's right—it will be included in the find request itself and FileMaker will look for records in which the omit flag equals `1`.

The easiest way to deal with this is to simply make the check box a Boolean calculation with an auto-entry setting of `yes` or `1` (whatever the value list controlling your check box is set to). In data terms, it serves as a constant, but in Find mode it does not affect the outcome of a Find request; it is always valid for all records. As such, you can use it as a variable to check against in your `Perform Find` steps without having to worry about clearing it from your Find requests. You still need to manage the process of what to do with the flag if your users enable it, but at least the user interface works as they (and you) would expect.

MODAL DIALOG DANGERS

What are the downfalls to using the Modal Dialog technique to control what data gets posted to my solution?

Using the modal dialog technique described in this chapter isn't a foolproof way to address atomicity in FileMaker Pro.

→ Atomicity specifies that a transaction needs to be completed either in its entirety or not at all. For more information on atomicity and multiuser development, **see** Chapter 11, "Developing for Multiuser Deployment," **p. 307**.

Users can close FileMaker Pro anytime they want. Depending on what assumptions you've made in your development and the scripts leading to opening such a dialog, your system might be left in a less-than-optimal state. We encourage you to create flags for when pop-up windows are opened and then confirm that they're then closed. In cases when this doesn't occur, you might create an error message or some other graceful way to alert you to this fact.

FILEMAKER EXTRA: USER INTERFACE HEURISTICS

We opened this chapter by saying we wouldn't preach to you about what makes a good interface and what doesn't. Well, we're breaking our word here. Although we won't argue about pop-up windows versus single-pane applications, or whether buttons should be 3D beveled or just text on the screen, here are a few guidelines we recommend to all of our clients, students, and developers alike:

- **Use real-world terminology**—You should strive to speak your customers' language. Use terms they'll find familiar. In some cases you may need to retrain them, but whenever possible, leverage the body of knowledge already in place in an organization to make your system more intuitive.

- **Impart meaning with more than just labels**—Text is only one of many things your users will see on a layout. They'll also see colors, shapes, headlines, subheads, footers, and so on. Use all the objects in your toolbox to impart meaning: Consider, for example, changing the background color of find layouts or perhaps making navigation buttons look different from functional buttons. Keep this in mind though: Don't rely too heavily on color. A great many people have varying degrees of colorblindness.

- **Give users the freedom to click around without fear**—Users should be able to cancel out of any destructive function (delete, for example) so that they can explore your application and learn by doing.

- **Be consistent**—We can't stress this enough. Whatever the colors, shapes, sizes, styles, and so on that you prefer, make sure that your layouts follow whatever set of rules you establish. Name fields and buttons consistently, place them in the same positions, and give your users a visual grammar for your system they can learn.

- **Manage errors**—Errors happen. Handle them behind the scenes whenever possible, but when they're unavoidable make sure that you present the users with a graceful error routine that informs them, proffers a course of action, and then returns them to what they were doing.

- **Focus your screens**—Less is more. Whitespace is your friend. Leave the important bits on your layouts and dialogs and remove the objects that can be pushed elsewhere. If you offer focus to users, you will help them understand what to do on a given layout.

- **Remember your power users**—Contrary to all the earlier advice, don't forget your power users. Offer keyboard shortcuts through "Are you sure?" dialogs, give them simple Table view access to your data, and don't bother them with wizards.

## CHAPTER 14

ADVANCED CALCULATION TECHNIQUES

In this chapter

WHAT'S AN ADVANCED CALCULATION TECHNIQUE?

Chapter 8, "Getting Started with Calculations," presented an introduction to FileMaker Pro calculation formulas. Our goals there were to give you a foundation in how and where calculation functions are used, and to present what we feel are the core functions and formulas FileMaker Pro developers need to know and use on a daily basis.

This chapter covers functions and usages that are more advanced or specialized in nature. Think of the core functions covered in Chapter 8 as the hammers, screwdrivers, and wrenches of a developer's toolkit. They're the tools you use every day. The specialized functions covered here are the metric socket sets, the low-angled block planes, and the self-leveling laser levels of your toolkit. These might not be things you use on every project, but they sure come in handy at times. The nice thing, of course, is that after you've made the "investment" in the specialized "tool," you'll have it handy for all future projects.

Certainly, our characterization of some functions or usages being part of a core and others being advanced is subjective and open to debate. We do want to stress that advanced doesn't necessarily mean difficult. Nor does it mean arcane or esoteric. We think that all the specialized functions presented here have very practical uses. In some cases, what's specialized isn't the function itself, but perhaps some usage of a core function that's not something you're likely to encounter on a routine basis.

We don't intend to present here a comprehensive list of functions. That can be found in the companion to this book, *FileMaker 8 Functions and Scripts Desk Reference*. Rather, similar to our approach in Chapter 8, we take a thematic approach and focus on demonstrating practical uses of a handful of functions.

LOGICAL FUNCTIONS

The category of functions known as the *logical functions* contains a strange hodgepodge of things. Chapter 8 discussed two of them: the If and Case conditional functions. The logical functions covered here include several that are new to FileMaker Pro 8.

THE Let FUNCTION

The Let function enables you to simplify complex calculations by declaring variables to represent subexpressions. These variables exist only within the scope of the formula and can't be referenced in other places. As an example, this is a formula presented in Chapter 8 for extracting the last line of a text field:

```
Right(myText; Length(myText) - Position(myText; "¶"; 1;
➥PatternCount(myText; "¶")))
```

With the Let function, this formula could be rewritten this way:

```
Let ([fieldLength = Length(myText) ;
     returnCount = PatternCount(myText; "¶") ;
     positionOfLastReturn = Position (myText; "¶"; 1; returnCount) ;
     charactersToGrab = fieldLength - positionOfLastReturn];
```

```
Right (myText, charactersToGrab)
)
```

The Let function takes two parameters. The first is a list of variable declarations. If you want to declare multiple variables, you need to enclose the list within square brackets and separate the individual declarations within the list with semicolons. The second parameter is some formula you want evaluated. That formula can reference any of the variables declared in the first parameter, just as it would reference any field value.

 If you experience unexpected behavior of a Let *function, the trouble might be your variable names. For more information, see "Naming Variables in* Let *Functions" in the "Troubleshooting" section at the end of this chapter.*

Notice in this example that the third variable declared, positionOfLastReturn, references the returnCount variable, which was the second variable declared. This capability to have subsequent variables reference previously defined ones is one of the powerful aspects of the Let function because it enables you to build up a complex formula via a series of simpler ones.

It is fair to observe that the Let function is never *necessary*; you could rewrite any formula that uses the Let function, without using Let, either as a complex nested formula or by explicitly defining or setting fields to contain subexpressions. The main benefits of using the Let function are simplicity, clarity, and ease of maintenance. For instance, a formula that returns a person's age expressed as a number of years, months, and days could be written as shown here:

```
Year (Get (CurrentDate)) - Year(birthDate) - (DayOfYear(Get(CurrentDate))
➡ < DayOfYear(birthDate)) & " years, " & Mod ( Month(Get(CurrentDate))
➡- Month (birthDate) - (Day (Get(CurrentDate)) < Day(birthDate)); 12) &
➡" months, and " & (Get(CurrentDate) - Date (Month(Get(CurrentDate))
➡- (Day (Get(CurrentDate)) < Day(birthDate)); Day (birthDate);
➡Year (Get(CurrentDate)))) & " days"
```

This is a fairly complex nested formula, and many subexpressions appear multiple times. Writing and debugging this formula is difficult, even when you understand the logic on which it's based. With the Let function, the formula could be rewritten this way:

```
Let ( [   C = Get(CurrentDate);
          yC = Year (C) ;
          mC = Month (C) ;
          dC = Day (C) ;
          doyC = DayOfYear (C) ;

          B = birthDate;
          yB = Year (B) ;
          mB = Month (B) ;
          dB= Day (B) ;
          doyB = DayOfYear (b) ;

          num_years = ( yC - yB - (doyC < doyB)) ;
          num_months = Mod (mC - mB - (dC <dB) ; 12) ;
          num_days = C - Date (mC - (dC < dB) ; dB ; yC) ] ;

          num_years & " years, " & num_months & " months, and " & num_days
          ➡& " days" )
```

14

Because of the extra space we've put in the formula, it's a bit longer than the original, but it's vastly easier to comprehend. If you were a developer needing to review and understand a formula written by someone else, we're sure you'd agree that you'd prefer seeing the Let version of this rather than the first version.

Besides simplicity and clarity, there are also performance benefits to using the Let function. If you have a complex subexpression that you refer to multiple times during the course of a calculation, FileMaker Pro evaluates it anew each time it's referenced. If you create the subexpression as a variable within a Let statement, the subexpression is evaluated only once, no matter how many times it is subsequently referenced. In the example just shown, for instance, FileMaker would evaluate Get(CurrentDate) eight times in the first version. In the version that uses Let, it's evaluated only once. In many cases, the performance difference may be trivial or imperceptible. But other times, optimizing the evaluation of calculation formulas may be just the answer for increasing your solution's performance.

The more you use the Let function, the more likely it is that it will become one of the core functions you use. To help you become more familiar with it, we use it frequently throughout the examples in the rest of this chapter.

Quick Calculation Testing Using Let

The Let function makes it much easier to debug calculation formulas. It used to be that if you wanted to make sure that a subexpression was evaluating correctly, you'd need to create a separate field to investigate it. Using Let, you can just comment out the second parameter of the Let function and have the function return one or more of the subexpressions directly. When you've got each subexpression working as intended, just comment out the test code and uncomment the original code.

TIP

NEW

It's not uncommon that you may want to set the same variable several times within a Let statement. A typical example occurs when you want to perform a similar operation several times on the same variable, without excessive nesting. For example, in FileMaker 7, a fragment of a Let statement that's involved in some complex text parsing might look like this:

```
result =     _TextColor( text; RGB( 255: 0; 0 ));
result1 =    _TextFont ( result; "TimesNewRoman");
result2 =    _Textsize ( result1; 14);
```

Here, we want to apply several text formatting operations to the value of text. We'd like to put them on successive rows, rather than building a big nested expression. We'd prefer to just keep naming the output result, but in FileMaker 7, we'll be prevented from setting a variable with the same name twice. In FileMaker 8 this behavior is permitted, and we could rewrite the code fragment as something like this:

```
result =     _TextColor( text; RGB( 255: 0; 0 ));
result =    _ TextFont ( result; "TimesNewRoman");
result =     _Textsize ( result; 14);
```

Although this is a great convenience when you need to do it, be aware that calculations and custom functions that use this technique will *not* execute correctly if the file is accessed via FileMaker Pro 7.

THE Choose FUNCTION

The If and Case functions are sufficiently robust and elegant for most conditional tests that you'll write. For several types of conditional tests, however, the Choose function is a more appropriate option. As with If and Case, the value returned by the Choose function is dependent on the result of some test. What makes the Choose function different is that the test should return an integer rather than a true/false result. The test is followed by a number of possible results. The one that's chosen depends on the numeric result of the test. If the test result is 0, the first result is used. If the test result is 1, the second result is used, and so on. The syntax for Choose is as follows:

```
Choose (test ; result if test=0 ; result if test=1 ; result if test=2 ....)
```

A classic example of when a Choose function comes in handy is when you have categorical data stored as a number and you need to represent it as text. For instance, you might import demographic data in which the ethnicity of an individual is represented by an integer from 1 to 5. The following formula might be used to represent it to users:

```
Choose (EthnicityCode; ""; "African American"; "Asian"; "Caucasian"; "Hispanic";
➥ " Native American")
```

Of course, the same result could be achieved with the following formula:

```
Case (EthnicityCode = 1; "African American"; EthnicityCode = 2; "Asian",
➥EthnicityCode = 3; "Caucasian"; EthnicityCode = 4; "Hispanic";
➥EthnicityCode= 5; "Native American")
```

You should consider the Choose function in several other situations. The first is for generating random categorical data. Say your third-grade class is doing research on famous presidents, and you want to randomly assign each student one of the six presidents you have chosen. By first generating a random number from 0 to 5, you can then use the Choose function to select a president. The formula would be this:

```
Let ( r = Random * 6;    // Generates a random number from 0 to 5
     Choose (r, "Washington", "Jefferson", "Lincoln", "Roosevelt", "Truman",
     ➥ "Kennedy"))
```

Don't worry that r isn't an integer; the Choose function ignores everything but the integer portion of a number.

Several FileMaker Pro functions return integer numbers from 1 to n, so these naturally work well as the test for a Choose function. Most notable are the DayofWeek function, which returns an integer from 1 to 7, and the Month function, which returns an integer from 1 to 12. As an example, you could use the Month function within a Choose to figure out within which quarter of the year a given date fell:

```
Choose (Month(myDate)-1; "Q1"; "Q1"; "Q1"; "Q2"; "Q2"; "Q2"; "Q3"; "Q3"; "Q3";
➥ "Q4"; "Q4"; "Q4")
```

14

The -1 shifts the range of the output from 1–12 to 0–11, which is more desirable because the Choose function is *zero-based*, meaning that the first result corresponds to a test value of zero. There are more compact ways of determining the calendar quarter of a date, but this version is very easy to understand and offers much flexibility.

Another example of when `Choose` works well is when you need to combine the results of some number of Boolean tests to produce a distinct result. As an example, imagine that you have a table that contains results on Myers-Briggs personality tests. For each test given, you have scores for four pairs of personality traits (E/I, S/N, T/F, J/P). Based on which score in each pair is higher, you want to classify each participant as one of 16 personality types. Using `If` or `Case` statements, you would need a very long, complex formula to do this. With `Choose`, you can treat the four tests as a binary number, and then simply do a conversion back to base-10 to decode the results. The formula might look something like this:

```
Choose( (8 * (E>I)) + (4 * (S>N)) + (2 * (T>F)) + (J>P);
    "Type 1 - INFP" ; "Type 2 - INFJ" ; "Type 3 - INTP" ; "Type 4 - INTJ" ;
    "Type 5 - ISFP" ; "Type 6 - ISFJ" ; "Type 7 - ISTP" ; "Type 8 - ISTJ" ;
    "Type 9 - ENFP" ; "Type 10 - ENFJ" ; "Type 11 - ENTP" ; "Type 12 - ENTJ" ;
    "Type 13 - ESFP" ; "Type 14 - ESFJ" ; "Type 15 - ESTP" ; "Type 16 - ESTJ")
```

Each greater-than comparison is evaluated as a 1 or 0 depending on whether it represents a true or false statement for the given record. By multiplying each result by successive powers of 2, you end up with an integer from 0 to 15 that represents each of the possible outcomes. (This is similar to how flipping a coin four times generates 16 possible outcomes.)

As a final example, the `Choose` function can also be used anytime you need to "decode" a set of abbreviations into their expanded versions. Take, for example, a situation in which survey respondents have entered SA, A, N, D, or SD as a response to indicate Strongly Agree, Agree, Neutral, Disagree, or Strongly Disagree. You could map from the abbreviation to the expanded text by using a `Case` function like this:

```
Case (ResponseAbbreviation = "SA"; "Strongly Agree";
      ResponseAbbreviation = "A"; "Agree" ;
      ResponseAbbreviation = "N"; "Neutral" ;
      ResponseAbbreviation = "D"; "Disagree" ;
      ResponseAbbreviation = "SD"; "Strongly Disagree" )
```

You can accomplish the same mapping by using a `Choose` function if you treat the two sets of choices as ordered lists. You simply find the position of an item in the abbreviation list, and then find the corresponding item from the expanded text list. The resulting formula would look like this:

```
Let ( [a = "¦SA¦¦A¦¦N¦¦D¦¦SD¦" ;
       r = "¦" & ResponseAbbreviation & "¦" ;
       pos = Position (a; r ; 1 ; 1) ;
       itemNumber = PatternCount (Left (a; pos-1); "¦") / 2];

       Choose (itemNumber, "Strongly Agree"; "Agree"; "Neutral"; "Disagree";
    ➥ "Strongly Disagree")
)
```

In most cases, you'll probably opt for using the `Case` function for simple decoding of abbreviations. Sometimes, however, the list of choices isn't something you can explicitly test against (such as with the contents of a value list), and finding one's position within the list may suffice to identify a parallel position in some other list. Having the `Choose` function in your toolbox may offer an elegant solution to such challenges.

THE GetField FUNCTION

When writing calculation formulas, you use field names to refer abstractly to the contents of particular fields in the current record. That is, the formula for a FullName calculation might be FirstName & " " & LastName. FirstName and LastName are abstractions; they represent data contained in particular fields.

Imagine, however, that instead of knowing in advance what fields to refer to in the FullName calculation, you wanted to let users pick any fields they wanted to. So you set up two fields, which we'll call UserChoice1 and UserChoice2. How can you rewrite the FullName calculation so that it's not hard-coded to use FirstName and LastName, but rather uses the fields that users type in the two UserChoice fields?

The answer, of course, is the GetField function. GetField enables you to add another layer of abstraction to your calculation formulas. Instead of hard-coding field names in a formula, GetField allows you to place into a field the name of the field you're interested in accessing. That sounds much more complicated than it actually is. Using GetField, we might rewrite our FullName formula as shown here:

```
GetField (UserChoice1) & " " & GetField (UserChoice2)
```

The GetField function takes just one parameter. That parameter can be either a literal text string or a field name. Having it be a literal text string, although possible, is not particularly useful. The function GetField("FirstName") would certainly return the contents of the FirstName field, but you can achieve the same thing simply by using FirstName by itself. It's only when the parameter of the GetField function is a field or formula that it becomes interesting. In that case, the function returns the contents of the field referred to by the parameter.

There are many potential uses of GetField in a solution. Imagine, for instance, that you have a Contact table with fields called First Name, Nickname, and Last Name (among others). Sometimes contacts prefer to have their nickname appear on badges and in correspondence, and sometimes the first name is desired. To deal with this, you could create a new text field called Preferred Name and format that field as a radio button containing First Name and Nickname as the choices. When doing data entry, a user could simply check off which name should be used for correspondence. When it comes time to make a Full Name calculation field, one of your options would be the following:

```
Case ( Preferred Name = "First Name"; First Name;
       Preferred Name = "Nickname"; Nickname) &
       " " & Last Name
```

Another option, far more elegant and extensible, would be the following:

```
GetField (PreferredName) & " " & Last Name
```

When there are only two choices, the Case function certainly isn't cumbersome. But if there were dozens or hundreds of fields to choose from, GetField clearly has an advantage.

14

BUILDING A CUSTOMIZABLE LIST REPORT

One of the common uses of GetField is for building user-customizable list reports. It's really nothing more than an extension of the technique shown in the preceding example, but it's still worth looking at in depth. The idea is to have several global text fields where a user can select from a pop-up list of field names. The global text fields can be defined in any table you want. Remember, in calculation formulas, you can refer to a globally stored field from any table, even without creating a relationship to that table. The following example uses two tables: SalesPeople and Globals. The SalesPeople table has the following data fields:

SalesPersonID

FirstName

LastName

Territory

CommissionRate

Phone

Email

Sales_2005

Sales_2006

The Globals table has six global text fields named gCol1 through gCol6.

With these in place, you can now create six display fields in the SalesPeople table (named ColDisplay1 through ColDisplay6) that will contain the contents of the field referred to in one of the global fields. For instance, ColDisplay1 has the following formula:

GetField (Globals::gCol1)

ColDisplay2 through 6 will have similar definitions. The next step is to create a value list that contains all the fields you want the user to be able to select. The list used in this example is shown in Figure 14.1. Keep in mind that because the selection is used as part of a GetField function, the field names must appear exactly as they have been defined—and any change to the underlying field names will cause the report to malfunction.

The final task is to create a layout where users can select and see the columns for their custom list report. You might want to set up one layout where the user selects the fields and another for displaying the results, but we think it's better to take advantage of the fact that in FileMaker 8, fields in header parts of list layouts can be edited. The column headers of your report can simply be pop-up lists. Figure 14.2 shows how you would set up your layout this way.

Back in Browse mode, users can now click into a column heading and select what data they want to appear there. This one layout can thus serve a wide variety of needs. Figures 14.3 and 14.4 show two examples of the types of reports that can be made.

Figure 14.1
Define a value list containing a list of the fields from which you want to allow a user to select for the custom report.

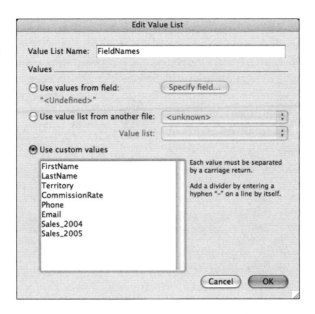

Figure 14.2
The layout for your customizable list report can be quite simple. Here, the selection fields act also as field headers.

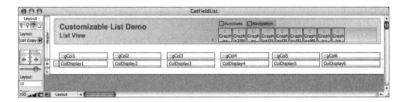

Figure 14.3
A user can customize the contents of a report simply by selecting fields from pop-up lists in the header.

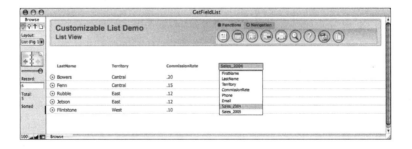

Figure 14.4
Here's another example of a how a user might configure the customizable list report.

14

EXTENDING THE CUSTOMIZABLE LIST REPORT

After you have the simple custom report working, there are many ways you can extend it to add even more value and flexibility for your users. For instance, you might add a subsummary part that's also based on a user-specified field. A single layout can thus be a subsummary based on any field the user wants. One way to implement this is to add another pop-up list in the header of your report and a button to sort and preview the subsummary report. Figure 14.5 shows what your layout would look like after adding the subsummary part and pop-up list. `BreakField` is a calculation in the SalesPeople table that's defined as shown here:

```
GetField (Globals::gSummarizeBy)
```

Figure 14.5
A subsummary part based on a user-defined break field gives your custom report added power and flexibility.

The Preview button performs a script that sorts by the `BreakField` and goes to Preview mode. Figure 14.6 shows the result of running the script when `Territory` has been selected as the break field.

Figure 14.6
Sorting by the break field and previewing shows the results of the dynamic subsummary.

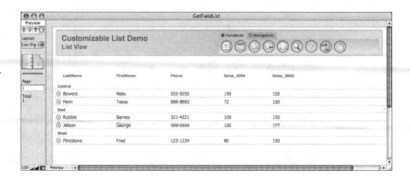

CAUTION

> To be fully dynamic, any calculations you write using the `GetField` function are probably going to need to be unstored. Unstored calculations will not perform well over very large data sets when searching and sorting, so use caution when creating `GetField` routines that might need to handle large data sets.

14

THE Evaluate FUNCTION

The Evaluate function is one of the most intriguing functions in FileMaker Pro 8. In a nutshell, it enables you to evaluate a dynamically generated or user-generated calculation formula. With a few examples, you'll easily understand what this function does. It may, however, take a bit more time and thought to understand why you'd want to use it in a solution. We start with explaining the what, and then suggest a few potential whys.

The syntax for the Evaluate function is as follows:

```
Evaluate ( expression {; [field1 ; field2 ;...]} )
```

The expression parameter is a text string representing some calculation formula that you want evaluated. The optional additional parameter is a list of fields whose modification triggers the reevaluation of the expression.

For example, imagine that you have a text field named myFormula and another named myTrigger. You then define a new calculation field called Result, using the following formula:

```
Evaluate (myFormula; myTrigger)
```

Figure 14.7 shows some examples of what Result will contain for various entries in myFormula.

Figure 14.7
Using the Evaluate function, you can have a calculation field evaluate a formula contained in a field.

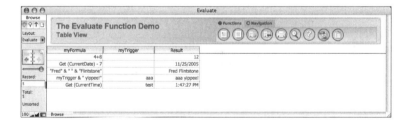

There's something quite profound going on here. Instead of having to "hard-code" calculation formulas, you can evaluate a formula that's been entered as field data. In this way, Evaluate provides an additional level of logic abstraction similar to the GetField function. In fact, if myFormula contained the name of a field, Evaluate(myFormula) and GetField(myFormula) would return exactly the same result. It might help to think of Evaluate as the big brother of GetField. Whereas GetField can return the value of a dynamically specified *field*, Evaluate can return the value of a dynamically specified *formula*.

USES FOR THE Evaluate FUNCTION

A typical use for the Evaluate function is to track modification information about a particular field or fields. A timestamp field defined to auto-enter the modification time is triggered anytime any field in the record is modified. There may be times, however, when you want to know the last time that the Comments field was modified, without respect to other

14

changes to the record. To do this, you would define a new calculation field called CommentsModTime with the following formula:

```
Evaluate ("Get(CurrentTimestamp)" ; Comments)
```

The quotes around Get(CurrentTimestamp) are important, and are apt be a source of confusion. The Evaluate function expects to be fed either a quote-enclosed text string (as shown here) or a formula that yields a text string (as in the Result field earlier). For instance, if you want to modify the CommentsModTime field so that rather than just returning a timestamp, it returns something like Record last modified at: 11/28/2005 12:23:58 PM by Fred Flintstone, you would need to modify the formula to the following:

```
Evaluate ("\"Record modified at: \" & Get (CurrentTimeStamp) & \" by \" &
➥Get (AccountName)" ; Comments)
```

Here, because the formula you want to evaluate contains quotation marks, you must *escape* them by preceding them with a slash. For a formula of any complexity, this becomes difficult both to write and to read. There is, fortunately, a function called Quote that eliminates all this complexity. The Quote function returns the parameter it is passed as a quote-wrapped text string, with all internal quotes properly escaped. Therefore, you could rewrite the preceding function more simply as this:

```
Evaluate (Quote ("Record modified at: " & Get (CurrentTimeStamp) & " by " &
➥Get (AccountName)) ; Comments)
```

In this particular case, using the Let function further clarifies the syntax:

```
Let ( [
    time = Get ( CurrentTimeStamp ) ;
    account = Get ( AccountName );
    myExpression = Quote ( "Record modified at: " & time & " by " & account ) ] ;

  Evaluate ( myExpression ; Comments )
)
```

EVALUATION ERRORS

You typically find two other functions used in conjunction with the Evaluate function: IsValidExpression and EvaluationError.

IsValidExpression takes as its parameter an expression, and it returns a 1 if the expression is valid, a 0 if it isn't. An invalid expression is any expression that can't be evaluated by FileMaker Pro, whether due to syntax errors or other runtime errors. If you plan to allow users to type calculation expressions into fields, be sure to use IsValidExpression to test their input to be sure it's well formed. In fact, you probably want to include a check of some kind within your Evaluate formula itself:

```
Let ( valid = IsValidExpression (myFormula) ;
    If (not valid; "Your expression was invalid" ; Evaluate (myFormula) )
```

The EvaluationError function is likewise used to determine whether there's some problem with evaluating an expression. However, it returns the actual error code corresponding to the problem. One thing to keep in mind, however, is that rather than testing the expression, you want to test the evaluation of the expression. So, as an error trap used in conjunction with an `Evaluate` function, you might have the following:

```
Let ( [result = Evaluate (myFormula) ;
       error = EvaluationError (result) ] ;
    If (error ; "Error: " & error ; result)
)
```

CUSTOMIZABLE LIST REPORTS REDUX

We mentioned previously that `Evaluate` could be thought of as an extension of `GetField`. In an example presented in the `GetField` section, we showed how you could use the `GetField` function to create user-customizable report layouts. One of the drawbacks of that method that we didn't discuss at the time is that your field names need to be user- and display-friendly. However, there is an interesting way to get around this limitation that also happens to showcase the `Evaluate` function. We discuss that solution here as a final example of `Evaluate`.

→ Another use of `Evaluate` is presented in "Passing Multivalued Parameters," **p. 438**.

To recap the earlier example, imagine that you have six global text fields (gCol1 through gCol6) in a table called Globals. Another table, called SalesPeople, has demographic and sales-related data for your salespeople. Six calculation fields in SalesPeople, called ColDisplay1 through ColDisplay6, display the contents of the demographic or sales data fields, based on a user's selection from a pop-up list containing field names. ColDisplay1, for instance, has the following formula:

```
GetField (Globals::gCol1)
```

We now extend this solution in several ways. First, create a new table in the solution called FieldNames with the following text fields: FieldName and DisplayName. Figure 14.8 shows the data that might be entered in this table.

Figure 14.8
The data in FieldName represents fields in the SalesPerson table; the DisplayName field shows more user-friendly labels that will stand in for the actual field labels.

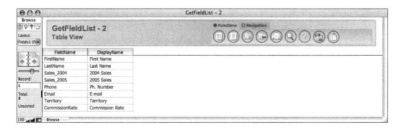

Earlier, we suggested using a hard-coded value list for the pop-up lists attached to the column selection fields. Now you'll want to change that value list so that it contains all the items in the DisplayName column of the FieldNames table. Doing this, of course, causes all the ColDisplay fields to malfunction. There is, for instance, no field called Ph. Number, so `GetField ("Ph. Number")` will not function properly. What we want now is the `GetField` function not to operate on the user's entry, but rather on the FieldName that corresponds to the user's DisplayName selection. That is, when the user selects Ph. Number in gCol1, ColDisplay1 should display the contents of the Phone field.

You can accomplish this result by creating a relationship from the user's selection over to the DisplayName field. Because there are six user selection fields, there need to be six relationships. This requires that you create six occurrences of the FieldNames table. Figure 14.9 shows the Relationships Graph after you have set up the six relationships. The six new table occurrences are named Fields1 through Fields6. Notice that there's also a cross-join relationship between SalesPeople and Globals. This relationship allows you to look from SalesPeople all the way over to the FieldNames table.

Figure 14.9
To create six relationships from the Globals table to the FieldNames table, you need to create six occurrences of FieldNames.

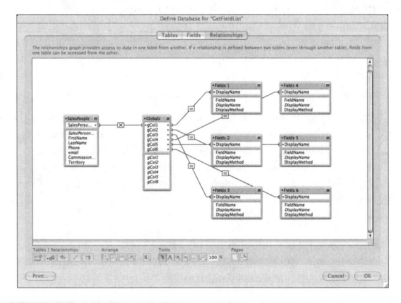

The final step is to alter the calculation formulas in the ColDisplay fields. Remember, instead of "getting" the field specified by the user, we now want to get the field related to the field label specified by the user. At first thought, you might be tempted to redefine ColDisplay1 this way:

```
GetField (Fields1::FieldName)
```

The problem with this is that the only way that ColDisplay1 updates is if the FieldName field changes. Changing gCol1 doesn't have any effect on it. This, finally, is where Evaluate comes in. To force ColDisplay1 to update, you can use the Evaluate function instead of GetField. The second parameter of the formula can reference gCol1, thus triggering the reevaluation of the expression every time gCol1 changes. The new formula for ColDisplay1 is therefore this:

```
Evaluate (Fields1::FieldName ; Globals::gCol1)
```

There is, in fact, still a slight problem with this formula. Even though the calculation is unstored, the field values don't refresh onscreen. The solution is to refer not merely to the related FieldName, but rather to use a `Lookup` function (which is covered in depth in the next section) to explicitly grab the contents of FieldName. The final formula, therefore, is the following:

```
Evaluate (Lookup (Fields1::FieldName) ; Globals::gCol1)
```

There's one final interesting extension we will make to this technique. At this point, the `Evaluate` function is used simply to grab the contents of a field. It's quite possible, however, to add a field called Formula to the FieldNames table, and have the `Evaluate` function return the results of some formula that you define there. The formula in ColDisplay1 would simply be changed to this:

```
Evaluate (Lookup (Fields1::Formula) ; Globals::gCol1)
```

One reason you might want to do this is to be able to add some text formatting to particular fields. For instance, you might want the Sales_2004 field displayed with a leading dollar sign. Because all the ColDisplay fields yield text results, you can't do this with ordinary field formatting. Instead, in the Formula field on the Sales_2004 record, you could type the following formula:

```
"$ " & Sales_2004
```

There's no reason, of course, why a formula you write can't reference multiple fields. This means that you can invent new fields for users to reference simply by adding a new record to the FieldNames table. For example, you could invent a new column called Initials, defined this way:

```
Left (FirstName; 1) & Left (LastName; 1)
```

You could even invent a column called Percent Increase that calculates the percent sales increase from 2004 to 2005. This would be the formula for that:

```
Round((Sales_2005 - Sales_2004) / Sales_2004 *100, 2) & " %"
```

Figure 14.10 shows the contents of the FieldNames table. Note that for columns where you just want to retrieve the value of a field (for example, FirstName), the field name itself is the entire formula.

Figure 14.10
The expression in the Formula field is dynamically evaluated when a user selects a column in the customizable report.

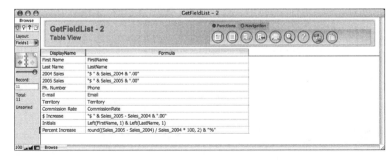

This technique is quite powerful. You can cook up new columns for the customizable report just by adding records to the FieldNames table. Figure 14.11 shows an example of a report that a user could create based on the formulas defined in FieldNames. Keep in mind that Initials, $ Increase, and Percent Increase have not been defined as fields anywhere.

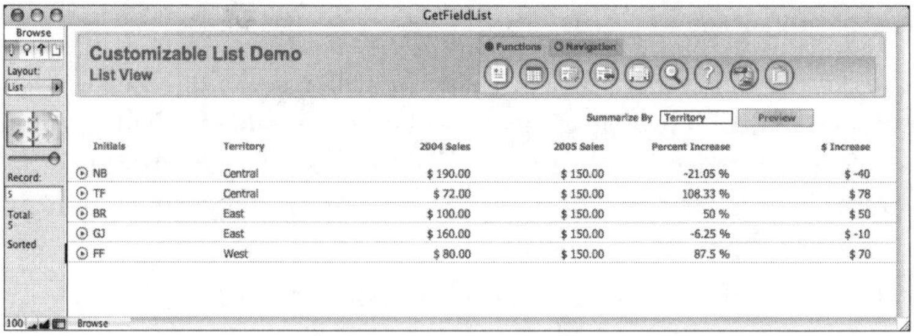

Figure 14.11
In the finished report, users can select from any of the columns defined in the FieldNames table, even those that don't explicitly exist as defined fields.

THE LOOKUP FUNCTIONS

In versions of FileMaker before version 7, lookups were exclusively an auto-entry option. FileMaker 7 added two lookup functions, Lookup and LookupNext, and both are useful additions to any developer's toolkit.

The two lookup functions operate quite similarly to their cousin, the auto-entry lookup option. In essence, a lookup is used to copy a related value into the current table. Lookups (all kinds) have three necessary components: a relationship, a trigger field, and a target field. When the trigger field is modified, the target field is set to some related field value.

It's important to understand the functional differences between the lookup functions and the auto-entry option. Although they behave similarly, they're not quite equivalent. Some of the key differences include the following:

- Auto-entry of a looked-up value is an option for regular text, number, date, time, or timestamp fields, which are subsequently modifiable by the user. A calculation field that includes a lookup function is not user modifiable.

- The lookup functions can be used anywhere—not just in field definitions. For instance, they can be used in formulas in scripts, record-level security settings, and calculated field validation. Auto-entering a looked-up value is limited to field definition.

- The lookup functions can be used in conjunction with other functions to create more complex logic rules. The auto-entry options are comparatively limited.

Lookup

The syntax of the Lookup function is as follows:

```
Lookup ( sourceField {; failExpression} )
```

The sourceField is the related field whose value you want to retrieve. The optional failExpression parameter is returned if there is no related record or if the sourceField is blank for the related record. If the specified relationship matches multiple related records, the value from the first related record is returned.

There are two main differences between using the Lookup function and simply referencing a related field in a formula. The first is that calculations that simply reference related fields must be unstored, but calculations that use the Lookup function to access related fields can be stored and indexed. The other difference is that changing the sourceField in the related table does not cause the Lookup to retrigger. Just as with auto-entry of a looked-up value, the Lookup function captures the sourceField as it existed at a moment in time. The alternative, simply referencing the related field, causes all the values to remain perfectly in sync: When the related value is updated, any calculations that reference it are updated as well. (The downside is that, as with all calculations that directly reference related data, such a calculation cannot be stored.)

LookupNext

The LookupNext function is designed to allow you to map continuous data elements to categorical results. It has the same effect as checking the Copy Next Lower Value or Copy Next Higher Value options when specifying an auto-entry lookup field option. Here is its syntax:

```
LookupNext ( sourceField ; lower/higherFlag )
```

The acceptable values for the second parameter are Lower and Higher. These are keywords and shouldn't be placed in quotes.

An example should help clarify what we mean about mapping continuous data to categorical results. Imagine that you have a table that contains information about people, and that one of the fields is the person's birth date. You want to have some calculation fields that display the person's astrological information, such as a zodiac sign and ruling planet. Birth dates mapping to zodiac signs is a good example of continuous data mapping to categorical results: A range of birth dates corresponds to each zodiac sign.

In practice, two small but instructive complications arise when you try to look up zodiac signs. The first complication is that the zodiac date ranges are expressed not as full dates, but merely as months and days (for example, Cancer starts on June 22 regardless of what year it is). This means that when you set up your zodiac table, you'll use text fields rather than date fields for the start and end dates. The second complication is that Capricorn wraps around the end of the year. The easiest way to deal with this is to have two records in the Zodiac table for Capricorn, one that spans December 22–December 31, and the other that spans January 1–January 20.

Figure 14.12 shows the full data of the Zodiac table. The StartDate and EndDate fields, remember, are actually text fields. The leading zeros are important for proper sorting.

14

Figure 14.12
The data from the Zodiac table is looked up and is transferred to a person record based on the person's birth date.

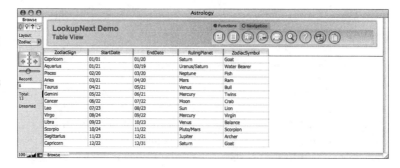

In the Person table, you need to create a calculation formula that generates a text string containing the month and date of the person's birth date, complete with leading zeros so that it's consistent with the way dates are represented in the Zodiac table. The DateMatch field is defined this way:

```
Right ("00" & Month (Birthdate); 2) & "/" & Right ("00"& Day (Birthdate); 2)
```

Next, create a relationship between the Person and Zodiac tables, matching the DateMatch field in Person to the StartDate field in Zodiac. This relationship is shown in Figure 14.13.

Figure 14.13
By relating the Person table to Zodiac, you can look up any information you want based on the person's birth date.

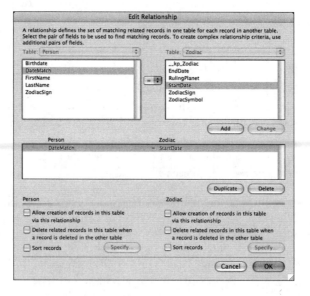

Obviously, many birth dates aren't start dates for one of the zodiac signs. To match to the correct zodiac record, you want to find the next lower match when no exact match is found. For instance, with a birth date of February 13 (02/13), there is no matching record where the StartDate is 02/13, so the next lowest StartDate, which is 01/21 (Aquarius), should be used.

In the Person table, therefore, you can grab any desired zodiac information by using the `LookupNext` function. Figure 14.14 shows an example of how this date might be displayed on a person record. The formula for ZodiacInfo is as follows:

```
"Sign: " & LookupNext (Zodiac::ZodiacSign; Lower) & "¶" &
"Symbol: " & LookupNext (Zodiac::ZodiacSymbol; Lower) & "¶" &
"Ruling Planet: " & LookupNext (Zodiac::RulingPlanet; Lower)
```

Figure 14.14
Using the `LookupNext` function, you can create a calculation field in the Person table that contains information from the next lower matching record.

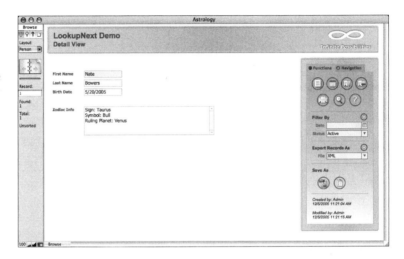

It would have been possible in the previous examples to match to the EndDate instead of the StartDate. In that case, you would simply need to match to the next higher instead of the next lower matching record.

An entirely different but perfectly valid way of approaching the problem would have been to define a more complex relationship between Person and Zodiac, in which the DateMatch was greater than or equal to the StartDate and less than or equal to the EndDate. Doing this would allow you to use the fields from the Zodiac table as plain related fields; no lookup would have been required. There are no clear advantages or disadvantages of this method over the one discussed previously.

NOTE

> Other typical scenarios for using `LookupNext` are for things such as shipping rates based on weight ranges, price discounts based on quantity ranges, and defining cut scores based on continuous test score ranges.

14

TEXT FORMATTING FUNCTIONS

In versions of FileMaker Pro before version 7, there was no way to affect the display of a field (that is, color, size, font, style) via calculation formulas. Developers had to come up with workarounds for seemingly simple tasks, such as having the contents of a field change color based on some conditional test. For example, a typical workaround was stacking two calculation fields on top of one another, each formatted with a different text color on the layout, and then having a conditional test in each turn it "on" or "off" to simulate the effect of the text changing color.

In FileMaker Pro 8, nine text formatting functions obviate the need for many of these old workaround options. They are each discussed in detail in our *FileMaker 8 Functions and Scripts Desk Reference*, but here we demonstrate some examples of how and why you might use these functions.

TEXT COLOR, FONT, AND SIZE

The `TextColor`, `TextFont`, and `TextSize` functions are quite similar. The first parameter of each is the text string you want to act on; the second parameter contains the formatting instructions you want to apply.

For example, perhaps you have a Tasks table, and you want to have any tasks due within the next week be displayed in red. To accomplish this task, you would define a calculation field called TaskDisplay with the following formula:

```
Case (DueDate <= Get (CurrentDate) + 7;
     TextColor (TaskName; RGB (255; 0; 0));    // Red
     TextColor (TaskName; 0))                  // Black
```

The TaskDisplay field displays the task name in either red or black, depending on the due date.

The second parameter of the `TextColor` function needs to be an integer from 0 to 16777215 (which is 256^3–1), which represents a unique RGB color. If you know the integer value of the color you want (for example, black is 0), you can simply use that integer. More typically, you'll use the `RGB` function, which returns the integer representation of the color specified. Each of the three parameters in the `RGB` function must be an integer between 0 and 255. The first parameter represents the red component of the color; the second, the green component; and the third, the blue. The `RGB` function determines the integer representation by the following formula:

```
((255 2) ^ Red) + (255 * Green) + Blue
```

TEXT STYLE

The next two text formatting functions are `TextStyleAdd` and `TextStyleRemove`. Each of these takes two parameters. The first is a text string to act on; the second is a style or styles to apply to the text string. If listing multiple styles, you need to separate them with a plus sign (+). The style names are keywords and should not appear in quotes. They also must be hard-coded in the formula; you can't substitute a field that contains style instructions. The valid styles for both `TextStyleAdd` and `TextStyleRemove` are listed here:

```
Plain

Bold

Italic
```

    Underline

    Condense

    Extend

    Strikethrough

    SmallCaps

    Superscript

    Subscript

    Uppercase

    Lowercase

    Titlecase

    WordUnderline

    DoubleUnderline

    AllStyles

To remove all styles from a chunk of text, you can either *add* Plain as a style, or *remove* AllStyles. Additionally, there are numeric equivalents for each of the text style keywords. Unlike the keywords themselves, the numeric equivalents can be abstracted as field values.

→ For a listing of the numeric style equivalents and some sample usage, see Chapter 6, "Calculation Functions," in *FileMaker 8 Functions and Scripts Desk Reference*.

REMOVING TEXT FORMATTING

In addition to functions for selectively adding formatting to text strings, FileMaker has functions for removing formatting from text. In addition to TextStyleRemove, mentioned previously, there are also functions called TextFontRemove, TextColorRemove, TextSizeRemove, and TextFormatRemove. The first three of these remove some specific styling attribute from the designated text. TextFormatRemove removes all formatting from the selected text in one operation.

For most of these functions, you can specify an optional second parameter that specifies exactly what value you want to remove. For example,

TextSizeRemove(text)

will remove all text sizing from text, causing all of text to return to whatever text size was specified for the field in Layout mode, whereas

TextSizeRemove(text; 14)

will remove only the 14-point size from text, causing any characters in a 14-point size to revert to the field default size.

TextFormatRemove, as mentioned, is the exception to this pattern. TextFormatRemove takes just one parameter, the text string to be reformatted, and strips all formatting from the field.

14

> **NOTE**
>
>
> The `TextFontRemove`, `TextColorRemove`, and `TextSizeRemove` functions are new in FileMaker 8.

You might have difficulty when applying text formatting functions within calculations that return something other than plain text. See "Text Formatting in Nontext Calculations" in the "Troubleshooting" section at the end of this chapter.

EXAMPLES INVOLVING TEXT FORMATTING FUNCTIONS

There are many practical, everyday uses for the text formatting functions. For instance, you might have a database where you've tracked books and articles pertaining to a research project. You could define a field called BibliographyDisplay that performs the appropriate bibliographic formatting of the data elements.

Another use is to create tools so that users can highlight and format field data without using the built-in menu commands. For this example, imagine that you have a simple layout with three text fields on it called Text1, Text2, and Text3. The end goal is to add buttons to the layout that perform some formatting action on a text snippet selected by the user, no matter in which field the user has highlighted a selection. For the example, the formatting options are limited to Bold, Underline, and Red, but you'll easily be able to extend it to perform any formatting you require. Believe it or not, you can do this with a single, one-line script!

Figure 14.15 depicts the layout, buttons, and some sample text. For now, the buttons don't do anything.

Figure 14.15
Users can highlight a section of text in any field on the layout and use the buttons at the top of the screen to format their selections.

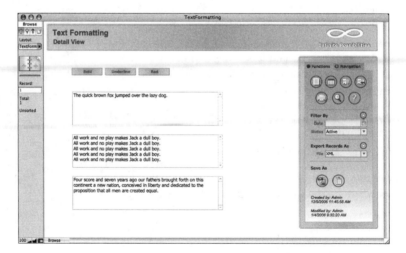

The script that does the formatting is called `Apply Format`. Its single step will be a `Set Field`. Normally with `Set Field`, you specify the field you want to alter. However, with the field unspecified, the currently selected field, where the user has highlighted some text, is affected. The formula needed to actually do the formatting is as follows:

```
Let ( [
     param = Get (ScriptParameter);  // will be Bold, Underline, or Red ...
     oldText = Get ( ActiveFieldContents );
     highlightedText = Middle (oldText; Get ( ActiveSelectionStart );
     ➡Get ( ActiveSelectionSize ));
     newText = Case (param = "Red" ;
          TextColor (highlightedText ; RGB (255 ; 0 ; 0));
          TextStyleAdd (highlightedText; param)
     ) ];

     Replace (oldText; Get ( ActiveSelectionStart );
     ➡Get ( ActiveSelectionSize ); newText)
)
```

The three buttons each use a script parameter to pass in a formatting request, enabling you to use this single script to do any and all formatting. Notice also that Get(ActiveFieldContents), Get(ActiveSelectionStart), and Get(ActiveSelectionSize) are used to identify and isolate the snippet highlighted by the user. Then the appropriate formatting is applied to that snippet, and the Replace function is used to swap it into the old text.

With the script written, all that's left is to go back to the three buttons and define them to call the Apply Format script. Each button needs to pass formatting instructions (Bold, Underline, "Red") to the script through the script parameter. Creating buttons to perform additional formatting would simply be a matter of duplicating an existing button and changing its script parameter.

Figure 14.16 shows the results after some formatting has been performed on the three text fields.

Figure 14.16
A single, one-line script is used to format the user's selection appropriately.

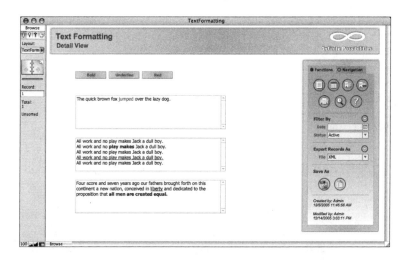

Even though the example is complete as it stands, you might want to add a nice additional bit of functionality to the Apply Format script. Currently, after the formatting is applied, the user's selection is no longer highlighted. If the user wants to perform multiple format operations, such as bold *and* red, she needs to manually rehighlight the desired text. Alternatively, you can use the Set Selection script step to leave the user's selection highlighted. The Set Selection script step needs to know three things: in what field to operate, what character number should start the selection, and what character number should end the selection. Just as with Set Field, if you don't explicitly specify a field on which to act, the currently selected field is used, which is exactly what's desired in this case. For the start and end positions, you can use the Get(ActiveSelectionStart) and Get(ActiveSelectionSize) functions. The problem is that in reformatting the field, those values are lost. Therefore, you need to capture those two values at the very beginning of the script in some way you can refer to later. One way to do this would be simply to create two global number fields (one for each value), but because we're discussing interesting applications of functions, let's look at a method for storing and passing both values as part of a single global text field. As the first step of the Apply Format script, add a Set Field that sets a script variable ($selectionParams) to the following:

```
"start = " & Get ( ActiveSelectionStart ) & " ; stop= " &
➡Get ( ActiveSelectionSize ) + Get ( ActiveSelectionStart ) - 1
```

After this step has executed, $selectionParams might contain something like the following:

```
"start = 16 ; stop = 23"
```

What we've done here is captured the two values in which we're interested, in a format that can be dropped into the middle of a Let function and evaluated with the Evaluate function.

As the final step of the script, the Set Selection script step needs to be told the starting and ending positions of the selection. The starting position would be "unpacked" from $selectionParams by the following formula:

```
Evaluate ( "Let ([ " & $selectionParams & " ]; start)")
```

The wonderful thing about this method is that you can pass any number of variables quite easily. When unpacking it for later use, you simply swap in the appropriate variable at the end of the Evaluate function.

ARRAY FUNCTIONS

Arrays are a powerful and extremely useful programming concept. If you've done any programming in languages such as C++, Perl, PHP, or Visual Basic, you're probably very familiar with both the concept of arrays and some uses for them. We think it likely, however, that most FileMaker Pro developers out there haven't had much experience with arrays and will benefit from both a formal and a practical discussion of them.

Abstractly, an *array* is essentially a structure that can hold multiple values. The values are ordered within the structure and can be referenced by their position or index number. Figure 14.17 shows a representation of a simple array. The array has been defined to hold up to seven values, but only four values are present. The first element in the array is the value red.

Figure 14.17
An array is a structure that can hold multiple values. Each value can be identified and referenced by an index number.

1	2	3	4	5	6	7
red	green	blue	white			

Arrays are useful for a wide variety of things, including storing lists of data, efficiently moving multiple values through a system, and dealing with variable-size data structures in which it's impossible to define separate fields for each individual data element.

FileMaker Pro doesn't have an explicit "array" data type, but fields defined to hold multiple repetitions can be regarded as arrays. More commonly, if you want to use arrays in FileMaker, you can create your own by placing into a text field multiple values separated by some delimiter.

> **NOTE**
>
> In FileMaker Pro 8, an "array notation" can be used to refer to data in a repeating field. `myField[3]`, for instance, refers to the data in the third repetition of `myField`. It's really just a shorthand notation for `GetRepetition(myField, 3)`, but it makes formulas much easier to read.

Return-delimited lists pop up all over the place in FileMaker Pro. Many functions and operations in FileMaker generate return-delimited lists, including most of the `Design` functions and the `Get (ExtendedPrivileges)` function. When a user selects multiple values in a check box–formatted field, FileMaker stores that data as a return-delimited list of the selections. Additionally, the `Copy All Records` script step generates a return-delimited list of the data elements on the current layout for the current found set (elements within a record are separated by the tab character).

WORKING WITH RETURN-DELIMITED DATA ARRAYS

FileMaker Pro 8 has five functions that greatly facilitate working with return-delimited data arrays such as the ones just described. These are `ValueCount`, `LeftValues`, `MiddleValues`, `RightValues`, and `GetValue`. Syntactically, they are very similar to the four "word" functions (`WordCount`, `LeftWords`, `MiddleWords`, and `RightWords`), as well as to the four "character" functions (`Length`, `Left`, `Middle`, and `Right`).

Briefly, the syntax of these functions is as described here:

- `ValueCount (text)`—Returns the number of items in a return-delimited list. Unlike its cousin the `WordCount` function, which interprets sequential word delimiters as a single delimiter, if you have multiple carriage returns in a row, even at the beginning or end of a list, `ValueCount` treats each one as a delimiter. For example, `ValueCount ("¶¶Red¶Blue¶Green¶¶White¶")` returns 7. It's immaterial whether the list contains a single trailing return; the `ValueCount` is not affected by this. Multiple trailing returns affect the `ValueCount`.

14

- **LeftValues (text; numberOfValues)**—Returns a list of the first *n* elements of a return-delimited text string. The list always has a trailing return, even if you are requesting just the first item of the array.

- **MiddleValues (text; startIndex; numberOfValues)**—Returns a list of *n* elements from the middle of a return-delimited array, starting from the position specified in the second parameter. As with LeftValues, the output of this function always contains a trailing return.

- **RightValues (text; numberOfValues)**—Returns a list of the last *n* elements from a return-delimited array. This function, too, always generates a trailing return at the end of its output.

 - **GetValue (listOfValues; valueNumber)**—Returns a single value from a return-delimited list of values. This value will not contain a trailing carriage return. This function is useful in cases in which you want to loop through a set of values and perform some operation using each value in turn.

 If you ever use arrays that use delimiters other than return characters, see "Working with Arrays" in the "Troubleshooting" section at the end of this chapter.

To demonstrate how you might use these functions in a solution, we present an example of iterating through a user's selections in a check box–formatted field and creating records for each selection in another table.

Imagine that you have a table containing information about kids coming to your summer camp, and that one of the pieces of information you are capturing is a list of sports in which the child wants to participate. When you originally set up the table, you simply created a check box–formatted field in the CamperInfo table for this information. You now realize that it's impossible to run certain reports (for example, a subsummary by sport) with the data structured this way, and that you should have created a separate table for CamperSport data. You'd like not to have to reenter all the data, so you want to create a script that loops through all the CamperInfo records and creates a record in the CamperSport table for each sport that's been checked for that camper.

There are many ways you can approach a challenge such as this. You might, for instance, temporarily set data from CamperInfo into variables, navigate to a layout based on the CamperSport table, create records, and populate data from the variables. You've chosen instead to use a portal from the CamperInfo table to the CamperSport table that allows creation of related records. This way, you avoid having to navigate between layouts for each camper, and the CamperID field is automatically set correctly in the CamperSport table.

STEPPING THROUGH AN ARRAY

A user's selections in a check box field are stored as a return-delimited array, in the order in which the user checked them. There are two ways you can step from element to element in such an array. One method is to iteratively "lop off" the first element of the array until there's nothing left to process. This requires first moving the data to be processed into a temporary location where it can be cut apart without harming the original data. The other method is to use a counter to keep track of what element is being processed. You continue processing, incrementing the counter as you go, until the counter has exceeded the number of elements in the array. To some extent, it's personal preference which method you use. Some developers had a preference for the first method in earlier versions of FileMaker Pro because it was simpler syntactically, but the newer "value" functions (introduced in FileMaker 7) make the second method very appealing now. Both versions of the script are presented here in Listings 14.1 and 14.2 so that you can decide for yourself which is preferable.

LISTING 14.1 METHOD 1: "LOP OFF" THE TOP ELEMENT OF THE ARRAY

```
Go to Layout ["CamperInfo" (CamperInfo)]
Go to Record/Request/Page [First]
Loop
    Set Variable [$sportArray; Value: CamperInfo::SportArray]
    Loop
        Exit Loop If [ValueCount ($sportArray) = 0]
        Go to Portal Row [Select; Last]
        Set Field [CamperSport::Sport; GetValue ($sportArray; 1)
        Set Variable [$sportArray; Value: Let (count =
        ➡ValueCount($sportArray); RightValues
        ➡( $sportArray; count-1))
    End Loop
    Go to Record/Request/Page [Next; Exit after last]
End Loop
```

Notice here that in line 8, the first element of the SportArray is pushed through the portal, where it becomes a record in the CamperSport table. In the next line, the $sportArray variable is then reset to be everything *after* the first line. It gets shorter and shorter with each pass through the loop, until finally there aren't any more items to process, concluding the inner loop.

LISTING 14.2 METHOD 2: WALK THROUGH THE ELEMENTS ONE BY ONE

```
Go to Layout ["CamperInfo" (CamperInfo)]
Go to Record/Request/Page [First]
Loop
Set Variable [$counter; Value: 1]
    Loop
        Exit Loop If [$counter > ValueCount (CamperInfo::SportArray)]
        Go to Portal Row [Select; Last]
        Set Field [CamperSport::Sport; GetValue (CamperInfo::SportArray; $counter)
        Set Variable [$counter; Value: $counter  + 1]
    End Loop
    Go to Record/Request/Page [Next; Exit after last]
End Loop
```

Again, the main difference with this method is that the inner loop steps through the elements of the SportArray field based on a counter variable.

THE "Filter"-ING FUNCTIONS

The Filter and FilterValues functions, introduced in FileMaker 7, are nifty tools for complex text comparison and manipulation. The following sections provide an example of each of them.

THE Filter FUNCTION

The syntax for the Filter function is as follows:

```
Filter (textToFilter; filterText)
```

The filterText parameter consists of a set of characters that you want to "protect" in textToFilter. The output of the Filter function is the textToFilter string, minus any characters that don't appear in filterText. For example:

```
Filter ("This is a test" ; "aeiou") = "iiae"
```

Here, the filter is the set of five vowels. Therefore, the output from the function contains all the vowels from the string "This is a test". The filter is case-sensitive, so if you wanted to include both upper- and lowercase vowels in your output, you'd need to make the filterText parameter aeiouAEIOU. The output is ordered according to the order in which characters in the filter are found in the first parameter. The order of the characters in the filter itself is irrelevant.

The Filter function is useful anytime you want to constrain the domain of possible characters that a user can enter into a field. The most common use of Filter, therefore, is as part of an auto-entry calculation for text fields. Figure 14.18 shows the auto-entry options dialog for a field called Phone. Note that the option Do Not Replace Existing Value of Field (If Any) has been unchecked. What this means is that the auto-entry calculation isn't triggered only when the record is created, but also when the Phone field is modified. Essentially, this means that whenever a user modifies the Phone field, his entry is replaced immediately by the result of the calculation formula specified.

Figure 14.18
The Filter function is often used as part of the auto-entry of a calculated value.

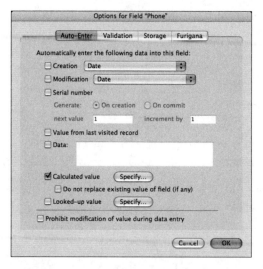

You can use the Filter function as part of the auto-entry calculation for the Phone field to remove any non-numeric characters that might have been entered by the user. The nice thing about the Filter function here is that you don't need to anticipate all the incorrect things a user can enter (text, punctuation, spaces), but rather, you can specify what the acceptable characters are. The actual function you use to reformat the user's entry in the Phone field depends on your needs and preferences, but one option would be the following:

```
Let ( [
   ph = Filter (Phone; "0123456789");
   len = Length (ph) ;
   areaCode = Case ( len = 10; Left (ph; 3); "");
   exchange = Case ( len = 10; Middle (ph; 4; 3); Left (ph; 3)) ;
   end = Right (ph; 4) ];

   Case (
       len =10 ;   "(" & areaCode & ") " & exchange & "-" & end ;
       len =7 ;    exchange & "-" & end ;

       "Error: " & TextStyleAdd ( Phone ; Bold)
   )
)
```

The formula starts by stripping out any non-numeric characters from the user's entry. Then, if the length of the remaining string is either 7 or 10, the number is formatted with punctuation and returned to the user. If it's not, the function shows the user an error message, complete with the original entry presented in bold text.

THE FilterValues FUNCTION

The FilterValues function is similar to the Filter function, except that it filters the elements in one return-delimited set by the elements in a second return-delimited set. When each of the sets consists of unique elements, the FilterValues function essentially returns the intersection of the two sets. In Figure 14.19, you can see that FilterValues returns the items common to the two sets. Had the two parameters been reversed and the formula been written as FilterValues (Set B; Set A), the only difference would have been the order of the elements in the resulting list.

> **NOTE**
>
> The result list always is ordered based on the first set. If an element appears multiple times in the first set (and it's included in the filter set), it appears multiple times in the result set.

FilterValues comes in handy anytime you want to see whether two lists contain any of the same elements. For instance, if you've defined any extended privileges as part of your security settings, you can see a list of all the privileges that have been granted to the current user with the Get (ExtendedPrivileges) function. If you have some routine that only users with PrivSetA or PrivSetC should have access to, you can use the formula FilterValues ("PrivSetA¶PrivSetC"; Get (ExtendedPrivileges)). If the result is not empty, the user has at least one of those two privilege sets.

14

Figure 14.19
The `FilterValues` function returns a list of all the items of Set A that are also in Set B.

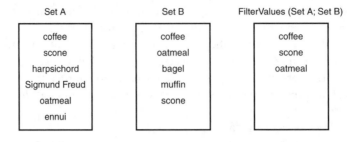

Set A	Set B	FilterValues (Set A; Set B)
coffee	coffee	coffee
scone	oatmeal	scone
harpsichord	bagel	oatmeal
Sigmund Freud	muffin	
oatmeal	scone	
ennui		

As another example, imagine that you are a third-grade teacher and that you have just given your students a 10-question True/False test. Rather than setting up a related table for their answers, you've just entered all their responses into a return-delimited text field. By also putting the answer key into a global text field, you can use the `FilterValues` function to determine the number of correct answers each student had. Figure 14.20 shows how this might look when you're finished. The formula for the NumberCorrect field is the following:

```
ValueCount (FilterValues (TestResults; AnswerKey) )
```

Figure 14.20
By using the `FilterValues` and `ValueCount` functions, you can count how many items in one array are contained within some other array.

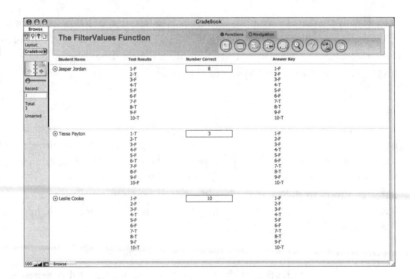

CUSTOM FUNCTIONS

In addition to all the wonderful and powerful calculation functions built into FileMaker Pro 8, you also can create your own custom functions. To create custom functions, you need to have a copy of FileMaker Pro 8 Advanced. Any custom functions you create using FileMaker Pro Advanced remain in the file and are fully usable when it's subsequently used by the regular FileMaker Pro 8 client application. You just can't edit the formula of the custom function unless you have FileMaker Pro Advanced.

As with other objects, such as scripts, tables, and user account information, custom functions live in a particular file. There is—unfortunately—no easy way to move or import custom functions defined in one file into another one. The implications of this are obvious: If you have a solution that consists of multiple files, you need to define custom functions redundantly in all the files that need to access them, thus complicating maintenance and troubleshooting. This fact shouldn't scare you off from using custom functions—they're really quite wonderful—but it's certainly a constraint you need to be aware of.

Custom functions that have been created for a particular file show up with all the built-in functions in the list of functions within the calculation dialog. To see just the custom functions, you can choose Custom Functions from the filter above the function list. Custom functions are used in a formula just as any other function. The function name and the names of its parameters are defined by the person who writes the custom function.

USES OF CUSTOM FUNCTIONS

There are several reasons for using custom functions in a solution. Custom functions enable you to abstract snippets of calculation logic so that they become reusable. Abstracting out bits of logic also makes your code easier to read and eliminates redundancy.

SIMPLIFYING COMPLEX FORMULAS

The best place to begin understanding the potential uses of custom functions is with a simple example. Imagine that for some reason you need to generate a random integer from 10 to 50. Knowing, as you do from reading Chapter 8, "Getting Started with Calculations," that the Random function returns a random number between 0 and 1, you eventually conclude that a formula that solves this particular problem is as follows:

```
Int(Random * 41) + 10
```

With the problem solved, you write your formula and go on your merry way. Now, imagine that the next day you come back and discover you need to write another function that requires a random integer from 1 to 6. After a bit more thinking, you come up with the following:

```
Int(Random * 6) + 1
```

About this time, you'd be wishing that the engineers at FileMaker, Inc., had thought to create a function that would return a random integer from x to y. Using FileMaker Pro 8 Advanced, you can in fact write your own custom functions for situations such as this. Rather than continuing to solve particular problems, you can solve the general case and never again need to divert your attention to the particular.

So, what would a generalized solution to the random-number problem look like? First, you'd need to have some way of abstractly representing the "from" and "to" numbers. Let's call these two numbers lowNumber and highNumber. Then the function that satisfies the general condition would be this:

```
Int (Random * (highNumber - lowNumber + 1)) + lowNumber
```

For any lowNumber and highNumber you feed this function, you get back an integer between the two. We'll look in a moment at how you would go about setting this up as a custom function, but for now, the important thing is the concept that custom functions, just like the built-in functions you use all the time, have inputs (which are called *parameters*) and an output. Let's say that you decide to call this function randomInRange. Now, to solve the first problem we looked at, finding a random integer from 10 to 50, you could just use the following function:

```
randomInRange (10; 50)
```

And to find a number from 1 to 6, you could use this one:

```
randomInRange (1; 6)
```

You've simplified your code by replacing a complex expression with a single function, thereby making it easier to read and maintain. You've abstracted that bit of logic out of whatever larger formula you were working on, leaving you with one fewer thing to think about.

CUSTOM FUNCTIONS AS SYSTEM CONSTANTS

There are a few different schools of thought about when you should write a custom function to abstract your programming logic, and when you should use existing tools to solve the problem. Some hold that you should always write custom functions. Even if you use a given custom function only a single time, you've made your code more modular, thus making it easier to track down and troubleshoot problems. Plus, if you do ever need that function again, it's there, ready and waiting.

Other developers find that they use custom functions more sparingly. Their attitude is this: If you find yourself solving a particular problem more than once, go ahead and write a custom function for it, and go back to change the original occurrence to reference the custom function instead. This process, often called *refactoring* as a general programming concept, has a certain pragmatism to it: Write a custom function as soon as it's more efficient to do so, but not sooner.

Whatever camp you find yourself falling into, you should be aware of two other common uses for custom functions. The first is for defining system constants. As an example, imagine that in your sales organization, the commission rate is 15%. In calculations in which you determine commission amounts, you might find yourself writing numerous formulas in which sales figures are multiplied by .15. If, heaven forbid, you ever need to change that figure to, say, .18, you'd need to sift through all your code to find all the instances where you had hard-coded the commission figure.

As an alternative, you might consider defining custom functions to represent systemwide constants such as these. In this example, you would simply have a custom function called CommissionRate that had no parameters and returned a value of .15. By abstracting out the hard-coded value, you're able to quickly and easily make global changes just by editing a single function. You should never refer directly to the magic number in a formula; use the custom function instead. Other examples of numbers and strings that should be abstracted out of your formulas include IP addresses, URLs, and colors.

There's a subtle pitfall here. Note that stored values that reference custom functions will *not* automatically update when a custom function definition changes. For example, if you have a system constant called commissionRate implemented as a custom function, and you then go on to create one or more stored calculations that reference commissionRate, the values in those calculations will not update if you later redefine commissionRate to be 18%. The same would hold true of data that's auto-entered into a field. If you wanted these stored values to take account of the new commission rate, you'd need to force the fields to explicitly refresh their contents somehow.

CREATING RECURSIVE FUNCTIONS

The final common situation in which custom functions are used is for making recursive functions. One of the limitations often lamented by developers over the years has been the fact that you can't create looping constructs within calculation formulas. That is, you can't instruct a regular calculation formula to keep doing something until some condition holds. Custom functions, on the other hand, can contain recursive logic, which mimics the effects of a looping control structure. This means that a class of problems can be solved only by the creation of custom functions. This stands in stark contrast to the "custom functions as vehicles for abstraction" idea discussed previously. As an abstraction tool, custom functions can always be replaced in a formula by the logic they've abstracted. No such substitution can be made when dealing with recursive functions. In those cases, using custom functions is not a convenience; it's a necessity. In the section that follows, we develop and discuss several recursive functions.

CREATING CUSTOM FUNCTIONS

Now that you understand what custom functions are and why you might want to use them, it's time to turn to the mundane subject of how to actually create them. First, recall that custom functions can be created and edited only with FileMaker Pro 8 Advanced, and that custom functions live in a specific file. To see a list of custom functions that have been defined in a particular file, and to define new ones, choose File, Define, Custom Functions. The resulting Define Custom Functions dialog is shown in Figure 14.21.

Buttons from this dialog enable you to create, edit, and delete a custom function. You also see the names of the parameters that have been defined for each function, as well as whether a function is available to all accounts or just those with the Full Access privilege set. When you go to create or edit a custom function, you're taken to the Edit Custom Function dialog, shown in Figure 14.22.

This dialog is similar in many ways to the standard calculation formula dialogs, so it shouldn't seem terribly unfamiliar. The main difference is the upper-left portion of the dialog, where instead of seeing a list of fields, you can instead name your function and its parameters. The restrictions for function and parameter names are the same as the those for field names: They can't contain any mathematics symbols (such as + - * / ^ =); they can't contain the words AND, OR, XOR, or NOT; they can't begin with a digit or period; and they can't have the same name as an existing function or keyword.

14

Figure 14.21
With FileMaker Pro 8 Advanced, you have access to a Define Custom Functions dialog.

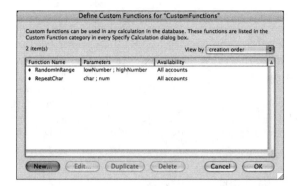

Figure 14.22
The parameters and formula for a custom function are defined in the Edit Custom Function dialog.

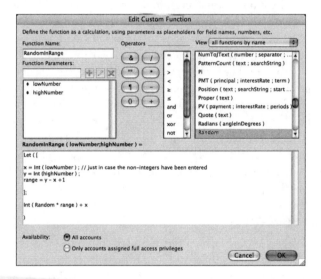

TIP

When naming your custom functions and parameters, we think it's best to follow the same naming conventions used in the built-in functions. The initial letter of each word in a function name should be capitalized, and the name should contain no spaces or other punctuation. Parameters should be in *camel case*, with the first letter in lowercase and the first letter of subsequent words capitalized (for example, `numberOfCharacters`, `textString1`). Some developers prefer that the function name itself should be in camel case as well.

There is no practical limit to the number of parameters you can define for a function, but most functions require anywhere from zero to a handful. The order of the parameters is important: When you use a function and specify the input parameters, they are interpreted as being in the order in which they are listed in the Edit Custom Function dialog.

NOTE

> If you find yourself writing a function that requires more than four or five parameters, that's a pretty good signal that you should break the function down into two or more smaller functions.

The other significantly new and different portion of this dialog is the Availability section at the bottom. By default, a function is available to all user accounts. Anytime a user or developer has access to a calculation dialog, he or she will see and be able to use all the unrestricted custom functions. The other option available to you is to restrict the use of the function to only those users who have been assigned the Full Access privilege set. The latter can be referred to as *private* functions, and the former can be thought of as *public* functions. We find it helpful to place an underscore at the beginning of the name of private functions so that they can be quickly and obviously identified. If access to a function has been restricted, users who don't have full access will not ever see or have access to use that function. If these users ever view a calculation dialog that references a private function (say, in a script), the name of the function is replaced with <Private function> in the calculation dialog. Declaring a function as private has no impact on what data is displayed or accessible to a user. The functions still do their jobs and work properly. It's just the functions themselves that can't be viewed or used.

You might want to restrict access to a function for several reasons. As you will see in some of the examples in the section that follows, often when you define recursive functions, you need to define two functions to accomplish one goal. In these cases, the first function is often a public function, whereas the other is restricted, thereby keeping users from accidentally calling it directly. Another reason to define a function as private is simply to keep from confusing novice developers. Your function may not be documented anywhere, and it might not contain adequate error trapping to handle improper parameter values. By making it private, you reduce the risk that the function will be used improperly.

EXAMPLES OF CUSTOM FUNCTIONS

We think the best way to learn how to write your own custom functions is to study examples so that you can get ideas about uses in your own solutions. Some of the sample functions that follow might have intrinsic value to you, but more important than the specific formulas are the ideas and techniques. To that end, following each of the examples presented in this section, we provide commentary about the syntax and/or use of the function.

```
Hypotenuse (leg1Length ; leg2Length) =
Let ( [
    a2 = leg1Length * leg1Length;
    b2 = leg2Length * leg2Length;

    c2 = a2 + b2] ;
    Sqrt (c2)
)
```

14

Although FileMaker Pro provides built-in functions for many common mathematical formulas and operations, a number of common equations are missing. The preceding Hypotenuse function uses the Pythagorean Theorem ($a^2 + b^2 = c^2$) to find the length of the hypotenuse of a right triangle given the lengths of the two legs.

Examples:

```
Hypotenuse (3 ; 4) = 5

Hypotenuse (5 ; 12) = 13
```

```
NthRoot (number ; root) =
Exp (Ln (number) / root )
```

This is another example of creating a custom function to provide an abstraction for a mathematical formula: There is a built-in function that returns the square root of a number, but no function that returns the nth root of a number. The NthRoot function uses logarithms to find this number.

Examples:

```
NthRoot (8 ; 3) = 2

NthRoot (64; 4) = 4
```

```
Quarter (myDate) =
Ceiling ( Month (myDate) / 3)
```

This function returns the calendar quarter (1–4) of myDate. This function exemplifies the idea of custom functions being used to substitute for code chunks, making your code easier to read and maintain. The Month function returns a number from 1 to 12, so taking the ceiling of that number divided by 3 yields an integer from 1 to 4.

Examples:

```
Quarter ("12/11/03") = 4

Quarter ("4/1/04") = 2
```

```
WeekEndingFriday (myDate) =
myDate + Mod (6 - DayOfWeek(mydate); 7)
```

Given a date, this function returns the date of the following Friday. This sort of functionality is often necessary in time-tracking systems so that you can summarize records by week. It would be easy to alter or extend this function to be referenced to some day other than Friday. To extend it, you would just specify a second parameter in the function and replace the hard-coded 6 (which is the DayOfWeek of any Friday) with a value derived from the parameter.

Examples:

```
WeekEndingFriday ("12/11/2005") = "12/12/2004"  // the 11th was a Thursday

WeekEndingFriday ("1/9/2006") = "1/9/2006" // the 9th was a Friday
```

```
RepeatText (text ; numberOfRepetitions) =
text & Case (numberOfRepetitions>1; RepeatText (text; numberOfRepetitions - 1))
```

This is the first example of a recursive function. The RepeatText function returns *n* repetitions of the text string passed in the first parameter. For instance, RepeatText ("t"; 3) returns the string ttt. If the concept of recursive functions isn't clear to you, this is a good place to begin experimenting. Figure 14.23 traces through exactly what the function is asked to do when it evaluates this simple example. RepeatText ("t"; 3) is first evaluated as t and the result of RepeatText ("t"; 2). Of course, the latter is then evaluated as t and the result of RepeatText ("t" ; 1), which is simply t. The iteration stops at this point because numberOfRepetitions is not greater than 1. This is known as the function's *exit condition*; without one, you have endless recursion (picture a dog chasing its tail endlessly), which fortunately FileMaker Pro is smart enough to recover from after some large number of iterations.

CAUTION

> Be sure that any recursive function you write has some exit condition that is guaranteed to be reached.

Figure 14.23
This diagram shows how the recursive custom function RepeatText ("t" ; 3) is evaluated.

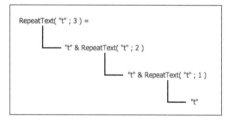

Possible uses of the RepeatText function include creating progress bars or bar graphs. If you ever tried to do this sort of thing in previous versions of FileMaker, you know what a kludgy workaround was required to get a repeating string of characters. Another use is for padding out spaces when generating fixed-length data formats. Say you need to pad out a FirstName field to 15 characters by adding spaces at the end. In previous versions of FileMaker, you would have used this formula:

```
Left (FirstName & "                  " ; 15)
```

Using RepeatText, you could simply use this:

```
FirstName & RepeatText (" " ; 15 - Length(FirstName))
```

Of course, if you have a lot of padding to do, you might decide to abstract this one more layer and build the PadCharacters function shown next.

14

Examples:

```
RepeatText ("¦" ; 10) = "¦¦¦¦¦¦¦¦¦¦"

RepeatText ("hello"; 3) = "hellohellohello"


PadCharacters (text ; padLength; characterToPad; side) =
Let ( [
    padString = RepeatText (characterToPad; padLength - Length(text));
] ;
Case (
  Length (text) > padLength ; Left (text; padLength);
  side = "start"; padString & text;
  side = "end"; text & padString
)
)
```

Building on the preceding example, the PadCharacters function pads either leading or trailing characters onto a string. We've used four parameters here to gain flexibility. The third and fourth parameters specify the pad character and whether the padding should be at the start or end of the string. If you knew you always wanted to pad leading zeros, you could define this function with just two parameters and then hard-code the location and character within the formula.

Notice that this function makes a call to the RepeatText function to generate the padString. We could have included the formula for RepeatText, but by abstracting it out, we centralize the code for RepeatText (making it easier to troubleshoot) while also making the formula easier to read.

Examples:

```
PadCharacters ("foo"; 8 ; "x"; "end") = "fooxxxxx"

PadCharacters ("123"; 10; "0"; "start") = "0000000123"


TrimChar (text; removeCharacter; location) =
 // valid locations are "start", "end", "all"
Let ( [
  leftChar = Left (text; 1);
  rightChar = Right (text; 1);
  remainderLength = Length(text) -1

] ;
Case (
  (location = "start" or location = "all") and leftChar = removeCharacter;
    TrimChar (Right(text; remainderLength) ; removeCharacter; location) ;
  (location = "end" or location = "all") and rightChar = removeCharacter;
    TrimChar (Left(text; remainderLength) ; removeCharacter; location) ;
   text
)
)
```

FileMaker Pro's built-in Trim function removes any leading and trailing spaces from a text string. There are times, however, when you need a more generalized way of removing a specific leading or trailing character from a string. The TrimChar function does just this. The first parameter is the string you want trimmed; the second is the character you want removed. The third parameter, location, is used to specify whether you want the character removed from the start or the end of the string, or from both. Valid inputs are start, end, and all.

This function works by checking whether the first or last character in the string needs to be lopped off. If so, the remainder of the string is fed back recursively to itself. Each iteration removes at most a single character; the "loop" continues until no more characters need to be removed, at which point the shortened text string is simply returned.

Examples:

```
TrimChar ("xxThis is a testxxx", "x", "all") = "This is a test"

TrimChar ("Another test¶¶¶", "¶", "end") = "Another test"


CrossProduct (array1; array2) =
_CrossProductGenerator (array1; array2; 1)
```

This, the final custom function example, looks at a more complex recursive function. In the recursive examples shown previously, the exit condition for the recursion was based either on an explicitly passed parameter reaching a certain value (RepeatChar), or on a condition no longer being true (TrimChar). There are other situations in which you want to be able to increment a counter with every iteration, and have the exit condition for the loop be based on that counter reaching some threshold. The interesting part is that because the counter needs to be passed along from iteration to iteration, it must be defined as a parameter. This means, however, that anyone using the function must initialize the counter for you, most likely setting it simply to 1.

The other solution is that you have a private function with a counter parameter that's called by a public function without one. In this case, the public function CrossProduct takes only two parameters, which are both expected to be return-delimited arrays. The function is defined merely to call another function, _CrossProductGenerator, which has three parameters. The first two inputs to _CrossProductGenerator are simply passed along based on the user's input. The third, however, is hard-coded to 1, hence initializing a counter used there.

The syntax for the private function is as follows:

```
_CrossProductGenerator (array1; array2; counter)
```

It has the following formula:

```
Let ( [
  array1count = ValueCount (array1);
  array2count = ValueCount (array2);
  limit = array1count * array2count;

  pos1 = Ceiling (counter / array2count) ;
  pos2 = Mod (counter - 1; array2count ) + 1;
```

14

```
    item1 = TrimChar (MiddleValues (array1; pos1; 1); "¶" ; "end");
    item2 = TrimChar (MiddleValues (array2; pos2; 1); "¶" ; "end")
] ;

Case ( counter <= limit ;
    item1 & item2 & "¶" & _CrossProductGenerator (array1; array2; counter + 1))

)
```

The cross product of two sets is a set containing all the two-element sets that can be created by taking one element of each set. For example, if Set1 contained {A, B} and Set2 contained {P, Q, R, S}, their cross product would consist of {AP, AQ, AR, AS, BP, BQ, BR, BS}. The number of elements in the cross product is the product of the number of elements in each of the two sets.

The _CrossProductGenerator function "loops," incrementing a counter as it goes, until the counter is no longer less than the number of elements expected in the result set. Each time it iterates, it figures out what element number to grab from each list. With Set1 and Set2 of the example, the function would iterate eight times. If you were on iteration 5, the function would realize that it needed to grab the second item from the first list (because Ceiling (5 / 4) = 2), which is B, and the first item from the second list (because Mod (4; 4) + 1 = 1), which is P. That's how BP becomes the fifth element of the result set.

Notice also that this function, besides recursively calling itself, also calls the TrimChar function created earlier in this section. From the section on working with arrays, you'll remember that the LeftValues, MiddleValues, and RightValues functions all return a trailing return after the item list; that trailing return needs to be removed before the item is processed.

Examples:

```
CrossProduct ("A¶B¶C" ; "1¶2¶3¶4") = "A1¶A2¶A3¶A4¶B1¶B2¶B3¶B4¶C1¶C2¶C3¶C4¶"

CrossProduct ("Red¶Yellow¶Blue" ; "-fish") = "Red-fish¶Yellow-fish¶Blue-fish¶"
```

→ For many more examples of custom functions, see Chapter 8, "Useful Custom Functions," in *FileMaker 8 Functions and Scripts Desk Reference*.

GetNthRecord

The quirkily named GetNthRecord is a new function in FileMaker 8, and one that merits its own discussion. In general, in FileMaker, if you are situated on one record and you want to see data from some other record, you need a relationship of some kind. This is intuitively so if you are on, say, a customer record, and want to see data from an invoice—you need some kind of relationship between Customer and Invoice to accomplish this task. But it's also been true if you want to see data from somewhere else in the same table.

But relational access has never covered all the possible scenarios in which you might want to access data from other records. Suppose that when you're situated on a customer record, you also want to know the names of the customers immediately before and after the current record? Suppose that when you're looking at a set of related invoices from the viewpoint of a customer, you want to get some specific information from the second related invoice record, or the third? It has always been *possible* to do these things in previous versions of FileMaker, but it has sometimes involved some cumbersome techniques.

GetNthRecord solves these problems, as well as a number of others. Its syntax looks like this:

```
GetNthRecord( fieldName; recordNumber )
```

Here, fieldName is the name of a field in the current table or a related table, and recordNumber is the number of the specific record from which to fetch data. Let's look at some examples.

```
GetNthRecord( CustomerName; 17 )
```

would return the value of the CustomerName field in the seventeenth record in the found set in the current table. The two expressions

```
GetNthRecord( CustomerName; Get(RecordNumber) + 1 )
```

and

```
GetNthRecord( CustomerName; Get(RecordNumber) - 1 )
```

would return the value of the CustomerName field from the records immediately succeeding and preceding the current record.

```
GetNthRecord( InvoiceLineItem::ProductName; 3 )
```

would return the product name from the third line item related to a given invoice.

These applications are useful enough, but when you use some other advanced calculation techniques, some very interesting things are possible. For example, you'll often see cases in which you want to collect or aggregate non-numeric data from some set of records. Say, for example, you wanted to extract the personal names from a found set of records and present them in a comma-separated list. In the past, it would have been necessary to write a looping script to run through all the records and collect the results into a list. In FileMaker 8, a recursive custom function that invokes GetNthRecord can accomplish the same thing more economically. Consider a function that looks like this:

```
allNames( recordNum, currentList)
```

Consider that it's defined as shown here:

```
Case( recordNum > Get ( FoundCount ); currentList;
allNames( recordNum + 1; currentList &
Case( recordNum > 1;  ", "; "" ) &   Evaluate( "GetNthRecord ( name ;" &
➥recordNum & ")" ) ) )
```

Initially, you'd need to call this function with a recordNum value of 1 and a currentList value composed of an empty string. From there, the function keeps calling itself until recordNum is equal to the current found count. With each fresh function call, the value of the name field returned by GetNthRecord is appended to the list, and the list is passed back into the function again for the next iteration.

Note that it was necessary to use the Evaluate function here. This is because a custom function cannot directly access record data, such as the name field. Without the Evaluate function, when you attempt to save the function definition, FileMaker warns you that the name

14

name is unknown. As a result, we need to build up the call to GetNthRecord as a text string, incorporating the current value of recordNum, and then pass that entire text string off to the Evaluate function.

As written, the function is designed to operate on data within the current table. It's rather limited in that sense, and we could certainly recast the function to be more extensible. It might be better to determine the total count of records from somewhere outside the function, and pass that in, along with the name of the field to be aggregated. Such a function might be called like this:

```
aggregateRecords( field; start; end )
```

And it might be defined something like this:

```
Case (start <= end ; GetNthRecord (field ; start ) &
➥Case( start < end; "¶"; "" ) & GetRelated (field ; start+1 ; end) ; "")
```

In this case, you need to decide for yourself what the end value would be; this is simply the total number of records you're trying to aggregate, and it could be the result of a Get(FoundCount) on the current file, or a Count() operation against a related file. The function needs to be called with a start value of 1, unless you want to begin aggregating from a later record for some reason. So a call to this function would look like this:

```
aggregateRecords( firstName; 1; Get(FoundCount) )
```

This would aggregate the firstName field across all the records in the current found set of the current table.

A recursive custom function, with or without an Evaluate, is probably one of the more complex pieces of coding you would need to do in FileMaker, but the results can be quite striking. GetNthRecord is one of the most important new functions in FileMaker 8, and we recommend you become familiar with all of its uses.

TROUBLESHOOTING

TEXT FORMATTING IN NONTEXT CALCULATIONS

I want some of my dates to come out in red. I created some calculations that apply text formatting to certain dates, but they just don't work.

For a calculation containing text formatting functions to work correctly, the calculation must have an output type of Text or Number. Calculations defined to output a data type of Date, Time, or Timestamp will not show the effects of text formatting calculations.

NAMING VARIABLES IN Let FUNCTIONS

Can I use spaces in the names of variables used in Let functions? Are the variable names case-sensitive? What happens if I name a Let variable the same thing as an existing field name, variable name, or function name?

First off, yes, you can use spaces in the names of variables used in Let functions. Variable names can't begin with numbers, nor can they contain certain reserved characters (such as ; ,

\ / + - * = ( ) [ ] < > & and "). You can, however, use characters such as $ and % in variable names.

Some complexity arises when we look at the possible use of script variables (variables beginning with $ or $$) within Let statements. We explore this complex topic in the following chapter. For now, suffice it to say that because various parts of a Let statement can work with script variables, you should avoid using $ or $$ in naming any of your Let variables.

→ For further discussion of the use of variables in Let statements, **see** "Accessing Variables from Within a Let Statement," **p. 452**.

Variable names within Let statements are not case-sensitive. You can use a particular name several times within a function, and names can also be reused in separate functions.

There are no restrictions against naming variables with the same names used for fields and functions. Be aware that any subsequent use of the name within the function refers to the local variable, not the field or function. With most functions, you don't need to worry about this, but names of functions that don't take parameters, such as Random, WindowNames, and Pi, should not be used for variables within a Let function. For instance, the formula Let (Pi = "Hello"; Pi) would return the string Hello, not the trigonometric constant pi that you might expect. As a rule, it's wise to avoid any overlap of names with reserved FileMaker names, or names of objects elsewhere in the system. Even if the logic works, it may be confusing and hard to read.

WORKING WITH ARRAYS

I use arrays that have pipe characters as delimiters. Can I use the "values" functions to extract elements from these arrays?

The five "values" functions (ValueCount, LeftValues, MiddleValues, RightValues, GetValue) operate only on return-delimited lists of data. If you have lists that are delimited by other characters, such as pipes or tabs, you'd first need to do a substitution to change your delimiter into a return. For example, if myArray is a pipe-delimited array, you could count the number of values in it with the following formula:

```
Let (tempArray = Substitute (myArray; "¦"; "¶"); ValueCount (tempArray))
```

Of course, one of the reasons you might not have used returns as your delimiter in the first place is that your data elements may possibly contain return characters. If that's the case, you can't swap in returns as your delimiters and expect the structure of the array to remain unchanged. Before turning pipe characters into carriage returns, you'd want to turn any existing carriage returns into something else—something that's guaranteed not to be found in an element and that's easy to turn back into a return character if necessary. You might, for instance, use the Substitute function to turn returns into the string ***RETURN***.

FILEMAKER EXTRA: CREATING A CUSTOM FUNCTION LIBRARY

If you or your organization uses custom functions across several solutions, you'll likely want to develop some sort of centralized library of the functions you've developed. That way, when you find yourself in need of a particular function, you won't have to rack your brain remembering where it was used before. Also, centralizing the function library is a way of creating a knowledge base that can help your organization leverage its past work and can aid in the training of new developers.

Your library can take many forms. One option, of course, is to create a FileMaker Pro file for your function library. Minimally, you'll want to include fields for the function name, its parameters, its formula, and a brief description. You might also use a container field to store a sample file for a particular function. Another "nice to have" would be a related table for storing information about where you've used the function.

As of the time of this writing, there's no way to move custom functions from one file to another using tools in the FileMaker product line, although cutting and pasting formulas to and from the library isn't terribly time-consuming. Custom functions are, however, part of the Database Design Report (DDR) that can be produced by FileMaker Pro 8 Advanced. If you're handy with XML, or are looking for a fun first XML project, you might want to use the XML output of the DDR to create your function library.

You also might want to investigate FMRobot, a tool sold by New Millennium Communications that can automate many development tasks, and that includes the capability to move custom functions between files.

Finally, if you always want to have a particular set of custom functions in your files, create a sparse template file that has them in it. Then, rather than creating new files from scratch, you can just duplicate and develop on top of your template.

14

## CHAPTER 15

ADVANCED SCRIPTING TECHNIQUES

In this chapter

WHAT IS ADVANCED SCRIPTING?

Chapter 9, "Getting Started with Scripting," presented an introduction to FileMaker Pro scripting techniques. It covered such topics as error trapping, linking scripts together via subscripts, conditional branching, looping scripts, and using custom dialogs. These are all essential scripting techniques you should become familiar with.

This chapter explores several additional scripting techniques, including working with script variables, script input/output techniques, and managing windows. Although we think that everyone can potentially benefit from learning these techniques, they do require a solid familiarity with general scripting techniques, calculation formulas, and the Relationships Graph. For this reason, we have opted to present these as advanced scripting techniques.

This chapter does not present a comprehensive overview of scripting techniques. Indeed, such an overview could require an entire book of its own. Rather, we have chosen techniques that highlight new features of FileMaker 8 and that we think will have the broadest appeal. This book's companion volume, *FileMaker 8 Functions and Scripts Desk Reference*, contains a comprehensive listing of script steps, along with notes and examples; refer to that source for additional information about script steps used throughout this chapter.

SCRIPT PARAMETERS AND SCRIPT RESULTS

NEW FileMaker 7 and now FileMaker 8 have each introduced features that allow you to write scripts that are more flexible and extensible than in the past. FileMaker 7 introduced script parameters, a means of passing inputs into a script. FileMaker 8 completes the picture by adding *script results*, the capability for a script to output a piece of data after it's finished executing. Together, we can think of these features as constituting a system for script input and output.

The capability to move data in and out of scripts is desirable because it means that scripts can be written more abstractly and thus can be reused. By "abstractly," we mean that scripts are written to solve general problems rather than specific ones. Using script input/output saves you time, reduces the number of scripts that are necessary in your files, and makes your scripts easier to maintain.

That being said, the use of script input/output is completely optional. FileMaker developers did quite well for years without script parameters and script results, and we can think of no scenario in which you couldn't still muddle through without them. Script input and output represent a considerable advance for FileMaker Pro scripting; the extent to which you want to take advantage of that depends on the needs of your users and the scope of your files.

Much of what there is to say about script input/output applies equally well to script parameters (inputs) and script results (outputs). We'll discuss script parameters first, and then delve into a consideration of script results.

SCRIPT PARAMETERS

Before we get into the details of how and why to use script parameters, a short example will give you a concrete sense of what script parameters are all about and why you want to learn this. Imagine that you want to create several navigation buttons that take users to a specified layout. One way to do this is to create a separate script that's hard-coded to go to a particular destination. You'd need as many scripts as you have destination layouts, and every time you wanted to add a new destination, you'd create a new script.

Another way to accomplish this task is to create a generic "Go to" script that navigates to a layout specified by the script parameter that was passed to it. Then, when setting up the buttons themselves, you would simply call the "Go to" script, specifying the destination as the parameter. This approach has the advantage of requiring only a single script. To add another destination in the future, you simply specify the new destination as the parameter. There is no need to add a new script or to edit the original "Go to" script.

It's clear from this example that extracting hard-coded values from a script and placing them instead into script parameters has a tangible benefit. Keep this example in mind as you read further about script parameters.

SPECIFYING SCRIPT PARAMETERS

Script parameters can be defined in several places: as part of a button definition, as an option for invoking a subscript within the Perform Script script step, or as part of the definition of a custom menu item. Figure 15.1 shows the first of these: the dialog for specifying which script should run when a button is clicked. The interface for specifying a subscript is exactly the same; it too gives you a place to specify a parameter when calling a script.

Figure 15.1
When attaching a script to a button, you can also specify an optional script parameter, which is passed into the script.

At the bottom of this dialog, you have the option of specifying a script parameter. The parameter can be some text string you type into the space provided, or you can enter a calculation formula as the parameter. Clicking the Edit button brings up a standard calculation formula dialog box. If you use a calculation formula as your script parameter, when the button (or subscript) is triggered, the formula is evaluated and the results are used as the parameter.

The actual string or formula you use as your parameter depends completely on what you're trying to accomplish. Later in this section, you'll see some sample applications of script parameters.

> Only scripts triggered by buttons or called as subscripts of other scripts can have script parameters passed to them. Scripts triggered through the Script menu, by an external source (such as via Custom Web Publishing), or as startup/shutdown scripts (under File, File Options) cannot have script parameters passed to them.

Retrieving a Script Parameter

The Get(ScriptParameter) function can be used to retrieve the value of the parameter passed to a script. If no parameter was specified, this function simply returns an empty string. The value of the script parameter can be accessed anywhere from within the script in this way. It can't be changed or altered in any way, and it expires as soon as the script is complete.

Any subscripts called by a script can have their own independent script parameters—they do not inherit the parameter of the script that calls them. As an example, say that the string abc was designated as the parameter to be passed to a script called Main Script. Assume further that Main Script called a subscript called Child Script as its second step, and that the parameter xyz was specified as part of the Perform Script step. Within Main Script, Get(ScriptParameter) will always return abc. Within Child Script, Get(ScriptParameter) will always return xyz.

The parameter passed to a script can be the result of a calculation, so by using Get(ScriptParameter) as the parameter, you can pass a script's parameter down to the subscripts it calls, as shown in Figure 15.2.

Passing Multivalued Parameters

The interface for specifying script parameters allows for only a single value to be passed to a script. For many situations, this is sufficient to achieve the desired outcome. Other times, however, you will find that you want to be able to pass multiple parameters to a script. Although this isn't directly possible, there are several methods to achieve such a result.

Parsing a Text Array

The simplest way to pass multiple values in a script parameter is to specify a delimited array as the script parameter. For instance, if you wanted to send a parameter that contained the values Fred, 123, and Monkey, you could send the string Fred¦123¦Monkey, or even Fred¶123¶Monkey.

Figure 15.2
If you want a subscript to inherit a parameter, set the parameter to `Get (ScriptParameter)`.

> **NOTE**
>
> The delimiter you use (here we've used pipe characters and carriage returns) is up to you; just choose something that you know won't be found in the data you're passing.

To retrieve a portion of the passed parameter, use the built-in text parsing functions of FileMaker Pro. If you've used carriage returns as your array delimiter, the `GetValue` function is the easiest way to extract a particular value. Say that you want to grab the third value (`Monkey`). From within your script, anytime you wanted access to this value, you would use the following formula:

```
GetValue (Get (ScriptParameter) ; 3 )
```

→ For more on text parsing functions, **see** Chapter 8, "Getting Started with Calculations," **p. 217**, and Chapter 14, "Advanced Calculation Techniques," **p. 391**. **See also** *FileMaker 8 Functions and Scripts Desk Reference*, Chapter 6, "Calculation Functions," for a detailed function reference.

The nice thing about using delimited lists to pass multiple values is that you can set them up very easily. Even if some of the values are derived as calculated results, it's still quite easy to set up a formula that concatenates all the appropriate pieces together. For instance, if you wanted to pass the current layout name and the current time as the two values of your script parameter, you would use the following formula:

```
Get (LayoutName) & "¶" & Get (CurrentTime)
```

The main drawback of this method is that the burden is on you, the developer, to know what each position in the array represents. Does the value `Monkey` represent a favorite animal, a password, or a Halloween costume? There's nothing in the parameter itself that offers any assistance. This can (and should!) be clarified with script and/or calculation comments.

USING THE Let FUNCTION

Another method for passing multiple values in a script parameter involves the Let and Evaluate functions. If you have a good understanding of those functions, you'll likely appreciate the elegance of this technique.

→ For more on the Let and Evaluate functions, **see** "Logical Functions," **p. 392**.

Imagine that you pass as your script parameter the following string:

```
"First Name = \"Fred\"; Favorite Number = 123 ; Favorite Animal = \"Monkey\""
```

What you have here is a set of name/value pairs, separated by semicolons. Immediately you can see one of the benefits of this method over the previous one: When you pass both names and values, the parameter becomes more meaningful. In 6 months when you need to troubleshoot or enhance your script, you won't have to rack your brain to remember what the elements in your parameter represent. Another benefit of this method is that the order of the values doesn't matter. They'll be retrieved by name rather than by their position within the parameter.

You'll notice that within the parameter, there are backslashes before all the internal quotation marks. This process, known as *escaping* your quotes, is necessary anytime you want to pass a string that contains internal quotes. For this technique, you need to escape the quotes surrounding any text values in your parameter; numeric values (such as the 123) do not need quotation marks and hence don't need to be escaped.

You might recognize that the parameter specified previously is structured similarly to the first parameter of a Let function. This isn't a coincidence. Recall that the Let function allows you to set variables within a calculation formula. Imagine you had the following formula:

```
Let ([First Name = "Fred"; Favorite Number = 123 ; Favorite Animal =
"Monkey"] ; Favorite Animal)
```

This formula sets three variables (First Name, Favorite Number, and Favorite Animal) and then returns the value of the Favorite Animal variable. It would, in fact, return Monkey.

By combining the Let and Evaluate functions, you can build a formula that pulls out a named value from within a script parameter. The Evaluate function executes a dynamically constructed calculation formula. Therefore, within your script, anytime you want to retrieve the value of the Favorite Animal, you would use the following formula:

```
Evaluate ( "Let ([" & Get(ScriptParameter)  & "]; Favorite Animal)")
```

As you can see, a string containing a Let function is dynamically assembled from the value of the script parameter. The Evaluate function is then used to execute it. To return one of the other variables within the script parameter, you would simply need to change the end of the formula to reference the proper variable name.

If you foresee a need to do much parsing of multivalue script parameters, you should consider creating a custom function to simplify the process even more. That way, you won't have to remember the syntax for the Let and Evaluate functions every time you need to retrieve a parameter value. Figure 15.3 shows the definition for a custom function called GetParam.

→ For more on creating custom functions, **see** "Custom Functions," **p. 420**.

Figure 15.3

The custom function `GetParam` abstracts the script parameter parsing routine even more.

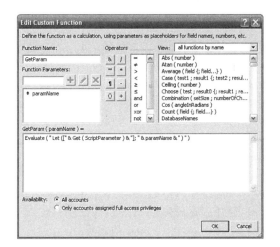

The `GetParam` function takes a single argument, `paramName`. The formula for the function is the same as the `Evaluate` formula shown previously, but with the `paramName` inserted in the place of the hard-coded parameter name:

```
Evaluate ( "Let ([" & Get(ScriptParameter)  & "]; " & paramName & ")")
```

Now, within your script, to retrieve the value of the `Favorite Animal`, you just need the following formula:

```
GetParam ("Favorite Animal")
```

This final abstraction provided by the `GetParam` custom function certainly makes the parameter parsing more convenient. After it's in place, you can pass and retrieve multivalued script parameters with ease.

PASSING STRUCTURED DATA ELEMENTS

The final method in this discussion for passing multivalued script parameters involves creating your own structured data elements. It's really a hybrid of the other two methods, in that it requires standard text parsing to retrieve an element (like the first method), but the elements are meaningfully named (as in the second method).

The syntax you create for naming elements is up to you. We generally prefer an XML-like structure because it's easy to use and organize. For instance, to pass the same three values discussed in the preceding section, you might specify the following as your script parameter:

```
"<First Name>Fred</First Name><Favorite Number>123</Favorite Number><Favorite
Animal>Monkey</Favorite Animal>"
```

This is, of course, simply another way of specifying element names and values. But you don't need to worry about escaping any quotes, as you do with a string that will be used in an `Evaluate` statement. To retrieve the value of a particular element of the script parameter, you would need to use standard text parsing functions. This is best accomplished with the creation of a custom function; you then need to write the parsing logic just once. The following

15

formula could be used as the definition for such a custom function; the function's only parameter is paramName:

```
Let ( [
    openElement = "<" & paramName & ">";
    closeElement = "</" & paramName & ">" ;

    startPos = Position (Get(ScriptParameter) ; openElement ; 1; 1) +
    ➥Length (openElement);
    endPos = Position (Get (ScriptParameter) ; closeElement ; 1; 1)] ;

Middle (Get(ScriptParameter) ; startPos ; endPos - startPos)
)
```

If this function were called GetParamXML, the value of one of the script parameter elements could then be retrieved with the function GetParamXML("First Name"). The custom function is hard-coded to parse out a value from a script parameter.

TIP

> You could easily turn this into a more generic XML parsing tool by passing a text string in which to search as another parameter.

STRATEGIES FOR USING SCRIPT PARAMETERS

Using script parameters can greatly reduce the number of scripts in a file and can make your database much easier to maintain. You should consider using script parameters in several common programming scenarios.

MODULARIZING SCRIPTS

The first—and most important—reason for using script parameters is to add a layer of abstraction to your scripts, thereby making them more modular and reusable. Rather than writing scads of single-purpose scripts, if you can generalize your scripts by using script parameters, you will need fewer scripts and your solution will be easier to maintain.

Practical Script Parameter Examples

Elsewhere in this book are several examples of script parameters being used to modularize scripts. For instance, in Chapter 10, "Getting Started with Reporting," one of the reporting techniques involved turning the column headings on a list view into buttons that would sort by the values in that column. All the buttons called a single script, passing in a different script parameter. Without script parameters, that routine would have required separate scripts for each column, each with a single hard-coded sort specification. Not only would that take longer to set up, but if the behavior ever needed to be modified, changes would need to be made to multiple scripts rather than a single, abstract script.

Script parameters were also central to the navigation routine described in Chapter 13, "Advanced Interface Techniques." There, a generalized navigation script was passed a destination layout as a script parameter.

You will know if you have encountered a situation that can potentially be simplified and strengthened by using script parameters if you find yourself writing several scripts that do basically the same thing, differing only in some specific value. In place of that specific value, use Get (ScriptParameter), and then have the buttons or other scripts that trigger the script specify the particular value.

For example, say that you've developed a system that contains a calendar, and that one of your layouts shows all the scheduled appointments for a given week. You'd like to be able to place a button above each of the seven days of the week (Sunday through Saturday) that users can click when they want to create a new appointment on that particular day. Assume that you have a field that contains the date of the Sunday of the week. Therefore, a script that would create a new appointment on Wednesday would do something like the following:

```
New Record/Request
Set Field [Appointments::AppointmentDate ; SundayDate + 3]
```

The scripts for creating appointments on the other days of the week would differ from what's shown in the preceding formula only by the constant that's added to the SundayDate. You could therefore write seven scripts, link them to your buttons, and move on to your next task.

We hope you can already see how and why script parameters can be used here. In the sample script, if you change the + 3 to + Get (ScriptParameter), you need only a single script to do the work of the seven that would be required without script parameters. Each of the seven buttons calls the generic version of this Add Appointment script, passing as a parameter an integer from 0 to 6 to differentiate them from each other. By using this method, you've replaced seven hard-coded scripts with a single generalized one.

PASSING DATA BETWEEN FILES

Another situation in which script parameters can be beneficial is for passing data between files. Using script parameters for this purpose saves you from needing to create extra fields and relationships in your files.

As an example, imagine that you have a file called Transactions and another called TransactionArchive (each with a single table with the same name as the file). You periodically archive old transactions into the archive file, but occasionally you have a need to pull a record back from the archive into the main production file. Further, you'd like to avoid placing a table occurrence from the archive file in the main file because the two need to be able to function independently.

Because you can call scripts in another file without having a relationship to that file, script parameters make an ideal transfer mechanism for moving data between unrelated files. In the sample scenario, you might set up a script in the TransactionArchive file that calls a subscript in the Transaction file, passing a multivalued parameter (using one of the methods described in the preceding section) that contains the pertinent data elements from the transaction. In the Transaction file, then, your subscript would create a new record and populate it, using the parsed-out parameter data.

In this example, importing the record from one file to the other would have been another solution within the defined constraints. Nonetheless, this example still clearly demonstrates the role that script parameters can play in moving data around. It's certainly preferable to

15

copying and pasting data, or even parking data in global fields for later retrieval (both of which were common techniques with versions of FileMaker before version 7).

PROTECTING SUBSCRIPTS

A final strategy for using script parameters is as a means of protecting subscripts from inadvertently being called improperly. Imagine that you have a pair of scripts, Script A and Script B, and that Script B is called as a subscript from Script A. As it stands, nothing would prevent another script from calling Script B, or even from Script B being called directly. In some cases, there may be undesirable consequences that can occur if subscripts are called directly.

To protect Script B, and ensure that it's called only as a subscript of Script A, you can pass a script parameter that authorizes Script B to run. It really doesn't matter what value you pass. You can check at the beginning of Script B to see whether the script parameter is set correctly. If it isn't, exit the script or show a warning dialog to the user.

CAUTION

Of course, any user who has access to the scripts in question can discover what parameter Script B expects, so this method isn't intended to be used as a security measure. It merely protects against accidental execution of subscripts (and direct invocation from the Web).

SCRIPT RESULTS

 Script results, a new addition in FileMaker 8, are, if you like, the flip side of script parameters. A script parameter lets you feed data into a script; a script result lets you pass data back out of a script. In the past, you might have done this by putting some data into a global field for other scripts to look at later. In FileMaker 8, you could opt to put the data into a global variable instead (variables are discussed in the following section). But the best choice is generally to use a script result.

To return a result from a script, you'll use the Exit Script script step, which has some new options in FileMaker 8. It's now possible, when using the Exit Script script step, to specify a result to be returned when the script exits. Much as when specifying the value for a Set Field or Set Variable script step, you can create a calculation expression that defines the result to be returned.

That takes care of how to return a script result. To access the returned result, you'll then need to use FileMaker 8's new Get(ScriptResult) function, a sort of a twin to Get (ScriptParameter). Get(ScriptResult) will hand back whatever result was returned by the most recently completed script or subscript.

Let's consider a full example. As we've suggested, one of the main reasons to use script input/output is to increase the reusability of your scripts. Consider a solution with a large number of reports. When allowing users to print reports, it's common to first display the report in Preview mode, pause the script, and then, on resuming, pop up a dialog box asking whether the user wants to print the report. The task of prompting the user for print confirmation may happen over and over again in a report-intensive solution. Using script results, you can write a single script to query the user, and then return the user's choice as a script result. Here's what such a script might look like:

```
Show Custom Dialog [ Title: "Print Confirmation"; Message: "Would you
➡like to print the report?"; Buttons: "Yes", "No" ]
Exit Script [ Result: Let (
       [
       msg = Get(LastMessageChoice) - 1;
       choiceText = Choose ( msg ; "Yes"; "No" )
       ];
    choiceText ) ]
```

Notice the difference in the Exit Script step. As part of this step, the script specifies that a calculated result be returned from the script. The calculation looks at the numeric result of the dialog box choice, converts it into text using the Choose function, and returns the corresponding text result.

To use this script's modular functionality, it needs to be called from another script. A script to display and optionally print a single report might look like this:

```
Go to Layout [ "Report" ]
Sort Records [ Specified Sort Order: Reporting::Region; ascending ]
➡[ Restore ]
Enter Preview Mode
Pause/Resume Script [ Indefinitely ]
Perform Script [ "Print Confirmation Dialog" ]
If [ Get ( ScriptResult ) = "Yes" ]
    Print [   ] [ No dialog ]
End If
Go to Layout [ original layout ]
Enter Browse Mode
```

This script performs all the usual sort of management common to previewing reports: navigating to a layout, sorting the records in some way, entering Preview mode, pausing for the user to look over the report. When the user resumes the script, though, the script goes straight into the confirmation subscript. Thereafter, the outer script uses Get(ScriptResult) to determine the result of the confirmation dialog, and prints the displayed report, or not, accordingly.

With such a script, instead of having a dozen print dialogs coded all over your system, you now have just one. If a user reports a problem with the print dialog, you now know where to start looking. And any changes or improvements made to the print confirmation process immediately benefit all reports that use this functionality.

Consider next a similar, but more complex, example. Suppose that your solution has a fairly complex dialog box that it needs to display on several occasions. For various reasons, FileMaker's built-in custom dialog tool is not quite enough for the task, so you'd like to design your own custom layout and pop it up in a new window as a kind of "super custom dialog."

Let's pretend your dialog is a typical software licensing dialog: It has a long software license in a scrolling text area and, underneath, buttons reading Agree and Disagree, as shown in Figure 15.4.

Figure 15.4
Using script results, you can create a modular custom dialog routine.

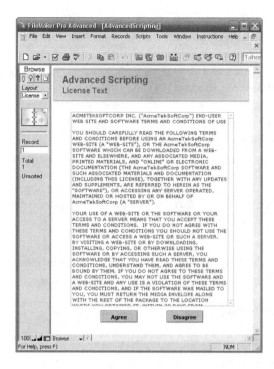

You'd like to create a script to show this dialog and then report whether the user clicked the Agree or Disagree button.

This sounds pretty straightforward, but something's not obvious. How do you determine which button the user pressed? With a standard dialog, you can use Get(LastMessageChoice); but this is a home-brew dialog, and FileMaker won't help you here.

Earlier in this chapter, you learned that you could attach a script parameter to a script when calling a script from a button. The Agree and Disagree buttons could each call a script, one with a parameter of Agree, the other with a parameter of Disagree. Still, that's not clearly helpful. This amounts to pushing data further down, into another subscript, when what you really want to do is pass the data backward, back up to whatever script invoked the license confirmation to begin with.

Here's where a little cleverness comes into play. Suppose that you write a one-line script, which we'll call Kicker, that looks like this:

```
Exit Script [ Result: Get(ScriptParameter) ]
```

All this script does is take whatever parameter is passed to it and "kick" it right back out as a script result (hence the quirky script name).

Now suppose that each of the two confirmation buttons calls the Kicker script; one with a parameter of Agree, the other with Disagree. Suppose further that each button is set to resume the currently executing script. And finally suppose that the overall license confirmation dialog script looks like this:

```
New Window [ Name: "Confirm Software License" ]
Show/Hide Status Area [ Hide ]
Go to Layout [ "License" (License) ]
Adjust Window [ Resize to Fit ]
Pause/Resume Script [ Indefinitely ]
Close Window [ Current Window ]
Exit Script [ Result: Get(ScriptResult) ]
```

The script creates a new, named window, and performs a number of basic window management tasks: hiding the status area, navigating to the layout containing the license text and the Agree/Disagree buttons, and resizing the window to fit its contents. The script then pauses, waiting for user input.

When the user clicks either button, the corresponding script parameter (Agree or Disagree) is passed down into the Kicker script. Kicker immediately kicks the value back as a script result, which means that the user's choice is now accessible via Get(ScriptResult). The buttons are set to resume the paused script, so after the user has clicked a button, the main script goes on executing: It closes the license window and then returns the user's choice (again!) as a script result to whatever outermost script invoked the license dialog.

This example may seem like a small bit of magic. How was it possible to move all that data around across as many as three scripts, without ever storing it anyplace? Well, that's some of the power of script input and output. Note also that the number of script steps it takes to accomplish all this is very small. Note finally that script input/output is not limited to operations that are one level deep. Here we took the result of a button press, passed it out to a calling script, and then turned right around and passed it "upstairs" once more. After you've mastered having script A call script B and get something back, you'll begin to see occasions when it makes sense to have A call B, have B call C, and have the result of C passed back along the chain until it comes back to A again. If you go more than three or four levels deep with this kind of data passing, you may be creating something more complex than is necessary. Still, it's important to realize that in some circumstances you may need to go a couple of levels deep. Not only is this possible with FileMaker's script input/output, but it's both powerful and straightforward.

FINAL THOUGHTS ON SCRIPT INPUT/OUTPUT

The script input and output capabilities of FileMaker 8 represent a major advance in the capability to construct streamlined, reusable routines within a FileMaker solution. Mastering the use of these techniques is critical to getting the most out of FileMaker 8. We recommend that you study these features carefully, and that you look fairly aggressively for opportunities to use them. Anytime a script does similar work with different input values, consider using script parameters. Anytime a script may be better structured as a tool that does some work, and then reports on the results, consider reporting those results via a script result. Your solutions will become cleaner, simpler, and more elegant.

SCRIPT VARIABLES

 Script variables are an extremely important addition to scripting in FileMaker 8. If you've worked with other languages or development environments, you're familiar with a variable as a type of named, temporary storage. For example, in the PHP programming language, you might write this:

```
$x = 7;
$y = 9;
$z = $x + $y;
```

Here $x, $y, and $z are all *variables*—temporary names to which values are then assigned (the $ in PHP indicates that these are variable names, and FileMaker 8, as you'll soon see, uses a similar convention for variable names). In later expressions, the variable names stand in for the values stored in them. So you'd expect that when the preceding program is run, the variable $z will end up storing a value of 16.

Often, as you build up a program or routine, you'll find yourself wanting to rely on named, temporary storage elements like these. In previous versions of FileMaker, the only place to cache such data has been within FileMaker's database structures, by putting the data into one or another kind of field.

Consider the simplistic example of a script that beeps 10 times in succession. Previously, you might have defined a field with global storage to act as a counter, and written the script like this:

```
Set Field [Loop::gCounter; 1]
Loop
    Beep
    Pause/Resume Script [Duration (seconds):1]
    Set Field [Loop::gCounter; Loop::gCounter + 1]
    Exit Loop If [Loop::gCounter > 10]
End Loop
```

This has always worked fine, but it has some drawbacks:

- Even though the counter field is used only in this script, it has to be defined within the field definitions for the table as a whole. It will always be there, cluttering up the list, even though it may apply to only a single script.
- The storage is not as temporary as you would like. The field gCounter will go on holding its value and being accessible after the script completes. This is one reason it's necessary to reset the field to 1 at the start of the script. If the script has been run previously, it might still have its old value of 11, or it might have some other value altogether if someone edited the field directly and stored it in the database.

Global fields are still useful for many things in FileMaker 8, as you'll see, but they're not ideally suited to the kind of temporary named storage we need for something like a loop counter. This is where FileMaker 8's variables come to the forefront. FileMaker 8 script variables are defined within scripts, so they don't appear in the list of defined fields. And script variables can be truly temporary, coming into existence within a specific script and disappearing when the script completes.

ABOUT LOCAL VARIABLES

A *local variable* is one that exists and has meaning only within a single script: exactly what you'd want for the loop counting example shown previously. If you were to rewrite the looping script using FileMaker 8 script variables, it might look like this:

```
Set Variable [$counter; Value:1]
Loop
    Beep
    Pause/Resume Script [Duration (seconds):1]
 Set Variable [$counter; Value: $counter + 1]
    Exit Loop If [$counter > 10]
End Loop
```

Local variables are named using a single dollar sign ($), and they're created and manipulated using the Set Variable script step. The options for the Set Variable script step are shown in Figure 15.5.

Figure 15.5
The capability to set variables is a powerful new feature in FileMaker 8.

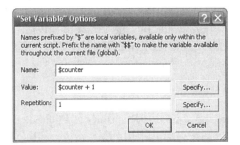

You'll notice that the Set Variable script step allows you to set the variable's value dynamically, using the Specify option. This means that a variable can be used to hold the results of any expression you can define using FileMaker's Calculation dialog. You could store the current username, the current date, or the results of an expression such as $counter + 1. You'll note also, by the way, that variables can be referenced from within such calculations just by using the variable name. For example, the following are perfectly valid calculation expressions:

```
$counter + 1
```

```
"Name: " & $userName
```

If a variable of the specified name is not currently defined, a reference to the variable returns an empty string (or a null result, if that term is more familiar). The first expression of the preceding two would give a result of 1, whereas the second would give a result of "Name: ", if the respective variables were not defined.

ABOUT VARIABLE SCOPE

You'll often hear computer-science types talking about the *scope* of a variable. It's a concept worth mastering. *Scope* can be defined as "that portion of a program for which a variable is

15

defined or has meaning." Variables in FileMaker have one of two kinds of scope: either *local scope* or *global scope*.

So far, the variables we've examined have local scope. It's most common to refer to them as *local variables*. A local variable exists and has meaning only within the context of a single script. Consider the example of the $counter variable discussed previously. This variable exists only within the script in which it's defined and manipulated. After the script completes, the $counter variable in effect disappears. Likewise, if you called a subscript from within that script, the subscript would not have access to the value of $counter contained in the parent script.

Because local variables exist only within the context of a single script, this can lead to subtle confusion. Consider a parent script that uses a $counter variable that then also calls a subscript. If you were to try to access the value of $counter within the subscript, you'd get a null value because you'd be trying to access a variable that had never been set within the context of the subscript. And if you were to try to *set* the value of $counter within the subscript, using the Set Variable script step, this would create a new variable, local to the subscript, with the same name, $counter. There would thus be a total of two $counter variables: one local to the parent script, one local to the subscript. The two exist simultaneously and independently; they don't conflict, and they don't affect one another.

LOCAL VARIABLES SUMMARY

So, to summarize what has been said about local variables in FileMaker 8:

- Local variables are set using the Set Variable script step.
- Local variables must have names beginning with $.
- Local variables can be referenced within calculation expressions.
- Local variables are limited in scope to the script in which they are defined (via the Set Variable script step). Neither any subscripts nor any parent scripts can access the value of a local variable.
- Local variables do not appear in the Define Database dialog.

ABOUT GLOBAL VARIABLES

Global variables, denoted with a double dollar sign ($$userName, $$currentLayout) share many features with local variables. The only difference is in their scope. Whereas local variables are limited in scope to a single script, global variables retain their value no matter what script is running, or whether a script is running at all. They can be used to store values that persist across any or all scripts, for the duration of a user's session.

The last point bears repeating. Whereas local variables have *script scope*, meaning that they are limited in scope to a single script, global variables have *file/session scope*. Like globally stored fields, global variables are unique to an individual user: Each user has his own copy of a global variable, so the variable $$userName can have a different value for each active user. And global variables also cease to exist when a user session ends. If you work with a global variable, quit FileMaker, and then open the same file again, the global variable will disappear, until some logic in the files creates it again.

Global variables also have scope only within a single file. There is no way to "reach across" to pull a global variable's data from one file into another. (Such a thing *is*, by contrast, possible with globally stored fields.) Global variables from other files cannot be accessed via relationships, because they don't appear in the field list.

So what good are global variables? When does it make sense to use them? We recommend that, by and large, you use global variables for *user session data*: data specific to one user that is intended to persist for just that user session. Examples include things like the name of the currently logged-in user, or user preferences such as a user's chosen default layout, or any other user-specific data you might be storing, such as a user's department or sales region.

It is also tempting to use global variables for general data transfer between scripts. For example, in a script that prompts the user for a dialog box choice, you might be tempted to store the user's choice in a global variable so that other scripts (a parent script, for example) could have access to the user's choice and act accordingly.

We can't stress too strongly that this is not a good use for global variables! FileMaker 8 provides a set of what we call *script (input/output) capabilities* that let you pass data into scripts, and now, in FileMaker 8, return results from scripts. If you simply need to move data from one script to another, script parameters and script results (discussed in the preceding section of this chapter) are the best way to accomplish that task. Using global storage, whether global variables or globally stored fields, for general data transfer between scripts will make your programs more fragile and less maintainable. Global storage, by definition, can be accessed from anywhere, so you can never quite be sure that you know where your data is coming from; it might have been modified by scripts other than those with which you're trying to communicate, perhaps even by accident.

In the dialog box example discussed previously, we chose to return the user's choice as a script result, rather than tossing it into a global variable. Using script results, we were able to avoid creating any temporary storage along the way.

Global variables cannot completely obviate the need for globally stored fields. Globally stored fields have several capabilities not shared by global variables:

- Globally stored fields can be accessed across files by using relationships.
- Globally stored fields can accept user input.
- Globally stored fields can be used to drive relationships.
- Globally stored fields can be used to store the content of an input field from a custom dialog.

For example, if you were implementing a *filtered portal* (a portal the contents of which change in response to user input), you would need to use a globally stored field to do so, both because you would need to capture user input, and because you would need to use that input to drive the portal relationship.

→ For more on filtered portals, **see** "Filtered Portals," **p. 489**.

OTHER WAYS TO WORK WITH VARIABLES

Variables in FileMaker 8 can be used in quite complex ways. When you're first starting out with variables, we recommend you try to stick to the following precepts until you feel you've mastered the basics:

- Use local variables for temporary storage that is used within the context of a single script.

- Use global variables to store user-specific session data (with the exceptions noted in the next point).

- Use globally stored fields to store user-specific session data that must be captured directly from the user, must drive a relationship, or must be shared heavily across files.

Now that we've said all of that, if you have mastered the basic concepts of variables, there are some advanced points to be made about them. If you feel you're ready, read on!

ACCESSING VARIABLES ACROSS FILES

We've said previously that there's no way to share global variables across files. This is not entirely true. Using FileMaker 8's new capability to return script results, you can have a script in file A return the value of a global variable from file A back to a script in file B. Consider the following one-line script:

```
Exit Script[Result: Evaluate( Get( ScriptParameter ) )]
```

This one-liner may appear puzzling at first. It simply takes whatever script parameter was passed in, uses Evaluate on it, and returns the result.

Now suppose that this script, living in file A, is called from file B with a parameter of "$$currentUserName" (quotes included!). The Evaluate function will evaluate the string "$$currentUserName", so if a global variable of that name exists in file A, Evaluate will return the value of that variable. This value in turn gets passed out of the script as a script result, and is returned to the calling function in file B.

The principal drawback to this technique is that it's scripted, so it doesn't give a means to access variables in other files in such a way that they could be used in calculation expressions. It's a highly specialized technique, but might come in handy from time to time.

ACCESSING VARIABLES FROM WITHIN A Let STATEMENT

If our editors had offered us a way to put a big yellow flag over an entire section, to signal "Caution! Slow Down! Dangerous Curves Ahead!" we would probably have applied it to this section. You may work with variables for a while before you need to delve into these techniques, but because the capability does exist in FileMaker 8, we discuss it here for completeness.

It's important to know that script variables can be referenced and used within a Let statement, both within the variables block of the Let statement and within the body of the Let formula itself. For example, the following Let statement incorporates the value of a global variable called $$currentUserName:

```
Let (
[ dayNm = DayName( Get(CurrentDate)) ] ;
"Hello, " & $$currentUserName & ", it is " &  dayNm )
```

In this example, we are only reading the value of $$currentUserName. But it's also possible to *set* the value of a variable from within the variables block of a Let statement, like this:

```
Let (
[
$$currentUserName = Get ( AccountName );
dow = DayOfWeek( Get(CurrentDate))
] ;

"Hello, " & $$currentUserName & ", it is " &  dow )
```

This operation will actually set the value of $$currentUserName, and because this is a global variable, the value of the variable will persist even beyond the bounds of the Let statement!

The same considerations apply to local variables (those denoted with a single $); they can be read from within a Let statement, and can be set or reset within the variable block of a Let statement.

The capability of reading and writing script variables from within a Let statement is intriguing, but we would argue that this technique is best used with caution, and only when you're certain that there's no better or equally practical way to accomplish your goals. There are actually several scenarios here, and each is slightly different:

- **Reading a global variable from within a Let**—Global variables are intended to be global, so this is in fact a somewhat reasonable thing to do.

- **Writing to a global variable from within a Let**—Again, global variables are supposed to be global, so this is not unreasonable; but we'd recommend that you strictly limit the places you do this. For a given global variable, it's best if you write to it only from a few, known locations. Otherwise it can be very difficult to track down when and how a global variable is being set. This is especially true for Let statements because a tool like the Script Debugger will let you follow a script but will not step through the inner operations of a Let statement.

- **Reading/writing local variables from within a Let**—We view this practice as potentially suspect and trouble-prone. The reason is that a local variable has meaning only within a single script. The implication is that any calculations or custom functions that use a Let to manipulate local variables then become tightly associated with a particular script or scripts. Because one of the main points of encapsulating logic into calculations or custom functions is to make them more reusable, it cuts very much against the grain to then make those formulas dependent on specific scripts.

The story is different, though, for Let statements within calculations that are defined on the fly within scripts, such as those you might enter in the Specify box of many script steps. These are transient, script-only formulas that it may make sense to bind closely to the script by referencing script variables.

15

ABOUT DYNAMIC FILE PATHS

There's another nice feature of variables in FileMaker 8 that's very much worth mentioning. Certain script steps, such as Export Records, as well as the new Save Records as Excel/PDF script step, allow you to specify the location of an output file by typing in a file reference. In FileMaker 8, that file reference may be taken from a variable, rather than being hard-coded.

If the usefulness of that isn't obvious, let it sink in for a moment. In the past, it hasn't been possible to create names for exported files on the fly: You either had to let the user enter a filename, or had to hard-code a single specific filename into the script step. If you wanted to name exported or saved files dynamically (say you wanted to include the current date in the filename), you were out of luck, unless you chose to use a third-party plug-in.

To save files to a dynamically specified file path, you'll need to create that file path in your script and put it into a variable. That variable can then be used in specifying a file path, as the following script example illustrates:

```
Go to Layout [ "Contacts" ]
Show All Records
Set Variable [ $filePath; Value: Let (
  [
    theDate    = Get(CurrentDate);
    theYear    = Year(theDate);
    theMonth   = Month(theDate);
    theDay     = Day(theDate);
    dateText   = theYear & "_" & theMonth & "_" & theDay;
    filePath   = Get ( FileMakerPath ) & "Export_" & dateText
  ];
  filePath ) ]
Save Records as PDF [ File Name: "$filePath"; Records being browsed ]
```

This script example uses no fewer than three new FileMaker 8 features: script variables, the capability to use script variables for dynamic file paths, and one of FileMaker 8's several new Get() functions, Get(FileMakerPath). Get(FileMakerPath) will return the path to the FileMaker application directory. This function is part of a family of new path functions in FileMaker 8 that also includes Get(DesktopPath), Get(DocumentPath), Get(PreferencesPath), and Get(SystemDrive). By using this suite of new functions, along with the new dynamic file path capability, you should now be able to save files with custom filenames to a wide variety of locations on a user's disk.

VIEWING YOUR VARIABLES

One final note on variables in FileMaker 8. We've made the point a few times that variables are beneficial in that they don't add clutter to the database schema: They don't appear in Define Database dialog, nor in the field lists that go along with operations such as Sort or Import Records. There's a disadvantage to this as well: There's currently no way to see a list of all the variables that are currently active in a FileMaker solution.

It is possible to view the values of individual variables in the FileMaker Pro Advanced Data Viewer, but you must enter the variable names one at a time, as with any other expression.

→ For more on the Data Viewer, **see** "Debugging Scripts," **p. 517**.

WINDOW MANAGEMENT TECHNIQUES

Among the many important features of FileMaker, the capability to have multiple windows showing data from the same table stands out as one of the most important. To aid developers with managing this feature, several window management script steps are present in ScriptMaker, including the following:

- New Window
- Select Window
- Close Window
- Move/Resize Window
- Set Window Title

There are also 11 Get functions that return data about the active window, ranging from its size and location to its name and the mode it's in. Another function that plays a role in window management is WindowNames, which returns a list containing the names of all the open windows, ordered according to the stacking order of the windows.

NOTE

> The window management script steps were introduced in FileMaker 7. In that release it was possible to get your windows mixed up if there were several windows open with the same name but based on different files. In FileMaker 8, many of the window management script steps, such as WindowNames, include an important new option to consider only windows from the current file.

These script steps and calculation functions provide you with tremendous ability to control the user experience. The amount of window management you do may vary widely from solution to solution, but having a good grounding in the options available to you is important.

THE ANATOMY OF A WINDOW

When you create, move, and resize windows, you have the opportunity to specify both a location for the window and its size. The unit of measure for all window manipulation is the pixel. Figure 15.6 shows the options for the Move/Resize Window script step.

For each parameter of the Move/Resize Window script step, you can either specify a literal number or supply a calculation formula whose result determines the parameter's value. If you leave any of the parameters empty, their values are inherited from the current active window. For instance, if you merely want to move the current window (without changing its size), you don't need to specify anything for the Height and Width parameters.

Figure 15.6
The Move/Resize
Window script step
enables you to specify
the exact coordinates
(in pixels) and size for
any given window.

Before you start creating and moving windows around the screen, however, it's important that you have a good understanding of the anatomy of a window. When you specify the Distance from Top value for a new window, for instance, is that the distance from the top of the screen, or from the top of the application window? Is it the distance to the window's title bar or to the layout itself? These are the types of questions this anatomy lesson answers.

Working from the outside inward, there are four important objects for managing windows. These are the screen, the desktop, the window, and the content area.

SCREEN

The screen is the backdrop against which all window actions take place. Screen resolution can, of course, differ from user to user. You can use the Get (ScreenHeight) and Get (ScreenWidth) functions to return the absolute height and width (in pixels) of the user's screen.

If multiple monitors are hooked up to a machine, these functions return the dimensions of whichever monitor contains the active window. If the active window straddles monitors, the active screen is considered to be the one that contains the majority of the window. You cannot programmatically alter the dimensions of the screen from within FileMaker Pro.

DESKTOP

FileMaker also has a pair of functions that return the dimensions of something called the *window desktop*: Get (WindowDesktopHeight) and Get (WindowDesktopWidth). In a nutshell, these represent the dimensions of the FileMaker application window.

On a Macintosh, the top menu bar, which is 22 pixels high, is not considered part of the application window. The desktop height, therefore, is 22 pixels smaller than the screen height. The desktop and screen widths should be identical.

The desktop size is slightly more complicated on Windows because an application can be maximized to fill the screen, or it can float free in its own window space. The two desktop functions return the *inside* dimensions of the application window. The application title bar and the FileMaker menu bar are not considered part of the window desktop on Windows. Scrollbars on the right and bottom of the application, however, are considered part of the window desktop. If you fully maximize FileMaker on Windows XP, and if the taskbar has its default size and location at the bottom of the screen, the desktop height is 80 pixels less than the screen height. That includes 46 pixels for the application title bar and menu bar and 34 pixels for the taskbar.

CAUTION

> Be aware that the dimensions are slightly different in Windows 2000/2003, and that many system settings can affect the exact pixel sizes for various screen elements. It's best to test on your own system.

You cannot programmatically set the dimensions of the desktop area, nor can you determine the placement of the desktop relative to the screen (which is interesting only on Windows when the application is not maximized).

WINDOW

The next type of object to discuss is the *window*. This is finally where you, as the developer, get to have some control over things. You can set the size, placement, and name of windows on the screen through various script steps. The size of the active window—its outside dimensions—can be obtained with the Get (Height) and Get (Width) functions. These dimensions include both the window's *frame* and its *content*. These concepts are discussed in depth later in this section.

When you position a window on the screen, you specify, in effect, the coordinates for the upper-left corner of the window. These coordinates are *not* relative to the overall screen dimensions. They are *mostly* relative to the window desktop. We say "mostly" here because a window positioned 0 pixels from the top and 0 pixels from the left is placed at the upper-left corner within the application window. If there are no active, docked toolbars, this window's position would, in fact, be relative to the window desktop. It's the potential presence of docked toolbars (either the Standard toolbar or the Text Formatting toolbar) that muddies the waters. Each of those can move the absolute position of (0,0) either downward or to the right, depending on where the toolbar is docked. Docked in the standard position at the top of the screen, each toolbar takes up 26 pixels on Mac and 27 pixels on Windows XP. The toolbars do not affect the size of the desktop area.

Further, the presence of the status bar (not to be confused with the status area) on Windows decreases the usable application window space by an additional 18 pixels. There's no way to test for the presence or location of the toolbars or the status bar, so it's impossible to know without experimentation the maximum size a window can be without exceeding the dimensions of the application window.

CAUTION

On Windows, a user may choose to use normal, large, or even extra large fonts under the display properties. The status bar does not change size, but the window and application title bars both increase in height dramatically. You should be aware that the pixel sizes for various objects provided here are not true constants.

CONTENT

Whereas the outside dimensions of a window are described by the `Get (Height)` and `Get (Width)` functions, the inside dimensions are described by the `Get (ContentHeight)` and `Get (ContentWidth)` functions. The content area is the most important to you, the developer, because it's the space your layouts inhabit.

It might be helpful to think of a window like a framed picture: Much as a picture frame surrounds a picture, a window's frame surrounds the content of the window. The content dimensions refer to the dimensions of the picture, not including the frame.

The size of the window's frame differs slightly on Mac and Windows. And because you specify window size, not content size, when creating or resizing windows, this means that to display a fixed content size, you need to use a variable window size.

On Macintosh, a window's title bar takes up 22 pixels, and its left and bottom scrollbars are each 15 pixels thick. If the status area is visible, this adds 69 pixels to the window's frame.

On Windows, if the current window is maximized, the window has no top title bar. If it's not maximized, the title bar requires 38 pixels on Windows XP, and 31 pixels on Windows 2000. The left and bottom scrollbars are each 16 pixels thick. If the window is not maximized, there's a further border on the left and right sides of the window that adds 12 more pixels to the width of the frame. Finally, the status area on Windows is the same as on a Mac—69 pixels.

The content dimensions tell you only the visible content area of the active window. That is, they don't take into account content that you need to scroll to see.

POSITIONING A WINDOW RELATIVE TO ANOTHER WINDOW

One common window manipulation routine involves having a new window pop up at a position on the screen relative to another window. This technique can make for very effective user interface management. Even if users move a window to another part of their screen, your pop-up window appears in the same position relative to the window that called it.

 You might have difficulty when creating pop-up windows for use on Windows PCs. See "Pop-up Window Issues on a Windows PC" in the "Troubleshooting" section at the end of this chapter.

The example discussed in this section is an expansion on the window pop-up technique discussed in the "Rich Dialog Windows" section of Chapter 13, "Advanced Interface Techniques." Refer to that section for more information on how to make the pop-up window behave like a modal dialog.

Figure 15.7 shows a layout from a basic contact management system; the portal at the bottom is used to collect notes associated with a particular contact.

Figure 15.7
A contact info layout with a portal into a Notes table becomes the anchor for a pop-up window.

Imagine that you want to create a workflow where users are not allowed to add new notes directly from the portal. Instead, you would like a pop-up window to appear in front of the portal when users click the Add Note button, regardless of where a user has positioned the contact info window. The end result of this is shown in Figure 15.8.

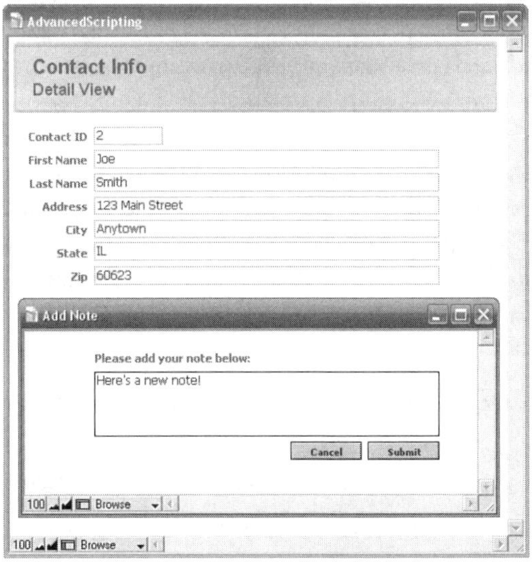

Figure 15.8
The Add Note window is positioned in front of the portal on the Contact Info layout, regardless of where that window has been positioned on the screen.

The trick to having the pop-up window follow the anchor window around the screen is referencing the position of the anchor window in the coordinates for the pop-up window. You still have to know the relative placement of the two windows. However, there's a systematic approach to this that can make the whole process quite simple.

Begin by creating a layout that contains the desired interface for the pop-up window. Use a rectangle (of any color) as the background for this layout. It's important that you use an actual rectangle rather than just changing the color of the layout part because the size of this rectangle determines the size of the pop-up window. Position the rectangle so that it's snug against the top and left borders of your layout. In the example shown in Figure 15.8, the background rectangle on the Add Note layout measures 463 pixels wide by 163 pixels high. Your layout should contain only a body part, and you should shrink the body up right to your background rectangle.

After the pop-up layout has been created, copy the background rectangle to your clipboard, switch over to the anchor layout (here, the Contact Info layout), and paste the rectangle onto this layout. Position it exactly where you want the pop-up window to be placed. Turn on the Object Size dialog (View, Object Size), and make a note of the top and left coordinates of the rectangle. In the example shown in Figure 15.8, these positions were 290 and 15, respectively. You can then delete the rectangle from your layout.

→ For more on using the Object Size palette, **see** "Positioning Objects on a Layout," **p. 109**.

CAUTION

> The values for the top and left pixel of an object returned by the Object Size dialog are relative to the page margins that have been defined for your layout. The margin settings can be set explicitly on the Printing tab of the Layout Setup dialog. If you want to know the absolute position of an object, set the top and left margins to both be 0. Or subtract the top and left margin settings from the values you noted in the Object Size dialog. Your goal is to know the position of the rectangle relative to the current window, so the margins, which aren't even visible in Browse mode, must be factored out.

In the script that generates the new window, you need to use the positions you've noted for the rectangle and the position of the current window to determine the location of the new window. Remember that you need to consider the size of the new window's frame as well, and that the frame size differs on Mac and Windows. The rectangle you placed on the anchor layout determines the size of the window's content area. The size of the window itself must be derived from this.

Taking all these factors together, the parameters you need for your new window are as listed here:

Height: 139 + Case (Get (SystemPlatform)) = -1 ; 37; 54)

Width: 457 + Case (Get (SystemPlatform)) = -1 ; 15; 27)

Top: 305 + Get (WindowTop)

Left: 46 + Get (WindowLeft)

You'll notice that the constants at the beginning of each of these formulas come from the size and position of the pop-up window that were noted earlier. The other constants in these formulas (the ones that were determined by checking whether the user is on a Mac or a Windows PC) are needed to translate from content size to window size. Recall from the preceding section that the size of the window's frame is different on each platform. The preceding calculations also make an assumption that the status area will be hidden in both the anchor window and the pop-up window. If that's not the case, you can easily adjust by adding and/or subtracting 69 (the width of the status area) to the width and distance from left values as necessary.

TIP

> If you plan to use pop-up windows often, consider creating custom functions for these formulas. You can have them adjust appropriately, based on platform and the visibility of the status area.

The remainder of the scripts used for the Add Note routine closely resemble those discussed in the "Rich Dialog Windows" section of Chapter 13.

The Add Note script itself is as follows:

```
Allow User Abort [Off]
If [PatternCount (WindowNames ; "Add Note")]
    Close Window [Name: "Add Note"]
End If
Set Field [Contact::gNote; ""]
New Window [Name: "Add Note"; other paramaters as given above]
Go to Layout ["Add Note" (Contact)]
Show/Hide Status Area [Lock; Hide]
Adjust Window [Resize to Fit]
Pause/Resume Script [Indefinitely]
```

On the Add Note layout itself, both the Cancel and the Submit buttons are specified to Resume the current script. The Cancel script simply closes the current window. The Submit button, which is defined to pass the current record's ContactID as a script parameter, runs the following script:

```
If [not IsEmpty (Get (ScriptParameter))]
    If [not IsEmpty (Contact::gNote)]
        Go to Layout ["ContactNotes" (ContactNotes)]
        New Record/Request
        Set Field [ContactNotes::ContactID; Get (ScriptParameter)]
        Set Field [ContactNotes::Note; Contact::gNote]
    End If
    Close Window [Current Window]
Else
    Show Custom Dialog ["Warning"; "Invalid script parameter."]
End If
```

There are many ways you could script the actual addition of the note record. This example navigates to a layout based on the ContactNote table. Because the user entered the new note into a global field, after the new record is created, the ContactNotes::Note field can be

15

directly set to the value of the gNote field. However, the ContactNotes::ContactID field, which is a foreign key relating back to the Contact table, needs to be set to the `ContactID` of whatever the active record was at the beginning of the routine. It could simply be placed in a field with global storage, but instead, we've elected to have the Submit button pass the `ContactID` as a script parameter to the `Submit Note` script.

 If you have issues with found sets not being retained when you create new windows, see "Creating New Windows Loses My Found Sets" in the "Troubleshooting" section at the end of this chapter.

Go to Related Record

`Go to Related Record` is one of the most useful and important script steps. In this discussion of scripting, we've focused for the most part on categories of tasks that you can perform with scripts rather than on specific steps, but `Go to Related Record`, which we'll refer to as GTRR, merits a discussion entirely its own.

The Go to Related Record Options dialog is shown in Figure 15.9. Essentially, GTRR lets you navigate to one or more records that are related to whatever record or records you're currently viewing. As we discuss in this section, there are several options for how and where that related set will be displayed. It may take a while for all the nuances of GTRR to sink in, but mastery of this script step is crucial for becoming an experienced script writer.

Figure 15.9
Go to Related Record is one of the most useful script steps. It's also one of the most complex.

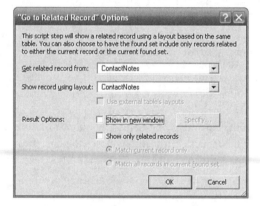

GTRR Basics

It might be helpful to think of GTRR as a way to move or jump from one point on the Relationships Graph to another point. But *from* where, and *to* where? In the GTRR options dialog (shown in Figure 15.9), the first thing you specify is the destination table occurrence for this move. The starting point for the move is determined by the script's *context*. We'll use the terms *origin* and *destination* to refer to these table occurrences.

Whenever a script executes, it does so in a context determined by the active window, the active layout, the active found set, and the active record. These things can, of course, all be changed during the course of a script through the use of a wide variety of script steps. The origin for a GTRR script step is determined by whatever layout is active at the point in the script at which the GTRR occurs. The active layout situates you at a particular point on the Relationships Graph. So, managing the origin of the jump is done not in the GTRR step itself, but rather through navigation (if necessary) to the appropriate layout beforehand.

As the destination for the GTRR, you can select any table occurrence on the graph, including table occurrences tied to external tables, table occurrences that aren't related to the origin, and even the origin itself. This last option produces a special result that's discussed in the "Jumping to Disconnected Table Occurrences" section a little later in this chapter.

The other pop-up list within the GTRR dialog is for specifying a layout to use for displaying whatever set of records is returned by the GTRR. Unlike the choice of a destination table occurrence, you are restricted in your choice to selecting among layouts that are tied to the same table (*not* table occurrence) as the destination table occurrence. That's a convoluted way of saying that you're expected to specify an appropriate layout to display the related set of records. We'll therefore refer to this layout as the *display layout*. If (and only if) the destination table occurrence is from an external file, you'll have the option to select the Use External Table's Layouts check box. The choices for the display layout consist of those layouts in the external table that are tied to the same table as the destination table occurrence.

Another option in the GTRR dialog enables you to specify that the related set of records appear in a new window. If you select this option, you have access to the same setup parameters that you do when using the New Window script step (window name, location, size). If you don't check the Show in New Window option, one of two things happens when the GTRR is executed:

- If the display layout is in the current file, that becomes the active layout.
- If the display layout is in a different file, another window must be activated (windows are file specific). If there are no windows for the required file currently open, a new window is created (regardless of whether you've checked this option). If there are windows belonging to the external file (even hidden ones), the frontmost of those in the stacking order becomes the active window.

The final option on the GTRR dialog is Show Only Related Records. Your choice here partially determines what found set the display layout contains. It's easier to discuss the possible implications of selecting this option in the course of a specific example, which we do in the example that follows. For now, know that in most cases, you'll want to enable this option.

FileMaker 8 adds an important and powerful twist to the Show Only Related Records option. If you choose this option, you now also have the choice to navigate to those records related only to the current record, or to records related to *any* record in the current found set. For example, if you've isolated a subset of customer records, it is now possible to use GTRR to navigate to a found set of all products ordered by any of those customers. This was possible in previous versions of FileMaker but required a fairly complex workaround.

GTRR—A SIMPLE EXAMPLE

As an example of GTRR in action, consider the scenario of a database that contains information about teachers and classes. Figure 15.10 shows the Relationships Graph from such a file; there is a one-to-many relationship from the Teacher table occurrence to the Class table occurrence. The relationship is defined to sort by ClassName. There are two layouts in the file—Teacher Detail and Class Detail—each tied to the obvious table occurrence.

Figure 15.10
The two table occurrences in this Relationships Graph are connected on the TeacherID field.

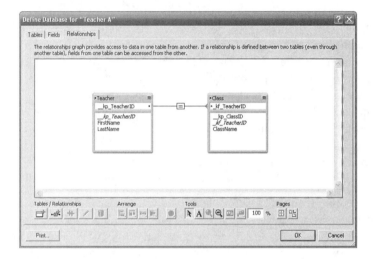

Say that you want to use a Go to Related Record script step to find all the classes taught by a particular teacher. To do this, begin by navigating to the record of the teacher you're interested in. Place a button on the layout that performs a Go to Related Record step. Because the button is on the Teacher Detail layout, the Teacher table occurrence is the context in which the GTRR will be performed; it acts as the origin for the coming jump. In the GTRR dialog, specify the Class table occurrence as the destination for the jump. Finally, specify Class Detail as the display layout.

The found set and the sort order that will actually be displayed on the Class Detail layout depend on three things: what other options have been specified for the GTRR, the existing found set on the Class Detail, and the relationship settings that link the origin and destination table occurrences. These are the possible outcomes:

- If you check the option to Show Only Related Records, and also choose the suboption to Match Current Record Only, the found set consists of just those classes related to the current teacher record. Those records are sorted according to the sort setting in the relationship, and the first class record in the set will be the active record.

- If the options to Show Only Related Records and Show in New Window are both unchecked, the found set on the Class Detail layout depends on whether the first related record was already part of the found set there. If it was, that record becomes the active record and the found set remains unchanged. If not, all records in the table are displayed, with the first related record as the active record. The sort order of the display layout (here, Class Detail) is not altered in either case. Be aware that it's only the presence of the first related record that matters. In fact, it's possible that other related records may not even be part of the found set following the GTRR step.

■ If the Show Only Related Records option is not checked, but Show in New Window is checked, all the records in the Class table will be in the found set, regardless of what found set existed there previously. The first related record is the active record.

■ If there are in fact no related class records for the given teacher, the found set and sort order on the Class Detail remain unchanged. Further, the display layout does not even become the active layout. Be on guard for this situation because if your scripts assume either that you have a particular found set or that you're on a particular layout following a GTRR, you might have problems. To trap for this situation, you can test for the existence of related records before the GTRR by using the Count function to determine the number of related records. Alternatively, you can check to see whether the GTRR step generates an error. Error 101, Record is missing, is returned if there are no related records. Finally, if you checked the option Show in New Window and there are no related records, be aware that a new window is not created.

PREDICTING THE FOUND SET

The preceding section contained an example of using GTRR to navigate to a set of classes related to a particular teacher. Because only one hop was involved in this GTRR, it was very easy to conceptualize what found set would be generated by the GTRR step. A GTRR, however, is not limited to short jumps such as this. In fact, the origin and destination table occurrences can be distantly connected on the Relationships Graph. When this is the case, it can sometimes be difficult to predict exactly what set of records will be returned. A few simple rules and examples should clarify this for you.

First of all, the origin and destination table occurrences must be connected on the graph for the GTRR to function. If they aren't, the user sees an error stating, This operation could not be completed because the target is not part of a related table. The actual error generated is error 103, Relationship is missing.

Assuming that there is some unique path from the origin to the destination, you really need to know just three rules to determine what found set will appear if you do a Go to Related Record script step:

■ Every relationship along the path is evaluated.

■ The found sets are cumulative.

■ The sort setting of the final hop determines the sort order.

To discuss more concretely how these rules can be applied, it is helpful to consider some examples. Figure 15.11 contains a Relationships Graph with five table occurrences. The Teacher and Advisor occurrences are both linked to the Teacher base table. The other table occurrences—Student, Enrollment, and Class—are linked to base tables of the same names.

In all the examples that follow, assume that the Show Only Related Records option is checked for all the GTRR steps, and that you have chosen to match only the current record. Starting from any of the table occurrences on the Relationship Graph shown in Figure 15.11, can you predict what found set you would end up with if you performed a `Go to Related Record`, targeting each of the other table occurrences?

Figure 15.11
From any table occurrence on this graph, you can jump to any other location on the graph using a `Go to Related Records` script step.

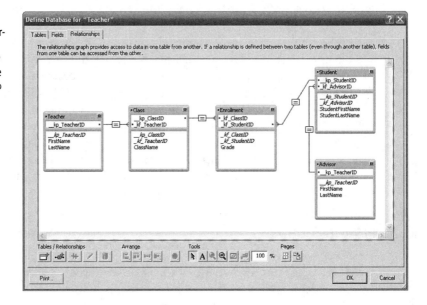

Imagine that you were on the Teacher Detail layout. In the preceding section, you saw how a GTRR directed at the Class table occurrence would find all of that teacher's classes. What if you did a GTRR directed at the Enrollment table occurrence from the Teacher Detail layout? There's a one-to-many relationship from Teacher to Class, and another one-to-many relationship from Class to Enrollment. The GTRR would need to traverse two hops: first to the set of classes taught by the teacher, and then to the enrollment records for those classes. The first hop might result in a set of, say, three classes. The second hop is the cumulative result of going to the related enrollments for each of the three classes. The end result would be a set of all the enrollment records for all the classes taught by that teacher.

What if you went one hop further, over to the Student table occurrence? The first two hops (Teacher to Class, Class to Enrollment) would again yield all the enrollment records for that teacher. The third hop, from Enrollment to Student, would yield the set of students that those Enrollment records represent. It's as if a GTRR were performed on each record of the found set of enrollments. The set of student records would represent all students enrolled in any of that teacher's classes.

Finally, what about a GTRR from the Teacher Detail layout all the way over to the Advisor table occurrence? Following the reasoning from the other examples, that would result in the set of teachers who are advisors for the students enrolled in any of that teacher's classes.

If any of the individual hops in a multi-hop GTRR yield a null set, the entire GTRR behaves the same as a single-hop GTRR that yields a null set. See the preceding section for a discussion of this possibility.

As stated in the third rule earlier, the sort order of the found set in a multi-hop GTRR is determined by the last hop. In this example, say that there was a sort defined for the relationship from Class to Enrollment. Even though a GTRR from Teacher to Enrollment would yield a sorted result, a GTRR from Teacher to Student would not, unless the relationship from Enrollment to Student was also sorted.

There's one final point to make about predicting the found set of a multi-hop GTRR. If you're ever in doubt about what records would appear or in what order, simply create a portal that displays records from the destination table occurrence. The same set of records that shows up in the portal would end up as the found set after a GTRR. Assuming that the portal itself wasn't sorted, the order of the records would even be the same.

JUMPING TO DISCONNECTED TABLE OCCURRENCES

There's one final behavior of the Go to Related Record step that's worth noting: It can be used to move a found set from one table occurrence of a base table to another. This even works for disconnected table occurrences. In a given window, all the layouts associated with a given table occurrence share the same found set and sort order. This is a good thing because it means that moving back and forth between, say, a list view and a form view based on the same table occurrence doesn't require any found set manipulation.

However, if two layouts are attached to different table occurrences, their found sets and sort orders are independent of each other, even if they're both occurrences of the same base table. Say you have two occurrences of a Teacher base table called Teacher 1 and Teacher 2 on your Relationships Graph (either related or unrelated to each other). Imagine that you're on a layout associated with Teacher 1 and that you've done a find for some subset of Teacher records.

Now what do you suppose would happen if from that layout you were to do a GTRR that specified Teacher 1 as the destination and a layout linked to Teacher 2 as the display layout? The origin and destination are the same table occurrence here, so the answer might not be completely intuitive. The effect of such a GTRR, assuming that you had checked the Show Only Related Records option, would be that the current found set and sort order would be *transferred* to the Teacher 2 layout.

So, by using the same table occurrence for both the origin and the destination of a GTRR, you can move the current found set to another layout and/or window. There's something about this behavior that defies intuition, but it's very handy nonetheless.

TROUBLESHOOTING

POP-UP WINDOW ISSUES ON A WINDOWS PC

Pop-up windows don't appear in front of the current window when the current window is maximized.

On the Windows platform, when a window is maximized to fill the application window, no other windows can also be visible on the screen. That is, only a single window can be maximized, and it must be the foreground window. This means that if you try to pop up a window in front of a maximized window, the background window cannot remain maximized. It instead reverts to its reduced state.

If you plan to build a user interface that makes use of multiple windows, be aware of this potential pitfall. It would be better in such cases to never have any windows maximized, even though this means you have to work within a reduced space. Users may still manually maximize a window, so test your routines thoroughly to see what effect this action would have. You'll likely need to add some control routines to your navigation scripts like `Adjust Window [Resize to Fit]` to get the windows back to the size at which you intend them to be viewed.

CREATING NEW WINDOWS LOSES MY FOUND SETS

Whenever I create a new window, all the found sets of the nonvisible layouts are reset to show all records. What causes this behavior?

When a new window is created, either manually from the Window, New Window menu command or via script, it inherits many characteristics of the currently active window. Specifically, it keeps the same size (except when opened via script and specified otherwise), active layout, found set, sort order, and active record. To all appearances, it's as if it's an exact duplicate of the currently active window.

In fact, only the settings of the active layout are retained when a new window is created. All layouts that are not visible (except those tied to the same table occurrence as the active layout) lose any sense of the found set, active record, and sort order. All records are displayed, unsorted, and the first record in the table is the active record.

FILEMAKER EXTRA: RECURSIVE SCRIPTS

Chapter 14, "Advanced Calculation Techniques," discusses how you could make custom functions recursive by including calls to themselves within their formulas. In a similar manner, you can use script parameters to create recursive scripts. Although this isn't something you need to do on a daily basis, there are some interesting applications for recursive scripts.

A recursive script is one that calls itself repeatedly until some exit condition is satisfied. Each time the script calls itself as a subscript, it passes a script parameter that can be used as part of an exit condition test. In many ways, recursive scripts are quite similar to looping scripts, and many of the tasks you can accomplish with one can be done as easily by the other.

As an example of a recursive script, consider this `Recursive Add` script:

```
If [Get (ScriptParameter) >= 100]
    Exit Script
End If
New Record/Request
Perform Script ["Recursive Add"; Parameter: Get (ScriptParameter) + 1 ]
```

This script adds 100 new records to the current table. It's first called without a script parameter, so the first time through, the script calls itself as a subscript, passing a parameter of 1. The parameter increments each subsequent time through, until eventually the exit criteria (`Get (ScriptParameter) >= 100`) is met.

If there are any steps in the script after the recursive subscript call, these are all executed, from the inside, out, after the exit criteria has been met. Try to predict what would happen if you added the following steps to the end of the preceding script:

```
Beep
Show Custom Dialog ["The parameter is:" ; Get (ScriptParameter)]
```

The 100 records would be created exactly as they were originally. But after they were all created, you'd hear a beep and see a message telling you that the script parameter value is `99`. After clicking OK, you'd then hear another beep and a message telling you that the parameter is `98`. This would continue for some time, and eventually the last message you'd see would be that the parameter is empty, which, of course, was the condition on the very first trip through the script.

As a final example of recursive scripting, consider the following script, which flags duplicates among a set of records. Assume that the set contains a list of names, which has been sorted by name before this script is called:

```
If [IsEmpty (Get (ScriptParameter))]
    Go to Record/Request/Page [First]
Else
    Go to Record/Request/Page [Next; Exit after last]
    If [Get (ScriptParameter) = Contacts::Name]
        Set Field [Contacts::DuplicateFlag; "Duplicate"]
    End If
End If
Perform Script ["Mark duplicates"; Parameter: Contacts::Name]
```

During each iteration through the script, the current record's name is compared against the value of the script parameter, which was set to the value of the previous record's name. The exit condition here is the `Exit after last` option on the fourth line; the script continues through the set of records, stopping only when there's no next record to go to.

CHAPTER 16

ADVANCED PORTAL TECHNIQUES

In this chapter

16

PORTALS IN FILEMAKER PRO

Portals are important tools in the FileMaker toolbox. In their most basic form they display data that pertains to the essential relationships in a given system. For example, a record for a neighborhood might show all the related house records in a portal, or a record for a class might show a portal of all the students enrolled in that class. Portals in cases like this reflect the primary relationships in a database. This is especially true if you make use of portal functionality allowing for the creation of related records; portals then can serve as the mechanism by which related records are created.

Portals can also serve a wide variety of user interface needs. They can be used to present a pick list for selecting records for various functions. They can be used to display ad hoc reports. They can even be used to present navigation or function options to users, display images, or offer alternative list views combined with form views of data. Portals can be used whenever a developer needs to display *n* rows of virtually anything on a layout.

This chapter begins by covering some basic portal details, but after we've moved through that information, we get to some more advanced techniques. We recommend this chapter for everyone, including beginners and advanced developers: Working with portals is a fundamental part of becoming adept with FileMaker, for whatever purpose.

PORTAL BASICS

As previously mentioned, a portal is a view into a related table. In each row of your portal, you will see fields from records as they relate to the current record to which the portal is tied.

Another way to think of portals is that they offer a view into another table from a specific perspective. The match criteria you've established determine the perspective, and, depending on how you've set things up, it is possible to change that perspective to useful ends.

FileMaker Pro 7 introduced new relationship operators, beyond the single equijoin (=), and portals have become even more flexible than in the past. However, a portal's basic function of displaying one record per row from a related table remains essentially the same. A Cartesian cross-product operator (x), for instance, relates all the records in one table to all the records in another table, regardless of key values. A portal based on such a relationship would therefore display all the records of the related table. Similarly, a < operator compares the match fields on either side of your relationship, and the rows in your portal will be displayed accordingly. As a final example, a ≠ operator enables you to exclude certain records from your portal.

→ To learn more about relationships and working with portals, **see** "Working with Related Data," **p. 166**.

One of the most important details to keep in mind is that the match field in the table from which you want to view records must be indexed (with a value index) for the relationship to properly resolve and display records in a portal.

→ To understand indexing, **see** "Storage and Indexing," **p. 86**.

Keep in mind that you can index calculations, as long as they do not reference related or unindexed fields themselves. It is entirely possible to relate to a calculation field in another table, rather than always relying on data input by users. You cannot create records through that relationship, however. Just as users cannot modify a calculation field, neither can FileMaker Pro itself. As you may recall, portals can be set to allow for the creation of related records. A user can click on the first empty row in a portal and enter data directly. FileMaker Pro then does the equivalent of a `Set Field` step and rightly places the match field value—key—in the analogous field on the other side of the relationship.

Indexing is not required for the match field in your current table. You can use global fields or unstored calculation values to create the bridge between two tables. We get into those techniques later in the chapter. The important thing to remember is that the match field in the "distant" or related table must be indexed for the relationship to resolve properly.

PORTALS VERSUS LIST VIEW/TABLE VIEW

Knowing when to use portals is often a matter of personal preference, user interface requirements, and data architecture. Quite often developers go through phases of infatuation with using various ways to display multiple records in a single view. The three tools for doing this are List views, Table views, and portals. Each has its own pros and cons, and we'd argue that the three are best used for very different purposes.

We encourage laziness (it breeds a need for efficiency), so we tend to favor Table view when a developer or user needs to access raw data with no regard to interface. You get a good bit of functionality for free, such as column sorting, column headers, and the capability to resize and reorder columns. The main downside to Table view is that you cannot add buttons or other visual objects to your rows. You also cannot rename or modify the appearance of column headers. Table view therefore is generally used for layouts that are accessible only to developers. They're usually not suitable for end users.

For cases in which control over the user interface is of paramount importance, List view and portals come into play. The key difference between the two, from a user's perspective, is that a List view can dynamically represent whatever found set your table currently has, and portals always display a set of related records.

List view displays records in their creation order unless a user or script explicitly sorts the records. Unless you've controlled and turned off or altered menu access, users can omit records, show all records, and otherwise manipulate the found set in an ad hoc manner to suit their needs. List views display the number of rows that will fit on a screen, expanding as much as a user has monitor space. When you're printing a List view of records, all the records can be printed; page breaks are placed between records as necessary.

Portals are differently focused. They are always driven by a specific relationship and always display a fixed number of related rows—only the content changes. They are always sorted (at a minimum in the order in which their related records were created, unless otherwise specified), so if you have a particularly large set of related data, your screen redraw speed may become an issue with hundreds of thousands of records. The obvious advantage of portals is that you can combine them on the same layout with data from other tables—both

16

with fields from a related record and with other portals. Unlike List views, portals are not particularly well suited to printing sets of records because the print output is limited to a specific number of related rows.

NEW PORTAL SETUP

To add a portal to a layout, use the Portal tool from the Status Area in Layout mode, and draw a rectangle that approximates how large you want your portal to be. You are then presented with the Portal Setup dialog, from which, at least, you need to choose a table occurrence on which to base the portal (see Figure 16.1).

Figure 16.1
These options enable you to govern how a specific portal behaves.

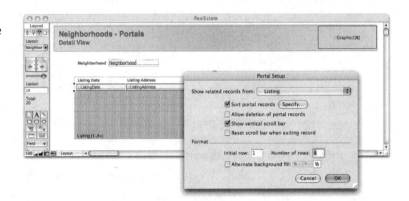

NOTE

Setting new portal options in the Portal Setup dialog does not affect other portals in your solution, regardless of whether others are tied to the same table occurrence.

TIP

When choosing from the list of table occurrences, note that it is not possible to create a portal showing records from an unrelated table. By definition, portals show related records. If you need to display records in an unrelated manner, create a Cartesian cross-product relationship to the table occurrence in question—but this is still a relationship. It will display all the records from that table.

As a helpful reminder, in Layout mode, the name of the table occurrence to which the portal is tied is displayed in the lower left, along with its row format options. We cover those options shortly.

SPECIFYING PORTAL SORTING

You can specify the order in which the related records are displayed by specifying sort criteria in the Portal Setup dialog (refer to Figure 16.1). It's thus possible to create two portals side by side, based on the same table occurrence, that offer two different sort views from the same related tables, as shown in Figure 16.2.

Figure 16.2
It is possible to establish different sort options for each portal in your database.

Note that the sort order is hard-coded to the portal. For users to change the sort order, they'd have to enter Layout mode and modify the Portal Setup dialog options. A technique for dynamic, user-based portal sorting is covered later in the chapter.

Note that the relationship from the current table occurrence to the destination table occurrence may also have a sort defined, but a portal sort, if defined, overrides the relationship sort. If the table occurrence is multiple hops away on the Relationships Graph, the last relationship is the one that determines the sort order.

ALLOWING PORTAL ROW DELETION

By enabling the Allow Deletion of Portal Records option, you enable users to select a portal row and delete a record by pressing the Delete or Backspace key. They are then prompted by FileMaker as to whether they want to delete the one related record in question.

You may instead want to overlay buttons attached to scripts in portal rows to delete related records so that you can more fully control the behavior of portals. This enables you to perform your own functions before deleting a record or to create your own calculation-based container fields to offer a different user experience. Given that it's not possible to alter FileMaker's default selection mask color, you may opt to use a container field to create row shading that is more to your liking.

In the same vein as never attaching anything but scripts to buttons for the purposes of control and maintainability, we almost never use the capability to delete records in portals with FileMaker's default behavior. We opt instead to place buttons (complete with an explicit icon or text indicating that it performs a delete function), attached to scripts, to do so.

Nonetheless, FileMaker's default portal row deletion capability is a handy feature to enable if you're working with a database that uses FileMaker's native user interface behaviors.

SETUP OPTIONS

FileMaker's Portal Setup options enable you to specify a starting row, how many rows (tall) a portal should be, whether to offer a vertical scrollbar, and whether to alternate row colors between that which you set for the portal itself and an alternative color.

The row choices are noteworthy. If you turn off your scrollbar, you can opt to display rows 1–8 in one portal, and rows 9–16 from the same relationship in another. Keep in mind that the end point is artificial; a child table can hold potentially millions of child records. With scrollbars turned on, a portal simply allows you to scroll from the initial row downward.

 To know what pitfalls to look for in starting a portal on a row besides the first one, refer to "Portal Rows Not Displaying" in the "Troubleshooting" section at the end of this chapter.

RELATIONSHIP PROPERTIES

Relationship properties have a direct bearing on a portal's behavior. These properties were covered in some detail in Chapter 6, "Working with Multiple Tables"; however, we'd like to draw your attention to some particular aspects of the Edit Relationship dialog, shown in Figure 16.3 and in the sections that follow.

Figure 16.3
Portal behavior is affected by the options you choose in the lower portion of the Edit Relationship dialog.

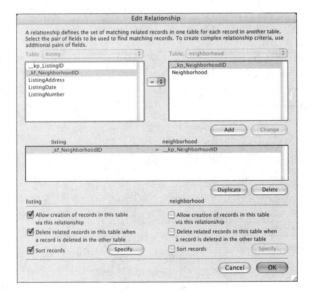

CREATING RELATED RECORDS

Notice in Figure 16.3 that one of the options you can specify for a relationship is Allow Creation of Records in This Table via This Relationship. When you check this option, a portal that's based on the relationship will contain a blank row under its related records (however many there are) that is readily available for data entry. When a user commits data in that blank row, FileMaker creates a record in the table into which the portal relates and pushes the value from the current parent record's match key into the related match field automatically.

This behavior is possible only with relationships that include the = operator (=, ≥, and ≤) in which FileMaker can determine exactly the foreign value to populate in the newly created record. In the case of greater-than-or-equal and less-than-or-equal operators, FileMaker pushes data into newly created records based on the equal-to value. You also need to be able to modify the field in question. If the relationship is tied to a calculation field, FileMaker Pro cannot automatically populate it with a value from a related record (see Figure 16.4).

Figure 16.4
Note that the match field, shown here in the third column, is populated automatically.

→ For more depth on relationships and relationship properties, **see** Chapter 6, "Working with Multiple Tables," **p. 157**.

CASCADING DELETION OF RELATED RECORDS

The next option is Delete Related Records in This Table When a Record Is Deleted in the Other Table. Choosing this option ensures that when a user deletes a record in one related table, all its related records are deleted as well. This cascading effect ensures that your database doesn't orphan records by allowing a user to delete records without their respective related records. A good example might be a contact person's record and related phone-number records. It is unlikely that you'd want to retain just the phone-number records after deleting the contact record to which related phone records belong.

The downside, of course, is that users may not realize that along with deleting the current record they are also going to delete all the records they see displayed in a portal, or, worse yet, that they will be deleting records they may not see onscreen currently.

→ For more detail on referential integrity and cascading deletion, **see** Chapter 6, "Working with Multiple Tables," **p. 157**.

RELATIONSHIP-BASED SORTING

The Sort Records option at the bottom of the Edit Relationship dialog enables you to define a sort order for that relationship. If set, it drives the order in which rows are displayed in portals based on this relationship. Portals themselves have their own sorting options and their options override whatever sort properties you set here; however, it's useful enough to consider this a default sort, if you want.

STICKY PORTALS

Portals in FileMaker 8, by default, maintain their scroll position even after a record has been committed or exited. In the past, FileMaker would "pop" back to the top of a portal after a user had finished entering data, regardless of how far down in a given related recordset a user might have scrolled. In FileMaker Pro 7, you could opt to change that behavior by turning off field frames. Happily, in FileMaker 8 this is no longer an issue. If you prefer to have a portal reset to the top each time a user finishes working with it, turn on the new feature in the Portal Setup dialog called Reset Scroll Bar When Exiting Record.

When this option is turned off, the scroll state of your portal is honored until you refresh the screen by changing modes, close the window in question, quit FileMaker Pro, perform a sort or script, or change records. All these actions result in a screen refresh. If you change from one record to another and return to the original, its portal position reverts to the top as well. Portals maintain their position when users actively edit fields in portal rows.

Scripted New Portal Records

It's quite common for developers to choose to disallow the creation of related records in portals. You might want to avoid the need for users to scroll to the bottom of a portal to create new related records. You may want to have your portal serve as a display-only tool, or you may simply have too many rows and don't want to force users through a bunch of unnecessary scrolling. Doing so means having to modify the relationship itself. You cannot simply turn on and off this behavior on a case-by-case basis at the portal level. (Consider that a feature request, FileMaker!)

If the option Allow Creation of Records in This Table via This Relationship setting is turned off, you've then got the task of figuring out how—other than driving users to the related table in question—to create new related records.

One approach to manage the creation of new records is to use a Set Field script step in combination with passing the necessary key match value via script parameter:

```
Go to Layout [ "Contact" (Contact) ]
New Record/Request
Set Field [ Contact::_kf_company; Get (ScriptParameter)
     // _kp_company should be passed as the parameter]
Commit Records/Requests [ No dialog ]
Go to Layout [ original layout ]
```

Note that this script makes no assumptions about the originating context from which it is called. This is an example of a nicely flexible script that simply creates related contact records and returns the user to the layout from which he came after calling the script.

"New Record Only" Relationships

You might not want to have to write scripts to create new related records for display in your portals. Scrolling to find them can still be an issue in some cases, and a script still requires a user action to be executed or performed.

An alternative is what we're calling "new record only" relationships. To establish them, you need to rely on the auto-entry options in FileMaker Pro, the triggering behavior of the Evaluate function, and the order in which FileMaker Pro performs certain tasks.

The technique described here enables you to use related fields through a relationship that allows creation of new records, just as if you were planning to allow users to scroll to the end of a portal, but that doesn't require you to scroll to the bottom of a portal to do so. The related fields you'll use provide a data entry area outside the portal that is always available to create new related records. When users type data into the fields, a new record is instantly created, but then on committing those new edits, the relationship is immediately invalidated so that these new record fields remain blank and ready for more data input.

This then obviates the need for scripting, and opens up some possibilities for user interface and working with portals. We'll often choose to place the layout objects for this technique in a pop-up window.

Consider the Relationships Graph shown in Figure 16.5, in which a neighborhood is related to many houses. The second of the two relationships is set to allow for the creation of related records. Note that we have created two foreign IDs in the related table occurrences and that the two relationships are different.

Figure 16.5
This Relationships Graph represents two equijoin relationships. The temp relationship is set to allow creation of related records.

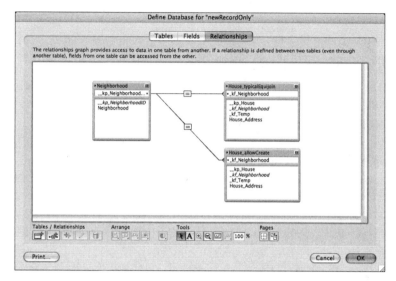

The rest of this technique relies on field definitions. The basic approach is that you allow the _kf_TEMPneighborhood field to be populated via the Allow Creation of Records in This Table via This Relationship setting, but then immediately set the field to zero when the record is committed.

This requires that two tasks happen: that the _kf_neighborhood gets set, and that, only after this field is set, _kf_TEMPneighborhood is cleared.

To accomplish the first task, set _kf_neighborhood to _kf_TEMPneighborhood, using an auto-entry calculation. An instant before the temp field is cleared, it will contain a proper value for this house record's neighborhood ID.

The second task, clearing the temp field, is accomplished if you set the auto-entry options for _kf_TEMPneighborhood, turning off the Do Not Replace Existing Value for Field (If Any), with this formula:

```
Evaluate (
    If ( IsEmpty (_kf_neighborhood); _kf_TEMPneighborhood; 0);
    _kf_neighborhood
)
```

Notice that the _kf_neighborhood is defined as a trigger for the Evaluate function. When _kf_neighborhood is populated, by its own auto-entry pointing to _kf_TEMPneighborhood, that event then triggers _kf_TEMPneighborhood 's auto entry—which then sets itself to zero. The technique assumes that you have no records in your neighborhood table with a _kp_neighborhood of zero. Because the second relationship based on the _kf_TEMPneighborhood is invalidated after this process is complete, you can place data entry fields on a layout, tied to your second temp relationship, that are then cleared after a new record is committed.

This is quite an advanced technique, but it is elegant in that it requires no scripting.

HORIZONTAL PORTALS

Working with user interfaces and creating new records together form a large part of working with portals. Another issue developers often face is the desire to have a portal scroll from left to right rather than vertically.

Horizontal portals are one of the grails which FileMaker developers seek. Although FileMaker 8 doesn't offer the capability to scroll through columns, rather than rows, of related records (or simply scroll horizontally to view more data in a related record row), you can easily display a fixed number of related records side by side without any fuss. Use the format options in the Portal Setup dialog to display related records to control different starting rows for multiple, side-by-side portals. An example is shown in Figure 16.6.

Figure 16.6
Notice that the right-most portal has a scrollbar. That ensures that however many related records this record has, they will all be accessible to your users.

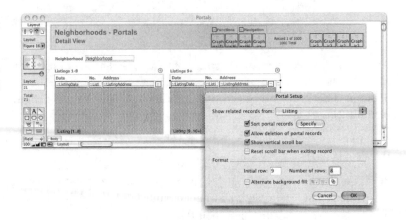

USING PORTALS TO CREATE CALENDARS

We often use the technique of placing seven portals next to each other to create calendar-like views within FileMaker. You can create a portal and relationship for each day of the week and include in the match values a _kf_dayofWeek value that ensures that only Mondays appear in the first portal, Tuesdays in the second, and so on. To your users this will feel like a completely natural calendar. You will need seven relationships—one for each day of the week—and will need a data table in which one record equates to a single day.

Be careful to ensure you have all your date records available. If you have missing records, you might get your days out of sync and display, say, Tuesday 14th to the right of Monday 6th. FileMaker will display records in each portal in order. If you have a Tuesday missing, for example, any Tuesday records that follow will appear to be out of sync with the other days of the week. This approach depends on your having data records for each full week that you choose to display in this way.

The obvious shortcoming to this technique is that you cannot use a scrollbar. Given that you have seven portals side by side, scrolling one portal would not behave intuitively for users (Saturday, for example, would scroll but none of the other days would). In these cases, we will often choose to create page-up/page-down routines that increment and decrement a "seed" date that controls the first records in each portal. If a user clicks your page-up button, the routine simply subtracts 7 from each date. Likewise, clicking the page-down button adds 7 to each date. To learn how to apply this technique, refer to "Filtered Portals" later in this chapter.

Note that a variance to this technique is to create a data table of week records, instead of days, with a field for each day. This is a significantly simpler data model that does away with the scrolling and syncing problem we discuss previously; however, it's a rare system that can be served without discrete day records. Your reporting capabilities will be significantly limited by week-based records.

SELECTION PORTALS

We've covered the basics of portals thus far, and discussed the idea that portals are used to display records from a related table and that the records themselves relate in a meaningful way. In other words, the related records shown in a portal correspond somehow to the active record—Parents to their own Children, Class to its attending Students, Company to its own Employees, Neighborhoods to Houses, and so on.

These relationships are often thought of as primary. They're the relationships that you depend on to define and determine a database's core architecture. Your users, likewise, will intuitively understand the process of entering data for, say, a class and then fleshing out its roster of students. There's a direct correlation between a primary data structure and the information that users expect to view, enter, and report on.

→ For a more in-depth discussion of data modeling, **see** Chapter 5, "Relational Database Design," **p. 129**.

We will now venture beyond the basic functions of data entry and display and explore other uses of portals. The other, advanced uses of portals mainly revolve around user interface choices in which you might opt for a more sophisticated approach in making selections. You may choose to relate to records in another table not for primary data purposes but for any number of others. We tend to refer to these cases as *utility relationships*. The following sections delve into some of the ways in which you can apply utility relationships.

BASIC SELECTION PORTALS

The first advanced technique we discuss is what we refer to as a *selection portal*. Selection portals are used to present choices to the user in lieu of a value list or menu of some kind.

This approach is necessary when a simple value list contains too many values to display practically or perhaps needs to display multiple columns of information as opposed to the two that FileMaker allows. In these cases we often choose to create a portal that displays options and permits a user to click on a row to select from among the choices presented.

Selection portals offer an alternative to the standard approach of using value lists to choose foreign key values: The only way two records in an equijoin become related is if they share a like value in match key fields. If you want, for example, to relate a real estate agent to a listing record, you can either manually enter the key for an agent into an AgentID field for the listing record, or assist data entry by providing a pop-up list or menu of options.

→ For a refresher in related value lists, **see** Chapter 3, "Defining and Working with Fields," **p. 67**.

Value lists, although a quick and easy means of giving users access to choose related records, can be limited: If you have hundreds of possible values, they can become cumbersome to scroll through. You're also able to utilize the contents of only two fields, the first of which needs to be the values for your match field (regardless of whether you choose to have it displayed). Figure 16.7 offers a pop-up window alternative to a value list that makes use of a portal.

Figure 16.7
This portal of options allows users to pick which related record they want to associate with their current record.

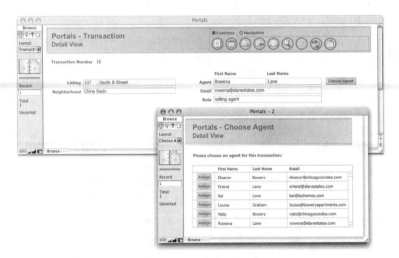

Selection portals address these issues, although they admittedly require more work to build. When a user wants to associate a record, as shown in Figure 16.7, he need only click, for example, the Rowena Lane row in the selection portal. Notice that the example shows the selection portal in a different pop-up window. This is a common way to display a selection portal for only as long as it is necessary. Clicking on a row above can also close the window in question.

The basic concept for selection portals is fairly straightforward. The goal here is to display all the possible relatable matches for a given record, and then through scripting capture and populate its match key into the appropriate foreign match key on the other side of the relationship. The work involves two elements: first, creating a portal that displays all the records from the other table and, second, writing a script that captures and populates the match field (foreign key) after a user has clicked on one of the portal rows available.

First define your data structure. In the example shown in Figure 16.7, agents can work with multiple listings, but a listing might have multiple agents as well: one representing the buyers and another representing the sellers. Notice that this now becomes a many-to-many relationship. At times there might be multiple agents on the buying or selling side as well. For the purposes of this example, use the Relationships Graph shown in Figure 16.8.

Figure 16.8
We've simplified the fields and relationships in this example to show just the primary data structure and a handful of fields necessary for the example.

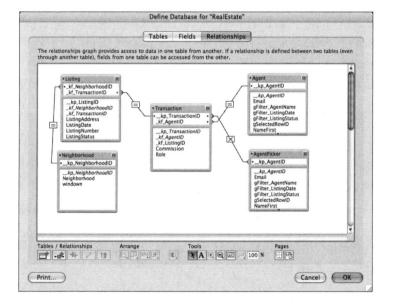

TIP

> To see this process work, first create an Agent layout and add a portal for all the listings associated with that agent. We recommend displaying your match key fields until you get comfortable with this technique.

Now you need a portal that shows all the listings in the table from which users can choose. For any portal, you always first need a relationship, so create a second table occurrence and second relationship. The example in Figure 16.8 related the _kp_agent to the _kp_listing via a Cartesian cross-product operator (x).

NOTE

Note that it doesn't matter what fields you choose as match fields for a cross-product join. The operator doesn't make any comparison and simply relates all records to all records.

A second portal can now be placed on your existing layout, or, in all likelihood, you would have these two portals displayed on a different layout expressly established for this picking process. You can even combine it with a pop-up window, as explained in Chapter 13, "Advanced Interface Techniques."

→ To review how to create a pop-up window, **see** "Rich Dialog Windows," **p. 369**.

After your cross-product selection portal is in place, you need to write a script to associate the related record your user will choose. The script, which will be tied to a button that's placed in the selection portal, needs to navigate to another layout to create the association. So that information about the current record and the selected portal row can be accessible on that other layout, you need to define the button to pass the agent and listing IDs as a script parameter. Use the following:

```
Select_Listing
    # assumes the user has clicked on the "assign" button for agents
    # establish context
    Go to Layout [ "Transaction" (Transaction) ]
    #
    # create the new record
    New Record/Request
    #
    # set the two foreign IDs required.
    # This script assumes that the button that launches the script passes the
    # script parameter:
    # Agent::_kp_agent & " " & select_Listing::_kp_listing
    Set Field [ Transaction::_kf_agent; LeftWords ( Get(ScriptParameter); 1 )]
    Set Field [ Transaction::_kf_listing; RightWords ( Get
    ➥(ScriptParameter); 1 ) ]
    #
    # commit and return to the original layout
    Commit Records/Requests [ No dialog ]
    Go to Layout [ original layout ]
```

→ To review script parameters and how to pass multiple parameters, **see** Chapter 15, "Advanced Scripting Techniques," **p. 435**.

This basic technique allows you to create a more complete user experience for your users and to expressly control the creation of related records. The advantages of this over a value list are that you can offer more than two fields of information to users, you can leave obscured the key values in your database, and generally the user interface can come across as more polished (depending, of course, on your artistic abilities).

PORTAL ROW HIGHLIGHTS

You are now exploring ways of working with portals that go beyond simply using them to display data that is related in a real-world sense. You're now establishing utility relationships that allow for other things beside basic structural relationships. In the example in the preceding section, you related your current record to all records in another table. In this example, we establish a condition by which a single portal row can be highlighted (see Figure 16.9). This is another technique to enhance usability and extend user interface.

Figure 16.9
The highlighting gives solid feedback to users that they are acting on the row in question; it allows you to establish a "selected" row.

> **NOTE**
>
> Notice that the Assign Selected button has been moved to the top of the portal, rather than placed on every row of the portal.

This technique involves setting a global field to the value of the primary key of whichever row the user clicks. You need three fields in all for this technique. We generally add them to the related table or a separate utility table, but keep in mind that you can use globals from any context. The following is a list of the fields you'll need for this technique:

- `gHighlightColor`—A global container field that holds a rectangle of the color you want to use as a highlight. You need only one such field in your database, regardless of how many portals you want to have use this technique.

- `gSelectedRowID`—A global number field that holds the primary key value of whichever row the user last clicked.

- `HighlightRow`—A calculation field that returns a container as its result:

    `If ( gSelectedRowID = _kp_relatedTable; gHighlightColor; "" )`

    To set the global field, you need only create a script like so:

    ```
    SelectRow_SetHighlight
        Set Field [ Listing::gSelectedRowID; relatedTable::_kp_relatedTable ]
        Commit Records/Requests [ No dialog ]
    ```

    This script presumes that the user has clicked on a portal row: The `_kp_relatedTable` is passed from that mouse click.

Notice that in cases in which `gSelectedRowID` equals the primary key of the related table, the calculation returns the value (in this case a colored rectangle) from `gHighlightColor`. Because you're using global fields, this solution works perfectly well in a multiuser environment. Whatever a given user has selected as her highlight row remains specific to her session.

The final element of implementing highlighted portal rows is to place the `HighlightRow` calculation field in the portal itself. Make the field exactly the size of the top row of the portal, and set its graphic format to Crop. (Make sure that your colored rectangle is larger than the portal rows you plan on having the highlight.) Attach the `SelectRow_SetHighlight` script to the field. In Browse mode a button does not need to be the topmost object on the screen to work. Move fields above it and your highlight color fills in nicely in the background. You would generally turn off access to the fields in your portal in Browse mode so that clicking on the portal row anywhere results in a highlight appearing, rather than a field being entered for data entry.

 If you're having difficulty getting the colored rectangle to display properly, refer to "Incomplete Highlighting Rectangle" in the "Troubleshooting" section at the end of this chapter.

One additional option when storing a selected row ID and creating a highlighted portal row is that it is possible to then also create a relationship specifically for that selected record. By relating `gSelectedRowID` to `_kp_listing`, you now have a relationship that will change as a user clicks portal rows.

Consider the implications: You can display related record fields directly on your current layout, based on the selected row (see Figure 16.10).

Figure 16.10
Notice that the information on the right corresponds to the related record selected by the portal on the left.

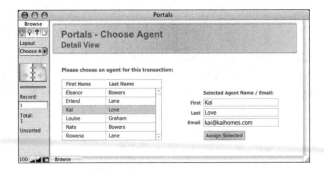

This is a great way to address a portal that is getting too crowded with fields. Instead of making each column smaller, or perhaps stacking fields in rows that might then get difficult to read, simply allow users to select a row in a portal and then display additional information about the selected, related record off to the side.

There's one flaw in the technique described. When users move from parent record to parent record, what happens to the row highlight? The `gSelectedRowID` would still remain associated to a record in the related table, even though a subsequent record may not include it in the selection portal. This could lead to confusion at best or, at worst, data integrity problems.

To ensure that a selected related record is visible only from its parent record, add a second predicate to the relationship so that it displays only related records from the current listing or transaction context. If the status area book icon is used to change records, the relationship will no longer be valid and no records will display.

To manage displaying related data in a safe, multiuser-conscious way, refer to "Multiuser Selected Data" in the "Troubleshooting" section at the end of this chapter.

MULTI-KEYS AND MULTI-ROW SELECTIONS

In addition to wanting to highlight a single row, as in the preceding example, you may encounter the need to have multiple rows selected at once. In the Agent Listings example, for instance, you may want to allow users to click multiple rows in the listing portal and assign them all at once to the agent in question.

This is a particularly handy way of allowing users to do multiple things at once: add a batch of listings to an agent, select multiple people for form letters, apply new dates to a series of records, and so on. There are dozens of possibilities.

The technique for this is nearly identical to that already presented. However, we rely on FileMaker Pro's capability to resolve multiple match values in a single field. These multiple match value keys are often called *multi-keys*.

Consider a company table related to an agent table, as shown in Table 16.1.

TABLE 16.1	PEOPLE
ID	**Name**
1	Eleanor Bowers
2	Erlend Lane
3	Kai Love
4	Nate Bowers
5	Rowena Lane

If you establish a relationship to this table by using a field—global or otherwise—FileMaker will recognize all return-delimited match key values as though they were individual values.

For example, if your company match field holds

1

3

then your valid, related records will be Eleanor and Kai's.

Likewise,

5

2

4

relates to Rowena, Erlend, and Nate. It doesn't matter to FileMaker in which order the values fall, simply that they are valid and delimited with a carriage return.

With a multi-key match, it is possible to show multiple rows as highlighted or selected in a given portal. You can use again the same three fields you'd use to set up a single row highlight:

- gHighlightColor—A global container field that holds a rectangle of the color you want to use as a highlight.

- gSelectedRowID—A global text field that holds multiple primary key values, return delimited, of whichever rows the user last clicked. Note that a number field no longer works. You cannot insert line breaks in a number field. Happily, in this case, FileMaker Pro can relate a text field to a number field. Be wary of problems with field types, but in this case there will be no problem.

- HighlightRow—A calculation field that returns a container as its result:

```
If ( FilterValues ( gSelectedMultiRows; _kp_listing ); gHighlightColor; "" )
```

If you are modifying the fields from the example given earlier in the chapter, notice that the test in the calculation is now using a FilterValues function that recognizes whether an ID is included in your global (as opposed to simply checking whether the two fields are equal).

When you're setting values in gSelectedRowID, a simple Set Field script step won't do the trick any longer. Doing so would replace the contents of the field and you'd be left with just one row selected. Your script needs to look like this:

```
SelectRow_SetHighlight
#
# if the ID already exists, remove it
If [ FilterValues ( Listing::gSelectedMultiRows; select_Listing::_kp_listing)]
Set Field [ Listing::gSelectedMultiRows;
    Let ( [
    selectedRowKey = select_Listing::_kp_listing & "¶"
    ] ;
    Substitute ( Listing::gSelectedMultiRows; selectedRowKey ; "")
    ) ]
    #
    # if the ID doesn't exist, append it to the end
    Else
Set Field [ Listing::gSelectedMultiRows;
    Let ( [
        selectedRowID = select_Listing::_kp_listing & "¶"
    ] ;
    Listing::gSelectedMultiRows & selectedRowID
    ) ]
End If
#
Commit Records/Requests [ No dialog ]
#
```

The mechanics of this script will result in your user adding and removing key values to your global match field as he or she clicks on multiple rows in your portal. Each row will highlight and in this manner you can have users choose multiple items from a given set of related records.

FILTERED PORTALS

Allowing users to select rows within portals allows portals to serve multiple functions: They can both display information to the user and, through selections, act on that data somehow. However, in this chapter thus far, we have dealt only with portals that are driven by fixed relationships. The data displayed remains constant and changes only when the data itself changes (when records are added to or deleted from a database).

A portal filter extends your capabilities to allow you to dynamically alter or constrain the rows of data displayed in a portal. Think of it somewhat as performing a find in List view.

16

For example, imagine a case in which you have hundreds of customers in a database and a portal displaying all customers. Your portal actively shows only a modest fraction of all customers in your system and forces users to scroll quite a bit. (Most users don't have monitors that can support a portal hundreds of rows tall.) To solve this usability problem, you can turn either to a List view, supported by Find mode to reduce the found set, or to a filtered portal.

Generally, filters enable users to dynamically specify match criteria—often a status or type field of some kind—and then view only portal rows that match those criteria. In the real estate example you've been following in this chapter, listings could be set as active, sale pending, or sold. Using a portal filter, you could allow users viewing a set of listings in a portal to specify a particular status and have the contents of the portal change to reflect their choice (see Figure 16.11).

Figure 16.11
In this example, choosing from the available value list alters the rows displayed in the portal.

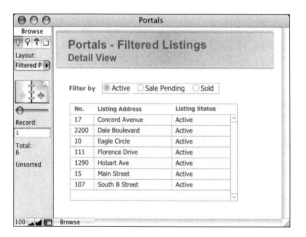

To create a simple filtered portal, first create a globally stored text field for holding the value a user chooses. In the example shown in Figure 16.11, a `gFilter_ListingStatus` will work well. When it's placed on a layout, we'd recommend attaching a value list with "active," "sale pending," and "sold" for ease of use.

The second element to this technique is modifying the relationship between agents and listings to take the filter into account. The relationship was originally set up with a cross-product operator so that all listings could be displayed. If you replace that with a match of gFilter_ ListingStatus to ListingStatus, only listings that match the currently specified status are considered related records (see Figure 16.12).

Figure 16.12
The assumption this relationship makes is that gFilter_ListingStatus will change based on user preference.

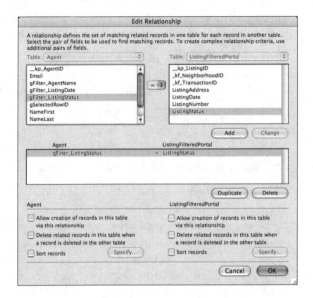

NOTE

gFilter_ListingStatus is a global and is therefore unindexable; however, from the perspective of its table, it is possible to use this field to relate to another table. Only the "far" table being viewed in a relationship requires an indexed match field (in this case, ListingFiltered).

By comparing the status field from the listing table with gFilter_ListingStatus, you have created a relationship that changes based on the value a user selects in gFilter_ ListingStatus. Keep in mind, if gFilter_ListingStatus is empty, so too will the portal be empty.

MULTIVALUE And FILTERED PORTALS

Consider a second scenario in which you might want to filter on two criteria. To accomplish this task, add a second criterion to your match relationship, as shown in Figure 16.13.

The relationship shown in Figure 16.13 filters on match values for both status and date fields. A filter acts on both fields. Notice the ≥ operator on the date. You can use a combination of match fields and relationship operators to display a wide range of related records.

This enables you to create a filtered portal with a range of possible, mutually inclusive filters. You can allow someone to select, say, all active listings for dates greater than 4/1/2006.

Figure 16.13
This example makes use of two match criteria.

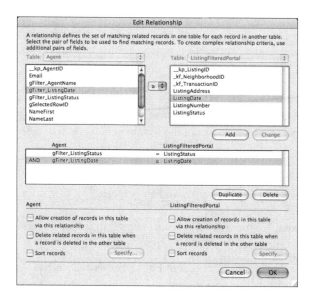

MULTIVALUE Or FILTERED PORTALS

A natural extension to the example you've been exploring is a case wherein you want the portal to match one or another criterion but not necessarily both criteria. For example, what if you alter the value list attached to gFilter_ListingStatus to include "all" as an option? Here you will want listings for an agent displayed based on his status, unless the user selects All, in which case all listings for a given agent should be displayed.

You need to apply the technique for a multi-key as discussed previously. In the earlier example, the multi-key was applied to the front end of the relationship. This time we apply it to the back end.

Create a calculation field in the listings table like so:

```
listingStatus & "¶" & "all"
```

Now change the listing side of the relationship from listingStatus to the new calculation field. This is the only change (beyond adding the "all" option to your filter value list) that you need to make to turn this into an Or filter. This relationship resolves where values in the status list include one of the three statuses or "all".

RANGED, MULTIVALUE Or FILTERED PORTALS

Multivalue Or filters can become quite powerful. Consider a new example: Imagine wanting to provide users with a filtered list of contact names from a pool of hundreds or even thousands of records in a contact table. Instead of creating a value list by which to filter, allow your users to type a few characters of text into a filter field. If a user enters co, your (presumed) contacts returned in the portal might be a list like this:

16

Coleen Neff

Corbin Daniels

Cordelia Henrich

If someone enters `col`, the list might return only Coleen Neff.

The way to approach this is to use the relationship operators for comparing ranges of text. Consider an example in which you have the following fields in a contact table:

- `gMatchField`—A text field stored globally where users type whatever portion of text by which they'd like to match.

- `NameFirst`—The first name of your contact person.

You now need to compare the text `co` against some set of values to get the record for Coleen Neff to appear from the list.

Consider that a `<` c is a valid expression in FileMaker Pro. By relying on text string comparisons, you can create a relationship comparing your `gMatchField` to `NameField`. If you create a calculation like

```
NameFieldzzz, calculation = [NameField & "zzz"]
```

and then create a calculation in which `gMatchField <= NameFieldzzz`, a portal using this sample comparison will display all names that are comparatively less than "Coleenzzz." This gets you only halfway there. "Anthony" and "Beth" are, for example, comparatively less than "Coleenzzz." You need to create a second calculation:

```
NameFieldaaa, calculation = [If (IsEmpty (gMatchField); "0"; gMatchField )]
```

In cases in which `gMatchField` has a value, say `"co"`, the comparisons now would be

- "Coleen" >= "co" and "Coleen" <= "cozzz"
- "Conrad" >= "co" and "Conrad" <= "cozzz"
- "Cordelia" >= "co" and "Cordelia" <= "cozzz"

In this example, "Anthony" and "Beth" would both not be valid match conditions. Both are comparatively less than "co."

The relationship driving a portal of this nature is shown in Figure 16.14.

Consider the `NameFieldaaa` field. When empty, it returns zero—a value that no text string will be less than. This then means that when `gMatchField` is empty, all the records in your contact table will be valid matches and all records will show in the portal.

You can opt to add further fields to drive the relationship in the portal by adding additional pairs of `gMatchField` and its two comparison fields. The relationship shown in Figure 16.15 demonstrates the case in which both `LastName` and `FirstName` fields can be used.

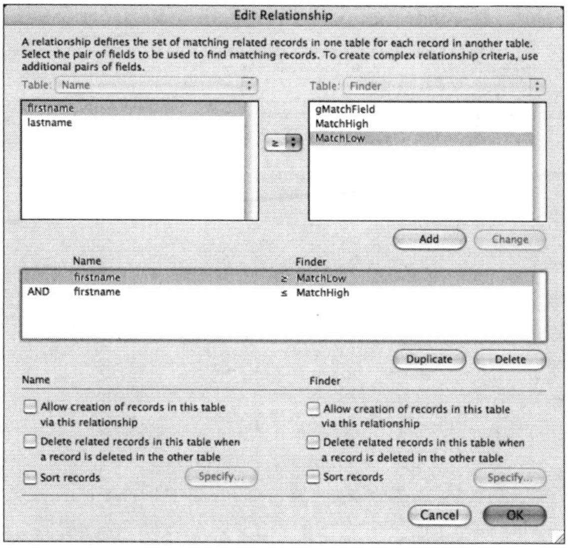

Figure 16.14
Notice that relationships can accept multiple And criteria.

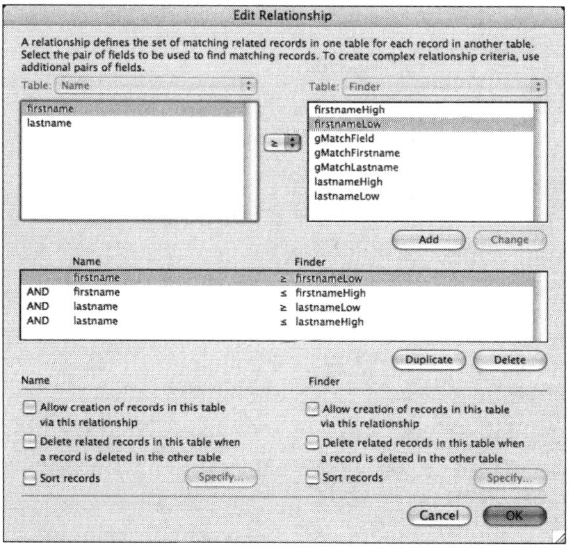

Figure 16.15
This relationship references two match fields. If a user types fractions of text in gMatch_firstname and gMatch_lastname, the portal filters on both values.

EXPLODED KEY FILTERED PORTALS

The last technique was one often used with prior versions of FileMaker Pro, before comparative operators were introduced into relationship definitions, and enables you to assemble a true Or condition for a relationship by making use of multi-key matching. It is an alternative to the earlier approach, but it has the added benefit of giving you the ability to add additional or custom values (like "all") into your match criteria. The technique still applies, and using a custom function to explode match values is even easier to utilize.

Consider the same example from the preceding section, in which you expect a user to type some fraction of text in a gMatchField text field and you want your filtered portal to display matches from a contact record's NameFirst field or NameLast field, or the domain from a ContactEmail field. In Figure 16.16, notice that matches are valid for all three data columns.

Figure 16.16
Notice that the filter is being applied to three fields: first name, last name, and email address. The records returned match the filter in at least one case.

To accomplish this task, use exactly the same multi-key technique. Rather than concatenating the values from one field, the match field concatenates the values from multiple fields. The calculation looks like this:

```
Let ( [
     atPosition = Position ( Email; "@"; 1; 1 ) + 1 ] ;
Left (FirstName; 4) & "¶" &
Left (FirstName; 3) & "¶" &
Left (FirstName; 2) & "¶" &
Left (FirstName; 1) & "¶" &
Left (LastName; 4) & "¶" &
Left (LastName; 3) & "¶" &
Left (LastName; 2) & "¶" &
Left (LastName; 1) & "¶" &
Left (Email; 4) & "¶" &
Left (Email; 3) & "¶" &
Left (Email; 2) & "¶" &
Left (Email; 1) & "¶" &
Middle (Email; atPosition; 4) & "¶" &
Middle (Email; atPosition; 3) & "¶" &
Middle (Email; atPosition; 2) & "¶" &
Middle (Email; atPosition; 1) & "¶" &
FirstName & "¶" &
LastName & "¶" &
Email & "¶" &
"all"
)
```

This calculation, if you can't already guess, resolves a match based on the first four characters of a contact's first name, last name, email address start, or email address domain (the characters following the @ symbol). Notice that the end of the calculation includes the full text of all three fields, along with an "all" to support users wanting to see all contacts in their databases.

Remember that the far side of a relationship requires an indexed field. This means you cannot include related data in your multi-key.

This calculation shows explicitly the values you need to assemble for a multi-key match field, and it's valuable to know how to do it as a straight calculation field; but we suggest building a custom function for assembling match fields. Using the recursive capabilities of custom functions and the fact that they are reusable throughout a solution, you can write one custom "explode text" function to take the parameters of however many fields you want to feed them, and never again have to write a calculation like the one we've shown here.

→ To learn more about how to build custom functions, **see** Chapter 14, "Advanced Calculation Techniques," **p. 391**.

DYNAMIC PORTAL SORTING

Developers often place column labels above portals, and one of the first things we've seen users do with a newly minted database is click those ever-so-tempting column headers expecting them to sort. As discussed previously in this chapter, you can sort portals either at the portal level or at the relationship level, but whichever method you choose, the portal will remain controlled by those baked-in sort options. Users cannot re-sort portals on the fly. One of the more common requests we get as developers is to allow users to sort by whatever column they want. Unfortunately, there's no way to programmatically define by which field a portal sorts. There is, however, a method for dynamically sorting a portal.

Using a calculation field, you provide FileMaker with the data by which you want a portal sorted. You need to create two new fields for your database: a control field, gSortPref, to hold the name of the field by which you want to sort, and a field for the actual sorting, sortCalc. We suggest you place sortCalc in the same table in which the rest of your portal fields sit. Your control field serves as a mechanism for choosing sort order. There are multiple ways to allow the user to change the values in it: You can use a value list, set by script when a user clicks on a column header, or perhaps a script available in the Scripts menu. However this field is managed, it's the end result that is important. Your sortCalc field depends on it. Here's an example of how sortCalc might be defined:

```
Case (
    gSortPref = "First Name" ; Name_first;
    gSortPref = "Last Name"; Name_last;
    gSortPref = "Email"; Email;
    "error"
)
```

If you set a portal to sort by sortCalc, notice that depending on what choice someone makes for gSortPref, the calculation returns the data by which the user expects to sort. If gSortPref = "First Name", the related portal data from sortCalc might look like this:

- Alex
- Beth
- Coleen

16

If `gSortPref = "Email"`, sortCalc's data would change to be this:

- beth@email.com
- gibson_alex@email.com
- neffy@email.com

By establishing this calculated field as the field by which your portal sorts, as the user chooses a sort preference, its data will update and the order in which rows appear should change. However, one remaining task to be done is managing screen refresh. Your user may change `gSortPref` and `sortCalc` updates accordingly, but your portal doesn't actually re-sort until the user changes layouts or modes, or performs one of a range of other possible actions. You could write a script to take the user into Preview mode and back into Browse mode, but to force the screen to refresh with a minimum of screen flashing, it's better to reset the key that controls the front of the portal relationship. Use a `Set Field ()` script step, and set the key field to itself. This forces the portal to refresh—because you've just altered one of the sides of its relationship—without requiring the user to navigate or change modes.

To establish sort buttons at the top of column headers, simply create as many buttons as there are fields in your portal, and then attach a script that, using `Set Field`, controls what parameter is passed to `gSortPref`.

An alternative technique would be to have `gSortPref` hold the actual name of the field by which you want to sort, and then instead of a `Case` statement, use a `GetField` function to populate `sortCalc`. This works well when all your fields are of the same type; however, both techniques fail when you are dealing with multiple field types—for example, `NameFirst`, `NameLast`, `BirthDate`, and `Age`. You still need a `Case` statement in that scenario.

MULTIPLE FIELD TYPE PORTAL SORTING

If you are using the technique just described, `sortCalc` needs to be a calculation that returns text, so numbers and dates sort by the rules that govern text. Unfortunately, it's not possible to dynamically control which data type a calculation returns, so the following data—1, 8, 9, 12, 82—sorts like so:

1

12

8

82

9

To get numbers to sort properly as text, you need to ensure that all of your numbers contain an equal number of digits. The numbers 01, 03, and 10 sort properly whereas 1, 3, and 10 do not.

Dates in your text calculation, likewise, sort like so:

1/12/2006

10/1/2006

10/10/2006

10/2/2006

3/1/2006

Remember that FileMaker stores dates internally as integers. This is the key to solving the puzzle. The idea here is that if the integer representations of dates are compared, the sort works properly. `sortCalc` needs to be set as the following, assuming that you have three fields that you want to display in your portal (`myNumber`, `myText`, and `myDate`):

```
Case (
    gSortPref = "Number" ; Right ( "000000000000000" & myNumber; 15 );
    gSortPref = "Text"; myText;
    gSortPref = "Date"; GetAsNumber( myDate );
    "error"
)
```

This calculation converts all your numbers into 15-digit numbers. It concatenates 15 zeros with whatever number has been entered into `myNumber`, and then truncates the result to 15 characters. This ensures that 1, 3, 10, and 999 respectively return 000000000000001, 000000000000003, 000000000000010, 000000000000999.

Quite likely, the integer representation of your date field already uses the same number of digits. Remember that dates are stored in FileMaker as integers. 4/1/2006 is 732402. To drop below or above six digits, you'll need to be working with dates approximately before 274 A.D. or after 2738 A.D. Most databases are a safe bet at six digits, but if you're calculating dates for a sci-fi novel or are dealing with ancient times, feel free to use an identical approach to add digits.

DESCENDING DYNAMIC PORTAL SORTING

It's possible to extend the technique discussed in the preceding section so that the portal can be sorted in either ascending or descending order. To accomplish this function, you need to sort by two fields—one ascending and one descending—instead of just one.

Recall how sorting by multiple fields works: FileMaker Pro sorts all like values from the first field in a sort request together, and then orders records with identical values in that first field by a second field. Table 16.2 shows an example in which a user sorted by last name, and then first name.

TABLE 16.2   CONTACTS ASCENDING

Last Name	First Name
Abrams	Alex
Abrams	Beth
Adams	Steve
Adid	Fereena
Adid	Samir

Recall also that sort fields can be set for ascending or descending behaviors. If you change the first name in Table 16.2 to sort descending, the list would look as shown in Table 16.3.

TABLE 16.3   CONTACTS FIRST NAME DESCENDING

Last Name	First Name
Abrams	Beth
Abrams	Alex
Adams	Steve
Adid	Samir
Adid	Fereena

You can use FileMaker Pro's capability to properly sort in descending order for your sortCalc field. To toggle between the two behaviors, ensure that the first field always contains identical values when a user wants to have a portal sort by the second field—in this case set to descending order.

The formula for your sortAscend field looks like this:

```
Case (
    gSortPref = "number-ascending" ;
        Right ( "000000000000000" & myNumber; 15 );
    gSortPref = "text-ascending"; myText;
    gSortPref = "date-ascending"; GetAsNumber( myDate );
    1
)
```

And the corresponding calculation for sortDescend is as follows:

```
Case (
    gSortPref = "number-descending" ;
        Right ( "000000000000000" & myNumber; 15 );
    gSortPref = "text-descending"; myText;
    gSortPref = "date-descending"; GetAsNumber( myDate );
    1
)
```

Notice that in the case that someone chooses one of the descending options, all the values in sortAscend equal 1. If you set up your sort dialog to first sort by sortAscend (ascending) and second by sortDescend (descending), your first field overrides the second when a user chooses one of the ascending options from gSortPref; otherwise, that field is set to all the same values, and by definition the values in sortDescend will apply, happily making use of the descending sort behavior built into FileMaker.

To put the finishing touches on your user interface, you might consider making icons that indicate when a portal column is sorted ascending or descending. The script that sets your gSortPref can also control which images appear in container fields to provide visual feedback to the user.

There is one caveat to the portal sorting technique described in this section: It depends on being able to change the data in the sortCalc field for each record being sorted. If another user has a record locked (by actively editing data in that record), the value in sortCalc will not update and one (or more) of the rows in question will not sort properly. We recommend checking for locked records in the script you use for your user interface for setting sortCalc.

TROUBLESHOOTING

PORTAL ROWS NOT DISPLAYING

I know I have a valid relationship established, but some (or all) of my portal rows aren't showing. What could be some of the issues?

You can opt to display only a specific set of rows via Portal Setup format options, but it is possible that you'd have a case of related records in your data that would never show up for a user. If you turn off vertical scrollbars and set a portal to show rows 4–8, rows 1–3 and 9+ won't display.

This applies to creating rows as well. If you've allowed the creation of related records and a portal's bottommost row is intended to allow such, your users cannot access that feature if the row falls outside your range of visibly formatted rows. As in the example of showing only rows 4–8, there would have to already be at least three related records in the database before the editable row would appear for users.

CREATING RELATED ROWS FOR NON-EQUIJOIN RELATIONSHIPS

How do I create records via relationships that aren't equijoins? The option is grayed out.

When you allow creation of related records in a relationship, you may have noticed that this works only for the equijoin (=) operator. In cases in which your primary relationship is driven by a different operator, we recommend still establishing an equijoin relationship with different table occurrences to create new records. If you're still not happy doing so (perhaps over concerns of cluttering your Relationships Graph), the only other alternative is to create a script that takes a parameter—the primary key of your parent table's current record—navigate to a layout attached to your child table occurrence, and use the create new record/request script step in combination with a manual Set Field [childTable::_kf_ ParentID; Get (ScriptParameter)] for the match key.

INCOMPLETE HIGHLIGHTING RECTANGLE

My row highlight is showing in its container field, but it doesn't fill the entire portal row well. Where should I first look to address this problem?

If you place an image in a container field, and then have a calculation display the contents of that container field in a portal row, even when Maintain Original Proportions is enabled, your rectangle may show whitespace on either side. This is further complicated if you are trying to put something more complex than just a colored rectangle in the highlight field. FileMaker's resizing of images can be unpredictable at times.

The best way around this situation in many cases is to simply make the image larger than you need it to be and set the graphic format to Crop.

MULTIUSER SELECTED DATA

I have used a regular field—not a global field—for storing the ID of the related record I want selected in a selection portal and related fields. In multiuser environments, this will break if two users are working with the same record at once. How do I work around that problem, while still not using globals that might display the wrong related data for a given record?

In cases in which the field tracking a portal row selection is a standard field, as opposed to a global field, you will run into problems in multiuser environments. Two users might be viewing the same record at the same time and make two different row selections on a portal. Only one state would be valid (the latter of the two), but no event or screen refresh would occur for the first user.

There are two ways to deal with this problem. To employ the first, make certain that users never end up working with the same record by either scripting a check-in/check-out approach or possibly building a one-record-only user interface for each user. This first approach is quite scripting and development intensive.

The second approach makes use again of multi-keys. To track what portal row is selected, keep track of your account name in a global field and populate a multi-key that concatenates `accountName` and `rowID` into the `selectionID` field. You need to use the `Substitute` function to parse in-and-out as multiple users work with the portal, but this is multiuser-safe as long as they don't run into actual record-locking problems.

FILEMAKER EXTRA: PORTALS AND RECORD LOCKING

Record and portal rows do not lock until a user begins actively editing a field or when a script performs an `Open Record/Request` script step.

At the point at which a user begins actively entering data (or modifying existing data), a record lock is established until such time as the user exits the record and commits or reverts the record.

It is important to keep this behavior in mind and to understand how it applies to portals. When a record is being modified and is related to other records viewed in a portal, it and the portal itself are locked; however, other users (or the same user in a different window) can navigate to one of the related records and edit it directly.

Portal rows and related records are created when the record is committed. FileMaker treats the entire set, including the parent record and all related child records, as a single transaction. It is possible to create a new parent record, tab from field to field entering data, tab into a portal and create a few rows (including potentially entering data into fields from a grandchild record), and either commit the entire batch at once or roll back and revert the entire batch. To support such functionality, FileMaker locks the entire portal for a given record.

Record locking used to be more of an issue for both users and scripts in versions before FileMaker 7. Although FileMaker 8 doesn't do away with record locking—nor would we want it to, for maintaining data integrity—the behavior you need to anticipate is far more localized than in version 6 and earlier.

CHAPTER 17

DEBUGGING AND TROUBLESHOOTING

In this chapter

WHAT IS TROUBLESHOOTING?

We hear about troubleshooting all the time. It conjures the image of a brainy technician, her utility belt bristling with tools, head stuck inside a rocket engine, muttering about how the condensers on the Apollo-96 tend to get "a little sticky" in the asteroid belt. One answer to the question "What is troubleshooting?" is simply "the art of detecting, diagnosing, and repairing problems." In our case, of course, we're concerned with problems that might appear during the operation of a piece of software.

This diagnostic flavor of troubleshooting is extremely important. This chapter introduces you to some of the broader systematic problems that can occur in a FileMaker system. We explain how to spot these and fix them, and we discuss some useful debugging tools that the FileMaker product line offers you.

We're also going to try to sell you on a broader interpretation of the idea of troubleshooting. The problem that's easiest to fix, of course, is the problem that never happens. So in addition to *reactive* troubleshooting—the art of finding and fixing problems *after* they happen—we're also going to spend some time talking about *proactive* troubleshooting. To us, this means designing systems that are simply less error-prone, and designing them in such a way that any errors that do appear are caught and handled in a systematic way. The better you become at this kind of proactive troubleshooting, the less often and less severely your reactive skills are likely to be tested.

STAYING OUT OF TROUBLE

Whether you're writing applications that only you will use, that your coworkers will use, or that a client has hired you to build, the best thing to do with trouble is to avoid it. When we think of software bugs, we think of users or developers cursing the foibles of machines and wishing that "the software (or the tools) just worked better." The truth is, the overwhelming majority of problems in software are caused by human mistakes, and often those humans are programmers. So, clearly, as programmers, we should avoid making mistakes! Let's look at some typical sources of programmer mistakes.

UNDERSTAND SOFTWARE REQUIREMENTS

On the one hand, the need to understand requirements might seem obvious, and on another it might seem a bit far afield from this chapter's topic, but as far as preventing software error, understanding requirements is at the top of the food chain. If you don't know what the software you're writing is supposed to do, it's very unlikely that it will work correctly. It might work correctly from a technical perspective; it won't necessarily crash, or scramble data. But from a user's perspective it'll be just as bad. If you misunderstood how your client calculates mortgage futures, from her perspective, the software is broken.

So *know what the program is supposed to do*. "Sort of" knowing isn't good enough, and guessing is even worse. There's often pressure—sometimes severe—to "just get started," even if all the requirements haven't been fully explored. Do not give in! FileMaker is a wonderful Rapid Application Development (RAD) tool. It's terrifically easy in FileMaker to sit down and just start banging out screens and scripts, and it gives a wonderful feeling and appearance of productivity. But if you haven't fully understood what you're doing, this feeling is an illusion.

Sometimes it's not possible or advisable to try to scope out *all* the requirements of a project before getting started. If you determine that your project is of this type, you need a different approach. In this case we recommend you explore and familiarize yourself with some of the latest thinking on what software engineers call *agile development*, which is the art of developing a complex piece of software in small, incremental stages, or *iterations*. One popular school of agile development is called "Extreme Programming."

The basic theory of Extreme Programming (or XP) is to break the work up into small pieces that meet two criteria. In the first place, each piece needs to be complete; that is, it needs to be large enough and inclusive enough that it constitutes a working piece of software in its own right. Think of a big program for a real estate management firm. Perhaps a portion of its requirements is a module that calculates different types of mortgages. Can this module be separated from the rest of the system and made independent? If so, you can build that module as a unit and then worry about what to build next.

The second requirement for such a unit is, of course, that it be small enough that it *is* possible to nail down all the requirements! If you can break a project up into pieces that are each complete, comprehensible, and as mutually independent as possible, you'll greatly increase your chances of success.

This book isn't intended to be a primer on software development methodologies, but remember this essential point: If you feel you don't quite understand what your program is supposed to do, please stop working and find out! Otherwise you're priming the pump for a later flood of software defects.

AVOID UNCLEAR CODE

As a programmer or software developer, relatively little of your time will be spent in writing new programs. Most of your time will be spent maintaining and extending old ones. This being the case, it's imperative that the programs you write be easy to extend and maintain. As much as possible, your programs should be both *readable* and *modular*.

Have you ever returned to a script you wrote six months ago, and find you have no idea what it does or how it does it? Of course you have; so have we all. And when we do this, we're in immediate violation of the "know what you're doing" rule. You *don't* know what you're doing, and you have to relearn it. You'd better have a good memory!

Much better is to write your program in a way that makes its functioning clear to whomever reads it, whether that's you or someone else. Two things in particular are important: giving descriptive names to the different components of your program (databases, tables, fields, layouts, and scripts, to name a few), and using comments liberally throughout your program.

CHOOSING GOOD NAMES

As much as possible, the names you choose should be descriptive and follow clear conventions where possible. We'll offer some suggestions, but they should be taken as just that:

suggestions. Think of them more as examples on which you could base your own naming conventions. The most important thing here is consistency: Try to adopt clear rules for naming things, and do your best to stick to them.

DATABASES AND TABLES   Each database file (a collection of tables) should be named for its overall function. If one file contains all the tables for an invoicing module, call the database Invoicing, not Module A.

For tables, we recommend that you name the table according to the type of thing that it stores. For intermediate join tables, you should give thought to the function of the table and then decide what thing it represents. So a join table between Student and Class could be called StudentClass, but is better called Enrollment. A join table between Magazine and Customer is called Subscription, a join table between Book and Library is Holding, and so forth.

TIP

> Additionally, we like our table names to be in the singular. So a table of customers is called Customer, a table of pets is called Pet, and so forth.

Some join tables don't really evoke a natural function, in which case you may need to fall back on a less descriptive name that just incorporates the names of each file: ProjectEmployee, for example, or OrderPayment.

Some tables are naturally line item files. The children of other files, which are generally accessed through portals, are characteristic of certain kinds of business documents. Order line items and invoice line items are common examples. Calling these OrderLine or InvoiceLine seems to make sense.

FileMaker 8 presents another naming challenge as well, with the existence of the table occurrences that populate the Relationships Graph. A number of developers feel that it's helpful to name these tables in some way that indicates their base table, so that if the same base table has multiple occurrences in the Graph, it's possible to discern this fact easily.

When it comes to field naming conventions, the debates among FileMaker developers often assume the character of holy wars (much like the arguments about bracing style among C programmers). We're not going to inject ourselves here and make any strong pronouncements—we'll just offer a few thinking points.

→ For additional discussion of field naming conventions, **see** "Field Naming Conventions," **p. 70**.

FIELDS   One of the main issues with fields in FileMaker is that they're a superset of what we normally think of as database fields. FileMaker fields include, of course, the classic fields, which are those that store static data, generally entered by users. But they also include fields with global storage, which are not data fields at all, but programming variables. They include calculation fields, which are in fact small functions, units of programming logic. And they include summary fields, which are actually aggregating instructions intended for display in reports.

You, as a developer, need to decide what things you need to be able to distinguish quickly in this thicket of fields, and devise a suitable naming scheme. Generally, we like to be able to pick out the following database elements quickly:

- User data
- Globally stored fields
- Structural database keys

Distinguishing globals and keys is easy. One common practice is to prefix global field names with a *g*, and keys with a *k*, plus another letter to describe the type of key: *kp* for primary keys, *kf* for foreign keys. When you sort your field list alphabetically, all the key names clump together and you have easy access to your fundamental structural elements.

> We often go one step further in naming key fields. For primary keys, we precede the field name with a double underscore (__), and then "kp" to signify a primary key. For foreign keys, we precede the field name with a single underscore and the designation "kf". The effect of this convention is to cause all the key fields to sort to the top of an alphabetized field list in FileMaker, and also for the primary key to sort to the very top, above all foreign keys. This makes it very easy to access the keys when building relationships in the Relationships Graph.

17

Making a broad distinction between user fields and developer fields is harder. Those that try to do this generally adopt some kind of overall field name prefix. It's not uncommon to see a scheme where all developer fields are prefixed with an additional *z*. This puts them all together at the end of the field list, and uses an uncommon letter that's unlikely to overlap with the first letter of a user field (well, except ZIP code, which is common, but you can fudge this by calling the ZIP a "postal code" instead). In a z-based scheme, globals might be prefixed with *zg* and keys with *zkp* or *zkf*.

There are those that swear by such naming schemes, and an equal number that swear *at* them. We recommend that you think very carefully before deciding you don't need *some* kind of field-naming scheme. Admittedly, such a scheme takes discipline to keep up. You should choose a scheme that at least makes certain things such as keys and globals clear; then you can decide whether you need more. Again, no matter which convention you choose, consistency is the important thing.

LAYOUTS   With naming layouts, again, we'd advocate that you have some clear naming scheme to distinguish between layouts your users interact with directly and those that you build for behind-the-scenes use. One general rule is to prefix the names of all "developer" layouts with `Dev_` or a similar tag.

As with table names, FileMaker 8 gives an additional twist to layout naming because layouts are each associated with an underlying table occurrence and base table. Some developers have argued that it's a good idea to include the base table name in all layout names, as an easy way to indicate what kind of records will display on the layout.

SCRIPTS   With scripts, it's hard to provide any clear guidelines, especially because—unlike the Create Database field listing—script names can't be sorted, and so you can't take great advantage of any clever naming scheme. You should try to keep your scripts grouped, using dummy divider scripts to create the groups. Other organizational tricks include adding prefixes to scripts, such as Btn: for scripts intended to be called by pressing a button, Nav: for scripts whose function is navigational, and so on. In some ways the script organization problem is more daunting in FileMaker 7 and 8 than in earlier versions because scripts that used to live in multiple files might all now live in one single file.

OTHER ELEMENTS   There are, of course, still other areas where improper names can sow confusion, such as the naming of value lists, extended privileges, and custom functions. Function and parameter naming are especially important, so we'll touch on that area as well.

It pays to take care when naming custom functions, custom function parameters, and also the temporary local variables you create in a Let statement. A few simple choices here can greatly add to the clarity of your code or greatly detract from it.

Suppose that you have a custom function intended to compute a sales commission, with a single parameter, intended to represent a salesperson's gross sales for the month. To be fully descriptive, you should call this parameter something like grossMonthlySales. That might seem like a lot to type, but if you call it something short and efficient like gms you'll be scratching your head over it in a few months' time. The longer name will stay descriptive.

> **NOTE**
> Notice the capitalization in grossMonthlySales. For custom function parameters, script variables, and Let variables, we like to use a style called *camel case*, popular among Java programmers, in which the first letter of the first word is lowercase and all other words in the name begin with uppercase. We don't use this convention for field names by the way—there we prefer title case.

→ For additional discussion of custom functions, **see** "Custom Functions," **p. 420**.

 We would apply similar naming considerations to the new local and global script variables available in the FileMaker 8 product line. These variables, of course, have a mandatory element in their names in that they must be prefixed with $ (for local variables) or $$ (for global variables). Beyond that, though, we follow the same guidelines: clear and, if necessary, somewhat verbose variable names, and a consistent casing convention such as camel case.

→ For additional discussion of script variables, **see** "Script Variables," **p. 448**.

USING COMMENTS WISELY

A *comment* is a note that you, the programmer, insert into the logic of your program to clarify the intent or meaning of some piece of it. You can use comments many different ways, but we strongly suggest you find ways that work for you, and use them.

FileMaker 8 offers a number of useful commenting facilities. Whereas in previous versions of the product you could add comments only to scripts, FileMaker 7 and 8 permit you to add them onto field definitions, and inside the body of calculations as well.

To add a comment to a field, just type your note into the Comment box in the field definition dialog. To view comments, you need to toggle the Comments/Options column of the field list—the list can display comments or options, but not both at once.

Comments can be useful for almost any field. They can be used to clarify the business significance of user data fields, or to add clarity to the use of global and summary fields. Figure 17.1 shows a field list with comments liberally applied.

Figure 17.1
Adding comments to your field definitions can provide useful clarification.

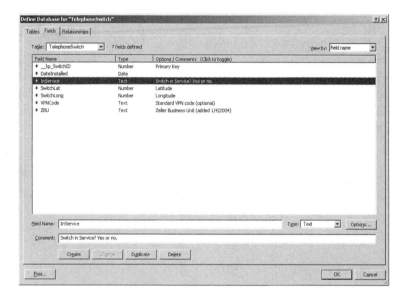

Also present in FileMaker 8 is the capability to insert comments into the text of calculations and custom functions. We recommend you make use of this new feature to clarify complex calculations.

Finally, FileMaker enables you to add comments to your scripts. Some developers have elaborate script commenting disciplines. They may create an entire header of comments with space for the names of everyone who's worked on it, the creation date, and even a full modification history. Figure 17.2 shows an example of such a commenting style.

Figure 17.2
Using script comments to keep a copious revision history for a script.

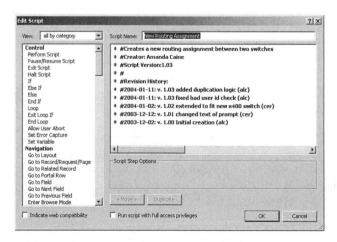

Other developers use script comments more sparingly, reserving them for places where the flow of the script is less than self-explanatory, or for guiding the reader through the different cases of a complex logic flow. Short, pointed comments throughout a lengthy script can add a great deal to its clarity.

Some developers scorn comments altogether, swearing that they can instantly understand their own programs even if they come back to them cold six months or a year later. Well, even if that were true (and it surely is for some people), it ignores the fact that you need to write programs to be read not only by you, but by anyone who comes after you. Someday, others will probably have to maintain and extend what you wrote. Of course, if they can't make heads or tails of it, they're much more likely just to conclude that it's simpler to scrap it and rewrite it.

TIP

> Commenting increases the longevity of your code, and we recommend you learn about the different commenting options that FileMaker allows.

→ For more information on how to use comments, **see** "Using Comments Effectively," **p. 843**.

WRITING MODULAR CODE

Modularity is one of those popular buzzwords for which it seems every programmer has a different interpretation. To us, a modular program is one that avoids unnecessary duplication of effort. Much as the concept of database normalization encourages that each piece of information be stored once and only once in a database, you should try to program in such a way that you avoid (as much as possible) writing multiple routines that do the same or similar things. Try instead to write that routine or piece of logic once and then draw on it in many places.

MODULARITY IN SCRIPTS   As a simple example, let's say you're working with a system that prints a lot of reports. Many of the reports need to be printed to a special printer, on legal-size paper, with certain paper-handling options specific to the printer. Well, naturally, you'll have scripts to print each of the reports, and you could simply have a Print Setup step in each script that sets up the printer and page handling correctly. But there are two problems with this. In the first place, you'll have to set up those print options for each and every script in which you want to use them. The more times you do this, the greater the odds that you'll make a mistake. Further, if you ever need to change those options, you need to track down every place you've set them up and change them there.

A better practice would be to write a single script called "Print Setup Report Legal" or something to that effect. All the script does is set the print options—nothing more. When you need to call up that set of print options, call the script. When you need to change the options, change the script. This way you have to write the logic once, and you only ever need to change it in one place.

FileMaker 7 and 8 offer several powerful features that can greatly increase the modularity of your code if used with discipline. Three of the most important are custom functions, script parameters, and script results (a new addition in FileMaker 8). These topics have been covered thoroughly in their respective chapters, but it's worthwhile to bring them up here again. You should thoroughly understand the mechanics and uses of custom functions and script parameters, and use them aggressively to make your code more general and extendable. (Bear in mind that custom functions can be created only with FileMaker Pro 8 Advanced, not with the regular FileMaker Pro 8 product.)

→ For more on custom functions, **see** "Creating Custom Functions," **p. 423**.

→ For more on script parameters and script results, **see** "Script Parameters, Script Results, and Script I/O," **p. 436**.

Like other areas in FileMaker, even seasoned developers can disagree on the best way to do things. Some developers use custom functions more aggressively, some less so. To finish off this section let's look at an example of the aggressive use of custom functions to make code more abstract.

MODULARITY USING CUSTOM FUNCTIONS   Let's say we're dealing with a simple problem: We have a system that deals with billing of some kind, and our client has asked that bills that are more than 30 days old appear with their date written in a red color in the billing list.

FileMaker's new text formatting calculations make that a snap. Let's say the table has a field called DueDate and another called DueDateDisplay. If the DueDate is less than 30 days ago, the DueDateDisplay field contains the date in a black color; otherwise it contains the date in a red color. It's easy enough to write a calculation for DueDateDisplay that does all these things:

```
Case( Get(CurrentDate) - DueDate <= 30; GetAsText(DueDate); TextColor
➥(GetAsText(DueDate); RGB ( 255 ; 0 ; 0 ) ))
```

Well, that works, but there are things that could be better about it. For one thing, it hard-codes quite a number of different elements: What if the rules change so that "past due" happens at 45 days? What if they want the color to be a different shade of red? If those things are being used in multiple places, you'll have to hunt them all down and change them. The second problem with this setup is that it works only for the specific field called DueDate. If you wanted to perform similar logic elsewhere, you'd have some duplication to do.

Let's tackle these issues one at a time, using custom functions. Chapter 14, "Advanced Calculation Techniques," discusses the possibility of using custom functions for system constants to abstract out hard-coded values. That's a good place to start. Define one custom function, called getOverDueLimit. That function takes no parameters, and always returns 30. The next thing is to define another custom calc called getOverdueHighlight, and define it to always return RGB(255;0;0).

So far, so good. This abstracts out some of the hard-coded values. Next, you need a generic way to determine whether a record is overdue. You could write a custom function called isOverdue(dateValue), defined as follows:

```
Case( dateValue + getOverdueLimit > Get(CurrentDate); 0; 1)
```

This function takes a dateValue, compares it to the current date and the value from getOverdueLimit, and returns a 0 or 1 depending on whether or not the date is overdue.

17

The next function is called `colorIfOverdue( dateValue, textValue, rgbColor)`. This function's job is to take a date, a piece of text, and a color, and apply the color to the text if the date is overdue. The definition looks like this:

```
Case( not IsOverdue ( dateValue ); textValue;
➡TextColor ( textValue ; rgbColor) )
// last parameter needs to be an RGB color value, i.e. the result of RGB(x,y,z)
```

(Notice, by the way, that this function uses a comment to clarify the data type of the third parameter.) This function draws on the previously created `isOverdue` function to do its work. Notice also that this function doesn't assume anything about the color to apply to the text, or even what the text is—it just applies *a* color to *a* text string based on a date.

With these custom functions created, it's finally time to do some work based on actual fields. So the `DueDateDisplay` field can now be redefined very simply as

```
colorIfOverdue ( GetAsText(DueDate); DueDate, getOverdueHighlight() )
```

It might seem like that was a lot of work, but look at the advantages. If you decide you want a different color for all your overdue highlights, you need to change only the definition of `getOverdueHighlight`. If you decide to let bills go 45 days instead of 30, you need to change only the definition of `isOverdue()`. And if you need additional fields to highlight according to whether a record is overdue, you don't need to replicate any of the core logic; just create another display field like `DueDateDisplay` that references a different base field, and you're in business.

That's an example of what we'd call fairly aggressive use of custom functions to achieve a high degree of modularity and flexibility. As with any technique, it's possible to overdo it. As a general rule of thumb, try to abstract out those elements of the logic that seem to have the most potential to change or be duplicated. As another general rule of thumb, additional layers of abstraction can make a program harder to understand at first glance. Make sure that you provide sufficient comments for later readers to understand your elegant abstraction.

PLANNING FOR TROUBLE

The previous sections suggested a few approaches you can follow to make your programming easier to troubleshoot. But errors *will* happen. As you build systems, you need to expect errors, and plan for how to handle them. Many programmers (too many) make the mistake of assuming that things will always work correctly. Their programs behave perfectly well, as long as nothing unexpected happens. But when a user enters data they didn't expect, or a network connection drops, suddenly the program ceases to behave gracefully, and its behavior becomes what we call (charitably) "undefined."

Let's take a simple example. You have a FileMaker system that periodically needs to import data from some other source. Imagine that the FileMaker system contains a table of manufacturers, and the manufacturer data is actually being fetched from an Oracle system via an XML Import. The update is intended to be a destructive update, meaning that the new data completely replaces the old. You want to perform all this work via a script, so you write the following (naï[um]ve) script:

```
Go to Layout ["Manufacturers"]
Show All Records
Delete All Records [No dialog]
Import Records [No dialog: http://my.mfg.com/mfg_update?code=3]
```

That *seems* right. Find all the current manufacturers, delete them, and import the new ones. But it's not right; it's dead wrong. What if the import step fails (for example, because the web server at http://my.mfg.com is down for maintenance)? Well, you've already deleted all your manufacturers, and now you have no way to fetch new ones, for who knows how long. Much better to go on with a slightly outdated manufacturer list than none at all.

The deletion step could fail as well—for example, if users had one or more records locked. If this happens and you don't catch it, you end up with duplicate manufacturers, which could be a serious problem.

The right way to do this is to perform the import *first*. If and only if it succeeds, you can then find the old records and delete them. The script should look like Listing 17.1.

LISTING 17.1   CORRECT IMPORT SCRIPT

```
Import Records [No dialog: http://my.mfg.com/mfg_update?code=3]
If[ Get( LastError ) <> 0 ]
    Exit Script
Else
    Show Omitted Only
    Delete All Records [No dialog]
End If
```

This still isn't perfect, but it's much better. To make it better still, you'd need to examine what the exact error was during the import to decide whether some records had been imported and needed to be deleted. But it prevents the worst case, which is an empty manufacturer table.

→ For more on FileMaker's XML Import feature, which we posited as a possible source for the data in this example, **see** "XML Import: Understanding Web Services," **p. 683**.

It's easy to produce other examples of this kind. They all boil down to the same logical error: the unwarranted assumption that a specific step is going to work. The only time that it's okay to make this assumption is if there's no significant penalty for being wrong. For example, imagine you have a script that finds all invoices over 30 days old and changes their status from Current to Past Due. It's possible that the search will fail and find no records. But in that case it's innocuous to go on and perform the Replace step—it will operate on a found set of zero records and will have no effect.

So, one of the most important ways to avoid software defects (the graceful term for bugs) is to be aware of all the possible failure points in your system, and, most importantly, *calculate the consequences of failure*. Good programmers do this instinctively. They have a clear sense of what will happen if some element of their program fails. The question is never a surprise to them, and they almost always know the answer.

TROUBLESHOOTING SCRIPTS AND CALCULATIONS

There are many specific areas of potential trouble in FileMaker, and we'll get to those in the next section. Here, though, we want to discuss some general principles for dealing with errors in scripts and calculations.

HANDLING ERRORS IN SCRIPTS

Many FileMaker actions can result in an error. Error in this context can mean any exceptional condition that needs to be reported to the user. This can be something as simple as a search that returns no records or a field that fails to pass validation, or it can be a more esoteric error involving something like a missing key field. In general, in the normal operation of FileMaker, these errors get reported to the user via a dialog box of some kind, often with some sort of choice as to how to proceed.

For example, as shown in Figure 17.3, if a user performs a search that finds no records, she gets a dialog alerting her to the error and she has the option to go back and redefine her search.

Figure 17.3
FileMaker generally provides a lot of feedback on error conditions, such as this "no records found" message.

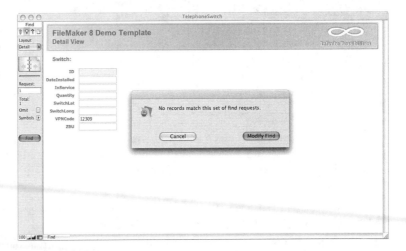

This is fine, up to a point. But you, the developer, may not want the user to see this default FileMaker dialog. You may want to present a different message, or none at all. Well, if your user performs her searches by dropping into Find mode, filling in some search criteria, and clicking the Find button, there's not much you can do. But if your user is performing a find via a script that you've written, you can intervene in such situations.

NOTE

Using the Custom Menus feature of FileMaker Pro 8 Advanced, you can now bridge the gap between applications that rely mostly on the native, menu-driven functionality of FileMaker and those that provide much of their functionality through scripts. Using Custom Menus, you can override selected menu items from the regular FileMaker menu set and attach your own scripted functionality to them. You could, for example, replace the generic Find command in FileMaker's View menu with a menu item called Find Customers, and tie that menu item to a specific, customized Find script of your own devising.

→ For more on custom menus, **see** "Working with Custom Menus," **p. 373**.

There's a very important script step called Set Error Capture. It's worth your while to become familiar with it. This step allows you to tell FileMaker whether or not to suppress error messages while your script is running. The use of the step is shown in Figure 17.4.

Figure 17.4

The Set Error Capture script step is useful for controlling how FileMaker errors are displayed to the user.

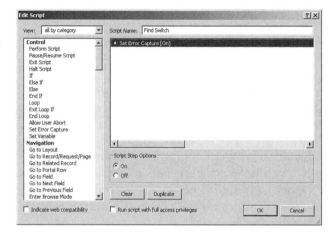

If this step is not present in a script, or if it's present and set to "off," FileMaker reports errors to the user directly. If your script performs a search, and no records are found, your users see the usual FileMaker dialog box for that situation (shown in Figure 17.3). However, if you have error capture set to "on," the user sees no visible response of any kind. After you've set the error capture state (on or off), this setting is carried down through all subscripts as well, unless you explicitly disable it by using Set Error Capture [Off] somewhere down in a subscript.

In general, you don't just turn error capture on and walk away. In fact, error capture obliges you to do a lot more work than you normally might. With error capture on, FileMaker error dialogs are suppressed, so it's up to you to check for errors and either handle them or inform the user of those that are important.

As an example of custom error handling, suppose that you've built a system that primarily stores text content in a variety of forms: press releases, biographies, articles, and so on. If a user does a search in one area and finds no results, you'd like to offer the option to search in other areas as well. Rather than let FileMaker intervene and show the standard No Records Found dialog, you want to pop up a custom dialog that allows the user to run a different scripted search on a different table or just give up. The script might look like the one in Figure 17.5.

Here, Set Error Capture is turned on and the script is configured to check whether the user's search found any records. If so, he's sent to the article list. If not, the custom dialog with other search choices is offered. If he picks a different type of search, the appropriate script runs; otherwise the script is exited and he is left where he was.

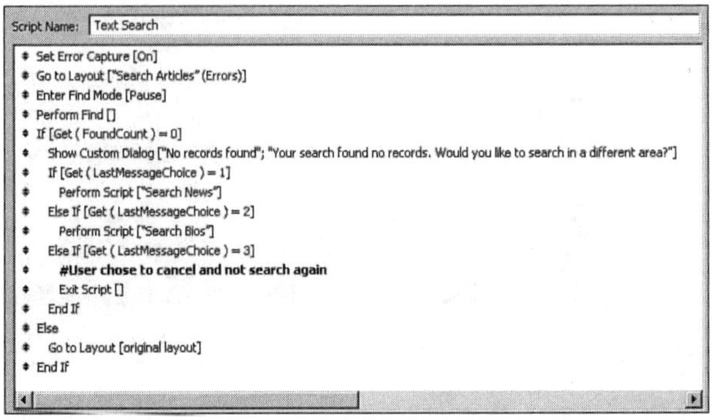

Figure 17.5
Within a script, you can use Set Error Capture to hide the usual error messages and display custom feedback to the user.

In addition to checking for specific conditions (such as a found count of zero), it's also possible to check more generically to determine whether the previous script step produced an error. This technique was shown in Listing 17.1, which used the Get(LastError) function. This function returns whatever error code was produced by the most recent operation. An error code of 0 means "no error." Otherwise, an error of some kind has occurred. In Listing 17.1, as written, it didn't matter too much exactly which error had occurred—it was enough to know that *some* error had happened.

→ For a complete listing and description of FileMaker error codes, **see** Chapter 11, "FileMaker Error Codes," in *FileMaker 8 Functions & Scripts Desk Reference*.

Get(LastError) can be tricky. It reports on the most recent action taken no matter whether the action was triggered directly by a user or by a script. Let's say you have the following script fragment:

```
Set Error Capture [On]
Perform Find[]
Go To Layout ["Search Results"]
If[ Get(LastError)<>0 ]
    Show Message ["An error has occurred"]
End If
```

This is not going to do quite what you would hope. If the Perform Find script step found no records, at that point the "last error" would be 401 (the code for "no records found"). But after the Go To Layout step runs, that error code no longer applies. If that step runs successfully (which it might not if, for example, the particular user didn't have privileges to view that layout), the last error code would now be 0. So, if you want to check for errors, check for them at the exact point of possible failure, not a couple of steps down the road.

Note also that the concept of "last error" is specific to each client session. This means that if another user, in his session, generates an error, this has no effect on the "last error" status in other sessions.

TRACKING DOWN ERRORS

Suppose that, despite your best efforts at defensive programming, some aspect of your system just doesn't work right. (Actually, you don't need to suppose. This *will* happen, and what's more, it'll happen after the software is delivered. That's not cynicism; it's just reality.)

When this happens, of course, you'll want to track the problem down and fix it. There are a couple of verbs you'll want to keep in mind: *reproduce* and *isolate*.

REPRODUCING ERRORS

The first thing to do with any problem is to render it reproducible. Bugs that occur only occasionally are a programmer's worst nightmare. Often the circumstances are clear and entirely reproducible: "If I hit Cancel in the search script, I end up on some goofy-looking utility layout, instead of back at the main search screen." At other times, the problem is more slippery: "Sometimes, when I mark an invoice as closed, the system creates a duplicate of that invoice!"

If the bug is not transparently reproducible, you need to gather as much data on the bug as you can. Who experienced it? What type of computer and what operating system? Has it been experienced by one user, or several? Does it appear consistently? Look for hidden patterns. Does it occur more at certain times of day? Only from specific computers? Only for a particular account or privilege set? Only during the last week of the fiscal quarter? And so on.

Reproducing the bug should be your first priority because you can't isolate it until it's reproducible, and isolating it is your best means of fixing it.

You might find that you, yourself, are unable to make the bug happen. This may be a sign that you are using the software differently from your users. Your usage pattern may never cause the bug to happen. One way to leap this hurdle is just to sit down with a user and watch him work. You might find that he's using a feature of the software differently than you had intended or expected, or that he performs functions in a different order. This may give you the clue you need.

What if, despite all these efforts, the bug remains elusive? You can see its tracks but can't catch it. Well, you have a few choices. One is to program around it. If users report that, very occasionally, they get duplicate invoices when they close an invoice, you can rewrite the invoice-closing script to check for duplicates and eliminate an extra one when it appears. This doesn't eliminate the bug, but it does repair the effects. This is a distinctly less-than-perfect solution, but if it solves the problem and makes the system work again, that's what counts. But the bug is still in there, possibly causing other mischief.

Another possibility is to try to do some kind of logging. For example, in the duplicate invoice case, you could add some logic to the Close Invoice script. In addition to all the work it normally does, it would also create an entry in a new Log table. It would write out the time the script was run, the username, the system IP address, and the platform. Then, at the end of the script, it would check for duplication and log the findings. Even if you were programming around the bug at this point, to buy time, you could still use this log information to try to pin down the bug. Let the system run for a month, and then look at the log and try to pick out any patterns in when the bug happens.

DEBUGGING CALCULATIONS

After you've reproduced the bug (you hope), it's time to *isolate* it. Let's think about calculations for a moment. Suppose that you have a complex calculation like the one in Listing 17.2.

This calculation expresses a person's age (the DOB field) as something like "38 years, 5 months, 9 days."

LISTING 17.2 COMPLEX CALCULATION EXAMPLE

```
Let (
 [ Today = Get(CurrentDate);
   DOBDay=Day(DOB);
   TodayDay = Day(Today) ] ;

GetAsText(Year(Today) - Year(DOB) - Case(Today< Date(Month(DOB);
➥DOBDay; Year(Today)); 1; 0)) & " Years, " &

GetAsText(Mod(Month(Today) - Month(DOB) + 12 -
➥Case(TodayDay <> DOBDay; 1; 0); 12)) & " Months, " &

GetAsText(TodayDay - DOBDay + Case(TodayDay >= DOBDay; 0; Day(Today- TodayDay)
< DOBDay; DOBDay; Day(Today - TodayDay))) & " Days")
```

Actually, as written, the calculation does have a bug, and will generally give the wrong value for the Days element. How do you debug this lengthy calculation?

NOTE

> Lengthy though this calculation is, FileMaker's Let statement makes the formula much more readable, and hence easier to debug.

One nice thing about this calculation is that it's actually three smaller calculations merged into one. To isolate the problem in this calculation, you need to examine each individual piece and see whether it gives the expected result. Here you could pull out just the piece that computes the Days value, like so:

```
Let (
 [ Today = Get(CurrentDate);
   DOBDay=Day(DOB);
   TodayDay = Day(Today) ] ;

/*
GetAsText(Year(Today) - Year(DOB) - Case(Today< Date(Month(DOB);
➥DOBDay; Year(Today)); 1; 0)) & " Years, " &

GetAsText(Mod(Month(Today) - Month(DOB) + 12 -
➥Case(TodayDay <> DOBDay; 1; 0); 12)) & " Months, " & */

GetAsText(TodayDay - DOBDay + Case(TodayDay >= DOBDay; 0; Day(Today- TodayDay)
< DOBDay; DOBDay; Day(Today - TodayDay))) & " Days")
```

In the preceding example, two subunits of logic have been commented out so that the calculation now performs only the logic of the third unit, relative to the Days figure. Selective commenting like this is a powerful debugging technique, especially if your calculations are nicely modularized using the Let function.

You'll find this subunit behaves the same way when isolated from the rest of the calculation, and now your problem has shrunk in size. It shouldn't take you long to find that the <> (not equals) in the second line is a slip of the hand, and should just be < (less than).

As a general rule, we recommend that you debug complex calculations by breaking them down into smaller pieces and using techniques like those above to test subunits of the calculation code. This suggestion contains a strong implication for how you should build complex calculations in the first place: Define and test the smaller pieces of functionality first, and then add additional pieces to the calculation. Or, if there's anything at all reusable in the smaller pieces, don't just fold them into a larger calculation, but define them as custom functions instead.

TIP

> For easy debugging of calculation fragments like the one shown previously, you have a couple of choices. If you're not using FileMaker Pro Advanced (and you probably should be!), you can define two new fields in the problem table: a `CalcSource` field (which holds a calculation fragment), and a `CalcEval` field (well, the names can be whatever you like) that's a calculation defined as `Evaluate(CalcSource)`. Anything you cut and paste from the problem calc into the `CalcSource` field will be evaluated by the `CalcEval` field. This beats defining entirely new fields to hold your calculation fragments.
>
> If you're using FileMaker Pro Advanced, the Evaluate Now feature of the FileMaker Advanced Data Viewer will let you evaluate any calculation or expression on the fly, and it can act as a kind of scratchpad for calculation testing.

The key to the idea of isolation is specifically to isolate the broken part. Pull out the pieces that are known to work. As you test each piece, remove it if it tests out correctly. As you do this, the area that contains the problem grows smaller and smaller.

DEBUGGING SCRIPTS

 The principle of isolation applies to scripts as well as to calculations. Your problem may lie inside one script, or you might have a complex chain of scripts and subscripts that's exhibiting failure. By far the best tools available for this are the Script Debugger and the Data Viewer, which are part of FileMaker Pro 8 Advanced. The Data Viewer is an extremely handy addition in FileMaker 8.

The Script Debugger vastly simplifies the process of script debugging, which once upon a time (prior to FileMaker 7) relied chiefly on the insertion of numerous Pause Script and Show Message script steps! But debugging scripts is still not an automatic process. In this section, we'll walk you through the tools and how to use them.

ABOUT THE SCRIPT DEBUGGER   The Script Debugger (and its close companion the Data Viewer) are tools that are available only in FileMaker Pro Advanced. This alone is reason enough to invest in Advanced. Trying to troubleshoot a complex script without reasonable debugging tools is a bit like trying to assemble a jigsaw puzzle with your eyes closed. It's not strictly impossible, but it's much harder than it needs to be.

Script debugging can be enabled or disabled from within FileMaker Advanced at any time by choosing Debug Scripts from the Tools menu. The next time a script is triggered, whether by clicking a button, opening a file, or some other means, the Script Debugger will appear. The Script Debugger interface is shown in Figure 17.6.

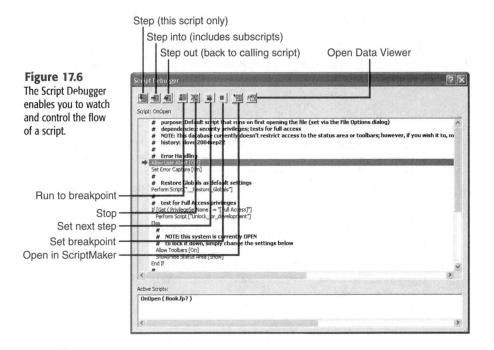

Step (this script only)
Step into (includes subscripts)
Step out (back to calling script)   Open Data Viewer

Figure 17.6
The Script Debugger enables you to watch and control the flow of a script.

Run to breakpoint
Stop
Set next step
Set breakpoint
Open in ScriptMaker

Using the Script Debugger, you can step through a script line by line as it executes. You can see when and whether it follows a certain logical path (which branch gets followed when it encounters an If statement, for example), when and how it breaks out of a loop, and which subscripts it calls, for example. Using the Data Viewer, you can see how record and calculation data change as the script runs (we'll say more about the Data Viewer later on).

Figure 17.6 shows the tools available in the Script Debugger. Most of them have to do with controlling the flow of the script. In general, you'll want to step through the script line by line (using the Step command), but you'll also often want to follow the execution path into subscripts (the Step Into command). Sometimes, when you're inside a subscript, you might want to finish with the subscript and start debugging step-by-step again back in the parent script (the Step Out command).

You can also stop the script altogether, open it in ScriptMaker, or use the breakpoint features to allow even more precise control over script execution. We discuss breakpoints in the following section.

PLACING BREAKPOINTS   The Script Debugger enables you to place a breakpoint in a script so that execution stops there and you can see what's happening. In theory, if you have a troublesome script or script chain, you could place a breakpoint at the very start and step through the script. But if this is a lengthy script chain, or one than contains a loop that might run many times, this may not be very time effective.

Consider a case where you have a complex set of scripts that call each other—let's say that there are three scripts total. Somewhere in the middle of that script, a date field on the current record is getting wiped out, but you don't know where.

In a case like this, you can use a classic isolation technique called *binary search*. If you have no idea where the problem is happening, place a breakpoint more or less in the middle of everything, say halfway through script #2. Turn on the Script Debugger, let the script run, and see whether the field has been wiped out by the time you stop at the breakpoint. If the problem has already occurred, move the breakpoint to around the midpoint of the first half of the script chain (that is, 25%) and try again. If it hasn't happened by the 50% mark, move the breakpoint to 75%. Repeat until you narrow the possible range to one or two lines. This may sound like it's not much of a time-saver, but using this technique can find the error in a script of over 1,000 lines using at most ten of these check-and-move operations.

TIP

> If you have to a debug a looping script, it's worthwhile to try to reduce the number of records on which the script runs. In general, if you need to debug the loop itself, one internal breakpoint should suffice at first, either at the beginning or end of the loop.

INSPECTING VALUES   One of the most important uses of a debugger is to watch certain values and see how they change. These could be database fields, global variables, or aspects of FileMaker state such as the current layout.

 FileMaker Pro 8 Advanced adds a new debugging tool called the Data Viewer. Using this tool, you can monitor any number of data values at a time. Previously, you might have had to create special debugging layouts to display the information you wanted, but the Data Viewer makes all that go away. You can display the Data Viewer at any time, though you'll probably use it most often while debugging scripts.

Like the Debug Scripts option, you can find the Data Viewer in the Tools menu of FileMaker Pro Advanced. The Data Viewer presents a list of expressions, along with the current value of each expression. This view is shown in Figure 17.7.

Figure 17.7
FileMaker's Data Viewer, with a list of expressions being monitored.

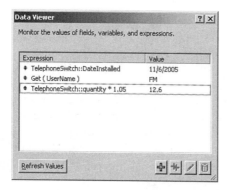

So, what's an *expression*? Probably the best way to think of it is anything you can type into a calculation dialog box. If you can type it into a calculation dialog window, click OK, and have FileMaker accept it without warning of any errors, it's a valid expression. For example, the following are all expressions:

```
CustomerID // the name of a field

Product::ProductID // the name of a related field

MyHighlight(InvoiceDate) // a call to a custom function

Quantity * 1.05 // a math expression involving a field
```

The Data Viewer has its own interface for defining expressions, shown in Figure 17.8. It's almost identical to the regular calculation dialog box but adds the button called Evaluate Now. Clicking it will put the expression's result into the Result box down below. This is quite a nifty "sleeper" feature. If you are trying to build a complex calculation, you can use the Data Viewer's Evaluate Now feature to test the calculation, or pieces of it, very rapidly—no need to define a custom function or calculation field, save the changes, and go look at data on a record layout. Like the Script Debugger, the Data Viewer is a floating window that will hover above your other windows as you work.

TIP

> Use the Evaluate Now feature of the Data Viewer (available only in FileMaker Pro 8 Advanced) as a calculation scratch pad for testing calculations or calculation expressions before reusing them in custom functions or calculation fields.

Figure 17.8
The Data Viewer's expression builder presents an interface very similar to the Define Calculation dialog box.

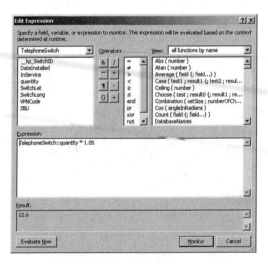

As an example of a typical use of the Data Viewer, consider the example of a script that mysteriously clears out a field. You'd like to step through the script line by line and find out when that happens. Your first step is to bring up the Data Viewer, create a new expression, and type the name of the field in question as your expression. When the expression appears in the Data Viewer window, it's being monitored, and you can turn on Debug Scripts (if it's not on already) and run your script. Using the various stepping operations, you can move slowly through the script, watching the expressions you're monitoring and seeing how they change. In this case, you can watch the field expression and pin down the exact step where the field gets cleared.

The Data Viewer is a critical tool in FileMaker troubleshooting, and we heartily recommend you become familiar with it.

NEW INTERACTIVE CALL STACK   There's one more convenient addition to the Script Debugger in FileMaker 8. It's sometimes called the *interactive call stack*. It's always been the case that, if you're debugging a script that in turn calls other scripts, the Script Debugger will show you any parent or grandparent that might have called the current script. This call chain, or *call stack*, as it's sometimes known, is shown near the bottom of the Script Debugger. Figure 17.9 shows this tool in use.

Figure 17.9
The interactive call stack enables you to flip backward to previous scripts in the call chain.

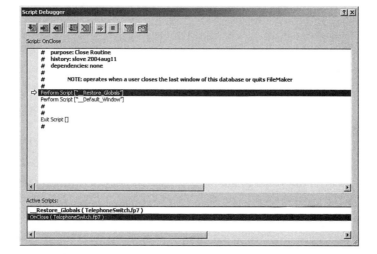

In FileMaker Pro 8 Advanced, not only can you see the call chain, but if you click on a script further up the call chain, the script will now display that script in the main window, along with a marker that shows where the flow of control left that script (usually at a `Perform Script` step). This is a handy convenience if you need to be reminded of what steps brought you to the current location in the current script.

TROUBLESHOOTING IN SPECIFIC AREAS: PERFORMANCE, CONTEXT, CONNECTIVITY, AND GLOBALS

The individual troubleshooting sections in each chapter of this book cover particular isolated "gotchas" that we've wanted to highlight. In this section, we want to do two things: We want to talk generally about broad areas of potential FileMaker trouble and how to diagnose them, and we want to talk about a number of specific areas that don't pop up in the other chapters, or at least don't get a comprehensive treatment.

PERFORMANCE

"The system is slow!" Performance is a critical part of the user experience. What can you do if things seem slow? Well, first of course, it's important to *isolate* the problem. Is just one area of the system slow, or one particular function? Or does the system generally seem sluggish? In general here, we're assuming that your solution is a multiuser solution hosted under FileMaker Server, but most remarks (except those entirely specific to Server) apply equally to Server and non-Server configurations.

GENERAL SLOWNESS

If a FileMaker application seems generally sluggish and slow to respond, the leading candidates are insufficient hardware (client, server, or both), improper server configuration, or insufficient network resources. The last two apply only when the files are being hosted on FileMaker Server.

Hardware is a straightforward issue. Read and understand the hardware requirements for the client and server computers. If you plan on having many users on the server, please don't skimp on the server hardware! Get the very best machine you can afford. Likewise, on the desktop, try to meet or exceed the stated standards.

If you're not hosting the files on FileMaker Server, but rather have a peer-to-peer configuration, and things seem slow, you should seriously consider moving to Server.

If you're working with FileMaker Server, you also need to make sure that your server settings are configured correctly for your situation. In particular, you'll want to look at things such as the percentage of cache hits, the frequency with which the cache is flushed, and the amount of RAM dedicated to the file cache size.

→ For a full treatment of FileMaker Server settings, **see** "Configuring and Administering FileMaker Server Using the SAT," **p. 788**.

If you're using Server and all the hardware seems reasonable, it's time to look at your network. You should know your network's exact topology. What connections are there, at what speeds? Where are the routers, switches, and hubs? What other traffic besides FileMaker traffic flows over the network? FileMaker is fastest over a LAN at speeds of 10 megabits and higher. In general it's better not to try to run FileMaker over a network link that's slower than T1 speed (1.544 megabits). All other things being equal, a fully switched network is better than not, and of course a 100-megabit LAN is better than a 10-megabit LAN, if they're both built correctly. FileMaker, like any networked service, also suffers from competition with other services running over the same wire.

You should also be familiar with your firewall situation. Does FileMaker traffic need to pass through any firewalls or packet filters? This can slow things down as well.

A last point is that FileMaker Server can be set to encrypt traffic between the client and the server. This encryption is somewhat processor-intensive and may impose a performance penalty. If you're experiencing slowness in a client-server environment, and you're using client-server encryption, you may want to disable the encryption and see whether that makes a difference. If so, you may need to consider investing in faster hardware.

SLOWNESS IN SEARCHING AND SORTING

Searching and sorting are among the operations that, in a Server configuration, are handled chiefly by the server. So it's possible the slowness in searching or sorting is symptomatic of some general networking issue of the type discussed in the previous section.

It's also possible that there's a problem with the search or sort itself. In terms of performance, the cardinal sin is to execute a search or a sort based on one or more *unindexed* fields. This, of course, means that there's no index for the field, which in turn condemns FileMaker to examining each and every record in the database—somewhat akin to trying to find a word in a dictionary where the order of the words is random.

As you might recall, some fields in FileMaker can be unindexed merely because the designer chose to leave them that way, perhaps to save space. For certain fields, this setting can be changed, and FileMaker can be permitted to index the field. Other fields, though, such as globals, or any calculation that references a global or a field in another table, *cannot* be indexed under any circumstances. If your search or sort includes such a field, the operation will never go quickly, and in fact its performance degrades linearly as the database grows in size.

NOTE

> You should allow an unindexed search only if you're sure that the set of searchable records is always going to remain fairly small, and there's no other way to achieve the result you need. In general, programming a search or sort on unindexed fields should be considered a design error and should be avoided.

Note too that "unindexable-ness" has a certain viral character to it, where calculations are concerned. Suppose that you have a calculation A, which references calculation B, which references fields 1, 2, and 3. For reasons of saving space, you decide at some point to eliminate the index on field 3. Immediately, calculations A, B, and C all become unindexed as well, for the simple reason that they now all depend on an unindexed field. Any searches or sorts that use these calculations will now potentially run quite slowly. Be aware of this issue of cascading dependencies when working with indexes.

→ For additional discussion of indexes, **see** "Storage and Indexing," **p. 86**.

SLOWNESS IN EXECUTING CALCULATIONS

If you have a calculation that seems to execute very slowly, there are a few avenues you can explore. In general, the greater the number of fields and other calculations that your calculation references, the slower it'll be. It's possible to build up quite lengthy chains of dependencies, or to have dependencies with a non-obvious performance impact. Consider the previous example, with a calculation C that references a calculation B that references a calculation A. Every time A or B changes, C gets re-evaluated as well. So the calculation contains more work than you might expect. It's very easy to create elaborate chains of such dependencies, so watch out for them. If you find such chains, see whether there are ways to restructure the chain, perhaps in a way that allows some of the intermediate data to be stored, or set by a script.

Likewise beware if your calculations reference any custom functions with recursive behavior. A recursive function is like a little looping script. How long it loops for any case all depends on the inputs. If you're referencing these in your calculations, be aware of this fact.

→ For more information on recursion, **see** "Creating Custom Functions," **p. 423**.

Finally, if your calculation references related fields, it will likely be slower than a calculation that looks only at fields in the same table.

SLOWNESS IN PERFORMING LOOKUPS

One issue that has come to light over the course of many conversions from FileMaker 6 or earlier to FileMaker 7 or 8 is a difference in the behavior of the Lookup auto-entry field option. To refresh your memory, a *lookup* is an auto-entry field option that copies data from a related table into the current table. Lookups might be used, for example, to copy a unit price from a product record into an order line item record.

In FileMaker 7 and 8, it's possible, and indeed advisable, to replace the Lookup option with a different auto-entry option that gives exactly the same results and behavior but is much faster with large record sets. The preferred method in FileMaker 7 and 8 is to use the "Calculated value" auto-entry option instead. The calculation should simply make a direct reference to the related field you intend to copy.

As an example, suppose that you have a table of order line items related to a table called Product. In the order line item, you have a field UnitPrice, defined as a lookup, where the data copied is simply the UnitPrice field from the Product table. A better choice is to define the field with a "Calculated value" auto-entry option, where the calculation simply reads `Product::UnitPrice`. The behavior is exactly identical to the behavior of the Lookup, but when the related record set (Product, in this case) is large, the performance is potentially much faster.

→ For more information on the lookup auto-entry option, **see** "Assigning Field Options," **p. 78**.

SLOWNESS IN SCRIPTS

You can do almost anything in a script, so in some sense a slow script could be caused by anything that could cause slowness elsewhere in FileMaker. But there's one additional point we want to make here: You can often speed things up by using some of FileMaker's complex built-in functionality from a script, rather than building things up from simpler script steps.

USE REPLACE RATHER THAN LOOP Assume you have a batch of records representing library books. Once a day you want to scan the book list, find all those that were due yesterday and are still checked out, and mark them overdue. Well, you could solve this with a loop: Find the right records, go to the first one, loop through the whole set, and perform a `Set Field` on each record. But there's a quicker and easier way: Use the `Replace Field Contents` script step. This step lets you specify a field and a value to put into the field. The value can be a hard-coded value, or the result of a calculation, possibly quite a complex one. (The latter technique is called a *calculated replace*—an essential tool in a FileMaker developer's toolkit.)

In any case, a Replace Field Contents, calculated or otherwise, has almost exactly the same effect as a Loop/Set Field combination, and is often much faster. In simple tests that we've performed, Replace seems to run about twice as fast as Loop.

GO TO RELATED RECORDS VERSUS SEARCHING   The `Go To Related Records` script step is one of FileMaker's most powerful tools. Using this step, you can navigate from a starting point in one table to a related set of records in some other table, via the relationships defined in the Relationships Graph. (Technically, you are navigating from one table occurrence to another via the graph.) This navigational "hop" can be much quicker than running a search in the desired table.

CREATING RECORDS   Under certain circumstances, creating records can be a slow process. Specifically, record creation will be slower the more indexes you have on a FileMaker table. Indexes on a table are updated every time a table record changes, and each index on that table may potentially need to be updated. As a general rule, indexes cause searches to run faster, but may cause record creation to be slower.

CONNECTIVITY AND RELATED ISSUES

There are many scenarios in which FileMaker's behavior may be affected by network and connectivity considerations. Unless you are working alone with a FileMaker database that lives on one single computer, and is used on only that computer, you're likely going to find yourself in a situation where FileMaker data is being distributed over a network. This situation offers a number of potential problems.

INABILITY TO CONTACT THE SERVER

What happens if you're running FileMaker Server and your users can't see your files? There could be any number of reasons for this turn of events, but this list contains a few of the most common reasons.

- **Server is down**—Verify that the server is running via inspection or a network utility such as `ping`.

- **Server is up, but FileMaker service is not responding**—Verify that *both* the FileMaker Server and FileMaker Server Helper processes are running. (Without the Helper process, clients cannot connect to the server.)

- **The server machine is working and the processes are running correctly, but the files have not been correctly set for network hosting**—Make sure that you have granted network access to the files for at least some users.

- **The files have been placed on the server but are not opened for sharing on the server**—Even if the files are on the server, with appropriate network hosting, it's still necessary to instruct FileMaker Server to open the files for sharing. If the files are marked Closed in the Files area in the Server Administration Tool, they are not open for hosted sharing.

- **Users may not have appropriate permissions to see the hosted files**—In the FileMaker Network Settings dialog, it's possible to specify that the file will be visible for network sharing only to users with certain privilege sets. Users with insufficient privileges could in theory have no privileges that would allow them to see any of the hosted files.

→ Making files available via network access is covered fully; **see** Chapter 25, "FileMaker Server and Server Advanced," **p. 779**.

- **Firewall problems**—If there's a firewall between your server and any of your users, the firewall needs to pass traffic on port 5003. If this port is blocked, users will probably not even be able to see the server, much less access any files on it.

CROSSTALK

If a user comes to you and says that all of last week's sales data has disappeared, there are a number of possible causes for this effect. It's possible, of course, that last week's sales data really *is* gone (in which case you'll want to price tickets to Nome). But it's also possible you've been bitten by a case of *crosstalk*.

Crosstalk had the potential to be a serious problem in previous versions of FileMaker. The File Reference feature that debuted in FileMaker 8 has taken a lot of the sting out of the problem, but the potential for trouble remains.

→ For a full discussion of file references, **see** "Working with Multiple Files," **p. 201**.

The trouble stems from the way FileMaker Pro resolves external file references. To access any content from another file, you must first create a file reference to it. You need to do this to add tables from an external file to the Relationships Graph, or to call a script from that file, or to use a value list from that file. In FileMaker 8, you create and manage file references explicitly. In versions of the product prior to FileMaker 8, FileMaker managed them for you, behind the scenes, making it easy to lose track of what you were doing. FileMaker also had an automatic search routine, so that if it couldn't find a file in the first place it looked, it might look elsewhere, and come up with the wrong copy of the file.

FileMaker 8 does not perform this sort of automated search for your files. Instead, it looks to the file references you've set up. If it exhausts the search path for a file, it stops looking. However, if you specify a multi-element search path for a file, you could still get into trouble.

Suppose that you're developing a system that has one file for Customers and another for Orders, each containing a cluster of tables to support its function. You're developing the files locally, on your own computer, so to bring the Order file into the Relationships Graph in the Customers file, you'd create a local reference in the Customers file, as shown in Figure 17.10.

Now suppose that you deploy the files to FileMaker Server. Now you'd like to add an element to the Order reference's search path that points to the copy of the file on the Server. You place it before the local reference, so that FileMaker looks to the server first, as shown in Figure 17.11. This has become a bit dangerous! If FileMaker can't find that file on the server, it looks for it on a user's local hard drive, and if it finds it, it opens it up and uses it. At the very least, you the developer need to be quite careful in this scenario about which version of the file you're working with.

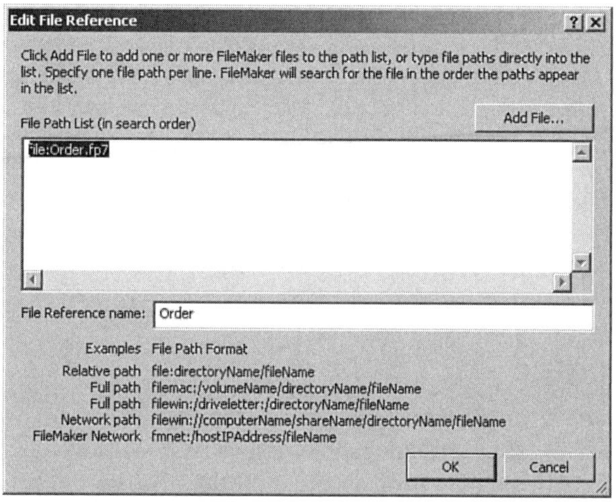

Figure 17.10
A file reference with
one local entry.

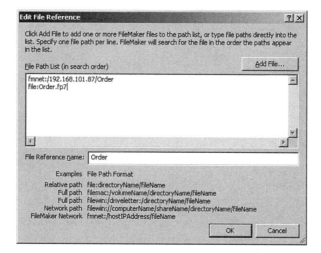

Figure 17.11
A file reference with
multiple search loca-
tions defined.

Other users aren't likely to have a copy of the file locally. But suppose that you had made a reference instead to a shared network drive? That could cause a real headache—the server goes down, the network drive is still in the search path, and clients begin to access and enter data into the nonserved copy.

Again, the elegance of file references makes this danger much less severe than in the past, but it still pays to be aware of the issue to avoid any pitfalls.

TIP

> If you've got a system that's being hosted on a network, and you are still doing development work on another copy of the system, there are several anti-crosstalk precautions you can take. In the first place, make sure to work in single-user mode. One useful practice is to add scripts to every file you create, to toggle between single-user and multiuser mode. In the case of multifile (not multi-table) solutions, it's possible to create a single master script that flips between single-user and multiuser mode for a whole file set. And the other precaution is always to archive your old working copies by some form of compression, so that they can't be accidentally opened and hosted on the network.

CONTEXT DEPENDENCIES

The idea of *context* covers a lot of ground. Speaking generally, it refers to the fact that many actions that occur in FileMaker don't happen in a vacuum. The effect of certain script steps, calculations, or references can vary depending on where you are in the system. *Where you are* means specifically what layout you're on, what window you're in, what mode you're in (Browse, Find, Layout, or Preview), and what record you're on in the current table. Each of these dependencies has its own pitfalls, and each one is discussed in the sections that follow.

LAYOUT DEPENDENCIES

Be aware, when writing scripts, that a number of script steps might not function as you intend, depending on what layout is currently active. Most of these steps require certain fields to be present on the current layout. These include the Go To Field, virtually all the editing functions (Undo, Cut, Copy, Paste, Clear, Set Selection, Select All, Perform Find/Replace), all the Insert steps, Replace Field Contents, Relookup Field Contents, and Check Selection. These are all script steps that act on a field on the current layout. You can run each of them without specifying a field, in which case they run on whatever field is current. They can also be run with a particular field specified. If you specify a field, and for some reason the script is invoked on a layout that doesn't contain the field, the desired action doesn't take place. Even if you don't specify a field, the odds are very strong that you have a specific layout on which you intend that script to be run. In general, these script steps are somewhat fragile and you should use them with care. If you do use them, you should be sure that your logic guarantees that the correct layout will be current when the script step runs.

TABLE CONTEXT

You're certainly familiar with table context if you've read much of the rest of this book. The topic was introduced in Chapter 6, "Working with Multiple Tables," and it plays an important role in most other chapters as well.

→ For a full discussion of table context, **see** "Understanding Table Context," **p. 164**.

FileMaker 8 databases can contain multiple tables. For many actions in FileMaker, then, it's necessary to specify which table is the current one. For new records, to what table does the new record get added? When I check the current found count, for which table am I checking it? And so forth.

Table context introduces a new kind of layout dependency, and one which, in our opinion, dwarfs the old layout dependencies of earlier versions of FileMaker. If you're not aware of table context and don't handle it correctly, your FileMaker solutions may appear to be possessed. They will almost certainly not behave as you expect, unless your system is extremely simple.

There are quite a number of areas in FileMaker 8 where table context comes into play. A brief recap of each of these is provided here.

CAUTION

> As with other kinds of dependencies, it's important to make sure that the context is correct for an operation before trying to perform that operation. This is a special pitfall for scripts, which can easily change context during script operation via a `Go To Layout` step. If your script steps are context sensitive, make very sure to establish the proper context first!

Table context is probably one of the trickiest areas of FileMaker: powerful, but full of pitfalls for the unwary.

LAYOUTS   A layout's table context is determined by the table occurrence to which it's tied. Table context governs which records the layout displays. Note that the link is to a table occurrence, not to a base table—this is significant if you'll be working with related fields, or navigating to related record sets (via the `Go to Related Record` step). In that case, the choice of table occurrence can make a difference in the contents of related fields.

→ For a discussion of table occurrences and their implications for related fields, **see** Chapter 6, "Working with Multiple Tables," **p. 157** and Chapter 8, "Getting Started with Calculations," **p. 217**.

IMPORTING RECORDS   When you import records into FileMaker, the target table is determined by the current table context, which is of course determined by the current active layout. Before importing records, manually or via a script, be sure to go to the appropriate layout to set the context correctly.

EXPORTING RECORDS   Exporting records is also context dependent. Furthermore, if you're exporting related fields and you're exporting from a base table with multiple table occurrences, the choice of table occurrence from which to export might also make a difference. As in the case of importing, make sure that you establish context before an export.

CALCULATIONS   Calculations can also be context dependent, in very specific circumstances. If a calculation lives in a base table that appears multiple times in the Relationships Graph (that is, there are multiple occurrences of that table in the Graph), *and* the calculation references related fields, then the table context matters. The Calculation dialog in FileMaker 8 has a new menu choice at the very top, where you can choose the context from which to evaluate the calculation. If the calculation matches the criteria just mentioned, you should make sure that you get the context right. In other cases, you can ignore it.

VALUE LISTS   Like calculations, value lists can also access and work with related data, via the options to Also Display Values From Second Field and/or Include Only Related Values. Here again, if the value list lives in a base table that appears with multiple occurrences, *and* it works with related data, the table context will be an issue and you should make sure it's set correctly.

17

SCRIPTS Every script executes in a particular table context, which is determined by the table context of the current layout in the active window. (FileMaker 8 can have several windows open within the same file, and they might even display the same layout.) A large number of script steps in FileMaker 8 are context dependent. If you fail to set the context correctly, or change it inadvertently during a script (by switching layouts or windows), you could end up deleting records in the wrong table, to take an extreme case. Interestingly, FileMaker 8 currently doesn't offer a Set Context script step. You need to establish your context explicitly by using a Go To Layout step to reach a layout with the appropriate context.

MODE DEPENDENCIES

A variety of actions in FileMaker depend on the current mode. In other words, things taking place in scripts (which is where these dependencies occur) don't happen in a vacuum; they depend on the current state of the application and the user interface. To take an easy example, some script steps don't work if the application is in Preview mode, including especially the editing steps such as Cut, Copy, and Paste, and others such as Find/Replace and Relookup. If you have a script that's trying to execute a Relookup step, and some other script has left the application in Preview mode, your Relookup won't happen.

> **NOTE**
> The Copy command does actually have one meaningful and useful behavior in Preview mode. If no target field is selected, a Copy command executed in Preview mode copies the graphic image of the current page to the Clipboard.

Most of these mode dependencies are really "Browse mode dependencies," because in general it's Browse mode that's required. But a few other mode-based quirks are also important to remember. A few script steps have different meanings in Find mode than in Browse mode. In Find mode, the Omit script step causes the current Find request to become an Omit request, whereas New Record and Delete Record create and delete Find requests respectively. These three steps work differently in Browse mode, where they respectively omit a record from the current found set, or create or delete a record.

If you're using such script steps, the answer's the same here as elsewhere: Explicitly set the context if you're using script steps that depend on it. In this case, you should use an explicit Enter Browse Mode script step when using steps that depend on this mode.

> **NOTE**
> Some FileMaker dogmatists go so far as to suggest that *every* script you write should begin with an Enter Browse Mode, unless otherwise required. We think this policy may be a bit much in practice, but the spirit of it is dead-on: Be aware of these dependencies, like others, and handle them explicitly.

Finally, there are also mode dependencies that occur outside the context of scripting. A number of FileMaker's presentation features are dependent on Layout mode. These include the capability to display data in multiple columns, the capability to show the effects of any sliding options you may have set, and the capability to show summary parts and summary fields.

→ To find full detail on these Preview-dependent layout features, **see** "Working with Objects on a Layout," **p. 106**, and "Summarized Reports," **p. 287**.

THE RECORD POINTER

In addition to all the other elements of context, there's one other important one. Quite a number of scriptable actions depend on what record you're currently on. You might remember that this is a function of two things: what layout you're on (which in turn translates to a table occurrence, which in turn translates to a base table), and which *window* you're in. FileMaker 8, you may remember, supports multiple windows open onto the same layout, each with its own found set.

Within each found set, FileMaker keeps track of something called the *record pointer*—in other words, on which record of the set you actually are. This is indicated both by the record number in the status area, and possibly by the small black bar that appears to the left of each record in list views. Figure 17.12 shows both of these indicators.

Indicates the position of the record pointer

Figure 17.12
The small black bar in a list view indicates the record pointer's position. The status area also shows the current record number.

The current record number

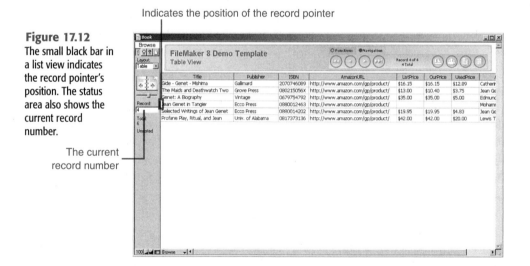

17

Some script steps *are affected* by the record pointer, whereas others *affect* it. Obvious cases of the former are `Delete Record` and `Set Field`. The record that gets deleted, and the field that gets set, depend on which record you were on to start with. These kinds of cases are clear and trivial.

Less clear are the steps that affect the record pointer—in other words, that move it. Say you have a found set of 7 found records and you navigate to number 5 and delete it. Which record do you end up on? Old number 6, or old number 4? Old number 6 is the answer: Deletion *advances* the record pointer (except, of course, when you delete the last record of a set). The omission of one or more records from the found set is treated like deletion as far as the record pointer is concerned.

What about adding or duplicating a record? Is the additional record created immediately after the current record? Just before it? At the end or beginning of all records? Well, it turns out to depend on whether the current record set is sorted. If the record set is unsorted, new or duplicate records are added at the very end of the found set. (More exactly, the set is then sorted by creation order, so of course the newest records fall at the end.) But if the record set is sorted, things are different. New records are created right after the current record. A duplicate is created at its correct point in the sort order, which could be immediately after the current record, or possibly several records farther along.

The bottom line is that you need to be aware of which script steps move the record pointer. This is a particular pitfall inside looping scripts that perform these kinds of actions, such as a looping script that deletes some records as it goes. If, on a given pass through the loop, you don't delete a record, you need a `Go to Record/Request/Page [Next]` to advance the record pointer; but if you delete a record on one pass, the pointer advances automatically, and unless you skip the "go to next record" step this time around, you'll end up one record ahead of where you want to be.

GLOBALS

Global fields (which in FileMaker 8 are more exactly called "fields with global storage" because "Global" is no longer really a field type) have long been a powerful feature of FileMaker Pro. But there are a few nonobvious facts about globals that can cause problems and confusion.

Unlike data values that are placed in record fields, the values of global fields are specific to each database user (if the databases are being run in a multiuser configuration). That is, if you have an invoicing system with an `Invoice Date` field, every logged-in user sees exactly the same invoice date for invoice record number 1300. By contrast, if you have a globally stored field called `gFlag`, it's possible that every single user could see a different value for that global field. If a global field gets set to a value of 1300 by one user, that value isn't seen by other users. They each have their own copy of the field, unlike a nonglobal data field.

It's helpful to remember that when a file containing globally stored fields is first opened, all global fields are set to the last values they had when the files were last open in single-user mode. This means that users in a multiuser environment can't save the values of global fields. When a user closes a file, all global fields associated with that file's tables are wiped clean. (In effect, they disappear.) If the same user reopens the file, all the globals will have reverted to the server defaults. This is an important troubleshooting point. If you are relying on global fields to store important session information such as user preferences, be aware that if the user closes the file containing those globals, all those session settings disappear, and reopening the file does not, by itself, bring those stored global values back.

From a troubleshooting perspective, it's important to remember that globals are volatile and session-specific.

FILE MAINTENANCE AND RECOVERY

A corrupted database system is every developer's nightmare, as well as every user's. Database systems are complex, and very sensitive to the integrity of their data structures. Errors in the way data is written to a database can damage a system, or in the worst case render it unusable. Periodic maintenance can help you avoid file structure problems. In the worst case, if one of your files does become corrupted, FileMaker has tools to help you recover from this situation as well.

FILE MAINTENANCE

As you work with a database file, the file can become slowly more fragmented and less efficient over time. Large deletions can leave "holes" in the file's data space. Heavy transaction loads can cause indexes to become fragmented. If your databases are large or heavily used, it's a good idea to perform periodic file maintenance.

The File Maintenance feature is available only in FileMaker Pro 8 Advanced (formerly FileMaker Developer). File maintenance can be performed only on files that are open locally. It can't be performed on files that are hosted. To invoke it, choose Tools, File Maintenance. You'll see a dialog like the one in Figure 17.13, which allows you to choose to compact the file, optimize the file, or both. We recommend you execute both of these steps when performing file maintenance.

Figure 17.13
Periodic file maintenance (a feature of FileMaker Advanced) is a good idea if your files are large or heavily used.

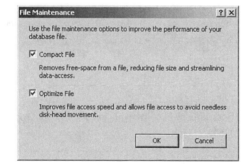

There isn't a firm rule of thumb for when and how often to perform file maintenance. A general rule might be that if you have a database file of more than 20–30 megabytes in size, or that is changed hundreds of times daily, it might be wise to perform a file maintenance every few months. If your file sizes rise into the hundreds of megabytes, or your activity rises into the thousands of records changed daily, you may want to perform maintenance monthly, or even more frequently.

FILE RECOVERY

It might occasionally happen that a FileMaker file becomes so badly damaged it cannot be opened. When this happens it's usually because the file's host (either the FileMaker client or the FileMaker Server) suffered a crash. If a file is damaged in this way, it's necessary to use the File, Recover command available in any copy of FileMaker Pro. This command tries to rebuild the file and repair the damage in such a way that the file can again be opened and its data accessed. The recovery process can take from a few seconds to many minutes or occasionally hours, depending on the size of the file and how many indexes it contains.

With previous versions of FileMaker, the recovery process was not intended to repair a damaged file fully. In the past it was necessary to issue extremely strong warnings, to the effect that *files that have been damaged badly enough to require recovery should not be put back into service*. Previously, the recovery process was intended primarily to bring the file back to a state in which the data could be moved into a clean copy of the file. You needed to create that clean copy by taking a recent backup (you do have a backup, don't you?) of the file, opening it, and choosing File, Save A Copy As, choosing to save it as Clone (No Records). This creates an empty copy of the file, containing all the structural elements such as table definitions, scripts, layouts, and the like. From there, you could run an import to fetch in the data from the recovered file.

 Things have changed a bit with the FileMaker 8 product line. In the past, there were really no reliable tools to tell you when a FileMaker database might contain some form of corruption. If you even suspected your database of corruption (and needing to recover a file was taken as reasonable evidence of corruption), it was deemed better to recover the data and rebuild or restore the structure.

FileMaker has always performed a consistency check on files it suspects of having something wrong with them. The consistency checker built in to FileMaker Server 8 is more thorough and aggressive than previous versions, and it's now our understanding that any file that passes FileMaker Server 8's consistency check can be considered safe to use. Nonetheless, old habits die hard, and we do advocate a bit of caution until the new tools are more completely field tested.

CAUTION

> Although we're excited at the prospect of better consistency checking and recovery tools in FileMaker 8, we recommend you continue to use caution in working with files that have been recovered.

FILEMAKER EXTRA: OTHER TOOLS OF THE TRADE

A number of the important tools you can use to avoid or diagnose trouble in your FileMaker systems were touched on in this chapter. Many of these are development practices, and a few, such as the Script Debugger, are available within the FileMaker product line. But there are also a number of third-party tools that can provide valuable diagnostics. As a rule, these tools analyze the structure and logic of a FileMaker system and produce output that warns you about potential difficulties with the files. Not all these tools were known to be available for FileMaker 8 at the time of this writing, but we fully expect them all to make to leap to 7 soon after the product is released. In general, these tools analyze an existing FileMaker file set and produce an interactive report (either in HTML or as a set of FileMaker databases).

- **Analyzer**—Analyzer, from Waves in Motion (http://www.wavesinmotion.com) is a tool that, well, analyzes your FileMaker solutions and produces a FileMaker-based report. Analyzer documents the entire internal structure of your system. Among the output it produces are notes about errors encountered within the system structure. The most common type of errors involves missing elements, such as missing fields, layouts, or related table occurrences, as well as relationships that are invalid or suspect.

- **Metadata Magic**—Metadata Magic, from New Millennium Communications (http://www.nmci.com), is a FileMaker plug-in that performs solution analysis and returns the results as a set of FileMaker databases, as does Analyzer. MdM is able to document a variety of problem areas in a FileMaker database. Of particular interest is its capability to note whether a file has been recovered, and if so, how many times.

- **Brushfire**—From Chaparral Software (http://www.chapsoft.com) produces an HTML-based report that, like the other two products mentioned here, shows complete details about the structure of a FileMaker solution, as well as highlighting possible trouble spots. Among its noteworthy features are the capability to find obsolete items that are no longer used or referenced, and the capability to find objects with improper names.

These tools are all worth serious consideration. Each has strengths and weaknesses. As a FileMaker developer it's worth your while to invest in at least one of this type of tool, or possibly several, depending on your needs.

17

## CHAPTER 18

CONVERTING SYSTEMS FROM PREVIOUS VERSIONS OF FILEMAKER PRO

In this chapter

Migration Choices

If you've never touched FileMaker Pro prior to version 7 or 8, the material in this chapter might not be of much use to you. On the other hand, anyone who has ever built or currently maintains systems in previous versions of FileMaker Pro faces a significant set of decisions regarding whether and how to migrate those systems to FileMaker Pro 8.

You've likely heard, read, or discovered on your own that the 2004 release of FileMaker Pro 7 brought tremendous changes to the FileMaker product line. The last time the product experienced such a fundamental change was in moving from version 2.1 to 3.0. If you were working with FileMaker back then (way back in 1995), you probably remember that a lot of unlearning, relearning, converting, and rebuilding had to take place. For the first time, in FileMaker Pro 3.0, the product contained such important tools as relationships and portals. It took quite a while for developers proficient with FileMaker 2.1 to fully understand relational database concepts and the benefits that portals and related fields offered over repeating fields and lookups. It was possible to convert solutions from 2.1 to 3.0 without loss of functionality, but to take advantage of the powerful new features required either extensive redevelopment or, in some cases, rebuilding the files from scratch. The same holds true of the migration from FileMaker 6.x to 7 or 8.

The features introduced in versions 4.x, 5.x, and 6 can perhaps be described as more evolutionary than revolutionary. Web publishing, plug-ins, and data exchange via ODBC all were important extensions to FileMaker, but none of them required fundamental mind-shifts, nor was there any concern that a converted solution might not function exactly as it had previously.

FileMaker 7, on the other hand, represented a revolutionary shift from its predecessors. The ability to place multiple tables in a single file, the addition of an entirely new security model, the ability to create relationships based on multiple match fields, the ability to have multiple windows open in a file, server-based web publishing tools, and custom functions are some of the biggest changes, but there are myriad subtle changes as well, ranging from being able to add comments to fields and calculation formulas to changes in how alphabetic characters placed in number fields are interpreted.

Because of the sweeping changes, conversion of existing solutions into FileMaker Pro 7 or 8 becomes a complex issue. There are circumstances where it will be a better idea to rewrite a solution completely rather than convert it; even if you do convert, you may need to do considerable development work and testing before the converted solution can be deployed. In the end, the effort to do either is well worthwhile. This chapter helps you identify the migration strategy that makes the best sense for your solution and how to go about it.

Conversion: What's New in 8?

FileMaker 8 builds on FileMaker 7's deep architectural changes with many new, powerful features, but the conversion picture, with respect to systems written in FileMaker 6 and before, stays more or less the same. Converting a system to FileMaker 8 entails the same range of considerations as converting to FileMaker 7. By contrast, FileMaker 7 and FileMaker 8 share a common file format; files are virtually interchangeable between the two. FileMaker 8 clients can access files served on a FileMaker 7 server, and vice versa; the only provision is that a FileMaker 7 client will not be able to use features specific to FileMaker 8.

In any case, all considerations in this chapter apply equally well to files being converted from FileMaker 6 and before into either FileMaker 7 or FileMaker 8. Occasionally, we might refer to "FileMaker 8" as shorthand for the more cumbersome "FileMaker 7 and/or 8." Rest assured that the fundamental distinction here is between FileMaker 6 or earlier (.fp3, .fp5) and FileMaker 7 or later (.fp7). This chapter deals with converting .fp3 and .fp5 files to a .fp7 system.

Note, however, that FileMaker 8 Advanced does offer a number of useful tools (such as the capability to copy and paste fields and tables) that can make post-conversion work, such as consolidating tables, easier.

Factors Influencing Your Migration Strategy

By the term *migration*, we mean simply the concept of moving a solution from version 6 of FileMaker or earlier to version 8. You can employ two primary strategies to effect a migration. The first is to *convert* your solution using the built-in routines in FileMaker 8. The other is to *rewrite* your solution as a fresh set of FileMaker Pro 8 files.

The decision about how (and indeed whether) to migrate your older solution will be informed by a number of factors, including your future needs, the benefits you hope to reap through migration, the complexity of your solution, and your timeline and available resources. You may decide that some of your solutions can simply be converted; other solutions may be better off being rewritten from scratch.

Migration Benefits

Of all the new features and benefits of FileMaker Pro 7 and 8, there will undoubtedly be some features that matter more to you than others in a decision to convert. For some people, support for Unicode may be a compelling reason to upgrade, whereas others may not find this feature relevant. Some people will choose to migrate to use the new security features; others for the new Instant Web Publishing. For existing solutions, determine what specific benefits you hope to achieve by migrating to FileMaker Pro 8; if you decide to migrate, you'll then need to determine whether those benefits can best be attained by conversion or rewriting. Sometimes the desired benefits will completely drive the migration strategy; other times they will play a lesser role in the decision.

Centralized security is a good example of a reason to rewrite rather than convert. Anyone who's maintained complex security settings in a 50-file solution will welcome the ability to assign accounts and privileges for all the tables in a file at once. When you convert a multifile solution from an eralier version of FileMaker, however, each file in the existing systems turns into a one-table file in the new system, and there's no easy way to consolidate tables into the same file (although FileMaker Pro 8 Advanced does offer some useful tools—such as the capability to copy and paste tables and fields—that can make consolidation a bit easier). So, after converting a 50-file solution, even if everything works flawlessly, you'll still need to manage accounts and privileges in 50 different places. If centralized security is a crucial feature for you, you may prefer to rewrite your solution as a single-file application in FileMaker 8.

 If you do attempt to consolidate tables, there are some potential issues you should be aware of. See "Repointing Table Occurrence References" in the "Troubleshooting" section at the end of this chapter.

Many other benefits will be just as achievable through straight conversion as through a rewrite. Examples of these include larger field and file size limits, the ability to put binary data into container fields, support for Unicode, and encrypted data transfer between FileMaker Server and client applications.

Another class of benefits can be achieved by a rewrite or through a hybrid of conversion and subsequent development. For instance, your solution may have work-arounds to get around limitations of previous versions of FileMaker. After conversion, those work-arounds will still be in place, but they may no longer be necessary; your converted solution may be FileMaker 8 *compatible* but it may not be FileMaker 8 *optimized*. Examples of features that you won't benefit from unless you rewrite or do post-conversion development include custom functions, script parameters, script variables, text formatting functions, new layout objects such as the tab control and calendar picker, and relationships based on complex match criteria.

COMPLEXITY

Complexity is such a subjective and nebulous concept that it's hard to pin down the effect of solution complexity on the decision to convert or rewrite. All other things being equal—which of course they never are—we feel the more complex a solution is, the more likely it is that you'll prefer to rewrite from scratch rather than convert.

To some extent, complexity can be measured by sheer numbers: number of scripts, number of files, number of relationships, and number of layouts. But there are qualitative measurements of complexity that may override the quantitative: Having a hundred simple navigation scripts is less complex than having a hundred scripts that do, well…complex things. Complexity also may involve interactions with external systems, or simply very complicated business logic.

So why is it better to rewrite than to convert a complex solution? If some features don't work properly in a complex system after conversion, it can be very time consuming to find and fix the problems. Further, it can be almost impossible in complex systems to systematically test every button and script to ensure that it functions as it's supposed to. It's possible that some conversion issues won't be easy to discover, resulting in problems well down the road.

When you create a system from scratch, you test components as you go, so it's less likely that there will be lingering issues after the system is deployed. Also, in a rewritten FileMaker 8 system, it's almost always possible to achieve your previous functionality with significantly fewer objects and global fields: fewer fields because you won't need as many unstored calculations; fewer scripts because of script parameters and the capability to define multiple different finds and sorts within a single script; fewer relationships because they're all inherently bi-directional.

It will also be easier and more efficient to maintain a complex solution in FileMaker 8 if it's been rewritten than if it's been converted. Figure 18.1 shows the Relationships Graph of a very large, complex file after conversion. Keep in mind, of course, that you'll have similarly impenetrable graphs in many —if not all—the files in your solution. Grooming all those graphs into something that can be efficiently maintained is time-consuming. A rewrite, on the other hand, gives you the opportunity to systematically plan how to arrange tables in your graphs; you can also choose the file architecture that's best for your solution rather than passively accepting the one-table-per-file architecture obtained through conversion.

NOTE

> Each relationship in the previous file is converted into a table occurrence in the new file, named by the relationship name from the old system.

Figure 18.1
After conversion, each file in your solution will have a hub-and-spoke design graph with the current file at the top center of the graph.

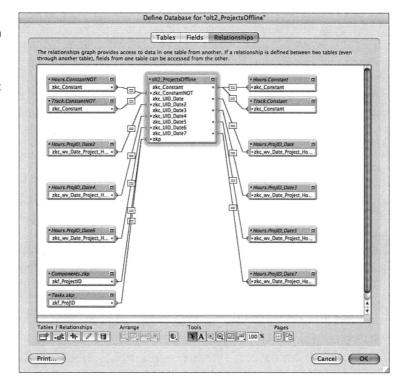

CONDITION OF THE EXISTING SYSTEM

The condition of your existing system can have an impact on your migration decision. Plenty of systems out there have grown more like weeds than well-tended gardens. Such systems exhibit inconsistent naming conventions, have fields, scripts, and layouts that are no longer needed, use inefficient and/or idiosyncratic processes, and usually have data integrity problems to boot.

Converting these systems often accomplishes little more than paving the cow path: It's using a new technology to do things the same, inefficient way they've always been done. Chances are that you'll end up disappointed in the new product because it doesn't solve any of your inveterate problems. It will also be very difficult to do proper post-conversion testing and development on such systems, as you'll always be plagued by the detritus from the old system.

On the other hand, if your solution has been well tended over the years, or has recently been overhauled, there's a good chance it will convert well and be easy to maintain going forward. A well-tended solution will have consistent, intuitive naming conventions, will have a minimum of unnecessary objects, and will have ample data protection in place. If that's not a description of your system, you may want to use the upgrade to FileMaker 8 as your excuse to do the rewrite that your system needs. Rather than blindly replicating the existing system, take the time to redesign and rebuild it correctly from the start.

FUTURE NEEDS

Your future needs for a particular solution may influence your decision whether to convert or rebuild. If you have a solution that does x, y, and z, and all you need to have it do going forward is x, y, and z, conversion might be the best path for you. In such cases, your primary motivation for conversion is likely something like the larger file size limit in FileMaker 7 or 8, or the ability to make schema and privilege changes without kicking users out of the system. Even if it takes kludgy work-arounds to do x, y, and z, if you don't foresee a likely need to do much future development or maintenance work on the system, it's probably just fine to leave those kludgy work-arounds in place.

At the other end of the continuum is a solution (and likely an organization) that's in constant flux. You need a system that's easy to maintain and is nimble enough to adapt to changing needs and conditions. Or maybe your current solution is phase one of a larger, grander application. If for these or any other reasons you foresee a need to do considerable post-conversion development for a solution, it's likely that you'll be better off rewriting your solution. If you don't, you'll probably end up with a stratified solution, where old features and objects are noticeably "B.C." (before conversion) and new work is noticeably "A.C." (after conversion). Such a system will invariably be more difficult to build upon and maintain than one developed entirely in FileMaker 8.

TIME AND COST

There's little question that rewriting a solution from scratch requires more time and/or cost than simply converting a solution. Be aware, too, that conversion itself carries time and cost requirements: You will always need to do significant testing before deploying a converted solution, and you'll often need to do some post-conversion maintenance as well.

Estimating the time and cost requirements for either migration strategy is difficult because you won't know what issues you'll face until after you're underway. Conversion is like a home remodeling job in many ways. After you tear down a few walls you may be faced with a bigger problem than you anticipated. Similarly troublesome, rewriting is prone to the "while-we're-at-it" factor (that is, "as long as we're rewriting the solution, let's hire a designer to create a new interface while we're at it," or "while we're at it, let's build those hooks into the accounting and shipping solutions we've always talked about adding").

Rewriting a solution from scratch certainly sounds like it will involve more significant time and cost than conversion. Keep in mind, though, that you have your original solution as a blueprint, and that you'll probably be able to copy significant portions of the system, including layouts, scripts, and calculation functions. It certainly won't require the same resources as it did to build the system originally.

When you think about the time and cost of migration, it's also important that you take a long view. What might be more time- and cost-efficient in the short term might have significantly higher costs in the long run because of inefficiency and lost productivity. For example, it may take longer to add new features in the future to a converted solution. Or, if your present system has inefficient processes, an initial time and cost outlay to rewrite your systems may result in a steady stream of cost savings in the future.

There's another way that time plays into your migration plan, and that's the timeliness of your need. If you have a solution that's on the verge of surpassing the old file size limit, or if you have been teetering along with an unstable, crash-prone solution, you probably want to migrate as quickly as possible. It's calendar time, not programming time, that matters the most to you, and conversion is your best course of action. Even if you decide that your solution needs to be rewritten in the future, you may opt to deploy a converted solution as a stopgap until a more permanent solution can be achieved.

THE BOTTOM LINE

You might have noticed that nowhere in the preceding discussion did we specifically recommend conversion or rewriting as absolutely preferable. We instead pointed out factors that might cause you to prefer one method to another. In the real world, of course, you must figure out how to weigh all these factors against each other. You might have a very clean, very complex system that won't need much future development. Or you might have a simple solution that's used by a hundred users, each with a separate password. There are no simple rules you can follow to determine which path is best, but to make an informed decision, it certainly helps to have all the issues on the table.

18

CONVERTING FILES

The actual conversion of files from previous versions of FileMaker is a very simple task. Even if you have decided to do a total rewrite of a solution, you will still end up performing a conversion so that you can salvage scripts and layouts. You'll probably also do another conversion to move the data to the new version. From here on out, though, we're going to assume that you've decided to migrate your solution via conversion, and will focus on the process and methods to accomplish this.

NOTE

> FileMaker 8 can directly convert files from versions 3, 4, 5, and 6. If you have files created in FileMaker Pro 1 or 2, you need to convert them first to version 3 or higher before converting to 8. (FileMaker 7 and 8 share a common file format and no conversion is necessary to move between them.)

It's quite likely—and even expected—that you will need to perform multiple conversions on a solution during the course of migration. Typically, the first conversion is a throwaway that you'll use for research and experimentation. We usually refer to this as the *alpha* conversion. We've found that each solution behaves a bit differently after conversion, and rather than theorizing and guessing what features will or won't convert well, just convert them and do some poking around. You may quickly discover you need to disable startup scripts that check for the presence of plug-ins, or that you can't open the solution because you don't remember the case of your passwords. (They're case sensitive in FileMaker Pro 8, but not in previous versions.) If necessary, make minor adjustments to the source files and make a new alpha conversion set. The goal at this stage is simply to have a set of FileMaker 8 files that you can open and dissect. These files will never see the light of day, so experiment freely.

Later in this chapter, we'll discuss some pre-conversion tasks that can make the migration process go more smoothly. When you've completed these tasks and are ready to proceed, you'll convert your files once again, this time creating what we call the *beta* conversion set. These are the files that will eventually be deployed as your new solution. Some solutions require significant post-conversion testing and tweaking. It's important that you make frequent backups of your beta files during this process so that if you make mistakes, you can roll back to a stable version without having to re-convert the files.

NOTE

The types of mistakes that can necessitate a rollback include things like deleting file references before you've re-specified any objects that use them, and removing tables or table occurrences from your files without accounting for the impact on scripts or layouts.

In cases where the testing and other post-conversion work takes days or weeks to perform, you are likely to need to do another conversion of your original system so that you can import fresh data before deploying the converted solution.

CAUTION

Be sure to take the old files offline during this conversion and data migration to prevent users from making additional modifications.

For this final conversion, the only thing you care about is the raw data; the solution doesn't need to function beyond letting you open the files and show all records. You can skip converting the indexes for this conversion; they won't be necessary for the final transfer.

It's also possible merely to export data from your old system and import into your new one. There's no way to import directly from the old files into FileMaker 8, though. The main drawback with exporting and importing is that you'll not be able to transfer any data in container fields. You will also lose text styling information that might have been applied to bits of text within individual fields. For these reasons, we prefer to do the final import from a freshly converted set of files.

Converting Single-File Solutions

There are a few ways to actually go about converting files. If you have a multifile system, it's important that you convert all the files at the same time so that links between the files are properly preserved. The method for converting multifile solutions is covered in the next section.

A single-file solution is one that has no links to other FileMaker databases, whether those links are relationships, external scripts, imports, or value lists. You can convert such files simply by launching FileMaker 8, choosing File, Open, and selecting your old file. When you do so, you see a dialog similar to the one in Figure 18.2, asking whether you'd like to rename the old file.

Figure 18.2
When converting a single file, you'll have the option to rename the existing file. There's no need to do so.

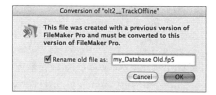

There's no particular need to rename the old file. During conversion, the old file is left unaltered and is still fully functional; a brand new, FileMaker 8 file is created for you. You have the opportunity to name the converted file and specify a location for it as well.

> **TIP**
>
> If your file contains a large amount of data, it may take considerable time to convert. For the alpha conversion, it's helpful to have all the data, but for the beta conversion, consider creating a clone of your file. This speeds up both your conversion and your post-conversion development work. Memory is also a consideration if you're converting a large system (in the 200MB range or above). We recommend multiple gigabytes of RAM for large conversions.

CONVERTING RELATIONAL SOLUTIONS

When you convert a multifile relational solution, it's important that you convert all the files at once. If you don't, and instead use the method outlined in the previous section to convert each file individually, you'll be forced to wade through potentially numerous "File Not Found" messages as each file converts and opens. Also, if you don't specify the correct filename for the converted files (by removing the Converted suffix appended by default), you may have a hard time fixing your file references later on.

To convert a set of files all at once, simply select them all and drag them on top of the FileMaker 8 application icon. You can achieve the same thing by choosing multiple files from the File, Open dialog. Hold down the (⌘) [Ctrl] key to do this.

You aren't prompted to rename your old files, nor to name your new ones. Instead, you are presented with the dialog shown in Figure 18.3, in which you're asked to select a directory in which to place the converted files. We recommend setting up a new directory for each set of converted files; if you simply place them in the same folder where your old files live, it gets a bit confusing, particularly if you're performing multiple conversions.

As with single-file conversion, your old files are unaltered during conversion and can still be used. Nonetheless, it's certainly good practice to make sure you have backups of your old system in case of accidents such as deleting or renaming the wrong files.

18

Figure 18.3
When converting multiple files, your new files are given the same names as the old ones. You aren't prompted for filenames the same way you are when converting single files.

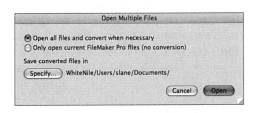

For each file in your old solution, the conversion routine creates a new FileMaker 8 file, named the same as the old file but with an `.fp7` file extension (this file extension is common to FileMaker 7 and 8). Each converted file contains a single table, named the same as the file. All the relationships are turned into external table occurrences on your Relationships Graph (with the exception of self-relationships, which are created as local table occurrences).

 If your databases don't open correctly immediately after conversion, see "Disabling Startup Scripts" in the "Troubleshooting" section at the end of this chapter.

PRE-CONVERSION TASKS

You can and should do a number of things before converting older solutions to FileMaker 8. Your pre-conversion tasks vary somewhat from solution to solution, but some categories of tasks are still common to most solutions.

Our comments here are aimed at people who are converting older relational (multifile) systems of some complexity. The purpose of doing any pre-conversion work at all is to make the post-conversion work go more smoothly; for single-file and simple relational solutions, you might not need to have rigorous conversion plans like this in place.

Also, by *conversion* here, we mean beta conversion rather than alpha conversion. In fact, many of the pre-conversion tasks that we discuss will cause you to want to make new alpha sets of the files. The simple difference between alpha and beta conversion files (as you'll recall from earlier in the chapter) is that alpha files are meant to be experimented with and thrown away, whereas beta files are intended to be turned into your new solution.

PREPARE FOR CONVERSION

Converting a solution entails much more than the physical creation of new, upgraded files; you need to prepare both yourself and your environment for the conversion. The process goes faster and smoother if you spend a bit of time up front planning out the details. The specific preparation tasks you should do include the following:

- **Set up a test environment**—Install FileMaker 8 on the machine that you plan to use to actually perform the conversion and do testing. If you are networking your solution, having FileMaker Server 8 installed on a nonproduction server is important during testing.

- **Acquire any necessary hardware and software**—You may need to upgrade machines and/or operating systems before you can deploy a FileMaker 8 solution. Be sure that you get the ball rolling on this task early on in your conversion process because it can cause deployment delays. If you use plug-ins in your solution, check with their vendors to learn about any compatibility issues.

- **Learn FileMaker 8**—We strongly recommend that you spend a fair amount of time learning FileMaker 8 and perhaps even develop a few new solutions entirely with it prior to converting your old systems. The learning curve is considerable; if a conversion project is your first exposure to the new FileMaker 7 and 8 features, it is certain to take you longer and be more difficult than if you had previous experience.

- **Read the conversion documentation**—FileMaker's website has a number of documents and white papers that discuss different aspects of conversion. Check http://www.filemaker.com/support/whitepapers.html for documents relevant to conversion.

DOCUMENT YOUR SOLUTION

The more familiar you are with a solution, the better your conversion will go. Even if you're the sole creator of a system, having up-to-date documentation comes in handy during the conversion process. We recommend having at least the following items:

- **An ER diagram**—If you've never taken the time to formally create an ER diagram of your system, now's the time. For a refresher on creating ER diagrams, please see Chapter 5, "Relational Database Design."

- **Printouts of field definitions, scripts, and layouts**—You may balk at the thought of actually printing out and organizing all these documents, and some people may indeed find that creating PDFs rather than printing works well for them. Many subtle changes take place during conversion, and it's very helpful when looking at a script or calculation formula to be able to compare it with the original. One nice thing about hard copies, of course, is that you can annotate them as you go. You may, for instance, check off buttons on screen shots of layouts as you test them, noting whether everything worked as planned or needs post-conversion attention. The printouts become both your testing plan and your post-conversion audit trail.

- **An access privilege matrix**—This is simply an overview of the privilege settings in your current files. Create it in a database, spreadsheet, or text document—it really doesn't matter.

If you use FileMaker Pro Advanced, you may want to create a Database Design Report of your old solution as part of your documentation process. Third-party tools such as MetaData Magic (from New Millennium Communications), Brushfire (from Chaparral Software), and Analyzer (from Waves in Motion) also are excellent documentation tools and are all highly recommended.

→ For more information on third-party documentation tools, **see** "Documenting Your FileMaker Solutions," **p. 841**.

FIX FILE REFERENCES

Whenever you link one FileMaker file with another, FileMaker uses a *file reference* stored in File A to locate File B. The operations that may require file references include defining relationships, performing external scripts, creating value lists based on the contents of fields in another file, performing an Open script step, and scripting an import from another file.

File references are visible and editable in FileMaker 7 and 8 for the first time. In previous versions, they existed, but were hidden "under the hood." When you convert files created in earlier versions, all the old file references are suddenly visible. You may be in for a bit of shock, in fact, when you examine file references in a converted solution and discover a hornet's nest you never knew existed.

ABSOLUTE PATHS

To understand how that hornet's nest was created and why it can be difficult to untangle, you must understand how FileMaker managed file references in previous versions of the product. Prior to FileMaker Pro 5.5, all file references were stored as *absolute* paths: When you define a link from File A to File B, FileMaker remembers the full path to File B. On Mac OS X, that might look like /Macintosh HD/Documents/myDatabases/File B. On Windows, the full path could be something like C:/myDatabases/File B. If the link were to a hosted file, the link might include the IP address of the hosted file, as in 192.168.100.87/File B. If the hosted file were on the same subnet as the person defining the link, then the IP address wouldn't be stored; an asterisk would appear in the file reference instead.

The main problem with absolute references is that they tend to cause problems when you move files from one machine to another or rename files or folders. In those cases, FileMaker would pop up a message to the user saying, in effect, "I can't find File B...where is it?" You would re-establish the reference by pointing to the moved or renamed file. But rather than replace the previous reference, FileMaker would store the new path as an additional search path for the given link. If you had a file that had been developed over the course of many years and/or on many different machines, you may have had dozens of absolute paths stored in your files. If you ever had problems in previous versions where FileMaker would seemingly irrationally open the wrong copy of a given file, it was likely because there was an obsolete file reference higher up in the search order.

Another problem with file references in previous versions of FileMaker is that different linking operations might produce entirely new references. For instance, say you had created a relationship from File A to File B while the files were both open on your local computer. A file reference containing the path to File B would be stored. Then you moved the files to a server where they were hosted with FileMaker Server, and from your desktop you created a script in File A that called a subscript in File B. An entirely new file reference was created for the external script call.

RELATIVE PATHS

FileMaker Pro 5.5 introduced the option to store only a *relative* path when creating links between files. This went a long way to solve the problems caused by renaming or moving files. Rather than locate File B with a full path reference, a relative reference simply indicates the path to get to File B *from* File A. For example, the relative path may be `../File B`, which would indicate that FileMaker should look for File B in File A's parent directory.

CONVERSION OF FILE REFERENCES

So what happens to all of these obsolete and redundant file references during conversion? The conversion routine does try to do some consolidating and eliminating of file references that are no longer needed, but in most cases, you'll still end up with a bit of a mess. As an example, Figure 18.4 shows the file references from a converted solution. The names of converted file references are simply set to the filename plus a counter if there are multiple references to a given file. Notice that there are no less than five separate references to the Mainmenu file. The fact that there isn't a "Mainmenu 3" or "Mainmenu 4" makes it clear that in fact the conversion routine did identify those as unneeded. The conversion log also explicitly identifies any file references that are removed during conversion.

Figure 18.4
In a solution that's been around for a few years, it's likely that you have a lot of redundant and obsolete file references.

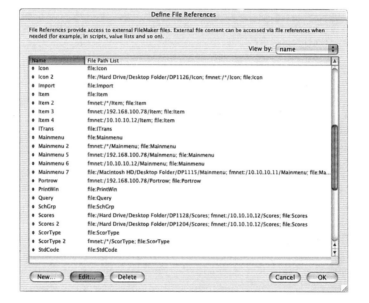

There are several potential problems that you may experience using a converted solution with file reference problems. The first is speed: FileMaker looks for files in the locations specified by the file references, in the order in which they appear. A complex solution with obsolete file references may take many times longer to open than one with *clean* file references. (The extra time is taken up as FileMaker scans fruitlessly through the obsolete references trying to find the file.)

After conversion, you can, of course, manually change all the obsolete paths to updated, relative paths. In a complex solution, this may require manually editing hundreds of references. After you're finished, you'll have solved the problem of obsolete references, but not that of redundant references.

The problem with redundant references is maintenance. If you have five file references that all point to the same file, every time you set up a link to a file, you have to choose which of those five references to use. If you ever need to update the reference, you need to update it in five places. That may be an acceptable short-term solution, but eventually, you'll want to eliminate the redundant file references.

Simply deleting redundant file references can have potentially disastrous consequences. Every link that uses that reference, be it an external table occurrence, a value list, or an external script call, will be broken and will need to be repaired manually. The proper way to remove redundant file references is as follows:

1. Pick one of the set that is to survive the consolidation.

2. Rename all the other file references in the set so that they include an easily identifiable text phrase. DELETE ME works well.

3. Run a DDR report using FileMaker Pro 8 Advanced.

4. Open the DDR report in a text editor or word processor and search for your text phrase to find all the objects that use a redundant file reference.

5. In your converted files, manually change the file reference used by these objects to the canonical reference for that set.

6. Run a new DDR report to make sure you haven't missed any references.

7. Delete the file references that are no longer needed.

Be sure to make a backup of your system before you start playing with file references; a small mistake such as deleting the wrong one can have far-reaching consequences.

METADATAMAGIC TO THE RESCUE

Cleaning up file references in a converted solution can be a very time-consuming and frustrating process. Thankfully, there's a tool called MetadataMagic, distributed by New Millennium Communications (www.nmci.com), which enables you to clean up file references in your system prior to conversion. The File Reference Fixer, one of the tools of MetadataMagic, provides several options for modifying file references. If you use the Auto-Fix function, only the most recently created relative path to a file is retained, and all internal links are updated to use that reference. Obsolete file references are then removed from the files.

In a complex solution, you may be better off using the Consolidate and/or Set Relative-Only functions. For instance, if you have files that span multiple FileMaker Servers or are located in multiple folders, the Consolidate function simply changes multiple and/or redundant references to a single file references.

If you clean up file references in your old solution, the conversion process takes less time and you're left without a severe post-conversion headache. Figure 18.5 shows the post-conversion file references of the same file depicted in Figure 18.4, but this time the file references were cleaned up before conversion with MetadataMagic.

It's easy to see the improvement here. All the file references are now simple relative paths, equally well suited for deployment as a single-user solution or by FileMaker Server. Before using File Reference Fixer, be sure to read the documentation and practice on a set of test files.

Figure 18.5
If you run File Reference Fixer before conversion, the file references in your new files are much easier to troubleshoot and maintain.

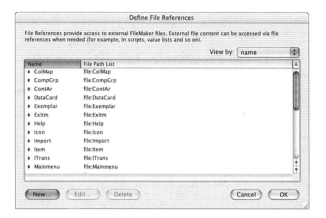

DO SOME HOUSEKEEPING

In addition to file references, other potential post-conversion problems can be avoided if you do a bit of pre-conversion work. You can actually identify much pre-conversion work by examining the alpha conversion files. You may, for instance, discover you have objects with illegal names, which are placed in between curly brackets during conversion. These can be changed in the original system so that by the time you're ready to do your beta conversion, they're no longer an issue. By doing as much work as possible in the pre-beta conversion stage, you'll reduce the amount of time and work required to get your converted files ready for production.

If there are scripts, layouts, relationships, passwords, value lists, or fields that you know are no longer used or needed, try to eliminate these before conversion. If there has been case inconsistency in the entry of passwords in your current system, take the time to standardize them. These efforts will be rewarded by shorter conversion time and having less to test after conversion. Any other housekeeping in the original files can only be beneficial, including organizing scripts, editing object names, and archiving old data.

POST-CONVERSION TASKS

As discussed in the previous sections, you can avoid many potential post-conversion problems by doing some pre-conversion work on your old system. However, a number of tasks can only be done post-conversion.

NOTE
> The actual tasks vary from system to system; many of the tasks listed here may not be applicable to your particular solution.

You should begin a list of post-conversion tasks during your exploration of the alpha files. You'll spot problems and potential areas of improvement. Anything that can't easily be fixed through pre-conversion work should go on your post-conversion task list. Keep in mind that you'll end up destroying the alpha files, so don't spend too much time or effort fixing problems. Some fixes are necessary just so you can continue your exploration; you may opt to do other fixes just so you can test out the results.

To know what tasks you'll need to do after conversion, you need to understand what actually happens to your files during conversion. The following sections look at five different aspects of your files: security, relationships, scripts, fields, and data. For each, we discuss what happens during conversion and what potential post-conversion tasks you need to perform.

TIP

> One vital post-conversion task that goes almost without saying is testing. Before deploying a converted solution, it's vital that you do sufficient testing to identify any problems.

 If your databases don't open correctly immediately after conversion, see "Disabling Startup Scripts" in the "Troubleshooting" section at the end of this chapter.

SECURITY

Depending on whether and how passwords and groups were set up in your solution, you may have some post-conversion work to do involving security. During conversion, passwords in your previous system are turned into accounts, and groups are turned into privilege sets. Accounts in FileMaker 8, of course, have both an account name and a password. For each account in a converted system, the account name and password will both be the same as the old password. So, a password of test123 in your old system turns into an account named test123 with a password of test123.

Post-conversion, you should change all the account names to something other than their default conversion value. Account names are visible on screen during login, so if you don't do this it will be very easy for people to discover their co-workers' passwords. Be sure that you distribute the new account information prior to deployment.

The conversion of groups into privilege sets is more complex than the conversion of passwords into accounts. The number of privilege sets may be more or less than the number of groups in the old system. The following list explains the rules for determining how groups relate to privilege sets:

- If there are multiple groups with identical settings, only the first group is converted and the others are discarded.

- If there are passwords not assigned to any groups, new privilege sets are created based on the properties of the passwords. The first one is named Privilege Set, the second Privilege Set 2, and so on. Any passwords with the same properties are assigned to the same privilege set.

- Any groups not assigned to any passwords (other than master passwords) are not converted into privilege sets.

- If a password is assigned to multiple groups that have different access privileges, a new privilege set is created that has the privileges of both groups. The name of the privilege set is a combination of the names of the groups used for its formation. For instance, if a password foo was associated with groups bar and baz, each of which had different access rights, the new account named foo would be associated with a privilege set named bar/baz.

■ Master passwords are associated with the "[Full Access]" privilege set.

> **TIP**
>
> Calls to the `Status(CurrentGroups)` function are turned into calls to the `Get (PrivilegeSetName)` function during conversion. However, if the older function call tests for the presence of literal text strings, you may need to change the strings to the new privilege set names; these aren't modified at all during conversion. For instance, if you used `PatternCount (Status (CurrentGroups), ("masterGroup"))` in a script or calculation formula, after conversion you need to manually edit this to be `Get (PrivilegeSetName) = "[Full Access]"`. Because accounts can be associated with only one privilege set (whereas passwords can be associated with multiple groups), the `PatternCount` function is no longer needed.

DEFAULT PASSWORDS

If you specified a default password in the document preferences in your old file, the converted solution has a default account specified in the File Options. As in previous versions of FileMaker Pro, you can force the account/password dialog to be shown by holding down the (Option) [Shift] key as the file opens.

(no password)

Older versions of FileMaker allowed you to specify a blank password as a valid way of gaining access to a file. As shown in Figure 18.6, this is represented in the password list as (no password). During conversion, a file with a blank password has the Guest account activated. It is associated with whatever privilege set is appropriate. When the Guest account is active, in the login dialog, users have the option of selecting the Guest Account radio button. It is grayed out if that account isn't active.

Figure 18.6
In older versions of FileMaker Pro (before version 7), you could specify no password as a valid password.

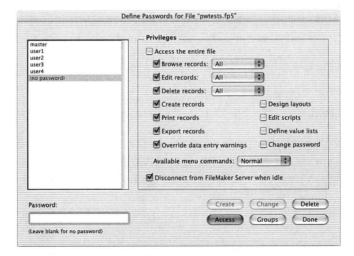

FILES WITH NO PASSWORD

If you convert a file that has absolutely no passwords in it, the converted file has an account named Admin with a blank password. It is assigned the [Full Access] privilege set, and is set as the default login under File, File Options. This is shown in Figure 18.7. A guest account is created as well, but it is inactive.

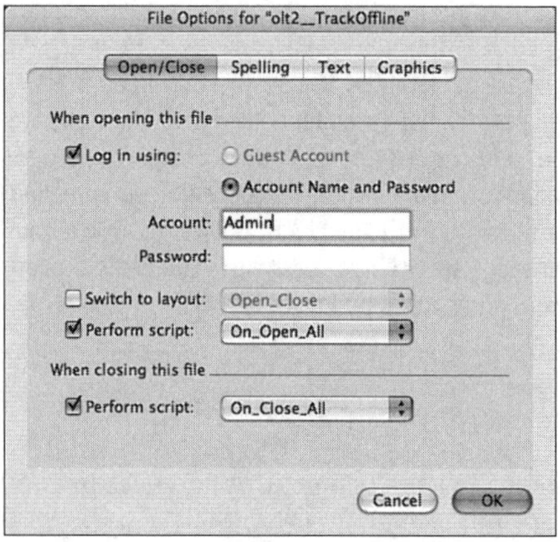

Figure 18.7
In the File Options dialog, you can specify an account to use as a default login.

EXTENDED PRIVILEGES

If a file was set to be Multi-User or Multi-User (Hidden) prior to conversion, all the privilege sets will have the fmapp extended privilege enabled when it is converted to FileMaker Pro 7. This is required for accounts to be able to open files hosted by FileMaker Server or shared peer-to-peer. You can certainly enable or disable this extended privilege after conversion as fits your deployment needs.

RELATIONSHIPS

During conversion, relationships are turned into table occurrences. For instance, if you have a relationship from File A to File B called "File B by someKey," when you convert these files, the Relationships Graph for File A will have an external table occurrence called "File B by someKey." The number of table occurrences in the converted file will be equal to the number of relationships in the old file. Settings from the relationship, such as cascading delete and the ability to add records through the relationship, will be retained in the converted solution.

As illustrated previously in Figure 18.1, the Relationships Graph in a converted solution is always in a hub-and-spoke configuration. The hub is a table occurrence associated with the file's base table; it is named the same as the table (and the file itself). All the other table occurrences are connected to the hub as spokes are connected to a wheel. All the layouts in the file are associated with the hub table occurrence, which means that it is always the context for all scripts, calculations, imports, and exports.

NOTE

> Remember that each file in a relational solution is turned into a file in FileMaker 8 during conversion. Each has its own hub-and-spoke Relationships Graph.

If you plan on doing any future development in your converted system, you'll likely want to spend some time organizing the Relationships Graphs. This may simply mean repositioning and resizing table occurrences to make particular relationships easier to locate. You might also consider using color as a means of organizing the graphs, or using the new Notes feature in FileMaker 8 to add descriptive notes to the graph. Finally, depending on what sort of conventions you used to name your relationships, you may want to change the names of the table occurrences to better reflect their purposes.

Down the road, consider making some more significant changes to the converted Relationships Graph. Many of the relationships from previous versions of FileMaker either could be implemented differently or are not required at all in FileMaker 8. For instance, many developers used relationships based on constants as a means for setting and retrieving global field values from other files. In FileMaker 8, fields with global storage can be accessed from any table occurrence, even ones disconnected from the current context. Likewise, relationships built with multiline and/or concatenated keys can be built in FileMaker 8 with join types other than equi-joins and/or multiple match criteria. These aren't changes you need to make prior to deployment, but they do make the converted solution easier to maintain and extend in the long run.

SCRIPTS

Many script steps in FileMaker 8 have slightly different parameters or behavior than in previous versions, and as such, you need to be vigilant in regard to a few potential post-conversion issues. The conversion routine actually adds steps to your scripts in some cases as a way to compensate for functional changes.

Some of the changes, and the issues that arise from them, include the following:

- The Go To Layout script step no longer has an option to Refresh Window. If you had checked this option, a Refresh Window script step is inserted during a conversion, directly after the Go To Layout step.

- The Refresh Window script step no longer has an option to Bring to Front. A Select Window [Current Window] step is added to scripts that had this option specified. This can cause some extra screen flashing in some instances, so you may need to remove Select Window steps to achieve the behavior you want.

- The Perform Script step no longer has the option not to perform subscripts. This was a feature that was infrequently used, so chances are that you won't miss it. In FileMaker 8, subscripts are always run. The conversion routine does nothing to account for this, nor does anything in the conversion log alert you of any Perform Script steps where the subscripts button was unchecked. If this was a feature you relied on in your solution, you may need to rework some of your scripts during post-conversion testing.

18

- In versions of FileMaker prior to 7, when an external script was called as the last step of a script, the external file's window would become active, having the effect of leaving the user in the other file. The same holds true of `Go to Related Record` steps. That's no longer the case. To accommodate this change, the conversion routine inserts a `Select Window` step following certain `Perform Script` and `Go to Related Records` steps. If a script ends with a call to an external subscript or with a `Go to Related Records` step, the conversion routine adds a `Select Window [Name: "NameOfOtherFile"]`. When these steps are not found at the end of a script, a `Select Window [CurrentWindow]` is added. The selection of another file's window, however, can be a bit fragile because the name of the window is hard-coded as the filename itself. If no window by that name exists, control isn't passed properly to the external file. You may need to edit the `Select Window` steps—or perhaps even delete some of them—for your script to function as it did previously. Having the wrong window in the foreground is probably the most frequent (and happily, most conspicuous) problem you'll face.

- There is no `Show Message` script step in FileMaker 8. During conversion, it is changed into a `Show Custom Dialog` step. The default title of the dialog is simply Message, and the message itself is the text of your old script. You need to make no post-conversion changes to these; simply be aware of the change that occurs.

- The settings stored on the Windows operating system for `Print` and `Print Setup` script steps may not convert properly. Be sure to test, and if necessary re-specify, these print settings after conversion. It may help to go back to your previous solution and take screen shots of the settings stored for particular scripts so that you can easily restore them post-conversion.

- The `Open File` script step in FileMaker 7 and 8 always activates the file being opened. In earlier versions, the `Open` script step would do this only if it were the last step in the script. Any additional steps after the `Open` step would cause the calling file to remain active. For example, say you have a script in File A that has two steps: `Open ["File B"]` and `Exit Record/Requests`. When performed in a previous version of FileMaker Pro, File A would remain the active file throughout the script. To retain this behavior, you need to add a `Select Window [Current Window]` after the `Open File` script step.

- FileMaker 7 and 8 require much greater attention to the opening and committing (saving) of records than previous versions did. Consequently, some of your scripts may require some post-conversion tweaking so they behave as desired. For instance, if a script ends with a step that modifies a record, such as a `Set Field`, the record isn't committed when the script ends. This may cause users not to see refreshed data until they manually commit the record. If the script in question was called as a subscript, there may be other unintended behaviors because the edited record would still be locked. The fix for this is to add a `Commit Record/Request` step at the end of any script that modifies data.

NOTE

> Because `Exit Record/Request` converts into `Commit Record/Request`, you can also fix many of these problems as pre-conversion tasks.

- In older versions of FileMaker, the `Go to Field` step would generate an error if the record was locked, so it was common to use this step as a test in scripts that needed to be able to modify records. In FileMaker 8, simply entering a field no longer attempts to place a lock on a record, so it doesn't generate errors that you can rely on. You should therefore find and change any `Go to Field` step that serves this need into an `Open Record/Request` step (which does explicitly try to lock the record).

- FileMaker 7 and 8 handles summary field sorting differently than older versions of FileMaker did. Instead of being able to specify only a single summary field as one of your sort criteria, in FileMaker 7 and 8 you can re-sort any number of sort criteria based on summary fields. During conversion, scripts that store sorts that include summary fields are altered so that the summary field is attached to the last nonsummary field in the sort criteria. For instance, say you have a summary report of customers and invoices where you sort by `CustomerName`, then by `InvoiceDate`, and finally by `TotalInvoiced` (a summary field). Your report would not list customers alphabetically, but rather from lowest to highest, based on the total you had invoiced. After conversion, your script's sort would have two criteria: `CustomerName` and `InvoiceDate`. The latter would be reordered by `TotalInvoiced`. You would need to manually adjust the sort criteria so that the `TotalInvoiced` summary was applied to the `CustomerName` field rather than `InvoiceDate` for your report to display the way it did previously.

- In older versions of FileMaker Pro, after sorting a set of records, the active record was always the first one in the sorted set. In FileMaker 7 and 8, the active record will remain whatever it was prior to sorting. Because this could have adverse impact on scripts that expect to be on the first record after a sort, a `Go To Record/Request/Page[First]` step is automatically added after every `Sort` script step during conversion.

- If you've specified scripts to execute when a file opens or closes, these preferences are retained in the converted file. Be aware, however, that they may be triggered at slightly different times in FileMaker 8. Startup scripts execute the first time that a window for a particular file becomes visible. For instance, if File A has relationships to File B, when File A is opened, File B appears in the list of hidden files in parentheses, meaning that there are no windows for that file, hidden or active. If you were to select that file from the list, the startup script for that file would run. Shutdown scripts run when the last window for a given file is closed. The `Close File` script step closes any windows for that particular file, thereby triggering the shutdown script. In both of these cases, however, if files that have relationships to the file you just closed are still open, the filename still appears in the list of hidden windows in parentheses. Thus, a file is not truly closed until all files that reference it are closed as well.

FIELDS AND FORMULAS

There are some subtle (and some not so subtle) differences in FileMaker 8 regarding fields and formulas. As with scripts, you'll find that the conversion routine does a good job at heading off many problems by modifying your code a bit. Still, a few things can go awry in a converted solution that you'll need to deal with during post-conversion testing.

- For the most part, conversion to FileMaker Pro 8 behaves the same as conversion to FileMaker Pro 7. There's at least one difference that you should be aware of. Conversion to FileMaker Pro 7 changed the order of operations for compound tests involving a Not operator. For example, say you had the following formula in FileMaker Pro 6:

  `If ( not IsEmpty (Nickname) and IsEmpty (FirstName), Nickname, FirstName)`

  This will be changed during conversion to FileMaker 7 into

  `If ( not (IsEmpty (Nickname) and IsEmpty (FirstName)) ; Nickname; FirstName)`

  These are very different functions and will return different results. The first looks to see whether there's a value in the Nickname field but not in the FirstName field; the latter tests whether there's a value in both fields. This conversion behavior was changed in FileMaker 8; the initial, intended logic will be retained by the conversion process.

- FileMaker 7 and 8 use new reserved words that didn't have the same significance in previous versions. For instance, Bold and Italic are potential parameters in the new TextStyleAdd and TextStyleRemove functions; you would be warned in FileMaker 8 that these are illegal filenames. If you used any reserved words or illegal names in your old system, anytime they were used in calculation formulas they are enclosed, upon conversion, with the symbols ${ } to avoid confusion with the reserved words. A field named Bold in your previous solution would appear as ${Bold} in formulas in FileMaker 8. The conversion log also lists this as a Poor field name.

- FileMaker 7 and 8 use a new shortcut evaluation method to speed up the processing of calculation formulas. This can cause problems in a converted system if you were relying on every portion of a formula being evaluated. As an example, say you have the formula `If (Length(myField) > 10 and Left (myField, 1) = "X", 1, 2)`. When FileMaker evaluates the first part of the test, `Length(myField) > 10`, if that does not return True, then it doesn't bother evaluating the other half of the test. It immediately knows that the False result must be returned. In older versions of FileMaker, external function calls to plug-ins were often placed in innocuous places in functions; it's possible they may not be invoked after conversion. For instance, in the formula `If ( 1 or External ("myPlugin", "someParameter"), 1, 2)`, the plug-in would never be invoked because the first part of the test is sufficient to establish which value should be returned.

- The Today function is not supported in FileMaker 7 or 8. During conversion, references to Today in scripts and validation checks are converted into Get (CurrentDate). If it's used in stored calculation fields, a new date field called Today is added to your database; it is set to auto-enter the creation date. Additionally, a new script called Update Today Field is added to the file; it's shown in Figure 18.8. This script is set as the file's startup script, or, if it already has a startup script, that script is modified so that it calls the Update Today Field script as its first step.

- The results returned by DatabaseNames and Status(CurrentFileName) included file extensions in previous versions of FileMaker Pro. In FileMaker 7 and 8, DatabaseNames and Get (FileName) do not return file extensions. You may need to edit scripts and fields that presume the presence of a file extension. For instance, you might have checked to see whether a file foo.fp5 was open by using the formula PatternCount (DatabaseNames, "foo.fp5"). This formula always returns 0 in FileMaker 7 and 8. Be aware also that no existing data is affected during conversion. If you have a field that auto-enters the results of Status (CurrentFileName) into the field (or even a stored calculation with the same formula), then after conversion all your data will still contain a file extension, but any new data you create won't. This sort of inconsistency should be avoided; it may have adverse consequences down the road.

Figure 18.8
The conversion routine automatically adds this script to your file if you have fields that use the Today function.

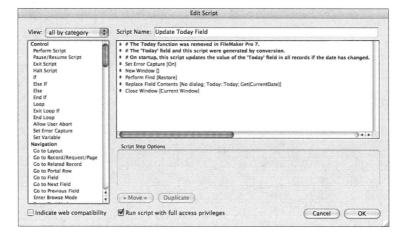

- The indexing rules have changed slightly. For instance, non-alphanumeric characters weren't indexed in previous versions but are in FileMaker Pro 7 and later. One of the consequences of the new indexing rules is that hyphens are considered word breaks for the first time. For instance, WordCount ("testA-testB") returns 2 in FileMaker 8 but only 1 in versions 6 and earlier. Some text parsing routines may need to be changed to account for this.

- Alphabetic characters, spaces, colons, and plus signs are not acceptable separators in date fields in FileMaker 8. If your older files use any of these as separators, your converted dates will be invalid. You can test for invalid dates after conversion by doing a find for ? in date fields. You can clean up invalid dates using a calculated Replace that uses the Substitute function. Similarly, if you have fields involved in relationships and the field data contain trailing spaces, the relationships might no longer resolve correctly. For example, a record in Table A that contained the value 123 used to find 123 as a related record, but it won't in FileMaker 8 until the trailing space is removed.

- Versions of FileMaker prior to 7 interpret text strings placed in a number field one of three ways. If the text string begins with the letters Y or T (representing Yes and True), it is considered to have a value of 1. Text strings beginning with an N or F (representing No and False) are considered to have a value of 0. With any other starting character, the value is considered blank. In FileMaker 8, all text strings are regarded as having no numeric value. Frequently, developers captured Yes/No radio button responses in number fields, knowing they could perform math as if these were 1 and 0. In a converted solution, any formula that relies on this behavior returns incorrect values. You can either edit these formulas so they explicitly regard Y and T as 1 and N and F as 0, or you can perform a Find/Replace action to modify your legacy data.

- With the exception noted in the previous bullet, text placed in number fields was ignored by older versions of FileMaker Pro. If, for instance, a number field called `myNum` contained a value of `23 skidoo`, `Length (myNum)` would return 2. In FileMaker 8, text functions recognize text characters found in number fields, so this function would return 9. To correct for this, all number fields used as parameters in text functions are wrapped with a `GetAsNumber` function, which strips out any nonnumeric characters. Don't be surprised if you see `GetAsNumber` sprinkled throughout your field definitions after conversion. It may not be needed, but it's a case of better safe than sorry.

- The contents of container fields are preserved during conversion, but depending on what platform you do the conversion, you may have some post-conversion work before they can be displayed properly cross-platform. In older versions of FileMaker Pro, when the Store Compatible Graphics option was selected in a file's document preferences, both Windows Metafile and PICT images were stored in a single container field. The Windows Metafile data is not immediately accessible if you use a Mac for the conversion. You can restore it by opening the files on a PC and viewing each record with a container field. If, on the other hand, you use a PC for the conversion, be sure that QuickTime is installed or else the PICT data is not preserved.

TIP

> If you think you may have issues with container fields, be sure that you test your alpha conversion files on both platforms. If it's convenient, perform the final conversion on a PC with QuickTime to avoid this issue altogether.

- The `Mod` function in FileMaker 7 and 8 handles negative numbers differently than older versions did. For example, in older versions, `Mod (-10, 3)` would return –1, but it returns 2 in FileMaker 8.

TROUBLESHOOTING

DISABLING STARTUP SCRIPTS

I've converted a solution, but it won't open properly.

Because of the changes that take place during conversion, there are many reasons your files may not open properly after conversion. The typical cause for this is a startup script that attempts to validate for conditions that no longer are true. For instance, a startup script may check that a certain plug-in is available. If you haven't installed the plug-in in FileMaker 8, or if the interface to it has changed, your script might not be able to get by the validation check.

Another typical problem in startup scripts is checking to see that some set of related files is open. The `DatabaseNames` function used to return file extensions of open files, but doesn't do this in FileMaker 7 or 8. Validating that `foo.fp5` is open, for instance, may cause a startup script to deny entry into the system.

If you experience problems opening a converted solution, try disabling the startup scripts in the pre-converted files and try again.

REPOINTING TABLE OCCURRENCE REFERENCES

After conversion, I've attempted to consolidate tables from multiple files into a single file, but the relationships, scripts, and portals all get pointed to the wrong fields when I repoint the table occurrence references.

One of the more difficult post-conversion tasks you can attempt is to consolidate tables from multiple files into a single file. In FileMaker 7, you would typically have begun by manually creating a new table in one of your files. The new table would be defined with fields named the same as those in one of your other files, the intention being to consolidate the second file into the first. Among other tasks, you would have to "repoint" relationships to table occurrences based on the new, consolidated table. On the Relationships Graph, when you repoint table occurrences from the external table to the new internal table, the match fields involved in the relationship may change, even if you've taken great care to keep all the field names exactly the same.

This happens because the match fields don't resolve by name, but rather by field ID. Therefore, if you create the fields in a different order, or have ever deleted fields, thereby leaving "holes" in your field IDs, the relationships won't match up correctly. This also affects portals and scripts that reference fields through the changed table occurrences.

 FileMaker 8 makes this type of consolidation a great deal easier. You can move tables between files in two ways: either by using the Import feature in the Define Database dialog, Tables tab; or by copying and pasting tables between files (you'll need FileMaker Pro 8 Advanced for this). Both of these methods will preserve the field IDs from the original file, and all relationships and references will continue to work as expected.

The moral of the story, of course, is that you should be using FileMaker 8, and we especially recommend you use FileMaker Pro 8 Advanced for conversion work.

After consolidating tables into a single file, be aware that you still need to move all your layouts, scripts, value lists, privilege settings, and data into the new file. None of these is a trivial activity. If consolidation of tables into a single file is one of the goals you hope to achieve from migrating to FileMaker 8, you may be better off rewriting your system.

FILEMAKER EXTRA: CONVERTING WEB-ENABLED DATABASES

If your existing solutions are web-enabled, then you have a few additional concerns when migrating to FileMaker 8. The web capabilities of FileMaker 8 are considerably different from previous versions; your migration plan depends mainly on the technology you used to web-enable your solution.

INSTANT WEB PUBLISHING

No Instant Web Publishing (IWP) configuration options are retained during conversion of a solution from FileMaker 6 or older to FileMaker Pro 7 or 8. IWP is so greatly improved in FileMaker 8 that the older configuration options are irrelevant and unnecessary. Where you were limited to a handful of layouts and themes before, IWP now has a status area that is very similar to that in FileMaker Pro itself, and it allows a user to potentially access any layout in a file. More than 70 script steps are IWP compatible (compared to about a dozen before), making IWP a very powerful and flexible Web technology. Even though no IWP settings are preserved during conversion, if you used IWP in your previous solution, you'll be up and running again within a matter of minutes.

Security in IWP is now handled just as it is for FileMaker users—via accounts and privilege sets—so you can easily create special accounts for Web users and restrict them to web-friendly layouts.

→ **See** Chapter 21, "Instant Web Publishing," **p. 633**, for more information on how to use IWP to web-enable a database.

CUSTOM WEB PUBLISHING

The other methods for web-enabling FileMaker solutions are often grouped under the banner of "Custom Web Publishing" (CWP). However, your migration path depends on what flavor of CWP you use.

CDML

CDML (Claris Dynamic Markup Language) is no longer supported in FileMaker 7 and 8. FileMaker has instead focused its CWP efforts on XML/XSLT. You can, thankfully, convert your CDML format files to XSLT stylesheets by using the CDML to XSLT Conversion Tool, which comes with FileMaker Server Advanced.

We strongly suggest that you use the conversion tool only after you have gained some proficiency working with XML and XSLT stylesheets. Even if the converted pages work flawlessly, without some knowledge of how they work, you'll be hard pressed to fix problems or extend the solution.

XML/XSLT

If you previously used the XML output from FileMaker as part of a custom web publishing solution, your previous code should require only minor programming changes to work with FileMaker 8. The biggest change you'll face will likely be understanding and setting up the new Web publishing components. There is, of course, no longer a FileMaker Unlimited or a Web Companion. All custom web publishing ties directly into FileMaker Server Advanced via the Web Publishing Engine.

There are also some changes to the query syntax and to the XML grammars that FileMaker can return; you can read about these in detail in Chapter 23, "Custom Web Publishing." You need to learn about the changes and make modifications to your code as necessary.

PHP

PHP has become a popular tool for web-enabling FileMaker Pro databases. Most people using PHP as part of their FileMaker Web publishing strategy make use of the FX.php class, developed and distributed for free by Chris Hansen (www.iviking.org). When PHP exchanges data with FileMaker, it does so via XML, but the FX class makes all of this transparent to the developer.

Because of the changes to the query syntax and XML grammars, you need to swap in an updated copy of FX.php for use with your converted files. If you rename files, layouts, or fields, you may have a bit of programming to do, but the changes should be minimal.

18

DATA INTEGRATION AND PUBLISHING

CHAPTER 19

IMPORTING DATA INTO FILEMAKER PRO

In this chapter

WORKING WITH EXTERNAL DATA

FileMaker Pro can work with data from a variety of other sources. It's possible to bring data directly into FileMaker from a number of different flat-file formats, as well as from remote databases and XML-based data sources. In many cases, you can open data files from other applications simply by dropping them onto the FileMaker Pro application as though they were native FileMaker files. FileMaker can also import data that resides on other computers (such as data from a remote database or a web-based XML data source), or even from devices such as a digital camera.

→ Additional information bearing on the topic of FileMaker data exchange can be found in Chapter 20, "Exporting Data from FileMaker," **p. 595**, and Chapter 22, "FileMaker and Web Services," **p. 669**.

FLAT-FILE DATA SOURCES

Flat file is a generic term that refers to a file containing data in row-and-column format. If you think of a spreadsheet that holds data about personal contacts, the spreadsheet will have some number of columns, for attributes such as first name, last name, address, and so forth, and some number of rows, each one representing a single contact.

The formats of flat files can vary. Some might separate one column from the next by tabs, and one row from the next by carriage returns (a tab-delimited file). Another might use commas to separate column values. Some might include a first row that gives a name for each column. Some might be in a plain text format that you could read with any text editor, whereas others might be in specialized file formats (such as FileMaker Pro or Microsoft Excel). In general, though, all flat-file data sources represent some variation on the idea of row-and-column data.

CHOOSING THE TARGET TABLE

As you can tell from the previous description, a flat data file maps well onto the concept of a database table. And indeed, in FileMaker Pro, we do import data into only one table at a time. FileMaker chooses this target table for you automatically, based on the prevailing table context.

Current Table Context

The current table context is determined by the active layout. You can examine the table context for a given layout by choosing View, Layout Mode, and then choosing Layouts, Layout Setup and inspecting the Show Records From menu. Be sure to switch back to Browse mode before trying to import records, though.

→ For a full discussion of table context, **see** "Understanding Table Context," **p. 164**.

INITIATING THE IMPORT

We give the example of importing tab-separated data because it's a good example of a typical text-based flat-file format. Many of the other text-based formats vary from tab-separated text only in small details. We'll note those differences further on. Here we'll walk through the process of importing from a tab-separated text file.

Like other types of data, a tab-separated data file can be imported in one of three ways:

- Choose File, Import Records, then navigate to the file and select it.
- Choose File, Open, then navigate to the file and select it.
- Drag and drop the file directly onto the FileMaker Pro application.

Importing and opening non–FileMaker files are very similar actions in FileMaker Pro. The main difference is that the "open" action creates a new FileMaker file (complete with data from the originating document), whereas the "import" action is used to bring data into an existing file. Importing can also be used to bring in images from a digital camera, or data from multiple files in a folder—neither of these is possible if you use either variation of the Open command.

THE IMPORT FIELD MAPPING DIALOG

When you're importing data, after you've chosen your source file you'll be presented with the Import Field Mapping dialog box, shown in Figure 19.1. This dialog lets you choose how the records in your source file will be imported, and in what order.

Figure 19.1
FileMaker's Import Field Mapping dialog. All importing processes pass through this dialog at some point.

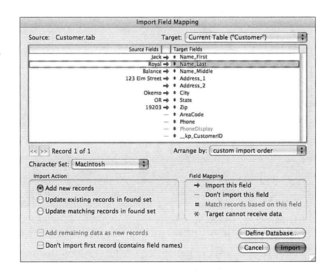

The Field Mapping dialog lists two filenames at the top, called Source and Target. Source is the file from which you're importing, and Target refers to the current table in the current file—in other words, the one that's receiving the imported data.

CHOOSING AN IMPORT ACTION

One of the things you need to choose in the Import Field Mapping dialog is called the Import Action. It's visible in the lower left of the dialog box. This choice tells FileMaker whether to try to *add* new records in the target table (one record per row of source data), or whether to try to *update* the existing FileMaker records with the source data. Updating on import is a topic in its own right, which we deal with later in this chapter. For now, we'll cover what happens when we want to create new FileMaker records based on the source data.

ALIGNING SOURCE AND TARGET FIELDS

You also need to decide which fields in the target are to receive data, and from which source columns they'll receive data. Figure 19.2 shows the field structure for a FileMaker table designed to hold customer information. It consists mostly of text fields, with the exception of the PhoneDisplay field, which is meant to create a formatted display from the AreaCode and Phone fields.

Figure 19.2
The field structure for a basic table of customer information.

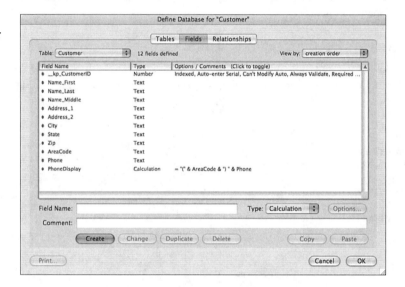

Assume that you want to import some data into this customer table. The source file is a tab-separated file containing first name, middle name, last name, address1, address2, city, state, and zip. (Notice the order is a little different from the field order on the FileMaker side.) To do this, you'd choose File, Import Records, File. From the Show menu choose Tab-Separated Text, and then navigate to your file and select it. The result is shown in Figure 19.3.

If we look at the way the source fields line up with the target fields, something isn't right. We have a record for someone named Jack Royal Balance. But this record will be imported into the system as Jack Balance Royal if nothing is changed in the import order. In the FileMaker creation order, middle name comes after last name, but in the source file, it comes before. It's not possible to manipulate the ordering of the fields on the left (the source fields), but you can use the black up-down arrows next to each target field to change the target ordering manually. In this case you'd just drag the Name_Middle field up one line to make it change places with Name_Last.

Figure 19.3
Another look at the Import Field Mapping dialog. Note that the source and target fields don't quite line up correctly. Jack R. Balance is about to enter the system as Jack B. Royal.

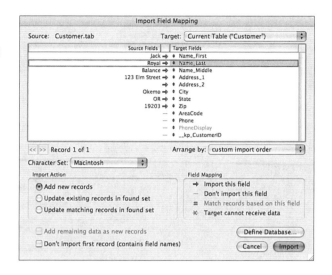

CAUTION

When you change the target field ordering by dragging a field manually, the field you drag *changes places* with the field you drop it on. Often you might want to drop the field you're moving between two others in the import ordering, so that it pushes all the fields underneath it down a step, but this is *not* how the manual ordering works.

DECIDING WHERE THE DATA GOES

After all the target fields are correctly aligned with the source fields, you need to make sure they're all set to receive data. Between the columns of source and target fields is a column of field mapping indicators. The possible indicators are shown in the Import Field Mapping dialog, in the section at the lower right called Field Mapping, which is shown in Figure 19.4.

The meaning of the different indicators is as follows:

- **Arrow**—Data from the source field will be imported into the target field.
- **Straight line**—Data from the source field will not be imported into the target field.
- **Equal sign**—The source and target fields are being used as part of a match criterion. This choice is available only if you've chosen one of the update import actions. We discuss the update options fully in the following section (see "Updating Records with Imported Data").
- **Red x**—This indicates that the target field *cannot* receive data. Typical causes are that the target field is a calculation or summary field.

To sum up, you'll want to make sure that all your target fields are aligned with the correct source fields, and that the mapping indicators are set so as to allow data to flow into the fields you intend to receive it.

Figure 19.4
FileMaker's Import
Field Mapping
indicators.

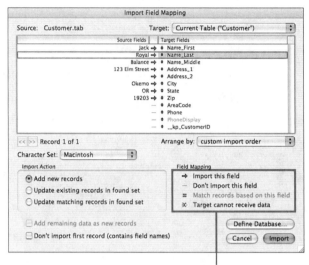

Field mapping indicators

WAYS OF AUTO-ALIGNING SOURCE AND TARGET FIELDS

In the Import Field Mapping dialog, you might have noticed a menu at the middle right called Arrange By. This menu simply governs the ordering of the target fields in the column on the right. It may be that you can line the target fields up with the source fields by putting the target fields in creation order, for example, or in alphabetical order by name. If you choose one of these options, FileMaker rearranges the target fields in the order you've chosen, and then does its best to set the mapping indicators accordingly. Most likely you'll need to do some manual adjustment of the result, but these choices can often eliminate a lot of tedious hand labor.

One very useful choice in this menu is the first one, called Matching Field Names. This choice is available only when the source file has some kind of data in it that attaches names to each of the source fields. Examples of such files are actual FileMaker files (of course), or flat data files with field names in the first row. If your source file contains field names that correspond to the names of target fields, you can choose this arrangement option and all the fields with identical names will simply line up, no matter what position they have in their respective files.

NOTE

This doesn't guarantee that the target fields will be able to accept data. If a source field has the same name as a field in the target table but the target field is defined as a calculation, the two will line up, but it will still be impossible to import any data into the target field (you cannot import into calculation fields).

SCANNING THE DATA BEFORE IMPORTING

When the Import Field Mapping dialog first opens, the Source column shows data from the first record in the source file. You may find that the first record's data is not enough to remind you of the appropriate field mapping, or you might want to scan through the source data for other reasons.

Directly under the source column, you'll notice forward-arrow and back-arrow buttons, and a display that shows the total number of inbound records, as well as the record you're currently viewing. You can use the forward and back arrow buttons to scan through the inbound data, either to verify that you have the correct mapping of source to target, or to examine it for other reasons.

PERFORMING THE IMPORT

After you've verified all your field mappings and made your choice of import action (so far we've looked only at adding records), pressing the Import button starts the import proper. When the import completes, FileMaker displays a dialog box telling you how many records were imported, and whether there were any errors in the import process.

Depending on how you have your field validation set up, the inbound data may or not be acceptable. Under certain circumstances, FileMaker may reject imported records for this reason. See "Imports and Validation" in the "Troubleshooting" section at the end of this chapter for more information.

Assuming that there were no serious errors and at least some records were imported, the newly imported records are isolated in their own found set after the import is complete. This is an important point because if there's something seriously amiss with the imported data you have an opportunity to delete the whole set and start over. Or, more optimistically, the records are all there in one set if you need to perform any other operations on them as a group, such as a batch Replace operation.

UPDATING RECORDS WITH IMPORTED DATA

When you import data into a FileMaker Pro table, you have a choice as to whether the source data should be used to create new records, or whether it should be added into records that already exist. (You can also choose to import the data into an entirely new table. This feature, new to FileMaker 8, is discussed in more detail later.)

As an example, suppose that you have a FileMaker file with a table of records about people. This table contains a name, address, Social Security number, and other information about each person. Let's say that you periodically want to import the most current address for each person, from some other source outside of FileMaker, and apply the most current address to each of your FileMaker records, without changing anything else about the record.

Assume that your table of personal data looks something like the data shown in Figure 19.5.

Then assume that you can get a data file from some other source, possibly governmental, that contains (among other things) a field for Social Security number and a few fields of address information. You'd like to match up the records in the source file with the records in your FileMaker table. Two records will be considered to match if they have the same Social

Security number. If there's a record on the FileMaker side that doesn't have a match in the source file, you'd expect it to be left alone. If there's a record in the source file that doesn't have a matching FileMaker record, you'd want to ignore the source record altogether.

All these goals are easily accomplished with FileMaker's import options. Figure 19.6 shows the necessary settings in the Import Field Mapping dialog.

Figure 19.5
Data structure for a table containing personal information.

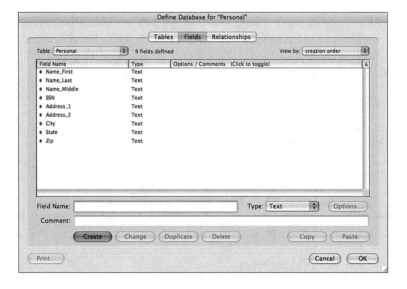

Figure 19.6
The Import Field Mapping dialog, preparing to import address data for records with matching Social Security numbers in the source.

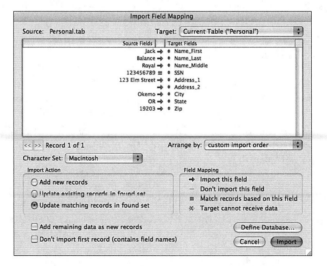

Here the action Update Matching Records In Found Set has been selected. This tells FileMaker that you're going to specify at least one pair of fields as matching fields. This pair of fields acts a lot like a match field in a FileMaker relationship: Each row (or record) in the source is matched with any corresponding records in the target.

FileMaker's Update Matching Records feature can be tricky. For an overview of some of the potential pitfalls, see "Matching Imports" in the "Troubleshooting" section at the end of the chapter.

In addition to choosing the Update Matching Records setting, it's also been chosen to bring in just the address fields. So these particular settings update just the address information, leaving all the other fields untouched.

As a final note on update importing, you should be aware that the update affects only records in the current found set on the target side. If a record on the target matches a record in the source, but the target record is outside the current found set, it is *not* affected by the import.

UPDATING RECORDS WITHOUT USING MATCH FIELDS

You've probably noticed that another update option is available in the Import Action section. It's called Update Existing Records in Found Set, and it's simpler than the Update Matching Records choice. When this action is selected, rather than matching records based on a match field or fields, FileMaker matches records based purely on their position: The first record in the source updates the first record in the current found set on the target side, the second source record updates the second found target record, and so on.

If the number of records in the source doesn't exactly equal the number of records in the target found set, FileMaker takes account of this. If there are more source records than target records, the extra source records are skipped. If there are more target records than source records, the extra target records are left untouched. In either case, FileMaker provides an extra message to tell you what happened.

The only exception occurs if you check the box labeled Add Remaining Data as New Records. In that case, if there are extra records on the source side, they are imported into the target as brand new records.

SPECIAL FLAT FILE FORMATS

All the flat file formats that are available for import into FileMaker have many similarities. They are generally text-based, row-and-column data files, suitable for import into a single target FileMaker table. Two of the possible formats are worth special mention.

IMPORTING FROM ANOTHER FILEMAKER PRO FILE

As you might expect, it's possible to import from other FileMaker Pro files. If you choose FileMaker Pro as your source format, you also need to specify a table in the source file from which you want to draw data. This choice is available in the Import Field Mapping dialog, as shown in Figure 19.7.

Importing from a FileMaker file can be particularly convenient in that it allows you to use the Matching Field Names option for lining up the source and target fields. Developers will often choose to open a source file within FileMaker, creating a new FileMaker file based on the originating document, and then use that new FileMaker file for importing, data cleanup, and so on.

→ For some other uses of the FileMaker-to-FileMaker import feature, **see** "FileMaker Extra: Exploiting the FileMaker-to-FileMaker Import," at the end of this chapter (**p. 592**).

IMPORTING FROM A MICROSOFT EXCEL FILE

FileMaker Pro has some special capabilities for importing data from Microsoft Excel documents. FileMaker is aware of multiple worksheets within an Excel document, and is also aware of any *named ranges* (a group of cells that's been given a specific name). When you select an Excel file for import, if it contains multiple worksheets or named ranges, FileMaker prompts you to select either a worksheet or a named range as the source for the data, as shown in Figure 19.8.

Figure 19.7
When importing from a FileMaker database with multiple tables, it's necessary to pick the source table from which you want to draw data.

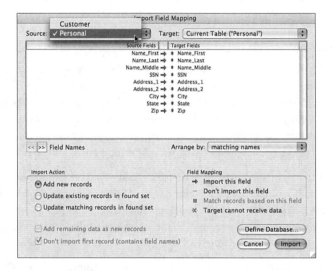

Figure 19.8
When you import data into FileMaker from an Excel document, you can import from a specific tab or a named Excel range.

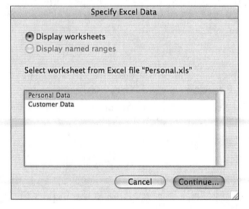

After you've chosen the specific part of the Excel document you want to import, the rest of the import proceeds.

If you're bringing Excel data into FileMaker by choosing File, Open, and selecting an Excel file to open, FileMaker creates a new FileMaker file, as it does when opening other "importable" file types. In this situation, FileMaker can apply a little extra intelligence to creating the new FileMaker file. If a column in the Excel file contains only one type of data (numbers, text, dates), FileMaker assigns a suitable field type to the resulting FileMaker field. If the data in the column are somehow "mixed"—that is, the column contains some data that look like numbers, and other data that look like dates, for example—then the resulting FileMaker field will be a Text field.

NOTE

> When importing from an Excel file, FileMaker brings in only the raw data it finds in the file. FileMaker does not import Excel formulas, only their results. FileMaker also does not import any graphics or charts, nor does it import notes. Programming logic, such as Visual Basic macros, is also not imported into FileMaker.

USING AN IMPORT TO CREATE A NEW TABLE

FileMaker 8 has added a nifty new capability to imports. In previous versions, you could only import data into an existing table within a file. In FileMaker 8, you may instead choose to create an entirely new table at the time of import, and have the imported data flow into the new table. Figure 19.9 illustrates the new feature.

Figure 19.9
FileMaker 8 enables you to create a new table from imported data.

19

The new table will behave in many ways like a table created by choosing File, Open and opening the data source directly (see the discussion of this behavior earlier in this chapter). This feature is particular useful, though, when importing from another FileMaker table. In this case, the entire schema of the table, including things like calculation and summary fields, is re-created. (Note that information such as value lists, custom functions, relationships, and security privileges will not be imported because they are attached at the file level rather than at the table level.) The newly created table will be an exact copy of the old one, including things such as field IDs (important if you're re-creating this table as a way of consolidating two formerly separate FileMaker files).

→ For a full discussion of consolidating multiple tables, **see** "Repointing Table Occurrence References," **p. 561**.

This capability, which is available in regular FileMaker Pro 8, is similar, though not identical, to the Import Table feature available only in FileMaker Pro 8 Advanced. The Import Table feature is limited to importing tables from other FileMaker files, but it can import many tables at once. Furthermore, the Import Tables function imports just the schema but no data, whereas with the Import As New Table feature, it's necessary to bring the data along—there's no way to copy just the schema of a table using this feature.

IMPORTING MULTIPLE FILES FROM A FOLDER

FileMaker can import data from several files at once. In this batch mode, FileMaker takes the data from a file and imports it into one or more fields in a FileMaker table. FileMaker can also bring in information about each file's name and directory path.

FileMaker can work with two types of data when performing a folder import: image files and text files. In the case of image files, FileMaker can bring the image data from each file into a container field so that each image can be viewed inside FileMaker. In the case of text files, FileMaker brings the entire contents of the file into a specified text field.

CAUTION

> FileMaker can store a maximum of 2GB of data in a single field. This may seem like a lot, and it *is* a lot compared to the limit of 64KB that was in force in previous versions of FileMaker! But it follows from this that you shouldn't import text or image files into FileMaker if any single imported file will be larger than 2GB.

IMPORTING TEXT FILES

Assume that you have a folder with a number of plain text files in it. Assume also that you have a FileMaker database that has a table in it with fields called TextContent, FileName, and FilePath. If you select File, Import Records, Folder, you'll see FileMaker's Folder of Files Import Options dialog box, shown in Figure 19.10.

In the upper area you can choose the folder from which to import data. You can also choose whether to confine the import to files at the first level inside the folder, or whether to drill into all the subfolders that might be below the top level.

After you've chosen a folder from which to import, choose the file type. To import from text files, choose the Text Files option and click Continue. You'll then see a folder import dialog box, similar but not identical to the regular Import Field Mapping dialog box, shown in Figure 19.11.

Figure 19.10
FileMaker kicks off the Import From Folder process with a special initial dialog box.

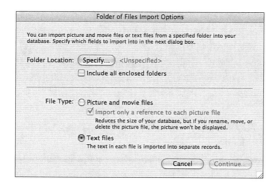

Figure 19.11
When importing from a folder of files, the source fields have a special name and meaning.

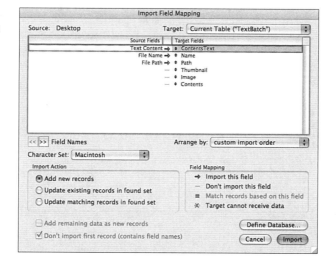

When you're doing a folder import, the names and contents of the source fields on the left are fixed: They depend on the type of file from which you're importing. When you're importing from text files, the source fields are called Text Content, File Name, and File Path. These fields contain, respectively, the actual text content of the field, the name of the individual file from which the data is coming, and the full name of the path to the file. As with any other data source, you can choose to import some or all of these fields, and you can choose how to map them to fields in the FileMaker table that's the target of the import.

Unlike imports from other kinds of flat-file data sources, FileMaker's batch text import brings the *entire* contents of each text file into a single FileMaker field.

After importing, you might have a data set that looks like the data seen in Figure 19.12.

Determining File Type

When you choose to import files from a folder, FileMaker scans the files in the directory to determine which ones are of the right type to import. So for each file in the folder, FileMaker decides whether it's an image file (if you're importing images) or a text file (if you're importing text). But how does it make this determination?

If you're familiar with the way file types are handled in Mac OS X and Windows, you know that the file's suffix (.html, .jpeg, and so on) often has a lot to do with it. Often, applications use the file suffix to determine whether an application "owns" that file type and can try to open it.

FileMaker's batch import determines file type differently, depending on platform. On Mac OS X, FileMaker looks first at the file's *type* and *creator*—special information (also called *metadata*) that Mac OS X stores with each file. If a file has no type or creator (for example, if it was created on a non–Macintosh platform), FileMaker falls back on the file suffix.

Windows, by contrast, has no file type metadata, so FileMaker simply relies on the file suffix to determine whether a file is eligible for a batch import.

What this means is that FileMaker has no other innate intelligence about file types. If you take an image or PDF file in Windows and give it a .txt file suffix, FileMaker considers it eligible for a text import and tries to bring its content into a text field. Likewise, if you strip out file type and creator on the Mac and manipulate the suffix, it's possible to confuse FileMaker about the file type.

To see a file's type and creator in Mac OS X, if you have the Apple Developer Tools installed, you can use the command-line tool /Developer/Tools/GetFileInfo to see file metadata, and /Developer/Tools/SetFile to change the metadata. Or you can use a shareware tool such as Xray (http://www.brockerhoff.net/xray/).

Figure 19.12
This is a sample data set resulting from a batch import of three text files from a folder.

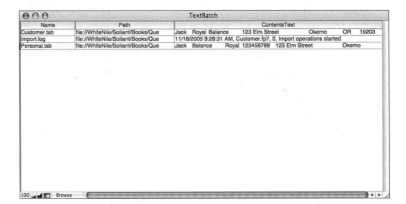

IMPORTING IMAGE FILES

Importing image files from a folder is quite similar to importing text files. See Figure 19.13 for a look at the folder-import options that apply to images. As with text files, you need to choose a source folder, and decide whether to drill down into any subfolders as well.

IMAGES OR REFERENCES?

In the past, FileMaker's usefulness as a tool for storing entire files (sometimes referred to as *asset management*) was somewhat limited by the 2GB maximum size of an individual FileMaker file. With FileMaker 7, the file size limit is reckoned in terabytes, so it's tempting to try to use FileMaker as a tool for managing large amounts of non–FileMaker data such as image files.

Still, image data can take up a great deal of storage space, and it may not make sense to try to store thousands of high-resolution images inside a FileMaker file. Accordingly,

FileMaker offers you the option (when importing images from a folder), to import only a *reference* to each file, rather than the entire contents of the image. If you choose to import a reference, FileMaker remembers where the image is stored on disk, and refers to it when necessary in a fashion similar to the way in which Mac OS and Windows work with short-cuts and aliases.

Figure 19.13
These are the special Import Field Mapping options for importing from a folder of images.

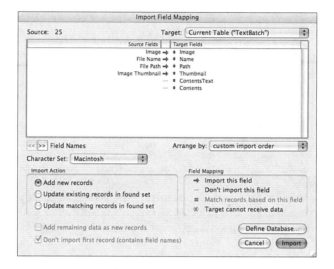

→ There are some additional considerations when using container fields in conjunction with FileMaker's Instant Web Publishing: **see** "Container Fields," **p. 607**.

The benefit of storing references is, of course, that they take up much less space in the database. The disadvantage is that if the original files are moved or renamed in any way, FileMaker will no longer be able to find them, and the images will not display in FileMaker nor be otherwise usable.

This is especially problematic if the file containing the images is hosted for multiuser access. Each user of the system needs to see the image directory via the same network path. Because Windows and Macintosh handle server paths differently, creating a unified server structure to work in both environments could be challenging.

In the end, the decision as to whether to import whole image files or just references is up to you, keeping in mind the tradeoff between the flexibility of having all images stored directly in the database, versus the increased capacity that comes from working with the file references alone.

IMAGES VERSUS THUMBNAILS

When you import data from text files, you can bring in up to three pieces of data: the filename, the full path to the file, and the text contents of the file. With image files, it is possible to bring in four pieces of data. As with text files, you can bring in the filename and file path. You can bring in the full contents of the image file (into a container field, presumably), and you can also bring in a smaller version of the image if you choose, called a

19

thumbnail. See Figure 19.12, shown previously, for a possible import configuration for a batch import of images.

Naturally, a full-sized image can take a lot of space, so FileMaker gives you the option of bringing in only a smaller thumbnail instead. You can bring in the thumbnail in addition to the larger image, or instead of it. (Of course, you could choose to import just the filename and path if that suited your purpose.)

> **TIP**
>
> FileMaker doesn't give you any control over how it creates thumbnails during the image import process. You may find that although you do want to store only a smaller copy of the image in the database, FileMaker's thumbnail process doesn't give you what you want. You might want the thumbnails a little smaller or larger, or with some kind of color adjustment. If so, you will want to experiment with creating your own thumbnails first, and import those instead.

Manipulating Images

With a tool such as Adobe Photoshop, it's possible to create batch-processing scripts (called *actions* in Photoshop) that can apply a series of transformations to every image in a folder. You might want to create an action to shrink every image to 120 pixels wide, 72 dots per inch, and save it as a high-quality JPEG with a two-pixel black border. You could then batch-import the resulting custom thumbnails. In doing so, you'd want to make sure to import the image data rather than the thumbnail data: If you asked FileMaker for the thumbnail data, your classy custom thumbnails would be further scrunched down into thumbnails of thumbnails—probably not the desired effect.

IMPORTING PHOTOS FROM A DIGITAL CAMERA

In Mac OS X, FileMaker is able to import photos from a digital camera, or a similar device such as a memory card reader. This procedure is fairly thoroughly covered in the manual, so we'll be content with a brief overview.

If you choose File, Import Records, Digital Camera on Mac OS X, with a compatible digital device connected to the computer and powered on, you'll see the dialog box shown in Figure 19.14. Here you'll have the opportunity to specify which photos you want to import from the camera or device, as well as the choice whether to import entire images or just image references. (See the earlier section titled "Images or References?" for details.)

> **TIP**
>
> If you choose the option to Specify Images in this dialog box, not only will you be able to select individual images for import, but you'll also be able to specify whether imported thumbnails should be small, medium, or large—an option that's not available when importing many images from a folder.

After you've decided on which photos to import, and whether to import them as images or full references, you'll proceed to the standard Import Field Mappings dialog. Just about everything here is as you expect it, but there's one possible difference, as you can see in Figure 19.15.

Figure 19.14
FileMaker has a variety of options for importing from a digital camera.

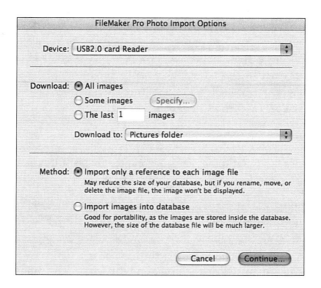

Figure 19.15
FileMaker can read and import EXIF data from a digital camera, in addition to the regular filename and path and image fields.

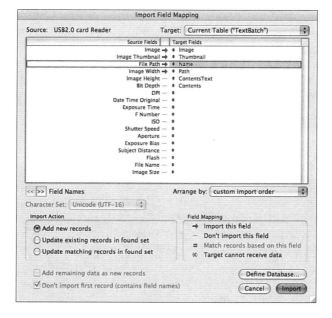

If the images you're importing contain EXIF (Exchangeable Image File) data, FileMaker can read and import that data as well. This data can include information such as the time of day, shutter speed, aperture, and film speed for the images, as well as many other pieces of data. The photos being imported in Figure 19.15 do contain EXIF data, as the long list of source fields shows; any or all of these fields are available for import. Many digital cameras capture EXIF data with each image.

IMPORTING FROM AN ODBC DATA SOURCE

In addition to importing data from resources on a local disk drive, such as individual flat files or folders of text or image files, FileMaker Pro can also access data sources that may be visible only over a network of some kind. One such type of remote data source is represented by remote databases, which FileMaker can access using a widespread technology known as *Open Database Connectivity (ODBC)*.

HOW ODBC WORKS

A full discussion of ODBC technologies is beyond the scope of this book. We'll have to be content with a fairly thorough overview.

Many database configurations are referred to as *client-server* configurations. Numerous *clients* (usually individual workstations) somehow connect to a database housed on a single master *server* (usually a powerful, centrally located computer). Each client interacts directly with the server to request data, or to submit changes to the database. Because there are ostensibly only two layers in this architecture (the client and the server), this kind of setup is also called a *two-tier architecture*.

FileMaker Pro, you may be aware, when coupled with FileMaker Server, represents a classic two-tier, client≠server architecture. FileMaker Pro is the client, of course, and FileMaker Server is, well, the server. FileMaker Pro and FileMaker Server communicate via a special FileMaker network protocol that isn't shared or understood by other applications. Figure 19.16 illustrates the FileMaker client≠server architecture.

Figure 19.16
A sketch of FileMaker's two-tier client≠server architecture.

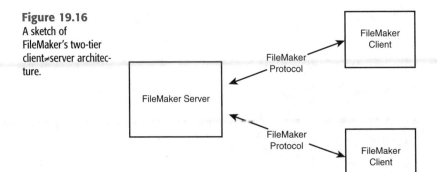

There are, of course, many other kinds of relational database servers in existence. Like FileMaker Server, each other product communicates using its own specialized protocol. But to overcome all this rampant disparity, a number of database and software vendors worked together to develop some more standard protocols for accessing database servers, so that rather than access databases a dozen different ways, clients can rely on a more consistent access method.

The result has been the ODBC standard. With ODBC, rather than having a client and a server communicate via a specific vendor protocol, the two sides can agree to communicate via ODBC instead. In this way, a client application that can use ODBC (such as FileMaker), can potentially communicate with any of the dozens of database products that use ODBC as well. Figure 19.17 illustrates the notion that a single client can communicate with many servers.

Figure 19.17
Using ODBC drivers and protocols, a single client application can communicate with many different types of ODBC-enabled servers.

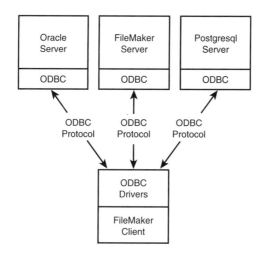

The ODBC standard is generally used with database servers that use the SQL (Structured Query Language) database language, but some non-SQL database servers (such as FileMaker Server, for instance) can also be accessed via ODBC.

→ This chapter covers techniques for bringing data *into* FileMaker via ODBC. Chapter 20, "Exporting Data from FileMaker," **p. 595**, covers how it's possible to extract data *from* FileMaker via ODBC.

INSTALLING ODBC

For a client and server to be able to communicate via ODBC, both sides need some special preparation. Many database servers can communicate via ODBC with no additional configuration. Some may require that special modules be added or certain settings be configured. For the purposes of this chapter we're going to assume that you need access to a server that has already been correctly configured for ODBC.

To participate in an ODBC communication, the client side must also be configured correctly. Generally, an individual client machine needs to have a special *driver* installed to allow it to communicate with a particular kind of database server. The driver is a piece of software, installed via the client's operating system, that knows how to talk to a particular kind of data source.

For example, if you want ODBC access to an Informix database from a client machine running Windows 2000, two things need to happen. First, the Informix server needs to be

19

configured for ODBC access. Second, you need an Informix ODBC driver that works under Windows 2000 to be installed on the client. If you want to perform similar access from a Mac OS X client, you need a separate Informix ODBC driver compatible with Mac OS X. ODBC drivers are not generally transferable, either across database servers or across operating systems: You need a driver that's specific both to the database you want to access and to the operating system you're working from.

CAUTION

One of FileMaker's most powerful appeals is that it's fully cross-platform (well, as long as the platforms under consideration are Mac or Windows). ODBC connectivity, by contrast, does not have as gleaming a record in the cross-platform arena. The Mac has historically lagged behind Windows in terms of ODBC support; it often used to take a long time, if ever, for the Mac to be able to use the latest ODBC drivers for a given database. The drivers for a version 8 of a certain database might appear on Windows, and not be followed by version 8 Mac drivers for months, or longer.

With the advent of Mac OS X, especially version 10.2 ("Jaguar"), the ODBC connectivity picture for the Mac is much improved. Mac OS X is of course a flavor of UNIX under the hood, opening the path for the porting and adoption of a wide range of UNIX-based ODBC tools.

The bottom line, though, is still buyer beware. If you want or need to delve into ODBC, be aware that there remain differences in the nature and extent of ODBC support on the different FileMaker target platforms.

CREATING A DSN

After your ODBC drivers are installed, the next step is to create one or more DSNs (Data Source Names) on the client computer(s). This is also somewhat beyond the scope of a book on FileMaker, but we'll touch on some of the major points.

NOTE

The exact mechanics of installing ODBC drivers vary depending on the particular drivers being installed and on the target operating system. Going into great detail on driver installation is outside the scope of this book. We're going to assume that your FileMaker client machine or machines have ODBC drivers installed on them for the databases or data sources you want to access via ODBC.

Both the Mac OS X (version 10.2 and greater) and Windows operating systems have built-in tools for working with ODBC drivers and DSNs. On the Mac, Apple ships a tool called ODBC Administrator, which can be found in the Application, Utilities folder. On Windows, there's a shortcut to the ODBC Data Administrator located in Start, Settings, Control Panel, Administrative Tools, Data Sources (ODBC).

To create a DSN to access a particular ODBC-based data source, you need to have a driver for that particular data source installed on the computer you're working from. Figure 19.18 shows the Mac and Figure 19.19 shows the Windows ODBC tools with a list of available drivers. Windows systems tend to have a great many ODBC drivers installed by default. Mac OS X, by contrast, doesn't install any ODBC drivers by default.

Figure 19.18
The Mac OS X ODBC Administrator.

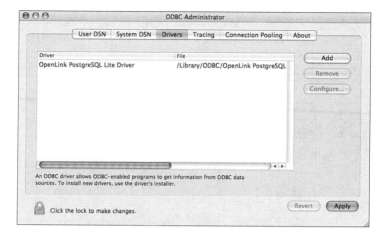

Figure 19.19
The Windows 2000 ODBC Data Source Administrator.

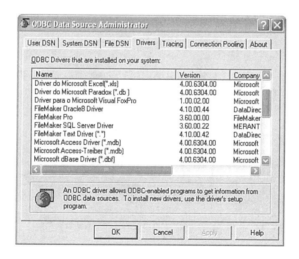

You need to create a DSN that uses the appropriate driver for the data source you're trying to work with. You probably also need to do some configuration of the DSN. Depending on the type of data source you're using, the DSN configuration can vary widely. To access a SQL database, for example, you'd generally need to configure the DSN with the hostname or IP address of the database server, a username, a password, and possibly the name of a specific SQL database. We show a sample DSN configuration screen in Figure 19.20, but in general, each DSN needs to be configured differently, and we can't give any general guidelines in a book of this nature. You'll need to consult the documentation for the particular ODBC driver you're using, and you may need to enlist the aid of someone, such as a database administrator, who's aware of the configuration settings for the data source you're trying to access.

NOTE

> You have a choice between creating a User DSN and creating a System DSN. These two kinds of DSNs differ only in who can access them: System DSNs are meant to be accessible to all users on a system, whereas a user DSN is meant to be accessible only to the user that created it. FileMaker can work with either type, though it respects the access restrictions: You'll be able to access a user DSN from FileMaker only if the DSN is accessible to you.

Figure 19.20
Defining a DSN for the PostgreSQL open source database in Mac OS X.

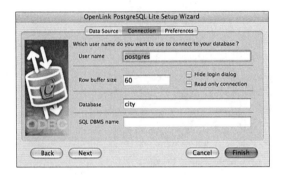

PERFORMING THE ODBC IMPORT

After you have a working DSN for the ODBC data source you want to access, importing from the data source is simply a matter of selecting File, Import Records, ODBC Data Source. You'll see a list of available DSNs, as shown in Figure 19.21.

Figure 19.21
When you begin an import from an ODBC data source, FileMaker prompts you to choose an ODBC DSN.

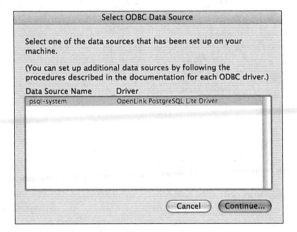

Here, two DSNs are available: a user DSN and a system DSN, both of which make connections to a PostgreSQL database. (PostgreSQL is an extremely powerful open source SQL database.)

If the data source to which you're connecting requires authentication, you might see a password prompt like the one shown in Figure 19.22.

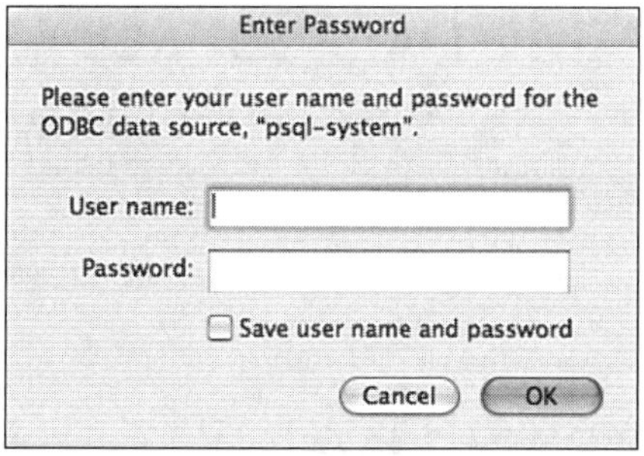

Figure 19.22
Some ODBC data sources may prompt you for authentication.

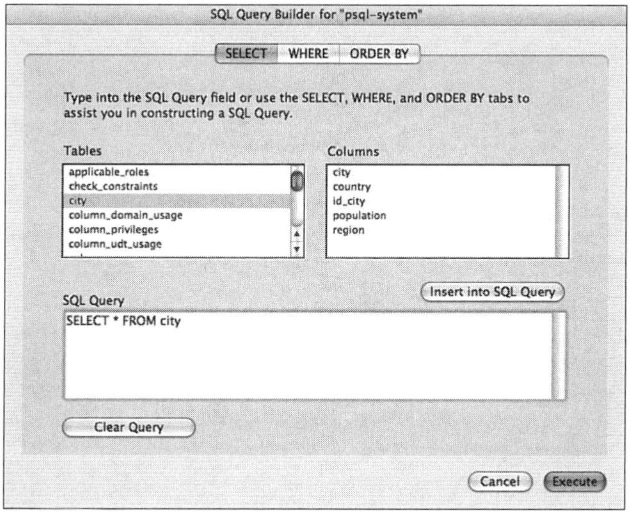

Figure 19.23
When importing from a SQL-based ODBC data source, you'll probably need to formulate a SQL query via a wizard like this one.

After you pass the authentication prompt, you'll likely see some additional dialog boxes, depending on the type of ODBC data source you're accessing. For SQL-based data sources, for example, you'll likely see a dialog that helps you formulate a SQL query, such as the one shown in Figure 19.23.

Here we're fetching data from a table called city in a remote PostgreSQL database. The SQL query instructs the ODBC driver to fetch all fields from the city table.

After this query is run, you'll be confronted with FileMaker's Import Field Mappings dialog, with which we've dealt extensively in this chapter. The dialog lets you map the fields from the SQL data source onto the fields in the FileMaker table.

Again, the options for ODBC import can vary widely depending on the particular driver and data source you're using. It's a bit beyond the scope of this book to provide a full overview of ODBC, SQL, or particular drivers. You may need to experiment a bit, or consult with the oft-mentioned local systems expert (in case it isn't you!) to arrive at the correct configuration for importing ODBC data.

IMPORTING FROM AN XML DATA SOURCE

Importing data from an XML data source is a large topic—so large, in fact, that we devote an entire chapter to it, in the more general context of discussing how FileMaker can interact with web services.

→ For a full explanation of FileMaker's XML import capabilities, **see** Chapter 22, "FileMaker and Web Services, **p. 669**.

USING A SCRIPT TO IMPORT DATA

Like most other actions in FileMaker Pro, importing data can be triggered from a script. It's possible to save your import settings in a script for later reuse as well.

A scripted import has a few steps and options that are slightly different from the regular File, Import Records method. To import records from within a script, choose the Import Records script step and add it to your script. ScriptMaker gives you several choices, as shown in Figure 19.24.

Figure 19.24
FileMaker enables you to save a number of options when you import records from within a script.

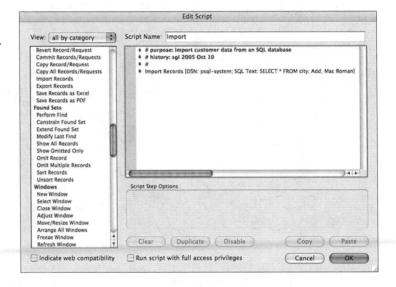

The Specify Data Source menu at the lower right gives you access to a set of options identical to those you see when you choose File, Import Records. Using this selection, you can save all the important information about your data source. For files, this means mainly the filename. For folders, it includes the file type, and the choice of whether to save references. For ODBC data sources, it includes the DSN information, password, and other data such as a SQL query.

The Specify Import Order button at the lower right gives you access to the Import Field Mapping dialog, where you can set any or all the relevant import mapping features.

Finally, as with other script steps in FileMaker, you have the choice of performing the import with or without dialogs. If you choose to run the import with dialogs, the user can re-specify any aspect of the data source or import order on the fly. If you choose to run it without dialogs, the import is a "canned" process that uses all the saved options you've specified.

TIP

> When performing a complex import, you may want to save drafts of the import into a script as you go. That way if you make a mistake or need to change things, you don't run the risk of FileMaker forgetting the import specification you worked so hard on.

CAUTION

> Note that a scripted import can go awry if your database structure changes after the script is configured. Adding fields should be no problem, but if you delete any fields, especially those involved in the import, your field mappings will be disrupted and data will no longer flow into the correct fields.

TROUBLESHOOTING

MATCHING IMPORTS

I can't get an import to work using the "update matching records" option. The outcome is never what I expect.

When you choose to "update matching records" when importing data into a FileMaker table, FileMaker tries to match records in the source to records in the target, based on the specified match field or match fields. We've been assuming that there will be at most one source record and one target record that share the same match criteria. But what happens if there are multiple matches on either or both sides?

Assume that you're doing a matching import based on a Social Security number. If there are several records in the source data with the same Social Security number, the data from the *last* of these records is used to update matching records in the target (assuming there are any).

On the other hand, if there are multiple records with the same Social Security number on the target side, they are *all* updated with whatever turns out to be the matching data from the source side. So all target records with the same value in their match field(s) are updated with the same data from the source, whether that means updating two target records or two thousand.

If you put both scenarios together, and multiple records in both the source and target share the same Social Security number, the outcome is as follows: Data from the *last* such record in the source will be used to update *all* the matching records in the target. If four matching records were in the source, and nineteen in the target, data from the fourth matching source record would be used to update all nineteen matching target records.

IMPORTS AND VALIDATION

I imported data, but some of it turned out to be invalid. I have field validation rules set up, but it seems as though FileMaker is ignoring them.

In previous versions of FileMaker, field validation and data imports didn't mix well. FileMaker simply didn't perform any field validation at all on data that was imported. Even if you marked a field as having to be not empty, for example, it was perfectly possible to import records that had no value in that field. This could be an annoying back door around your carefully constructed validation rules.

The situation is better in FileMaker 8 (and in FileMaker 7 as well), but there are still pitfalls. Everything depends on your field validation settings. When you apply validation to a field in FileMaker 8, you can choose to validate the data Only During Data Entry, or Always. If you select the first option, the behavior is similar to previous versions of FileMaker: Imported data is *not* checked for validity, and it's up to you to handle the consequences. On the other hand, if you choose Always for the data validation on a field, imported records *are* checked. If this is the case, any record that does not pass a validation check is rejected, and the dialog box that appears at the end of the import tells you how many records were rejected (though not *which* ones, unfortunately).

FILEMAKER EXTRA: EXPLOITING THE FILEMAKER-TO-FILEMAKER IMPORT

You saw earlier that it's possible to import data into one FileMaker table from another. Those tables can be in the same FileMaker file or different ones. This capability has a number of useful and interesting applications.

DUPLICATING A FOUND SET

Occasionally, you'll encounter situations where you want to duplicate a found set of records. Of course, as with most things in FileMaker, there are several approaches. You could write a script that would start at the beginning of the found set and loop through it, duplicating as it went. But you'd quickly find you had some tricky record-position issues to deal with. (Duplicating records can change which record is the current one, so it can be hard to keep your place when looping through a found set.)

One general rule for speeding up FileMaker operations goes something like this: *Where possible, replace scripts, especially looping scripts, with built-in FileMaker operations.* FileMaker's Replace command is much quicker than a script that loops over a group of records and performs a Set Field step on each record. FileMaker's Delete Found Records command is quicker than a script that loops over a set of records and deletes each one. And so on.

Another choice is to export these records to a separate table, then import them right back into the original table again. A single script can control both the export and the import, and the logic is much easier to read and understand.

Duplicating Between Tables

Suppose that you have a simple order tracking database. The database has tables for customers, orders, order lines, and products. Each order, of course, has one order line per product on the order.

Suppose also that users have said that they want to create new orders by checking off a number of products from a list and then having a new order be created with one line for each selected product. So a user would check off Screwdrivers, Milk, and Roofing Tar in a product list, click a button that says Make Order, and see a new order with lines for the three selected products.

Again, you can do a number of things with scripts, but one elegant solution is to gather up the selected products into a found set and then simply import that found set (well, the relevant fields from it, anyway) into the Order Lines table, thus creating one new order line per selected product.

Moving, Consolidating, and Re-creating Tables

With the added capability to create a new table when importing data into FileMaker 8, it has also become possible to use the FileMaker-to-FileMaker import to perform some important migration tasks. If you're converting files from FileMaker 6 or earlier to FileMaker 8, and you intend as part of your conversion to consolidate several older files into one new file with several tables, this feature can help. Creating a new table via import will preserve all aspects of the table schema. Still, if you're performing consolidation as part of a conversion, we recommend you invest in FileMaker Pro Advanced and its more heavy-duty features for copying and pasting schema elements.

→ For a full discussion of consolidating multiple tables, **see** "Repointing Table Occurrence References," **p. 561**.

19

EXPORTING DATA FROM FILEMAKER

GETTING OUT WHAT YOU PUT IN

Much of this book concentrates on tools for data entry—for getting data into a database system. But that information often needs to be extracted again. Sometimes the extraction takes the form of a report of some kind. At other times the best choice is simply to export the data into some specific format so that another program can import that data and work with it using different tools than might be available in FileMaker. Reasons for exporting might include the following:

- Perhaps you know someone who is compiling a quarterly report in Excel and needs some numbers from your FileMaker system.

- Perhaps the new accounting system needs transaction data from FileMaker, and likes to receive it in an XML format.

- Perhaps you've been storing low-resolution images for an upcoming ad campaign in FileMaker, but you would like to make all the images available on a CD that can be used without FileMaker.

In this chapter we cover various means for getting data out of FileMaker. We discuss the traditional concept of exporting to other file formats, and we also cover the related topic of making FileMaker data available via an ODBC or JDBC connection. There are still other methods of extracting data from FileMaker, such as various web publishing methods, and the new Save Records as Excel and Save Records as PDF features, all of which are covered fully in other chapters.

→ For more on saving and sending records as Excel or PDF files, see "Delivering Reports," **p. 298**.

→ Additional information bearing on the topic of FileMaker web publishing can be found in Chapter 21, "Instant Web Publishing," **p. 633**; Chapter 22, "FileMaker and Web Services," **p. 669**; and Chapter 23, "Custom Web Publishing," **p. 699**.

THE BASIC MECHANICS OF EXPORTING

The basic principles of exporting data from FileMaker are straightforward. You first pick a single table from which to export. (You cannot independently export data from two tables at once, although you can export related fields to any extent you want, a topic discussed in more depth later in this chapter.) You then choose an output file format and file location, and pick specific fields from your chosen table for export. Before you export, there are a few extra options you can choose that govern grouping and formatting of the exported data. That's all there is to it. Let's look at each step a bit more closely.

CHOOSING A SOURCE TABLE

As with much else in FileMaker 8, the starting point for a data export is determined by the user's *context* in the current system—specifically by the currently active layout, which in turn is tied (via its table occurrence) to an underlying data table (aka source table). So the currently active layout controls implicitly which table is the source table for the export.

CHOOSING AN OUTPUT FILE FORMAT

After your context is established, you'll need to choose File, Export to begin the export process. The next step in that process is to choose an output file format and file destination. FileMaker offers you a choice of 12 export formats, as shown in Figure 20.1. Some of these are plain-text formats, such as tab-delimited text, which could be read in any text editor; others are binary file formats that require more specific software to open, such as FileMaker Pro. This chapter goes into greater detail on available file formats in a later section.

Figure 20.1
FileMaker Pro can export data to various formats.

 FileMaker 8 sports a couple of new additions to this dialog: the choice to automatically open the file after saving it, and the choice to automatically create an email with the file attached. These choices parallel those available with the new Save as Excel and Save as PDF features; the goal in all cases is to make the final delivery of the data faster and easier.

SELECTING FIELDS TO EXPORT

After you've selected an output file type and destination, you'll be prompted to choose some fields to export, via the dialog shown in Figure 20.2.

 With FileMaker 8, when working with field lists, you often have the ability to limit your consideration to only those fields on the current layout, a feature known as *field list filtering*. By default, the fields displayed in the list at the left are limited to those found on the current layout, as indicated by the Current Layout menu setting. It's possible to switch the view to show all fields in the current table. As in previous versions of FileMaker, it's also possible to select fields from any related table for export.

→ For more information on exporting related fields, **see** "Exporting Related Fields," **p. 602**.

Figure 20.2
Most fields can be exported from a FileMaker database, but container fields cannot.

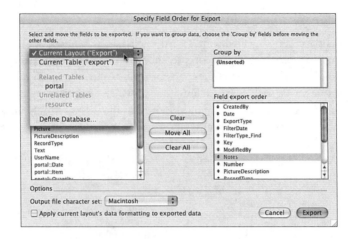

In addition to selecting fields for export, it's also possible to select grouping options for the fields, and to choose whether to format the exported data according to the current layout formats. These options, too, are discussed in more detail later in this chapter.

→ For more information, **see** "Exporting Grouped Data," **p. 604**, and "Formatting Exported Data," **p. 602**.

At any point in the field selection process, you can use the small up/down arrows beside each selected field name to change the order in which the fields are exported: Click the arrow and drag to move the field, or use (⌘-up/down) [Ctrl+up/down] if you prefer the keyboard. After you have a satisfactory field list, click Export, and the data will be exported to the file format and location of your choice.

EXPORTING ISSUES TO CONSIDER

Although the basic mechanics of exporting are simple, there are a couple of key points that bear remembering:

■ To export data from a file, a user must have sufficient privileges to do so. This is governed by selections within the user's privilege set. The user must have the Allow Exporting check box checked within the settings for her privilege set. Additionally, the user will not be able to export any records for which she does not have at least the capability to view the record.

→ For more information on privileges and security in FileMaker, see Chapter 12, "Implementing Security," **p. 325**.

■ Data will be exported only from records in the user's current found set. To export data from all records in a table, it's necessary to first run Show All Records to ensure that no records are omitted from the found set. Regardless of the found set, any records that the user's privileges prevent her from viewing cannot be exported.

■ There are certain practical limits on which fields you can export. Container fields can be exported only if the target file format is a FileMaker Pro file (we discuss other strategies for exporting files in container fields later in the chapter). And there are certain fields, such as summary or global fields, that it may not always make sense to export, even though it's technically possible.

→ For more information, **see** "Working with Large Fields and Container Fields," **p. 607**, and "Formatting Exported Data," **p. 602**.

EXPORT FILE FORMATS

FileMaker's Export Records feature can create export files in various formats. Many of these are text-based, and a few are binary. In this section we give an overview of available file types, with some specific notes on each. Each format has its own quirks and limitations. We attempt to call out the main features of each format, but you'll need to experiment to see just how a specific data set translates to a chosen file format.

CHARACTER TRANSFORMATIONS

When exporting data, FileMaker often performs substitutions on certain characters that tend to cause confusion when they appear embedded in field contents. For example, FileMaker permits you to embed a tab character in field data, but because the tab character is frequently used as a field separator in text-based data, FileMaker transforms these internal tabs to spaces when exporting. In the same vein, carriage returns within fields sometimes get transformed to the vertical tab character (ASCII code 11). The specific transformations that occur depend on the output file format; see the notes on each format outlined in the following sections for further details.

CAUTION

The transformation of carriage returns to vertical tabs is a significant problem if your data will need to be handled as XML along the way because the ASCII 11 character (vertical tab) is not a valid character in XML. When you export data as XML, FileMaker does not make this transformation—it simply eliminates the internal carriage returns. But if you export in a non-XML format, yet need the exported data to be processed via XML at some point, be aware that these embedded vertical tabs will cause the file to be rejected by XML parsers.

20

One other common transformation occurs when repeating fields are exported (for those formats that support it). Multiple repetitions of a field are often exported with the individual repetition data separated by the group separator character (ASCII code 29). Common transformations are listed in Table 20.1.

TABLE 20.1 CHARACTER TRANSFORMATION INFORMATION FOR EXPORTING FILEMAKER DATA

Character	Transformation
Tab-separated text	One of the most common data interchange formats, the tab-separated text format exports each record as a single line of text, terminated by a carriage return. The contents of individual fields are separated by the tab character. The repetitions of repeating fields are run together into a single string, with repetitions separated by the group separator character (ASCII code 29).
Comma-separated text	Comma-separated text (or values, commonly referred to as CSV) is another very common text interchange format. As with tab-separated text, records are separated by carriage returns; but individual records are separated by commas, and field contents are enclosed in quotation marks. (Quotation marks already present in the data are turned into pairs of quotation marks, so "data" becomes ""data"".) The repetitions of repeating fields are run together into a single string, with repetitions separated by the group separator character.
SYLK	The SYLK (Symbolic Link) file format is a text-based file format designed to be read by a software program. Generally it's been used for interchange between programs such as spreadsheets. The SYLK format doesn't accommodate repeating fields—only the first value in a repeating field will be exported. SYLK can preserve internal tab characters but eliminates internal carriage returns.
DBF	Originally the underlying file format for Ashton-Tate's dBASE software line, DBF is a binary file format that can be read by various software programs. Unlike many of the other export formats, the DBF format preserves FileMaker field names to some extent. Field names are converted to uppercase, spaces are converted to the underscore character, and the overall field name is limited to 10 characters. This can lead to field name duplication. The DBF format allows no more than 254 characters of data in a field and, like SYLK, does not support exporting more than the first repetition of a repeating field.
DIF	DIF (Data Interchange Format) is a text-based data format originally used with the VisiCalc program. DIF preserves field names during export, without either truncating or transforming them as DBF does. DIF preserves all repetitions of a repeating field, with repetitions separated by the group separator character.
WKS	WKS, the underlying file format for Lotus 1-2-3, is a purely binary data format, meaning it cannot be read sensibly with a text editor. Like most export formats, it has some limitations. Data is limited to 240 characters per field. Date and time values are not exported as raw data, but rather as date and time functions, if they are within a supported range of 1900 to 2099. Dates outside that range are exported as text. WKS does not support exporting more than the first repetition of a repeating field.

20

Character	Transformation
BASIC	BASIC (.bas) is a file format used for BASIC source code. Like the other text-based file formats, it has its export quirks. Internal tab characters are preserved. Internal return characters are converted to spaces. Internal double quotes are converted to single quotes. All field repetitions are preserved, with repetitions separated by the group separator character. Field length is limited to 255 characters.
Merge	The Merge format is intended for use with word processors and other applications that support mail-merge or similar functionality. Field names are fully preserved, as are internal tab characters. Internal returns are exported as vertical tabs. All repetitions of a repeating field are exported.
HTML Table	As the name suggests, this export format writes data from the selected records into a basic HTML table. Field names are output as column headers. Internal tabs are preserved, as are internal carriage returns. Field repetitions are exported into a nested table.
FileMaker Pro	This export format will create a new FileMaker Pro file with a field structure that matches the fields being exported. This is the only file format into which it's possible to export data from container fields. Not all FileMaker field types are preserved; summary fields become number fields, and calculation fields become data fields of the appropriate type (whatever the output type of the calculation is defined to be).
XML	FileMaker can export its data into two different XML formats, or *grammars*, called FMPDSORESULT and FMPXMLRESULT. You may choose whether to export raw XML, or to apply a style sheet as the XML is exported. When you choose to export as XML, a dialog box will prompt you for those choices, as shown in Figure 20.3.
Excel 〔NEW〕	FileMaker 8 can export data to a file in the native Excel format. When doing so, you can specify certain parameters of the result file, such as the name of the target worksheet, and whether to use the field names as column headers, as shown in Figure 20.4. Internal tabs and carriage returns are converted to spaces. Only the first repetition of a repeating field is exported. FileMaker fields will be assigned the appropriate Excel data type in their resultant columns where possible. (For an example of where this is not possible, consider FileMaker data that falls outside the range of dates supported by Excel.)

20

Figure 20.3
You have additional choices to make when exporting to XML.

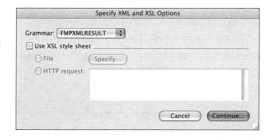

→ For more information on FileMaker's XML grammars, **see** Chapter 22, "FileMaker and Web Services," **p. 669**.

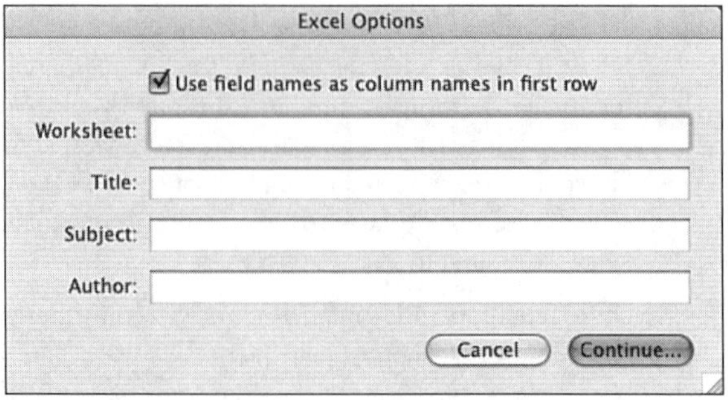

Figure 20.4
You have additional options when using the new capability to export to Excel.

FORMATTING EXPORTED DATA

FileMaker maintains a distinction between the way data is stored in a field and the way it is displayed. For example, although all dates are stored internally as simple integers, they may be displayed in many different date formats, such as "1-3-2006." Or a number, stored internally with 17 digits of precision, may be displayed with just 3 or 4 digits. None of these display options has any effect on the data stored in the field—they simply affect the way the data is shown to the user.

On FileMaker layouts, these formatting options are governed by choices made via the Format menu, in Layout mode. Some of these formatting options can be made to carry through to data when it's exported. To do so, when specifying fields for export, check the box labeled Apply Current Layout's Formatting to Exported Data. When this choice is selected, any formatting options applied via the Number, Date, or Time formatting dialogs are preserved. Text formatting, even character-based formatting such as uppercasing, is not preserved. Date and time formatting may both be applied to a timestamp field, and will be carried through on export.

CAUTION

> Not all export types support formatting data based on the current layout. The DBF and DIF file formats offer no support for additional formatting. The WKS format allows additional formatting for time and number fields, but not for date fields.

EXPORTING RELATED FIELDS

All exporting in FileMaker takes place from the context of a single table. In general, then, it's not possible to export data from several tables independently in one stroke. It *is* possible, though, to export data from tables related to the current one, whether immediately or more distantly.

Doing so is a simple matter of choosing fields from related tables when specifying fields for export. Consider a typical ordering system, in which a table holding order records is related to a table holding customer records via some sort of customer ID. The system probably doesn't store the customer name in the order table because this violates some principles of good data modeling. In FileMaker, the customer name probably is stored in a Customer table, and displayed on an order record via related fields.

Because the customer name is stored in a related field or fields, if you want to export the customer name along with the order, it will be necessary to export the related fields as well. Figure 20.5 shows what this might look like.

Figure 20.5
You can export fields from the current table, or from any related table as well.

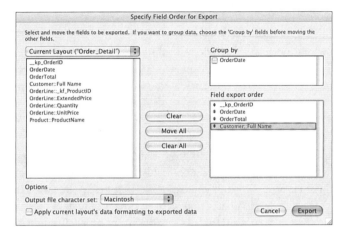

TIP

NEW

Notice a useful aspect of FileMaker's new field list filtering feature: Because the related fields for the customer's first and last name are displayed on the current layout, they are automatically available for export in the default (layout-based) field list—no need to go hunt for them in the field list for the related table.

The case of orders and their parent customer records is fairly clear-cut. Because there is only one customer record per order, the export produces one row per order, with the associated unique customer data as part of the row. But what if you try to export related fields from a child table, one that exists in a many-to-one relationship with the current table? Suppose that you shift to a detail layout showing individual orders, and export fields from that layout, including fields from related order lines? The result might not be what you'd expect, and may or may not be useful. Figure 20.6 shows a sample of such data, displayed in Excel.

Notice that although only five orders were exported, there are 10 rows in the output. FileMaker has output one row for each related record. The first row contains all data from the parent record (the order) along with data from the first related line item. Subsequent rows include only data from the line item, and leave the columns for data from the order record blank.

20

	A	B	C	D	E	F	G
1	__kp_OrderID	OrderTotal	Customer::Full Name	Product::ProductName	OrderLine::UnitPrice	OrderLine::Quantity	OrderLine::ExtendedPrice
2	33	2300.6	Dennis Copley	Thorium Spanner	1.69	140	236.6
3				CyberCrunch	8	160	1280
4				Quarterstaff	5.6	140	784
5	34	13065	Mary Jo Lickliighter	CyberCrunch	8	600	4800
6				Shelf Bracket	14.5	570	8265
7	35	1760	John Shaw	CyberCrunch	8	220	1760
8	36	5883	Janet Swanson	CyberCrunch	8	190	1520
9				Shelf Bracket	14.5	270	3915
10				Quarterstaff	5.6	80	448
11	38	4751.5	Irfon Kohn	Thorium Spanner	1.69	350	591.5
12				CyberCrunch	8	520	4160

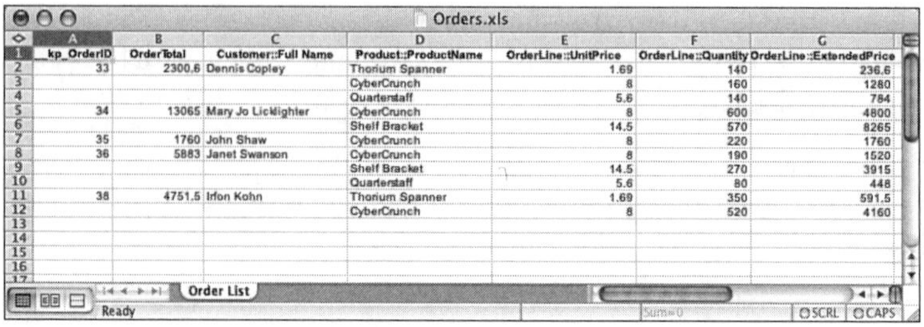

Figure 20.6
You can export fields from child tables, in which case you may get records with partial data.

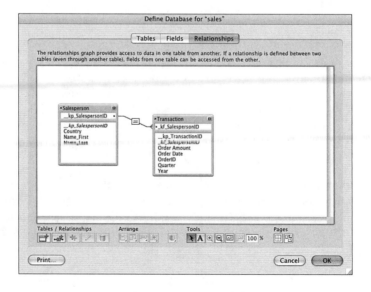

The behavior of exports that include related fields, then, depends on the number of records related to the current record being exported. When only one related record exists, one row will be output. If multiple records exist, a row will be output for each related record.

Exporting Grouped Data

A typical export will output some data from each record in the current found set (or, as discussed in the section "Exporting Related Fields," you may sometimes get multiple sets of information per current record, if you export related fields). But what if you don't want data for each and every record? What if you want to export only data that summarizes information from the current recordset, such as you might see in a subsummary report? FileMaker makes this possible as well.

Consider the example of a system that tracks sales and salespeople. Each salesperson has a country, and many associated transactions. You'd like to export a data set that contains one row per salesperson, with the following data: salesperson name, country, and total transaction volume. Assume that the initial database structure is as shown in Figure 20.7.

Figure 20.7
You might want to export summary data from a database of sales transactions.

20

To output summary data, it's necessary to have one or more summary fields defined. In this case what's desired is a count of transactions per salesperson. Here, you could define a summary field, called, say, TransactionCount, defined as shown in Figure 20.8.

Figure 20.8
To export summarized data, you need to define one or more summary fields.

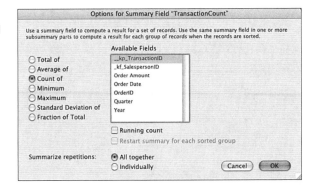

The field is a defined as a Count. The count is performed against a field that is known to contain data always, such as a primary key field.

→ For more information on summary fields and summary reporting, see "Working with Field Types," **p. 69**, and "Summarized Reports," **p. 287**.

It now just remains to use this summary field in an export. The process is similar to that required for preparing a subsummary report for display. First, isolate the transactions to be summarized (for example, to summarize across all transactions, you would perform Show All Records). Next, sort by the field that would be the break field if you were displaying the data in a subsummary report. Here you want to group by salesperson, so you would sort based on _kf_SalespersonID. Finally, you'd begin the export, and set your export options as shown in Figure 20.9.

Figure 20.9
It's necessary to choose grouping options when exporting summarized data.

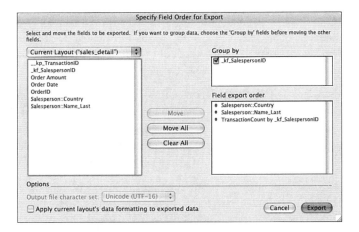

This export is set to group by the salesperson ID. The export contains some related fields from the Salesperson table, as well as the summary SalespersonCount field, and an entry called TransactionCount by _kf_SalespersonID. That extra field, rather than the raw TransactionCount field, is the one you want; it's triggered by adding TransactionCount to the export order, after which the TransactionCount field can be removed from the export order, leaving the group count field behind.

If you were then to export this data to Excel, the result would look something like what's shown in Figure 20.10.

Figure 20.10
When you export summarized data, the output contains one row per summary group.

Using more complex sorts and summary field choices, more complex summarized exports are possible.

EXPORTING TO FIXED-WIDTH FORMATS

Many computer systems exchange data in some form of *fixed-width* format. This term refers to formats in which an individual field always contains a certain number of characters of data. Data that's too wide for the field width is sometimes truncated to fit. Data that takes up less space than the field width allows is *padded* with a padding character, such as a zero or a space, to bring it up to the specified width. For example, the number 797 in a 10-character fixed-width format might be rendered as "0000000797" (left-padded with zeroes). The name Tomczak displayed in a 15-character fixed-width format might be displayed as "Tomczak   " (right-padded with spaces). Fixed-width formats also sometimes simply run all the columns together into a single big fixed-width string. There's no need for internal field separators—because the exact width of each field is known, it's easy to determine where each field's data starts and stops.

If you need to export FileMaker data to a fixed-width format, you'll need to do a bit of work by hand; FileMaker has no built-in support for exporting to a fixed-width format. At a minimum, you'll need to define some calculations to perform padding and concatenation. If you want to build a more permanent framework for working with fixed-width data, you can consider developing a small library of custom functions to do some of the work.

Padding data is a straightforward activity using FileMaker calculations. Say you have a number field called OrderTotal. To left-pad this number with zeroes and enforce a fixed width of 10 characters, you would use the following calculation:

```
Right( "0000000000" & OrderTotal; 10)
```

If you think about that for a moment, it should be clear how it works. The calculation tacks 10 zeroes onto the *left* of the numeric value, and then takes the *rightmost* 10 characters of the result. Likewise, to right-pad a text field called FirstName with spaces to a width of 10 characters, the calculation would look like this:

```
Left( FirstName & "          "; 10)
```

Finally, if you needed to run a set of these fields together into a single fixed-width row, a calculation that concatenated all the individual padding calculations together using the & operator would suffice. You could also create a single row-level calculation without bothering with individual calculations for each field:

```
Right( "0000000000" & OrderTotal; 10) & Left( FirstName & "          "; 10)
```

Calculations such as these will work fine for simple or occasional fixed-width exports. FileMaker also ships with an XSL style sheet, called `fixed_width.xsl`, that can be applied to a FileMaker data set on export to produce a fixed-width export. The style sheet supports only a single fixed width for all output columns. For more complex needs, you can build a tool of some sort to streamline the process.

WORKING WITH LARGE FIELDS AND CONTAINER FIELDS

Most of the formats discussed so far are predominantly text-oriented; that is, either they treat exported data as text, or at the very least they describe its attributes using text-based formats. But FileMaker has extensive capabilities for handling binary data as well, via the container field type. FileMaker can import files in batches, as discussed in the preceding chapter. FileMaker also has tools that allow you to create a batch export of binary files as well. The key to most such exporting operations is the Export Field Contents command, found in the Edit menu. You can manually enter a single field on a FileMaker layout and choose Edit, Export Field Contents, and the contents of that one field will be exported to a file of the appropriate type: a text file for most field types, or the actual file contents of a container field. (For example, exporting from a container field containing a file called `hurricanes.dbf` will produce exactly the `hurricanes.dbf` file.) The Export Field Contents option is not available for a container field unless the field contains something—either an embedded file or a reference to a file.

→ For more information on the batch import of images, **see** "Importing Multiple Files from a Folder," **p. 578**.

When used via the menu, Export Field Contents exports the contents of one selected field from one record. To create something like a batch export of images, it's necessary to write a script that uses the `Export Field Contents` script step. Scripted exports are a powerful technique that's covered in the next section.

SCRIPTED EXPORTS

All the techniques covered so far involve manual export operations, in which the user drives the process by hand, including the selection of output file type and filename, and the selection of fields for export. Exporting, though, is often an operation you want to be able to perform repeatedly, on demand. You may need to export a membership list to a text file periodically, or create a file containing information on this month's invoices to send to an accounting system that doesn't interact with FileMaker. In such circumstances it's typical that you'll want to export the same set of fields, for different data sets at different times. In these cases, it makes sense to consider using a script to perform the export.

All aspects of exporting can be scripted, from the selection of the records to be exported, to the determination of output file type, filename, and location, to the choices of specific fields and export options. Consider the script shown in Figure 20.11.

Figure 20.11
Exporting can be fully automated by using a script.

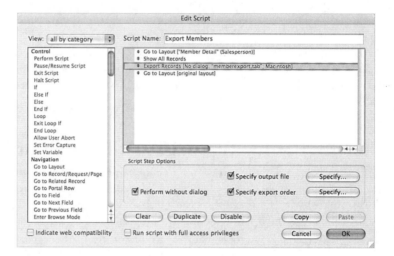

This script first establishes its context by navigation to the Member_Detail layout. The layout establishes context and thus governs which source table the exported records will be drawn from. The script then performs Show All Records so that all member records currently in the system will be exported. The Export Records script step performs the bulk of the actual work, and the script then returns the user to his original layout (the layout from which he invoked the script).

The Export Records script step is quite powerful, capable of automating all export settings. The available script step options are shown in Figure 20.11. You can set the output file and file type, as well as any additional XML or Excel options; you can set the export order, including related fields and grouping options; and you can choose to perform the import without displaying dialogs to the user.

Using the Specify Output File dialog, you can configure not only the file type and filename, but the file location as well. The Output File Path List, shown in Figure 20.12, works much like a file reference. Here you can specify one or more possible output locations for the file. As with a file reference, FileMaker will search through these locations one by one until it finds one that exists in the current environment. This makes it possible to create an export script that works correctly across different computer configurations, such as on an office machine and on a laptop on the road, or across both Mac and Windows configurations.

Figure 20.12
You can define a file reference to specify the location of the exported file. The file reference is stored with the script.

NOTE

In FileMaker 8, the Output File Path List can also be drawn from a script variable, which means that the paths need not be hard-coded, but can be determined dynamically at runtime.

→ For more information on dynamic file paths, see "Script Variables," **p. 448**.

In the Specify Output File dialog, you'll also specify the file type of the output file. If that file type is associated with additional options (as, for example, the XML and Excel file types are), additional dialogs will prompt you for those options. Once chosen, all of these options will be saved with the script, and can also be returned to and edited later.

Next, you'll have the opportunity to specify and save all the settings that can be made via the Specify Field Order for Export dialog (shown previously in Figure 20.9). This includes fields, field order, grouping and formatting options, and the output file character set. These are exactly the options you're familiar with from performing a manual export.

Finally, when using the Export Records script step, you can choose whether to display any dialogs to the user during the export process. Unless you plan for your user to interact with the export options in some way, such as tweaking the list of fields or field order, you may well want to check this box so that the export "just happens." In the case of the script shown in Figure 20.11, the user would see a short pause, perhaps a progress dialog that

20

tracks the progress of the export, and then the file would simply appear in the location designated in the export settings. A more elegant script might check for errors in the export, and then report the results to the user.

The Export Field Contents script step can also be used, especially when exporting container fields. The available export options are similar to those for the Export Records script step. The chief difference is that because Export Field Contents exports data from only one field and record at a time, it would need to be invoked from within a looping script of some sort in order to export data from all records in the current found set.

ACCESSING FILEMAKER DATA USING ODBC AND JDBC

So far, the techniques detailed in this chapter have involved pushing data out of FileMaker into static export files. It's also possible to pull data out of FileMaker from the outside, using the ODBC or JDBC technologies. ODBC (Open Database Connectivity) is an open standard for accessing databases from various client applications. JDBC (often taken to stand for Java Database Connectivity) provides standardized database access for Java-based applications. We'll refer to the two technologies together as xDBC from time to time for convenience.

→ For more information on importing data into FileMaker via ODBC, **see** "Importing from an ODBC Data Source," **p. 584**.

It's possible to grant xDBC access to FileMaker data in a couple of ways. FileMaker Server Advanced can be configured to provide xDBC access to hosted files. An individual copy of FileMaker Pro or FileMaker Pro Advanced can also be configured to provide local xDBC access to any files hosted by the client. There are two differences between these methods:

- FileMaker Server Advanced can support up to 50 simultaneous xDBC connections. The client version of FileMaker can support no more than 5.

- FileMaker Server Advanced permits xDBC connections from remote computers. The FileMaker client can accept xDBC connections only from client applications running locally (on the same computer).

Regardless of which specific means of access you use, a number of things are constant during setup of an xDBC connection. In the first place, it's necessary to configure the data source to accept xDBC connections. In the second place, it's necessary to configure the client application environment correctly, which generally means installing and configuring a driver of some sort. We'll first look at configuring the FileMaker Pro client for local ODBC access, and then consider how to configure FileMaker Server Advanced for remote ODBC access. First, though, we'll look at how to configure individual databases to permit xDBC access by either means.

GETTING YOUR DATABASES READY FOR ODBC/JDBC ACCESS

Like other means of external access, such as access via FileMaker Mobile, or access via XML, access via xDBC requires that a specific extended privilege be enabled in each file to be accessed. Any privilege set that has the Access via ODBC/JDBC extended privilege enabled will permit all accounts using that privilege set to access the file via xDBC. As with other external access methods, it may make sense to create a special user for xDBC access, and limit xDBC to that user alone. Figure 20.13 shows the extended privilege in question.

Figure 20.13
You must enable the
fmxdbc privilege in at
least one privilege set
to grant ODBC/JDBC
access to a database.

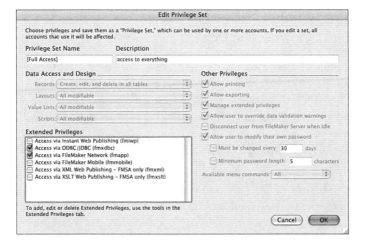

If this extended privilege is not enabled, xDBC access to the file will not be possible, regardless of any other configuration that has been performed. If you're having trouble accessing a file by xDBC or another remote access method, first check to make sure that the extended privileges in the file are in order before delving into complex troubleshooting of other parts of your configuration.

CONFIGURING FILEMAKER PRO FOR LOCAL ODBC/JDBC ACCESS

You can use FileMaker Pro or FileMaker Pro Advanced to permit local access to hosted databases. Other ODBC-capable applications on the same computer will then be able to access data in your files. To do this, first open the files you want to host. Make sure that the appropriate extended privileges are enabled in each file, and assigned to the correct users. Then open the ODBC/JDBC settings dialog (Edit, Sharing, ODBC/JDBC on Windows, FileMaker Pro or FileMaker Pro Advanced; or Sharing, ODBC/JDBC on Mac OS). Make sure that ODBC/JDBC sharing is set to On in the upper area of the dialog. The lower half of the dialog simply represents an alternative way to enable the fmxdbc extended privilege in each of the open files. If you have already configured all your privileges, there should be no need to make any changes in this area of the dialog.

After the FileMaker files are hosted and configured correctly, it's necessary to configure client application access. Prerequisites to ODBC client access are that the FileMaker ODBC driver be installed locally, and that there exist at least one DSN (Data Source Name) configured to use the FileMaker ODBC driver.

20

NOTE

It's possible to get a bit lost in the abundance of drivers and configuration options. When we refer to the "FileMaker ODBC driver" or "FileMaker JDBC driver," we're referring to drivers provided by FileMaker, Inc., on the FileMaker install disks, that provide other applications access to FileMaker data via ODBC or JDBC. You'll need to explicitly install these drivers from the FileMaker install media—they are not installed by default when you install FileMaker Pro or FileMaker Pro Advanced.

The preceding chapter went into some detail on installing ODBC drivers and configuring DSNs. It's recommended that you read that chapter if you need a bit of background on those topics. The ODBC and JDBC drivers are available on the FileMaker install media, along with detailed installation instructions. Rather than repeating the install instructions, we'll assume that you've installed the drivers on your platform of choice, and proceed to look at how to configure a working DSN to access FileMaker data.

CONFIGURING A DSN FOR FILEMAKER ACCESS (WINDOWS)

As with the process of configuring DSNs in general, the steps to reach a working DSN differ on Mac and Windows. On Windows, open the Control Panel, and then open Administrative Tools and choose the Data Sources (ODBC) tool to open the ODBC Data Source Administrator window, shown in Figure 20.14.

Figure 20.14
On Windows, ODBC settings are configured via the ODBC Data Source Administrator.

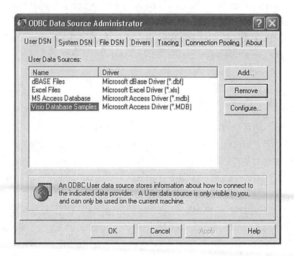

Click the Add button to create a new DSN. You should see the Create New Data Source dialog, shown in Figure 20.15.

The FileMaker ODBC driver is technically best known as the DataDirect SequeLink 5.4 driver. If you don't see that driver as an available choice when configuring, it may mean that the driver has not been installed, or that there was a problem with the installation.

 If you installed the driver on Windows but don't see it in the ODBC data administrator, see "ODBC Driver Missing on Windows" in the "Troubleshooting" section at the end of this chapter.

Figure 20.15
It's necessary to create a DSN to access data via ODBC.

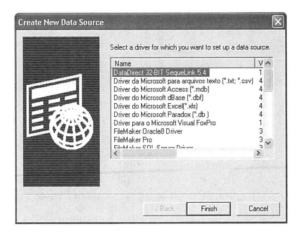

When the DataDirect SequeLink driver is available, click Finish, and you'll be taken to the setup dialog shown in Figure 20.16.

Figure 20.16
The new DSN will need several settings configured.

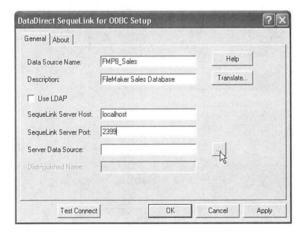

The Data Source Name field is for your own information; name it anything you like (it's best to avoid spaces). You can likewise enter anything you like for the description. Because the FileMaker data source is local (in other words, on the same machine as the DSN), you should enter localhost for the server host. For the port, enter 2399. This is the standard port for accessing FileMaker via xDBC, both on the client and on the server, and it cannot be changed.

Finally, you need to make a selection in the Server Data Source field. Whether you're hosting via the client or via FileMaker Server Advanced, you may be making several files available, and you need to specify which file you intend to access. (This means that you need one DSN for each file you want to access via xDBC, unless the files are joined via relationships.) Clicking the button to the right of the Server Data Source field will allow you to choose a file to access, as shown in Figure 20.17.

20

Figure 20.17
Specify the particular data source you want to access with this DSN.

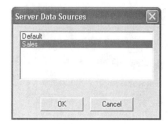

Note that if you know the file's name, you can simply type it into the box, minus any .fp7 extension. Choosing via the dialog has the useful side effect of testing the ODBC connection. If the connection is not functioning correctly, no list of files will appear.

Even if the data source is correctly broadcasting the availability of files, you'll also want to test access to the specific chosen file. To do so, click the Test Connect button (shown previously in Figure 20.16), and then enter the username and password for the chosen file in the resulting dialog, as shown in Figure 20.18.

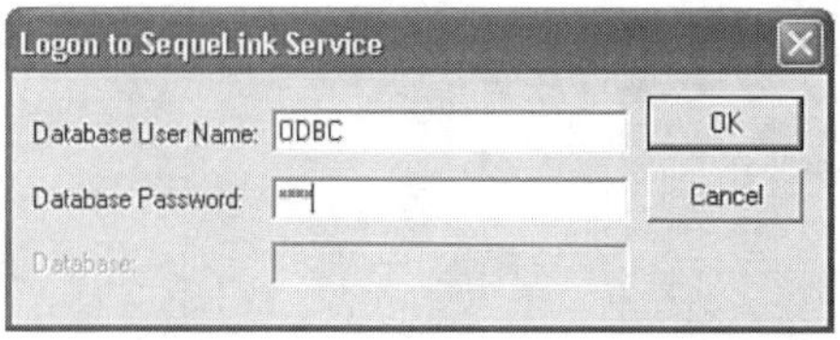

Figure 20.18
It's a good idea to test your connection to the data source after you're done configuring the DSN.

If there are no problems with configuration or passwords, you should see a message stating that the test was successful. If you get an error, such as a TCP/IP error, check to make sure that the file is correctly enabled for ODBC access. If the test was successful, you can click OK to return to the ODBC Data Source Administrator window, shown in Figure 20.19.

Figure 20.19
When you're done configuring the DSN, it will be available for use.

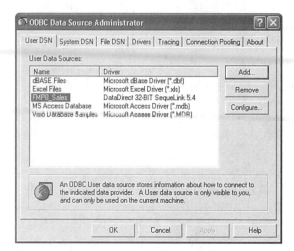

CONFIGURING A DSN FOR FILEMAKER ACCESS (MAC OS)

The process for configuring a FileMaker DSN on the Mac OS is generally similar, but ODBC is a bit less tightly integrated into the Mac OS. As a result, you have a bit more work to do.

First, you'll need to have an ODBC administration tool installed. Mac OS ships with Apple's ODBC Administrator. OpenLink makes a somewhat more full-featured replacement for the Apple utility. You should consider downloading and installing the OpenLink utility if you're planning to do much with ODBC on the Mac OS. The utility is free; examine the OpenLink web site (www.openlinksw.com) and search out the latest version of the iODBC SDK.

Presumably you've also already installed the FileMaker ODBC driver, according to the instructions that came with the installer files on the FileMaker disk. Unlike on Windows, simply installing the driver won't automatically make it available for use. You need to take another step and register the driver as well. To do so, open the ODBC Administrator, click on the Drivers tab, and then choose Add. You'll be able to give the driver a descriptive name of your own choosing. You'll also need to specify the full path to the location of the installed driver file. This path depends on whether you installed the driver to be accessible just to a single user, or to all users on the system. This choice, and the specific paths it entails, are discussed in the driver install instructions. Unless you have specific reasons for limiting driver use to just one user, it's simpler to install it as a system driver, available to all users. In that case, the install location will be `/Library/ODBC/SequeLink.bundle/Contents/MacOS/ ivslk18.dylib`, as shown in Figure 20.20.

Figure 20.20
You'll need to do a little extra driver configuration on the Mac OS.

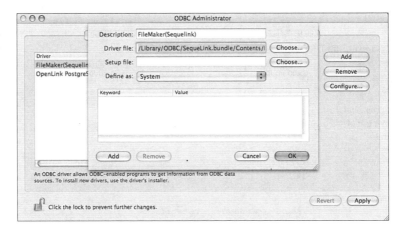

After the driver is installed and configured, you can go ahead and create a DSN that uses that driver. As on Windows, you can create either a User DSN or a System DSN. Switch to the appropriate tab of the ODBC Administrator, depending on which you plan to create. Click Add, and then pick the FileMaker driver you just configured. You'll see the Generic ODBC Driver Setup dialog, shown in Figure 20.21. The SequeLink driver has a fairly bare-bones interface on the Mac OS. Rather than having specific slots already set aside, it's necessary instead for you to specify the names of the configuration parameters yourself.

Figure 20.21
You'll need to set several driver keywords manually when creating a DSN for the Mac OS.

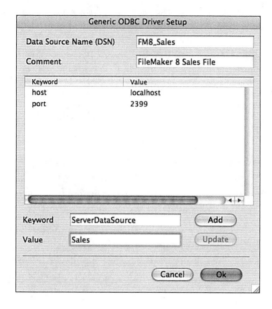

Specify host, port, and ServerDataSource as keywords, and also specify the appropriate values. The host and port should be localhost and 2399, respectively; the ServerDataSource is the name of the database you want to access, minus any file extensions.

If you're using the OpenLink ODBC Administrator, you'll have access to a Test button that lets you test the connection, as shown in Figure 20.22.

Figure 20.22
The iODBC Data Source Administrator gives you a useful Test button.

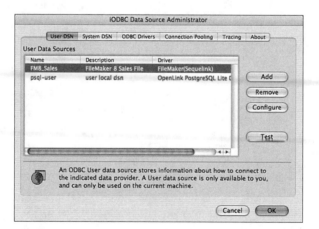

USING MICROSOFT EXCEL AS A LOCAL ACCESS ODBC CLIENT

In a typical local access scenario, an application needs to extract data from a copy of FileMaker running on the same machine. Microsoft Excel is an easy example, especially because it has a full-featured toolset for external data access. The techniques discussed in this section work equally well on the Mac OS and on Windows, assuming that you have configured a DSN on the local machine to access FileMaker, as described in the preceding two sections. This functionality relies on the presence of Microsoft Query. It's installed by default under certain circumstances, but you may need to install it separately if it's missing.

To access FileMaker data from Excel, open a new Excel workbook. Choose Data, Import External Data, New Database Query. The Choose Data Source dialog, shown in Figure 20.23, will open.

Figure 20.23
To access FileMaker data via ODBC, you'll need to choose an appropriate data source.

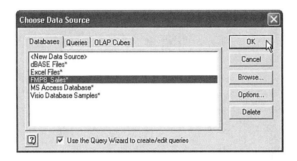

Select your FileMaker DSN (FMP8_Sales in this case), and click OK. You'll be prompted to enter a username and password.

After you enter the correct username and password for ODBC access to the file, the Query Wizard dialog, shown in Figure 20.24, will open.

Figure 20.24
The Microsoft Excel Query Wizard may (temporarily) spare you from having to write any SQL.

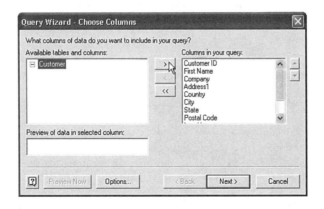

ODBC database access is based around the SQL query language. Most databases accessible via ODBC support SQL natively. Although FileMaker does not support SQL natively, the FileMaker ODBC driver effectively emulates a subset of SQL, allowing you to write SQL queries to access FileMaker data via ODBC. This means that you'll find some basic familiarity with SQL helpful in order to be able to perform these operations. Still, using the various query wizards that are often part of the ODBC client application, you can make quite a lot of progress without writing any SQL yourself.

Microsoft's Query Wizard allows you to choose from a list of "tables" on the left of the dialog. Take careful note: These will in fact be the names of table *occurrences* from the designated FileMaker file. A simple operation might consist of selecting a single table occurrence, and then clicking the > button to move all of its fields over to the right at once. This would select all columns of data from the underlying source table. Subsequent screens in the Query Wizard allow you impose filter criteria on the records being returned (a WHERE clause, if you're familiar with SQL) and to specify a sort order (an ORDER BY clause in SQL). Finally, you'll have the option of specifying what to do with the selected data, as shown in Figure 20.25.

Figure 20.25
After you've specified a query, the Microsoft Query Wizard lets you decide where to put the resulting data.

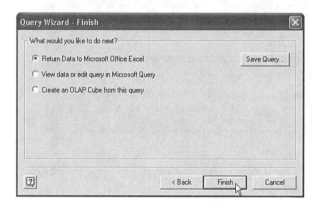

Microsoft Excel, like many client applications, also enables you to store queries for future use, much like storing an import or export routine in a FileMaker script. If this query is one you foresee reusing, it would be wise to save it for later use via the Save Query button, also shown in Figure 20.25.

 If you have persistent troubles connecting to FileMaker as an ODBC data source, see "ODBC Connection Checklist" in the "Troubleshooting" section at the end of this chapter.

CONFIGURING FILEMAKER SERVER ADVANCED FOR xDBC ACCESS

If you want your FileMaker data to be available via ODBC to various client applications on different computers, even on different networks, you'll need to serve your files via FileMaker Server Advanced. As when hosting files for local access, you'll need to have the privileges in each file configured correctly for xDBC access first.

Hosting a file via FileMaker Server or FileMaker Server Advanced is straightforward, and is covered in Chapter 25. Here we'll concentrate on what specifically needs to be configured on the server itself.

→ For more information on configuring FileMaker Server, **see** "FileMaker Server and Server Advanced," **p. 779**.

NOTE

Remember that you'll need FileMaker Server Advanced to host xDBC connections. FileMaker Server alone cannot host xDBC connections.

To configure the server to accept xDBC connections, open the Server Administration Tool (SAT). On Windows, you'll need to connect to the server using the SAT, right-click the server and choose Properties, and then choose the Clients tab and click the Server Advanced Settings button, as shown in Figures 20.26 and 20.27.

Figure 20.26
It's necessary to use FileMaker Server Advanced to provide ODBC/JDBC connectivity to remote computers.

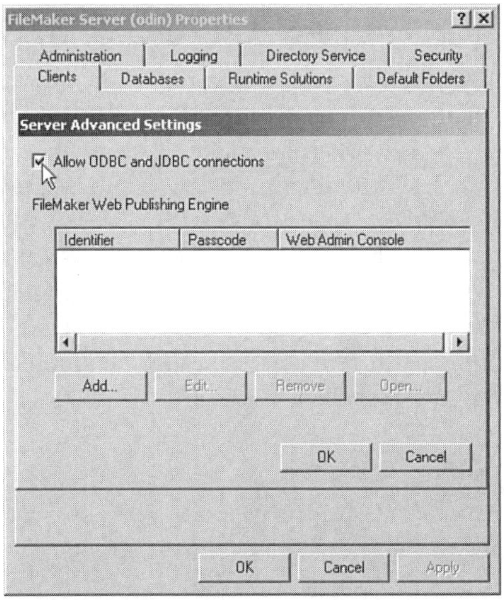

Figure 20.27
Configuring ODBC/JDBC connectivity is a matter of clicking a single check box.

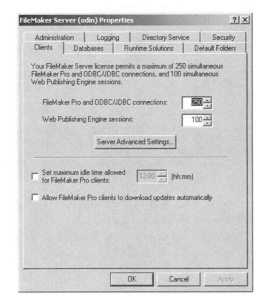

20

On the Mac OS, you'll likewise need to connect to the server using the SAT, and then choose the Configure area and select the Clients tab, as shown in Figure 20.28.

Figure 20.28
Configuration of ODBC/JDBC connectivity is similar on the Mac OS.

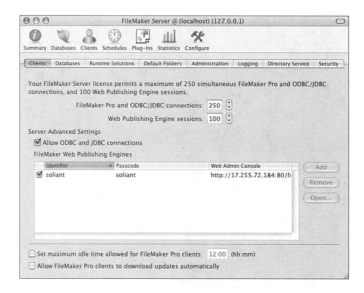

Regardless of platform, you'll need to check the check box labeled Allow ODBC and JDBC Connections. After this check box is checked, any database hosted on the server that is correctly configured for xDBC (that is, it has one or more privilege sets that have the `fmxdbc` extended privilege) can now be accessed by xDBC client applications. (Those clients still depend on a correct local client configuration, including driver installation and configuration, and DSN creation, as detailed in previous sections.)

USING FILEMAKER PRO AS AN ODBC CLIENT

So far, the discussion of xDBC technologies has centered on the question of how xDBC client applications, such as Microsoft Excel, can reach into FileMaker files and extract data. As already shown in Chapter 19, FileMaker Pro can itself act as a client to other ODBC systems. In Chapter 19, which dealt with importing data, we considered how FileMaker could extract data from non-FileMaker systems via ODBC. There's a flip side to this capability as well: FileMaker can also push data into other database systems via ODBC. Properly configured, FileMaker can add, delete, and edit records in remote database systems. With appropriate permissions it's even possible to add entire tables to remote databases, or create new databases altogether. Although this slightly strains the definition of exporting, it's an important capability that warrants discussion.

THE Execute SQL SCRIPT STEP

For FileMaker to interact with ODBC-based database systems in a way that involves activities besides querying for data, it's necessary to use the Execute SQL script step. Interacting with SQL data sources via ODBC is fairly complex. We'll work through an example of connecting to a PostgreSQL database from a client copy of FileMaker running under the Mac OS. For simplicity, the PostgreSQL server will be installed on the same computer as the client copy of FileMaker. The techniques illustrated are readily transferred to other database server products, and apply on Windows as well as on the Mac OS. That said, ODBC connectivity is all about specifics, and if you want to have FileMaker connect to, say, Sybase, from the Windows platform, there may be specific configuration steps you'll need to take that won't be covered here.

The basics, though, apply quite widely. You need, of course, an ODBC data source: some data source configured to allow access to its data via ODBC. The data source needs to be accessible, either on the same machine or over an accessible network. On the client machine (the machine running FileMaker), an ODBC driver for the data source needs to be installed, and there needs to be a DSN configured to communicate with that data source. Note that the driver/DSN configuration needs to take place on each machine that will access the ODBC data source via FileMaker. This is so even if the FileMaker files being used are hosted centrally via FileMaker Server; again, *each* machine that will need access to the ODBC data will need a correct driver and DSN configuration. (If you were sufficiently motivated, for example, if you had 300 desktops to configure, you could create an installer program to automate the process, although you'd need to know a lot about how ODBC gets installed and configured on your target platforms.)

In the example we've chosen to follow, several things need to happen. We need an installed copy of the PostgreSQL database, configured to accept connections via ODBC. (Much as FileMaker Server Advanced needed a setting enabled in order to allow ODBC access, many SQL-based database servers need a little extra configuration for ODBC as well.) To configure the client machine, we'll need an ODBC driver for PostgreSQL (one that runs on the Mac OS, in this case).

NOTE

It should be possible to make this example work equally well on the Mac OS or on Windows. On the Mac, we like to install PostgreSQL from the installer provided by Marc Liyanage at http://www.entropy.ch. Installers for PostgreSQL on Windows are available at http://www.postgresql.org. For a graphical administration tool, we like pgAdmin III, a free tool also available on both Mac OS and Windows: http://www.pgadmin.org. Finally, you'll need an ODBC client driver. OpenLink software (http://www.openlinksw.com) will provide drivers for Mac OS and Windows on a 30-day trial basis, and Actual Technologies has a different set of drivers for the Mac only, also available on a trial basis: http://www.actualtechnologies.com/product_opensourcedatabases.php.

20

Assume that we have a simple customer table in our SQL database, with the following fields:

```
__kp_customer_id
name_first
name_last
addr_1
```

```
addr_2
city
state
zip
```

Assume that, although the customer information is maintained in the main SQL database, we want to track some additional information about each customer in a FileMaker database. Our FileMaker database will have the same core fields as the SQL database, and some extra FileMaker fields as well. By and large, changes to the core customer record should be made in the SQL system, but we'd like to enable FileMaker users to make changes to core customer data and push those changes back into the SQL system. The Execute SQL script step will let us do all of this.

ADDING A RECORD TO AN SQL SYSTEM

To add a record to an SQL system, it's necessary to use the INSERT command. A typical statement might look like the following:

```
INSERT INTO customer (name_first, name_last, addr_1, city, state, zip)
➥VALUES ('Jack', 'Valance', '501 East Street', 'Norwich', 'AK', '11111');
```

The SQL statement specifies the column (field) names into which we're going to insert data, and the data values to be inserted as well.

It's simple enough to perform this operation from FileMaker using the Execute SQL script step (assuming, as always, the existence of a properly configured SQL data source and the proper client-side driver configuration). The Execute SQL script step requires two pieces of information: the name of an appropriate DSN, and the text of an SQL command to send to the data source. The SQL command may be entered as static text or derived from some calculation. The capability to create SQL from a calculation is extremely helpful, as you'll see. Settings for the Execute SQL script step are shown in Figure 20.29.

Figure 20.29
Using the Execute SQL script step, you can add records to remote SQL data sources.

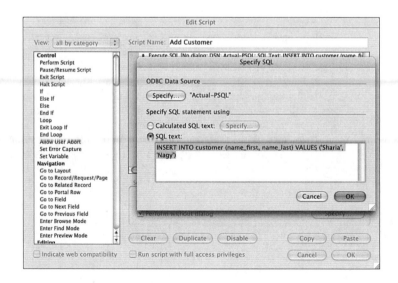

Using the capability to create calculated SQL statements, you could define a calculation in the FileMaker system that would create the correct INSERT statement on-the-fly. The calculation might look something like this:

```
"INSERT INTO customer (name_first, name_last, addr_1, addr_2, city, state, zip)
➡VALUES ('" & name_first & "', '" &
name_last & "','" &
addr_1 & "', '" &
addr_2 & "','" &
city & "', '" &
state & "', '" &
zip & "')"
```

Most of the values involved are text values, so it's necessary to enclose the values in single quotes, hence the somewhat convoluted syntax of the calculation.

SYNCHRONIZING RECORDS USING SHARED KEYS

The INSERT statement lets us insert records into remote databases. But if we really want to keep data in synch between the FileMaker record and its remote SQL twin, we'll need to do a bit more work. If we later make changes to the record in FileMaker, we'll want to push those changes up to the SQL system. To do that, we need an identifier for the remote record—a primary key. There are several schemes we can use to accomplish this task. Here's one approach.

Our SQL data source defines a primary key called __kp_customer_id. There's a similar field in the FileMaker table. We're probably not going to be able to keep those two fields in lock-step. Instead, we'll let each system generate its own primary keys, and then we'll have to "cross-store" the keys; we'll store the PostgreSQL primary key in the FileMaker system, and we'll also store the FileMaker primary key in the PostgreSQL system. To that end, we'll add a field called _ka_postgresCustomerID in FileMaker, and a similar field called _ka_filemaker_id in the PostgreSQL system. (The "ka" syntax, if you're curious, signifies an "alternate key.")

Consider first what needs to happen when we insert a record via FileMaker. We'll need to be sure to also push the FileMaker primary key to the SQL back end. After the new record is created, we then also need to fetch back the SQL primary key and store it in the FileMaker record. (We'll do that using an ODBC import, of the sort we covered in Chapter 19.)

Our new INSERT calculation will look like this:

```
"INSERT INTO customer (_ka_filemaker_id, name_first, name_last,
➡addr_1, addr_2, city, state, zip) values ("&
  __kp_customerID & ",'" &
  name_first & "', '" &
  name_last & "','" &
  addr_1 & "', '" &
  addr_2 & "','" &
  city & "', '" &
  state & "', '" &
  zip & "')"
```

20

This calculation makes sure that the FileMaker primary key is added to the SQL record as an additional or alternate key.

So we now know that any new record added to the SQL back end via FileMaker will also have sent along the primary key from the FileMaker side. As the record is inserted into PostgreSQL, an SQL primary key will also get created. We need to pull that key back and store it in the FileMaker record. (This might seem redundant, but it's a wise choice if we want to be able to synchronize records in both directions.)

Suppose that we insert a new customer record into the SQL database with a __kp_customerID of 6. That value of 6 will be inserted into the _ka_filemaker_id field on the SQL side. Consider the following SQL statement:

```
SELECT __kp_customer_id, _ka_filemaker_id from customer where _ka_filemaker_id = 6
```

You might wonder why we want to fetch back the FileMaker ID. After all, we already know it. The idea here is to use this SQL statement as part of an import that uses the "update matching records" capability of FileMaker. We'll use the FileMaker key as our match field, and leave the PostgreSQL key as the only field that actually gets imported. The import settings are shown in Figure 20.30.

Figure 20.30
Using a matching import, you can synchronize the primary keys between a FileMaker table and an SQL data source.

The logic of our insert process now looks like this:

1. Create and commit the record in FileMaker.

2. Insert the FileMaker record, along with its primary key, into the SQL back end.

3. Use an import with the Update Matching Records in Found Set choice enabled to bring the SQL primary key back into the FileMaker record.

We now have identical copies of the record in each database, each with its own primary key and that of the other system.

USING THE UPDATE STATEMENT TO REFRESH RECORDS

The act of inserting the record into the SQL back end, and then importing back the PostgreSQL key, creates a link between the two records, based on the shared keys. From here, it's straightforward to later update the remote record with new information from FileMaker. The syntax for the UPDATE statement in SQL looks like this:

```
UPDATE customer SET city='Millersville' WHERE __kp_customer_id=6
```

It's the WHERE clause of this statement that tells the SQL data source which record or records to update. It happens that the expression __kp_customer_id=6 matches only a single record on the SQL side. A broader statement such as WHERE state='PA' would cause all records with a state of PA to be updated with the specified values.

Armed with this knowledge, you'll find it a straightforward matter to implement an Update button on your customer detail layout that pushes the current state of the FileMaker record to the SQL back end. You can once again define a calculation that creates an UPDATE statement tailored to the data in the current FileMaker record, and use an Execute SQL script step to run the UPDATE command against the SQL data source, updating the record on the PostgreSQL side.

DELETING RECORDS FROM AN SQL DATA SOURCE

Deleting records from an SQL data source is straightforward as well. All it takes is a statement like this:

```
DELETE FROM customer WHERE __kp_customer_ID=8
```

No need to specify anything else about the record—the primary key is enough to identify the record for deletion.

Several cautions are in order. SQL data sources, unlike FileMaker, have no particular user interface and hence don't offer interactive features such as the capability to confirm a deletion. As soon as you issue a DELETE command, the relevant record or records are deleted. You won't be asked whether you really meant to do that!

Also, the business rules for deletion bear consideration. If a customer record is deleted in FileMaker, should the record in the SQL data source be deleted as well?

In any case, the mechanics of deletion are similar to those for inserting and updating: Create a calculation that will produce an SQL DELETE statement for a given record, and then run that command via the Execute SQL script step. How and when the deletion is triggered is a separate question, best determined on the basis of business rules.

DEFINING NEW STRUCTURES IN AN SQL SOURCE

As a final topic in FileMaker-SQL interaction, you should know that it's possible, using SQL commands, to alter the schema of an SQL data source on-the-fly. This would be the

20

equivalent of opening the Define Database dialog in FileMaker and adding (or deleting!) fields or entire tables. Consider the following statement:

```
CREATE TABLE region ( region_id serial NOT NULL, region varchar, geo varchar )
```

This would create a new table in the SQL database, called region, with three fields. The first field, region_id, is defined to be of type serial, which is a PostgreSQL extension that creates an auto-incrementing numeric field like FileMaker's serial number auto-entry option. The second and third fields are of type varchar, meaning "variable length character," akin to FileMaker's text fields. (Note also that the region_id has a NOT NULL constraint, meaning that it cannot be empty.)

It's also possible to add columns (fields) to a table on-the-fly:

```
ALTER TABLE region ADD COLUMN market_area varchar(30);
```

Similar statements exist to alter the data type of columns, drop columns, and even create entire databases on the fly. These are powerful capabilities that could potentially have many uses. All of these commands can be invoked over an ODBC connection, assuming that the ODBC user has sufficient privileges.

One final point about such commands (often called DDL commands, for *Data Definition Language*): FileMaker supports many DDL commands on *inbound* ODBC connections. The significance of this is that external client applications can also use DDL commands to create and edit table structures within FileMaker. FileMaker's ODBC interface does not support a full range of SQL DDL commands, but many of the basic ones, such as CREATE TABLE, are supported.

TROUBLESHOOTING

ODBC DRIVER MISSING ON WINDOWS

I'm sure that I installed the ODBC driver correctly on Windows, but when I go into the ODBC Administrator, the DataDirect SequeLink 5.4 driver is not there. What happened?

This happens from time to time, especially on Windows XP. It's common enough that it's specifically mentioned in the install instructions provided with the driver. To fix it, you'll need to edit the Windows Registry. Choose Run from the Start menu, type regedit, and then click OK. The Windows Registry Editor will open. Select the Registry entry called

```
HKEY_LOCAL_MACHINE\SOFTWARE\ODBC\ODBCINST.INI
```

Within that key you'll see entries for many individual drivers. Click each driver to view its contents. The first entry for each driver should be called (Default), and it should have some value, even if that value is only (value not set). If instead it has no value at all, select the key and press Delete. After you confirm the deletion, the key will be restored to a value of (value not set). Do this for the DataDirect SequeLink Driver, and then return to the ODBC Administrator to verify that the driver is now visible.

ODBC Connection Checklist

I can't connect to my FileMaker databases via ODBC. It seems like there are a lot of moving parts. What could I be doing wrong?

There *are* a lot of moving parts. Here are the things you should verify:

- The FileMaker database must have at least one account where the fmxdbc privilege is enabled for that account's privilege set.
- If the file is being shared locally, the local copy of FileMaker needs ODBC/JDBC Sharing set to On.
- If the file is being served remotely, it needs to be served via FileMaker Server Advanced, with ODBC/JDBC connectivity enabled on the server.
- If the file is being served remotely, port 2399 must be accessible on the host machine. Firewalls that block that port will not permit client access from outside the firewall.
- The FileMaker ODBC driver must be correctly installed and configured.
- There needs to be at least one DSN defined that uses the FileMaker ODBC driver and references one of the hosted files. Such a DSN needs to be present on any machine from which ODBC client access will occur.

FileMaker Extra: Accessing FileMaker Data via JDBC

The discussion in this chapter has focused largely on ODBC. In our experience, JDBC connectivity is less commonly sought for FileMaker than ODBC connectivity. It is an important capability, though, so we cover it here in some detail.

JDBC is a technology used by Java-based applications to connect to various databases. Like ODBC, it depends on the existence of drivers, each specific to a particular database. Unlike ODBC, because Java is cross-platform, the drivers are generally not platform specific (a very small class of drivers may be platform specific but these are rarely encountered). In this section we'll cover how to install and test the driver and the JDBC connection, and we'll look at using a JDBC-based tool to inspect an xDBC-enabled FileMaker database.

Testing for Java and Installing the Driver

The first step, whether on Mac or PC, is to verify that you have Java installed. Java should be installed by default on the Mac OS, and is often found installed on Windows as well. On either platform, drop to the command line (Terminal on Mac OS X, cmd.exe on Windows) and run this command:

```
java -version
```

You should see a response like this:

```
java version "1.4.2_09"
Java(TM) 2 Runtime Environment, Standard Edition (build 1.4.2_09-232)
Java HotSpot(TM) Client VM (build 1.4.2-54, mixed mode)
```

Such a response indicates that your system has a Java Virtual Machine (JVM) installed and is capable of running Java programs.

If instead you get a response that tells you the `java` command can't be found, your system does not have a JVM and you'll need to download and install one. See http://java.sun.com for information pertaining to your specific operating system.

The next step is to install the FileMaker JDBC driver. The installer is included along with other additional files on the FileMaker install media. Look for a folder named JDBC Client Driver Installer. Inside the folder, double-click on `sljcinstaller.jar`. This will start the driver installer. You can choose any location for the driver. On the Mac OS, `/Library/Java/Extensions` is a good place. On Windows, you can create your own directory in a place of your choosing.

CONFIGURING A DATABASE FOR JDBC ACCESS

Configuring databases for JDBC access is no different from configuring databases for ODBC access. The two types of access share a unified extended privilege (`fmxdbc`) that determines xDBC access to the file. For purposes of initial testing, you may want to practice JDBC access on a single machine, by using FileMaker Pro or FileMaker Pro Advanced to act as the JDBC host (as described earlier in this chapter for ODBC local hosting).

TESTING JDBC CONNECTIVITY

When configuring ODBC for the first time, you tested ODBC connectivity by configuring a DSN, and then using the operating system's capability to test that DSN to verify that the FileMaker data source was running and accepting ODBC configurations.

JDBC works a bit differently (among other things, there are no DSNs with JDBC). The FileMaker JDBC install includes a JDBC testing application you can use to test your JDBC configuration.

The testforjdbc application is installed in whatever directory you chose for the JDBC client driver install. Inside that directory is a directory named `testforjdbc` containing, among other things, command scripts to start the testforjdbc application. On Windows, you can double-click one of the batch scripts `testforjdbc.bat` or `testforjdbc14.bat`. (The latter is only for systems that are running Java 1.4 or later, which is most current systems.) On the Mac OS, you'll need to run your selected script from the command line. Assuming that you installed to `/Library/Java/Extensions`, you would open Terminal (usually found in `Applications/Utilities`) and type the following:

```
sh /Library/Java/Extensions/testforjdbc/testforjdbc14.sh
```

Regardless of how you launch it, your chosen script should start the Java-based testforjdbc application.

The interface is fairly bare-bones. Your first task is to make sure that the FileMaker JDBC driver is registered with the Java environment. To register the driver, choose Driver, Register Driver, and in the resulting dialog box type the following driver name:

```
com.ddtek.jdbc.sequelink.SequeLinkDriver
```

Then click OK. You should see a message in the JDBC/Database Output box in the middle of the window that says `registerDriver()` `succeeded`, as shown in Figure 20.31.

Figure 20.31
Each Java application needs to register the FileMaker JDBC driver before using it.

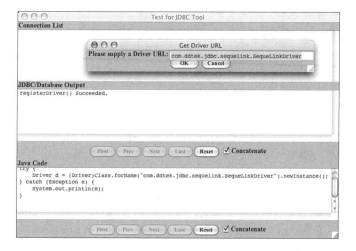

After the driver is registered, it's time to try to connect to the FileMaker file as a JDBC data source. JDBC-based programs make a connection by issuing a call via a URL-like syntax. An example might be as follows:

```
jdbc:sequelink://localhost:2399;user=user;password=password;serverDataSource=Sales
```

This *connection string* (as it's often known) tells a JDBC program to make a connection to a SequeLink data source (SequeLink is the name for both the ODBC and the JDBC drivers for FileMaker), running on the same machine on port 2399. The connection string further specifies that we try to connect to the data source called Sales, using a username of `user` and a password of `pass`. The `serverDataSource` in this case corresponds to a single FileMaker file.

You can make a connection in the testforjdbc program by choosing Connection, Connect to DB, and entering a connection string appropriate to your machine (your username, password, and database name are all you should have to change in the preceding string). The relevant dialog is shown in Figure 20.32.

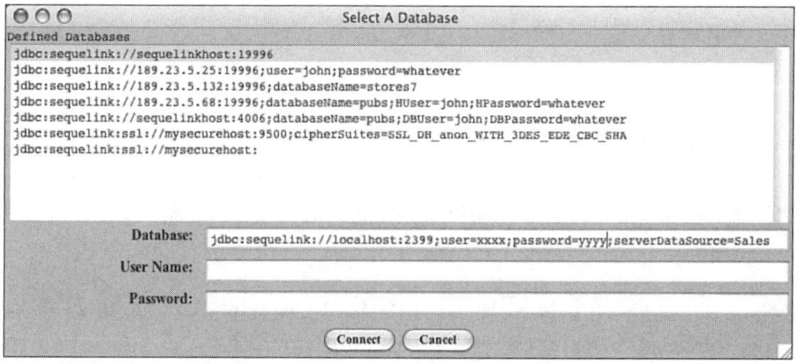

Figure 20.32
JDBC connections are made via a URL-like connection string.

If you see a message in the JDBC/Database Output window stating that getConnection() succeeded, everything is fine. You'll see a new Connection window (mostly blank). This lets you know that your connection was successful.

INSPECTING YOUR DATABASE USING JDBC

If you wanted to, you could go on using the testforjdbc program to inspect and manipulate your FileMaker database via JDBC. As you'll find, though, it's not a very friendly tool. If you want to experiment a bit more with JDBC, you may want to grab a more intuitive tool. One such tool is DbVisualizer, from Minq Software. You can download a time-limited evaluation copy from http://www.minq.se/products/dbvis. DbVisualizer is written in Java, so it looks and works identically on Mac and Windows. We'll walk quickly through the setup and configuration of a JDBC connection to FileMaker using DbVisualizer.

First, of course, you need a FileMaker database hosted somewhere and available for JDBC access. After the data source is ready, open DbVisualizer. You'll first need to register the driver (just as with testforjdbc), so choose Tools, Driver Manager. Next choose Driver, Create Driver (the menu will be within the window itself, not part of the application-level menus). The driver creation interface is shown in Figure 20.33.

Figure 20.33
In DbVisualizer, you need to first configure the FileMaker JDBC driver for use.

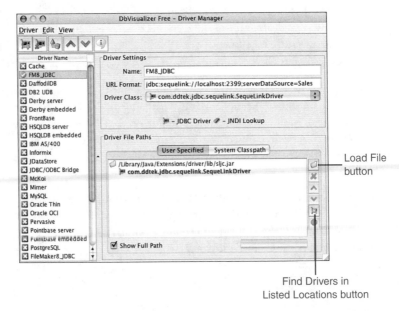

Fill in a name of your own choice for the driver. It's also helpful to fill in the URL format; DbVisualizer will display this format to you when you try to make a connection later. Each JDBC driver tends to have a slightly different URL syntax, so it's helpful to have this here as a reminder.

Next you need to find the driver itself. To do so, click the Load File button. Navigate to the file driver/lib/sljc.jar within the location where you installed the FileMaker JDBC driver. After you've found and selected that file, click the Find Drivers in Listed Locations button. DbVisualizer should scan the file and find a driver called com.ddtek.jdbc. sequelink.SequeLinkDriver. As a last step, in the Driver Settings area of the screen, choose that driver from the Driver Class menu. The final configuration should look roughly like what's shown in Figure 20.33.

Next you'll need to create a database connection using the new driver. Choose Database, Create Database Connection from the main application menu bar. You may be prompted as to whether you want to use the Connection Wizard; choose No (DbVisualizer has no installed wizard options for the FileMaker JDBC driver). You'll see the connection configuration screen, as shown in Figure 20.34.

Figure 20.34
The next step with DbVisualizer is to configure the connection to the data source.

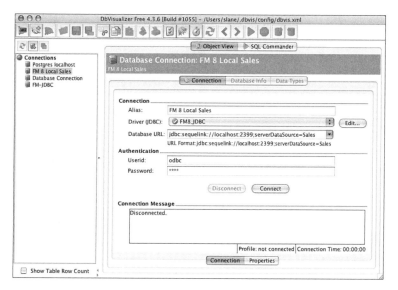

Choose a descriptive alias for the connection (probably something that mentions the name of the specific database being connected to). Select the driver you configured in the earlier steps (in this example it's called FM8_JDBC). Next you'll need to supply a correct connection string (database URL), just as with the testforjdbc program. Finally, you'll need to enter the username and password, and click the Connect button.

If the connection succeeded, you should see some additional information under the name of the database connection in the panel at the left of the window. Specifically, you might be interested in opening the Tables object and choosing a table occurrence from those present in the database. You could then choose the Info tab to see some general information about the table, or the Data tab to see the actual row data, as shown in Figure 20.35.

20

NOTE

Many of the options you can choose in DbVisualizer may give you scary-looking JDBC errors when you're working with FileMaker databases. This is not because anything has really gone wrong, but because the FileMaker JDBC driver doesn't support certain JDBC operations, especially those intended to extract metadata from the database (that is, information about the database: stored procedures, column types, and the like). If you see such an error, don't worry, just keep exploring until you get a sense for which DbVisualizer features are supported by the FileMaker JDBC driver.

Figure 20.35
You can use DbVisualizer to inspect your data directly.

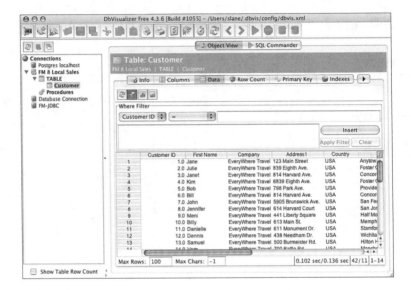

The intrepid may also experiment with using SQL directly against the database, via the SQL Commander tab, as shown in Figure 20.36. This is a great way to brush up on your SQL, and to learn which SQL features are and are not supported by the FileMaker JDBC driver.

Figure 20.36
You can also use DbVisualizer to experiment with running SQL queries against FileMaker.

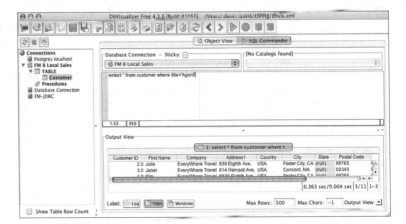

INSTANT WEB PUBLISHING

In this chapter

AN OVERVIEW OF INSTANT WEB PUBLISHING

Instant Web Publishing (IWP) has been a feature of FileMaker Pro since its introduction years ago in version 4.0. In its earlier incarnations, IWP was never quite the robust tool that one hoped it would be. Its main benefits were that it was extremely simple to enable and configure, and that it turned FileMaker layouts into web pages without any CGI programming or HTML coding. There were, however, many limitations, particularly with the number of layouts you could use and with script behavior, making IWP unsuitable for all but the most basic of web applications.

With FileMaker Pro 7, IWP took a great leap forward, retaining its amazing ease of setup and use, but adding enough features and flexibility that, for the first time, it could be used as part of a serious business application. We think that the new IWP will revolutionize the way FileMaker Pro systems are developed and deployed. Whether you're new to FileMaker Pro development or just haven't looked at IWP in a while, it's well worth your time to investigate and learn about this tool.

WHAT IS IWP?

Broadly speaking, Instant Web Publishing is one of several options for sharing data from a FileMaker database to the Web. The other options include exporting static HTML, exporting XML and transforming it into HTML with a style sheet, and Custom Web Publishing (CWP), which involves doing HTTP queries against the Web Publishing Engine and transforming the resulting XML into HTML.

→ For more on XML export, **see** Chapter 22, "FileMaker and Web Services," **p. 669**.

→ For more on Custom Web Publishing, **see** Chapter 23, "Custom Web Publishing," **p. 699**.

The goal of IWP is to translate to a web browser as much of the appearance and functionality of a FileMaker Pro database as possible, without requiring that a developer do any additional programming. FileMaker layouts are rendered in the user's browser almost exactly as they appear to users of the FileMaker Pro desktop application. To give you an idea of what this looks like from the user's perspective, Figures 21.1 and 21.2 show an example of a layout rendered both in FileMaker Pro and through IWP in a web browser.

IWP is more, though, than simply rendering your layouts as web pages. IWP users have much, if not all, of the same application functionality as do FileMaker Pro users. They can run scripts and view, create, edit, and delete data just like traditional FileMaker Pro users.

IWP IMPROVEMENTS IN FILEMAKER PRO 7

Although FileMaker has moved on to version 8, we know there are still a significant number of systems out there that have yet to move from FileMaker 6 to 7. For that reason, we recap here the main IWP improvements in FileMaker 7, and then go on to discuss the additional enhancements to IWP in FileMaker 8 in the following section.

There were numerous improvements to IWP in FileMaker Pro 7. For those readers who have used IWP in previous versions, we'll run through some of the most significant changes.

Figure 21.1
Using Instant Web Publishing, the layouts that you create in FileMaker are dynamically turned into web pages for you.

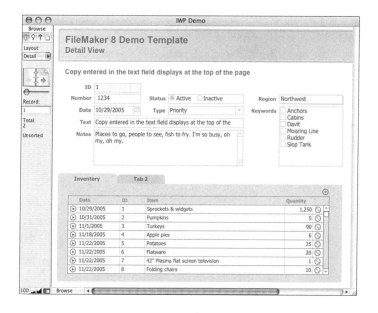

Figure 21.2
Instant Web Publishing renders FileMaker layouts almost flawlessly as web pages.

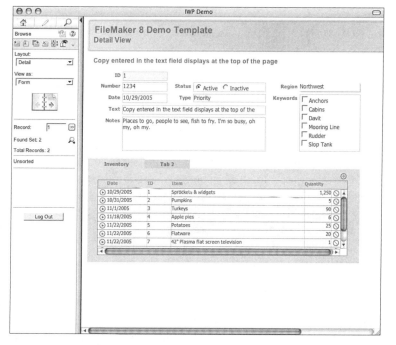

First, there is no longer a configuration wizard where you pick themes and views that determine the look and functionality of a status area. Instead, IWP in FileMaker 7 and 8 has a status area that looks and functions similarly to its FileMaker counterpart. And there are no restrictions on the number of layouts that can be accessed. The only layout restrictions are those that you, the developer, choose to put in place. We'll discuss this concept more in the "Designing for IWP Deployment" section later in this chapter.

21

Another major difference between the old and the new IWP is script support. Previous versions of IWP had severe restrictions on the type and length of scripts that could be run from a browser. Now, more than 70 script steps are supported, and there are no length constraints. We discuss script support in detail later in this chapter as well.

Perhaps the biggest change to IWP in FileMaker 7 and 8 is how it's deployed. In earlier incarnations, IWP was part of the Web Companion, which meant that a client copy of FileMaker Pro or FileMaker Pro Unlimited acted as the web host. That client was able to share files that it had opened as a guest of FileMaker Server. Frequently, this architecture proved to be unstable and required a fairly high degree of maintenance.

FileMaker Pro can still act as the host for IWP sharing (for up to five concurrent users), but now, FileMaker Server Advanced can also be a web host. Not only does this server-side architecture allow greater stability and a greater number of connections, but you can also use FileMaker Server's SSL encryption capabilities to better secure your data.

Finally, IWP in FileMaker 7 and beyond is session-based. We'll explore this concept more closely later in the chapter; the session capability is one of the ways that IWP is able to function very similarly to the FileMaker desktop application. It allows IWP to have a semblance of persistence in an otherwise stateless environment.

IWP IMPROVEMENTS IN FILEMAKER PRO 8

With FileMaker 8, rather than taking a radical leap forward, IWP takes a few nice evolutionary steps.

Authentication is now via an HTML form, rather than via the HTTP authentication used previously. With HTTP-based authentication, the user sees a dialog, presented by the browser, prompting for login information. In FileMaker 8, IWP displays an HTML page with fields for account name and password, and a submit button—this is generally thought to be a bit more elegant than the plain HTTP dialog. In addition, the forms-based login allows for the use of a wider range of characters in account names and passwords: Using HTTP authentication, account names and passwords were limited to characters in the ISO-Latin-1 character set, but this is not so with forms-based authentication. In addition, forms-based authentication is potentially more secure because the login credentials are not cached by the browser as they are with basic HTTP authentication. (This additional security can, however, be compromised by the fact that many browsers have a feature permitting you to save forms-based information for later use.) The new forms-based login is shown in Figure 21.3.

It's now also possible to create your own IWP home page, rather than being limited to the default home page displayed by IWP. The IWP home page is generally used as a portal with links to all the databases currently available under IWP. In a later section we'll discuss how to create your own IWP home page.

The other updates to IWP in FileMaker 8 are a bit more minor. IWP now exactly respects the tab order set in FileMaker 8 (rather than tabbing according to the stacking order, as in FileMaker 7). It's also worth noting that many of the new interface features in FileMaker 8, such as the tab control, tool tips, and calendar picker, are fully supported in IWP. (Custom menus are a notable and probably obvious exception.)

21

Figure 21.3
Instant Web
Publishing in
FileMaker 8 uses an
HTML-based login
mechanism.

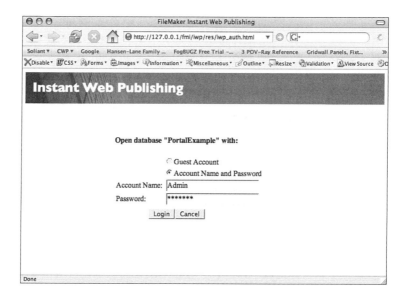

SCENARIOS FOR IWP

There are two primary scenarios in which IWP is a deployment option you may want to consider: first, for providing remote users access to your files, and second, for creating or integrating with a database-driven website. In each case, IWP is a less costly and an easier-to-implement choice than alternative options. We think it's helpful before diving into the implementation details to have a good understanding of how IWP stacks up against these alternatives.

REMOTE USERS

First, let's consider the idea of providing remote users access to a FileMaker database. By *remote*, we mean any users who are not physically connected to the same local area network as the FileMaker Pro (or FileMaker Server) application that is hosting a given file. It is certainly possible for remote users to use FileMaker's built-in networking to connect to a hosted database, which is of course what users on the local area network would do. The benefits of this are that there are no functionality differences experienced between remote and local users and that you don't have any additional costs or development work. The remote users need to have a copy of the FileMaker Pro desktop application, and that's it. The drawback of this as an option for remote users is performance. A networked FileMaker solution is highly network intensive and needs lots of bandwidth to operate well. Remote users may find client/server performance to be unacceptable, especially when using large files and for reporting functions.

One alternative you might consider is setting up Citrix with Terminal Services, or even just Terminal Services by itself, for your remote users. These are both instances of a *remote desktop access* technology. Essentially, when remote users start a remote desktop access session, their FileMaker Pro applications are running locally on the same network as FileMaker Server, and are hence very fast. All that are shipped across the network are keystrokes,

21

mouse clicks, and screen images. Remote desktop access is an appropriate solution when you have multiple offices or lots of remote users who need to access a centralized FileMaker database, but it comes with a fairly steep price tag and requires not insignificant amounts of configuration and maintenance.

NOTE

> Check out http://www.microsoft.com/windowsserver2003/technologies/terminalservices/default.mspx for more information on Terminal Services. Check out http://www.citrix.com for more information on using Citrix.

Other remote access technologies are also worth considering, such as Timbuktu and gotomypc.com. These can be excellent low-cost solutions for organizations with just a few remote users, but they do not allow multiple simultaneous client connections to a single remote computer.

Instant Web Publishing offers a reasonable alternative both to FileMaker's built-in networking and to remote access products as a means of providing database access for remote users. It provides significantly faster access to data than using FileMaker's networking, and it comes with much lower cost and maintenance requirements than a Citrix deployment. There are limitations of IWP that need to be weighed against these benefits, but for its functionality, speed, cost, and ease of use, it's certainly worth trying.

CREATING A DATABASE-DRIVEN WEBSITE

There are two general techniques for incorporating data from a FileMaker database into a website. On the one hand, you can create static views of data by exporting HTML or XML from your database. This works especially well for read-only sites where the content doesn't change often. For instance, you might want to publish data from an event database on your website. It might be suitable simply to find and export some portion of the data on a periodic basis, and then to move the resulting HTML document to your website.

→ Exporting XML and transforming it into other formats via XSLT is covered in Chapter 22, "FileMaker and Web Services"; **see** "Transforming XML," **p. 676**.

On the other hand, the alternative to publishing static data is publishing dynamic data, which means that the web user is somehow interacting with the database in real-time. This allows up-to-the-second data accuracy and also enables users to easily add, edit, and delete data directly from their browsers.

Creating dynamic connections from web pages to a FileMaker database can be a complex and time-consuming task. This process is often referred to as *Custom Web Publishing (CWP)*. For now, it's enough that you know a few of the pros and cons of CWP. On the plus side, using CWP, you can create robust, complex, and professional web applications. The drawback of CWP is the same as with most web application development: It's a fairly complex skill to learn and is therefore costly in terms of time and/or money.

→ To learn more about Custom Web Publishing and how it compares to IWP, **see** Chapter 23, "Custom Web Publishing," **p. 699**.

Instant Web Publishing offers a reasonable alternative to CWP as a means for building a dynamic web application. You can design layouts in your FileMaker solution that fit nicely with the rest of a site, or you can even create a whole website out of FileMaker layouts if you're so inclined. With IWP, you don't need to learn HTML or any middleware languages, and maintaining your site is as simple as editing scripts and layouts within FileMaker. However, these strengths of IWP also become its weaknesses when you're attempting to develop especially complex web applications. You have no ability to modify how IWP behaves at a low level: It does what it does, and that's it. You can't look under the hood at the code and manipulate it, nor is it easy to mingle IWP-based web pages and data with data or interface elements from other web environments.

GETTING STARTED WITH IWP

After you've decided that IWP is something you want to try, there isn't too much you'll need to do to get started. There are two ways to deploy IWP. You can use the regular FileMaker Pro desktop application, in which case you're limited to publishing a maximum of 10 database files to at most five concurrent users. Alternatively, you can use FileMaker Server Advanced, which allows for significantly more files and users. The configurations for these options are covered in detail in the next section.

The host machine—whether running FileMaker Pro or FileMaker Server Advanced—of course needs to have an Internet (or intranet) connection. Ideally, it will be a persistent connection (for example, T1 or DSL). The host machine also needs to have a static IP address. If you don't have a static IP address on the host machine, remote users can have a difficult time accessing your solution. Finally, any databases you want users to access via IWP need to be open on the host machine.

> **TIP**
>
> Consider setting up a domain name for the IWP host machine. This enables your users to go to something like databases.mycompany.com instead of a difficult-to-remember IP address. Your ISP or a networking specialist can help you with that task. If you ever need to change machines or IP addresses, you can repoint the domain name to the new address without your users being affected by the change.

To access your IWP-enabled files, remote users need to have an Internet connection and a compatible browser. Because IWP makes heavy use of Cascading Style Sheets (CSS), the browser restrictions are important, and are something you need to consider carefully if you intend to use IWP as part of a publicly accessible website.

On Windows, the supported web browsers are Internet Explorer 6.0, Internet Explorer 7.0, and Firefox 1.0. On Macintosh, users need Safari 1.1 (Mac OS 10.2), Safari 1.2 (Mac OS 10.3), Safari 2.0 (Mac OS 10.4), or Firefox 1.0. Obviously, these options may change with new releases of browsers and new versions of operating systems, so consult the www. filemaker.com website for the latest configuration guidelines. Whichever approved browser is used, JavaScript needs to be enabled, and the cache settings should be set to always update pages.

21

CAUTION

> Some organizations forcibly disable JavaScript in all browsers. If you, or any of your remote users, work for such an organization, be aware of this and its ramifications for your web publishing strategy: IWP will not work unless JavaScript is enabled in the browser.

ENABLING AND CONFIGURING IWP

To publish databases to the Web via IWP, you need to enable and configure IWP on the host machine, and you need to set up one or more database files to allow IWP access. Each of these topics is covered in detail in the sections that follow.

CONFIGURING FILEMAKER PRO FOR IWP

Using FileMaker Pro, you can share up to 10 databases with up to five users. To share more files or share with more users, you need to use FileMaker Server Advanced as your IWP host. FileMaker Pro can serve only files that it opens as a host. That is, it's not possible for FileMaker Pro to open a file as a guest of FileMaker Server Advanced and to further share it to IWP users.

Figure 21.4 shows the Instant Web Publishing setup screen in FileMaker Pro. In Windows, you get to this screen by choosing Edit, Sharing, Instant Web Publishing. On Mac, choose FileMaker Pro, Sharing, Instant Web Publishing. The top half of the Instant Web Publishing dialog box relates to the status of IWP at the application level; the bottom half details the sharing status of any currently open database files. The two halves function independently of one another and are discussed separately here. For now, we're just concerned with getting IWP working at the application level and therefore limit our discussion to the options on the top half of the Instant Web Publishing dialog box.

Figure 21.4
To enable Instant Web Publishing in FileMaker Pro, simply select On on the IWP configuration screen.

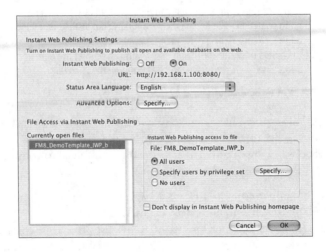

Turning Instant Web Publishing on and off is as simple as toggling the Off/On selection. Selecting On enables this particular copy of FileMaker Pro to act as an IWP host. You can choose the language that will be used on the IWP Database Homepage and in the status area. You can also configure a handful of advanced options, as shown in Figure 21.5.

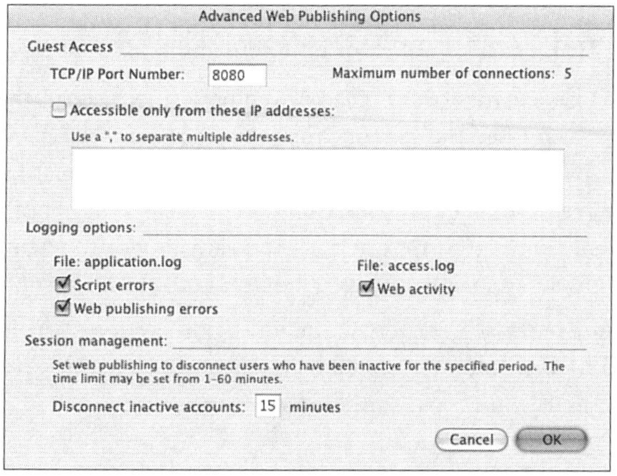

Figure 21.5
On the Advanced Web Publishing Options dialog box, you can configure the port number, logging options, IP restrictions, and session disconnect time.

PORT NUMBER

By default, IWP is configured to use port 80 on the host machine. If another application, such as a web server, is already using that port, you see an error message and are asked to specify a different port to use. FileMaker, Inc., has registered port 591 with the Internet Assigned Numbers Authority (IANA), so that's the recommended alternative port number. The only downside of using a port other than 80 is that users need to explicitly specify the port as part of the URL to access IWP. For instance, instead of typing **127.0.0.1**, your users would need to type **127.0.0.1:591** (or whatever port number you specified).

NOTE

If you are using Mac OS X, you may be asked to type your computer's pass phrase if you attempt to change the port number when configuring IWP within the FileMaker client.

SECURITY

If you know the IP addresses of the machines your IWP users will use when accessing your solution, you can greatly increase your solution's security by restricting access to only those addresses. Multiple IP addresses can be entered as a comma-separated list. You can use an asterisk (*) as a wildcard in place of any part of the IP address (except for the first part). That is, entering **192.168.101.*** causes any IP address from 192.168.101.0 to 192.168.101.255 to be accepted. Entering **192.*** allows access to any user whose IP address begins with 192.

If you don't set IP restrictions, anyone in the world who knows the IP address of your host machine and has network access to it can see at least the IWP Database Homepage (which lists IWP-enabled files). And if you've enabled the Instant Web Publishing extended privilege on the Guest privilege set, remote users could open the files as well. This is, of course, exactly the behavior you'd want when IWP is used as part of a publicly accessible website.

21

LOGGING

You can enable two activity logs for tracking and monitoring your IWP solution: the application log and the access log.

The application log tracks script errors and web publishing errors:

- **Script errors**—These errors occur when a web user runs a script that contains non–web-compatible script steps. See the section "Scripting for IWP," later in this chapter, for more information about what particular steps are not web compatible. A script error can also occur if a user attempts to do something (via a script) that's not permitted by that user's privilege set. Logging script errors—especially as you're testing an existing solution for IWP friendliness—is a great way to troubleshoot potential problems.

- **Web publishing errors**—These errors include more generic errors, such as "page not found" errors. The log entry generated by one of these generic errors is very sparse and may not be terribly helpful for troubleshooting purposes.

The access log records all IWP activity at a granular level: Every hit is recorded, just as you'd find with any web server. As a result, the access log can grow quite large very quickly, and there are no mechanisms that allow for automatic purging of the logs. Be sure to check the size of the logs periodically and to prune them as necessary to keep them from eating up disk space. (A knowledgeable system administrator can configure both Windows and Mac OS X to periodically trim or rotate logs to prevent uncontrolled log growth.)

> **NOTE**
>
> Each of the two logs can be read with any text editor, but you may find it helpful to build a FileMaker database into which you can import log data. It will be much easier to read and search that way.

ENDING A SESSION

The final option on the Advanced Web Publishing Options dialog box is the setting for the session disconnect time. As mentioned previously, IWP establishes a unique database session for each web user. This means that as a user interacts with the system, things such as global values, the current layout, and the active found set are remembered. Rather than just treating requests from the Web as discrete and unrelated events, as was the case in previous incarnations of IWP, the host maintains session data on each IWP user.

Because only five sessions can be active at any given time when FileMaker Pro is being used as an IWP host, it's important that sessions be ended at some point. A session can be ended in several ways:

- A user can click the Log Out button in the status area.
- The Exit Application script step ends an IWP session and returns the user to the Database Homepage.
- You can terminate a session after a certain amount of inactivity. The default is 15 minutes, but you can set it to anything from 1 to 60 minutes.

Are your IWP sessions not ending when you think they should? See "Problems Ending IWP Sessions" in the "Troubleshooting" section at the end of this chapter.

Clicking on the house icon in the status area to return to the Database Homepage does not end a session. If a user reenters the file from the Database Homepage without ending his session, he returns to exactly the same place he left, even if a startup script or default layout is specified for the file.

Configuring FileMaker Server Advanced for IWP

One of the best features of the FileMaker product line is the capability to do web publishing directly from files hosted by FileMaker Server Advanced. Using FileMaker Pro as an IWP host works well for development, testing, and some limited deployment situations, but for many business applications, you'll find that you want the added power and stability that come from using FileMaker Server Advanced for this purpose.

Using FileMaker Server Advanced as your IWP host provides several significant benefits. The first is simply that it scales better. With FileMaker Pro, you are limited to 5 concurrent IWP sessions; with FileMaker Server Advanced, you can have up to 100 IWP sessions. FileMaker Server Advanced can also host up to 125 files, compared to FileMaker Pro's 10. Even more important, you have the option to use SSL for data encryption when using FileMaker Server Advanced as the web host. FileMaker Server Advanced is a more reliable web host as well. It is more likely that the shared files will always be available for web users, that they'll be backed up on a regular basis, and that the site's IP address won't change when you use FileMaker Server. (Even in organizations that use dynamic addressing for desktop machines, servers are typically assigned static IP addresses.)

Chapter 25, "FileMaker Server and Server Advanced," covers in detail the various components and installation options of FileMaker Server and the Web Publishing Engine. Chapter 23, "Custom Web Publishing," also contains a good deal of installation and configuration information. Here, we'll assume that you have all the required components in place and will merely touch on the relevant configuration screens in the FileMaker Server *Web Publishing Administration Console (WPAC)*. WPAC is a web-based configuration tool that allows you to attach a Web Publishing Engine to a FileMaker Server and configure it. As shown in Figure 21.6, you turn on Instant Web Publishing for FileMaker Server simply by toggling the On/Off buttons on the Publishing Engine configuration page. This page is—by design, of course— quite similar to the IWP configuration dialog in the FileMaker Pro desktop application.

On the General Settings page, as shown in Figure 21.7, you can specify logging and session disconnection settings. These are analogous to their FileMaker Pro counterparts, which were discussed in depth in the preceding section. Refer to that section if you need additional information about what is contained in the logs or the significance of the session disconnection setting. The logs are written as text files in the following directory on the web server:

Mac OS X: `/Library/FileMaker Server 8/Web Publishing/logs`

Windows: `\Program Files\FileMaker\FileMaker Server 8\Web Publishing\logs`

21

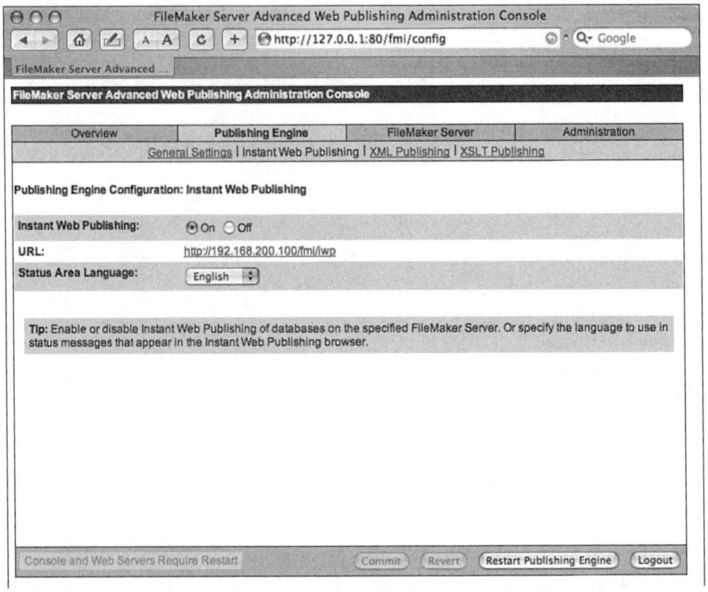

Figure 21.6
Use the Web Publishing Administration Console to allow FileMaker Server Advanced to host IWP-enabled databases.

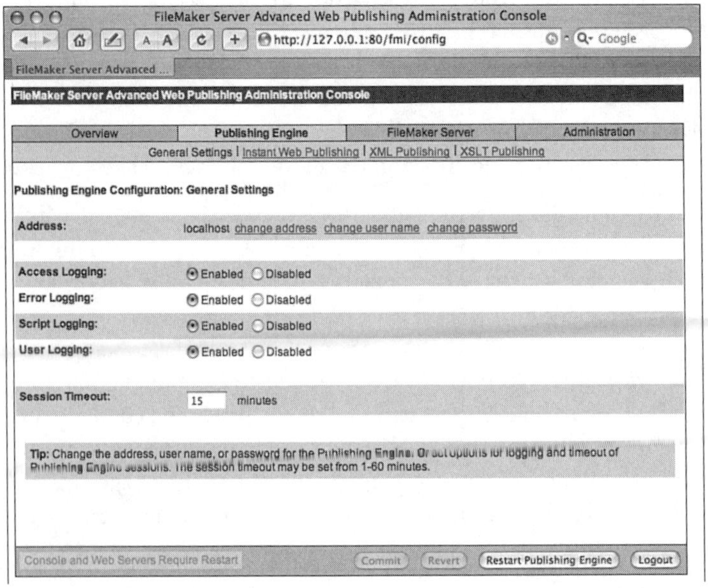

Figure 21.7
Logging and session disconnection options are specified on the General Settings page.

You can see a list of the databases that are accessible via IWP on the server by going to the FileMaker Server Published Databases page, shown in Figure 21.8. For a database to be IWP-accessible, one or more privilege sets needs to have the fmiwp extended privilege enabled. There's no configuration or setup that you need to do in WPAC nor to the files themselves before hosting them with FileMaker Server. In fact, even while a file is being hosted by FileMaker Server, a user with the privilege to manage extended privileges can use FileMaker Pro to open the file remotely and edit the privilege sets so that the file is or isn't IWP accessible.

Figure 21.8
WPAC lists all the web-accessible databases on the server, but you don't need to do any configuration here at the file level to allow something to be shared to IWP.

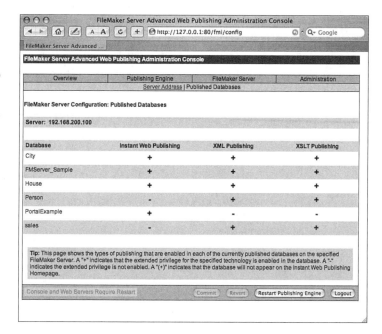

NOTE

If you want a file to be accessible via IWP, but not to show up on the Database Homepage, you need to open the file with FileMaker Pro (open it directly, that is, not simply as a guest of FileMaker Server) and go into the Instant Web Publishing configuration screen. After you are there, select the file and then check the Don't Display in Instant Web Publishing Homepage check box. You do not need to actually enable IWP or add any extended privileges to privilege sets to have access to this setting.

SHARING AND SECURING FILES VIA IWP

Security for Instant Web Publishing users is managed the same way it's managed for FileMaker Pro users: via accounts and privileges. Accounts and privileges also dictate which database files are accessible via IWP. To be shared via IWP, a particular file needs to be open, and one or more privilege sets in that file needs to have the fmiwp extended privilege enabled. This is true regardless of whether you plan to use FileMaker Pro or FileMaker Server Advanced as the web host.

You assign the fmiwp extended privilege to a privilege set in any of three ways:

- Go to File, Define, Accounts & Privileges. On the Extended Privileges tab, you'll see a list of the various extended privileges and be able to assign fmiwp to any privilege sets you want.

→ For more information on what extended privileges are and how to assign them to a privilege set, **see** "Extended Privileges," **p. 342**.

- Also in File, Define, Accounts & Privileges, on the Privilege Sets tab, you can select fmiwp as an extended privilege for the currently active privilege set.

- On the Instant Web Publishing setup screen (refer to Figure 21.4), the bottom half of the screen shows a list of open database files. When you select a particular database, you can manage the fmiwp extended privilege right from this screen. If you select All Users or No Users, the fmiwp extended privilege is granted or removed from all privilege sets in the file. You can also select Specify Users By Privilege Set to select those privilege sets that should have access to IWP. Although the words *extended privilege* and *fmiwp* never appear on this screen, it functions exactly the same as the Extended Privilege detail screen. This screen is intended to be more user friendly and convenient, especially when working with multiple files.

NOTE

> To assign extended privileges in any of these ways, a user must be logged in with a password that grants rights to Manage Extended Privileges.

The other sharing option you can configure on the Instant Web Publishing setup screen is whether the database name appears on the Database Homepage. In a multifile solution, you may want to have only a single file appear there so that users are forced to enter the system through a single, controlled point of entry.

NOTE

> Any changes made in the sharing settings and privileges for a file take effect immediately; you do not need to restart FileMaker or close the file.

When users type the IP address (or domain name) of the IWP host in their browsers, the first thing they'll see is the IWP Database Homepage, an example of which is shown in Figure 21.9). The Database Homepage lists, in alphabetical order, all files on the host machine that have at least some privilege sets with the fmiwp extended privilege enabled. The Database Homepage cannot be suppressed, though it can be customized or replaced, as explained later in this chapter.

Users aren't prompted for a password on their way to the Database Homepage. The password prompt occurs (unless you are logged in as a guest, as described in the following bulleted list) when users first try to interact with a database. IWP now uses an HTML forms-based interface for entering a username and password. To be authenticated, users must enter an active, valid username and password, and their accounts must be associated with a privilege set that has the fmiwp extended privilege enabled.

You should know a number of things about how accounts and privileges are authenticated under IWP:

- As in regular FileMaker authentication, the password is case-sensitive (although the account name is not).
- IWP ignores any default login account information that has been set up under File Options.

Figure 21.9
The Database Homepage provides users with a list of accessible files.

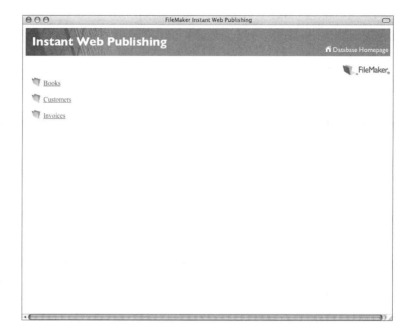

- IWP does not support the Account option to require users to change their passwords after the next successful login. Changing passwords is not a feature supported by IWP. If this option has been set, the web user who tries to log in with that username and password receives an Error 211, Password Has Expired, and cannot enter the system.

- If the Guest account has been activated and given the fmiwp extended privilege, users might not be prompted for a username/password to access the database. To skip the login screen, though, it's necessary that the fmiwp extended privilege be assigned only to the [Read-Only Access] privilege set (the privilege set used by the Guest account). Anyone automatically logged in in this fashion will have the privileges of the Guest account. Such a configuration would typically be used only for websites that need to be accessed by the general public.

 If you're having difficulty getting past the password prompt from the IWP home page, see "Logging into an IWP-Enabled Database" in the "Troubleshooting" section at the end of this chapter.

TIP

> You can create a script that uses the new account management script steps to create your own customized login routine. Users would use Guest privileges to get to your login screen, and then your script would use the Re-login step to reauthenticate them as different users.

After a user is authenticated as a valid user of the file, that user's privilege set then controls which actions can be performed, just as it does for users of the FileMaker Pro desktop

21

application. Field and layout restrictions, record level access, creation and deletion of records—all of these are managed exactly the same for IWP users as for FileMaker Pro users. The capability to make use of this unified security model is truly one of the best features of FileMaker IWP and makes it much simpler to deploy robust and secure IWP solutions.

→ For more information about setting up user accounts and privileges, **see** Chapter 12, "Implementing Security," **p. 325**.

You will likely want to restrict your IWP users to some set of IWP-friendly layouts. If you have users who sometimes access your file via FileMaker (when they're in the office) and sometimes via IWP (from home), consider setting up two separate accounts for those people: one that has the fmiwp extended privilege and one that doesn't.

DESIGNING FOR IWP DEPLOYMENT

The preceding section discussed how to enable IWP at the application level and how to set a file so that users can access it via IWP. Although this is enough for IWP to function, there are usability issues to consider as well. Not all layouts and scripts translate well to the Web, and some FileMaker features simply don't work via IWP. This section discusses the constraints that you, as a developer, must be aware of when deploying an IWP solution. We also discuss a number of development techniques that can make an IWP solution feel more like a typical web application.

CONSTRAINTS OF IWP

Most of the core functionality of FileMaker Pro is available to IWP users. This includes being able to view layouts, find and edit data, and perform scripts attached to buttons. There are, however, a number of FileMaker features that are not available to IWP users. It's important to keep these points in mind, especially when trying to port an already existing solution to the Web:

- IWP users have no database development tools. This means IWP users can't create new files; define tables, fields, and relationships; alter layouts; manage user privileges; or edit scripts.

- IWP users can't use any of the FileMaker Pro keyboard shortcuts. Be sure that you leave the status area visible or provide your users with ample scripted routines for tasks such as executing finds and committing records.

- There is no capability to import or export data from an IWP session. In general, any action that interacts with another application, the file system, or the operating system is not possible via IWP.

- IWP has no Preview mode. This means that sliding, subsummary reports, and multicolumn layouts, all of which require being in Preview mode to view, are not available to IWP users. Similarly, printing is not supported. IWP users can choose to print the contents of the browser window as they would any other web page, but the results will not be the same as printing from FileMaker Pro. (That is, headers and footers won't appear on each page, page setups will not be honored, and so on.)

- There are a few data-entry differences for IWP users. For instance, web users can't edit rich text formatting in fields. That is, they can't change the style, font, or size of text in a field. They can generally, however, see rich text formatting that has already been applied to a field.

- Most window manipulation tools and techniques do not translate well to IWP. The user's browser can show only the contents of the currently active window in the virtual FileMaker environment. That environment can maintain multiple virtual windows and switch between them, but a user can't have multiple visible windows in the browser, and cannot resize or move windows except to the extent allowed by the browser (in other words, the users can manually resize their browser windows, but precision movement and placement of windows using script steps such as Move Window is not supported in IWP).

- None of the FileMaker Pro toolbars are available via IWP. IWP does offer its own toolbars in the status area, however, and these contain some of the same functionality found in the FileMaker Pro toolbars.

- Spell-checking is not available via IWP.

- Many graphical layout elements are rendered differently, or not at all, on the Web. This includes diagonal lines, rounded rectangles, rotated objects, ovals, and fill patterns. The sections that follow discuss this topic in greater detail.

- IWP users can't edit value lists through a web browser.

- There is no built-in way for users to change their passwords via IWP, even if they have the privilege to do so. If you need this sort of functionality, you need to use the account management script steps and come up with your own scripted routine.

SCRIPTING FOR IWP

One of the greatest recent advances in Instant Web Publishing is script support. In versions of FileMaker before version 7, only a handful of script steps could be executed from the Web, and scripts could be no more than three steps long. Under those severe restrictions, it was quite difficult to build anything but the most basic web applications.

IWP in FileMaker 7 and 8 supports more than 70 script steps, and scripts can be of any length and complexity. Also, because IWP is now session-based, scripts that are executed from the Web operate within what might be thought of as a virtual FileMaker environment. This means that changes to the environment (active layout, found set, and so on) are persistent and affect the browser experience, which is a good thing.

Even though IWP script support has come a long way, there are still some behaviors, constraints, and techniques you should be aware of.

UNSUPPORTED SCRIPT STEPS

Given the great number of supported script steps, it's easier to talk about what's not supported under IWP. In general, anything that requires that the user interact with a dialog box is unsupported, as are any steps that interact with the operating system or other applications.

21

The list of unsupported steps is shown in Table 21.1.

TABLE 21.1 UNSUPPORTED SCRIPT STEPS

Script Category	Script Step
Navigation	Enter Preview Mode
Editing	Perform Find/Replace
Fields	Insert from Index
	Insert Picture
	Insert QuickTime
	Insert File
	Export Field Contents
Records	Import Records
	Export Records
Windows	Adjust Window
	Move/Resize Windows
	Arrange All Windows
	Freeze Window
	Refresh Window
	Scroll Window
	Show/Hide Text Ruler
	Set Zoom Level
Files	All steps unsupported
Spelling	All steps unsupported
Open Menu Item	All steps unsupported
Miscellaneous	Show Custom Dialog
	Allow Toolbars
	Beep
	Speak
	Dial Phone
	Send Mail
	Perform AppleScript
	Send Message
	Execute SQL
	Send Event
	Flush Cache to Disk

Additionally, the option to perform with a dialog is not supported in a number of supported script steps. These include Delete Record/Request, Replace Field Contents, Omit Multiple Records, and Sort Records. These steps are always performed without a dialog via IWP, regardless of which dialog option has been selected in ScriptMaker.

ScriptMaker itself has an option that makes identifying unsupported script steps quite easy. When you check the Indicate Web Compatibility check box, all the unsupported script steps are dimmed. This affects both the list of script steps and the steps in whatever script you're viewing. Figure 21.10 shows an example of what script step dimming looks like. The Indicate Web Compatibility check box has no effect other than showing you which steps are not supported; how you choose to use that information is up to you (although unsupported script steps are dimmed out, you can still add them to a script). Additionally, its status is not tied to any particular script. That is, it is either turned on or off for the entire file, and it remains that way until a developer changes it. We point this out explicitly because the check box right next to it, Run Script with Full Access Privileges, is a script-specific setting.

Figure 21.10
When writing scripts that will be used via IWP, turn on the Indicate Web Compatibility check box to dim out incompatible script steps.

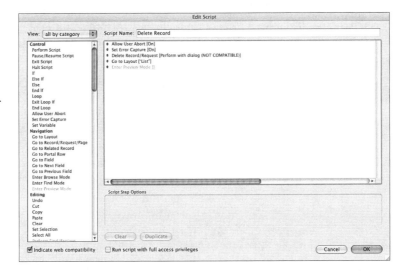

ERROR CAPTURE

The outcome of running a script (from the Web) that contains unsupported script steps depends on whether the Allow User Abort setting has been turned on or off. If it's not explicitly specified, a script executes on the Web as if Allow User Abort had been turned on. So not specifying any setting is the same as explicitly turning it on.

If user abort is on (or not set at all), script execution halts when an unsupported step is encountered. Steps before the offending script step are performed as normal. If you've chosen to log script errors, the offending step is logged as an error in the application log. The user does not see any error message or have any knowledge that anything is amiss.

If user abort has been turned off, a script will simply bypass any unsupported scripts and attempt to perform subsequent steps. It's performed as if the offending step were simply not there. No error is logged to the application log when this occurs.

Script steps with the unsupported "perform with dialog" options discussed earlier are not affected at all by the error capture setting. These script steps will always be performed as if Perform Without Dialog had been checked, regardless of error capture.

21

COMMITTING RECORDS

If a script run via IWP causes a record to be altered in any way (such as using a Set Field script step), be sure that you explicitly save the change by using the Commit Record/Request step sometime before the end of the script. If you don't, your web user will be left in Edit mode and, provided that the status area is visible, will have the option to Submit or Cancel the changes, which is likely not an option you want to offer at that point. Canceling would undo any changes made by the script.

STARTUP AND SHUTDOWN SCRIPTS

If you have specified a startup script for a file, it is performed for IWP users when the session is initiated. Similarly, IWP also switches to a particular layout on startup if you've selected that option.

The shutdown script is performed when the user logs out, even if the logout is the result of timing out.

CAUTION

> The startup script executes only once per session, when the user navigates there from the Database Homepage (or follows an equivalent link from another web page). The startup script is not run if a file is activated through the performance of an external script.

PERFORMING SUBSCRIPTS IN OTHER FILES

A script can call a subscript in another file, but that file needs to be open and enabled for IWP for the subscript to execute. Calling a subscript does not force open an external file, as happens in the FileMaker Pro desktop application.

If your subscript activates a window in the external file, the IWP user sees that window in the browser. Unless you provide navigation back to the first file, a user has no way of returning, except by logging out and logging back in. You should make sure that any record changes are fully committed before navigating to a window in another file. It's possible that the record will remain in an uncommitted, locked state, even though the IWP user has no idea this has occurred.

TESTING FOR IWP EXECUTION WITHIN A SCRIPT

If you have a solution that will be accessed by both FileMaker Pro desktop users and IWP users, chances are that they'll use some of the same scripts. If those scripts contain unsupported script steps, you might want to add conditional logic to them so that they behave differently for IWP users than they do for FileMaker users. You can do this by using the Get (ApplicationVersion) function. If the words Web Publishing are found within the string returned by this function, that means the person executing the script is a web user. It's not possible to discriminate between an IWP user and a CWP user with this function; you simply know you have a web user. The actual syntax for performing the test is as follows:

```
PatternCount (Get (ApplicationVersion); "Web Publishing")
```

LAYOUT DESIGN

Most layouts you design in FileMaker Pro will be rendered almost perfectly in a web browser via Instant Web Publishing. IWP does this by using the absolute positioning capability of Cascading Style Sheets, Level 2. The CSS requirements of IWP are the reason there are browser restrictions for its use. We've already mentioned a few layout elements that don't translate well to IWP—we'll recap them here as well—but there are several additional things to keep in mind when creating or modifying layouts for IWP use.

GRAPHIC ELEMENTS

Rounded rectangles, ovals, diagonal lines, rotated objects, and fill patterns are not rendered properly in the web browser and should be avoided. In some cases, IWP displays altered versions of the objects; in other cases the objects simply do not show up.

Figure 21.11 shows a test layout in FileMaker that we filled with various shapes and objects; Figure 21.12 shows how it renders in a web browser. As you can see, IWP does a great job with vertical and horizontal lines of varied widths, with rendering nonstandard fonts, with overlapping text, and with stylized boxes. However, it completely ignored the circle and diagonal line, and altered the rotated text, rounded rectangle, and fill pattern. Also, multi-column check box and radio button fields don't maintain their columnar alignment.

Figure 21.11
It's important to be aware of which layout elements don't render properly via IWP.

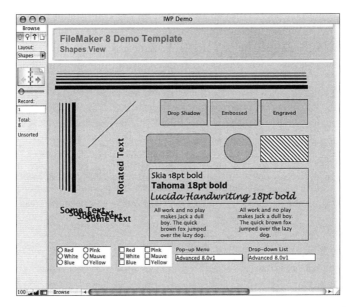

Figure 21.12
Most elements of the test layout render properly in a browser, but a few are displayed either differently or not at all.

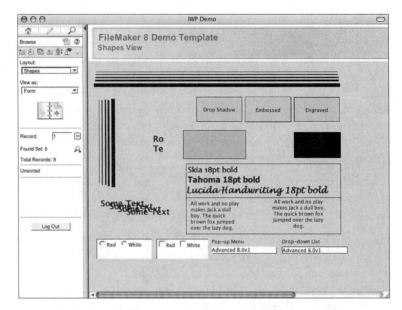

TAB ORDER

In IWP in FileMaker 7, the tab order you set for a layout within FileMaker did not carry over to the web browser. Instead, tab order in the browser was determined by the stacking order of the fields on the layout, with the backmost field being first in the tab order. There was no quick and easy way to see or edit the stacking order within FileMaker; mostly you needed to use the Arrange, Send Backward and Arrange, Bring Forward commands to rearrange things manually.

Happily, this has changed with IWP in FileMaker 8. IWP will now respect the tab order established in FileMaker.

> **CAUTION**
>
> IWP does not support the field behavior options to go to the next field by using the Return or Enter key rather than the Tab key. Navigation from field to field in IWP occurs only via the Tab key, just as it would for any browser-based form.

"VIEW AS" OPTIONS

Web users have the same ability that FileMaker desktop users have to switch between View As Form, View As List, and View As Table on a given layout, unless you restrict that ability at the layout level. To do so, go into the Layout Setup options, shown in Figure 21.13, and simply uncheck any inappropriate views. The additional Table view options that can be specified all translate well to IWP, except for resizable and reorderable columns.

Figure 21.13
In Layout Setup, you can specify the views to which a user should be able to switch for a given layout.

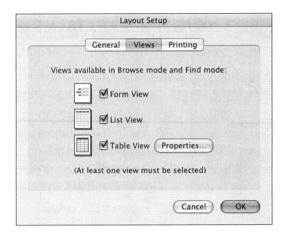

You should be aware of a few special characteristics of List and Table views in IWP. By default, View As List shows a set of at most 25 records, and View As Table shows a set of at most 50 records. You cannot change these settings. Also, while in List or Table view, whenever a user clicks on a record to edit it, the active record jumps to the top of the set. This can be slightly disconcerting for users who are habituated to working with lists of records in FileMaker. For instance, if a user is viewing records 6–10 of a set as a list, and clicks on record 8, record 8 jumps to the top, and the screen then displays records 8–12.

→ To learn how to build your own Next and Previous navigation routine for use with List and Table views when the status area is hidden, **see** the "FileMaker Extra: Building Your Own Next and Previous Page Buttons" section of this chapter, **p. 666**.

LAYOUT PARTS

IWP can render any and all parts that compose a layout. There are a few differences, however, between how and when parts display in IWP and how and when they display in the FileMaker desktop application.

First of all, in Form view, the vertical size of a part displayed via IWP is the size that the part was defined to be. It doesn't stretch to fill the vertical space. This is different from how FileMaker Pro behaves. In FileMaker Pro, the last visible part expands to fill any remaining vertical space. Say, for instance, that you have a layout that consists of only a single, colored body part. Via IWP, if a user resizes a browser window so that it's larger (vertically) than the body part, the space between the bottom of the part and the bottom of the browser is a white void. This also means that if your layout has a footer part, it won't necessarily (indeed, won't likely) be displayed at the very bottom of the browser window.

View As List in a browser also has some differences from its FileMaker counterpart. In FileMaker, a header or footer part is locked on the screen at the top or bottom. The area in between displays as many body records as space permits. In FileMaker, leading and trailing grand summary parts display in List view, but title header, title footer, and subsummary parts do not (in Browse mode).

As we've mentioned, in a browser, List view always contains 25 records (except, of course, when the found set is fewer than 5 or if the active record is one of the last four of the found set). The header and footer are not fixed elements as they are in FileMaker. If the 25 records of the list take up less than the full browser window, the footer simply shows up in the middle of the screen; if they take up more than the full window, a user would need to scroll to see the footer. Another major difference is that title header, title footer, and subsummary parts are all visible in the browser at all times (in List view). Even if the database is sorted properly, however, subsummary parts do not show correct values—they show the same values that a leading or trailing grand summary would show. For this reason, it's unlikely to be a good idea to allow your IWP users access to layouts that contain subsummary parts.

CONTAINER FIELDS

You should know about a few special restrictions and considerations when using container fields in an IWP solution. Most important, there is no capability to add or edit data in a container field via IWP; these fields are strictly view-only. Entry and updating of pictures, sounds, QuickTime movies, files, and objects is available only to regular FileMaker Pro users.

The visibility and/or accessibility of a container field's contents are dependent on the types of objects they are and how they were entered into the container field in the first place:

- Graphic images that have been directly stored in a container field (that is, not stored as a reference) are visible through a browser. Images should be stored as pictures, not as files.

- Graphic images that have been stored as a reference are visible to IWP users only if the images are stored in the web folder of the FileMaker Pro application (if FileMaker Pro is the IWP host) or if they are stored in the root folder of the web server (if FileMaker Server is the IWP host).

- QuickTime movies can't be accessed directly from the web browser. If you insert them as files rather than as QuickTime, however, a user can play or download them.

- Files stored directly in a container field are rendered to an IWP user as a hyperlink. Clicking on the link begins a download of the file. No icon or other graphic representation of the file is visible to web users.

- Sounds that have been stored directly in container fields cannot be played via IWP.

APPLICATION FLOW

We've discussed many of the technical limitations and details of how various FileMaker features translate to the Web. We turn now to more practical development matters. There are certain routines and development habits that work well in the FileMaker desktop application that don't work as well from a web browser. The following sections discuss how the constraints of IWP will influence how you develop solutions.

Web-based applications generally have a different application flow than FileMaker applications, and you may consequently find that you need to rethink some things when you share a solution to IWP. By *application flow*, we mean broadly how a user actually interacts with the application. For instance, one of the typical flows for web applications is search->hitlist->detail. Think about google.com or amazon.com and how those sites make heavy use of this pattern. A user enters search criteria; sees a list of matching records, usually in groups of 10 or 20 at a time; and then drills down to a detail record by clicking on a link from the hitlist.

Such an application flow is rare in FileMaker solutions. More often, users spend most of their time on a detail record. They drop into Find mode when they need to locate records. They then flip through the records one by one, or perhaps they switch to a List view where they can scroll through to locate a particular record. An application flow like this can indeed work via IWP; our point is merely that it's not a traditional web application flow. Depending on your solution and your users' experiences, they may expect a more weblike flow.

When it comes down to it, we've discovered that it's actually easier to make FileMaker mimic the web flow than the other way around.

TIP

> If you're designing a new solution and you know that you'll have IWP users, you might consider thinking about how you would develop the solution if it were a web application. Because there are more constraints placed on designing for the browser, anything you build for the browser should work well for FileMaker users as well.

EXPLICIT RECORD COMMITS

Many of the application flow differences described in the preceding section stem from the fact that HTTP—the underlying protocol of the Web—is a stateless protocol. This means that every request a browser makes to a web server is separate and independent from every other request. Put differently, the web server doesn't maintain a persistent connection to the web client. After it has processed a request from someone's browser, it simply stands by waiting for the next request to come in. To make HTTP connections appear to be persistent, web programmers need to add information to each request from a single client, and then let some piece of web server middleware keep track of which client is which, based on this extra request data. This technique is referred to as *session management*.

The client/server connection between FileMaker Pro and FileMaker Server is persistent. The two are constantly talking back and forth, exchanging information and making sure that the other is still there. FileMaker Server is actively aware of all the client sessions. When FileMaker Server receives new record data from any client on the network, it immediately broadcasts that information to all the other clients. And when a user clicks into a field and starts editing data, FileMaker Server immediately knows to consider that record as locked, and to prevent other users from modifying the record.

The fact that IWP is now capable of performing session management means that FileMaker maintains information about what's happening on the Web in a virtual FileMaker environment. Even though this doesn't change the fact that HTTP is stateless, using sessions gives IWP a semblance of persistence. Essentially, the server stores a bunch of information about each IWP user; each request from a user includes certain session identifiers that enable the

21

server to recognize the IWP guest and to know the context by which to evaluate the request. One of the benefits of this session model is that IWP users can lock records, and they are notified if they try to edit a record that a regular FileMaker Pro user has locked.

Still, the statelessness of the Web makes the application flow for something even as basic as editing a record much different in IWP than it is in FileMaker. In FileMaker, of course, a user just clicks into a field, makes some changes, and then clicks out of the field to commit (save) the change. On the Web, editing a record involves two distinct transactions. First, by clicking on an editable field or using the Edit Record button in the status area, the user generates a request to the server to return an edit form for that record and to mark the record as locked. As we discussed earlier in this chapter, Edit mode in the browser is distinctly different from Browse mode.

The second transaction occurs when the user clicks the Commit button in the status area (or clicks a similar button you've provided for this purpose). No actual data is modified in the database until and unless the record is committed explicitly.

This transaction model for data entry may feel very alien to users who are accustomed to working with a FileMaker interface. As you evaluate the web-friendliness of existing layouts or build new layouts for IWP users, try to make the application flow work well as a series of discrete and independent transactions. One common way to do this is by having tightly controlled routines that users follow to accomplish certain tasks. For instance, rather than letting users just create new records anywhere they want, create a "new record" routine that walks users through a series of screens where they enter data and are required to click a Next Screen or Submit button to move forward through the routine.

LOOKUPS AND PORTAL FILTERS

Because of the transactional nature of the Web, two common FileMaker development tools—lookups and portal filters—don't work well in IWP.

Consider first how a lookup works in FileMaker. When a value in a trigger field is edited (usually by a user), the values of one or more target fields change. For instance, when you're creating an invoice, it's typical to enter a Product ID for a line item and have a description and price for that item appear as soon as the user exits the field. It's not important here whether the description and price are actually looked up or are simply related fields. The point is that from a user perspective, exiting the field caused something to happen.

→ For more on lookups, **see** "Auto-Entry Field Options," **p. 78**.

When using IWP, to trigger an action such as a lookup or the display of related data, a user must actually submit the change as an edit to the trigger field and then wait for a reply. It works, but it's a far cry from being able to just Tab out of a field and have data appear.

Portal filters exhibit the same behavior. The typical portal filter works by having a user choose some value in a field that anchors one end of a relationship. After the selection is made, the portal data immediately updates to reflect the matches to the filter. When using IWP, the user would again need to explicitly submit the entire record, including the filter value, for the portal to refresh.

→ For more information about creating portal filters, **see** "Filtered Portals," **p. 489**.

As a more weblike alternative to triggered events like these, you might consider calling explicit attention to the fact that something needs to be submitted before the user can continue with entry. For instance, Figure 21.14 is an example of a layout for creating a new invoice. Notice that as step 1, users are asked to enter a customer ID and to click Submit. After this is done, the related customer data is displayed, and the user moves on to step 2, where they're asked to enter the product code of an item to add to the invoice. Behind the scenes they're actually entering a value into a global field at that point; the Add button creates a related line item record, filling in the description and quantity, and then returns users to Edit mode so that they can enter another product. By leaving users almost perpetually in Edit mode, you'll cut in half the number of transactions they have to trigger explicitly during repetitive data entry like this.

Figure 21.14
If you have a routine that requires triggered events, make the submission of the triggers a very explicit part of the process. That is, draw more attention to the triggered events rather than less.

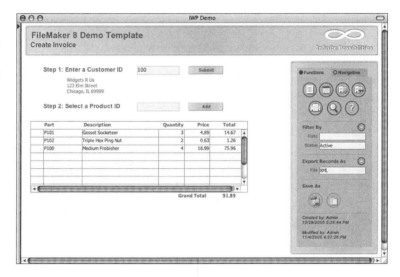

HIDING THE STATUS AREA

As when designing a solution for FileMaker users, you have the option to leave the status area visible for your IWP users or to hide it from them. And as with regular FileMaker, unless you lock it open or closed, users can toggle it themselves.

By default, the status area is visible for your IWP users. The script step Show/Hide Status Area enables you to programmatically control the visibility of the status area. Typically, if you want to hide the status area, you do so as part of a startup script.

There are certainly benefits to having the status area visible. Most important, the status area provides a wealth of functionality for the IWP user. Navigation, complex searching, and a host of record manipulation tools are all features that come for free in the status area. Also, the status area heightens the "FileMaker-ness" of the user experience. If one of your goals is to make your IWP deployment feel like FileMaker to your users, the status area can certainly help you accomplish this goal.

21

There are also reasons that developers want to hide the status area from users. The first is simply to constrain users' activities by forcing them to use just the tools you give them. This is generally why developers hide the status area for FileMaker desktop deployments as well. Hiding the status area also makes your application more weblike. If you are using IWP alongside an existing website or plan to have the general public access your site, you'll probably want to hide the status area. Public users are more likely to expect a web experience than a FileMaker experience.

If you do decide to hide the status area, you must provide buttons in your interface for every user action you want or need to allow, including committing records, submitting Find requests, and logging out of the application. Because users have no keyboard shortcuts—including using the Enter key to do things like submit Find requests and continue paused scripts—and no pull-down menus, you'll probably need even more buttons than you would when designing without the status area for FileMaker users.

PORTALS

Instant Web Publishing does an astonishingly good job of displaying portals in a browser, complete with scrollbars, alternating row colors, and the capability to add data through the last line of a portal (providing, of course, that the underlying relationship allows it). Another nice thing about portals in IWP is that you can edit multiple portal rows at once and submit them together as a batch.

When designing an IWP application that requires displaying search results as a list, consider whether you can use a portal instead of a List view. A portal gives you flexibility as far as the number of records that are displayed, and you can use the space to the left or right of it for other purposes. Figure 21.15 shows an example of what a search results screen might look like if you used a portal instead of List view.

Figure 21.15
For many search results screens, a portal makes a good alternative to using List view to display the found records.

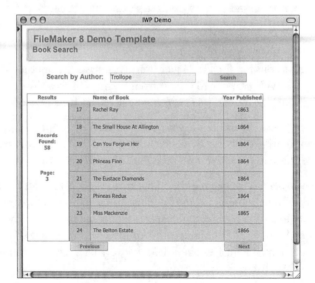

The best way we've found for having a portal display an ad hoc set of records (such as those returned by a user search) is to place all the record keys of the found set into a return-delimited global text field (using the Copy All Records script step), and then to establish a relationship between that field and the file's primary key. Because you can let the portal scroll, you don't strictly need to create Next and Previous links, but it would make your application more weblike if you did. One option to do this is to take the return-delimited list of record IDs and extract the subset that corresponds to a given page worth of IDs. The MiddleValues function comes in handy for this task. You'd simply need to have a global field that kept track of the current page number. Then the function

```
MiddleValues (gRecordKeys; (gPageNumber-1) * 8 + 1; 8)
```

would return the eight record IDs on that page. Substitute a different number of records per page in place of 8, of course, if you want to have a hitlist with some other number of records on it. The scripts to navigate to the next and previous pages then simply need to set the page number appropriately and refresh the screen.

NOTE

To see the example from this section in action, locate PortalExample.fp7 on the CD-ROM accompanying this book.

CREATING LINKS TO IWP FROM OTHER WEB PAGES

The IWP Database Homepage provides a convenient access point for entering web-enabled databases. It's possible also to create your own links into a file from a separate HTML page, which is perhaps more desirable for publicly accessible sites. To do this, you simply create a URL link with the following syntax:

http://*ip address:port number*/fmi/iwp/cgi?-db=*database name*&-loadframes

CAUTION

This syntax is different than it was in versions of FileMaker prior to version 7, so be sure to update external links if you're upgrading an IWP solution from FileMaker 6 or earlier.

If you are using FileMaker Pro itself as your IWP host (as opposed to FileMaker Server Advanced), you can place static HTML files and any images that need to be accessible to IWP users in the web folder inside the FileMaker Pro folder. The web folder is considered the root level when FileMaker Pro acts as a web server. If you had, for example, an HTML page called foo.html in the web folder, the URL to access that page would be the following:

http://*ip address:port number*/foo.html

If you develop a solution that uses FileMaker Pro as the host and later decide to migrate to FileMaker Server Advanced, you should move the entire contents of the web folder (if you've put any documents or images there) to the root folder of your web server.

CREATING A CUSTOM HOME PAGE

 In FileMaker 7, if you accessed IWP via the default path (as opposed to navigating directly to an IWP-enabled database via a hard-coded path like those described in the preceding section), you would always be taken to the same IWP home page (depicted earlier in Figure 21.9). With FileMaker 8, you can override the default page with a page of your own devising. The new file must be called `iwp_home.html`. It can be used when serving files via IWP either from FileMaker Pro (in which case it belongs in the web directory inside the FileMaker Pro application folder) or from FileMaker Server Advanced (in which case it belongs in the `FileMaker Server/Web Publishing/iwp` folder).

There are several approaches to creating such a file. You could devise your own file from scratch, creating your own look and feel, and populate that file with hard-coded links to specific databases, as described in the preceding section. Or, if you want a file that dynamically assembles a list of all available databases, the way the default home page does, you'll want to customize the default page. An example of that default page can be found on the FileMaker Pro product CD. (For the curious, it can also be found in the FileMaker application folder: On Windows it's found in `Extensions/Web Support/Resources/iwpres`, and on Mac OS it's found in `Extensions/Web Support/FM Web Publishing/Contents/Resources/iwpres`. On Mac OS, `Extensions/Web Support/FM Web Publishing` is an OS X package, not a directory, so you'll need to right-click on it and select Show Package Contents in order to drill deeper.) The default page makes heavy use of JavaScript and in particular of JavaScript DOM function calls, so familiarity with those technologies will be desirable if you want to customize the IWP home page.

USING AN IWP SOLUTION

The focus of this chapter is on what a developer needs to know to create and share databases to the Web using Instant Web Publishing. One crucial piece is an understanding of what IWP looks like and how it functions from the user's perspective.

BROWSE MODE

If you've hidden the status area from your users, you have complete control over what a user can do and how it's done. With the status area active, however, a user has access to a great many built-in features, including the capability to perform complex finds, sort records, navigate to other layouts, and manipulate data. Even so, you can still constrain a user's options by placing restrictions on the privilege sets assigned to IWP users.

TIP

> To avoid a user navigating to a non–IWP-friendly layout, edit the layout options of the IWP-enabled privilege sets. Mark any layouts you want users to avoid as No Access.

Figure 21.16 shows the status area a user sees while in Browse mode. Unless you explicitly lock the status area either open or closed, a user can toggle it open and closed while in any mode.

Figure 21.16
The IWP status area in Browse mode contains a number of record manipulation and navigation tools.

While in Browse mode, providing that they have the proper privileges, users can create, edit, duplicate, and delete the current record. They can also sort, find all, omit one record, omit multiple records, and show only the omitted records. Any buttons whose functionality is not permitted by the users' privilege sets are dimmed and inactive.

EDIT MODE

As we've discussed, one of the biggest differences between the user experience in IWP versus the FileMaker Pro desktop application is the explicit distinction between being in Browse mode and being in Edit mode. A user can enter Edit mode in a few ways:

- By clicking on any field (except container and calculation fields) where the Field Behavior is set to allow entry while in Browse mode
- By running a script that opens a record and doesn't commit it
- By clicking the Edit Record button in the status area

Buttons on a layout are active regardless of whether a user is in Browse, Edit, or Find mode. Executing a script via a button does not change the mode unless a mode-changing step is in the script.

CAUTION

> The Enter Browse Mode script step does not return an IWP user from Edit mode to Browse mode. Use the Commit Record/Request script step for this purpose.

21

FIND MODE

Users can enter Find mode in IWP either by clicking on the magnifying glass icon in the status area or by clicking on a button of your creation that leaves them in Find mode. The status area as it appears in Find Mode is shown in Figure 21.17. Users can enter their search criteria and execute the find by clicking on the appropriate buttons in the status area. Just as in the FileMaker Pro desktop application, users can create multiple Find requests, pick from a set of find operators, choose to omit found records, and extend or constrain the current found set.

Figure 21.17
In Find mode, the IWP status area contains all the tools necessary for users to create complex ad hoc searches.

CAUTION

> If you are using the Perform Find, Constrain Found Set, or Extend Found Set script steps to execute a find, be aware that if no records are found, IWP does not display an error message to users. You need to trap for that error yourself and take appropriate action, such as navigating to a layout that has a "No records found" message.

SORTING RECORDS

The Sort button in the status area takes users to a pop-up Sort dialog that looks and functions much like its FileMaker Pro counterpart. It's shown in Figure 21.18. The only way to get to this dialog is through the status area; there's unfortunately no way you can write a script to get here.

21

Figure 21.18
The Sort dialog in IWP appears as a pop-up window.

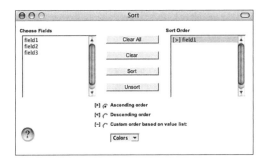

Unlike the Sort dialog in the FileMaker Pro desktop application, which lets users choose any field from the current layout's table, the IWP Sort dialog allows them to choose only from fields that are physically present on the current layout.

TROUBLESHOOTING

PROBLEMS ENDING IWP SESSIONS

FileMaker Pro thinks that there are active IWP sessions, but I know that all the users have closed their browsers.

Closing the browser window or quitting the browser application does not end a session, so be sure to train your users to click the Log Out button (or an equivalent button that you provide). One of the problems you could run into is that an IWP user might quit his browser but still have a record lock. Until the session times out, no other user can modify that record.

If you experience this problem, try reducing the session timeout setting to something like five minutes.

LOGGING IN TO AN IWP-ENABLED DATABASE

I keep trying to log in to a file from the IWP home page, but I can't get past the prompt for a user-name and password.

IWP's new forms-based login will let you know if you've tried to log in with a bad user-name/password combination. Keep in mind that passwords are case-sensitive and that IWP users must belong to a privilege set that has the fmiwp extended privilege enabled.

A related problem is the error message that users see if their accounts have been set to require a password change on the next login. If a user ever mentions seeing a dialog box saying Password Has Expired when trying to log in to an IWP database, this is almost invariably the problem.

FILEMAKER EXTRA: BUILDING YOUR OWN NEXT AND PREVIOUS PAGE BUTTONS

When a user views records via a browser as a list or table, the flipbook navigation tool in the status area changes its behavior slightly. Rather than moving from record to record, as it does for Form views, it performs Next Page/Previous Page navigation, jumping by either 25 records (for List view) or 50 records (for Table view). If you have hidden the status area from your users, you need to create your own Next Page/Previous Page buttons and place them in the header or footer part.

The concept is fairly simple: You need a script that jumps ahead or backward by some number of records. One thing you need to consider, however, is what should happen when the user is already on the first or last page. That is, if you are on record 1 and try to go backward, what happens? And, if you're viewing records 26–50 of a set of 50 records and you click Next, what happens?

It turns out that you don't need to worry too much about the first case. If you feed the Go To Record/Request/Page script step a negative number or 0, you simply end up on record 1, which is perfectly acceptable behavior. However, in the latter case, if you're viewing records 26–50 of 50 found, and you try to jump to record 51, you end up on a page consisting only of record 50. It's not the end of the world, but it's also not what users expect. It would be better if the Next Page script were smart enough to know when it would exceed the record count, in which case it shouldn't do anything at all.

You can create different scripts for the Next and Previous buttons, and you can hard-code the jump size to either 25 or 50 depending on whether it's a List or Table view. You can also use script parameters and conditional logic to do everything, including the check for exceeding the found count, in a single, one-line script. That step would be Go To Record/Request/Page [By Calculation], and it would use the following formula:

```
Let ( [
  curRec = Get ( RecordNumber );
  jumpSize =
  Case (
    Get ( LayoutViewState ) = 1; 25;  // it's in List view
    Get ( LayoutViewState ) = 2; 50; // it's in Table view
    1) ;    // it's in Form View
  direction =
  Case (
    Get (ScriptParameter) = "Next"; 1;  // jump forward
    Get (ScriptParameter) = "Prev"; -1 );  // jump backward
  newRec = curRec + (jumpSize * direction) ] ;

  Case ( newRec > Get ( FoundCount ) ; curRec ; newRec)
)
```

You might want to add one other finishing touch to your Next and Previous buttons. It's common that the Previous link appears dimmed out when you're on the first page, and that the Next link behaves similarly when you're on the last page. One way to accomplish this is to use the TextColor function to conditionally gray out the link text in those situations. The logic needed is virtually the same as in the preceding navigation script. For the Next link, for instance, you could define an unstored calculation field with the following formula:

```
Let ( [
  curRec = Get ( RecordNumber );
  jumpSize =
   Case (
     Get ( LayoutViewState ) = 1; 25;  // it's in List view
     Get ( LayoutViewState ) = 2; 50; // it's in Table view
     1) ;     // it's in Form view
  newRec = curRec + (jumpSize ) ] ;

  Case ( newRec > Get ( FoundCount ); TextColor ("Next"; RGB (120;120;120));
  ➥TextColor ("Next"; 0))
)
```

You can simply place this field in the header and define it to be a button, or you can place it on top of a graphic element to make it look like a button. If you do the latter, you need to be sure to group the two elements as a single button to avoid having them function independently. Do not use Merge fields for the text because calculated text colors in Merge fields do not show up properly via IWP.

The logic for the Previous link is similar. Rather than testing whether the new record number would exceed the found count, instead test whether it would be less than 1.

21

FileMaker and Web Services

ABOUT WEB SERVICES

So what is a Web service? It's certainly a popular buzzword, but what does it mean? Well, loosely speaking, the term refers to the capability of computers that are remote from each other to exchange information and messages over the World Wide Web (which we'll generally refer to simply as "the Web").

As an example, let's say there's a computer out there somewhere on the Internet that knows the current temperature at various points all over the world. If you send that computer a latitude and longitude, in the correct format, the remote computer sends back the nearest current temperature it can find. Such a transaction is shown in Figure 22.1.

Figure 22.1
A desktop PC queries a remote server for temperature data over the Web and receives an answer in XML format.

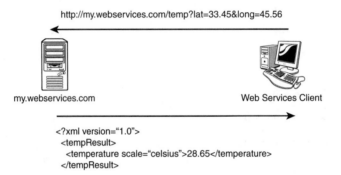

http://my.webservices.com/temp?lat=33.45&long=45.56

my.webservices.com

Web Services Client

```
<?xml version="1.0">
  <tempResult>
    <temperature scale="celsius">28.65</temperature>
  </tempResult>
```

You'll notice a couple of things about this picture. The machine making the request, which we've called the Web Services Client, has sent its request in the form of a URL (a *uniform resource locator*, the standard way of making a request for content over the Web). And the responding computer has sent the requested information back in a tagged message format that you might recognize as XML.

The important thing about this transaction is that it doesn't require any specialized communication protocols to exist between the two machines. The request and response both use standard HTTP, the well-established protocol that powers the entire Web. And the data returned by the server is presented as XML—a standardized and widely accepted way to present data.

So that's our definition: A *Web service* is a means of exchanging information and messages between two computers, which uses XML data sent over the Web via HTTP. Not all Web services involve sending XML over HTTP. But many do, and it's a suitable way to think about Web services for the purpose of working with FileMaker Pro.

Before you can delve very far into how FileMaker works with Web services, though, you need to learn some of the basics of how FileMaker can work with XML data. For the first half of this chapter we discuss how FileMaker interacts with XML, and in the second half, we apply that knowledge to working with actual Web services.

FileMaker and XML

Before you can appreciate FileMaker's Web service capabilities, you need to learn more about the things FileMaker can do with XML data. To put it briefly, FileMaker can both *import* and *export* data as XML. This capability has several interesting uses: For one thing, it means FileMaker can participate in Web services transactions, as you'll see in this chapter. For another, it means FileMaker can exchange data with other applications via XML. Before we delve deeper, though, a brief overview of XML may be useful.

The Basics of XML

XML is a large topic, on which many books have been written. We'll have to content ourselves with a quick overview; you can find further reading suggestions in this book's companion volume, the *FileMaker 8 Functions and Scripts Desk Reference*.

XML is a text-based means of representing data, which is at the same time *rich* and *portable*. By "rich," we mean that the data is more than mere text: An XML document is capable of describing its own structure, so that in looking at an XML document you can tell a chapter heading from a bullet point, or a personnel ID from a health-insurance deductible. By *portable*, we mean that XML documents are stored as plain text and can be read by a wide variety of programs on a wide variety of computers and operating systems.

As an example, consider the XML document that appears in Listing 22.1. This is a short document containing information about motors. You'll notice the document is full of tags (called *markup*) that might look superficially familiar to you if you've seen some HTML before. You'll notice that the tags always occur in pairs, with some content between them, and you'll notice that the tags seem to describe the data they contain. These tag pairs are known in XML jargon as *elements*.

Listing 22.1   A Small XML File Containing Motor Data

```
<?xml version="1.0" encoding="UTF-8" ?>
<motors>
    <motor>
        <model>Rotary 17</model>
        <weight>1200</weight>
        <part_number>M3110A-3</part_number>
        <volume>312</volume>
    </motor>
</motors>
```

This XML document is rich, in the sense that it contains two kinds of information: It contains raw data, but it also contains tags telling a reader what the data *means*. In this document, M3110A-3 is not just a string of numbers and letters; it's specifically a part number.

The document is also portable in the sense that it's stored as plain text, meaning you don't need a special "motor processing" application to read it. Any tool or program that can read plain text can work with this data.

XML documents have to follow some simple rules. Each must begin with an XML declaration, like the first line of Listing 22.1. Each must have a single outermost, or document, element—in Listing 22.1, the document element is called `motors`. Each tag must be properly closed—if you have a `<model>` tag, you'd better have its closing counterpart, called `</model>`. And, although tags may be nested (for example, in Listing 22.1, the `weight` element is completely enclosed within the `motor` element), it is not permissible for tags to overlap. Therefore, something like

```
<model>Rotary<weight>500</model></weight>
```

would not be allowed because the `weight` tag, rather than being completely enclosed in the `model` tag, instead overlaps it.

XML documents that follow these few simple rules, as well as some rules about allowable characters, are said to be *well-formed*.

> **NOTE**
> XML is a rigorous standard, with plenty of technical documents that describe it in exact detail. In this book we opt for clarity over rigor, so we encourage you to get hold of additional resources to explore the full details of XML concepts such as well-formedness. The description we've given is fairly complete, but the last word can be found at `http://www.w3.org/TR/2004/REC-xml-20040204/#sec-well-formed`.

FILEMAKER'S XML GRAMMARS

XML syntax rules, as you may have noticed, don't say anything about *how* to mark up your data. XML doesn't force you to use a `motor` element when talking about motors, nor would it specify what other elements a motor element should contain. If you're designing an XML document, the exact structure of the document, as far as what data it contains and how that data is marked up, remains up to you, the document designer.

FileMaker is capable of presenting its data as XML, and when it does so, it uses its own, FileMaker-specific set of elements to describe its data. FileMaker can actually present its data in either of two XML structures, called *grammars*; you, as the user or developer, get to choose which one suits your current situation best.

> **NOTE**
> FileMaker can actually present its data in as many as four XML grammars, but two of these are only meaningful in the context of Custom Web Publishing, which is the subject of the next chapter.

EXPORTING FILEMAKER DATA AS XML: THE FMPDSORESULT GRAMMAR

Suppose that you have some product data in a FileMaker table, which looks like Figure 22.2.

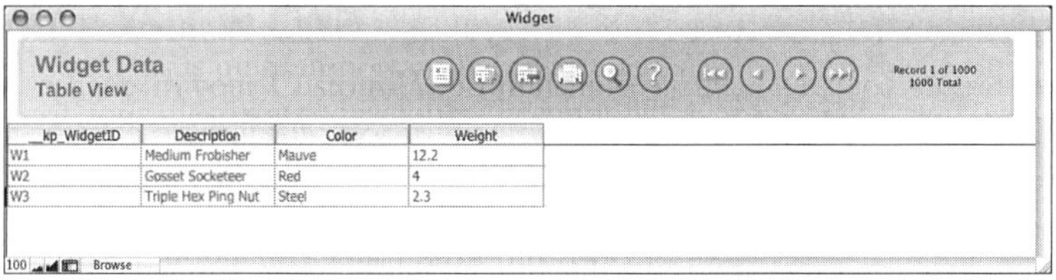

Figure 22.2
Some sample widget data in a FileMaker table.

To export these records as XML, choose File, Export Records, and then choose a file type of XML in the following dialog. When you do this, before seeing the familiar Export dialog, you see an XML options dialog, as shown in Figure 22.3.

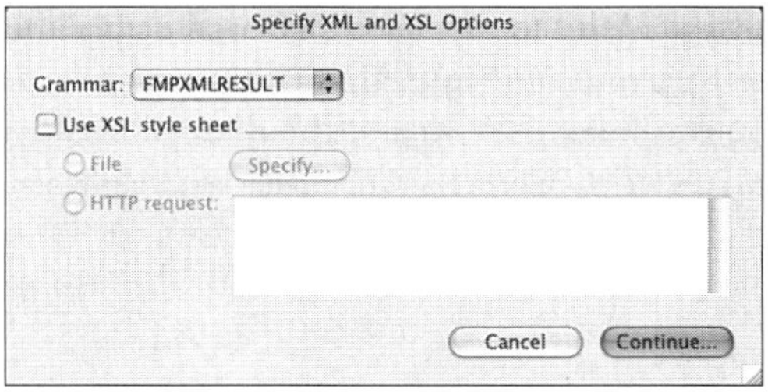

Figure 22.3
FileMaker's XML/XSL export options dialog.

Here you can choose which of FileMaker's XML grammars to apply. (You can also apply an XSL stylesheet to the output, which is an important topic we'll deal with in its own section later in this chapter.) If you're trying this for the first time, you might want to choose FMPDSORESULT. From there, you'll see the familiar Export dialog, where you can choose which fields to export, and in what order.

If you open the resulting exported file, you'll see something like the document in Listing 22.2.

LISTING 22.2   RECORDS EXPORTED USING FILEMAKER'S FMPDSORESULT GRAMMAR

```xml
<?xml version="1.0" encoding="UTF-8" ?>
<!-- This grammar has been deprecated - use FMPXMLRESULT instead -->
<FMPDSORESULT xmlns="http://www.filemaker.com/fmpdsoresult">
  <ERRORCODE>0</ERRORCODE>
  <DATABASE>Widget.fp7</DATABASE>
  <LAYOUT/>
  <ROW MODID="1" RECORDID="1">
    <WidgetID>W1</WidgetID>
    <Description>Medium Frobisher</Description>
    <Color>Mauve</Color>
    <Weight>12.2</Weight>
  </ROW>
  <ROW MODID="1" RECORDID="2">
    <WidgetID>W2</WidgetID>
    <Description>Gosset Socketeer</Description>
    <Color>Red</Color>
```

continues

22

LISTING 22.2   CONTINUED

```
    <Weight>4</Weight>
  </ROW>
  <ROW MODID="0" RECORDID="3">
    <WidgetID>W3</WidgetID>
    <Description>Triple Hex Ping Nut</Description>
    <Color>Steel</Color>
    <Weight>2.3</Weight>
  </ROW>
</FMPDSORESULT>
```

FileMaker has applied its own XML structure to the exported data—in this case the FMPDSORESULT structure. An FMPDSORESULT document has a document element (the top-level element) called <FMPDSORESULT>. That element in turn contains elements for ERRORCODE (generally 0 unless there was some error in the export process), for DATABASE (to tell us which database file the data was drawn from) and LAYOUT, as well as one <ROW> element for each record in the table from which we're exporting. The <ROW> elements in turn contain additional elements, named for the fields that were selected for export.

About the FMPDSORESULT Grammar

You might have noticed, in Listing 22.2, that the second line of the generated XML contains a warning: "This grammar has been deprecated—use FMPXMLRESULT instead." *Deprecation* is a term used in computer language design to indicate that a language's designers are actively discouraging you from using an element or feature. This is generally because the language designers believe that newer features represent an improvement on the deprecated feature. The old feature continues to work (as does FMPDSORESULT in FileMaker 7), but you are discouraged from using it and encouraged to use a different or newer feature instead.

Although FMPDSORESULT is now formally deprecated, we chose to use it here anyway because of its value in teaching XML. It's a verbose grammar that creates XML element names based on FileMaker field names. This makes it very easy for an XML novice to see how the FileMaker data maps onto the XML output, and this makes FMPDSORESULT a useful teaching tool.

So, what's wrong with FMPDSORESULT? Three things, all of them tied to the fact that FileMaker generates the element names for this grammar directly from FileMaker field names. In the first place, if your FileMaker field names are of any length, the XML element names are similarly long, and the generated files can become massive. Second, the element structure of an FMPDSORESULT document obviously varies depending on the FileMaker field names that lie behind it. All such documents will have an FMPDSORESULT element, containing one or more ROW elements, but within each ROW element there's no way to predict what the subelements will be. This makes it impossible to validate these documents via a single Document Type Definition document, or DTD. (We don't deal with DTDs much in this book, but many XML environments and workflows make significant use of them, and the ability to conform to a single DTD is useful.)

The third and most serious problem with FMPDSORESULT, though, is that it can generate XML that is literally invalid. To take a simple example, XML element names may not begin with a number. There's no such restriction on FileMaker field names. A FileMaker file with a field named 2004Results will generate an FMPDSORESULT XML document with elements called <2004Results>. That's not a valid XML element name, and any XML parser that tries to process a document containing such a name will generate an error.

So, pay careful attention to the fact that this grammar is deprecated. Although we used it in this section for teaching purposes, we recommend that you begin using the FMPXMLRESULT grammar as soon as you feel comfortable with this more complex grammar.

EXPORTING FILEMAKER DATA AS XML: THE FMPXMLRESULT GRAMMAR

The FMPDSORESULT grammar is considered to be FileMaker's more readable export grammar. It's a bit more legible to humans, but it's not the one FileMaker uses most heavily. That honor is reserved for the other grammar, called FMPXMLRESULT. If you were to export the widget data as XML with this grammar, you'd see something like the document in Listing 22.3.

LISTING 22.3   DATA EXPORTED USING FMPXMLRESULT GRAMMAR

```xml
<?xml version="1.0" encoding="UTF-8" ?>
<FMPXMLRESULT xmlns="http://www.filemaker.com/fmpxmlresult">
  <ERRORCODE>0</ERRORCODE>
  <PRODUCT BUILD="11-08-2005" NAME="FileMaker Pro" VERSION="8.0v2"/>
  <DATABASE DATEFORMAT="M/d/yyyy" LAYOUT="" NAME="Widget.fp7"
➡RECORDS="3" TIMEFORMAT="h:mm:ss a"/>
  <METADATA>
    <FIELD EMPTYOK="YES" MAXREPEAT="1" NAME="WidgetID" TYPE="NUMBER"/>
    <FIELD EMPTYOK="YES" MAXREPEAT="1" NAME="Description" TYPE="TEXT"/>
    <FIELD EMPTYOK="YES" MAXREPEAT="1" NAME="Color" TYPE="TEXT"/>
    <FIELD EMPTYOK="YES" MAXREPEAT="1" NAME="Weight" TYPE="NUMBER"/>
  </METADATA>
  <RESULTSET FOUND="3">
    <ROW MODID="1" RECORDID="1">
      <COL>
        <DATA>W1</DATA>
      </COL>
      <COL>
        <DATA>Medium Frobisher</DATA>
      </COL>
      <COL>
        <DATA>Mauve</DATA>
      </COL>
      <COL>
        <DATA>12.2</DATA>
      </COL>
    </ROW>
    <ROW MODID="1" RECORDID="2">
      <COL>
        <DATA>W2</DATA>
      </COL>
      <COL>
        <DATA>Gosset Socketeer</DATA>
      </COL>
      <COL>
        <DATA>Red</DATA>
      </COL>
      <COL>
        <DATA>4</DATA>
      </COL>
    </ROW>
    <ROW MODID="0" RECORDID="3">
      <COL>
        <DATA>W3</DATA>
      </COL>
      <COL>
```

continues

LISTING 22.3 CONTINUED

```
        <DATA>Triple Hex Ping Nut</DATA>
      </COL>
      <COL>
        <DATA>Steel</DATA>
      </COL>
      <COL>
        <DATA>2.3</DATA>
      </COL>
    </ROW>
  </RESULTSET>
</FMPXMLRESULT>
```

The most obvious difference from the FMPDSORESULT grammar is that whereas FMPDSORESULT provides element names within each row that correspond to field names, FMPXMLRESULT wraps all the database data in generic-looking <COL> and <DATA> elements. There's also a <METADATA> element, which you can see contains subelements for each field that give a lot of information about the field, such as its data type, whether it's a repeating field, and whether it's allowed to be empty. The data within the <ROW> elements then matches up to the field descriptions in the <METADATA> section based on position: The value Mauve in the first row is the third data element, and when you consult the <METADATA> section you can see that this means it corresponds to the Color field.

TRANSFORMING XML

By itself, the capability to turn FileMaker data into XML is not terribly useful. The reason is that FileMaker emits the XML in one of its specialized grammars. Even though other applications can *read* the file containing the exported data, they might not be able to make much sense of the FMPDSORESULT and FMPXMLRESULT grammars. In fact, this is a general issue with XML-aware applications: They all work with different formats and structures of XML.

Let's say there exists a tool (call it WidgetPro) that can read information about widgets from an XML file, as long as the XML file looks like what's shown in Listing 22.4.

LISTING 22.4 THE WIDGETPRO XML FORMAT

```
<?xml version="1.0" encoding="UTF-8" ?>
<widgetset>
    <widgetrecord index="1">
        <id>789</id>
        <widget_description>Large Flanger</widget_description>
        <widget_color>blue</widget_color>
        <widget_weight>45</widget_weight>
    </widgetrecord>
    <widgetrecord index="2">
        <id>790</id>
        <widget_description>Granite Auger</widget_description>
        <widget_color>Slate</widget_color>
        <widget_weight>715</widget_weight>
    </widgetrecord>
</widgetset>
```

We can get widget data from FileMaker, and we can get it as XML, but the two XML documents have different structures—the same data, but expressed with different tag names and tag structures.

This is an important point to understand about XML: XML is not in itself a language or a file format. Using XML, the same data can be described ("marked up," as it's often said) in many different ways. For applications to share data via XML, it's not enough for each application to support reading and writing data in its own, specific XML format. There has to be some means to translate between different forms of XML as well. In the widgets example, this means that we need to take the "FileMaker widget XML" and make it look like "WidgetPro widget XML." This leads to the concept of *XML transformations*.

Figure 22.4 illustrates the idea of an XML transformation. From the FileMaker Pro database of widget information, we first need to export the widget data in an FMPXML structure. Next, we need to *transform* that XML so that it looks like WidgetPro's XML structure instead. Finally, we bring the transformed XML into WidgetPro. Figure 22.4 sketches what this process would look like.

Figure 22.4
An XML transformation pipeline. FMPXMLRESULT (emitted by FileMaker) is transformed into WidgetPro XML (accepted by WidgetPro).

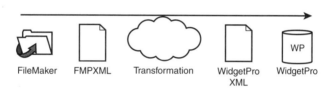

FileMaker   FMPXML   Transformation   WidgetPro XML   WidgetPro

INTRODUCING XSL STYLESHEETS

It turns out that XML already has a transformation technology available for us. That technology is called XSL, which stands for eXtensible Stylesheet Language. The *stylesheet* turns out to be the transformer. In much the same way that a word processing or page layout stylesheet can take ordinary text and transform it into formatted text, an XSL stylesheet can take one form of XML and transform it into another (or into any other text-based format, actually), as shown in Figure 22.5.

Figure 22.5
An XML transformation pipeline that uses an XSL stylesheet to accomplish the transformation.

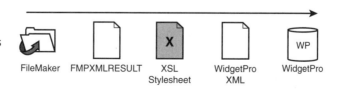

FileMaker   FMPXMLRESULT   XSL Stylesheet   WidgetPro XML   WidgetPro

> **NOTE**
>
> You might often see the terms XSL and XSLT (which stands for *XSL Transformations*) used interchangeably. Technically they're distinct; XSLT is in fact a subset of XSL. But when people speak of XSL they're generally referring to XSL transformations, so we won't make a major point of distinguishing between the two terms.

So what is an XSL stylesheet? It's a series of commands that describe how to transform XML input into some new form. The new form can also be XML (and often is), but it's possible to use a stylesheet to transform your XML into other text-based formats as well: tab-separated text, HTML, or more complex formats such as PDF and RTF. Interestingly, the XSL transformation language is itself a variety of XML, so XSL stylesheets are also valid XML documents in their own right.

Here's an example of an XSL stylesheet that would transform the "FileMaker widget XML" into "WidgetPro XML" (see Listing 22.5).

LISTING 22.5   AN XSL STYLESHEET

```
<?xml version="1.0" encoding="UTF-8" ?>
<xsl:stylesheet version="1.0"
➥xmlns:fmp="http://www.filemaker.com/fmpxmlresult"
➥xmlns:xsl="http://www.w3.org/1999/XSL/Transform"
➥exclude-result-prefixes="fmp">
  <xsl:output indent="yes" method="xml"/>
  <xsl:template match="fmp:FMPXMLRESULT">
    <widgetset >
      <xsl:for-each select="fmp:RESULTSET/fmp:ROW">
        <widgetrecord index="{position()}">
          <xsl:for-each select="fmp:COL">
            <xsl:choose>
              <xsl:when test="position()='1'">
                <id>
                  <xsl:value-of select="fmp:DATA"/>
                </id>
              </xsl:when>
              <xsl:when test="position()='2'">
                <widget_description>
                  <xsl:value-of select="fmp:DATA"/>
                </widget_description>
              </xsl:when>
              <xsl:when test="position()='3'">
                <widget_color>
                  <xsl:value-of select="fmp:DATA"/>
                </widget_color>
              </xsl:when>
              <xsl:when test="position()='4'">
                <widget_weight>
                  <xsl:value-of select="fmp:DATA"/>
                </widget_weight>
              </xsl:when>
            </xsl:choose>
          </xsl:for-each>
        </widgetrecord>
```

```
        </xsl:for-each>
      </widgetset>
    </xsl:template>
</xsl:stylesheet>
```

Our goal, remember, is to take the original XML output from FileMaker (Listing 22.3) and translate that output into a new form of XML that contains much the same information, but in a different structure (Listing 22.4).

The stylesheet in Listing 22.5 contains two kinds of statements: On the one hand there are XSL commands (which you can tell by their xsl: prefix), and on the other hand are the actual XML tags that the stylesheet will output. The stylesheet's job is to pick through the original XML document and decide which pieces of it to output, and in what order.

Analyzing a Stylesheet

If you've never read through an XSL stylesheet before, this section may be useful. We'll go through the stylesheet in Listing 22.5 line by line to illustrate its inner workings.

The XML Declaration

```
<?xml version="1.0" encoding="UTF-8" ?>
```

Every XML document begins with an XML declaration—and XSL stylesheets are XML documents. Simple enough.

The Stylesheet Statement

```
<xsl:stylesheet version="1.0"
➥xmlns:fmp="http://www.filemaker.com/fmpxmlresult"
➥xmlns:xsl="http://www.w3.org/1999/XSL/Transform">
```

The xsl:stylesheet statement announces the document as an XSL stylesheet. The stylesheet statement also declares two XML *namespaces* (that's what the xmlns stands for). Namespaces are an important XML concept, but like most of the finer points of XML, namespaces are a bit too complex a topic for us to spend much time on in this book. Suffice it to say that both the namespaces declared here are necessary. The second namespace, which is abbreviated xsl, is common to all XSL stylesheets, and is used to distinguish all the XSL stylesheet commands from other forms of XML. (These commands, again, begin with the same xsl: prefix that's specified by the namespace.) And the fmp namespace declaration is crucial as well because it matches the namespace declaration that appears at the start of any XML document output by FileMaker. We'll have a bit more to say about the FileMaker namespace farther on.

NOTE

Notice also that the stylesheet declaration includes a statement called exclude-result-namespaces. This rather important command prevents namespaces declared in the source document from being carried through to the output document. In general, we recommend you use this command in the <xsl:stylesheet> element of your

continues

continued

> stylesheets to strip all FileMaker-specific namespaces from your output. The `exclude-result-namespaces` attribute uses a space-delimited list of namespace prefixes to decide what to strip out. In Listing 22.5 just one namespace is being stripped, so it says `exclude-result-prefixes="fmp"`. If there were multiple namespaces to strip (as there often are in FileMaker's Custom Web Publishing), you would say something like `exclude-result-prefixes="fmp fml fmr fmrs"`. This would exclude all four namespaces from the stylesheet's output.

→ FileMaker's Custom Web Publishing is covered in depth in Chapter 23, "Custom Web Publishing," **p. 699**.

SPECIFYING THE OUTPUT TYPE

```
<xsl:output indent="yes" method="xml"/>
```

The `xsl:output` statement tells the XSL processor what type of document is being output. If you're trying to produce XML output, you need to include a statement like this one so that the XSL processor adds the appropriate XML declaration to the final document. The output statement also includes an attribute called `indent`—when this is set to `yes`, the XSL processor tries to format the XML output in a pleasing and readable way.

USING A TEMPLATE TO FIND THE RESULT SET

```
<xsl:template match="fmp:fmpxmlresult">
        <widgetset>
        [... code omitted ...]
        </widgetset>
```

The concept of a *template* is crucial to XSL. Templates are a way for the stylesheet writer to specify which parts of the source document she's interested in. In this case, we're telling the processor we want to find the element called `<FMPXMLRESULT>` in the source document and do something with it. You'll notice that this template takes up all the rest of the stylesheet—so the rest of the stylesheet tells what to do with the `<FMPXMLRESULT>` after we've found it.

Just inside the `xsl:template` statement is some actual XML, in the form of a `<widgetset>` tag. This tag is matched by the `</widgetset>` tag at the very end of the template instruction (almost at the end of the document). These two tags, unlike the `xsl:` commands, aren't instructions at all—they represent XML that will be output. So the `xsl:template` here is saying "When you find a `<RESULTSET>` tag, output a `<widgetset>` ... `</widgetset>` tag pair, and then go on to do some other things inside it."

Of course, inside the `<widgetset>` tag we want the stylesheet to emit XML that describes the individual widget records, which is what the next part of the stylesheet does.

USING `xsl:for-each` TO LOOP OVER A RESULT SET

```
<xsl:for-each select="fmp:RESULTSET/fmp:ROW">
        <widgetrecord index="{position()}">
```

The `<xsl:for-each>` tag is a *looping construct*. Right now, we're inside the XSL template that matches an `<FMPXMLRESULT>` tag, so the command tells the XSL processor to find all `<ROW>` elements that are children of `<RESULTSET>` elements inside the `<FMPXMLRESULT>`. The additional commands inside the `<xsl:for-each>`...`</xsl:for-each>` tag pair furnishes instructions on what to do with each `<ROW>` element that we find.

For each `<ROW>` in the original FileMaker XML, we want to output a `<widgetrecord>` element, and that's what the next line does. Additionally, the `<widgetrecord>` element needs to have an attribute called `index`, which shows the numerical position of the widget, in sequence. The `position()` function that's used in that line gives the position of the current element. (We wrap the function call in curly braces so that the XSL process knows it's a command, and not literal text to be output with the XML.)

USING xsl:choose TO DETERMINE OUTPUT

```
<xsl:for-each select="fmp:COL">
                  <xsl:choose>
                    <xsl:when test="position()='1'">
                        <id>
                            <xsl:value-of select="fmp:DATA"/>
                        </id>
                    </xsl:when>
                    [other columns omitted for brevity]
```

At this point, we're inside the `<ROW>` element in the original FileMaker XML, and from an output standpoint, we're inside the `<widgetrecord>` element in the output XML. (Read that sentence a few times if it doesn't sink in right away!) Given what we know the output is supposed to look like, all that's left is to find the four data elements from this `<ROW>` in the FileMaker XML, and output each one wrapped in a tag that correctly names its data field.

This is a little trickier because in the FileMaker XML, a `<ROW>` contains only `<COL>` elements, with no mention of the actual field name in question. (You might recall that field names, in the `FMPXMLRESULT` output grammar, appear near the top of the document in the `<METADATA>` section.) We have to loop through all the `<COL>` elements inside the row, and for each one, we decide how to output it based on its position in the group.

Once again we use `<xsl:for-each>` to loop over a set of elements, in this case all the `<COL>` elements inside the current `<ROW>`. For each `<COL>` element we process, we need to make a choice as to how to output it. If it's in the first position, we output it as an `<id>` element; if it's in the second position, we output it as a `<widget_description>` element, and so forth.

If we were trying to program this type of multiple choice in a FileMaker calculation, we'd use a `Case()` statement, or perhaps a `Choose()`. Here we use the XSL equivalent, which is called `<xsl:choose>`. Like FileMaker's `Case` statement, `xsl:choose` lets you choose among several options, each one corresponding to a logical test of some kind. The `<xsl:choose>` element contains one or more `<xsl:when>` statements. Each one corresponds to a particular choice, and each choice is associated with a logical test. In the code we showed in the preceding section, the first test inside the `<xsl:choose>` element is the test for columns whose position equals 1. In this case, we go on to output the `<id>`...`</id>` tag pair, with the data value inside it. To do this, we use the `<xsl:value-of>` element, which can pull out a piece of the source XML document to output. In this case, each `<COL>` element in the FileMaker source XML has a `<DATA>` element inside it, and it's that element we want to grab and add to the output.

The rest of the `<xsl:when>` statement contains the remaining tests, for the columns in positions 2, 3, and 4 of the output. At this point, we're done! The rest of the code consists of emitting closing XML tags that match the opening tags we've already sent, and of closing up our XSL constructs, like `<xsl:for-each>`.

APPLYING AN EXPORT TRANSFORMATION TO FILEMAKER XML

FileMaker lets you use XSL stylesheets to transform your data when moving data into or out of FileMaker with XML. Let's consider the export example first. If you have a table of FileMaker data (such as the widget data we've been using), and you choose to export the data as XML, you'll see the dialog box shown in Figure 22.6.

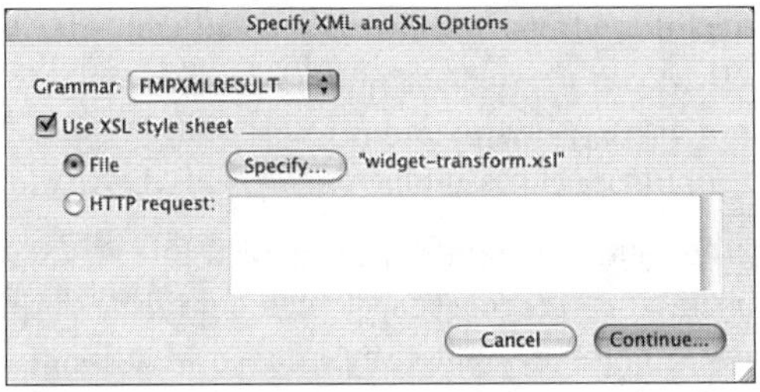

Figure 22.6
When exporting XML from FileMaker, you may also choose to apply a stylesheet to transform the outbound XML.

Here you can choose your XML export grammar, as we've already seen, but you can also choose whether to apply an XSL stylesheet to transform the XML as it's being output. If you want to apply a stylesheet, you can pick a local file (in other words, a file resident on your local hard drive or on a mounted server volume). You can also pick a stylesheet file that's available over HTTP (namely, on a web server somewhere).

Working with Remote Stylesheets

The HTTP feature was a very smart choice on the part of FileMaker's development team. It's very important in a multiuser FileMaker deployment, where many users use the same solution files hosted by a single server. If the only option for stylesheet use was to use a file from the user's locally accessible hard drive or drives, you'd either have to distribute the stylesheet to all system users and make sure that they put it in the right location on their hard drives, or you'd have to have a common server volume that all users would have to mount. With the capability to pull a stylesheet from a web server, you can create one single stylesheet and place it on a central web server, and let it be accessed by all users.

One important qualification to this capability is that FileMaker currently supports remote access to stylesheets via only the HTTP protocol. HTTPS (secure HTTP) is not currently supported.

Using XSL stylesheets in the export process in this way, you can transform FileMaker data into a wide variety of output formats: other variants of XML, or HTML, or XML suitable for import into applications such as Excel or Quark Xpress, or even a complex text format such as PDF.

XML IMPORT: UNDERSTANDING WEB SERVICES

In addition to FileMaker's capability to export data via XML, either with or without an XSL stylesheet, FileMaker also has the capability to work with remote XML data sources, often referred to under the umbrella term "Web services." This is a capability that was added in FileMaker version 6 and is a significant addition to FileMaker's XML strengths. Using this capability, you can bring data from a variety of remote data sources directly into FileMaker, as we'll discuss in the sections that follow.

FILEMAKER'S XML IMPORT CAPABILITY

The concept of XML exporting ought to seem fairly straightforward: Take some FileMaker data, pick an XML grammar for the export, and optionally apply an XSL stylesheet to transform the XML data as it heads out. But what about the concept of *importing* XML? What does this mean, and what is it good for?

Stated simply, FileMaker can import any XML data that conforms to the FMPXML grammar. FileMaker reads the <METADATA> section of the document to determine the field structure, and reads the individual row and column data to figure out the actual data values that should be imported.

To demonstrate this for yourself, find some suitable FileMaker data and export it as XML, using the FMPXMLRESULT grammar, without applying any XSL stylesheet to it. Starting from the same file and table, go back and re-import the file you just exported, treating it as an XML data source—you'll see that FileMaker correctly reads the field structure and data from the XML document. Or, to test it in a different way, drag the new XML file onto the FileMaker application icon to open it. FileMaker should, without intervention from you (except for choosing a filename for the new file), open the XML file, read its structure, and create a new FileMaker file with a new table containing the correct fields, field types, and data values.

NOTE

One of the things developers have often wanted from FileMaker is a way to save a file's field structure as a text document, and then use that text document to move the field structure somewhere else and re-create it. The capability to open an XML document and have it create a new FileMaker file might seem to make that possible, but there are caveats. The XML export doesn't preserve important information about your field structure, such as the definitions of calculation fields and summary fields. In the XML output, these fields are treated simply as their underlying data types, so a calculation that produces a number is treated in the XML metadata as a simple number field, without preserving the calculation's definition.

So, FileMaker can import any XML data file that conforms to the FMPXMLRESULT grammar. Additionally, as you might have seen, this XML data stream can come from a local file, or it can come from a file available over HTTP—in other words, a file from somewhere on the Web. This is where things get interesting, so let's delve further into the concept of a Web service.

 If you try to import data that doesn't conform to the FMPXMLRESULT *grammar, FileMaker gives you an error. For more information, see "Wrong XML Format" in the "Troubleshooting" section at the end of this chapter.*

NOTE

As was the case with using remote stylesheets for XML export, FileMaker is also unable to work with data from an HTTPS data source when importing XML. If the data source from which you want to import is available only over secure HTTP, FileMaker isn't able to import it.

WEB SERVICES REVIEWED

We started this chapter by saying that *Web services* was a term referring to the sharing of data between computers via the Web's HTTP protocol, and that the data was often exchanged in XML format. Imagine you have two computer systems that need to exchange data. One is a large student information system that resides on a mainframe computer. The other is a system that generates complex forms for each student, to conform to governmental guidelines. Periodically, the forms application needs to consult the mainframe application to see whether any new students have been added so that those students are accounted for in the forms system.

There are many ways to make this kind of sharing happen. The mainframe programmer could export a file of new students every night, in some plain-text format, and the forms programmers could write routines to grab the file and process it in some way. Or the mainframe could be made accessible via a technology such as ODBC, and the forms application could be configured to make ODBC requests to the mainframe.

→ For more information on ODBC, **see** Chapter 19, "Importing Data into FileMaker Pro," **p. 567**, and Chapter 20, "Exporting Data from FileMaker," **p. 595**.

Another option, though, is to make it possible to send queries to the mainframe via HTTP, and get XML back in response. This is simpler than either of the previous scenarios: It doesn't require any complicated processes such as writing and then fetching an actual file, nor does it involve the client-side complexities of ODBC transactions. It uses the widely (almost universally) available HTTP protocol, and requires only that one side be able to generate a form of XML and the other side be able to read it. Don't get us wrong—Web services transactions can still be plenty complicated, but standards such as XML and HTTP make them less complex than they might be otherwise. Refer to Figure 22.1 for a sketch of a possible Web services transaction.

Let's say that, in our example, the forms application was written in FileMaker. And let's assume the mainframe student information system was accessible as a Web service, meaning that you could send a request via HTTP and get back a listing of new students in some XML format (that would likely *not* conform to the FMPXMLRESULT grammar). To import that data into FileMaker, you could perform an XML import, use the URL of the student information system as the data source, and apply an XSL stylesheet that would transform the new student XML into FMPXMLRESULT. The concept is sketched out in Figure 22.7. To retrieve student data from this mainframe, make a request to a URL that's able to produce an XML representation of the student, and then bring that XML back through a stylesheet into FileMaker.

Figure 22.7
This is a graphical representation of the process of retrieving data via XML.

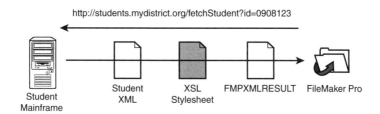

http://students.mydistrict.org/fetchStudent?id=0908123

Student Mainframe Student XML XSL Stylesheet FMPXMLRESULT FileMaker Pro

A Stylesheet for XML Import

For the sake of argument, assume that we have an XML *data stream* representing new students. (We use the term "data stream" rather than "file" as a reminder that the data need not come from a file, but can also come from a networked data source over HTTP.) Listing 22.6 shows what that data might look like.

LISTING 22.6   SAMPLE XML FILE CONTAINING DATA

```xml
<?xml version="1.0" encoding="UTF-8"?>
<newStudentSet count="4" date="11/1/2003">
    <student id="414">
        <nameFirst>Jonathan</nameFirst>
        <nameLast>Middlesex</nameLast>
        <nameMiddle>A</nameMiddle>
        <address>123 Oak Way</address>
        <city>Bensenville</city>
        <state>AK</state>
        <zip>09080-1001</zip>
        <county>Hightower</county>
        <district>Sparta</district>
        <school>Bensenville Junior High</school>
        <grade>4</grade>
        <parents>
            <parent>
                <nameFirst>Sharon</nameFirst>
                <nameLast>Middlesex</nameLast>
                <relationship>Parent</relationship>
            </parent>
            <parent>
                <nameFirst>Martin</nameFirst>
                <nameLast>Middlesex</nameLast>
                <relationship>Parent</relationship>
```

continues

LISTING 22.6   CONTINUED

```
            </parent>
        </parents>
    </student>
</newStudentSet>
```

It's a simple enough structure, consisting of a `<newStudentSet>` filled with one or more `<student>` elements, where each `<student>` has a number of fields associated with it. The only wrinkle has to do with parent information: Clearly a student can have more than one parent, so each student contains a `<parents>` element with one or more `<parent>` elements inside it. We'll have to think about what to do with that.

That's the XML file that the hypothetical data source can put out. But remember, for FileMaker to import this XML data, it has to be structured in the FMPXMLRESULT format. Such a structure would look Listing 22.7.

LISTING 22.7   DATA IN THE IMPORTABLE FMPXMLRESULT FORMAT

```
<?xml version="1.0" encoding="UTF-8" ?>
<FMPXMLRESULT xmlns="http://www.filemaker.com/fmpxmlresult">
    <ERRORCODE>0</ERRORCODE>
    <PRODUCT BUILD="8-11-2005"  NAME="FileMaker Pro" VERSION="8.0v2"/>
    <DATABASE DATEFORMAT="M/d/yyyy" LAYOUT="" NAME="Student.fp7" RECORDS="1"
          TIMEFORMAT="h:mm:ss a"/>
    <METADATA>
        <FIELD EMPTYOK="YES" MAXREPEAT="1" NAME="NameFirst" TYPE="TEXT"/>
        <FIELD EMPTYOK="YES" MAXREPEAT="1" NAME="NameLast" TYPE="TEXT"/>
        <FIELD EMPTYOK="YES" MAXREPEAT="1" NAME="NameMiddle" TYPE="TEXT"/>
        <FIELD EMPTYOK="YES" MAXREPEAT="1" NAME="Address" TYPE="TEXT"/>
        <FIELD EMPTYOK="YES" MAXREPEAT="1" NAME="City" TYPE="TEXT"/>
        <FIELD EMPTYOK="YES" MAXREPEAT="1" NAME="State" TYPE="TEXT"/>
        <FIELD EMPTYOK="YES" MAXREPEAT="1" NAME="Zip" TYPE="TEXT"/>
        <FIELD EMPTYOK="YES" MAXREPEAT="1" NAME="County" TYPE="TEXT"/>
        <FIELD EMPTYOK="YES" MAXREPEAT="1" NAME="District" TYPE="TEXT"/>
        <FIELD EMPTYOK="YES" MAXREPEAT="1" NAME="School" TYPE="TEXT"/>
        <FIELD EMPTYOK="YES" MAXREPEAT="1" NAME="Parents" TYPE="TEXT"/>
    </METADATA>
    <RESULTSET FOUND="1">
        <ROW MODID="0" RECORDID="1">
            <COL><DATA>Jonathan</DATA></COL>
            <COL><DATA>Middlesex</DATA></COL>
            <COL><DATA>A</DATA></COL>
            <COL><DATA>123 Oak Way</DATA></COL>
            <COL><DATA>Bensenville</DATA></COL>
            <COL><DATA>AK</DATA></COL>
            <COL><DATA>09080-1001</DATA></COL>
            <COL><DATA>Hightower</DATA></COL>
            <COL><DATA>Sparta</DATA></COL>
            <COL><DATA>Bensenville Junior High</DATA></COL>
            <COL><DATA>Sharon Middlesex(Parent),
            ➥Martin Middlesex (Parent)</DATA></COL>
        </ROW>
    </RESULTSET>
</FMPXMLRESULT>
```

Web services scattered through the ether are unlikely to emit XML that conforms to the FMPXMLRESULT grammar. So before bringing that data into FileMaker, we need to transform it into FMPXMLRESULT. And the tool for doing that is, of course, an XSL stylesheet. This is exactly the reason FileMaker lets you apply a stylesheet to *inbound* XML (in other words, on import). Odds are that the XML data source does not produce the FMPXMLRESULT grammar directly, so it's our job to translate the source XML into the form that FileMaker can read.

We need an XSL stylesheet to make that transformation. The stylesheet needs to make sure to output all the initial information found in an FMPXMLRESULT file, such as database name, and all the metadata describing the field structure. Then, in the context of a <RESULTSET>, we need to output the actual student data.

Listing 22.8 shows what the stylesheet for transforming student data prior to importing it into FileMaker should look like.

LISTING 22.8   AN XSL STYLESHEET

```
<?xml version="1.0" encoding="UTF-8" ?>
<xsl:stylesheet version="1.0" xmlns:xsl="http://www.w3.org/1999/XSL/Transform">
 <xsl:output indent="yes" method="xml"/>
 <xsl:template match="newStudentSet">
   <FMPXMLRESULT xmlns="http://www.filemaker.com/fmpxmlresult">
     <ERRORCODE>0</ERRORCODE>
     <PRODUCT BUILD="8-11-2005"  NAME="FileMaker Pro" VERSION="8.0v2"/>
     <DATABASE DATEFORMAT="M/d/yyyy" LAYOUT="" NAME="Student.fp7"
     ➥RECORDS="{@count}" TIMEFORMAT="h:mm:ss a"/>
     <METADATA>
       <FIELD EMPTYOK="YES" MAXREPEAT="1" NAME="NameFirst" TYPE="TEXT"/>
       <FIELD EMPTYOK="YES" MAXREPEAT="1" NAME="NameLast" TYPE="TEXT"/>
       <FIELD EMPTYOK="YES" MAXREPEAT="1" NAME="NameMiddle" TYPE="TEXT"/>
       <FIELD EMPTYOK="YES" MAXREPEAT="1" NAME="Address" TYPE="TEXT"/>
       <FIELD EMPTYOK="YES" MAXREPEAT="1" NAME="City" TYPE="TEXT"/>
       <FIELD EMPTYOK="YES" MAXREPEAT="1" NAME="State" TYPE="TEXT"/>
       <FIELD EMPTYOK="YES" MAXREPEAT="1" NAME="Zip" TYPE="TEXT"/>
       <FIELD EMPTYOK="YES" MAXREPEAT="1" NAME="County" TYPE="TEXT"/>
       <FIELD EMPTYOK="YES" MAXREPEAT="1" NAME="District" TYPE="TEXT"/>
       <FIELD EMPTYOK="YES" MAXREPEAT="1" NAME="School" TYPE="TEXT"/>
       <FIELD EMPTYOK="YES" MAXREPEAT="1" NAME="Grade" TYPE="TEXT"/>
       <FIELD EMPTYOK="YES" MAXREPEAT="1" NAME="Parents" TYPE="TEXT"/>
     </METADATA>
     <RESULTSET FOUND="{@count}">
       <xsl:for-each select="student">
         <ROW MODID="0" RECORDID="{position()}">
           <COL><DATA><xsl:value-of select="nameFirst"/></DATA></COL>
           <COL><DATA><xsl:value-of select="nameLast"/></DATA></COL>
           <COL><DATA><xsl:value-of select="nameMiddle"/></DATA></COL>
           <COL><DATA><xsl:value-of select="address"/></DATA></COL>
           <COL><DATA><xsl:value-of select="city"/></DATA></COL>
           <COL><DATA><xsl:value-of select="state"/></DATA></COL>
           <COL><DATA><xsl:value-of select="zip"/></DATA></COL>
           <COL><DATA><xsl:value-of select="county"/></DATA></COL>
           <COL><DATA><xsl:value-of select="district"/></DATA></COL>
           <COL><DATA><xsl:value-of select="school"/></DATA></COL>
           <COL><DATA><xsl:value-of select="grade"/></DATA></COL>
```

continues

22

LISTING 22.8   CONTINUED

```
            <COL><DATA><xsl:for-each select="parents/parent">
                <xsl:value-of select="nameFirst"/>
                <xsl:text> </xsl:text>
                <xsl:value-of select="nameLast"/>
                <xsl:text> (</xsl:text>
                <xsl:value-of select="relationship"/>
                <xsl:text>)</xsl:text>
                <xsl:if test="position() != last()">
                  <xsl:text>, </xsl:text>
                </xsl:if>
              </xsl:for-each></DATA></COL>
        </ROW>
      </xsl:for-each>
    </RESULTSET>
  </FMPXMLRESULT>
 </xsl:template>
</xsl:stylesheet>
```

We won't spend as much time dissecting this stylesheet as we did with the last one. The mechanics should be pretty easy to discern. After the usual declarations, we declare a template that matches to the source document's `<newStudentSet>` element. (It's the root element, so there will be only one.) That's the occasion to output all the header-type information particular to the FMPXMLRESULT grammar, including the field structure metadata. We then go on to output a `<RESULTSET>...</RESULTSET>` tag pair, and do some more work inside that.

Within the `<RESULTSET>` tags, we use an `<xsl:for-each>` to loop over all the `<student>` elements inside the `<newStudentSet>`. For each one, we output the corresponding `<ROW>` element. Each `<ROW>`, in turn, is a collection of `<COL><DATA>...</COL></DATA>` tag pairs. We output one of these for each inbound field, and insert the correct data into it, using `<xsl:value-of>`.

The only thing at all noteworthy is the treatment of the parent information. The inbound student information is not completely "flat." The nested `<parents>` element almost implies a new table, in relational database terms. We could choose to handle it that way, and bring the parent information into a separate table, but we chose instead to flatten the parent data into a single field. This was more to illustrate a particular technique than because it's actually a good idea to do that. Whether it really is a good idea depends on the application.

In any case, the technique here is to loop over the individual `<parent>` elements, using `<xsl:for-each>`. For each parent, we output the first name, last name, and the family relationship in parentheses. You might notice that we use the `<xsl:text>` command liberally, to output the spaces between words and the parentheses around the relationship. The reason for this is that XML treats certain characters, such as white space, specially. White space, in particular, XML ignores. Wrapping it in an `<xsl:text>` tag ensures that the processor treats it as real white space and outputs it as such.

The last wrinkle here is that we want the parent list to be comma separated. So we write a little piece of logic that requests that a comma and its following white space be output, but only if the current `<parent>` element is not the last one in the group. The check is performed with `<xsl:if>`.

As you can see, the stylesheet isn't too complicated. The hardest part is getting all the FMPXMLRESULT-specific elements and attributes correctly included.

TIP

> It's irritating, if not impossible, to remember all the specifications for the FMPXMLRESULT grammar every time you need to write a new import stylesheet. To save yourself the trouble, first make sure that the FileMaker table you're using to receive the data is correctly built and has the right structure. Then add a sample record or two to the table, and export the table as FMPXMLRESULT. The result is exactly what any inbound XML needs to look like (well, the data itself is likely to be different!). You should be able to copy large chunks of this XML output and paste them into your stylesheet to get yourself started.

After you've written the stylesheet, you would apply it in the course of the import. If everything goes smoothly, the stylesheet is successfully applied, it emits pure FMPXML, and this is cleanly imported into FileMaker.

 If your stylesheet contains a programming error, FileMaker presents an error dialog and tries to alert you as to where in the stylesheet the problem occurred. For more information, see "Errors in Stylesheets" in the "Troubleshooting" section at the end of this chapter.

You might need to do a bit of work to make sure that the fields line up correctly on import. The easiest way to ensure this is to write your XSL stylesheet in such a way that the field names in the resulting `<METADATA>` section of the XML are exact matches for your FileMaker field names. If that's the case, you need to specify only that fields should import based on matching names. If for any reason there's a discrepancy between the field names that are used in the resultant FMPXMLRESULT and the field names in the target table, you have to specify the import matching by hand.

→ For more details about specifying import field mappings, **see** "The Import Field Mapping dialog," **p. 569**.

 Of course, the import may not go smoothly. See "Correct Stylesheet, Failed Import" in the "Troubleshooting" section at the end of this chapter for some tips on how to handle stylesheets that don't perform as expected.

WORKING WITH WEB SERVICES

The previous section, on importing XML via a stylesheet, tells you more or less all you need to know to work effectively with Web services in FileMaker. The only other thing you need is a real Web service to work with.

It can actually be a bit difficult to find interesting Web services to play with. Many of the really meaty Web services, because they're providing useful information, charge an access or subscription fee of some kind. (These might include Web services that provide current weather information from satellites, or financial information, for example.) Many of the free

22

Web services, by contrast, are either of limited scope, or else represent hobby work, student programming projects, and the like.

Happily, there are a few exceptions. We're going to take a look at Amazon.com's Web service offerings. Amazon, of course, has a user interface, presented via HTML, that you can use to conduct Amazon searches by pointing and clicking with your mouse in a Web browser. But Amazon has also been a pioneer in offering XML-based Web services that let you do the same thing, allowing you to integrate Amazon data into other applications.

Suppose that you have a FileMaker database containing information about books. For each book you'd like to be able to check whether it's available from Amazon, and if so, at what price. With FileMaker's XML Import capability, you can do this fairly easily.

ACCESSING THE AMAZON WEB SERVICES

Working with Amazon's Web services is straightforward, but you need to do a couple of things first. You should visit http://www.amazon.com/webservices; there, you'll be able to download the Web services developer's kit, which provides useful documentation, and you'll also be able to apply for a *developer's token*, which is a special personal key you'll need to send along with your Web service requests for validation. (There's no charge for either the developer's kit or the token.)

NOTE

> If you don't want to take the trouble to apply for your own developer's token, you can use one that we requested for use in this book. That token is D1AT17BPIA1PX7.

Types of Web Services

As you browse the Internet looking for Web services, and as you look at the Amazon material, you may see a lot of references to different types of Web services, using terms such as SOAP and XML-RPC. Here's what you need to know about this: Although all the Web services we're interested in work by sending and receiving XML over an HTTP protocol, there are several different ways to do this. HTTP requests are divided into broad categories, called GET and POST. A GET request passes information in the URL: If you've ever seen a long, ugly-looking URL in your browser, like `http://my.ecommerce-site.com/cartApp.astj?userID=ED45jUiJJ&sessKey=6a45Rtfe4`, you're looking at information being sent via a GET request. On the other hand, if you've ever filled out an HTML form and clicked the Submit button, odds are the data was being sent behind the scenes, in what's called a POST request.

Web services may work with either GET or POST requests. FileMaker's XML Import feature, however, can make only a GET request. But a number of the most common Web services techniques work exclusively via POST.

SOAP is an example of such a Web services protocol. SOAP transactions send a complex XML request to the server via a POST operation. Many Web services are available only via SOAP. A good example is the Google Web service, which lets you interface directly to the Google search engine. Because Google is SOAP-based, there is no direct way for FileMaker to interact with the Google Web service at the moment.

In looking for FileMaker-ready Web services, you're looking for Web services that support simple XML over HTTP via GET requests.

The developer's kit comes with documentation that shows how to formulate various types of HTTP requests for data. Here's a sample URL:

```
http://xml.amazon.com/onca/xml3?t=xxx&dev-t=D1AT17BPIA1PX7
➥&PowerSearch=title:Genet&mode=books&type=lite&page=1&f=xml
```

This searches Amazon for books with the word "Genet" in the title. Try entering the above URL in Firefox or Internet Explorer 5 or greater (which render the resulting XML nicely), and you'll see what the returned results look like. This returns data in Amazon's lite format, which has less information than the corresponding heavy format.

Amazon's XML format, whether lite or heavy, is clearly not FileMaker's FMPXMLRESULT. So if you want to bring this book data back into FileMaker via an XML import, you need a stylesheet to transform it appropriately on the way in.

WRITING A STYLESHEET TO IMPORT AMAZON DATA

Let's say we have a book database with the field structure shown in Figure 22.8.

Figure 22.8
Field structure for a database of book information.

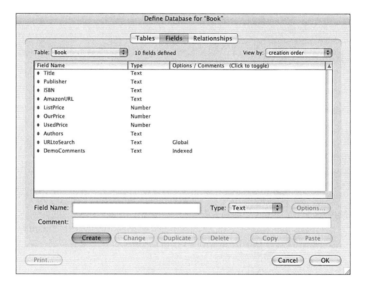

We can bring Amazon data into this FileMaker structure by performing an import from an XML data source and applying a stylesheet to the inbound data. The stylesheet looks and works a lot like the one in Listing 22.8. We show it here, for completeness, as Listing 22.9.

LISTING 22.9   STYLESHEET FOR TRANSFORMING AMAZON XML INTO FMPXMLRESULT XML

```
<?xml version="1.0" encoding="UTF-8" ?>
<xsl:stylesheet version="1.0" xmlns:xsl="http://www.w3.org/1999/XSL/Transform">
  <xsl:output indent="yes" method="xml"/>
  <xsl:template match="ProductInfo">
    <FMPXMLRESULT xmlns="http://www.filemaker.com/fmpxmlresult">
```

continues

LISTING 22.9   CONTINUED

```
<ERRORCODE>0</ERRORCODE>
<PRODUCT BUILD="11-08-2005"  NAME="FileMaker Pro" VERSION="8.0v2"/>
<DATABASE DATEFORMAT="M/d/yyyy" LAYOUT="" NAME="Student.fp7" RECORDS="10"
➥ TIMEFORMAT="h:mm:ss a"/>
<METADATA>
  <FIELD EMPTYOK="YES" MAXREPEAT="1" NAME="Title" TYPE="TEXT"/>
  <FIELD EMPTYOK="YES" MAXREPEAT="1" NAME="Publisher" TYPE="TEXT"/>
  <FIELD EMPTYOK="YES" MAXREPEAT="1" NAME="ISBN" TYPE="TEXT"/>
  <FIELD EMPTYOK="YES" MAXREPEAT="1" NAME="AmazonURL" TYPE="TEXT"/>
  <FIELD EMPTYOK="YES" MAXREPEAT="1" NAME="ListPrice" TYPE="NUMBER"/>
  <FIELD EMPTYOK="YES" MAXREPEAT="1" NAME="OurPrice" TYPE="NUMBER"/>
  <FIELD EMPTYOK="YES" MAXREPEAT="1" NAME="UsedPrice" TYPE="NUMBER"/>
  <FIELD EMPTYOK="YES" MAXREPEAT="1" NAME="Authors" TYPE="TEXT"/>
</METADATA>
<RESULTSET FOUND="10">
  <xsl:for-each select="Details">
    <ROW MODID="0" RECORDID="{position()}">
      <COL>
        <DATA>
          <xsl:value-of select="ProductName"/>
        </DATA>
      </COL>
      <COL>
        <DATA>
          <xsl:value-of select="Manufacturer"/>
        </DATA>
      </COL>
      <COL>
        <DATA>
          <xsl:value-of select="Asin"/>
        </DATA>
      </COL>
      <COL>
        <DATA>
          <xsl:value-of select="url"/>
        </DATA>
      </COL>
      <COL>
        <DATA>
          <xsl:value-of select="ListPrice"/>
        </DATA>
      </COL>
      <COL>
        <DATA>
          <xsl:value-of select="OurPrice"/>
        </DATA>
      </COL>
      <COL>
        <DATA>
          <xsl:value-of select="UsedPrice"/>
        </DATA>
      </COL>
      <COL>
        <DATA>
          <xsl:for-each select="Authors/Author">
```

```
            <xsl:value-of select="."/>
            <xsl:if test="position() != last()">
              <xsl:text>, </xsl:text>
            </xsl:if>
          </xsl:for-each>
        </DATA>
      </COL>
    </ROW>
  </xsl:for-each>
 </RESULTSET>
 </FMPXMLRESULT>
 </xsl:template>
</xsl:stylesheet>
```

This is extremely similar to the earlier stylesheet, even down to the treatment of book authors, which occur in nested groups: Here, we loop over authors in the same way we looped over parent records, flattening them into a single text field.

BUILDING A MORE FLEXIBLE INTERFACE TO A WEB SERVICE

The previous section concentrated on the stylesheet that you would use to import data from Amazon. But so far, we've just assumed that FileMaker is issuing some hard-coded URL to perform an Amazon search. In fact, we probably want our users to be able to compose their own queries and submit them to Amazon.

There's no great mystery to this. The Amazon developer's kit documents the different types of search strings that the Amazon Web service can accept. (If we're just searching for books, a lot of the more interesting options can be found as part of the overall "power search" option.)

So far, we've imported XML only from data sources we specified via a hard-coded URL. It's also possible, though, when importing XML into FileMaker via a script, to draw the XML from a data source specified by a calculation. Figure 22.9 shows the relevant dialog choice.

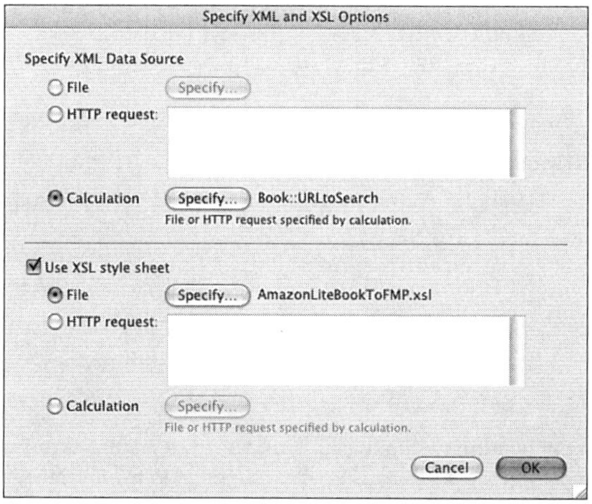

Figure 22.9
When importing XML into FileMaker via a script, you can use a calculation to create the source URL on the fly.

22

This makes it possible to compose the Amazon URL on the fly based on user input. For example, if we wanted to search for books by Naguib Mahfouz, published by (say) Anchor, the Amazon URL would look like this:

```
http://xml.amazon.com/onca/xml3?t=xxx&dev-t=D1AT17BPIA1PX7&PowerSearch=
➥author:Mahfouz and publisher:Anchor&mode=books
➥&type=lite&page=1&f=xml
```

(In the real URL, you would use your Seller ID, if you had one, instead of the nonsense string xxx.) To compose this URL dynamically, you'd need to offer the user a couple of global fields in which to type. Assume that the user called gAuthorSearch and gPublisherSearch. You could then define a calculation field that would look something like this:

```
http://xml.amazon.com/onca/xml3?t=XXX&dev-t=D1AT17BPIA1PX7
➥&PowerSearch=author:" & gAuthorSearch & " and publisher:"
➥& gPublisherSearch & "&mode=books&type=lite&page=1&f=xml"
```

And, as shown in Figure 22.9, you can instruct FileMaker to derive the URL from a calculation, which could point directly to this dynamic field. This snippet is really useful only as an example of how you might go about this conceptually. In reality, you'd need to do some work to build a really nice interface to Amazon. You'd want to add fields for all the types of Amazon searches (there are about seven). You'd also want to provide for the fact that the user might choose to search on some but not all criteria, making it a good idea to omit the unused search types from the URL. You'd have to account for the fact that it's possible for searches to have multiple words, in which case they need to be enclosed in quotes. And you'd want to account for the different search types Amazon allows, such as searching by exact match or initial match.

USING FILEMAKER AS A WEB SERVICES SOURCE

So far in this chapter, we've mainly discussed how to get data *from* Web services *into* FileMaker. But it's possible to do this the other way around as well. Let's say that you have some order data in FileMaker Pro. Let's also suppose that there's a central mainframe computer that needs to have access to the FileMaker orders, as they're completed.

There are a number of ways to skin this particular cat, but let's suppose for the sake of example that the mainframe system is capable of requesting data from a Web service. In other words, the mainframe can make a request for data over HTTP, and expects to get some form of XML in return.

The strategy for handling this with FileMaker is straightforward. First, you need to make the relevant FileMaker database available over the Web. This means you need to have a copy of FileMaker Server with the appropriate web publishing technologies enabled, and you need to have the particular database in question available for Web access.

→ For more information on configuring web publishing on your FileMaker Server, **see** "Configuring FileMaker Server Advanced for IWP," **p. 643**, as well as "Setting Up the Server-side Components for CWP," **p. 704**.

Assuming that your FileMaker databases are correctly configured for Web access, the procedure for allowing FileMaker to act as a Web services server is relatively straightforward. All that's necessary is to make potential Web services clients aware of the correct URLs to use. You'll provide one or more URLs that will publish FileMaker data to an XML format. You could provide a URL that would provide raw XML in one of FileMaker's built-in XML grammars. For example:

```
http://192.168.123.101/fmi/xml/fmresultset.xml?-db=products-lay=sales&-findall
```

Or you could provide a URL that would first format the outbound XML with a stylesheet, like this:

```
http://192.168.123.101/fmi/xsl/my_template/my_stylesheet.xsl?-grammar=
➥fmresultset&-db=mydatabase &-lay=mylayout&-findall
```

As you'll learn in Chapter 23, "Custom Web Publishing," it's possible to include access validation logic in your stylesheets that could (for example) check to make sure that Web services requests came from only a select set of IP addresses, or perform some other kind of validation.

In general, though, using FileMaker as a Web services provider falls under the heading of Custom Web Publishing, which we cover thoroughly in Chapter 23.

TROUBLESHOOTING

WRONG XML FORMAT

I'm trying to import an XML file someone gave me, but I can't even get to the Import Field Mappings dialog. FileMaker says there's an unknown element in the document.

FileMaker can import only XML that's in the FMPXMLRESULT grammar. If you got the XML document from some source other than FileMaker, it's very unlikely to conform to FMPXMLRESULT. You'll need to apply a stylesheet to the XML as you import it to transform it into valid FMPXMLRESULT XML.

ERRORS IN STYLESHEETS

FileMaker says there's a parse error in my XSL stylesheet.

There's a lot of programming in an XSL stylesheet—and XSL and XML are fairly unforgiving languages. A single bracket out of place in your stylesheet, and the XML parser rejects it as being ill-formed. You need to be able to track down the syntax error and fix it. A good XML development environment, such as Oxygen (Mac/Windows) or XMLSpy (Windows only), can be a big help in tracking down such problems.

CORRECT STYLESHEET, FAILED IMPORT

My XML development tool tells me my stylesheet is valid and correct, but when I use it in the process of importing XML into FileMaker I still get strange errors from FileMaker.

It's perfectly possible to write a stylesheet that's correct in itself, but does not produce correct output. When you're importing into FileMaker, the inbound data has to be in correct

FMPXMLRESULT format. Any deviation from that format, and FileMaker rejects the data. You might have written a stylesheet that is correct and runs perfectly without an error, but that nonetheless doesn't produce correct FMPXMLRESULT output as you intended. Here again, you need to figure out what went wrong and how to fix it.

There are other possible errors as well. For example, if you are fetching either your XML data or an XSL stylesheet from an HTTP server, you get an error if that server isn't available to you when you try to perform the import.

Unfortunately, FileMaker isn't much of an XML debugger. If you run into either of the errors we just discussed, FileMaker gives you a fairly terse error message, which may possibly lead you to the line of the file that produced the problem. If the problem is that you produced bad XML from your stylesheet, you may not even get that much information.

This is no fault of FileMaker's. XML development is a big area and it's not in the scope of FileMaker's capabilities to be a full-fledged development environment for generating and debugging XML files. But if you're at all serious about using FileMaker and XML together, you'll want to invest in such a tool.

An XML development tool generally consists of an XML editor that provides a lot of assistance in writing XML and XSL files. It may include features such as tag balancing (automatically closing tags when it seems right to do so), command completion (for example, being able to finish your XSL commands for you after you type a few letters), automatic indentation, and, of course, document validation and debugging.

To use such a tool to develop an export stylesheet for FileMaker, for example, you could first do a sample XML export from your FileMaker database into a test file. You could bring this FileMaker XML file into your XML development tool. Then you could write up your XSL stylesheet, have the tool check its syntax to make sure that it's technically correct, and then have the tool apply the stylesheet to the FileMaker XML. You could then inspect the result for correctness.

We strongly recommend you look into such a tool if you plan on doing much XML work with FileMaker. The Oxygen XML editor, for Mac or PC, is fairly full-featured (http://www.oxygenxml.com). On the PC, Altova's XMLSpy is highly regarded (http://www.altova.com).

FILEMAKER EXTRA: WRITE YOUR OWN WEB SERVICES

We generally think of Web services as being something that someone else has, and that we want access to. But Web services have many other uses as well. They can provide a powerful way to extend the capabilities of your FileMaker application.

For example, suppose that you needed to compute a Fourier transform, based on some measured signal data. FileMaker has no built-in facility for such analysis—computing the transform requires complex mathematics. (Well, with enough diligence, you might be able to write a FileMaker script to perform a discrete Fourier transform. But its cousin, the fast Fourier transform, requires mathematical operations FileMaker can't perform.)

NOTE

> Don't worry if Fourier transforms don't ring a bell; this is just a data example. A Fourier transform is an advanced mathematical technique for taking a complex signal, such as a sound or radio wave, and decomposing it into a series of simpler signals.

FileMaker already provides a number of extension mechanisms to developers. Many problems can be solved with a custom function. Those that can't may be addressed by a plug-in already in existence.

→ For more details about installing and using FileMaker plug-ins, **see** "Plug-ins," **p. 771**.

Web services provide another way to extend FileMaker's capabilities. They are, in our view, easier to write than plug-ins, which require knowledge of a low-level programming language such as C++, and knowledge of how to program in each specific client environment supported by FileMaker 7, namely Windows and the Mac OS. Web services, by contrast, can be written in the lighter-weight scripting languages, which we feel are easier to learn, and because they execute in a server environment, they don't require that you have any knowledge of how to program specifically for the Mac or Windows.

Of course, this points up one of the hurdles involved in writing your own Web service: You still have to know how. Web services can be written in a wide variety of programming languages, such as PHP, Perl, JSP, ASP, Visual Basic, Tango, Lasso, or any of many other Web scripting languages, not to mention hard-core languages such as Java, C, and C++. There's literally no limit to the kinds of work you can perform with Web services written in these languages. The only catch is, again, you have to know how.

Of the languages discussed, we feel the Web scripting languages are probably the most approachable. PHP is a superb general-purpose Web scripting language. JSP has a Java base, whereas ASP and Visual Basic are particular to a Windows server environment. Tango and Lasso were once exclusively FileMaker-aware Web tools, but have since grown into more general-purpose languages. All these languages presume some familiarity with the fundamentals of computer programming, and familiarity with the specific language in question.

Let's return again to the hypothetical example. Let's say you're importing signal data from an electronic instrument of some kind. You have the raw data, and you want to compute a discrete Fourier transform of the samples. Our strategy for doing this is twofold: First we write a Web service capable of doing the math, and then we call that Web service from FileMaker, hand it our data, and get our results back in return.

In a book of this kind, we can't explain in detail how to write the kind of Web service that would do this. Conceptually, if you know a language like PHP, you can write a PHP program, designed to be accessed over the Web, which expects to receive a vector of numbers in the request. You would call the Web service via a URL, which might look something like this:

```
http://webservices.my-company.net/DFT.php?samples=
➥"1.0, .45, 3.2, -.23, 1.76, 1.55, 2.01, 1.23, .34, -.78, - .64, -.09"
```

22

The samples represent the actual data you are sending to the Web service for processing. You would compose the URL dynamically in FileMaker, much as we demonstrated for the Amazon example earlier in this chapter. The URL accesses the Web server at webservices. my-company.com, requests access to the discrete Fourier transform program, and passes the DFT program a series of sample values. The DFT program processes the information and returns some information. For the purposes of getting the resulting data back into FileMaker, we want to work through the FileMaker XML Import feature, so the DFT program should output XML of some sort—either straight FMPXML that we can import back into FileMaker, or some other XML flavor that we can transform with a stylesheet.

So what's DFT.php? Well, it would be a program, written in the PHP language, that knows how to compute a discrete Fourier transform from a vector of numbers, and output the results in XML. You might choose to write the program in straight PHP. For more advanced math, though, such as the more complex fast Fourier transform, you might choose to use PHP to call a code library on the Web server computer, which would perform the complex math in a very fast language such as C.

The one downside to using Web services in this way (besides the need to learn one or more additional languages) is that the Web service functionality doesn't really live "in FileMaker"; it lives on a server someplace, so if you are creating standalone FileMaker applications that are meant to work in a single-user, nonhosted environment, or possibly an environment with no network or Internet connection, home-brew Web services are probably not the way to go.

There are relatively few limits to the kinds of programming tasks you can accomplish in FileMaker, just by hooking FileMaker up to the appropriately written Web service. Of course, those services are not trivial to produce in practice. But if you have the knowledge to do so (or access to someone with such knowledge), the potential uses are almost limitless.

To recap, Web services can provide a way to extend the capabilities of FileMaker. The range of possible functionality is much wider than that afforded by custom functions, and programming Web services is, in general, easier than programming FileMaker plug-ins (which requires writing platform-specific compiled code).

CHAPTER **23**

CUSTOM WEB PUBLISHING

In this chapter

ABOUT CUSTOM WEB PUBLISHING

Custom Web Publishing is one of two technologies you can use to dynamically publish your FileMaker data on the World Wide Web. (The other is Instant Web Publishing, which you can read about in Chapter 21.) Custom Web Publishing in FileMaker 7 replaced the technology that was known as CDML (Claris Dynamic Markup Language) in earlier versions of FileMaker Pro.

One of the most significant recent advances in FileMaker web publishing technologies is that, since FileMaker 7, it's been possible to publish FileMaker data to the Web without using a copy of the FileMaker Pro client. In earlier versions of the product, it was necessary to use FileMaker Unlimited, which was a specially enabled version of the client software. In the FileMaker 7 and 8 product lines, the web publishing technologies are built directly into the Server products and run as true standalone server-side processes.

NOTE

> In FileMaker 8, it's still possible to use Instant Web Publishing to publish data from a client copy of FileMaker Pro. IWP can also be used in the server-only mode as well, though, and can support many more users in a server configuration.

NOTE

> As you can read in more detail in Chapter 25, "FileMaker Server and Server Advanced," the FileMaker Server product line has two different flavors: FileMaker Server and FileMaker Server Advanced. It's necessary to purchase FileMaker Server Advanced to gain the capability to do server-side web publishing.

Server-side web publishing works through an intermediate server called the Web Publishing Engine (which we'll call the WPE for short). The WPE is installed in a way that binds it to a web server (Apache and Internet Information Server are the supported web servers), and is able to make calls directly against a copy of FileMaker Server. Figure 23.1 shows the flow of a server-side CWP request (this flow actually applies to both Instant and Custom Web Publishing).

Figure 23.1
The Web Publishing Engine mediates between a web server and a copy of FileMaker Server.

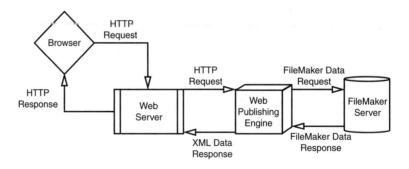

The WPE is responsible for accepting a request for FileMaker data that comes in over the Web and for relaying that request to a copy of FileMaker Server. The WPE then receives the server's response and (this is important!) converts the data into an XML format before sending it back.

The last part bears repeating: Custom Web Publishing is completely XML-based. Requests to the CWP engine can return either raw XML—meaning that it's presented in one of FileMaker's built-in XML grammars—or they can return the results of an XSLT transformation applied to the XML. This leads to the possibility of transforming the XML into HTML, PDF, or any other text-based format before the data is returned to the client.

→ You can read about FileMaker's XML grammars in "FileMaker's XML Grammars," **p. 672**, and you'll learn more about them in the course of this chapter as well.

CUSTOM WEB PUBLISHING VERSUS INSTANT WEB PUBLISHING

If you've read about Instant Web Publishing already (in Chapter 21), you'll be aware that the IWP capabilities of FileMaker 8 are quite extensive—so extensive, in fact, that you might wonder whether IWP would suffice for all your web publishing needs. It certainly seems simpler than working with a lot of XML and XSL data files.

But CWP has a number of important advantages over IWP. Here are some of the most significant ones:

- IWP works very hard to replicate the look and feel of your FileMaker layouts, so it is guaranteed to work with only a few browsers (recent versions of Internet Explorer and Firefox, as well as Safari on Mac OS X). By contrast, if you are publishing XML data as HTML, you can create HTML that is compatible with as wide (or narrow) a range of browsers as you choose.

- If you are converting previous solutions that were written in CDML, FileMaker offers a conversion path from CDML to FileMaker 8's CWP, via the CDML Conversion Tool that is discussed later in this chapter.

→ For more on converting from CDML to CWP, **see** "The CDML Converter," **p. 749**, later in this chapter.

- With CWP, it's straightforward to integrate FileMaker data with other websites, or provide FileMaker data to others in the form of a web service. CWP makes a strong distinction between the raw data (which is returned as XML) and the final presentational form (which can result from applying an optional XSLT stylesheet). By contrast, in IWP, data and presentation are combined in a way that makes it all but impossible to use the data itself in other contexts.

- CWP is best for sites that need to conform to the conventions of the World Wide Web. IWP presents data in a FileMaker-driven way: It's fairly easy, using IWP, to reproduce a fairly complex FileMaker layout on the Web, but it would be quite difficult to, for example, display a set of search results in a two-column list, or break a large set of search results up into multiple results pages—both of which are common presentation styles on the Web.

- IWP has a number of built-in limitations. For instance, it cannot reproduce FileMaker's Preview mode, so it can't be used to display subsummary reports on the Web. Also, the IWP list and table views are limited to displaying 5 and 20 records at a time, respectively. These are limits that CWP can overcome.

In general, IWP is best for making some portion of the functionality of an existing FileMaker database accessible to remote users. IWP's chief strength is in bringing the FileMaker experience into a web browser. The most likely targets for this technology are remote users of a FileMaker system who may not be able to be in the same building or same site as the server, but require ready access. This is likely to cater to a relatively small group of users (hundreds, say, rather than the thousands and tens of thousands that a public website can reach).

CWP, on the other hand, is best when FileMaker data needs to be presented in a non-FileMaker style, either as familiar-looking web pages or in some other text-based form. It enables you to make FileMaker data available over the Web as raw XML, to integrate FileMaker data into an existing website, or to build a new website around FileMaker data while preserving all the conventions of web presentation.

CUSTOM WEB PUBLISHING VERSUS XML EXPORT

At first view, Custom Web Publishing might sound a lot like the XML Export capability we discussed in Chapter 20, "Getting Data Out of FileMaker." There are some similarities, but there are also many significant differences. The main ones are these:

- XML export is a "push" technology rather than a "pull" technology. New data becomes available to potential clients only when you decide to publish the data by performing a new export, possibly manually, possibly via an automated script. CWP is a server-side technology that can be made available on demand, enabling clients to pull new data at any time by accessing a specific URL that you provide.

- Using CWP, you can publish your FileMaker data in a new XML grammar, called `fmresultset`. This new grammar has the richness of the `FMPXMLRESULT` grammar, while being easier to work with for stylesheet writers. The grammar is available only through CWP.

- CWP is a server-side technology, which means you don't need a copy of the FileMaker client to take advantage of CWP. All necessary programming occurs on the server side. On the other hand, exporting XML can take place only from a client application.

To sum up: Use XML export for occasional exports of FileMaker data as raw or transformed XML that you trigger through a client copy of FileMaker Pro. Use CWP when you want to provide live, on-demand access to FileMaker data via a web interface.

GETTING YOUR DATABASES READY FOR CUSTOM WEB PUBLISHING

To get your FileMaker databases ready for Custom Web Publishing, you need to do a few specific things with access privileges in each file you want to share via Custom Web Publishing.

If you're familiar with previous versions of FileMaker Pro, you'll recall that the various publishing options for a database (web sharing, local ODBC, remote ODBC) were all accessed via a file's sharing options. Enabling or disabling a sharing method was simply a matter of checking or unchecking a sharing option.

Access to a FileMaker database via either XML or XSLT is handled via the security and privilege system. You can allow or deny XML or XSLT access to a file based on whether a user has the appropriate privilege, as well as controlling that user's rights and privileges down to the record or field level.

Unfortunately, with this flexibility comes some additional work. To enable Custom Web Publishing in a file, you must enable the correct extended privileges for each type of CWP access you want to allow. To allow access to data from the file as raw XML, enable the extended privilege with the keyword `fmxml`. To allow access via XSLT, enable the extended privilege with the keyword `fmxslt`. Figure 23.2 illustrates the use of these extended privileges.

Figure 23.2
You'll need to enable certain extended privileges to enable Custom Web Publishing with XML and XSLT.

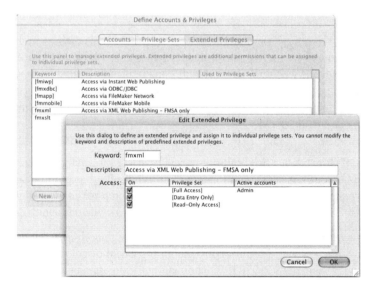

> **NOTE**
>
> In FileMaker 7, it was necessary to create these extended privileges by hand. In FileMaker 8, the set of default extended privileges is expanded to include these two privileges. They're off by default, but it's no longer necessary to create them by hand.

NOTE

In versions of FileMaker Pro before version 7, web sharing in any of its forms could not be enabled or disabled while a database was being served by FileMaker Server. In FileMaker 7 and later, the extended privileges for CWP can be enabled or disabled on the fly.

23

To recap, each database that you want to share via CWP needs to have the appropriate extended privileges created and added to one or more privilege sets.

 If you expect to see a database served via Custom Web Publishing and it doesn't appear, check to make sure that the appropriate extended privileges are enabled. See the section on "Getting the Right Privileges" in the "Troubleshooting" section at the end of this chapter.

SETTING UP THE SERVER-SIDE COMPONENTS FOR CWP

Three distinct server-side components make up the CWP publishing chain. Requests for FileMaker data via CWP come first to a web server—either Apache (on Mac OS X) or Internet Information Server (on Windows). The web server then routes that request to a Web Publishing Engine, a standalone piece of software that sits in between the web server and FileMaker Server. The Web Publishing Engine processes the web request, makes the appropriate call to a copy of FileMaker Server Advanced, and formats the returned data into XML, which it then sends back to the client via the web server.

In theory, all three server-side components (web server, Web Publishing Engine, and FileMaker Server), can be run on the same machine. Depending on your needs, this may or may not be a good idea. We recommend that you use at least two machines for your CWP setup: one for the web server and another for FileMaker Server. The Web Publishing Engine can be installed on either of those two machines. If you want, you can spread the deployment across three machines, and have the Web Publishing Engine sit on its own machine in the middle. We see the biggest gain in moving from a one-machine setup to either of the two-machine configurations.

 If you have any firewalls anywhere in your network architecture, be aware of this: If any machine in your Custom Web Publishing setup is separated from the others by a firewall, certain ports in that firewall may need to be open. See "Dealing with Firewalls" in the "Troubleshooting" section at the end of this chapter.

INSTALLING THE WEB PUBLISHING ENGINE

We're going to assume that you already have a web server running (Apache and IIS, again, are the only choices here), and a working installation of FileMaker Server 8 Advanced.

There are actually two separate items to install: The web server module and WPE administrative console constitute one piece and the WPE itself the other. Unless you're installing the WPE on a machine different from the web server, you can install all these components at once, on the same machine. If the web server and WPE are on different machines, you need to install the web server module and the admin console on the web server machine, and then install the WPE on whichever other machine you've designated for that purpose. Figure 23.3 shows how these components work together.

Figure 23.3
FileMaker's Custom Web Publishing consists of a number of server-side components. The Web Publishing Engine may or may not be installed on the same machine as your web server.

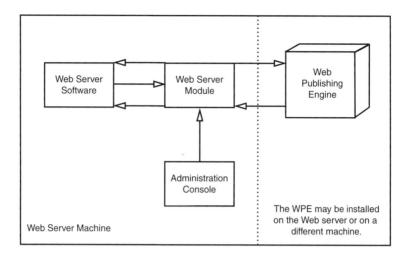

The web server module is an add-on to your web server (Apache or IIS) that allows the web server to communicate with the Web Publishing Engine. The Administration Console is a web-based application, installed on the same machine as the web server, that allows you to configure and control a WPE via a web browser.

N O T E

> For best results, shut down your web server processes (not the server machine itself, but the web server processes) before installing the web server module and admin console.

CONFIGURING THE WEB PUBLISHING ENGINE

The Web Publishing Engine is configured via the Administration Console, which is a web-based application that gets installed when you install the web server module on the web server of your choice. After you've completed that install, and you've also installed a Web Publishing Engine (either on the same machine as the web server or elsewhere), you can configure the Web Publishing Engine by opening a browser and pointing it to `http://<server-ip>/fmi/config/`.

SETTING UP AUTHENTICATION

When doing this for the first time, you'll be prompted to configure administrative access to the Console, via a screen like the one shown in Figure 23.4.

When this is done, you'll be prompted for the IP address of the Web Publishing Engine, as shown in Figure 23.5. (If the Web Publishing Engine is on the same machine as the web server, just enter the word **localhost**.)

The third step is to configure authentication for the Publishing Engine. This authentication is separate from the administrative access you configured in step one. The screen is shown in Figure 23.6.

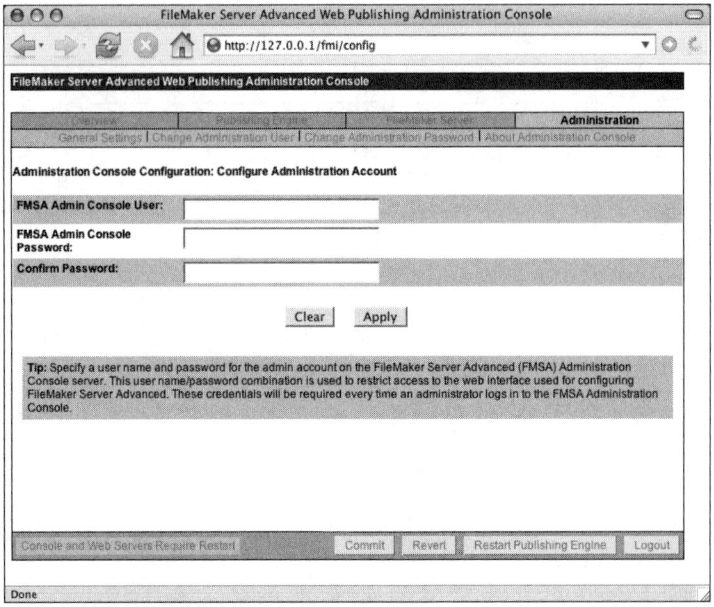

Figure 23.4
You'll need to configure the Administration Console with a username and password when you access it for the first time.

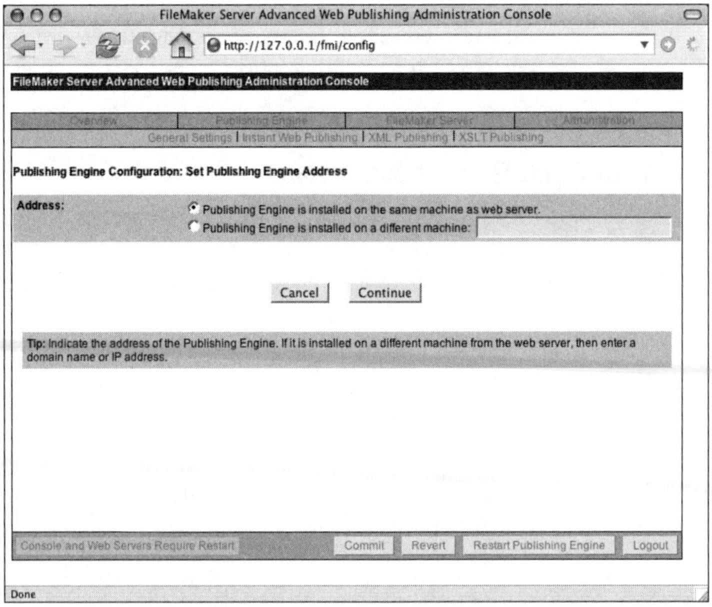

Figure 23.5
You need to specify the address of the machine on which your Web Publishing Engine is located.

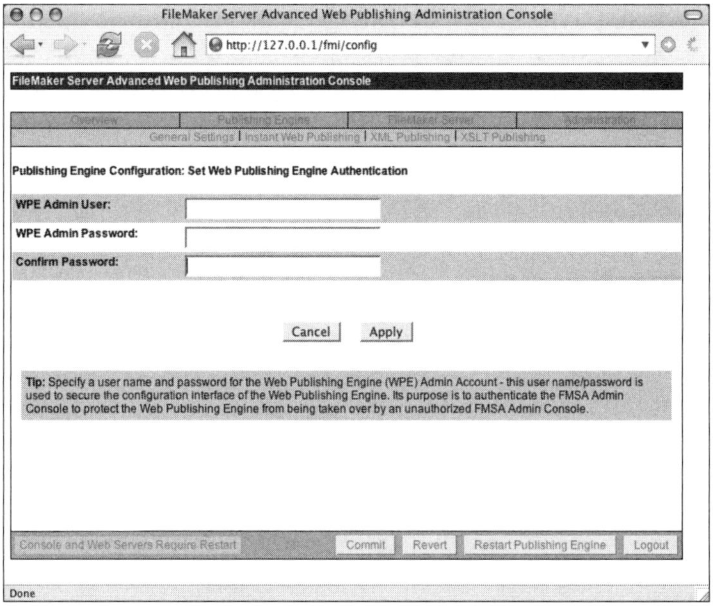

Figure 23.6
You need to set a username and password that are specific to one Publishing Engine.

At this point, you'll be asked to configure the connection to an instance of FileMaker Server, as shown in Figure 23.7. If you want to postpone this step of the configuration, you can. We'll cover the details farther on, under "Configuring the Connection with FileMaker Server."

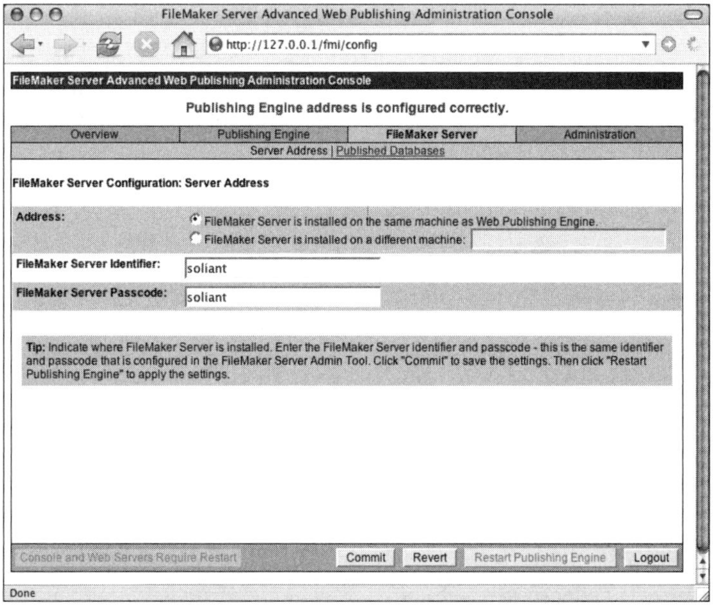

Figure 23.7
The Web Publishing Engine must be configured to work with one specific instance of FileMaker Server.

CONFIGURING DIFFERENT TYPES OF ACCESS TO THE WEB PUBLISHING ENGINE

You need to configure the Web Publishing Engine for each different type of Web access you want to support. The Publishing Engine tab of the Administration Console has four subtabs: one for General Settings and three more for the three flavors of Web access. Chapter 21 discusses how to configure the Web Publishing Engine for Instant Web Publishing.

→ For more information on configuring the WPE for Instant Web Publishing, **see** "Configuring FileMaker Server 8 Advanced for IWP," **p. 643**.

The configuration screen for XML access is so simple we won't show it here. It consists of a single radio button that turns XML access on or off. If XML access is off, it isn't possible to serve XML data from the Web Publishing Engine, regardless of any privileges the attempting user may have.

The same is true for XSLT access. The configuration screen for XSLT-CWP is more complex and is shown in Figure 23.8.

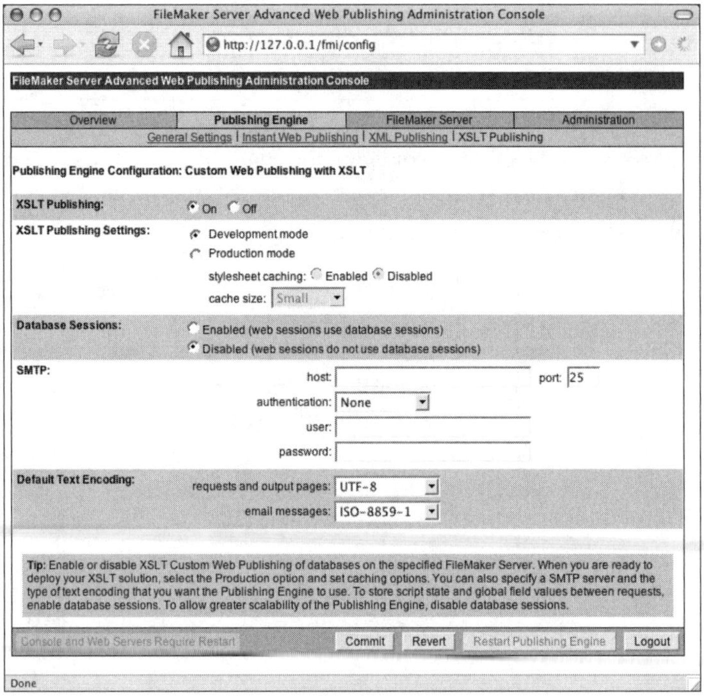

Figure 23.8
You might need to consider many options when configuring the Web Publishing Engine for XSLT access.

This screen, of course, allows you to enable or disable XSLT publishing. As with XML and IWP publishing, you can globally disable the publication of data via XSLT from the Web Publishing Engine.

Next, you can choose between Development and Production modes. In development mode, the Web Publishing Engine returns HTML screens with detailed error messages, including a specific error number and the exact position in the XSL stylesheet that generated the error (if known). In Production mode, your users don't see these formidable messages, but instead see a friendlier, more generic message.

Next, you can enable stylesheet caching. This option is available only in Production mode. It causes the Web Publishing Engine to store stylesheets in memory after they're initially accessed, which speeds up repeated uses of the stylesheet. You can also set the cache's maximum size. We recommend enabling this option whenever you go to Production mode (unless you feel strapped for RAM, in which case you probably need a beefier server for the Web Publishing Engine anyway). We recommend setting the cache to the maximum size necessary for the solutions you'll serve, but no larger. The Small option covers up to 25 stylesheets, Medium covers 25–100 stylesheets, and Large is for more than 100.

> **TIP**
>
> During development and debugging, you should turn stylesheet caching off. With caching turned on, any changes you make to your stylesheets won't be reflected until the cached copy expires.

Your next choice is whether to use database sessions. This is a complex concept that is covered more fully later in this chapter, in the section titled "About Sessions."

Next, you can specify a mail server that will be used for any emails you send from your stylesheets. FileMaker's Custom Web Publishing offers you the capability to have your web application send emails. If you create such a web application, this area is where you'd specify the parameters of the SMTP server you're using for outbound mail.

Last, you have the opportunity to set the default text encoding for stylesheets and emails. Text encoding is a large topic that we don't cover fully in this book. The FileMaker defaults are generally adequate for an American or Western European environment. If you're working in an Asian environment, you may need to change these settings.

Configuring the Connection with FileMaker Server

The Web Publishing Engine and FileMaker Server now need to be made aware of each other. There's work to be done on both sides. In the Administration Console, you need to specify the IP address of the FileMaker server. You also need to give your Web Publishing Engine an *identifier* and an optional *passcode*. The Web Publishing Engine uses these two keys to identify itself when it makes requests to FileMaker Server.

FileMaker Server, in turn, needs to be configured to accept requests from a specific Publishing Engine. To do this, you need to open the Server Administration Tool and connect to the relevant FileMaker Server.

→ For more information on the Server Administration tool, **see** "Configuring and Administering FileMaker Server Using the SAT," **p. 788**.

Of course, you need to have FileMaker Server set up to allow Web Publishing Engine sessions. The relevant dialog from the Server Admin Tool on Windows is shown in Figure 23.9.

Figure 23.9
FileMaker Server also needs to be configured to accept connections from a specific Web Publishing Engine.

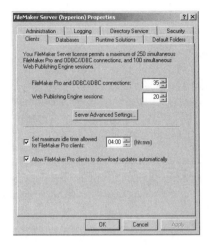

After you click the Server Advanced Settings button, you can configure the server to accept connections from a specific Web Publishing Engine. Click the Add button and enter the identifier and optional passcode that you entered on the corresponding screen when configuring the Web Publishing Engine, as depicted in Figure 23.10.

Figure 23.10
Use the same passcode and identifier you used when configuring the connection within the Web Publishing Engine's configuration screen.

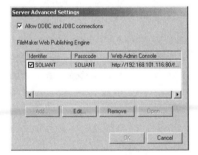

In the Mac OS, the connection to the Web Publishing Engine is configured from a single all-in-one screen, as shown in Figure 23.11.

After you enable the connection to the server from both sides, you should be able to access the FileMaker Server tab in the Administration Console. Then go to the Published Databases subtab and see a list of all databases on the chosen server that are enabled for some form of web publishing, as shown in Figure 23.12.

SAVING YOUR CHANGES

As you move through the Administration Console, remember to click the Commit button where necessary to save your changes. (Somewhat confusingly, not all screens have a Commit button. In some cases your entries are saved when you click Continue.)

Figure 23.11
The Web Publishing Engine connection is configured on a single screen in the Mac OS.

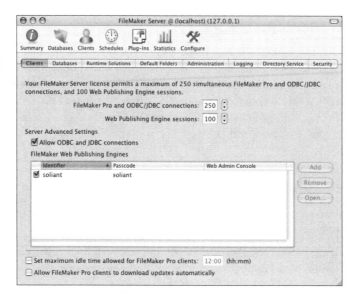

Figure 23.12
The Administration Console lets you see at a glance which databases are enabled for Custom Web Publishing.

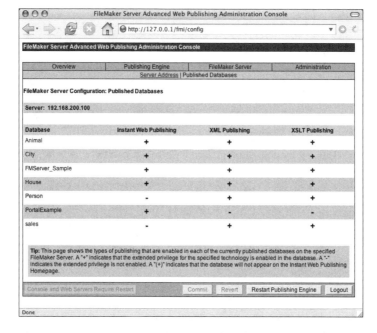

Certain changes require you to restart the Publishing Engine. If a screen requires this, you have a Restart Publishing Engine button available at the lower right. Additionally, some changes require that you restart the entire web server. If this is the case, a red message to this effect appears at the lower left of the window.

PUBLISHING FILEMAKER DATA AS XML

Custom Web Publishing falls into two broad categories: CWP with XML and CWP with XSLT. The former technique allows you to publish FileMaker data as raw XML over the Web. The latter technique is XML-based as well, but involves applying additional *transformations* to the XML to turn it into other data formats such as HTML. Because XML publishing is the basis for both of these flavors of CWP, we begin with a thorough discussion of FileMaker data publishing with XML.

INTRODUCTION TO XML PUBLISHING

To publish FileMaker data as XML via the Web Publishing Engine, you need several things:

- A web server with the appropriate web server module and the Administration Console installed.

- A running copy of the Web Publishing Engine, with XML publishing enabled. (See the previous section, "Configuring the Web Publishing Engine.")

- A copy of FileMaker Server Advanced that's configured to work with the Web Publishing Engine.

- One or more FileMaker databases that are enabled for XML access via the appropriate extended privilege, and are being served by the server mentioned in the preceding bullet.

If—and only if—all these pieces are in place, you can draw XML data from a served database by opening a web browser and entering a URL like the following:

```
http://192.168.100.101/fmi/xml/fmresultset.xml?-db=Animal&-lay=web&-findall
```

This URL, 192.168.100.101, is the address of the web server that we've configured to work with the Web Publishing Engine. The path to `fmresultset.xml` indicates that we want the results returned in the `fmresultset` grammar. URL also instructs the WPE to access a database called Animal, via a layout called Web, and then find all records and return them in the select `fmresultset` grammar.

> **NOTE**
>
> Note that it's not necessary to include the filename suffix (`.fp7`) when referencing the database name in the URL.

If you indeed had a database called Animal open under FileMaker Server, and if it had privilege sets with the extended privilege for XML enabled, and it had a layout called Web, the Web Publishing Engine would return an XML document to your browser. If you're using a browser capable of displaying XML (which includes Firefox, Safari, and Internet Explorer), you'd see something like the code in Listing 23.1.

LISTING 23.1   XML FORMATTED WITH THE `fmresultset` GRAMMAR

```
<?xml version="1.0" standalone="no"?>
<!DOCTYPE fmresultset PUBLIC "-//FMI//DTD fmresultset//EN"
➥ "/fmi/xml/fmresultset.dtd">
```

```
<fmresultset xmlns="http://www.filemaker.com/xml/fmresultset" version="1.0">
    <error code="0">
    </error>
    <product build="12/10/2003" name="FileMaker Web Publishing Engine"
    ➥ version="7.0v1" />
    <datasource database="animal" date-format="M/d/yy" layout="web"
    ➥ table="Animal" time-format="h:mm:ss a" total-count="17" />
    <metadata>
        <field-definition auto-enter="no" global="no" max-repeat="1"
        ➥ name="date_birth" not-empty="no" result="date" type="normal" />
        <field-definition auto-enter="yes" global="no" max-repeat="1"
        ➥name="id_animal" not-empty="yes" result="text" type="normal" />
        <field-definition auto-enter="no" global="no" max-repeat="1"
        ➥ name="id_father" not-empty="no" result="text" type="normal" />
        <field-definition auto-enter="no" global="no" max-repeat="1"
        ➥ name="id_mother" not-empty="no" result="text" type="normal" />
        <field-definition auto-enter="no" global="no" max-repeat="1"
        ➥ name="name" not-empty="no" result="text" type="normal" />
        <field-definition auto-enter="no" global="no" max-repeat="1"
    ➥ name="weight_birth" not-empty="no" result="number" type="normal" />
        <field-definition auto-enter="no" global="no" max-repeat="1"
    ➥ name="weight_current" not-empty="no" result="number" type="normal" />
        <field-definition auto-enter="no" global="no" max-repeat="1"
        ➥ name="HerdID" not-empty="no" result="text" type="normal" />
        <field-definition auto-enter="no" global="no" max-repeat="1"
        ➥name="gender" not-empty="no" result="text" type="normal" />
    </metadata>
    <resultset count="17" fetch-size="17">
        <record mod-id="6" record-id="1">
            <field name="date_birth">
                <data>4/23/1994</data>
            </field>
            <field name="id_animal">
                <data>A1</data>
            </field>
            <field name="id_father">
                <data></data>
            </field>
            <field name="id_mother">
                <data></data>
            </field>
            <field name="name">
                <data>Great Geronimo</data>
            </field>
            <field name="weight_birth">
                <data>107</data>
            </field>
            <field name="weight_current">
                <data>812</data>
            </field>
            <field name="HerdID">
                <data>H1</data>
            </field>
            <field name="gender">
                <data>Male</data>
            </field>
        </record>
        [ ... multiple additional records ...]
    </resultset>
</fmresultset>
```

23

In general, when you want to access XML data from an appropriately configured FileMaker file, you do so by entering a URL in the following format:

```
<protocol>//<server-ip>[:<port>]/fmi/xml/<grammar>.xml?[<query-string>]
```

Protocol indicates a web protocol, either HTTP or HTTPS.

Server-IP is the IP address of the web server that serves as the point of entry to the Web Publishing Engine. Note that if the Web Publishing Engine is installed on a different machine from the web server, you must specify the IP address of the web server machine here—providing the address of the Web Publishing Engine does not work.

Port is an optional part of the URL. In general, your web server will be running on the default HTTP port of 80 or the default HTTPS port of 443. If for any reason you've configured your web server to run on a different port than the protocol default, you need to specify that port number here. This port has nothing to do with any of the WPE-specific ports (in the 16000 range) or the FileMaker Server port (5003) that you may have encountered in the Web Publishing Engine documentation; it refers strictly to the port on which your web server accepts incoming requests.

Grammar refers to one of three FileMaker xml grammars: FMPXMLRESULT, FMPXMLLAYOUT, or fmresultset.

NOTE

> Note that only the first one of these is available via XML export: The second two are available only via Custom Web Publishing. The FMPDSORESULT grammar that's available with XML export is not available with Custom Web Publishing.

Query-string refers to a series of one or more specific pieces of information you pass to the Web Publishing Engine to form the substance of your request. Among the pieces of information you would pass in the query string are the name of the database to access, the name of the layout you want to work with, and the name of a database *action* (such as "find all records", expressed in the sample URL by the `findall` command).

In general, then, you'll use specially formatted URLs to access FileMaker data as XML via Custom Web Publishing. These URLs can be manually entered in a web browser, or they can be linked from a web page, or they can be used by other processes or applications that want to consume FileMaker data as XML.

UNDERSTANDING QUERY STRINGS

A lot of the action in a Custom Web Publishing URL occurs inside the *query string*—that odd-looking set of commands at the end of the URL. Here again is the example URL from the previous section:

```
http://192.168.100.101/fmi/xml/fmresultset.xml?-db=Animal&-lay=web&-findall
```

The query string is the portion of the URL that comes after the question mark. A query string consists of multiple *name-value pairs*, with each name-value pair taking the form *name=value*. If there are multiple name-value pairs in a URL, additional pairs are separated from the first one by an ampersand character (&).

In the sample URL, we've passed three name-value pairs. Table 23.1 shows the names and their corresponding values.

TABLE 23.1   NAME-VALUE PAIRS IN A SAMPLE CWP URL

Name	Value	Meaning
-db	Animal	Which FileMaker database to access
-lay	Web	Which layout in the specified database to use
-findall	(No associated value)	What action to perform

In general, any Custom Web Publishing URL needs to specify at least a database name, a layout name, and a database action to perform. (In fact, the database name and layout name can also be omitted in the case of a few specialized database actions). So, at a minimum, you will usually provide a -db value, a -lay value, and the name of some database action.

A few more notes on query string syntax: The *order* of the name-value pairs within the query string doesn't matter, as long as all the required pairs are present. The initial dash (-) in the various names *is* significant, however, and can't be omitted. You'll notice that the database action consists of a name without a value (which is perfectly legitimate in an HTTP URL query string); database actions always consist of a name with no value attached.

If you have spaces in your field, layout, or database names, this might cause trouble. See "Dealing with Spaces" in the "Troubleshooting" section at the end of this chapter.

PERFORMING SPECIFIC SEARCHES WITH CWP URLS

The CWP URLs we've looked at so far are simply querying a FileMaker database table, finding all records, and returning the results as raw XML according to the selected XML grammar. But what if you want to query different tables within the chosen database, or select only certain records rather than all records, or apply a sort order to the results? All these things are possible with CWP.

SPECIFYING THE TABLE

One of the reasons it's so important to supply a layout name with your CWP URLs (via the -lay parameter) is that the active table is determined by the active layout, via that layout's *table context*. You may recall that, in the Layout Setup dialog for each layout, there's a choice labeled Show Records From. This enables you to select a table occurrence that will provide the layout's table context. When you specify a layout in a CWP URL, you are implicitly setting the active table as well. All commands in the query string are considered to be applied to whatever table underlies the chosen layout.

→ For a refresher on the idea of table context, **see** "Understanding Table Context," **p. 164**.

FINDING SPECIFIC RECORDS

The Custom Web Publishing URL can also be used to search for specific records. To do this, use `-find` as the database action, instead of `-findall`. You also need to specify one or more search criteria, which are also supplied as name-value pairs.

For example, if you're working with a database of animals, and there's a field called *name* for the animal's name, you can use the following URL to search for any animals named Hector:

```
http://192.168.100.101/fmi/xml/fmresultset.xml?-db=animal&-lay=web
➥&name=Hector&-find
```

NOTE

The database in question has only a single table, also called Animal, and that table is the table context for the web layout.

This code snippet specifies a database action of `-find`, and adds one more parameter to the query string. We say `name=Hector` to cause the Web Publishing Engine to search for only records where the name is Hector. If there are any such records, they'll be returned in the chosen XML grammar. If there are no matching records, we get back a response that looks a bit like Listing 23.2.

LISTING 23.2   SAMPLE ERROR RESPONSE

```
<?xml version="1.0" encoding="UTF-8" standalone="no" ?>
<!DOCTYPE fmresultset (View Source for full doctype...)>
<fmresultset xmlns="http://www.filemaker.com/xml/fmresultset" version="1.0">
    <error code="401" />
    <product build="12/10/2003" name="FileMaker Web Publishing Engine"
    ➥ version="7.0v1" />
    <datasource database="" date-format="" layout="" table="" time-format=""
    ➥ total-count="0" />
    <metadata />
    <resultset count="0" fetch-size="0" />
</fmresultset>
```

You can see that in the case where no records are found, the XML returned by the Web Publishing Engine contains an error code appropriate to the situation. In this case, the code is a standard "no records found" error. (Note that the exact format of the error response varies depending on which XML grammar you specified in the URL.)

SPECIFYING AN EXACT MATCH WHEN SEARCHING

In the previous example, the search appeared to be for all animals named Hector. This is not exactly true. The previous URL will have exactly the same effect as entering Find mode in the regular FileMaker client, typing **Hector** into the name field, and performing the search. FileMaker, when searching text fields, searches on a "starts with" basis, so this search actually finds animals named Hector, Hector II, Hectorax, and so on. To specify that you want an exact match, rather than a "starts with" match, you need a bit more precision. In FileMaker's regular Find mode, you'd type `=Hector` in the search field, with the equal sign indicating an exact match. In a CWP URL, you'd write:

```
http://192.168.100.101/fmi/xml/fmresultset.xml?-db=animal&-lay=web&name=Hector
➥&name.op=eq&-find
```

Another parameter has been added to the query string here. The new parameter specifies what kind of *operator* we want to apply to one of the search fields. The syntax for this new parameter is

```
<field-name>.op=<operator>
```

Here, `field-name` is the field to which you want to apply the operator, and `operator` is a short character string indicating one of nine different possible operators. Here, the operator we've chosen is eq for an exact match. Other possible operators are cn for *contains*, bw for *begins with* (the default), and ew for *ends with*. So, if you wanted to find all animals with a name ending in *tor*, you could use this URL:

```
http://192.168.100.101/fmi/xml/fmresultset.xml?-db=animal&-lay=web&name=tor
➥&name.op=ew&-find
```

This query string instructs the Web Publishing Engine to treat the search on the name field as an "ends with" search.

NOTE

> The operators available to you in Custom Web Publishing are similar to, but not identical to, the list you would find in the FileMaker client if you entered Find mode and clicked on the symbol list in the status area. FileMaker Find mode and the Custom Web Publishing find syntax each contain operators that are not available in the other. Table 23.2 lists all the operators available in Custom Web Publishing.

TABLE 23.2 COMPARISON OPERATORS FOR THE -find **COMMAND**

Operator	Significance	FileMaker Find Equivalent
eq	Equals	`=value`
cn	Contains	`*value*`
bw	Begins with	`value*`
ew	Ends with	`*value`
gt	Greater than	`>value`
gte	Greater than or equal	`>=value`
lt	Less than	`<value`
lte	Less than or equal	`<=value`
neq	Not equal	(Omit check box)

PERFORMING A NUMERICAL COMPARISON SEARCH

Consider a database that contains some numerical fields. The Animal database used as an example so far contains a field called `weight_birth` for an animal's birth weight. Suppose that you want to find all animals with a birth weight less than 100 pounds. The following URL would do it:

```
http://127.0.0.1/fmi/xml/fmresultset.xml?-db=animal&-lay=web&weight_birth=100
➥&weight_birth.op=lt&-find
```

Here, 100 is specified for the `weight_birth` search field, but we go on to say that the *operator* for that search field is the less-than operator, symbolized by the code `lt`.

SEARCHING ON MULTIPLE CRITERIA

Suppose that we want to construct a more narrowly tailored search. You want to find all *male* animals with a birth weight less than 100. (This is the equivalent of filling in two fields in FileMaker's Find mode, instead of just one.) You'd use a URL like the following:

```
http://127.0.0.1/fmi/xml/fmresultset.xml?-db=animal&-lay=
➥web&weight_birth=100&gender=Male&weight_birth.op=lt&-find
```

Here we've simply added one more search field: `gender=Male`. This constitutes a further limit on the search you saw in the previous example. This search finds only records for male animals with birth weight less than 100.

CREATING MULTIPLE FIND REQUESTS

The preceding example showed how to use multiple criteria to narrow a search. But what if you want to use multiple criteria to *broaden* a search? We've searched for animals with birth weight less than 100. What if you also want to find, in the same search, any animals who have a current weight less than 500? (You might recognize this as the equivalent of creating additional Find requests in the regular FileMaker Pro software.)

To explain this kind of search, you need to introduce the concept of a *logical operator*. In the search demonstrated previously, for a record to be included in the search, *all* the search criteria in the query string had to be true. That is, an animal would not be included in the search results unless it was both male *and* had a birth weight less than 100. This kind of search is thus often referred to as an *and* search or an *all-true* search.

On the other hand, when you think about also finding animals with current weight less than 500, you have a situation where an animal will be included in the search results if *any* of the search criteria are true. In other words, a record will be found if the animal had a birth weight of less than 100, *or* it has a current weight of less than 500. This type of search is thus often called an *or* or an *any-true* search.

By default, the Web Publishing Engine treats all searches as *and* searches. To perform an *or* search, you'd use a URL like this one:

```
http://127.0.0.1/fmi/xml/fmresultset.xml?-db=animal&-lay=web&weight_birth=100
➥&weight_current=500e&weight_birth.op=lt&weight_current.op=lt
➥&-lop=or&-find
```

Here you supply two search criteria. You also need to supply the field-level operator for each search field. In both cases, you're performing a *less-than* search, so you need to specify an operator of lt for each field. The new element in the query string is the -lop parameter, which stands for *logical operator*. -lop can have a value of *and* (the default) or *or* (the one we're using here). The -lop parameter here instructs the Web Publishing Engine to treat the search as an *or* search.

> **NOTE**
>
> In FileMaker proper, you can construct a search that's a complex mixture of *and* and *or* searches by entering multiple Find requests, each with more than one field filled in. Such searches can't readily be reproduced with Custom Web Publishing: The -lop command can be applied only to all the search fields taken together. There is also no way to invoke the additional FileMaker search options of Constrain or Extend Found Set.

SPECIFYING A SORT ORDER FOR SEARCH RESULTS

When you make a request to the Web Publishing Engine, you can specify how the results should be sorted. You can specify one or more fields to sort on, as you can in the regular FileMaker application, and you can specify whether each sort field should be sorted in ascending or descending order. Consider a URL that will find all records in the Animal table, and ask that the records be sorted by name:

```
http://192.168.101.100/fmi/xml/fmresultset.xml?-db=Animal&-lay=web
➥&-sortfield.1=name&-findall
```

The new query string command here is called -sortfield. You'll notice we also added the suffix .1 to this parameter. This indicates the sort field's *precedence*. The concept of precedence is meaningful only if you have more than one sort field, as you'll see in a moment. Despite this fact, you can't omit the sort precedence, even for a one-item sort, or the records won't be sorted at all.

Suppose that you wanted the records to be sorted by gender, and within each gender to be sorted by current weight from highest to lowest. You'd do that like this:

```
http://127.0.0.1/fmi/xml/fmresultset.xml?-db=Animal&-lay=web
➥&-sortfield.1=gender&-sortfield.2=weight_current&-sortorder.2=
➥descend&-findall
```

Here two sort fields are specified. The first sort is by gender, the second by weight_current. There's also a new parameter, called -sortorder. Like -sortfield, -sortorder also takes a numeric suffix. Here, it's used to indicate which sort field is being referred to. By default, each field will be sorted in ascending order. If you supply a value of descend for the second sort field, you ensure that the animals will be sorted, within each gender group, from heaviest to lightest.

APPLICATIONS OF CUSTOM WEB PUBLISHING WITH XML

The current section shows how to use the Web Publishing Engine to query a database and publish the results as raw XML in one of several XML grammars. But what use is this capability, exactly?

Well, the most obvious significant use is to allow FileMaker to act as a web service provider. In Chapter 22, "FileMaker and Web Services," we cover how to use FileMaker to pull data from other web services on the Internet. But FileMaker can also act as a web service. If you provide a web service client with an appropriate URL, remote services and programs can query your FileMaker database via the Web Publishing Engine and extract whatever information you choose to let them see.

Additionally, the URL query syntax discussed in this section is also at the heart of the more sophisticated form of Custom Web Publishing that's made possible by the application of XSLT stylesheets, which is the topic of the next section.

USING XSLT WITH CUSTOM WEB PUBLISHING

The previous section discusses how to use FileMaker to produce plain XML, distributed over HTTP. This section builds on the previous one and demonstrates how to use XSL transformations (XSLT) to manipulate that raw XML further.

ABOUT SERVER-SIDE XSLT

The previous section demonstrates how to query a FileMaker database via the Web Publishing Engine, and return the results as some form of raw XML. But, as you'll know if you've worked with XSLT before, or if you've already read Chapter 22 of this book, XML becomes even more interesting when you begin to transform it with XSLT stylesheets.

→ For an overview of XML and XSLT basics, **see** "FileMaker and XML," **p. 671** and "Transforming XML," **p. 676**.

If you've already read Chapter 22, you'll have become familiar with the distinction between *client-side* and *server-side* XSL transformations. When using FileMaker's XML export capability, it's the client copy of FileMaker that performs any XSL transformations you specify, hence the term *client-side transformation*. On the other hand, with Custom Web Publishing, the transformation is performed by the Web Publishing Engine (server-side), and only the transformation result is sent back to the client (in this case a web browser).

In the world of Custom Web Publishing, all XSLT transformations are server-side transformations. Stylesheets are placed in one or more predetermined locations within the Web Publishing Engine install hierarchy and accessed by the Web Publishing Engine as necessary.

WHERE TO PUT YOUR STYLESHEETS

When using Custom Web Publishing with XSLT, your stylesheets live on the same machine as the Web Publishing Engine. All the stylesheets you write need to be located at or beneath a certain point in the Web Publishing Engine directory hierarchy. On Mac OS X, the root directory is /Library/FileMaker Server 8/Web Publishing/xslt-template-files. On Windows, the root directory is located by default at c:\Program Files\FileMaker\ FileMaker Server 8\Web Publishing\xslt-template-files, but you have the option to change the install directory on Windows, so be aware of where you installed your Web Publishing Engine and plan accordingly.

Getting Started with XSLT in CWP

To use XSLT stylesheets in your Custom Web Publishing project, you need several things. A number of them are also prerequisites for using Custom Web Publishing with plain XML. The only significant additional points are that the Web Publishing Engine must be configured with XSLT publishing enabled (see the section titled "Configuring the Web Publishing Engine" earlier in this chapter), and all FileMaker databases that you want to make accessible must have the fmxslt extended privilege assigned via a privilege set to one or more activated user accounts (see the section titled "Getting Your Databases Ready for Custom Web Publishing" earlier in this chapter) .

A Simple Stylesheet to Display Search Results

Suppose that, rather than have data come out of FileMaker Server as raw XML, you'd like to return it in nicely formatted HTML. For convenience, let's continue working with the example of a simple listing of herd animals. A simple database lists the animals, and you'd like them to appear in a browser formatted as shown in Figure 23.13.

Figure 23.13
We'd like to produce a simple HTML listing from a database.

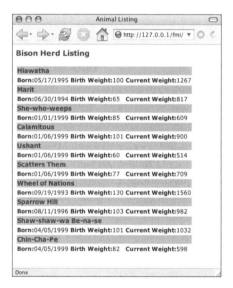

So you need an XSLT stylesheet that will transform FileMaker's XML into formatted HTML.

You'll probably remember that, before you can write a stylesheet to transform FileMaker XML, you need to know in what grammar that XML will be presented. When you're using Custom Web Publishing, you can request the XML from the Web Publishing Engine in whichever one of the available FileMaker grammars you prefer. Here you're going to request the data in the fmresultset grammar and write the stylesheet accordingly. (For an example of this CWP-only grammar, see Listing 23.1.) A stylesheet that will do this is shown in Listing 23.3.

LISTING 23.3 CSS-FORMATTED HTML STYLESHEET

```
<?xml version="1.0" encoding="UTF-8"?>
<xsl:stylesheet version="1.0"
➥ xmlns:fmrs="http://www.filemaker.com/xml/fmresultset"
➥xmlns:xsl="http://www.w3.org/1999/XSL/Transform">
 <xsl:output doctype-public="-//W3C//DTD HTML 3.2 Final//EN"
 ➥ indent="yes" method="html"/>
 <xsl:template match="/fmrs:fmresultset">
  <html>
   <head>
    <title>Animal Listing</title>
    <STYLE MEDIA="screen" TYPE="text/css">
      H3 { font-weight:800; font-size:12.5pt;
      ➥ font-family:verdana,helvetica,arial; color:#333333;}
      .name { font-weight:800; font-size:10pt;
      ➥ font-family:verdana,helvetica,arial; color:#333333;
      ➥background-color:silver }
      .label {font-weight:800; font-size:9pt;
      ➥font-family:verdana,helvetica,arial; color:#000099;}
      .data {font-weight:300; font-size:9pt;
      ➥ font-family:verdana,helvetica,arial; color:#000000;}
    </STYLE>
   </head>
   <body>
    <H3>Bison Herd Listing</H3>
    <table border="0">
     <xsl:for-each select="/fmrs:fmresultset/fmrs:resultset/fmrs:record">
      <tr>
       <td class="name" colspan="3">
        <b>
         <xsl:value-of select="fmrs:field[@name='name']/fmrs:data"/>
        </b>
       </td>
      </tr>
      <td>
       <span class="label">Born:</span>
       <span class="data">
        <xsl:value-of select="fmrs:field[@name='date_birth']/fmrs:data"/>
       </span>
      </td>
      <td>
       <span class="label">Birth Weight:</span>
       <span class="data">
        <xsl:value-of select="fmrs:field[@name='weight_birth']/fmrs:data"/>
       </span>
      </td>
      <td>
       <span class="label">Current Weight:</span>
       <span class="data">
        <xsl:value-of select="fmrs:field[@name='weight_current']/fmrs:data"/>
       </span>
      </td>
     </xsl:for-each>
    </table>
   </body>
  </html>
 </xsl:template>
</xsl:stylesheet>
```

The mechanics of the stylesheet are straightforward enough. It declares a namespace called fmrs, to match up with the fmresultset namespace. It does an initial template match on the fmresultset element, where it outputs all the initial HTML elements, including a small CSS stylesheet. After this is done, it uses <xsl:for-each> to loop over all the <fmrs:record> elements, and outputs two formatted HTML table rows for each record: one containing the name, the other containing the other three fields of interest. You'll notice that the fmresultset grammar is easier to work with than the FMPXMLRESULT grammar because you can reference field names directly, instead of having to refer to them by their position within the <METADATA> element.

FORMAT OF THE XSLT URL

The previous section demonstrated a simple server-side stylesheet, but it didn't explain exactly how the stylesheet would be applied to XML coming out of FileMaker Server. Just as with XML Custom Web Publishing, you invoke the stylesheet from a web browser, via a specially formatted URL. For the previous section's stylesheet, a sample URL might be

```
http://192.168.101.100/fmi/xsl/animal/animal-fmresult.xsl?-lay=web
➥&-db=Animal&-grammar=fmresultset&-findall
```

The general format of an XSLT URL is somewhat similar to that for XML. It looks like this:

```
<protocol>//<server-ip>[:<port>]/fmi/xsl/[<path>/]<stylesheet.xsl>
➥[?<query string>]
```

Many of these elements have the same significance as in the plain XML URL. Rather than reference the /fmi/xml path on the server, though, we reference /fmi/xsl. We follow this immediately with the name of the stylesheet, but note that this assumes that the stylesheet is immediately inside the root XSL directory in your Web Publishing Engine installation directory. You have the option, though, of creating additional subdirectories inside that root directory, and if you do this, you need to reference those intermediate folders in the path as well. In the URL shown previously, we've created a subdirectory inside the XSLT root directory, called animal, and inside that directory is the stylesheet, called animal-fmresult. xsl. So you need to include the intermediate /animal folder in the path in the URL.

After the name of the stylesheet, a query string is supplied that's very similar to the XML query string (because you can request the identical actions and search options). One difference, though, is that you need to pass a parameter called -grammar, and set it to be equal to the name of the grammar you intend to use. The earlier stylesheet was written with the fmresultset grammar in mind, so this needs to be specified in the URL. It's an error to omit the -grammar parameter. And of course, if you specify a grammar different from the one the stylesheet expects, you'll get unexpected results.

NOTE

It's actually possible to omit the entire query string when using XSLT with Custom Web Publishing! The reason is that XSLT-CWP has a special command for embedding the query parameters inside the stylesheet itself. You'll see more on this in the following section.

EMBEDDING QUERY PARAMETERS IN A STYLESHEET

One of the difficulties with allowing your FileMaker data to be accessed via a URL is that a canny user can easily experiment with the URL elements to try to create effects other than those you intended—for example, displaying forbidden records, or even sending a command to delete a record.

Custom Web Publishing has a method for embedding query parameters in the body of a stylesheet. To do this, you use a special XML construct called a *processing instruction*. A processing instruction is a command to a specific XML processor. If you pass a processing instruction that your processor doesn't understand, it is ignored.

To embed query parameters in a stylesheet, you could add a line like the following to a stylesheet:

```
<?xslt-cwp-query params="-grammar=fmresultset&-db=Animal&-lay=web&-findall"?>
```

What this processing instruction means is that any values for -grammar, -db, -lay, or the database action that are passed via the URL will be overridden by the values supplied in this processing instruction. So, no one can ever point the page to a different database, or demand a different database action (such as record deletion!).

CAUTION

> You should be aware that this query string in the processing instruction does not simply *replace* the query string that might be present in a URL. It *overrides* it, one parameter at a time. What this means is that if the URL contains a parameter (such as a search field or sort order) that isn't mentioned in the processing instruction, that parameter will still be in force. If you want to block any possibility that a user can supply a rogue query parameter, you need to specify that parameter explicitly in your static processing instruction.

It's a good idea to use this technique wherever you can to increase the security of your databases and your web application. Also, embedding at least the expected grammar in the stylesheet prevents you from ever having a mismatch between the grammar you choose in a URL and the one for which the stylesheet is written.

BUILDING WEB APPLICATIONS WITH XSLT-CWP

All the examples shown so far consist of one query at a time. And so far the examples have all been oriented toward displaying search results. In this section, we'll demonstrate some techniques for building multiscreen sites that allow you to navigate smoothly between different views of your data, and allow you to create, edit, and delete records as well.

BUILDING A "VIEW DETAIL" LINK

Suppose that you envision something more interesting—for example, the capability to click a View link in the list view and come to a new screen with more detailed information on the record.

To do this, the View link needs to consist of another Custom Web Publishing URL, one that links to a stylesheet that searches for one specific record, and displays information about it. That URL will look like this:

```
<a href="animal-detail.xsl?-recid=2&-find">View</a>
```

(This assumes, by the way, that the `animal_detail.xsl` file is in the same directory as the list view file, so as to be accessible via a relative URL.) What's new in this URL is the `-recid` parameter. FileMaker stores a unique identifier of its own for each database record. This identifier is internal to FileMaker and is in addition to any primary key fields you may define. In Custom Web Publishing, the `fmresultset` grammar (among others), contains the record ID for each returned record (it's in the `record-id` attribute of the `<record>` element)—so you have access to the record ID in your stylesheets. Additionally, if your XSL URL contains the `-recid` parameter, and a database action of `-find`, the Web Publishing Engine attempts to find that specific record, which is exactly the behavior you want.

Figure 23.14 shows how you might like the new web page to look.

Figure 23.14
You might like to add a simple View link to the HTML list.

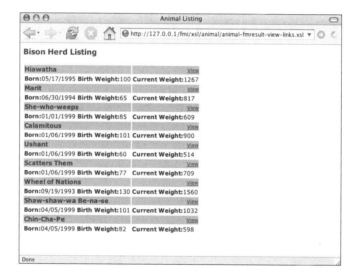

The strategy, then, is to retool the earlier record list stylesheet so that it contains links to the detail stylesheet. Each link needs to reference a specific record ID. Second, a stylesheet needs to be written for the detail view.

The first thing to consider is the modified stylesheet that includes a View link. It's presented as Listing 23.4.

LISTING 23.4   STYLESHEET FOR A LIST WITH A VIEW LINK

```
<?xml version="1.0" encoding="UTF-8"?>
<xsl:stylesheet version="1.0"
    xmlns:fmrs="http://www.filemaker.com/xml/fmresultset"
    xmlns:xsl="http://www.w3.org/1999/XSL/Transform">
```

continues

23

LISTING 23.4 CONTINUED

```
<?xslt-cwp-query params="-grammar=fmresultset&-db=Animal&-lay=web
➥&-findall"?>
<xsl:output doctype-public="-//W3C//DTD HTML 3.2 Final//EN"
➥ indent="yes" method="html"/>
<xsl:template match="/fmrs:fmresultset">
    <html>
        <head>
            <title>Animal Listing</title>
            <STYLE MEDIA="screen" TYPE="text/css">
  H3 { font-weight:800; font-size:12.5pt;
          ➥font-family:verdana,helvetica,arial; color:#333333;}
    .name { font-weight:800; font-size:10pt;
          ➥font-family:verdana,helvetica,arial; color:#333333;
          ➥background-color:silver }
    .label {font-weight:800; font-size:9pt;
          ➥font-family:verdana,helvetica,arial; color:#000099;}
    .data {font-weight:300; font-size:9pt;
          ➥font-family:verdana,helvetica,arial; color:#000000;}
    .edit-cell {  border-color:silver; background-color:silver;
          ➥text-align:right; font-weight:300; font-size:8pt;
          ➥font-family:verdana,helvetica,arial; color:#000099;}
    </STYLE>
</head>
<body>
 <H3>Bison Herd Listing</H3>
 <table border="0">
  <xsl:for-each select="/fmrs:fmresultset/fmrs:resultset/fmrs:record">
   <tr>
    <td class="name" colspan="2">
     <b>
      <xsl:value-of select="fmrs:field[@name='name']/fmrs:data"/>
     </b>
    </td>
    <td class="edit-cell">
     <a>
      <xsl:attribute name="href">animal-detail.xsl?-recid=
          ➥<xsl:value-of select="@record-id"/>
     </xsl:attribute>View</a>
    </td>
   </tr>
   <td>
    <span class="label">Born:</span>
    <span class="data">
     <xsl:value-of select="fmrs:field[@name='date_birth']/fmrs:data"/>
    </span>
   </td>
   <td>
    <span class="label">Birth Weight:</span>
    <span class="data">
     <xsl:value-of select="fmrs:field[@name='weight_birth']/fmrs:data"/>
    </span>
   </td>
   <td>
    <span class="label">Current Weight:</span>
    <span class="data">
     <xsl:value-of select="fmrs:field[@name='weight_current']/fmrs:data"/>
    </span>
```

```
        </td>
      </xsl:for-each>
    </table>
   </body>
  </html>
 </xsl:template>
</xsl:stylesheet>
```

The code is similar to Listing 23.3. The main difference is in the added link, which is placed in its own table cell (we added some additional CSS styling for this cell as well). The text View is wrapped in an <a>...</a> tag pair. To output the href attribute, we use the <xsl:attribute> tag. For the href, we provide the name of the stylesheet we'll be using to view the record detail, which we've named animal_detail.xsl. We've also added a query string that picks the record-id attribute out of the current <record> element and adds a database action of -find.

Now consider what animal_detail.xsl might look like. It's a straightforward stylesheet, and appears as Listing 23.5.

LISTING 23.5   STYLESHEET TO PRODUCE A DETAIL VIEW

```
<?xml version="1.0" encoding="UTF-8"?>
<xsl:stylesheet version="1.0"
  ➥ xmlns:fmrs="http://www.filemaker.com/xml/fmresultset"
  ➥ xmlns:xsl="http://www.w3.org/1999/XSL/Transform">
 <?xslt-cwp-query params="-grammar=fmresultset&-db=Animal&-lay=web&-find"?>
 <xsl:output doctype-public="-//W3C//DTD HTML 3.2 Final//EN"
   ➥ indent="yes" method="html"/>
 <xsl:template match="/fmrs:fmresultset">
  <html>
   <head>
    <title>Animal Detail</title>
    <STYLE MEDIA="screen" TYPE="text/css">
     H3 { font-weight:800; font-size:12.5pt;
          ➥font-family:verdana,helvetica,arial; color:#333333;}
     TH { text-align:left;}
     .name { font-weight:800;  font-size:10pt;
          ➥font-family:verdana,helvetica,arial; color:#333333;
          ➥background-color:silver }
     .label {font-weight:800; font-size:9pt;
          ➥font-family:verdana,helvetica,arial; color:#000099;}
     .data {font-weight:300; font-size:9pt;
          ➥font-family:verdana,helvetica,arial; color:#000000;}
    </STYLE>
   </head>
   <body>
    <H3>Bison Record Detail</H3>
    <table border="0">
     <xsl:for-each select="/fmrs:fmresultset/fmrs:resultset/fmrs:record">
      <tr>
       <td class="name" colspan="2">
        <b>
         <xsl:value-of select="fmrs:field[@name='name']/fmrs:data"/>
        </b>
```

continues

23

LISTING 23.5   CONTINUED

```
        </td>
      </tr>
      <tr>
      <th>
       <span class="label">Born:</span></th>
       <td> <span class="data">
        <xsl:value-of select="fmrs:field[@name='date_birth']/fmrs:data"/>
       </span>
      </td></tr>
      <tr>
      <th>
       <span class="label">Gender:</span></th>
       <td> <span class="data">
        <xsl:value-of select="fmrs:field[@name='gender']/fmrs:data"/>
       </span>
      </td></tr>
      <tr>
      <th>
       <span class="label">Birth Weight:</span></th>
         <td> <span class="data">
        <xsl:value-of select="fmrs:field[@name='weight_birth']/fmrs:data"/>
       </span>
      </td></tr>
      <tr><th>
       <span class="label">Current Weight:</span></th>
         <td> <span class="data">
        <xsl:value-of select="fmrs:field[@name='weight_current']/fmrs:data"/>
       </span>
      </td></tr>
     </xsl:for-each>
    </table>
   </body>
  </html>
 </xsl:template>
</xsl:stylesheet>
```

It was relatively easy to take the list view stylesheet and move a few things around to get the stylesheet shown in Listing 23.5. In addition to changing the styling and formatting of the data somewhat, and adding the Gender field, the only other significant change is in the setup of the static query parameters, where we've changed the database action from -findall to -find. Remember that the stylesheet still uses any additional parameters coming in unless the static parameters override them. Because we don't override the inbound -recid, the stylesheet accepts it and uses it as the basis for the database search.

USING TOKENS TO SHARE DATA BETWEEN STYLESHEETS

Suppose that you wanted to build a list-and-detail page arrangement like the one in the previous section, but you wanted to add the capability to page through records in detail mode. You'd like to have a Next and a Previous link on the detail screen so that you can flip between records without having to go back through the list view. The web page might appear as in Figure 23.15.

Figure 23.15
A detail view of an animal record with links added to allow paging between records.

Well, the links to do this will presumably look just like the links used to get from the list view to an individual detail view. Those links, again, look like this:

```
<a href="animal-detail.xsl?-recid=2&-find">View</a>
```

The Next and Previous links will look just like this, but will reference the record IDs of the next and previous records. You might think at first glance that you need to pass these record IDs from the list stylesheet over to the detail stylesheet, but this doesn't quite work. After you begin paging through the records in detail view, you'll quickly use up the record IDs that were passed in, and you won't know where to go next.

To do this correctly (well, *more* correctly), you need to change the way the detail page works. Previously we accessed the detail page with a -recid parameter and a -find action, instructing the Web Publishing Engine to search for one specific record ID, and display just that record. What you want to do now is ask instead for a -findall action, but only *display* the one chosen record. Because you'll have access to all the records in the set, you'll still be able to pull out the next and previous record IDs to use in the Next Record and Previous Record links.

To do things this way, you don't want to pass in the record ID as a -recid parameter anymore. The action specified for the detail page is going to be a -findall, so passing an explicit -recid could be confusing (to a programmer if not to the software!). You need another means to pass along the record ID.

To do this, you can use a CWP tool called a *token*. A token is a named piece of information (much like a variable) that you can pass in a CWP URL and that the target stylesheet can then extract. A URL that included a token for the specific record ID to show might look like this:

```
<a>href="animal-detail-links.xsl?-token.rec-to-show=3
```

Tokens in the URL are denoted by the -token parameter, with a suffix that gives the token its own unique name. You need to provide a -token parameter and a unique name for each token you want to pass.

NOTE

There's no limit to the number of tokens you can pass, or to the size of the data you can pass with them, except for that imposed by the HTTP standard. If you're passing tokens via the URL itself (an HTTP GET request), you're probably limited to at most a few hundred characters in the URL. If you're passing the tokens via a form, there should be no limit to the number of tokens nor the amount of data passed.

To do this in the list/detail arrangement, you need to modify the View links in the list page to include a token for the current record ID. Then you need to modify the detail page to cause it to find all records, limit the display to the record ID corresponding to the passed token, and generate Next and Previous links based on the record IDs of the records before and after the record displayed.

Listing 23.6 contains a code fragment showing how you can rewrite the View link from Listing 23.5 to pass the current record ID as tokens.

LISTING 23.6   A RECORD DETAIL LINK CONTAINING A RECORD ID TOKEN

```
<a>
  <xsl:attribute name="href">animal-detail-links.xsl?-token.rec-to-show=
  ➥<xsl:value-of select="@record-id"/>
  </xsl:attribute>View
</a>
```

Now that you have a link that passes along the current record ID as a token, you need to add some code to the detail view that will extract these tokens, as well as some code to generate Next and Previous links based on the current record ID. This is actually a bit tricky. It turns out that the Web Publishing Engine provides a way for you to access *any* request parameter from within a stylesheet. You could use this technique to access a token value, or the specific values of search criteria, or the name of the requested database—anything that was sent in the query string that was part of the calling URL.

The Web Publishing Engine passes all this information to every stylesheet via an *XSL parameter*. XSL parameters look a lot like function parameters: They're values that are passed in to your stylesheet from the outside and are available to you under specific names.

→ For details on functions and function parameters, **see** "Exploring the Calculation Dialog Box," **p. 221**.

Suppose that you access the detail stylesheet with this URL:

```
http://192.168.101.100/fmi/xsl/animal/animal-detail.xsl?-token.rec-to-show=3
```

If you then issue the following command within the stylesheet:

```
<xsl:param name="request-query" />
```

this creates an XSL variable, called $request-query, which contains the following XML document fragment:

```
<query action="anima-detail.xsl" xmlns="http://www.filemaker.com/xml/query">
    <parameter name="-token.rec-to-show">3</parameter>
</query>
```

Note that the <query> element defines a new namespace! To access this document fragment, you need to add a matching namespace declaration at the top of your stylesheet. Assume you add the following namespace declaration:

```
xmlns:fmq="http://www.filemaker.com/xml/query"
```

You can then access your token via an expression of the following type:

```
$request-query/fmq:query/fmq:parameter[@name = '-token.rec-t0-show']
```

NOTE

> As we get into more advanced Custom Web Publishing, we'll be getting into more
> advanced XSLT as well. We'll touch on a number of the major significant XSLT topics as
> we go, but this book is no substitute for a solid grounding in XSLT, and you'll need that
> grounding to get the most out of Custom Web Publishing. XSL variables and XSL parame-
> ters are somewhat more advanced XSL concepts. We recommend you study them thor-
> oughly in the XML reference guide of your choice. See the *FileMaker 8 Functions and
> Scripts Desk Reference* for a list of recommended readings.

To see how to use these tokens in the detail page, it's best just to see the whole page and
then look at it piece by piece. It's shown as Listing 23.7.

LISTING 23.7 STYLESHEET SHOWING A SINGLE RECORD WITH NEXT AND PREVIOUS LINKS

```
<?xml version="1.0" encoding="UTF-8"?>
<xsl:stylesheet version="1.0" xmlns:fmq="http://www.filemaker.com/xml/query"
 xmlns:fmrs="http://www.filemaker.com/xml/fmresultset"
 xmlns:xsl="http://www.w3.org/1999/XSL/Transform">
<?xslt-cwp-query
params="-grammar=fmresultset&-db=Animal&-lay=web&-findall"?>
<xsl:output doctype-public="-//W3C//DTD HTML 3.2 Final//EN" indent="yes"
   method="html"/>
<xsl:param name="request-query"/>
<xsl:variable name="rec-to-show">
 <xsl:value-of select="$request-query/fmq:query/fmq:parameter
 [@name = '-token.rec-to-show']"/>
</xsl:variable>
<xsl:variable name="document-path">
➥http://127.0.0.1/fmi/xsl/animal/animal-detail-links.xsl</xsl:variable>
<xsl:template match="/fmrs:fmresultset">
 <html>
  <head>
   <title>Animal Detail</title>
   <STYLE MEDIA="screen" TYPE="text/css">
   H3 { font-weight:800; font-size:12.5pt;
    font-family:verdana,helvetica,arial; color:#333333;}
    TH { text-align:left;}
    .name { font-weight:800; font-size:10pt;
    font-family:verdana,helvetica,arial;
    color:#333333; background-color:silver }
    .label {font-weight:800; font-size:9pt;
    font-family:verdana,helvetica,arial; color:#000099;}
    .data {font-weight:300;
    font-size:9pt; font-family:verdana,helvetica,arial;
    color:#000000;}
    record-link { text-align:center; font-weight:300;
    font-size:8pt; font-family:verdana,helvetica,arial;
    color:#000099;}
    </STYLE>
  </head>
  <body>
   <H3>Bison Record Detail</H3>
   <table border="0">
```

continues

Listing 23.7 Continued

```
<xsl:for-each select="/fmrs:fmresultset/fmrs:resultset/fmrs:record
➥[@record-id=$rec-to-show]">
 <xsl:variable name="rec-previous">
  <xsl:value-of select="preceding-sibling::fmrs:record/@record-id"/>
  </xsl:variable>
 <xsl:variable name="rec-next">
 <xsl:value-of select="following-sibling::fmrs:record/@record-id"/>
 </xsl:variable>
 <tr>
  <td class="name" colspan="2">
   <b>
    <xsl:value-of select="fmrs:field[@name='name']/fmrs:data"/>
   </b>
  </td>
 </tr>
 <tr>
  <th>
   <span class="label">Born:</span>
  </th>
  <td>
   <span class="data">
    <xsl:value-of select="fmrs:field[@name='date_birth']/fmrs:data"/>
   </span>
  </td>
 </tr>
 <tr>
  <th>
   <span class="label">Gender:</span>
  </th>
  <td>
   <span class="data">
    <xsl:value-of select="fmrs:field[@name='gender']/fmrs:data"/>
   </span>
  </td>
 </tr>
 <tr>
  <th>
   <span class="label">Birth Weight:</span>
  </th>
  <td>
   <span class="data">
    <xsl:value-of select="fmrs:field[@name='weight_birth']/fmrs:data"/>
   </span>
  </td>
 </tr>
 <tr>
  <th>
   <span class="label">Current Weight:</span>
  </th>
  <td>
   <span class="data">
    <xsl:value-of select="fmrs:field[@name='weight_current']/fmrs:data"/>
   </span>
  </td>
 </tr>
 <tr>
  <td class="record-link">
```

```
        <xsl:if test="$rec-previous !=''">
         <a>
          <xsl:attribute name="href"><xsl:value-of select="$document-path"/>
          ➡?-token.rec-to-show=<xsl:value-of select="$rec-previous"/>
          ➡</xsl:attribute>Previous Record </a>
        </xsl:if>
       </td>
       <td class="record-link">
        <xsl:if test="$rec-next !=''">
         <a>
          <xsl:attribute name="href">
          <xsl:value-of select="$document-path"/>
          ➡?-token.rec-to-show=<xsl:value-of select="$rec-next"/>
          ➡</xsl:attribute>Next Record </a>
        </xsl:if>
       </td>
      </tr>
     </xsl:for-each>
    </table>
   </body>
  </html>
 </xsl:template>
</xsl:stylesheet>
```

This stylesheet shows off quite a number of new XSLT-CWP techniques. We go through them one by one.

In the first place, we've added a new namespace declaration:

```
xmlns:fmq="http://www.filemaker.com/xml/query"
```

As we said before, this is mandatory if you're going to be able to access individual request parameters, as you'll see shortly.

Next, we've changed the statically encoded database action from -find to -findall. This is in keeping with our new strategy, which is to fetch all the records and then sift through them to find a particular one.

CAUTION

> In general, fetching all records here would not be a good idea. You'd want to use some combination of the -max and -skip parameters to fetch the records in groups. See Table 23.3 for some notes on -max and -skip.

Next, we declare one stylesheet *parameter* and two XSL *variables*, as shown in Listing 23.8.

LISTING 23.8   EXTRACTING A TOKEN FROM A REQUEST

```
<xsl:param name="request-query"/>
 <xsl:variable name="rec-to-show">
  <xsl:value-of select="$request-query/fmq:query/fmq:parameter
  [@name = '-token.rec-to-show']"/>
 </xsl:variable>
 <xsl:variable name="document-path">
 ➡http://127.0.0.1/fmi/xsl/animal/animal-detail-links.xsl</xsl:variable>
```

The `<xsl:param>` statement provides access to the data passed to the stylesheet under the name `request-query`. The following `<xsl:variable>` statement reaches into the XML that's contained in the `request-query` variable, and digs out the parameter called `-token.rec-to-show`, which is the token passed from the list view. This value is now available under the name `rec-to-show`. Finally, we set up another variable, called `document-path`, which contains the path to the detail stylesheet. We need to use it in several places later, and it's always a better idea to pull out such "magic values" and keep them in one place, instead of having to update them in several places if something changes.

The next change is in the `<xsl:for-each>` selector used to pick out the record of interest. In the previous version, we simply looped over all instances of the `<record>` element, knowing there would only be one. Here, because the action is `-findall`, all the records are available, and we need to make sure to select only the one we're interested in. We do it like this:

```
<xsl:for-each select="/fmrs:fmresultset/fmrs:resultset/fmrs:record
➥[@record-id=$rec-to-show]">
```

The expression in square brackets is known in XSL as a *predicate*. It's a logical test that has the effect of limiting the previous expression to just those elements that match the predicate expression. So, rather than selecting all `<record>` elements, it selects only those whose `record-id` attribute is equal to the `rec-to-show` variable (which we already set equal to the token passed from the list view).

At the same spot, we take the opportunity to look at the records before and after the one we're displaying, and store their respective record IDs in different XSL variables, as shown in Listing 23.9.

LISTING 23.9   USING THE SIBLING AXES

```
<xsl:variable name="rec-previous">
    <xsl:value-of select="preceding-sibling::fmrs:record/@record-id"/>
    </xsl:variable>
    <xsl:variable name="rec-next">
    <xsl:value-of select="following-sibling::fmrs:record/@record-id"/>
    </xsl:variable>
```

To make this technique work, we use some special XSL *axes* called *preceding-sibling* and *following-sibling*. These expressions enable us to step back or forward one record within the `<resultset>` element, and then reach in and grab the `record-id` attribute. If we're on the first or last `<record>` element, these expressions won't find anything, and we'll end up with a blank value, which is fine.

All that's left is to write some code that creates the Next and Previous links, based on whether the next and previous record IDs are empty (see Listing 23.10). If not (meaning we're on the first or last record), no link is generated.

LISTING 23.10   XSL CODE FOR NEXT AND PREVIOUS LINKS

```
<tr>
        <td class="record-link">
         <xsl:if test="$rec-previous !=''">
          <a>
           <xsl:attribute name="href"><xsl:value-of select="$document-path"/>
           ➡?-token.rec-to-show=<xsl:value-of select="$rec-previous"/>
           ➡</xsl:attribute>Previous Record </a>
         </xsl:if>
        </td>
        <td class="record-link">
         <xsl:if test="$rec-next !=''">
          <a>
           <xsl:attribute name="href">
           <xsl:value-of select="$document-path"/>
           ➡?-token.rec-to-show=<xsl:value-of select="$rec-next"/>
           ➡</xsl:attribute>Next Record </a>
         </xsl:if>
        </td>
        </tr>
```

To generate each link, we use `<xsl:if>` to test whether the relevant record ID is empty or not. If it's empty, we output nothing. Otherwise we output an HTML link with a URL based on our `document-path` variable, which also passes the correct record ID in the `-token.rec-to-show` parameter.

This example introduced a fair number of additional XSL constructs, such as stylesheet parameters, XSL variables, and some of the more advanced expression axes. It also introduced a number of concepts peculiar to XSLT-CWP, such as token passing and the capability to extract request parameters within a stylesheet. We recognize that these are advanced concepts, so we suggest you start by understanding the supplied demo files and begin modifying them to experiment with these techniques.

USING A STYLESHEET TO DELETE A RECORD

So far, all our actions have involved searching for records. But it's also possible to send the Web Publishing Engine a URL with a query string that contains a command to create, edit, or delete a record as well.

Suppose that you have a list view in HTML, like those you've already looked at, and you want to add a link to each row that enables to delete the record. Let's also say you want to see some kind of confirmation screen before you actually perform the delete, and you further want some way to know the deletion has been performed. This can be done with three separate web pages: the list view, a page that shows a yes/no confirmation message, and a page that confirms that the deletion has actually occurred. The flow of the pages might look like Figures 23.16, 23.17, and 23.18.

Figure 23.16
A new list view of animals with a Delete link.

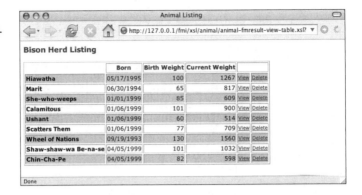

Figure 23.17
A small screen to prompt the user to confirm the deletion.

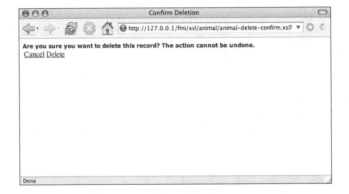

Figure 23.18
A final screen to confirm the deletion and enable the user to return to the list.

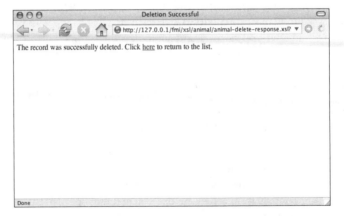

To accomplish this, you need a link in the list view that passes the user over to delete-confirm.xsl, and passes the record ID as a token. The delete-confirm.xsl page does very little: It just interrogates the user as to whether to proceed with the deletion. If the user decides not to delete, she's returned to the main list view. If she decides to go ahead with it, she's brought to delete-response.xsl, which is the page that actually performs the deletion and informs the user of the results.

Take a look at the code for the three pages. First is the code for the list view. We've modified the page so that it presents the records in an ordinary table grid, with View and Delete links at the end of each line. We've also added a little code to color alternate rows. The code is shown in Listing 23.11.

LISTING 23.11   STYLESHEET FOR A TABLE WITH VIEW AND DELETE LINKS

```
<?xml version="1.0" encoding="UTF-8"?>
<xsl:stylesheet version="1.0"
xmlns:fmrs="http://www.filemaker.com/xml/fmresultset"
xmlns:xsl="http://www.w3.org/1999/XSL/Transform">
<?xslt-cwp-query params="-grammar=fmresultset&-db=Animal&-lay=web&-findall"?>
 <xsl:output doctype-public="-//W3C//DTD HTML 3.2 Final//EN"
   indent="yes" method="html"/>
<xsl:template match="/fmrs:fmresultset">
 <html>
  <head>
   <title>Animal Listing</title>
   <STYLE MEDIA="screen" TYPE="text/css">
     H3 { font-weight:800; font-size:12.5pt;
     font-family:verdana,helvetica,arial; color:#333333;}
     .label {font-weight:800;  font-size:9pt;
     font-family:verdana,helvetica,arial; color:#000099;}
     .data {font-weight:300; font-size:9pt;
         font-family:verdana,helvetica,arial;
     color:#000000;}
     .number-data {font-weight:300; font-size:9pt;
       font-family:verdana,helvetica,arial;
     color:#000000; text-align:right;}
      .view-cell { text-align:right; font-weight:300; font-size:8pt;
      font-family:verdana,helvetica,arial; color:#000099;}
   </STYLE>
  </head>
  <body>
   <H3>Bison Herd Listing</H3>
   <table border="1">
    <tr>
     <th>
      <xsl:text> </xsl:text>
     </th>
     <th class="label">Born</th>
     <th class="label">Birth Weight</th>
     <th class="label">Current Weight</th>
     <th colspan="2">
      <xsl:text> </xsl:text>
     </th>
    </tr>
    <xsl:for-each select="/fmrs:fmresultset/fmrs:resultset/fmrs:record">
     <tr>
     <xsl:if test="position() mod 2 = 1">
       <xsl:attribute name="bgcolor">#cccccc</xsl:attribute></xsl:if>
      <td class="data">
       <b>
        <xsl:value-of select="fmrs:field[@name='name']/fmrs:data"/>
       </b>
       <td class="data">
```

continues

23

LISTING 23.11   CONTINUED

```
      <xsl:value-of select="fmrs:field[@name='date_birth']/fmrs:data"/>
     </td>
     <td class="number-data">
      <xsl:value-of select="fmrs:field[@name='weight_birth']/fmrs:data"/>
     </td>
     <td class="number-data">
      <xsl:value-of select="fmrs:field[@name='weight_current']/fmrs:data"/>
     </td>
    </td>
     <td class="view-cell">
      <a>
       <xsl:attribute
         name="href">animal-detail.xsl?-recid=<xsl:value-of select=
         ➥"@record-id"/>
       </xsl:attribute>View</a>
     </td>
      <td class="view-cell">
      <a>
       <xsl:attribute
         name="href">animal-delete-confirm.xsl?-token.recid=<xsl:value-of
         ➥ select="@record-id"/>
       </xsl:attribute>Delete</a>
      </td>
     </tr>
    </xsl:for-each>
   </table>
  </body>
 </html>
 </xsl:template>
</xsl:stylesheet>
```

There's not a great deal that's new in this stylesheet, other than the reformatting into a table layout, and the addition of the Delete link. You'll notice that this link points to a page called animal-delete-confirm.xsl, and passes the record ID of the current record across to that page in a token called -token.recid.

With that in mind, now look at the code for the deletion confirmation page, which is presented in Listing 23.12. This page performs no database actions; it merely confirms that the user wants to perform the specified deletion.

LISTING 23.12   A STYLESHEET FOR A DELETION CONFIRMATION PAGE

```
<?xml version="1.0" encoding="UTF-8"?>
<xsl:stylesheet version="1.0"
 xmlns:fmq="http://www.filemaker.com/xml/query"
  xmlns:fmrs="http://www.filemaker.com/xml/fmresultset"
   xmlns:xsl="http://www.w3.org/1999/XSL/Transform">
    <?xslt-cwp-query params="-grammar=fmresultset&-process"?>
    <xsl:output doctype-public="-//W3C//DTD HTML 3.2 Final//EN"
    indent="yes" method="html"/>
    <xsl:param name="request-query"/>
    <xsl:variable name="rec-to-delete">
```

```
<xsl:value-of select="$request-query/fmq:query/fmq:parameter
➥[@name = '-token.recid']"/>
 </xsl:variable>
 <xsl:template match="/fmrs:fmresultset">
<html>
  <head>
  <title>Confirm Deletion</title>
  <STYLE MEDIA="screen" TYPE="text/css">
   .label {font-weight:800; font-size:9pt;
   font-family:verdana,helvetica,arial; color:#000099;}
  </STYLE>
  </head>
  <body>
  <span class="label">Are you sure you want to delete this record?
     The action cannot be undone.</span>
  <table>
   <tr>
   <td>
    <a href="http://127.0.0.1/fmi/xsl/animal/
    ➥animal-fmresult-view-table.xsl">Cancel</a>
   </td>
   <td>
    <a>
    <xsl:attribute
    name="href">http://127.0.0.1/fmi/xsl/animal/animal-delete-response.xsl?
    ➥-recid=<xsl:value-of select="$rec-to-delete"/>
    </xsl:attribute>Delete</a>
   </td>
   </tr>
  </table>
  </body>
 </html>
  </xsl:template>
</xsl:stylesheet>
```

This stylesheet is a little different from those you've worked with thus far, in that it doesn't perform any database action. This is signified by the statically encoded -process action in the <?xslt-cwp-query?> processing instruction. The -process command tells the XSL processor to process the stylesheet without interacting with FileMaker Server at all. This is useful in stylesheets that don't need to touch a database: It keeps the load on the server from being heavier than it needs to be.

This stylesheet contains code to extract the -token.recid from the query parameters. The code is identical to that in Listing 23.8.

The stylesheet presents an HTML page that asks the user whether he wants to perform the deletion, and gives two choices, each one formatted as an HTML hyperlink. The first link, Cancel, takes the user back to the list view and performs no action. The second, Delete, passes the selected record ID along to a page called animal-delete-response.xsl.

Let's now look at the code for the third page, presented as Listing 23.13.

LISTING 23.13 A STYLESHEET FOR A DELETION RESPONSE PAGE

```
<?xml version="1.0" encoding="UTF-8"?>
<xsl:stylesheet version="1.0"
xmlns:fmrs="http://www.filemaker.com/xml/fmresultset"
xmlns:xsl="http://www.w3.org/1999/XSL/Transform">
  <?xslt-cwp-query params="-grammar=fmresultset&-db=Animal&-lay=web&-delete"?>
  <xsl:output doctype-public="-//W3C//DTD HTML 3.2 Final//EN"
      indent="yes" method="html"/>
  <xsl:template match="/fmrs:fmresultset">
 <xsl:variable name="error-code">
   <xsl:value-of select="fmrs:error/@code"/>
 </xsl:variable>
 <xsl:variable name="doc-title">
   <xsl:choose>
   <xsl:when test="$error-code !=0">Deletion Error</xsl:when>
   <xsl:otherwise>Deletion Successful</xsl:otherwise>
   </xsl:choose>
 </xsl:variable>
 <html>
   <head>
   <title>
     <xsl:value-of select="$doc-title"/>
   </title>
   <STYLE MEDIA="screen" TYPE="text/css">
     .label {font-weight:800; font-size:9pt;
     font-family:verdana,helvetica,arial; color:#000099;}
   </STYLE>
   </head>
   <body>
   <xsl:choose>
     <xsl:when test="$error-code !=0">
     <span class="label">Sorry, there was an error deleting the records.
       (Error code =
     <xsl:value-of select="$error-code"/>)</span>
     </xsl:when>
     <xsl:otherwise>The record was successfully deleted.</xsl:otherwise>
   </xsl:choose> Click <a
 href="http://127.0.0.1/fmi/xsl/animal/animal-fmresult-view-table.xsl">here
   </a> to return to the list. </body>
 </html>
   </xsl:template>
</xsl:stylesheet>
```

There are a few new twists in this stylesheet. By the time this page is reached, the user has confirmed that she does indeed want to perform a deletion. The ID of the record to delete has been passed to the page, this time in the standard -recid query parameter. We've statically coded the rest of the query parameters, including the database name, layout, and the database action, which now is called -delete. The -delete action looks for an inbound -recid, and if it finds it, it tries to delete that record.

There's something new in this stylesheet that really should be present in every stylesheet you write, namely error handling. In general, it's a bad idea to assume that a database operation will succeed. Even for a simple search, the search might contain no valid criteria, or you might misspell a database name, or the connection between the Web Publishing Engine and

FileMaker Server could be down. Any of these circumstances would cause your stylesheet to generate an error.

CAUTION

For stylesheets (or indeed any kind of program!) that are going to be deployed in production, careful error checking is mandatory. You should develop some standard techniques for checking errors in your XSLT-CWP stylesheets.

The error test here is pretty simple. We create an XSL variable called `error-code` and populate it with whatever error code the underlying XML contains. (In the `fmresulset` grammar, this can be found at `/fmrs:fmresultset/fmrs:error/@code`, assuming that the namespace has been abbreviated as `fmrs`.) This code will be either 0 (no error) or some nonzero numeric value, indicating an error of some kind.

Based on the error code, we create another variable, called `doc-title`, because we want to cause the page to appear with different titles, depending on whether the deletion worked.

Finally, in the body of the stylesheet, we use an `<xsl:choose>` construct that checks the error code variable and decides which confirmation message to display. In all cases we present the user with a link back to the list view.

USING STYLESHEETS TO CREATE AND EDIT RECORDS

It's also possible, using techniques similar to those we demonstrated for record deletion, to make stylesheets that can create records (with the `-new` action) or edit them (with the `-edit` action). Space prevents us from giving detailed examples (a full treatment of Custom Web Publishing could fill a book of its own!) but we can discuss them generally.

Both record creation and record editing can be thought of as requiring two different pages. The first page consists of a data entry form where the user either enters or updates some data. As in the deletion example in Listing 23.13, the other page is responsible for actually performing the database action and reporting on the result. (The deletion example contained a third intermediate page where the user was prompted for confirmation of this more dangerous database action.)

To form a better idea of how record creation and editing work, we recommend that you use the Site Assistant to generate a full suite of XSLT stylesheets for a simple database, and then inspect those of the generated stylesheets that handle adding and updating records. The Site Assistant generates three stylesheets that handle these actions: `addrecord.xsl`, `editrecord.xsl`, and `browserecord.xsl`. Here's an overview of what these generated pages do:

- **`addrecord.xsl`**—Displays an HTML form enabling the user to add values for all fields of an animal record. The form's action targets the `browserecord.xsl` page, and sends along the `-db`, `-lay`, and `-grammar` parameters, as well as the `-new` command. Sending the `-new` command ensures that the `browserecord.xsl` stylesheet will take care of creating the new record before trying to display it.

TIP

> We recognize that it's odd to think of the browse page as being the place the *creation* of the record happens, but this is a common occurrence in web programming. Often a destination page needs to do *two* things: take an action, and then report on the result. The `addrecord.xsl` page can't actually create the record because the user's data entries aren't known at the time the page is loaded.

- **`editrecord.xsl`**—This page displays an HTML form populated with the current values of an animal record. This page is accessible only from the `browserecord.xsl` page, and is accessed with a `-find` command and a specific `-recid`. This page actually performs no editing (just as `addrecord.xsl` didn't actually add the record). All this page does is find the record and display the field contents in an HTML form. When the user presses the Save Record button, this sends all the edited information over (once again) to the `browserecord.xsl` page, along with the `-edit` command and the specific `-recid`.

- **`browserecord.xsl`**—This is something of a hybrid page. It can be targeted in two different ways. When the page is targeted from the `addrecord.xsl` page, the URL contains a `-new` command, causing `browserecord.xsl` to create a new record based on the field values that also got sent over from `addrecord.xsl`. When the page is targeted from `editrecord.xsl`, the URL contains an `-edit` command, the specific `-recid` of the record to edit, and the field values for the updated record. Regardless of whether it's performing a `-new` or an `-edit` action, `browserecord.xsl` then displays the new or updated record.

What Happens Where in Web Programming

If you're new to web programming, you may find it confusing that none of these pages seems to do what its name suggests. Again, this is because of the one-step-at-a-time nature of web interactions. When adding a record, you want to perform three steps: specify the data, add the record, view the result. Of those three, only the first can be performed on the Add page. The record can't be created until the user presses Save Record on the Add page. By that time, the user is headed off to the destination page (`browserecord.xsl`), so in addition to displaying the record, `browserecord.xsl` also needs to be responsible for creating it. If you wanted your stylesheet names to follow a "truth in advertising" concept, you could perhaps name them thusly: `addform.xsl`, `editform.xsl`, and `add-or-edit-and-then-browse.xsl`!

We've depicted the relationships among these three pages in Figure 23.19, which should help to clarify how commands and data flow among the three pages.

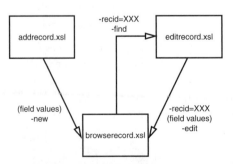

Figure 23.19
The flow of data and commands among the three Site Assistant pages.

OTHER CUSTOM WEB PUBLISHING COMMANDS AND PARAMETERS

In addition to the commands covered so far, XSLT-CWP has a lengthy list of other commands and parameters that you can pass as part of the query string. This section lists and explains them briefly. For a more detailed reference, see this book's companion volume, *FileMaker 8 Functions and Scripts Desk Reference*.

OTHER QUERY COMMANDS

As you know, each Custom Web Publishing URL contains a query string, and that query string can supply at most one database command. Commands covered so far include -find, -findall, -delete, -new, and -edit. Commands are supplied as a single name with no associated value. Table 23.3 contains the full list.

TABLE 23.3   CUSTOM WEB PUBLISHING DATABASE ACTION COMMANDS

Command Name	Command Effect
-dbnames	Returns an XML document containing the names of all databases available on the given FileMaker Server that are enabled for Custom Web Publishing.
-delete	Deletes a specific record. Requires that a -recid parameter be sent to identify the record to delete.
-dup	Duplicates a specific record. Requires that a -recid parameter be sent to identify the record to duplicate.
-edit	Updates a record, according to whatever name-value pairs are passed with the request (generally taken from an HTML form). Requires a -recid parameter indicating which record to edit.
-find	Performs a search, either based on field values sent as name-value pairs, and/or on a specified -recid. Can be modified by optional parameters for sort order, field operators, and logical operators.
-findall	Finds all records in the database.
-findany	Finds a random record.
-layoutnames	Requires a -db parameter to specify a database to query. Returns an XML document with a list of names of all the layouts in the specified database.
-new	Creates a new record based on whatever name-value pairs accompany the request.
-process	Can be used only with XSLT stylesheets, and causes the stylesheet to be processed without any interaction with FileMaker Server.

continues

23

23

TABLE 23.3   CONTINUED

Command Name	Command Effect
-scriptnames	Like -layoutnames, but provides a list of all script names in a database.
-view	Requires that -db and -lay be specified. If the requested grammar is FMPXMLLAYOUT, this command retrieves detailed layout information for the specified layout (this includes things such as the contents of value lists). If the FMPXMLRESULT or fmresultset grammar is specified, this retrieves just the metadata section of the XML document.

OTHER QUERY PARAMETERS

In addition to a single database command, Custom Web Publishing URLs can contain other parameters. Some are mandatory, such as -db, and (generally) -lay and -grammar. Others, such as -lop and -sortfield, are particular to specific commands. Table 23.4 shows a list of the most important ones. For an exhaustive list, see this book's companion volume, *FileMaker Functions and Scripts Desk Reference*.

TABLE 23.4   OTHER CUSTOM WEB PUBLISHING URL PARAMETERS

Parameter Name	Parameter Effect
-db	Name of the database on which to act. Mandatory for all commands except for -dbnames and -process. Do *not* include a filename extension (such as .fp7) when using this parameter.
-encoding	Use this to specify the encoding for an XSLT stylesheet.
-field	Use the -field parameter with the name of a *container* field to request the contents of the container field.
fieldname	Use plain unadorned field names as query parameters when sending data for use with the -new, -find, and -edit commands. See "Performing Specific Searches with CWP URLs," earlier in this chapter.
Fieldname.*op*	Sets the comparison operator for *fieldname* when performing a search. (See the table of operators earlier in this chapter.)
-grammar	For XSLT stylesheets, specifies the grammar of the underlying XML.
-lay	Specifies which layout (and hence which table context) to use for the request. Mandatory with all commands except –process, –dbnames, –layoutnames, and –scriptnames.
-lay.response	Enables you to use one layout for processing the command contained in a URL, and a different layout for generating the XML that comprises the response. For example, you might want to process your request (an Add, say) via a layout with certain hidden fields on it, but process the response via a layout that omitted those fields. Data could thus be added to the hidden fields, but that hidden data would then be omitted from the response.

Parameter Name	Parameter Effect
-lop	Used with the -find command, specifies whether to treat the search as an *and* search or an *or* search.
-max	Used with the -find command, specifies the maximum number of records to return. Sending a parameter of -max=all permits all records to be returned. (This is the default.)
-modid	FileMaker's modification ID is an internal number that increments every time a record is changed. Use the -modid parameter to ensure that the record you're editing has not been edited since the time you last checked the modification ID. This is useful for prohibiting different users' changes from overwriting each other.
-recid	Specifies which record should be affected by a given action. This parameter is mandatory with -edit, -delete, and -dup, and can also be used with -find.
-script	Use this parameter to run a FileMaker script during the processing of the request. By default the script runs after the query command and any sorting have occurred. For example, you run a script in your FileMaker solution after each new record is created, you can create a URL with the -new command that also includes the -script parameter for that post-creation script.
-script.prefind	If your command URL involves any kind of find request, use this parameter to request a script to be run before the specified search takes place.
-script-presort	If your command URL involves any kind of find request and a sort, use this parameter to request that a script be run after the specified search takes place, but before sorting.
-skip	Used with the various search commands, specifies that records should be returned starting elsewhere than at the first record. If you specify -skip=10, the records are returned starting with the eleventh record.
-sortfield.[1-9]	Specify any of up to nine different fields to sort by.
-sortorder.[1-9]	For a given sort field, specify whether it should sort ascending or descending.
-styletype	Used in conjunction with -stylehref. Use these two parameters to specify a client-side stylesheet for additional processing. The most common choices would likely be CSS and XSLT. For these choices, you would specify -styletype=text/css or -styletype=text/xsl.
-stylehref	Use this in conjunction with -styletype to specify the location of a stylesheet for client-side processing. Note that this option and the previous one are effective only when the user's client (generally a browser) supports some form of client-side stylesheet processing.
-token.[string]	Use to pass additional data from one stylesheet to another. See "Using Tokens to Share Data Between Stylesheets," earlier in this chapter, for more detailed information.

23

ABOUT THE FILEMAKER XSLT EXTENSIONS

All XSL transformations need to be performed by an XSL *processor* of some kind. An XSL processor should conform to some standard flavor of XSL (currently 1.0). But XSL processors are also free to add their own extensions; like proprietary extensions to web browsers, this practice stands to increase the range of actions you can perform with a given XSL stylesheet, but risks the creation of stylesheets that work well with only one XSL processor. Stylesheets for CWP work well in only a FileMaker environment anyway, so this is not a serious concern.

The Web Publishing Engine's XSLT processor obviously adds some extensions because it's capable of triggering FileMaker database actions. But it also has a host of other extended capabilities. Some of these you've seen already, such as the capability to access all the parameters of the HTTP request that invoked the stylesheet. With similar syntax, you can get access to the user's IP address, username, and password, as well as the address of the server from which the stylesheet is being served.

FileMaker also provides XSL extensions to handle a host of other common web programming tasks. There's a rich library of string-manipulation functions, as well as a set of functions to send email, a set of functions to create and maintain user sessions, and functions to deal with HTTP headers and cookies. Unfortunately, a full treatment of all these areas is beyond the scope of this book, but the documentation that accompanies FileMaker Server Advanced describes these functions fairly thoroughly.

The point to be aware of here is that FileMaker's XSL implementation is actually a full-featured web programming language as well, and has many of the features of powerful modern web programming languages such as Perl, PHP, or JSP. After you're familiar with the basics of combining XSL stylesheets with FileMaker database actions, you can delve further into the other rich features of the CWP XSL implementation.

ABOUT SESSIONS

If you've read Chapter 21, "Instant Web Publishing," you've already read some discussion of the concept of *sessions*. To recap briefly: The connection between a web browser and the Web Publishing Engine is very much *unlike* the connection between a client copy of FileMaker and the FileMaker Server. FileMaker Server can at any time reach out and push data to any connected client. It knows at all times what its connected clients are, where they are in the system, and at what network address they can be found. A web server, by contrast, retains no memory of a client from one connection to the next.

This is not a good thing for database work! I need my website to remember the contents of my shopping cart as I shop around the site. This is possible only with *session management*. Session management is generally a middleware feature. Web programming languages such as PHP and JSP offer the programmer different means of managing sessions. In general, under session management, each incoming web request is associated with a key of some kind. The key may be passed in the URL (if you've ever seen a long ugly string like `?jsession=A9238Ajasdj9mAEd` in a web URL, odds are you're looking at a session key), or it may be passed behind the scenes in an HTTP cookie. (FileMaker's Custom Web Publishing session implementation lets you choose between these two methods.)

Whatever the means, the middleware on the web server has a way of associating that key to other information about the client. In the shopping cart example, the key might hook up to a database record that stores the actual contents of your cart as you navigate around the site.

FileMaker's Custom Web Publishing, like other middleware solutions, enables you to manage sessions for your users behind the scenes. You would use this capability any time you wanted to store important information about the user that would be carried from screen to screen. An experienced HTML programmer could get away with passing a lot of data from page to page via the URL, or via an HTML form. But there are limits to the amount of data than can be passed by URL, and there are limits to the *type* of data that can be passed by either method—generally just plain text strings.

FileMaker's session implementation is quite elegant because it allows you to pass around XML fragments behind the scenes. This allows for much richer data structures than you could pass with regular HTML.

In addition to passing around XML information by means of sessions, FileMaker's session implementation allows you to keep track of the state of the FileMaker client session as well. This is the distinction described previously in the "Setting Up the Server-Side Components for CWP" section: The XSLT configuration screen allows you to enable or disable database sessions. Database sessions are an additional capability on top of regular session management. In addition to "sessionizing" user information of your choice, they enable you to also keep track of FileMaker-specific information such as global fields or the current script state.

So, for example, if your stylesheets modify a global field, and you have database sessions enabled, the global field retains its new value, for the specific current user, as that user navigates from page to page. Or, if you used a script to change some aspect of the user's state (for example, by using the `Relogin` script step to change the user's privileges), this state is maintained across sequential requests.

Session management is a large topic and we don't have space to do it justice. The FileMaker documentation helps you get a better grip on the specific functions and commands that Custom Web Publishing uses for session management. As for the issue of whether to configure the Custom Web Publishing to use database sessions, your decision will depend on how you construct your XSLT-CWP solution. If you intend to make heavy use of global fields, or call scripts from your stylesheets that would change the state of a user's privileges, you should configure the Web Publishing Engine to enable database sessions.

TROUBLESHOOTING

GETTING THE RIGHT PRIVILEGES

I can connect to my Web Publishing Engine and FileMaker Server via the Administration Console, but I don't see the databases I expect to see.

Make sure that for every database you want to make available via XML-CWP or XSLT-CWP, you have attached the appropriate extended privilege (`fmxml` or `fmxslt`) to at least one privilege set.

DEALING WITH FIREWALLS

My web requests mysteriously time out, as though something were blocking them.

If you can get to the Administration Console, but your Custom Web Publishing URL requests appear to get no response, you may have a firewall in your way. If you suspect a firewall may be involved, consult your network administrator to explore this question. If it turns out that your machines are set up such that your web server is on one side of a firewall, and your Web Publishing Engine machine or FileMaker Server machine is on the other, you need to open certain ports in the firewall. The rules are these:

- When the web server and Administration Console are on one machine, and the Web Publishing Engine on another, traffic must be able to flow between the two machines on ports 16016 and 16018.
- When the Web Publishing Engine is on a different machine from FileMaker Server, traffic must be able to flow between the two machines on port 5003.

DEALING WITH SPACES

The Web Publishing Engine doesn't seem to see my entire URL. I enter a long URL and the web server appears to truncate it and reports that the shorter URL can't be found.

If (despite the cautionary notes in this chapter) you have left any of your databases, fields, or layouts with spaces (or indeed any other nonalphanumeric characters) in their names, your Custom Web Publishing URLs may very well break. If a web server or browser encounters a space in a URL, it might assume the URL ends there. Other nonalphanumerics have different but equally irritating effects.

If you must work with URLs with spaces in them, you can get by with replacing all spaces with the string `%20` whenever you need to write out a URL. Your stylesheet then might generate an HTML page with the following link:

```
<a href="http://192.168.101.100/fmi/xsl/process-this.xsl?
➥-db=Too%20Many%20Spaces&-lay=Spaces%20Here%too&-findall
```

If at all possible, we strongly encourage you to use only alphanumeric characters for database, layout, and field names and to avoid the use of whitespace. Extend this caution to script names if you are planning to call scripts from the Web.

FILEMAKER EXTRA: ABOUT THE CUSTOM WEB PUBLISHING TOOLS

FileMaker Server Advanced comes with a couple of extremely useful tools for kick-starting your work with FileMaker XSL. These are the CDML Converter and the Site Assistant. They're not installed automatically—you need to install them separately if you want to use them.

The CDML Converter

The CDML Converter is designed to do what its name implies. It does its best to take a set of FileMaker-based web pages written in CDML (which was the custom Web publishing option in versions of FileMaker Pro before version 7) and convert these files to a set of XSLT-CWP stylesheets. As of FileMaker Pro 7, CDML is no longer an available web publishing option for FileMaker, so if you want to use an existing CDML solution with FileMaker 7 or later, you need to convert it somehow, and the CDML Converter is probably the best place to start.

The CDML Converter converts all your CDML files into XSLT-CWP stylesheets. A reasonable conversion path exists for most CDML constructs, but not all CDML is converted correctly. There are, for example, a few CDML commands that the Web Publishing Engine no longer supports, such as `-dbopen` and `-dbclose`. CDML also, like XSLT-CWP, supported custom functions for sending email, but these tags won't be converted correctly and you'll probably need to rewrite your email functionality with the new XSLT-CWP tools.

As the CDML Converter converts your CDML files, it writes out a conversion log describing the conversion process. If there were any errors during conversion, the Converter writes an entry into the log describing the error. It also adds a comment to the affected XSLT file, if possible, pointing you to the exact location and description of the error.

The documentation that accompanies FileMaker Server Advanced has a thorough description of the CDML conversion process, and a detailed list of all potential trouble areas. To ensure the smoothest conversion of your CDML files, we recommend you read the conversion specification carefully before beginning. Take note of any potential trouble areas. The documents offer specific guidance in rewriting any CDML trouble spots.

Whether or not you do any rewriting, it's a good idea to verify that your CDML files actually work (under FileMaker 6 or whichever version they're built for). After you have a working CDML system that you've vetted for possible conversion problems, make a copy of the system and try out the CDML Converter. From there, you'll want to refer to the conversion log, inline comments, and the detailed conversion documentation to iron out any remaining difficulties.

The Site Assistant

The Site Assistant is likely to have much wider application for you than the CDML Converter. Think of the Site Assistant as an XSLT wizard of sorts. You point the Site Assistant to a hosted database, tell it what kinds of stylesheets you want to generate (search, edit, summary report, and so on), and where to put the files. It then generates the files, and you're free to use them as is, or modify them further. If so instructed, the Site Assistant generates a home page with links to the different stylesheets, and can add navigational elements to each page as well. If you have the Site Assistant generate a full suite of pages for a database, you'll end up with a fairly full-featured little website that allows you do almost anything you need to via XSLT-CWP.

Using the Site Assistant is simple. When run, the Site Assistant asks to be pointed to a running Web Publishing Engine. After you give it the Web Publishing Engine's address, it queries the Web Publishing Engine for a list of hosted databases that have XSL publishing enabled. You then choose one, and continue to the next screen. This first step is shown in Figure 23.20.

Figure 23.20
Choosing a database for use with the Site Assistant.

After you've picked your file, you're presented with a screen that allows you to choose up to seven different kinds of stylesheets. The screen is shown in Figure 23.21.

Figure 23.21
Choosing which stylesheets you'd like the Site Assistant to generate.

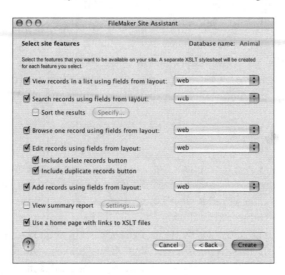

Most of these choices involve specifying a layout against which the stylesheet should run. Remember that this also amounts to choosing the affected *table* because each layout's table context determines the target table.

There are a few pitfalls to be aware of when using the Site Assistant. The generation process really works well only when all your actions involve the same base table. If your database contains multiple tables, you need to make sure that all the layouts you reference are based on the same table.

There are also a few mutual dependencies among stylesheets. If you choose Search Records Using Fields From, you should also select View Records in List. The generated search stylesheet tries to use the list stylesheet to display its search results, but unless you ask the Site Assistant to generate that stylesheet, it won't exist.

In addition to generating a stylesheet for each of your chosen options, the Site Assistant generates a utilities file called, appropriately enough, `utilities.xsl`. Even if you never use the Site Assistant again, it's worth your while to generate this file and inspect it carefully. It includes a number of powerful techniques for working with XSLT-CWP. If you can thoroughly understand the XSLT techniques contained in this file, you'll have some very useful additions to your XSLT-CWP toolkit.

In general, we recommend that you try to get to the point where you write your own files from scratch. The one place we feel otherwise is with subsummary reports. Subsummary reporting is famously irritating to do in XSL—so much so that the XSL 2.0 proposal contains specific features for making it easier. For subsummary reporting, we recommend you rely heavily on the files generated by the Site Assistant. Learn how the selected options translate into the final HTML page, and learn which pieces of the page are specific to the Site Assistant's mini-site functionality (which you can replace) and which ones are at the core of the report.

One caveat, though: The Site Assistant's generated subsummary reports support only one level of summary grouping. To create reports that are two or more levels deep, you need to read the wizard-generated files carefully, understand the applied techniques, and extend them to your multilevel report.

Learning How to Program with CWP

In general, we're not big fans of wizards. They tend to both obscure the way things actually work and impose a limit on the flexibility and power of the underlying tools. We find them to be most useful as a basis for quickly generating an example that you can then dissect by hand to see how things actually work.

One danger with wizards, though, is that because they're automated, they often tend to assume that you're *not* going to inspect or modify the results. So they often use quite advanced techniques to generate pleasing functionality. Think of how most typical graphical web design tools generate JavaScript rollovers: The rollovers work beautifully, but the tool usually generates some extremely dense JavaScript. If you want to use the tool's output without modifications, you're in great shape. If you want to use the output as a basis for learning, you need to deal with some advanced code.

This is more or less the case with the XSL stylesheets generated by the Site Assistant. The generated stylesheets are quite powerful, and are packed with complex functionality—especially the record list view and the subsummary reports. But they do *not* generate simple XSL! You need to have a good grasp of intermediate-to-advanced XSL to be able to read the output.

But of course, you need to be a strong XSL programmer in any case to get the best use out of Custom Web Publishing. If you're an XML/XSL novice, here's the learning path we'd recommend:

1. Write some simple queries that use plain old XML-CWP. In other words, get accustomed to writing the query strings that the Web Publishing Engine uses to bring back FileMaker data. Experiment with various search criteria and sort fields.

2. Write some simple stylesheets to process search results. We recommend beginning with stylesheets that display search output in a variety of list formats.

3. Generate a set of stylesheets with the Site Assistant. Pay special attention to the files that perform database actions other than searches. Read and understand the `utilities.xsl` file.

4. Experiment with adding capabilities to the Site Assistant files.

5. Read up on the advanced features of XSLT-Custom Web Publishing in the supplied documentation and expand your knowledge. Practice with features such as email, cookies, and sessions.

Custom Web Publishing is a rich programming environment, and this chapter only scratches the surface. As you progress with CSP, you'll want to deepen your mastery of XSL and XML by reading, experimenting, and participating in online forums.

Deploying a FileMaker Solution

CHAPTER **24**

DEPLOYING AND EXTENDING FILEMAKER

In this chapter

FILEMAKER DEPLOYMENT OPTIONS

One of the strengths of FileMaker is that a solution can be deployed in various ways. With this flexibility, FileMaker can fit many different needs, and it can change and adapt as your organization evolves. This chapter offers a brief overview of the ways a FileMaker database can be deployed. Several of these methods are discussed in depth in their own chapters elsewhere in the book, but we bring them all together here to give you a broad view of the deployment landscape. We also go into detail here on a couple of specific deployment possibilities, those surrounding the creation of runtime solutions and the use of plug-ins.

Your deployment decisions depend on a number of factors. How many users will need access to the database? Where are they located? Are they all on the same local area network? Do other systems or applications need access to the data? Some of the deployment decisions may involve additional investment in hardware, or learning new skills. Some deployment options depend on others. There's no way to do Custom Web Publishing, for example, without using FileMaker Server Advanced. Finally, most of the deployment options are not mutually exclusive. You might have both FileMaker Pro clients and web clients accessing the same files hosted by FileMaker Server.

SINGLE USER

The most basic way of deploying a solution is as a single-user application. In any organization that uses a lot of FileMaker, there are likely dozens or hundreds of single-user databases scattered on computers throughout the organization. The typical single-user solution is something that a knowledge worker cooked up to meet an ad hoc need. Perhaps it's a database for the office football pool or to keep track of gifts from a baby shower. Maybe someone needed a tool to clean up the ugly data sent by a customer. In many cases, the creator of such a database could have met the need with another tool, such as Microsoft Excel, but chose FileMaker Pro instead because of its simplicity and attractive user interface.

Single-user solutions like these are typically not well planned out, nor constructed according to rigorous development standards. These databases usually grow organically, have little or no security, and have sparse or idiosyncratic user interfaces. Single-user databases are typically a developer's first foray into the world of FileMaker; these solutions frequently exhibit the evolving skills of the creator.

There are a few risks to be aware of with single-user solutions. First, it's unlikely that such solutions have been integrated into a rigorous backup strategy. If you, or users in your organization, store important data in or fulfill important business needs through single-user solutions, be sure to periodically burn a backup on CD or copy it to an external device, or to some networked volume that you're sure is being backed up on a periodic schedule.

Another common risk of single-user deployments is that they may not be suitable for evolution into workgroup- or organization-wide solutions. It's trivial to share the files peer-to-peer, or to move them to a FileMaker Server for hosting, but if a solution was originally designed with only a single user in mind, you may end up with a difficult-to-maintain and/or fragile solution.

→ For more information on good multiuser design, **see** Chapter 11, "Developing for Multiuser Deployment," **p. 307**.

PEER-TO-PEER HOSTING

Peer-to-peer deployment enables a small number of workers to share a solution, without the cost of setting up and maintaining a dedicated server. You can turn any single-user solution into a peer-to-peer solution simply by turning on FileMaker networking and adding the fmapp extended privilege to one or more privilege sets.

→ To learn more about extended privileges, **see** Chapter 12, "Implementing Security," **p. 325**.

Peer-to-peer deployment is often found in small organizations or departments in which only a handful of users need access to shared data. The database usually physically lives on one person's machine or on a file server. The first person to open the file is known as the *host*; other users who access it are *clients*. Provided that they have proper privileges for the file, both the host and clients can modify field definitions, access privileges, scripts, and layouts. Development teams therefore often use peer-to peer sharing during construction of large systems.

Several of the risks of single-user deployments also pertain to peer-to-peer deployments. Files are likely to be backed up sporadically rather than systematically; development standards are frequently nonexistent or not enforced. Solutions that are shared peer-to-peer often fly under the radar of IT departments as well, which might be a good or bad thing depending on your perspective. It's nice for you, as the creator or user of a system, to be in control of your own project, but our experience is that IT departments generally prefer that shared systems be centrally controlled and managed.

Using peer-to-peer sharing, you are restricted to sharing up to 10 databases with up to five concurrent users. If you need to expand beyond these constraints, you need to use FileMaker Server to deploy your solution.

CAUTION

> Because the host of a peer-to-peer shared solution is a user's workstation, you may face stability and performance concerns. For instance, the user's machine may crash, she might need to disconnect clients to reboot her machine, or she may perform actions in other applications that cause slow client performance. FileMaker Server is the remedy to all these problems.

FILEMAKER SERVER

FileMaker Server is the correct deployment option for most business-critical solutions. Databases hosted by FileMaker Server are always open, and can therefore be accessed by guests without concern that the host is unavailable (which is a concern with peer-to-peer sharing). FileMaker Server allows access for up to 250 concurrent FileMaker Pro clients.

FileMaker Server also has several built-in tools to aid with database administration. For instance, you can (and should!) schedule regular backups. You can also do things such as disconnect idle guests to free up resources and enable clients to automatically download updates of plug-ins. Data exchanged between FileMaker Server and clients can be encrypted with SSL, making FileMaker Server a secure deployment option as well.

→ For more information on these and other features of FileMaker Server, **see** Chapter 25, "FileMaker Server and Server Advanced," **p. 779**.

The connection between FileMaker Server and FileMaker Pro clients is network intensive, so this deployment option is most appropriate when all the clients are connected to the server via a fast local area network (LAN). Wide area network (WAN) client connections are possible, but performance may not be sufficient to meet users' needs and expectations. In cases in which remote users need access to your FileMaker data, you may need to consider web publishing, or using a remote access tool such as Citrix/Terminal Services (discussed later in this chapter) as part of your deployment strategy.

WEB PUBLISHING

A FileMaker database can be deployed to web users in several ways. One method is to simply export data as either HTML or XML so that it can be statically accessed through a web server. For dynamic interaction with your database, the deployment options are Instant Web Publishing (IWP) and Custom Web Publishing (CWP).

Both FileMaker Pro client and FileMaker Server Advanced can provide access to databases via IWP. FileMaker Pro supports up to 5 concurrent IWP connections; FileMaker Server Advanced supports up to 100. In both cases, setup is straightforward. With IWP, your existing FileMaker layouts are dynamically rendered as web pages. Most scripts will function correctly as well, meaning that designing a solution for IWP deployment requires no web programming skills. Because of the browser restrictions for using IWP, we don't recommend using IWP for public websites. It's a more proper deployment option for remote users who would otherwise be connecting to your databases via a slow FileMaker Pro client connection.

→ For more information on Instant Web Publishing, **see** Chapter 21, "Instant Web Publishing," **p. 633**.

Custom Web Publishing is an appropriate deployment option when you need to integrate FileMaker data into an existing website, to provide FileMaker data to other applications in the manner of a web service, or when you simply require more flexibility than IWP affords. CWP requires that a database be hosted by FileMaker Server Advanced. You must also set up a Web Publishing Engine and have a suitable web server available (Apache or Internet Information Server). Using CWP, appropriately formatted HTTP requests can be interpreted by the Web Publishing Engine and passed on to FileMaker Server. The server responds to these requests via XML, which can be transformed into HTML with an XSL stylesheet or simply parsed by some other middleware application. Unlike IWP, CWP requires some knowledge and experience with web application development.

→ For more information on Custom Web Publishing, **see** Chapter 23, "Custom Web Publishing," **p. 699**. For more information on Web Services, **see** Chapter 22, "FileMaker and Web Services," **p. 669**.

ODBC/JDBC

ODBC (which stands for Open Database Connectivity) and JDBC are standards that were developed to facilitate data exchange between disparate data sources. FileMaker can access remote data via ODBC/JDBC (sometimes referred to jointly by FileMaker as "xDBC"), and it can act also as an ODBC/JDBC data source for other applications. The latter is a deployment option you should consider if you need your FileMaker data to feed other applications in your organization.

TIP

> ODBC and JDBC are standards, not languages or applications. Different applications are compliant with these standards to varying degrees. SQL (Structured Query Language) is the language used to exchange data via ODBC/JDBC. The term "xDBC" is used for convenience in the FileMaker documentation to refer to both technologies jointly.

24

To make FileMaker data available via xDBC, you must be using the Windows version of FileMaker Pro or FileMaker Server Advanced. Configuring a database to be accessible via xDBC is similar to configuring it to be accessible via the Web: You need to add the `fmxdbc` extended privilege to one or more privilege sets, and you need to turn on ODBC/JDBC sharing. After doing this, you need to set up data source names (DSNs) for other applications to use when accessing your FileMaker databases. After everything has been configured properly, other applications can send SQL queries to FileMaker.

You might want to consider xDBC as part of your deployment strategy for many reasons. For instance, you might set up report templates and charts in Microsoft Excel that pull data from FileMaker via ODBC. Similarly, you can design Java applets that interact with FileMaker databases via JDBC. Other potential uses include integration with JSP pages, ASP or ASP.NET pages, and query tools.

→ For more information on using ODBC/JDBC with FileMaker, **see** Chapter 20, "Exporting Data from FileMaker," **p. 595**, and Chapter 19, "Importing Data into FileMaker Pro," **p. 567**.

CITRIX/TERMINAL SERVICES

As discussed previously, the connection between FileMaker Server and FileMaker Pro clients is network intensive. Users outside your local area network may not find client/server performance to be satisfactory for their needs.

One solution to the remote user deployment dilemma is to use remote access software, such as Citrix and Terminal Services. The hardware and software licensing costs for such a solution are not inconsequential, but neither are the performance benefits it provides. Remote users establish a network connection to the Citrix/Terminal Services server, which in turn opens a FileMaker Pro client connection to FileMaker Server. The only data flowing between the remote user and the Citrix server are screen refresh information, keystrokes, and mouse clicks. Because the Citrix server and the FileMaker Server are located on the same local area network, the client performance is outstanding.

24

TIP

> There are several less expensive remote access options you may want to consider, including Timbuktu, PCAnywhere, and gotomypc.com. These don't offer all the features of Citrix/Terminal Services, such as local printer mapping, nor do they allow for multiple concurrent remote connections. On a budget, though, or for the occasional remote access need, these are excellent tools.

RUNTIME SOLUTIONS

For some solutions, the best deployment option is as a bound, runtime solution. A *runtime solution* can be distributed to users who can run it without having a copy of FileMaker Pro on their machine. Runtime solutions are created with the Developer Utilities, which are available only in FileMaker Pro 8 Advanced.

A typical example of a solution that might be deployed as a runtime solution is a product catalog. Perhaps you've developed a gorgeous FileMaker database of all your products, and you want to send it to all your customers on a CD. You could create a runtime version of the files and do just this. Your customers would be able to browse and search for items, maybe even print or email orders to you, all without having a copy of FileMaker on their machines.

The downside to runtime deployment is often version control. After you distribute stand-alone copies to myriad users, if you need to make a change to the solution, you might need to distribute new copies to those users. Moving data from the old solution to the new solution can be a bit troublesome, for both you and your users. If version control of distributed solutions is likely to be a problem for you, consider web-enabling your database or providing remote access via Citrix/Terminal Services as an alternative deployment method.

TIP

> If you need to distribute a runtime solution to both Mac and PC users, you must bind a separate version for each platform, and you therefore need access to both a Mac and a PC during development.

Runtime solutions are primarily designed to be run as single-user applications. A runtime solution can't be shared peer-to-peer. You can, however, host a runtime solution with FileMaker Server; users would need FileMaker Pro to access it, just as they would for any other hosted file. This does take away one of the main points of a runtime solution, which is the capability to distribute it widely to users who don't have FileMaker—but it may be useful if you want to create a solution with two distribution models. One model would be to release it as a standalone, non-networkable solution, the other to release it as a networkable solution that does require FileMaker Pro and FileMaker Server.

Another deployment option that's available via the Developer Utilities is to create a *kiosk* from your FileMaker solution. When run as a kiosk, a solution takes up the entire screen. Users don't even have access to the Status Area or any menus, which means you must provide buttons for every action they might perform.

The runtime options are discussed in more detail in the section "Creating a Runtime Application," later in this chapter.

Deploying to Handheld Devices

If you have users who are on the road a lot, or who are just hooked on handheld devices, a deployment option you may want to consider is FileMaker Mobile. FileMaker Mobile enables you to easily synchronize data between a FileMaker database and a handheld device.

When a database is deployed to FileMaker Mobile, you can specify which fields should be available and how they should appear to users (for example, text field, check box field, pop-up list). None of your FileMaker layouts or scripts is actually available on the handheld device.

FileMaker Mobile is limited in certain ways in comparison to FileMaker Pro. Databases deployed to a handheld may contain only a single table, with no more than 50 fields and no more than 5,000 records, and text and number fields are limited to 2,000 and 255 characters of data.

FileMaker Mobile is not the only option for using handheld devices with FileMaker. Citrix makes an ICA client for Pocket PC, which means that if you have a wireless network available to you, you can use a FileMaker solution directly from a handheld device. The display on a handheld device has a different form factor than regular monitors, so you'd likely need to design handheld-friendly layouts.

A final option for handheld deployment is via the Web. Using Custom Web Publishing and wireless web protocols such as WML and WAP, you can design handheld solutions that interact with FileMaker databases and run in a web browser on a wireless device.

Customized Deployment Options

FileMaker Pro Advanced allows you to perform a range of functions on a grouped set of files; you'll find them in the Developer Utilities under the Tools menu. This function of FileMaker Pro Advanced focuses largely on modifying your files in preparation for specific types of deployment. These options vary from renaming files to building a kiosk. Review Figure 24.1 for an overview of the options available.

The mechanics of the dialog are fairly simple: Add all the files in a given solution to the dialog (they need to be closed for you to do so) and then specify a destination project folder. FileMaker creates new files anytime you use these utilities, so it needs to know where to put them.

You can opt to save your Solution Utility settings. Often solutions require multiple Developer Utilities settings. By using the Load Settings and Save Settings buttons, you'll be able to save yourself the trouble of having to reenter all the various settings. This is quite helpful: This dialog includes a number of options, and development and testing often requires running through the process multiple times.

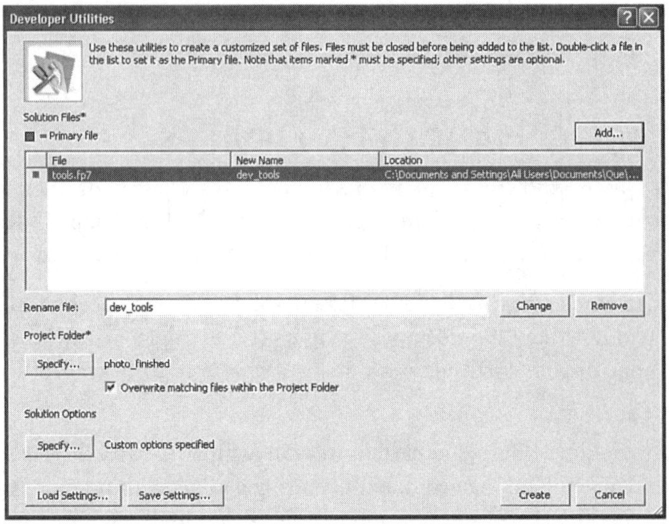

Figure 24.1
In the Developer
Utilities dialog you're
able to work with a
group of files and
apply various options
or rename them.

RENAMING FILES

This might sound trivial, but don't let the apparent simplicity here deceive you. Multifile solutions in FileMaker depend on filenames to maintain internal references. If you arbitrarily rename one of the files in a given solution via your operating system, FileMaker prompts you with a File could not be found error when it next tries to resolve a reference to that file. You risk breaking table occurrence references, script references, value list references, and more by renaming your files manually. We very strongly recommend against manually renaming files.

TIP

> If you run across a file that shows signs of having been incorrectly renamed or lost altogether, the Database Design Report is a great place to turn to root out "file missing" problems.

→ To explore issues of file references in converting files from prior versions of FileMaker Pro, **see** "Fix File References," **p. 548**.

Rename your files by using the Developer Utilities dialog. Notice, as in Figure 24.2, that you will need to add all the files for a given solution to the dialog. This is important: You need to add both the file you want to rename and all those files that reference it. Then set new names for however many files you need to change. For example, suppose that you have a system composed of 10 linked files. Load all the files into the Developer Utilities dialog.

Rename just the one file you intend to rename. When you click Create, FileMaker generates new files in your destination project folder, leaving the old files unchanged. In the 10-file example, the one file would have its named changed, and all 10 files would have any references to that file updated to use the new name.

Figure 24.2
The files in this example have been prepared for renaming.

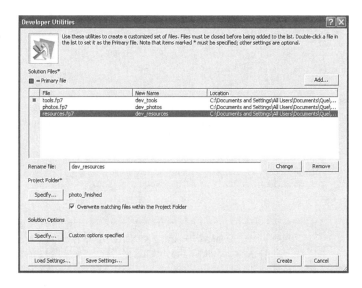

 To learn how to manually address filename and reference problems, refer to "File Reference Errors" in the "Troubleshooting" section at the end of this chapter.

SOLUTION OPTIONS

Using the Specify button under Solution Options, you'll find a range of actions that FileMaker Pro Advanced can perform as it creates a new solution (and a new set of files). All these options generally pertain to readying your files for deployment; you would not necessarily use them during development, but rather at the end when you're preparing files for hand-off to users (see Figure 24.3).

 If you've used the Developer Utilities in previous versions of FileMaker (FileMaker Developer 7 and before), you'll notice that three of the solution options are missing: Custom Scripts Menu Name, Custom Script for Help Menu Item, and Custom Script for About Menu Item. These features have been superseded by the new Custom Menus development feature in FileMaker Pro 8 Advanced.

CREATING A RUNTIME APPLICATION

FileMaker Pro Advanced enables you to bind a set of files into a *runtime application*—one that includes the FileMaker engine and does not require that the user buy a copy of FileMaker Pro to make use of the solution you've built. This is a great way to create distributable software with FileMaker Pro, and FileMaker, Inc.'s licensing terms allow you to do so without further obligation.

Figure 24.3
Solution options enable you to prepare a set of files for deployment with options beyond simply posting to a server.

> **NOTE**
>
> FileMaker Pro Advanced's licensing details for runtime solutions can be found in the Licensing PDF you'll find in the root folder of your FileMaker Pro 8 Advanced installation.

You'll need to keep some conditions in mind. A bound runtime version does not support further development; a runtime solution does not include Layout mode, ScriptMaker, and the Define Database functions, thus disallowing further editing of the files. A runtime solution works only with the files bound with it; it may not be linked to other databases, either other runtimes or files hosted via FileMaker Server. Finally, a runtime solution is single-user only. If end users want to share the files, they need to turn to FileMaker Server and standard copies of FileMaker Pro.

> **NOTE**
>
> It's sometimes thought that a runtime file is necessarily read-only, but this isn't the case. Assuming that the database user has the correct permissions, a runtime can be used to create, edit, and delete records just as with the regular FileMaker client. (The misconception may stem from the fact that bound files are often distributed on CD, and such files are indeed read-only until they're copied off the CD to a writable medium such as a hard drive.)

Let's look in more detail at the process of creating a runtime solution. As with any other use of the Developer Utilities, you'll first need to choose the files you want to include in the bound solution, and load them into the Developer Utilities dialog window. Next, specify a project folder where the resulting solution files will be written (in their own directory).

Next you'll need to click Specify under Solution Options, and then choose a series of binding options, as shown in Figure 24.4.

Figure 24.4
When creating a runtime solution, there are several options you must first set.

Here's a brief rundown on these options:

- **Runtime Name**—The runtime name will be used to name the resulting solution directory, and it will also be the name of the master file created for the runtime (more details on the master file follow this list).

- **Extension**—To distinguish the runtime files from regular FileMaker files (which in many senses they still are), the binding process adds a custom file extension to each of the solution files. You may choose your own extension; otherwise, a default extension of .USR will be applied.

  The extension for FileMaker-bound runtime solutions determines, in both Mac OS X and Windows, what application becomes associated with your individual solution files—which by definition is the runtime application you're in the process of creating. These file extensions simply help identify the application that should open your files and differentiate them from other FileMaker Pro documents.

  Mac OS X uses four-character extensions (creator codes), and FileMaker simply inserts an uppercase *F* after the first character (usr becomes uFsr). On Mac OS X, we recommend registering your creator code with Apple: http://developer.apple.com/dev/cftype/find.html.

  On Windows a somewhat incomplete check can be found directly via http://shell.windows.com/fileassoc/0409/xml/redir.asp?Ext=fp7 (where the last three letters are the extension you want to investigate). Another source of information can be found at http://filext.com/.

- **Bindkey**—To have the runtime application recognize its associated files, the *bind key* in a given file needs to match the bind key of the application. This simple pairing ensures that a given application will authorize use of specific FileMaker Pro files. Notice in Figure 24.4 that FileMaker Advanced inserts a timestamp by default as a bind key.

> **TIP**
>
> To replace or add a file to a solution that has already been bound, use the same bind key when preparing that new file, and users will be able to drop the file in question directly into their solution folders. You need not replace the entire solution.

Consider cases in which you'd want to be able to add files to a solution to upgrade functionality or address bugs. This introduces the complex issue of upgrade paths in a FileMaker Pro solution. You need to remember that after someone begins using your solution, he will be adding and storing data in your files. If you were to simply replace those files with no concern for exporting or managing that data, users would open their applications and discover an empty shell waiting again for the first records to be created.

- **Closing Splash Screen**—When users close your solution, they will see a small closing splash screen. You can determine how long the screen will be visible (2–12 seconds).
- **Custom Image**—By default, the closing splash screen shows a FileMaker logo. You can instead include an image of your own for display on the closing splash screen. If you choose to include a custom closing image, size it for 382×175 pixels at 72 dpi. JPEG and GIF both work best in cross-platform environments; we don't recommend any other file type.

After you've chosen your solution options, you can click OK to start the process of creating the solution. The solution files are written into a directory with the same name as the runtime name you established previously. It's a common misconception about the runtime binding process that the result is one single, monolithic file. Try the process for yourself and you'll see that this is not the case (remember, it creates a new set of solution files, so no need to worry about hurting your current files). Sample results for Mac OS X and Windows are shown in Figures 24.5 and 24.6. On the Mac you'll get a fairly sparse file set, whereas with Windows you'll get dozens of supporting DLLs. Don't be surprised by the differences between the two platforms, and keep the following caution in mind.

> **CAUTION**
>
> Creating a bound runtime solution is a platform-specific process. A solution bound on the Mac OS cannot be used on Windows, and vice versa. The binding also needs to occur on the target platform. To create a bound solution for the Mac OS, you'll need to run FileMaker Pro 8 Advanced on a Mac, and likewise for Windows. It's not possible to create both Mac and Windows runtimes in a single pass, from a single machine.

Figure 24.5
A bound solution on the Mac OS results in a fairly small file set.

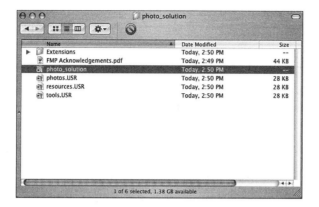

Figure 24.6
Binding a solution on Windows generates a rather large number of files.

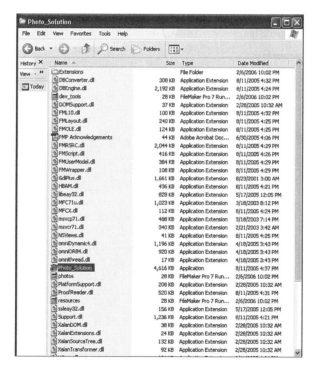

Regardless of platform, each bound solution contains a master file, of which you'll want to take special note. The file has the name *solution_name.extension*, where *solution_name* is the solution name you chose when binding, and *extension* is the custom extension you chose. If you were creating a solution called Sales, and chose the default .USR extension, the master solution file would be called Sales.USR.

Besides the master file, there will also be a single additional file for each of the FileMaker files that went into the solution. Each will be named with your chosen file extension. So if your Sales solution was made up of files called Contact, Company, and Order, the bound solution would contain the following files: `Sales.USR` (the master file), `Contact.USR`, `Company.USR`, and `Order.USR`.

The master file is significant because this is the file that must be run in order to gain access to the solution. For example, if you were packaging the runtime onto a CD, the CD might contain your solution directory, but also a shortcut to the master file at the root level of the CD. You'd rather users not have to rummage around in a directory full of files to find the right one.

The individual database files (as opposed to the master file) are actually not much changed by the binding process. The database files within the application remain FileMaker Pro files, accessible from FileMaker Pro proper (assuming that you haven't disabled such access via the Remove Admin Access solution option that is covered later in this section). You could continue to work with these files in FileMaker Pro or FileMaker Advanced, add features, and simply redeploy the altered files without having to re-create a runtime solution each and every time a change is called for. Likewise, you can have some users make use of the runtime applications and still others access separate copies of the files (or share files) with full versions of FileMaker Pro. It's rare that you'd build a database that could be used in both single-user and multiuser modes, but the point here is that it's possible.

Note that this somewhat mitigates the point that bound solutions are platform-specific. This is true of the solution as a whole, but the constituent database files remain for all intents and purposes FileMaker files, and can be edited as such on either platform.

TIP

> Some bound runtime solutions require a good bit of data entry prior to their being ready to distribute to a wide audience. It can be convenient to host the files—just as they are—on FileMaker Server to allow multiple people to enter data. The fact that the FileMaker files themselves are unaltered by the binding process means you can swap them between a bound runtime application and FileMaker Pro or Server as needed.

REMOVING ADMIN ACCESS

Removing admin access often goes hand-in-hand with creating a runtime solution, but it doesn't necessarily have to. To prevent anyone—including yourself—from changing the files in a given solution (regardless of whether you intend to bind them into a runtime), it is possible to remove all admin (or better, perhaps, "developer") access to a set of files.

CAUTION

> There's no going back after you've removed the access—so be certain you have all the kinks worked out of your solution, and keep your original files backed up!

You'll remove access to the dialogs for Define Database, Value Lists, File References, Accounts & Privileges, and Custom Functions. Access to Layout mode and ScriptMaker are also removed.

In addition, removing admin access removes any accounts set up explicitly with the [Full Access] privilege set. This is quite important because it actually modifies the account and privilege settings of your files. Your "developer" account will be removed. If you have written scripts that depend on a certain account being there, you need to be careful in how you accomplish such functions. You also need to ensure that you *yourself* have a password that will allow you into the solution after you've run this process.

It's possible to define an account and assign a custom privilege set that has the equivalent of full access without assigning it to the built-in [Full Access] set, but keep in mind that, again, the capability to use all editing functions will be removed from the files. Those menu options, regardless of the account you used to sign in, will be grayed out.

→ For a complete understanding of security in FileMaker, **see** Chapter 12, "Implementing Security," **p. 325**.

> **TIP**
>
> We recommend, at a minimum, making certain there's a good way to export all data from a solution before removing admin access. Just write a scripted routine that saves all records to XML files. This at least ensures that you can extract data from a locked-down version of your solution.

24

DEVELOPING KIOSK SOLUTIONS

Kiosks are good ways to present users with a completely encapsulated user experience. As an example, one of our favorite projects was building a kiosk-based wine recommendation service for grocery stores using touch-screen input.

Kiosk mode allows FileMaker Pro to open full-screen, with no toolbars or menus. On Windows and Mac OS X, the taskbar and Dock, respectively, become unavailable as well. This has the effect of taking over the entire computer environment and allowing you to build complete appliances that serve a specific purpose. If you combine kiosk mode with an alternative means of data input—touch-screen input, bar-code readers, or other devices—the result can be something that very much departs from what you might think of as a database.

Securing Kiosk Mode

Kiosk mode does not completely lock down a computer. On Windows, users can still use Alt+Tab to access different running processes. The way to avoid this is to simply establish FileMaker Pro as the only running application. Also, on Windows a Ctrl+Alt+Delete calls forward the Windows Task Manager, and the Windows key on current keyboards brings forward the Start menu. You need to take additional steps to lock down Windows.

If you plan on deploying many kiosks, this would be tedious, but you can use a system utility such as gpedit on Windows XP to lock access to various elements such as the Alt key and Start menu.

Another approach is to use a third-party utility such as Win Control: http://www.salfeld.com/software/wincontrol/index.html.

On Mac OS X, this is not as much an issue. Kiosk mode properly takes control of the computer environment, but there are still backdoors, not the least of which is simply pulling the power cable of the computer in question.

In general, though, keep in mind that kiosk mode is meant to facilitate a storefront experience especially geared toward touch-screen input, and it is not focused on delivering a specific level of security.

When preparing a solution for kiosk mode, you need to consider several unique issues, not the least of which are important user interface elements. Because FileMaker's menus are inaccessible in kiosk mode, a vital requirement is to offer users a means for at least exiting the application. Without a scripted quit routine, users have to force-quit the application and may lose data as a result.

Being able to exit the application, though, is just the first requirement. Any function you'd like users to be able to perform needs to have been scripted and attached to a layout object (such as a button—FileMaker 8's new Custom Menus feature won't help here). You can opt to leave the FileMaker Status Area open if you want, but none of FileMaker's native keyboard shortcuts will work (for, say, creating or deleting records).

Most kiosks offer a complete set of scripted functions attached to a custom-crafted user interface, and very rarely do developers opt to leave the Status Area open. Therefore, you need to create scripts and buttons for navigating from layout to layout, for creating records, for managing any importing or exporting of data, and for dealing with upgrading the files themselves, if necessary.

After a kiosk is deployed to end users (it need not be a kiosk—it could just be a copy of a FileMaker database you're distributing widely), you leave the world of modifying and managing workgroup solutions and enter the world of commercial development, where your ability to tweak things becomes exponentially more difficult. This suggests that a solution needs to be completely tested and perfect before it goes out the door—or else you need to craft and implement an upgrade strategy that allows you to pass new functionality to your users without leaving them lost, with no means of preserving whatever data they may have input. This strategy could be as simple as exporting all data from the old version and importing into the new, or you could build a distributed file system in which it's possible to replace certain files without altering the data itself.

→ For ideas on user interface approaches, **see** Chapter 13, "Advanced Interface Techniques," **p. 353**.

POLISHING YOUR CUSTOM SOLUTION

When distributing a custom solution, you can better tailor its look and feel by creating a custom menu scheme that reflects and supports the identity of your application. In previous versions of FileMaker, you were limited to customizing the name of the Scripts menu, and to attaching your own scripts to the Help and About menu items. With FileMaker Pro 8 Advanced, you can implement a completely customized menu scheme. (Note that this will not be of any use in a solution destined for kiosk mode because kiosk mode removes menu access, as explained in the preceding section.)

A custom menu scheme allows you a very high degree of control over your solution: You could write a complete help system that might include opening a FileMaker Pro file or interface in itself. Users might then be able to perform find requests and employ other familiar approaches to using your system. The About menu could be as simple as a window with an image or a logo that is brought forward, or you could get as fancy as a QuickTime movie that is played within a container field.

→ For more information on custom menus, **see** "Working with Custom Menus," **p. 373**.

The opportunity FileMaker Pro Advanced gives you is to truly customize a solution so that it takes on an identity of its own.

TIP

> This might seem a minor point, but we've found that if you take pains to give your solutions a name and add even simple levels of customization, end users will more easily accept the system that they will then presumably spend a good percentage of their work lives using.
>
> It's also somewhat helpful in getting users and IT folks to differentiate FileMaker Pro–the technology–from your specific solution. If you name and modestly customize it, you foster a better sense of differentiation by creating an identity other than "the FileMaker database."

ERROR LOG

As Developer Utilities runs, it can keep track of any errors it encounters. To generate a log, simply turn on this option in the Solution Options. A text file named `LogFile.txt` is created in your solution folder. Some of the Developer Utilities processes run into errors that don't prompt dialogs, and thus it's a good idea to check the log before wrapping up a solution for end users.

These are the errors you'll find in the log:

- `Updating File Specs for this destination file skipped due to a previous fatal error.`
- `Destination file could not be created, and all further processing on it was skipped. File:`
- `Skipped runtime generation, due to missing or damaged resources.`
- `Destination folder could not be created, and all further processing was skipped. Folder name:`

As you can see, these messages aren't particularly illuminating and generally indicate that you have a significant problem with the interaction between your OS and FileMaker's processes. In testing for these conditions, a full hard drive was the cause for some of these issues. If you see such messages, verify that it's possible and practical to create a solution directory in the place you've chosen (meaning, check for a full disk, restrictive permissions, and the like), and verify that the source files open correctly and don't appear corrupted.

PLUG-INS

Plug-ins extend FileMaker Pro's capabilities and are quite varied. Their offerings range from charting functionality, OS-level file manipulation, and bar code readers to scientific math functions, credit-card authentication, help systems, telephony, and more.

NOTE

We encourage you to visit FileMaker's website to explore a wide range of plug-ins. Just go to http://solutions.filemaker.com and click Plug-ins in the For Developers area at the lower right.

We won't describe specific plug-ins here; a wide range of professionally supported plug-ins are available, many of which we use frequently in our consulting practice, but we could write an entire book on that topic alone. For the purposes here, we cover briefly the concepts you need to keep in mind for all plug-ins.

Plug-ins are written and compiled in accordance with FileMaker Pro's plug-in API. They're not something many FileMaker developers will ever need to create, and you generally do not have access to the code from which they're built.

If you want to delve into writing your own plug-ins, you need to be an expert in either the C or the C++ language. (We don't recommend a FileMaker plug-in as your first C++ project!) You also need a development environment, such as CodeWarrior for the Mac or Visual Studio for Windows, and the plug-in API documentation and sample files that ship with FileMaker Pro Advanced. Plug-ins are platform specific, so if you want your plug-in to work on both Mac and Windows, you need to do at least some reengineering to get your code to compile and run correctly on both Mac and Windows.

As in all third-party software products, we recommend you get to know a given plug-in well and test it along with the rest of your solution before deploying. Another obvious consideration is cost: Some of your clients might benefit from utilizing a plug-in, but remember that this is third-party software that may require a purchasing license.

UNDERSTANDING PLUG-INS

Plug-ins work by adding external functions to your calculation functions list. Generally, but not always, they take a single text parameter (although the parameter may be internally delimited, containing several values). The result of the plug-in operation is then delivered back in the form of a calculation result.

```
An actual external call might look like this:
```

```
XMpl_Add( numberInput1; numberInput2 )
```

If you use this plug-in function, it returns two numbers added together. To make use of the function, you generally have to store its result someplace; often in the context of a script step that puts the value into a field or variable:

```
Set Variable [$sum; XMpl_Add( numberInput1; numberInput2 )]
```

The name of the plug-in function is a string specific to the plug-in you're working with. Its syntax is governed by the plug-in, and (if it follows proper FileMaker, Inc., conventions) includes the name of the plug-in as well. In this case, the example is drawn from FileMaker's included sample plug-in (described further in the next section), and XMpl_ is the prefix FileMaker chose. Likewise, the expected parameters passed as text vary widely from none to complex data arrays. FileMaker Pro 8's data storage limit of 2GB per field means that we could be facing some quite complex programming within the realm of a single text field. One of our favorite charting plug-ins (xmCHART, found at www.x2max.com) requires that a complex array of information be passed both to format and then populate the charts it returns.

The results of a plug-in are returned as a calculation result, but often some other action may be performed as well. For example, a dialog may appear. Often the calculation field simply serves as a means for passing error conditions.

For example, a plug-in might copy an image file from one directory to another. Or it might display a dialog of some kind. Or it might create a chart image and place it on your clipboard. The possibilities are nearly endless and we recommend, again, exploring available plug-ins to understand specific cases.

USING FILEMAKER'S SAMPLE PLUG-IN

The installation disk for FileMaker Pro Advanced includes a sample plug-in, including the C++ library and code necessary for building it. It offers some basic functions that should get you thinking about what plug-ins are capable of:

- **XMpl_Add**—Adds two numbers together. This is totally superfluous because you'd always use a calculation to do so, but it serves as the most basic example of a plug-in function.

- **XMpl_Append**—Appends the contents of one text field to another. You can continue to add parameters to the function. It simply appends all those that you pass it. This function is redundant with the & operator.

- **XMpl_NumToWords**—Converts a number (1111) to words (One Thousand, One Hundred and Eleven).

- **XMpl_StartScript**—Initiates a script as specified by filename and script name.

- **XMpl_UserFormatNumber**—Reformats a number based on user preference. The plug-in's default is a standard (111) 222-3333 North American phone number.

The sections that follow discuss the process of installing and configuring plug-ins in FileMaker.

INSTALLING PLUG-INS

There are two distinct types of plug-ins: purely client-based, or client-based with a server-side component. Deployment is consistent between the two: To enable a plug-in, it needs to be placed in the Extensions folder with the FileMaker application folder for each client, regardless of whether it has a server-side component. In addition to the client-side installation, server-side plug-ins need to be deployed to the Extensions folder on the server as well. (This is true for both Windows and Mac OS X platforms.)

 If your plug-in is not responding, refer to "Plug-in Not Responding or Not Installing" in the "Troubleshooting" section at the end of this chapter.

DEPLOYING PLUG-INS VIA FILEMAKER SERVER

FileMaker Server offers auto-update functionality that copies a plug-in from the server machine onto a client computer when a requisite plug-in is either out-of-date or missing altogether on the client. This saves a great number of headaches and makes it possible to seamlessly fold a plug-in into a workgroup solution.

The functions that manage auto-update are called by scripts and require, ironically, that the Auto-Update plug-in be installed and enabled on all client computers. (Fortunately it is installed and enabled by default with FileMaker Pro and FileMaker Pro Advanced.)

➔ For a full discussion of using plug-ins with FileMaker Server, **see** "Automatically Updating Plug-ins," **p. 802**.

CONFIGURING AND ENABLING PLUG-INS

To enable a particular plug-in, visit the Preferences dialog within your FileMaker Pro (or FileMaker Pro Advanced) application. Notice that to use a given plug-in you need to explicitly enable it (by marking its respective check box), as shown in Figure 24.7.

Figure 24.7
Plug-ins are enabled and configured via the Preferences dialog.

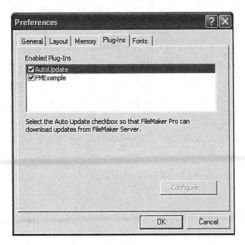

Notice also that your AutoUpdate plug-in is enabled in this list as well. It is here that you can find all the plug-ins available for a given client.

Some plug-ins offer configuration choices (see Figure 24.8). Every plug-in is different; here we're using the sample plug-in that ships with FileMaker Pro Advanced, FMExample.

If you've just installed a plug-in, you may need to close and restart your FileMaker Pro client to gain access to its external functions. (An exception is the case in which a plug-in is downloaded and installed by the Auto Update function, as discussed in Chapter 25. In that case the plug-in is immediately enabled for use.)

Figure 24.8
FileMaker's
FMExample plug-in
gives users the option
to specify a number
format for one of its
functions in its config-
uration attributes.

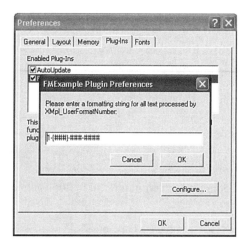

TROUBLESHOOTING

PLUG-IN NOT RESPONDING OR NOT INSTALLING

My plug-in isn't working. Where do I start to diagnose and fix the problem?

Issues with plug-ins can be difficult to troubleshoot. If a plug-in isn't responding, check first to see that you have the latest version, and make sure that it is enabled on your client computer. Restarting FileMaker Pro (or Developer) after adding a plug-in to the Extensions folder is also a necessary first step.

Beyond that, your testing has to encompass the functionality of the plug-in itself. You may, for example, be struggling with a plug-in written for a prior version of FileMaker Pro.

When using the Auto Update feature, one of the most common mistakes to make is forgetting to turn on the Auto Update option at the server itself.

FILE REFERENCE ERRORS

I renamed my files, but still seem to have problems with missing files. How can I manipulate my file references by hand?

If you encounter problems with file references, where you get "file missing" error messages when FileMaker Pro opens your database solution or you notice such in your DDR, we recommend first working with the Define File References dialog, (Define, File References, under the File menu). You may be able to simply re-point a file reference to repair some issues. In other cases you may need to manually reestablish connections; to identify all such places where that will be necessary, refer to the DDR.

Again this is a symptom of a file having been manually renamed at the OS level. The Rename Files function in FileMaker Developer is a great way to rename files all you like; we encourage you to use it whenever this is necessary.

FILEMAKER EXTRA: THE LIMITS OF CUSTOMIZATION

Using the tools in FileMaker Pro Advanced, you can customize your solutions to a considerable degree. However, there are still some limitations on what you can accomplish in using FileMaker Pro Advanced to create something like a "shrink-wrap" software experience. This section explores some of those limitations and what you can do to overcome them.

LACK OF MULTIUSER CAPABILITY

As we mentioned previously in this chapter, FileMaker solutions that are bound into runtime applications cannot be shared among multiple users. Each copy of a bound runtime application can be installed and used on only one computer, and multiple copies of the same runtime application can't share data.

There is an exception to this rule. If you have a copy of FileMaker Server and you configure it to allow the hosting of runtime solutions, you can then share a bound solution such that users with the FileMaker Pro software can open and work with the files. This technique, of course, removes much of the reason for creating a bound runtime in the first place because one goal is to allow the distribution of FileMaker-based software to users who don't have a copy of FileMaker Pro.

MENU CUSTOMIZATION

In the preceding edition of this book, we had to report that there were limited options for menu customization in FileMaker. With the release of Custom Menus, all that is changed. FileMaker menus are vastly more customizable than they were in FileMaker 7 and before. Still, even the new Custom Menus feature has its limits. Menus can be enabled or disabled only in sets. And there is very little programmatic control of menus and menu sets, aside from the `Install Menu Set` script step. There's no way to add items to a menu via a script, for example, nor have menus generated dynamically from database data.

Further customization of menus *is* possible, though, using third-party plug-ins. SecureFM with MenuMagic, from New Millennium Communications (www.nmci.com), allows even more fine-grained control over menus, as does MenuControl from Dacons (www.dacons.net).

NOTE

> As with all plug-ins, you'll want to look at these carefully and weigh whether they have the features you need. Plug-ins aren't guaranteed in any way by FileMaker, Inc., so do your homework!

LACK OF EVENT TRIGGERS

The term *event triggers* refers to the capability to associate program logic (such as running a script) with specific kinds of user interaction events (such as tabbing out of a field while doing data entry). In a system that supports event triggers, it would be possible to specify that a particular script be run every time a user exited a field, or every time a user submitted or deleted a record.

FileMaker doesn't yet support event triggers (although we hope developers are toiling away on them behind the scenes!), but this doesn't mean that such functionality can't be achieved. Again, you'll want to look into a plug-in that can accomplish some or all of this task. Several useful candidates are listed in the Scripting section of the FileMaker, Inc., plug-ins list (http://solutions.filemaker.com/solutions/index.jsp, and then follow the Plug-ins link). Each of these plug-ins will have its strengths and limitations, so here again, due diligence is called for.

24

## CHAPTER 25

FILEMAKER SERVER AND SERVER ADVANCED

In this chapter

ABOUT FILEMAKER SERVER

You'll use FileMaker Server to make your FileMaker Pro databases available to many users at once across a network. On its own, the FileMaker Pro software can host files for networked access from up to five users at a time, in what's called a *peer-to-peer* configuration. In practice, except for developmental configurations, or production deployments to very small groups, peer-to-peer sharing is unlikely to be a suitable choice for making files available to multiple networked users. Unless you're in that rather small minority of situations, you'll want to look at FileMaker Server instead.

THE FILEMAKER SERVER PRODUCT LINE

Two separate products are available under the name FileMaker Server:

- **FileMaker Server**—FileMaker Server is used to provide concurrent access to as many as 250 networked users running FileMaker Pro client software.

- **FileMaker Server Advanced**—You'll need FileMaker Server Advanced if you want to make FileMaker data available via ODBC, JDBC, Instant Web Publishing, or Custom Web Publishing. FileMaker Server Advanced supports networked access from up to 250 FileMaker Pro or ODBC/JDBC clients, as well as an additional 100 web clients.

→ For a discussion on ODBC and JDBC, **see** Chapter 20, "Exporting Data from FileMaker," **p. 595**.
→ To find out about Instant Web Publishing, **see** Chapter 21, "Instant Web Publishing," **p. 633**.
→ Custom Web Publishing is discussed in Chapter 23, "Custom Web Publishing," **p. 699**.

The essential distinction here is between Server and Server Advanced. Server allows connections from only FileMaker Pro clients. To allow access from ODBC, JDBC, or web clients, you need to purchase Server Advanced.

Installing and working with the components of FileMaker Server Advanced is covered extensively in other chapters. This chapter focuses on the administration and configuration tools and techniques that pertain to the core Server product.

FILEMAKER SERVER VERSUS PEER-TO-PEER DATABASE HOSTING

There are some major differences between FileMaker Server and peer-to-peer database hosting. We alluded to the differences between these methods in the preceding chapter. The limitations of the peer-to-peer sharing method are fairly severe: With peer-to-peer sharing, no more than ten database files may be served, to no more than five clients at a time. The peer-to-peer method uses a regular copy of FileMaker Pro as the database host, so a deployment of this type also forgoes important features of FileMaker Server, especially the capability to make regular, scheduled backups of the databases. Although such schedules could be created with operating-system-level scripting technologies, it's much simpler to use FileMaker Server's built-in tools.

Additionally, peer-to-peer configurations tend to be run on less capable hardware than Server-based configurations. In some cases, we've even seen peer-to-peer configurations hosted on an individual's personal workstation, in constant daily use for many tasks. Neither lower-end hardware nor constant competition for machine resources is a good foundation for a robust multiuser deployment.

If you do choose to begin with a peer-to-peer configuration for multiuser database sharing, we recommend that you still treat this situation as a server-type deployment as far as possible. Give the database host its own dedicated machine on which to run—one that people won't casually use for other daily tasks; make sure that you have a reliable solution for regular backups; make sure that the machine at least meets the minimum specifications for the FileMaker Pro client software, and add a bit more RAM if you possibly can.

Backing Up Open Files

If you're backing up hosted FileMaker files by hand, please be aware that you should never make a copy of a FileMaker file while it is open—even if it's not hosted and is in use by only a single user. FileMaker can guarantee that a database file is in a fully consistent state on disk only if the file has been closed properly by the server process. Otherwise, there might be database transactions that exist only in RAM that have not yet been committed to disk.

In versions of FileMaker prior to version 7, a database that had been copied from an open file would display a warning the next time it was opened, stating that the file had been closed improperly and was being checked for consistency. This warning no longer necessarily appears in FileMaker 8 when you open a file that has been copied from an open file. Don't let this fact lure you into thinking that it's now okay to copy an open file. It's not.

As you'll read in a later section, FileMaker Server's built-in backup capability handles the details of closing the files before backing them up. If you're working in a peer-to-peer setting, you don't have that luxury. You'll need to make sure that any automated solution you put into place takes into account the need to close each database file before backing it up.

25

The extremely limited scalability and lack of backup automation capabilities ought to discourage you from using FileMaker's peer-to-peer sharing for production use. For the cost of a handful of copies of the FileMaker Pro client, you can host your databases on a solid server platform (FileMaker Server) that can handle 125 database files (potentially comprising thousands of tables) and up to 250 users.

FILEMAKER SERVER CAPABILITIES

We've talked about some of the features that set the FileMaker Server product line apart as a hosting solution: much greater scalability than the plain FileMaker Pro software, and the capability to perform automated tasks such as backups. There are quite a number of other distinguishing features as well. Here are some of the most important:

- **Centralized Remote Administration**—FileMaker Server comes with the Server Administration Tool (SAT), which is an application that can be used to administer one or several instances of FileMaker Server, potentially all running on different machines from the machine where the SAT is installed.

 - **Consistency Checker**—FileMaker Server 8 performs consistency checking on files as it opens them. A file that's been closed improperly (for example, by being copied from an open file), or a file that's never been opened by FileMaker Server 8 will be subjected to a consistency check. If the check fails, a message will be written to the application log and the file will not open.

- **Plug-in Management**—FileMaker Server can be configured to download plug-ins to FileMaker Pro clients in response to programmed requests from the clients, ensuring that clients will always have the latest versions of plug-ins installed on their own machines.

- **External Authentication**—FileMaker Server can be configured to check user credentials against a networked authentication source, such as a Windows Active Directory server or a Mac OS X Open Directory server.

- **Secure Transfer of Data**—When FileMaker Pro clients are used in conjunction with FileMaker Server, the transfer of data can be encrypted with SSL (Secure Sockets Layer).

In addition to these features, FileMaker Server offers a large number of other important functions as well, such as the capability to send messages to guests, to disconnect idle guests, to limit the visibility of database files based on user privileges, to be run in a scripted fashion from the command line, and to capture a variety of usage statistics and server event information for logging and analysis. All of these features are discussed in the sections to come.

FILEMAKER SERVER REQUIREMENTS

Like any piece of server software, FileMaker Server has certain minimum hardware and software requirements. You'll achieve the best results with a dedicated server; as with any piece of server software, it's best if FileMaker Server is the only significant server process running on a given machine. Forcing FileMaker Server to compete with other significant processes, such as mail services or domain controller services, is likely to hurt Server's performance.

File Sharing and FileMaker Server

A special word is in order about file sharing and file servers. FileMaker, Inc., recommends that all file sharing should be disabled on a machine running FileMaker Server. This has long been the official position, and in the past, a number of different reasons have been advanced for this. For instance, FileMaker Server uses its own techniques for managing concurrent access to files, and it's been said that contention between FileMaker Server's file access and the operating system's file sharing could lead to file corruption.

Another troublesome fact about file sharing is that it opens the possibility that users could mount the volume containing the hosted database files on their own computers, and open the files directly with FileMaker Pro, at the same time that other users were accessing the files via Server. This is a clear recipe for disaster and is almost certain to lead to file corruption.

In practice, it's often been difficult to disable file sharing completely on the server machine. It's often desirable to have at least part of the server machine published as a share point to move new FileMaker databases up to the server or to copy local backups to remote storage.

At the very least, if you feel you *must* have an operating system–level share point somewhere on the server, make very sure that the OS-level file sharing does not directly cover the directories where the live FileMaker files are kept. (Later sections in this chapter discuss the location of those files.)

And as a best practice, try to disable OS-level file sharing altogether on the server machine, and use one of the many good remote administration tools available instead—tools such as Terminal Services (Windows), Apple Remote Desktop (Mac OS), or Timbuktu (cross-platform commercial).

The server machine, in addition to being dedicated as far as possible to FileMaker Server, and having the minimum amount of file sharing enabled (preferably none), also needs the things discussed in the following sections.

STATIC IP ADDRESS(ES)

The server machine needs to be enabled for TCP/IP networking with one or more static IP addresses. (Much earlier versions of FileMaker Server supported the IPX/SPX protocol in addition to TCP/IP, but this has not been the case for several versions of Server.) Note, by the way, that FileMaker Server 8 is capable of *multihoming*, meaning that it can take full advantage of multiple physical network interfaces, each with its own IP address. FileMaker Server listens on all available network interfaces. As far as we know, it's not possible to configure FileMaker Server to ignore one or more of the available interfaces; if the interface is available, FileMaker Server tries to bind to port 5003 on that interface and begins listening for FileMaker traffic. (The FileMaker client/server port number, 5003, is also not configurable.)

FAST HARD DRIVE

Like any database, FileMaker Server is capable of being extremely disk-intensive. For some database operations, particularly those involving access to many records—such as a large update or a report—the speed of the server's hard disk may be the limiting factor. RAID (Redundant Array of Inexpensive Disks) technologies (whereby multiple physical disks are combined into a single *disk array*, for greater speed, greater recoverability, or both) are becoming ever cheaper, and some sort of RAID array may well be the right answer for you. (It probably goes without saying, but we're talking about a hardware-based RAID, not a software-based RAID.) Otherwise, consider a high-RPM SCSI disk, or one of the relatively new Serial ATA disks.

25

FAST PROCESSOR(S)

This is a fairly obvious requirement for a server machine. But it's worth noting that FileMaker Server 8 can take full advantage of multiple processors.

LOTS OF RAM

Again an obvious requirement. FileMaker Server 8 is capable of using up to 800MB of RAM for its cache. Maximum cache RAM is determined as a fraction of installed RAM: the formula is roughly (physical RAM $-$ 128) $\times$ .25. This means that in order to be able to use 800MB of cache memory, you'll need 4GB of RAM installed. This limitation on cache RAM was introduced in FileMaker Server 7.0v3. FileMaker Server can use only 2GB of RAM directly. Larger amounts of RAM will increase the available cache, and are also desirable if you're running components of FileMaker Server Advanced on the same machine as Server itself. (Those components can be installed on the same machine as Server, or a different machine, as discussed in Chapter 23.)

FAST NETWORK CONNECTION

FileMaker is a client/server application, which means that FileMaker Pro clients remain in constant contact with a database host such as FileMaker Server. FileMaker Server constantly *polls* (attempts to contact) any connected clients to determine what they're doing and whether they're still connected. In addition, although Server 8 is capable of handling a few more tasks than its predecessors, it still needs to send quite a lot of data to the client for processing in certain kinds of operations. All this means that FileMaker is an extremely network-intensive platform that benefits greatly from increased network speed. Best results will be achieved on fast network connections of T1 speed or greater. A 10Mbps LAN is an improvement, and 100Mbps is even better. Of course, there's no point in spending money on machines with Gigabit Ethernet interfaces if the intervening network and the individual client machines don't support such a high speed.

SUPPORTED OPERATING SYSTEM

FileMaker Server 8 supports the following operating systems: Mac OS X Server, Mac OS X client, (10.3.9 or 10.4.x for both), Windows XP Professional Service Pack 2, Windows 2000 Server Service Pack 4, and Windows 2003 Server Standard Edition Service Pack 1. On the Mac OS X side, Mac OS X Server is listed as the recommended choice. FileMaker, Inc., has indicated that this means it has not tried to verify the acceptability of the regular Mac OS X operating system for loads greater than 50 connected FileMaker users.

DATA CENTER ENVIRONMENT

Although not strictly a requirement for running FileMaker Server, proper care and housing of server equipment is a necessity, one that's often overlooked, especially in the small- and medium-sized business sectors, some areas of education, and among nonprofit groups. These are all key groups of FileMaker users, ones that do not always have sufficient resources to build and maintain anything like a data center. Ideally, a server of any kind should be housed in a physically secure and isolated area, with appropriate cooling and ventilation, with technical staff on hand 24 hours a day to troubleshoot any issues that arise, and with automated monitoring software that periodically checks key functions on the server and notifies technical personnel by email or pager if any services are interrupted. Some organizations are fortunate enough to be able to house their FileMaker servers in such an environment. But even if you can't provide all those amenities, you can see to the key areas. The server should minimally be up off the floor, well ventilated, and under lock and key if possible. And some sort of monitoring software is nice, and need not break the bank: the open source package Nagios (http://www.nagios.org) is a popular and powerful open-source monitoring package.

NOTE

> Nagios runs on UNIX but can monitor servers running on almost any platform. Many server monitoring packages exist for Windows deployment as well.

INSTALLING FILEMAKER SERVER

FileMaker Server consists of several components. When you install the product, you may choose to install the FileMaker Server software, the Server Administration Tool (SAT), or both. You may install either component without the other: FileMaker Server can run on a machine that does not have the SAT installed, and the SAT can be used to administer multiple instances of FileMaker Server, none of which needs to be installed on the same machine as the SAT.

The installation process is straightforward and is well covered by the supplied documentation and by the installer screens. On Windows, all installed files, both FileMaker Server itself and the SAT, are installed in a directory called `Program Files\FileMaker\FileMaker Server`. On the Mac OS, the FileMaker Server components are installed in `/Library/FileMaker Server`, and the SAT and documentation are installed in `/Applications/FileMaker Server 8`. The default install location can be changed on Windows, but not on the Mac OS.

RUNNING FILEMAKER SERVER

Installing FileMaker Server installs two separate components, both of which run as services: FileMaker Server and the FileMaker Server Helper. These appear as two separate services (Windows) or processes (Mac OS). FileMaker Server does not function correctly without the FileMaker Server Helper service also running. (Installing FileMaker Server Advanced will cause additional services to be added.)

STARTING AND STOPPING FILEMAKER SERVER

When you install FileMaker Server, you can choose whether to have these services start automatically (in which case they are started every time the server itself starts up) or manually (in which case you need to start the services by hand). On Windows you can start and stop the services with the tools available in the Services console. On the Mac OS, there's a new option in the SAT that lets you start and stop the FileMaker Server services.

On Mac OS X, there is no tool that corresponds to the Windows Services console. If you chose to have the services start automatically, a directory called `/Library/StartupItems/FileMakerServerHelper` will be created on the server machine. This directory contains a simple shell script that controls automatic starting of the service on Mac OS X. To see the specific command-line syntax for starting and stopping the server, read the startup script, which is contained in `/Library/StartupItems/FileMakerServerHelper/FileMakerServerHelper`.

25

Currently the command to start the FileMaker Server services looks like this:

```
/Library/FileMaker\ Server/Tools/fmserver_helperd
```

And the command to stop the services looks like this:

```
/Library/FileMaker\ Server/Tools/fmserver_helperd stop
```

 In the event you need to write scripts to start and stop the FileMaker Services on the Mac OS, knowing about the specific paths may be helpful. Otherwise, though, just avail yourself of the new Services Administration Tool in FileMaker Server 8 for the Mac OS: Choose Server, Local FileMaker Server Administration, and you'll see a dialog that allows you to selectively start and stop the services. You might need to authenticate as an administrator to start or stop the services.

HOSTING DATABASES

FileMaker Server can host up to 125 FileMaker databases. When the server starts, it looks for files in the default database file directory, and in the alternate database directory if one has been specified. (We discuss how to specify the alternate directory later.) It also tries to open any databases found in the first directory level within either of those two top-level directories. Databases in more deeply nested directories are not opened. The main database directory can be found at `Program Files\FileMaker\FileMaker Server\Data\Databases` (Windows) and `/Library/FileMaker Server/Data/Databases` (Mac OS X).

Care should be taken to place these directories on hard drives that are local to the server machine. It's not at all a good idea to host files from a mapped or networked drive. In such a configuration, every database access needs to be translated into a network call and passed across the network. At the very least this approach is likely to cause significant loss of performance.

USING THE SERVER ADMINISTRATION TOOL

You'll administer FileMaker Server using the Server Administration Tool, a separate piece of software that can administer multiple instances of FileMaker Server, local and remote. You can't configure FileMaker Server without using the SAT, although you can perform many routine administrative tasks from the command line.

When you open the SAT, you are prompted to connect to a server. You can choose a server that's available on your local network, a server you've stored in a list of favorite servers, or a server that's registered with an LDAP server. (We cover the LDAP registration process later in the chapter.) The connection screen is shown in Figure 25.1.

Assuming that the server you specify exists and is available, after you've connected, you'll see the main SAT interface. When working with the SAT, on Windows you have a choice between using a wizard-like interface (reached by clicking the server name in the left SAT pane) and using the more specialized tool available in the left SAT pane. The wizard-like interface is useful for simple configuration, but a number of features can be accessed only by using the tools in the left pane. For quick access to all configuration options, right-clicking the server name opens the Server Properties dialog. Figure 25.2 shows the Server Properties dialog in the Windows version of the SAT.

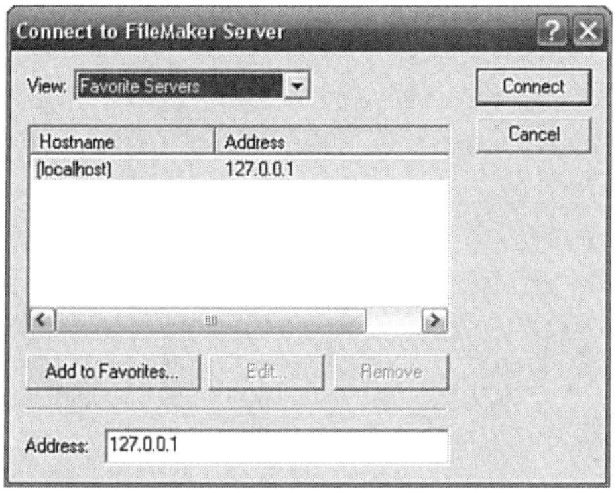

Figure 25.1
When you open the SAT, you must first connect to a specific FileMaker server.

Figure 25.2
Right-click the server name and select Properties to have quick access to all of FileMaker Server's configurable properties (Windows SAT only).

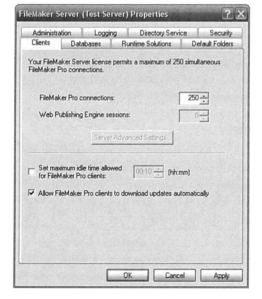

25

When using the SAT on Mac OS X, there is no equivalent to the various wizards available on Windows. All configuration options can be reached by clicking the Configure tool at the upper right of the SAT window, which gives access to a set of configuration tabs that parallel those in the Properties box in Windows. Figure 25.3 shows the Configuration window on Mac OS.

Figure 25.3
Select the Configure icon to have quick access to all FileMaker Server's configurable properties when using the Mac OS version of the SAT.

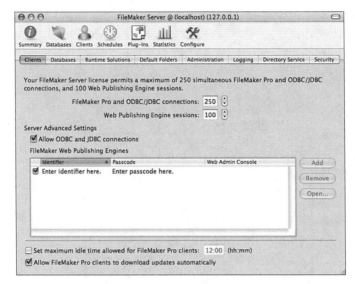

CONFIGURING AND ADMINISTERING FILEMAKER SERVER USING THE SAT

You use the SAT to set up and maintain a number of important properties of a FileMaker Server installation. We cover here what we consider to be the most critical areas. The supplied documentation provides comprehensive coverage of the remaining features.

SERVER ADMINISTRATION SETTINGS

On the Administration tab of the SAT you can set some options that control administrative access to the server. In particular, you can choose the method by which administrators must authenticate, as well as specify whether remote administration of FileMaker Server is possible, as shown in Figure 25.4.

You should always require a password for server administration (this should go without saying). You have the option, though, of using a non-FileMaker authentication source. You can instruct FileMaker Server to authenticate administrators against a user group called fmsadmin. You can choose to look for such a group among the accounts that are local to the specific machine, or to look among the accounts for whatever domain the server machine participates in, if any.

Also on this tab you can control whether to allow remote administration of this instance of FileMaker Server. If this box is unchecked, FileMaker Server can be administered only by a copy of the SAT running on the same machine. You need to enable this option if you want to administer FileMaker Server from a copy of the SAT running on a remote machine.

Figure 25.4
Use the Administration area of the SAT to control administrative access to the server.

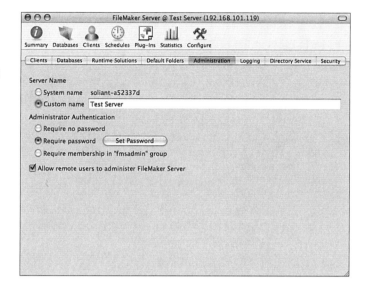

RESOURCE USAGE SETTINGS

The SAT has a number of settings that control the resources that FileMaker Server sets aside for certain tasks. On the Clients tab of the SAT, you can specify the maximum number of FileMaker Pro and web clients that can be connected at one time, and on the Databases tab you can control the maximum number of files that FileMaker Server will try to open. (The Clients tab was shown previously in Figure 25.2. The Databases tab is shown in Figure 25.5.) All these numbers have a hard upper limit: 250 for simultaneous FileMaker Pro or ODBC/JDBC users, 100 for simultaneous web connections, and 125 for the maximum number of open files. If you know that your loads will be lower than those figures, though, you can lower the numbers. If you'll never need to have more than 50 files open, or more than 25 users, you can set these thresholds lower. Doing so frees up resources, such as RAM, that FileMaker Server would otherwise need to keep in reserve for the possible higher loads. As a general rule, you should set these three numbers as low as you can.

You can also specify the amount of RAM to set aside for a database cache. This value is configured on the Databases tab. The SAT lets you know what it thinks the maximum allowable cache size is, based on total available RAM. FileMaker Server 8 has a hard cap of 800MB of cache RAM. A good rule of thumb is to set the cache to half the allowable maximum to start, and then raise it if your cache hit percentage dips too low (consistently below 90% or so).

It's tempting to think you should just set the database cache to the largest possible size, but this isn't always the best option. Setting aside too large a cache can take RAM from other areas, such as the operating system, without necessarily being beneficial to FileMaker Server.

Figure 25.5
Use the Databases area to control file hosting and cache size limits.

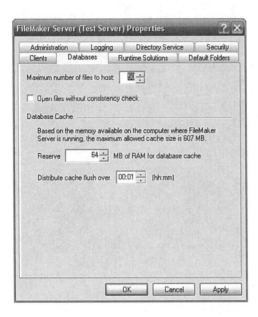

CLIENT CONNECTIVITY SETTINGS

The Clients tab of the SAT also lets you specify additional connectivity options for an installation of FileMaker Server Advanced. Here you can allow or disallow ODBC and JDBC connections, and configure connections to a Web Publishing Engine. These options are fully explored in other chapters.

→ For a discussion of ODBC and JDBC, **see** Chapter 20, "Exporting Data from FileMaker," **p. 595**.

→ To find out about Instant Web Publishing, **see** Chapter 21, "Instant Web Publishing," **p. 633**.

→ Custom Web Publishing is discussed in Chapter 23, "Custom Web Publishing," **p. 699**.

MANAGING CLIENTS

Using the SAT, you can see a list of all currently connected FileMaker Pro clients. You can also see which databases they currently have open. Any administrative sessions (that is, connections from the SAT) are shown. ODBC, JDBC, and web connections are not shown. The display of connected clients is shown in Figure 25.6.

From this display, by (Control-clicking) [right-clicking] on an individual user, or by selecting the user and going to the <u>A</u>ction menu, you can choose to send that individual user a message (asking him to log out, for example, or to call you to discuss the large number of files he has open). You can also choose to disconnect the user from the server. You also have the option to send a message to all users, or to disconnect all users, if you choose.

Figure 25.6
Use the SAT to monitor connected clients.

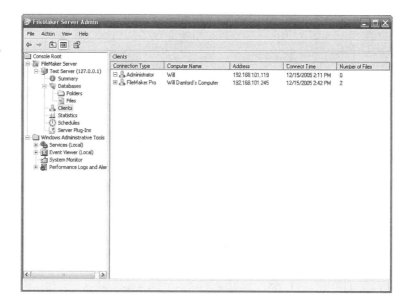

MANAGING DATABASES

The Databases area of the SAT is somewhat similar to the Clients area. Here, you can see a list of all open databases, grouped by directory if you so choose. (On Windows, choose the Files node within the Databases area to see files without directory groupings; on the Mac OS, choose Action, Database, Hide Folders.) See Figure 25.7 for a look at the database monitoring area on Windows. By (Control-clicking) [right-clicking] a database in the list, or selecting a database in the list and then choosing an option from the Action menu, you can open a closed database (making it available to clients). You may also close or pause an open database. The Pause option does not fully close the database (which would forcibly disconnect any users who might be connected to the database), but it does prevent the database from being read or written to until the Resume command is given for that database. The Pause command also synchronizes the database cache, rendering the database file consistent on disk so that it can be backed up.

When working with databases in the SAT, you also have the option to close, open, pause, or resume all databases at once.

Figure 25.7
Use the database monitoring area to inspect hosted databases.

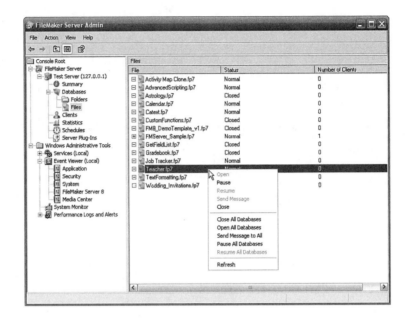

ADMINISTRATION FROM THE COMMAND LINE

So far we've looked at how to configure and administer FileMaker Server with the Server Administration Tool. But many of these tasks can be accomplished at the command line as well, with a command-line utility called `fmsadmin` that's installed alongside FileMaker Server. If you're comfortable at the command line, you can perform many administrative tasks without going through the graphical SAT. Like the SAT, the `fmsadmin` tool can administer instances of FileMaker Server that are running remotely, as well as those running on the same machine.

CAUTION

> This section assumes that you're fairly familiar with working at the command line on your chosen platform. It also assumes that you have some familiarity with setting system paths, writing batch scripts, and executing scheduled tasks.

Command-line administration is accomplished by passing arguments to the `fmsadmin` command. Consider the following code:

```
fmsadmin send -m "You have work to do!"
```

This command sends the message "You have work to do!" to all clients connected to the database on the local machine.

ABOUT SYSTEM PATHS

If you've worked much at the command line, you know that tools such as `fmsadmin` are easier to use if they're somewhere in the system path. If the command is not somewhere in the system path, it can be invoked only if the full path to the command is specified, as in this example:

```
/Library/FileMaker\ Server/Tools/fmsadmin send -m "You have work to do!"
```

(This is a Mac OS–style path, and the backslashes in the path are necessary to escape the spaces in the FileMaker Server install directory path on the Mac OS.) Alternatively, you can call the command when you've navigated to its installed location by saying

```
./fmsadmin send -m "You have work to do!"
```

where the dot (.) indicates the current working directory. Neither of these is very desirable, so it's best for the `fmsadmin` command to be available via the system path.

On Mac OS X Server, this happens automatically. On Mac OS X Server, `fmsadmin` is installed in `/usr/bin`, which is generally part of the system path. On regular Mac OS X, as well as Windows, `fmsadmin` is installed outside the default system paths. In this case, there are two choices: either copy it to a location within the default system path, such as `/usr/bin` on Mac OS or `C:\WINNT` on Windows, or edit the system path to include the `fmsadmin` install directory. The latter choice is probably the better option because it keeps the system path directories unencumbered.

The correct way to edit the system paths varies depending on operating system, and each operating system generally provides several ways to accomplish this goal. On Windows, you can choose Start Menu, Settings, Control Panel, and then open the System icon, select the Advanced tab, click the Environment Variables button, and then select and edit the path variable in the System Variables window. On Mac OS, you can edit a file such as `/etc/profile` to add your custom path commands. (Which file you edit depends on which command shell you and your users are using. If you're not very sure which file to edit, it's best to consult with a system administrator.)

A third option, on the Mac OS, is to create a *symbolic link* to the `fmsadmin` command from someplace on the system path. This installs a file in the system path that points to the true install location of `fmsadmin`. Such a command would look like this:

```
ln -s /Library/FileMaker\ Server/Tools/fmsadmin /usr/bin/fmsadmin
```

COMMAND LINE REFERENCE

The FileMaker Server documentation doesn't document the command line syntax very well (an odd lapse in what's otherwise a very good document). Instead, it refers you to the online help. Table 25.1 contains a list of all the commands and options you can use with `fmsadmin`.

→ For a more detailed command-line reference for FileMaker Server, see Chapter 14 of *FileMaker 8 Functions and Scripts Desk Reference*.

25

TABLE 25.1 `fmsadmin` COMMANDS AND OPTIONS

Name	Meaning	Usage
BACKUP	Back up databases	`fmsadmin BACKUP [FILE...] [PATH...] [-diopuwy]`
CLOSE	Close databases	`fmsadmin CLOSE [FILE...] [PATH...] [-imptuwy]`
DELETE	Delete a schedule	`fmsadmin delete schedule [SCHEDULE #] [-ipuwy]`
DISABLE	Disable plug-ins or schedules	`fmsadmin DISABLE TYPE [PLUG-IN #] [SCHEDULE #] [-ipuwy]`
DISCONNECT	Disconnect a client	`fmsadmin disconnect client [CLIENT #] [-impuwy]`
ENABLE	Enable plug-ins or schedules	`fmsadmin ENABLE TYPE [PLUG-IN #] [SCHEDULE #] [-ipuwy]`
LIST	List clients, files, plug-ins, or schedules	`fmsadmin LIST TYPE [-ipsuwy]`
OPEN	Open databases	`fmsadmin OPEN [FILE...] [PATH...] [-ipuwy]`
PAUSE	Pause databases	`fmsadmin PAUSE [FILE...] [PATH...] [-ipuwy]`
RELOAD	Reload preferences	`fmsadmin RELOAD [-ipuvwy]`
RESUME	Resume paused databases	`fmsadmin RESUME [FILE...] [PATH...] [-ipuwy]`
RUN	Run a schedule	`fmsadmin RUN SCHEDULE [SCHEDULE #] [-ipuwy]`
SEND	Send a message	`fmsadmin SEND [-cimpuwy] [CLIENT #] [FILE...] [PATH...]`
STATUS	Show status of guests and files	`fmsadmin STATUS TYPE [-ipuwy] [ID #] [FILE]`
STOP	Shut down the server	`fmsadmin STOP [-fimptuwy]`

COMMAND OPTIONS

Command options are additional parameters you can add to a command invocation to alter its behavior. The `fmsadmin` tool supports a number of standard options, and also several options that apply only to certain specific commands. The Usage column in each of the previous descriptions lists possible command options in square brackets. Many options have a long form that appears preceded by a double hyphen. The long form can be used to increase readability, for example, in scripts. See Table 25.2 for the available options.

TABLE 25.2   COMMAND OPTIONS

Option	Description
General Options	
`-h, --help`	Print the usage page
`-i address, --ip address`	Specify the IP address of a remote server
`-p pass, --password pass`	Password to use to authenticate with the server
`-u user, --user user`	Username to use to authenticate with the server
`-w seconds, --wait seconds`	Specify time in seconds for command to time out
`-v, --version`	Print the version information
`-y, --yes`	Automatically answer "yes" to all prompts
Command-Specific Options	
`-d PATH, --dest PATH`	Specify a destination path for a backup
`-f, --force`	Close databases or shut down the server forcefully, without waiting for clients to disconnect gracefully
`-m message, --message message`	Specify a text message to send to clients
`-o, --offline`	Perform an offline backup
`-s, --stats`	Return additional detail about clients or files
`-t secs, --grace-time secs`	Specify time in seconds before clients will be forcibly disconnected

25

SCRIPTING FILEMAKER SERVER ADMINISTRATIVE TASKS

Using the capabilities of the fmsadmin tool, an experienced system administrator can use command-line scripts to control many aspects of FileMaker Server functioning. These scripts may be executed manually, or run at scheduled times via a system utility such as cron (Mac OS) or the Task Scheduler (Windows). As you'll see further on, in the section "Scheduled Tasks," FileMaker Server can also be configured to run system scripts on a schedule.

Using scripted administration, you can even perform a few tasks that cannot directly be performed via the SAT. Suppose that you have a database system with several distinct files. The database is partitioned into different files because different tables in the database have widely differing usage patterns. One very large table is read-only, and consists of data that's imported nightly from another system. Other tables are smaller, but are updated constantly and contain critical data. You'd like to back up the smaller tables once an hour, but the larger table can be backed up as infrequently as once a day. If you establish a FileMaker

Server backup schedule via the SAT, each schedule must back up an entire directory at a time—you can't pick and choose among files within a directory. It would be easy enough to put the large file in one directory, the smaller files in another, and establish FileMaker Server–based backup schedules. If this organization is not desirable, though, you need to write two backup scripts—one for the large file, another for the smaller files—and use the operating system's task scheduling facilities to run them at different times. Each script would be fairly simple. They might look like this:

```
#hourly backup script for the transaction files
fmsadmin backup transaction.fp7 customer.fp7 orders.fp7

#daily backup script for the products file
fmsadmin backup product.fp7
```

You could also extend the scripts to use other operating system facilities. For example, you could compress the files after they had been backed up, or notify an administrator via email if the backup failed—neither of which is possible with FileMaker Server backups established via the SAT.

WORKING WITH EXTERNAL SERVICES

FileMaker Server can take advantage of certain external services to help centralize the management of information such as server location and user authentication credentials. If you or your organization maintains such services, you can configure FileMaker Server to use them. You can use external services to centralize two types of information:

- Information about the location of machines running FileMaker Server. You can use one or more directory servers to maintain information about the names and locations of FileMaker servers throughout your organization, rather than having your users keep track of server names or addresses.

- Information about user credentials. You can use the authentication services built into Windows and the Mac OS to map users' network credentials directly onto FileMaker accounts and privileges.

REGISTERING WITH AN LDAP SERVER

Suppose that you work with a large organization, where the network is divided into several subnets, and there are a number of instances of FileMaker Server running on different machines throughout the network. For a user on one subnet to access a FileMaker server on another, the user must know the machine name or IP address of the server, and must add that information to her list of favorite servers.

Rather than ask users and administrators to keep track of multiple machines and machine names, it's possible to use a *directory server* to maintain this information in a central location. The FileMaker Pro or FileMaker Advanced client and the SAT can both be configured to look for available servers via a directory server. As soon as the client or the SAT is configured to work through a directory server, any new FileMaker servers registered with the directory server automatically become visible to those clients.

FileMaker Server is capable of registering itself with directory servers that implement LDAP (Lightweight Directory Access Protocol). Such servers include Active Directory (Windows), Open Directory (Mac OS), and OpenLDAP (UNIX/Linux).

Configuring the interaction with a directory server has three steps:

1. Configure the directory server.
2. Configure an instance of FileMaker Server to register itself with the directory server.
3. Configure one or more copies of FileMaker Pro, FileMaker Advanced, or the SAT to search the directory server for available instances of FileMaker Server.

The registration process is relatively complex, and is best attempted by administrators with experience in managing the type of directory server in question. We'll walk through the critical steps in this section, without pretending to give a full introduction to the complex world of LDAP.

LDAP is a very flexible and very complex protocol. There are probably a great many ways to configure an LDAP server in such a way as to enable registration of FileMaker Server instances. We'll show you just one way, which involves creating a new *organizational unit (OU)* on the LDAP server and registering servers beneath it. We use Windows Active Directory to illustrate the process.

CONFIGURING AN ACTIVE DIRECTORY SERVER

To register a FileMaker Server with an Active Directory server, begin by adding a new organizational unit to the server. Choose Start, Programs, Administrative Tools, Active Directory Users and Computers. In the new window, right-click on the name of the LDAP server machine and choose New, Organization Unit. This operation is shown in Figure 25.8. Give the new OU a name; we call ours `fmp-ldap`.

Figure 25.8
To set up a FileMaker registry under Active Directory, begin by creating a new OU.

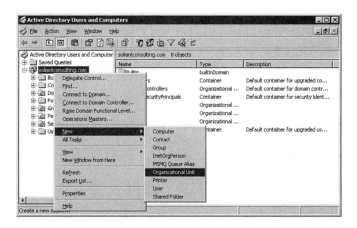

You need to associate a user with the new OU. You may want to create a new user just for this purpose. In that case, right-click the Users directory and choose New, User. This operation is shown in Figure 25.9. Take note of the username and password; they'll be necessary later when accessing the directory server remotely.

Figure 25.9
You'll probably want to create a new user to whom you want to delegate rights over the new OU.

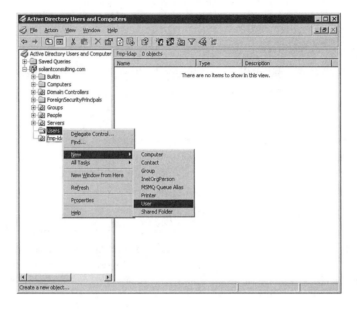

You next need to delegate certain privileges over the new OU to the user you just created. Right-click on the OU name and choose Delegate Control. You then see the Delegation of Control Wizard. On the second screen, choose the new user you just created. On the following screen, labeled Tasks to Delegate, choose the Create a Custom Task to Delegate radio button. On the following screen, choose to delegate control of This Folder, Existing Objects in This Folder, and Creation of New Objects in This Folder. On the next screen, titled Permissions, choose Full Control in the Permissions area. On the screen that follows, click Finish to complete the act of delegation. That completes the configuration of the Active Directory server.

NOTE

It is probably possible to create a workable configuration by delegating less than Full Control to the user in question. If you create a user specifically for this purpose, though, and grant him minimal or no rights elsewhere on the server, there is probably little risk in giving that user full rights to the OU.

REGISTERING WITH AN ACTIVE DIRECTORY SERVER

With the Active Directory configuration complete, you next need to register one or more FileMaker servers with the directory server. You use the SAT to do this. In the SAT, connect to the server you want to register and go to the Directory Service tab. Figure 25.10 shows the necessary configuration. Here are the important settings:

- **Directory Server Name**—The host name or IP address of the Active Directory server you just configured.

- **LDAP Port**—Use the default port of 389 unless your server has been configured differently.

- **Distinguished Name**—It's important to get this exactly right. In Figure 25.10 Active Directory is configured with an OU, so the distinguished name looks like `ou=<your OU name>` and then a series of `dc=` directives, which refer to the individual components of the machine name. If your machine name is adserver.mycompany.com and your OU is named `fmp-ou`, the distinguished name would be `ou=fmp-ou,dc=adserver,dc=mycompany,dc=com`.

- **Login Settings**—Choose to use Windows authentication. For the account name, it's important to use the form `<account-name>@<server-name>`.

Figure 25.10
You need to do a bit of work to fill in all the items necessary to register FileMaker Server with an LDAP server.

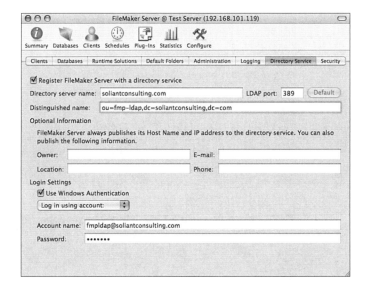

After you've filled these settings in, the SAT automatically tries to register the FileMaker server with the Active Directory server. This is the moment of truth!

One good way to check on the success of this operation is to look at the event log for the server you're trying to register. A registration failure generates only one or two events—one of them an error. A common error is one of insufficient privileges. This error may mean that you didn't supply the right logon credentials (bad username or password). It may also mean that you didn't delegate sufficient privileges over the OU to the chosen user. Such an error is shown in Figure 25.11.

Figure 25.11
Configuring your delegated user with insufficient privileges over the OU is a common source of problems.

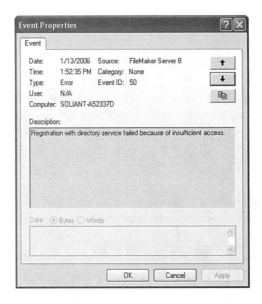

If registration did succeed, you should see quite a long list of events as each piece of information about the directory service is communicated to the server, culminating in an event with EventID 206, "Registration with directory service succeeded."

Successful registration also is visible on the Active Directory server, although it can take a while for the change to be visible there. Each registered server appears below the OU in which you registered it. The result is shown in Figure 25.12.

Figure 25.12
After FileMaker Server is successfully registered with the Active Directory server, the FileMaker server appears under the OU in Active Directory.

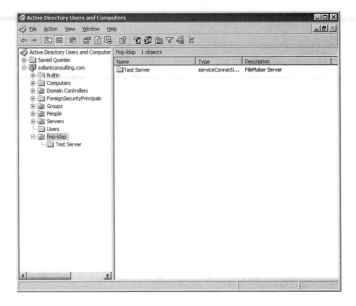

TIP

In the Mac OS version of the SAT, you can set up a preferred LDAP configuration. Choose FileMaker Server Admin, Preferences, and then choose LDAP Directory Service from the pop-up menu in the resulting dialog. You are given a screen where you can enter a default server address, port, search base, and login credentials.

LOOKING FOR SERVERS VIA LDAP

After you've successfully registered your FileMaker server with the Active Directory server, you can then use the Active Directory server when looking for hosts from FileMaker Pro, FileMaker Pro Advanced, or the SAT.

In FileMaker Pro, for example, if you choose File, Open Remote, you can then choose Hosts Listed by LDAP from the View menu. You can then click the Specify button to specify a directory service to connect to. Fill in the service information in the Specify LDAP Directory Service dialog. Possible settings are shown in Figure 25.13.

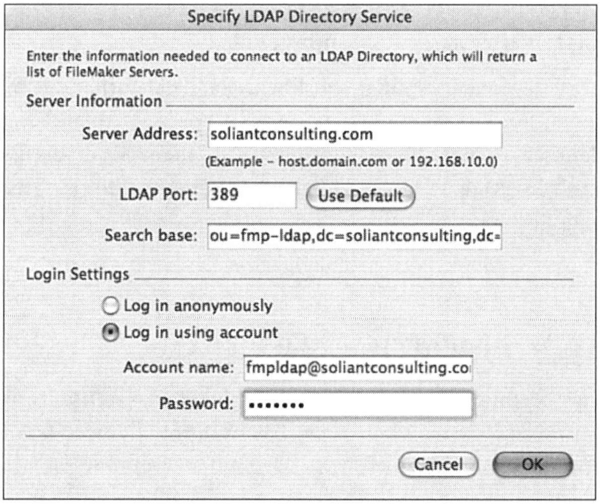

Figure 25.13
Use settings similar to those already used to register the server to look for registered FileMaker servers.

The settings are very similar to those you used when registering a FileMaker server. For Search Base, fill in the same string you supplied in the Distinguished Name field in the SAT when registering the FileMaker server earlier.

If all has gone well, the Open Remote File dialog should now show a list of all FileMaker servers registered with the chosen directory server. From here, you may work directly with those servers, or click Add to Favorites to add them to your list of preferred servers. These choices are shown in Figure 25.14.

Figure 25.14
After you've successfully connected to an LDAP server, you should see a list of all FileMaker servers registered with that directory service.

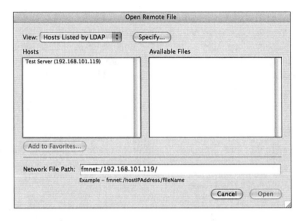

 There are quite a few things that can go wrong in the complex process of configuring and connecting to an LDAP server. To learn about some of them, see "Trouble with LDAP" in the "Troubleshooting" section at the end of this chapter.

USING EXTERNAL AUTHENTICATION SERVICES

You can configure FileMaker Server to work with external authentication services. If your organization maintains a directory of usernames and passwords, and you'd like to be able to reuse these credentials, it's possible to configure FileMaker Server to do so. The mechanics of configuring both FileMaker Pro and FileMaker Server to do this are covered in Chapter 12, "Implementing Security."

→ For a discussion of how to configure external authentication, **see** "External Authentication," **p. 346**.

AUTOMATICALLY UPDATING PLUG-INS

Using plug-ins has become commonplace in FileMaker Pro solutions, both big and small. One of the perceived issues with plug-in use has traditionally been the difficulty of distributing them to client machines. Even with the advent of server-side plug-ins in FileMaker Pro 7, every client machine that needs to make use of plug-in functionality must have the plug-in installed and enabled.

→ For a full discussion of using plug-ins with FileMaker Pro, **see** "Plug-ins," **p. 771**.

FileMaker Server has a feature called Auto Update that simplifies the distribution of plug-ins to client machines. The concept is very simple. Place your plug-ins in a designated folder on the server. When a user makes a client connection to a file hosted by FileMaker Server, you can have a script execute that checks the user's machine to see whether she has version such-and-such of such-and-such plug-in. If she doesn't, the script can automatically download the plug-in from the server. The plug-in is placed in the appropriate directory (the Extensions folder within the FileMaker Pro folder) and enabled. The server thus provides automatic updates to client machines that request them, obviating the need to manually distribute plug-ins.

There's a bit of setup and scripting you have to do to make use of this feature, but it's certainly not more than an hour's work per solution. The time you'll save not having to run around to all the machines on your network updating plug-ins is certainly worth the investment of an hour.

There are essentially three tasks that you need to perform to use the Auto Update feature. These are

- Prepare FileMaker Server
- Prepare FileMaker Pro
- Add scripts to your solution files to perform the auto update

These tasks are covered in detail in the following sections.

PREPARING FILEMAKER SERVER

To prepare FileMaker Server to provide automatic downloads of plug-ins, you must enable the option and put the plug-ins in the appropriate folder on the server.

You can turn on Auto Update within the Client Connections Assistant of the Server Administration Tool. It's simply a matter of checking a check box. There's only one check box on the screen, so you shouldn't have any trouble locating it. That same check box can be accessed on the Clients tab of the FileMaker Server Properties window, shown previously in Figure 25.2. You do not need to restart FileMaker Server after enabling the Auto Update feature.

The other task you need to do on the server is to place the plug-ins in an appropriate directory. Inside the Database directory, you should have a folder called AutoUpdate. That's where your plug-ins go. You create a folder within the AutoUpdate directory for each plug-in that you want to be downloaded to client machines. Name the folder the same as the plug-in itself, sans extension.

CAUTION

> Note that plug-in files often have different names on Mac and Windows. If this is the case, each plug-in file needs to be treated as its own plug-in, with its own directory tree within the AutoUpdate folder. See the example using the UPLOADit plug-in later in this chapter for further details.

Within that folder, create a folder for each version of the plug-in that you want to make available. You can name the folders anything you like, but it's recommended that you simply use the version number of the plug-in. For example, within the MyPlugin folder, you might have a folder called 1.0 and another named 1.1.

Finally, place the actual plug-ins within the appropriate version folder. If you have both Mac and Windows users, you need to place both the Mac OS X and Windows versions of the plug-in in this same version-specific directory. If you are using a Windows version of FileMaker Server and need to allow Mac OS X clients to download plug-ins, be aware that you must compress the Mac version of the plug-in as a `.tar` archive. (See the "Mac Plug-ins on a Windows Server" sidebar that follows to learn how to do this.)

Mac Plug-ins on a Windows Server

If you need to make Macintosh versions of your plug-ins available from a Windows version of FileMaker Server, you need to bundle the Mac plug-in as a `.tar` archive and place the archive on the server. This ensures that Macintosh-specific file information is not lost during the transition of the file from one platform to another.

Tar, which stands for *tape archiver*, was originally developed to create tape backups on UNIX systems. It's now commonly used for bundling files for all sorts of purposes. You can use the Terminal application on Mac OS X to create a `.tar` archive that contains your plug-in.

From the command-line prompt in the Terminal application, navigate to the directory where the plug-in is located on your machine by using the `cd` command. (You can learn more about changing directories by typing in **man cd** at the command prompt.)

Say that the plug-in you are working with is called `foo.fmplugin`. You want to turn this into an archive called `foo.fmplugin.tar`. To do this, you would type the following at the command line:

```
tar -cf foo.fmplugin.tar foo.fmplugin
```

Take the `.tar` file and place that in the appropriate directory on your Windows server. The archive is automatically unbundled when Mac clients download the archive.

CAUTION

> If you are using a Mac OS X version of FileMaker Server, you need to make sure that any plug-ins you place on the server are owned by the `fmsadmin` group and have group read permissions.

A sample plug-in is installed with FileMaker Server so that you can see the directory and naming structures that you need to follow. There's also a sample FileMaker Pro database that contains scripts to download the sample plug-in. These are both valuable resources the first time you go about setting up an auto-upload routine.

To give you an additional, more real-world example, we walk through the steps you'd take to build an auto update routine for a different plug-in. The plug-in that we've chosen as our guinea pig is UPLOADit, from Comm-Unity Networking Systems (www.cnsplug-ins.com). There's nothing special about this choice; we merely wanted to use something other than the sample plug-ins that ship with FileMaker. You follow the same steps for any plug-in that you use.

When you download UPLOADit, you'll get a folder full of demo files, instructions, and of course, the plug-ins themselves. The Mac version is called UPLOADit_OSX.fmplugin, and the Windows version is called UPLOADit_Win.fmx. The tasks you would need to undertake to prepare FileMaker Server to download these to client machines are as follows:

1. Create directories in the `AutoUpdate` folder on the server (`\FileMaker Server\Data\Databases\AutoUpdate\`) called `UPLOADit_OSX` and `UPLOADit_Win`. You need to have both because the plug-ins have different names on the two platforms.

2. Create a directory within each of these folders called simply 1.0.

3. If FileMaker Server is running on Windows, bundle the Mac version of the plug-in into a .tar archive called UPLOADit_OSX.fmplugin.tar (see the previous sidebar titled "Mac Plug-ins on a Windows Server").

4. Copy the .tar archive and the Windows version of the plug-in to the appropriate 1.0 folder.

After those steps have been taken, and assuming the Auto Update feature of FileMaker Server has been enabled, client connections to the server can now begin requesting the UPLOADit plug-in. The actual download process is covered in the following sections.

PREPARING FILEMAKER PRO

For a FileMaker Pro client to download plug-ins from FileMaker Server, the client needs to have the AutoUpdate plug-in installed and enabled. This plug-in is part of the typical installation of FileMaker Pro, so unless you've disabled the plug-in for some reason, chances are that the client application will be all prepared to download plug-ins.

As with all plug-ins, the AutoUpdate plug-in should be placed in the Extensions folder within the FileMaker Pro application directory. To confirm that the plug-in is enabled, go to the Plug-ins tab of the Preferences dialog, which is shown in Figure 25.15.

Figure 25.15
The AutoUpdate plug-in must be enabled on a workstation for it to be able to retrieve downloads of other plug-ins from FileMaker Server.

As part of the routine for performing the actual download—which is described in detail in the next section—you'll write a script that checks that the AutoUpdate plug-in is installed and active. If it's not, you can show users a dialog telling them to call the database administrator or giving them instructions on how to obtain and enable the AutoUpdate plug-in.

PERFORMING THE AUTO UPDATE

The actual downloading of a plug-in from the server to the client machine is triggered by a script executed on the client machine. The AutoUpdate plug-in, which was discussed in the preceding section, has three functions, which all play a role in an auto-update routine. These three functions are

- FMSAUC_Version (0)—Returns a string containing the name and version number of the AutoUpdate plug-in itself. Currently, this value is "FileMaker Auto Update Plugin Version 8.0".

- FMSAUC_FindPlugin (*plug-in_name*)—Returns a space-delimited list of the folder names on the server within the directory specified by the *plug-in name* parameter. The list, however, returns only folders that contain the specified plug-in. If there's no folder in the AutoUpdate directory on the server that's named the same as the specified parameter, this function returns a -1.

- FMSAUC_UpdatePlugin (*plug-in_name_and_version*)—This is the function that actually obtains the plug-in from the server. A string containing both the plug-in name and version should be used as the parameter. If the plug-in downloads with no error, the function returns a 0. Table 25.3 shows the other values that may be returned.

TABLE 25.3   ERROR CODES RETURNED BY FMSAUC UpdatePlugin

Error Code	Description
-1	The file to be downloaded is missing from the temporary folder.
-2	The Extensions\Saved folder to contain the backup of the outdated plug-in or support file couldn't be created.
-3	The file to be replaced on the client computer couldn't be deleted from the Extensions folder.
-4	The file to be replaced couldn't be moved to the Extensions\Saved folder.
-5	The downloaded file can't be copied to the Extensions folder.
-6	The download file must be a plug-in file.
3	The AutoUpdate plug-in is disabled in the FileMaker Server Administration Client Connections Assistant, FileMaker Server Properties (Windows), or Configure, Clients (Mac OS).
5	The download file can't be found in the AutoUpdate folder on the FileMaker Server computer.
6	An error occurred on the computer running FileMaker Server as the file was being downloaded.
100	The external function definition for FMSAUC_UpdatePlugIn contains an invalid or empty parameter.
101	The function call from the client computer to the computer running FileMaker Server failed. The server computer might be running a previous version of FileMaker Server.

To download a plug-in from the server, a user must first open a client session to a file that resides on the server. Plug-in downloads will not work from a peer-to-peer hosted file.

A typical auto-update routine consists of three tasks:

- Checking to see what version of the plug-in, if any, already resides on the client's workstation
- Checking whether the server has a more recent version
- If necessary, downloading the plug-in to the client workstation

If a certain plug-in is required for a file to operate as designed, you will want to have the auto update routine be part of the file's startup script. That way, if for some reason the user isn't able to retrieve the plug-in, you can prevent her from entering the system. Whether you write the routine using just a single script or split it into three (or more) subscripts that are called from a master script is a matter of personal preference. In the example that follows, we use a single script because it's a bit easier to follow the logic. First, however, we briefly discuss each of the parts of the routine independently.

CHECK WHAT'S ALREADY ON THE WORKSTATION

Every plug-in should contain a function that returns the name and version number of the plug-in itself. By calling that identity function, you'll know not only whether the user's workstation already has the plug-in, but also what version of the plug-in it has (thereby possibly obviating the need to download the plug-in again). You need to manually install and enable the plug-in on a workstation so that you can find out what this function is supposed to return when everything is up to date.

In the case of the UPLOADit plug-in that is serving as our example, this function is called `Upld-Version`, and the version we're working with returns the string `UPLOADit v.1.0.0`. A quick call to this function at the beginning of your auto-update routine informs you whether the workstation already has everything it needs. If it returns nothing, or if it returns a different version number, the script needs to proceed with the update routine.

Of course, if the user's workstation doesn't have the AutoUpdate plug-in installed and enabled, there's no chance that a download can occur. You therefore need to check the version number of that plug-in as well; you do this with the function `FMSAUC_Version (0)`. As long as this function returns something—indeed, anything—then the plug-in is active and you can proceed. If not, you'll want to provide users with some feedback on what they need to do (such as calling the database administrator).

CHECK WHAT'S ON THE SERVER

You can check what version(s) of a plug-in are available for download from the server by using the function `FMSAUC_FindPlugin`. The parameter you pass should be the name of a folder you've set up on the server to contain plug-ins. If a folder with the specified name can't be found, the function returns a `-1`. If it is found, the function returns a string containing a space-delimited list of the version numbers of the plug-ins of that name that are available.

The version number string returned by this function contains the names of the folders you've created within the plug-in's directory; these may or may not correspond to the actual version numbers of the plug-in. That is, you can name the folder anything you want. As long as it's in the plug-in's directory and contains the specified plug-in, the folder name is included in the response generated by the FMSAUC_FindPlugin function. For the example plug-in, the functions FMSAUC_FindPlugin ("UPLOADit_OSX") and FMSAUC_FindPlugin ("UPLOADit_Win") would both be expected to return 1.0.

There's one other thing to know about the list of version numbers returned by the FMSAUC_FindPlugin function. It returns only the names of folders that actually contain a version of the plug-in that's appropriate for the client's operating system. That is, if you have a Mac version of the plug-in in a folder called 1.0.1, and a Windows version in a folder called 1.0.2, Mac clients see only the 1.0.1 directory and Windows clients the 1.0.2 directory. If both directories contain versions for both platforms, the function returns the string 1.0.1 1.0.2.

CAUTION

> Because the FMSAUC_FindPlugin function returns a space-delimited string, you must avoid using spaces in the names of the folders you create on the server. It is impossible to parse one folder name from another if they contain spaces.

After you've determined the version numbers that are available on the server, you need to compare them to what the client already has to determine whether a new version should be downloaded. There are many ways you can go about comparing the local and remote version numbers, and there's no single right way that will work in all cases. You'll probably need to extract the numeric portion of the local version, using the GetAsNumber function or one of the text-parsing functions. Set up the name of the version folders on the server to facilitate easy comparison with what's actually returned.

TIP

> It's rare that you'll ever need or want to have multiple versions of a plug-in available on the server. If you have only one version, then you can simply check whether the local version equals the server version.

Download the Plug-In

If the workstation either doesn't have the plug-in, or if your comparison of the local and server versions reveals that the local version needs to be updated, you'll use the FMSAUC_UpdatePlugin function to download the plug-in to the workstation. The parameter you pass to this function should contain both the plug-in name and the version number, separated by a space. For instance, to download the Mac version of the UPLOADit plug-in, you would use the following function:

```
FMSAUC_UpdatePlugin ("UPLOADit_OSX 1.0")
```

If desired, you can use FileMaker's string manipulation functions to dynamically build a string to pass as this parameter, using the results from the FMSAUC_FindPlugin function. If you know the name and version number you want, though, you can also hard-code it as has been done here.

If the user's machine already has a version of the plug-in, it is automatically moved to a directory named Saved (within the Extensions folder). The new plug-in is placed in the Extensions folder and is enabled for immediate use. There should be no user intervention necessary before, during, or after the download.

It's good practice to include a final check at the end of your update routine to ensure that the plug-in is indeed active. This would consist of another call to the version function of the particular plug-in. Assuming that all's well, your startup script can proceed with any other desired tasks.

PUTTING IT ALL TOGETHER

The preceding sections have discussed the tasks and principles involved in a typical auto-update routine. It should nonetheless be helpful to see a complete sample script from start to finish. The example again uses the UPLOADit plug-in and assumes a directory structure on the server as described in the "Preparing the Server" section. Because the names of the Mac and Windows versions of the plug-ins are different, it's necessary to have some conditional logic that takes the client platform into consideration. Finally, in this script we're simply interested in getting the version 1.0.0 plug-in on the user's machine. You could add more complex logic to automatically test for updates; this script would need to be edited slightly if an updated plug-in became available.

```
Set Variable [ $localVersion; Value: Upld-Version ]
If [ RightWords ($localVersion; 1) ≠ "1.0.0" ]
    If [IsEmpty (FMSAUC_Version (0))]
        Show Custom Dialog [ Title: "Warning"; Message: "You do not have the
        ➥ Auto Update plug-in installed on your workstation.  Please
        ➥ call Jasper, the database administrator, immediately";
        ➥ Buttons: "OK" ]
        Halt Script
    End If
Set Variable [ $remoteVersion;
    Let ([paramName = Case ( Get (SystemPlatform) = -2;
            "UPLOADit_Win" ; "UPLOADit_OSX");
        versionString = FMSAUC_FindPlugin (paramName) ];
        RightWords (versionString; 1)) ]
    If [ IsEmpty ($remoteVersion) ]
        Show Custom Dialog [ Title: "Warning"; Message: "The UPLOADit plug-in
        ➥ could not be found on the server.  Please call Jasper, the
        ➥ database administrator, immediately"; Buttons: "OK" ]
        Halt Script
    End If
Set Variable [ $error;
    Let ( [pluginName = Case (Get (SystemPlatform) = -2;
            "UPLOADit_Win"; "UPLOADit_OSX");
        version = $remoteVersion;
        paramName = pluginName & " " & version] ;
        FMSAUC_UpdatePlugin (paramName)) ]
```

25

```
If [$error ≠ 0 ]
    Show Custom Dialog [ Title: "Error Downloading Required Plug-in";
    ➥ Message: "There was an error encountered during an attempt
    ➥ to download a plug-in required by this database.  ERR = " &
    ➥ AutoUpdatePlugin::gError; Buttons: "OK" ]
    Halt Script
End If
End If
```

As you can see, this script has three error traps in it. You'd want to change the error handling to be appropriate for your solution. We've just put Halt Script steps in here, but you may want to exit the application or take the user back to a main menu layout.

SCHEDULED TASKS

FileMaker Server has a built-in capability for executing scheduled tasks. The three types of tasks that can be scheduled are database backups, execution of batch scripts, and sending messages to connected users.

The Server Administration Tool is used to create scheduled tasks. On Windows, you use the Task Scheduling Assistant, which walks you through a series of seven screens, prompting you for a few bits of information about the schedule on each screen. On Mac OS X, you can click the New button while viewing the schedule list, or you can select Action, Schedules, New Schedule. The new task dialog on Mac OS X is shown in Figure 25.16.

Figure 25.16
When creating a new task, you specify information such as the type of task and the frequency with which it should be executed.

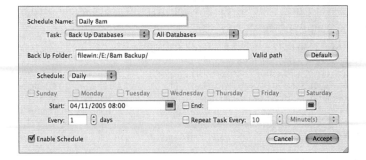

The information you are asked to provide when setting up a schedule is quite obvious and intuitive; we don't need to go over every option here. There are, however, a few important facts and tips that are worth knowing. First, you can create no more than 50 scheduled tasks. We've never seen anyone get anywhere near this limit, so it shouldn't be an area of concern for you. Second, new tasks are set to be enabled by default. Finally, if you need to create many similar scheduled tasks, it's best to create one and then duplicate it, changing each copy as appropriate to get the desired variation (backup schedules that vary only by the day of the week, for example).

You can see a list of all the tasks that are scheduled by navigating within the SAT to the Schedules screen, which is shown in Figure 25.17.

Figure 25.17
The Schedules screen contains a list of all the schedules and shows information such as the task's name, status, and next and last execution times.

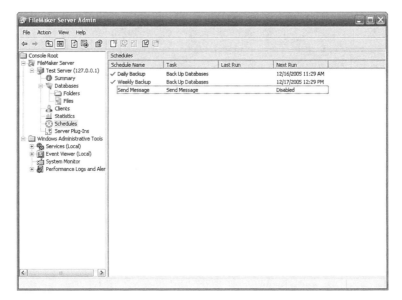

From the schedule list you can see a lot of useful information about the status of your scheduled tasks. For instance, you can see the date and time the task was last executed, as well as the date and time of the next scheduled execution. A check mark at the beginning of the line indicates that a task is enabled.

TIP

> If you ever need to suspend task execution because of system maintenance or other troubleshooting activities, it's better to simply disable any tasks that are waiting to be run rather than to delete them.

You can edit any task's options by double-clicking on it from the task list. If you right-click (Windows) or Control-click (Mac), you will see a list of other actions you can perform. These include running the task immediately, enabling or disabling the task, and duplicating the task. You can also delete a task this way.

If you schedule tasks in such a way that one task isn't finished by the time the next one is ready to begin, the second task is delayed until the first one has finished executing.

SCHEDULING BACKUPS

The most commonly scheduled tasks are database backups. The frequency of backups is dependent on your business needs. Some organizations back up their data once a day; others back up every hour during the day. The general rule of thumb is that your backup frequency should be based on how much data you're willing to lose. If you always base your assumptions on worst-case scenarios, you'll probably be well covered in the event such a scenario comes about.

When you set up a backup schedule, you can specify whether all databases should be backed up or just those in a particular folder. Typically, you'll choose to back up all the databases. The main reason to back up just those in a particular directory is if you have some number of very large files that don't change often, such as a data archive or large lookup table. You can place those databases in their own directory and back them up on a less frequent basis than your main production files. This results in less time required to perform the backup, but more importantly, the backups take up less hard drive space.

You also must specify a directory in which the backup files are placed. When you install FileMaker Server, a folder called Backups is automatically set up for you within the Data directory. You can use that directory for your backups, or specify another valid directory path if that's preferable.

TIP

> If space permits on your hard drive, it's a good idea to have multiple destination folders set up for your backups so that they don't overwrite one another. For instance, if you back up daily, you should have a Monday folder, a Tuesday folder, and so on, and set up separate schedules for each day's back up. This ensures that you always have several backups of varying ages if there's ever a problem. Sometimes you'll discover a data problem days after it occurs, so being able to go back to older backups comes in handy.

25

If the drive to which you are backing up runs out of space during the backup, the backup is aborted, any partial files that have been created are deleted, and an error is written to the server logs. Be sure to periodically check (once a month, at least) that your backups are being created as expected and that you have adequate drive space.

FileMaker Server 7 and 8 perform backups slightly differently than previous versions of FileMaker Server did. It used to be the case that databases were put into a paused state during a backup. Users would commonly experience a coffee-cup icon if they attempted to access a paused database.

FileMaker Server now performs a live backup that requires significantly less time when the databases are unavailable. At the beginning of the backup process, FileMaker Server flushes the cache so that any data saved in memory is written to disk. Then it creates a dirty copy of the file. Users can still access and modify the original file while this copy is being made. After that's finished, the live database is paused and compared to the dirty copy; incremental changes are made to the copy so that it reflects the current state of the live file. The pause required for the incremental update is usually quite short and may not even be perceptible to users.

RUNNING SCRIPTS

In addition to database backups, you can also use FileMaker Server to schedule the execution of script files. On Windows, script files might be batch files or something like a WinBatch executable file. On Mac OS X, script files might be AppleScript applets or UNIX batch files. Scripts must be placed within the Scripts directory, which is located in the Data folder.

Script files are typically used to perform activities such as copying backup files to remote drives and compressing copies of backup files. Pretty much anything that you can do from the command line on either platform can be done through a batch file. You can even use FileMaker Server's command-line interface commands to have your batch scripts act on FileMaker Server itself. See the section called "Administration from the Command Line" in this chapter to learn more about the types of activities this enables.

SENDING MESSAGES TO USERS

The final type of task that can be scheduled directly from FileMaker Server is sending messages to users. Messages can be sent either to all users connected to the server or just those using databases in a certain folder.

Sending messages via the server is useful for notifying users of scheduled downtime for the server or to remind them of periodic events.

MONITORING FILEMAKER SERVER

If you administer one or more machines running FileMaker Server, you'll want to take advantage of some of the tools that are available for monitoring resource usage and application events. We look at each of these areas in turn.

WORKING WITH USAGE STATISTICS

If you click the Statistics icon in the SAT, you'll see a table of information concerning six key usage parameters on the server. For each parameter, you can see the current, average, low, and peak values. Here's a list of what's monitored.

- **Network KB/Sec**—Average data transfer per second. This number tells you the extent to which the raw network bandwidth of the machine is being used up.

- **FileMaker Pro Clients**—This tells you the number of connected FileMaker Pro clients. It's useful to see it here in the summary view, but clicking the Clients icon in the SAT gives you more detailed information on connected clients.

- **Files**—This tells you the number of open files. Again, clicking the Database icon gives more detailed information.

- **Disk KB/Sec**—This gives you some idea of how much data is actually being written to disk over a given period. This is to some degree a measure of the extent to which the database files are being changed. If the files are being predominantly read from, the disk write activity should be low. If the files are constantly being written to, disk activity will be high. Keep an eye on this number if you expect that hard disk performance may be a bottleneck.

- **Cache Unsaved %**—Like many database servers, FileMaker Server sets aside an area of RAM (of a size configured by the administrator) to use as a cache. When a user makes a request for data, FileMaker Server checks first to see whether the data is in the cache, and if so, it fetches it from the cache, more quickly than it could fetch it from disk.

25

Over time, the contents of the cache are written out to disk. The period over which this occurs is governed by a setting on the Databases tab of the server properties (Windows) or Configure icon (Mac OS). The setting is called Distribute Cache Flush Over. For example, if that value were set to one minute, FileMaker would attempt to write the whole cache out to disk over the course of a minute. The Cache Unsaved % should ideally be around 25% or lower. If it's much above that, you may want to shorten the length of the cache flush period. Having too much data unsaved in the cache increases the odds of data corruption in the event of a crash.

- **Cache Hit %**—This number indicates how often FileMaker Server is finding the data it's looking for in the cache. Here you want to see a number over 90%. Much less than that, and FileMaker is looking to the disk too often. In that case, it's a good idea to increase the size of the RAM cache (also on the Database tab under Properties [Windows] or Configure [Mac OS]). If the RAM cache is already as high as it can allowably go, you may want to consider adding more RAM to the machine, unless you've already reached the limit of 800MB of cache memory, which will be reached at 4GB of system RAM.

WORKING WITH APPLICATION EVENTS

FileMaker Server uses the event-logging facilities of the operating system on which it's installed. On the Windows platform, FileMaker Server events can be viewed with the Windows Event Viewer, whereas on the Mac the events are written to a file called `Event.log`.

WORKING WITH APPLICATION EVENTS ON WINDOWS

On Windows, you can access the Event Viewer from the left pane of the SAT by choosing Windows Administrative Tools, Event Viewer, FileMaker Server 7. The Event Viewer is shown in Figure 25.18.

In this view you'll see a list of application events, sortable by any column. Double-clicking an event brings up additional detail about the event. Icons in the left margin indicate events that constitute errors.

Right-clicking on the log name enables you to manipulate the log in a variety of ways, such as clearing it or exporting it. Choosing Properties enables you to set some important logging parameters, such as the maximum size of the log and the filtering conditions that govern how the log is displayed. These choices are shown in Figure 25.19.

WORKING WITH APPLICATION EVENTS ON MAC OS X

On the Mac, events are written to the file `/Library/FileMaker Server/Data/Logs/Event.log`. This is a plain-text file that you can view with any text editor. You can also view it in the Console application to get a live view of the log while the server is running. The Mac OS X event log is shown in Figure 25.20.

Figure 25.18
It's a good idea to become familiar with the server event log.

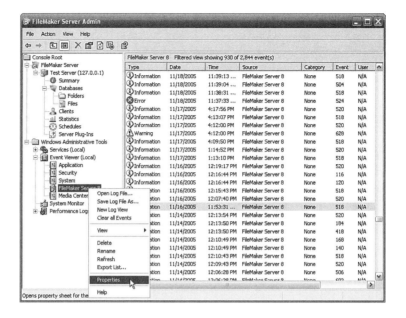

Figure 25.19
On Windows, you can configure a number of useful parameters pertaining to event logging.

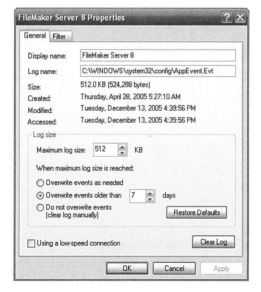

The FileMaker Server event logging model is fairly verbose. It logs all current configuration options when it starts up. It logs each database as it opens, and each client connection on a per-client per-file basis. The event log should always be one of the first sources of information that you draw on when troubleshooting a problem with FileMaker Server.

Figure 25.20
On Mac OS X, the event log is a plain-text file.

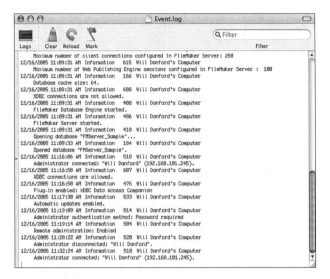

TROUBLESHOOTING

TROUBLE WITH LDAP

I think I configured my Active Directory server correctly, but when I try to use the SAT to register a server there, I get an error message reading "insufficient access privileges" in the server event log.

There are several possible reasons for this. It's possible that you've specified an incorrect username or password in the Directory Services tab of the SAT. When connecting to Active Directory, make sure that the username is in the form <username>@server, and make sure to verify the password as well.

It's also possible that you've delegated insufficient privileges over the organization unit you created. You shouldn't run into this problem if you grant your chosen user full access over the OU.

I tried to register with an with an LDAP server running Active Directory but I got a "Server Down" message in my FileMaker Server event log.

This indicates that connection to the server has failed for some reason. First verify that you have the correct server name. Next, verify that you know on what port the directory service is running—389 is the default port for LDAP, but a server administrator can change the port. If the server name and port are configured correctly in the Directory Service tab of the SAT, make sure that any and all intervening firewalls are configured to pass traffic on the correct directory service port.

PROBLEMS WITH AUTO UPDATE

I tried to get Auto Update working but I just can't seem to get it right.

There are quite a few steps to getting Auto Update to work successfully. For more information, check the supplied documentation—there's a document that deals specifically with Auto Update. The sample files on the disc for this book also include a file that demonstrates Auto Update logic.

FILEMAKER EXTRA: BEST PRACTICES CHECKLIST

Much of the work of server maintenance and administration consists of diligently following a routine. For each server or service you maintain, there should be a checklist of necessary tasks. Some of these you need to do only once, when you set things up. Others are recurring tasks that should be attended to carefully. In this section, we present a series of considerations for setting up and maintaining a FileMaker Server installation.

If you're working with network staff or administrators who don't have previous experience with FileMaker, offer them this list as a handy overview of the essentials of maintaining a FileMaker Server.

DETERMINE NETWORK INFRASTRUCTURE

You'll want to run FileMaker traffic over the fastest network possible. Before doing anything about a server machine proper, make sure that you have a handle on prevailing networking conditions. What's the topology of the network over which FileMaker will run? Is it fully switched, or are hubs involved? What's the minimum speed of links within the network? With what other services will FileMaker traffic be competing? Knowing the answers to all these questions can help you make the right hardware choices, and will give you a leg up on diagnosing any later problems that appear to be network-related.

PURCHASE HARDWARE

We discussed ideal hardware characteristics earlier in the chapter. Simply put, buy the best machine you can afford. Get a machine with one or more fast processors (ideally, 2GHz and up), a healthy dose of RAM (1GB and up), fast disk storage (SCSI or Serial ATA, and consider a hardware RAID configuration), and a networking capability that matches the prevailing speed of your network. Expandability is also a good idea: Additional drive bays, external hard drive connectivity, and multiple slots (for additional or upgraded networking capability, for example) are all desirable.

All this might sound expensive, but hardware power these days is reasonably priced. For example, at the present time (early 2006), $3,300 will get you a PowerMac G5 with dual 2.3GHz dual-core processors, Mac OS X Server, 2GB of RAM, and a 250GB Serial ATA drive. And $3,500 will get you a Dell PowerEdge SC1425 with dual 3GHz dual-core Xeon processors, Windows Server 2003, 2GB RAM, and two 160GB Serial ATA hard drives. If you want to spend less, you could reduce the amount of available hard drive space, use a bit less RAM (but not much less!) or drop back to a single processor.

INSTALL SOFTWARE

Use the latest version of an approved operating system, with all relevant patches and updates. Avoid enabling any other services on the machine except for those strictly necessary for system administration. In particular, avoid file sharing as much as possible. If it can't be avoided, make *sure* that you do not enable file sharing for those areas that contain the hosted database files—otherwise you run the risk of file corruption.

Install FileMaker Server and make sure that all appropriate updates are applied. Make sure that your version of FileMaker Server is compatible with both the operating system and, if applicable, the service pack level of the operating system. Make sure that all drivers are up to date, especially drivers for critical things such as disks. Make sure that the BIOS and firmware for the machine are up to date as well.

It's a good idea, if possible, to put the FileMaker Server data on its own volume, separate from the volume containing the applications and operating system.

Here are a few more useful tips for operating system configuration:

- Disable any disk-indexing software.
- Configure any virus-scanning software so that it does not scan the FileMaker data files for viruses.
- On Windows, turn off Volume Shadow Copy.
- On Windows, set the network throughput in File and Print Sharing to Maximize Data Throughput for Network Applications.
- On Windows, set your virtual memory paging files to a specific size, rather than allowing them to grow as needed.

CONFIGURE FILEMAKER SERVER

Configure FileMaker Server to a level appropriate for your expected usage (see the detailed notes earlier in the chapter). Bear in mind that it's worthwhile to try to use only those resource levels (for example, maximum numbers of connected clients and hosted files) that you think you'll need. Here are some other quick rules of thumb:

- Set the cache to half the allowable maximum, and increase it if the cache hit rate dips much below 90%.
- Set the cache flush interval to 1 minute. Fast modern hard drives can flush most or all of even an 800MB cache in that period.

DEPLOY DATABASES AND SCHEDULE BACKUPS

Decide on your database directory structure—that is, how you'll group databases into directories on the server. Decide whether to use an alternate database directory (but make sure that it's on a local hard drive, not on a networked volume!). Regardless of your choice, establish backup schedules that provide you and your organization with an appropriate level of security. How much data can you afford to lose? Decide on the answer and back up accordingly. Remember that local backups by themselves are not sufficient security: You should make provisions to transfer this data to offline storage such as a tape backup.

MONITOR USAGE STATISTICS

Keep a careful eye on usage statistics, especially early on when usage patterns are being established. Be alert for signs of inappropriate configuration, such as a low cache hit percentage or a high amount of unsaved data in the cache. Make sure that your network bandwidth continues to be adequate.

MONITOR EVENT LOGS

Check the application event logs periodically to make sure that things are operating smoothly. If you want to be especially proactive, and have some facility with operating system scripting, write a batch script that scans the event log for errors and emails you if errors appear in the log.

PERFORM REGULAR FILE MAINTENANCE

It's probably a wise idea to periodically run the File Maintenance tool, available in FileMaker Pro Advanced, on your files. How often to run it depends on how heavily used your files are. A good rule of thumb is to perform file maintenance once per month. If your databases experience thousands or tens of thousands of transactions a month, you might want to optimize your files as often as every couple of weeks.

KEEP CURRENT WITH SOFTWARE UPDATES

It should go without saying, but you'll want to keep current with all updates and patches to your operating system, and to all software packages installed on the server, including, of course, FileMaker Server itself.

FILEMAKER MOBILE

FILEMAKER MOBILE 8 OVERVIEW

The latest version of FileMaker's mobile data application provides a solution for those users who need to take their data with them in a simple yet highly usable format on either Palm OS– or Pocket PC–based devices. FileMaker Mobile 8 consists of two applications: one, the application that you use on your computer to prepare a database to be published or synchronized to a handheld device and, two, the application used on your handheld device to access data there. You will also use FileMaker Pro 8 or FileMaker Pro 8 Advanced to manage security settings within the database file with which you want to synchronize.

Simply put, FileMaker Mobile 8 allows you to synchronize a data table in a FileMaker file (note that you can work with only one table per file) with a handheld form-based interface and access your data on the go. You can then resynch your data when you return to your desk and ensure that any changes you made on your handheld device are then represented within your FileMaker solution and vice versa.

 FileMaker Mobile 8 introduces a significant new feature: Developers and users can now synchronize their mobile databases with a FileMaker file hosted on another computer, either through FileMaker Server (versions 7 or 8) or via peer-to-peer sharing.

FILEMAKER MOBILE COMPONENTS

FileMaker Mobile 8 consists of three software components:

- The computer-based application that allows for the configuration of data tables to be shared on a mobile device.

- The mobile device application that presents the shared data and allows their records to be searched, edited, deleted, added, and sorted.

- The synchronization module that allows for the mediated synchronization of the mobile data tables and their associated computer-based data tables. This engine synchronizes FileMaker-to-FileMaker Mobile data tables in the same process that synchronizes a user's other mobile applications, such as their contact manager and calendar.

SYSTEM REQUIREMENTS

FileMaker Pro Mobile 8 is compatible with computers running Windows and Mac OS X, as well as with Palm OS– and Pocket PC–based mobile devices. (Note that the listed hardware and software requirements are minimum requirements. More recent versions and higher capacities are also compatible.) FileMaker Mobile also requires FileMaker Pro 7 or 8 (or FileMaker Developer 7 or FileMaker Pro 8 Advanced).

USING FILEMAKER MOBILE ON YOUR HANDHELD DEVICE

The use of FileMaker Mobile is as simple as configuring an existing FileMaker Pro data table and synching it with your handheld device. After the data is on your handheld, the application provides the basic functions of searching and sorting of the data, as well as the addition, modification, and deletion of individual records in your data set. There isn't any development work to be done, and note that only your data is copied to your handheld; none of the layouts in your desktop FileMaker Pro database will be transferred.

There are, however, a fair number of options for controlling the functionality of the application on your handheld, as well as the means for customizing the display characteristics of the data in your handheld database. The mobile application offers two primary views of your data: List and Form. The use and formatting of these views is covered in more detail later in this chapter.

Note that FileMaker Mobile does not present all the layout options you're used to in FileMaker Pro. The forms it presents are fairly simple; having access to one's data on the road is really what this product is all about.

One alternative to FileMaker Mobile, for users of portable devices running the full Windows operating system, is to install a copy of FileMaker Pro on the handheld. This option will provide FileMaker's full set of functionality, but the synchronization of data becomes far more challenging. A developer would need to write heavily scripted routines to manage the process, or you'd need to invest in a third-party tool like WorldSync's SyncDeK product. A second alternative would be running with a Citrix ICA client.

NOTE

> For developers hoping to synchronize data between two FileMaker solutions, we recommend you look into WorldSync's SyncDeK product. Although this entails additional setup and cost, it is an excellent option and provides powerful features.

INSTALLING ON YOUR HANDHELD DEVICE

Assuming that you have all the hardware components required for the use of the FileMaker Mobile 8 application, its installation is worth some discussion:

1. Cradle or connect your handheld device, and then run the FileMaker Mobile 8 install script contained on the provided install disk.

2. Launch your handheld desktop management software (this will vary between Palm and Pocket PC platforms) and select the option to install files. Select FileMaker Mobile 8 and then synchronize your handheld.

3. Launch the FileMaker Mobile 8 application on your computer and enter the appropriate installation code for at least one handheld license. Note that later in the application, after installation is complete, you can add additional licenses in order to synchronize with multiple devices.

   The installation process also allows you to choose from among a collection of starter solutions that you want to add to your handheld. If you select one or more of these solutions, the software will install mobile databases to your handheld device (queued for the next time you synch). The FileMaker databases configured for synchronization with their mobile analogs will have been installed in a folder in the Documents directory on your computer.

4. Synchronize again and you will have successfully installed FileMaker Mobile 8 on your handheld and computer.

At this point, the application is ready to be used on your Palm or Pocket PC handheld. You can either use one of the sample databases provided or configure a database to be synched with your handheld device. Database files are discussed in the next section.

USING MOBILE DATABASE FILES

The mobile version of FileMaker has many of the same features and functions as its more full-featured PC- or Mac-based version.

After launching FileMaker Mobile 8 on your handheld, you will be directed to a menu of available mobile databases, as shown in Figure 26.1. If you left a database open and turned off your device, you will return to it. When working within a database, you can always navigate to the menu of available databases by clicking the FileMaker icon in the lower-left corner of every screen in FileMaker Mobile 8.

Figure 26.1
The main menu of FileMaker Mobile 8 presents you with a list of available mobile databases.

After FileMaker Mobile is launched, it will present data from a table in either a List view or a Form view, as shown in Figure 26.2, and allow you to search and sort within either view. The List view presents all the fields in a horizontal grid (very similar to the Table view within FileMaker Pro), whereas the Form view presents fields in a vertical arrangement. As with FileMaker on your computer, List view presents multiple records, whereas Form view presents just one record. You can navigate between the two views by selecting the List/Form View icons at the bottom of the application screen. Also, if data entry is not enabled in List view (more about that later), clicking on a record's data will navigate to the Form view for that record.

Figure 26.2
Each mobile database can be viewed in either a List view or a Form view on your handheld device.

Using the FileMaker Mobile application should feel familiar to any experienced FileMaker user. You can create new records (by clicking the omnipresent New button at the bottom of each view, or by using the menu at the top of the screen), duplicate existing records, and delete records by selecting the appropriate menu items from the Record menu. Your found set can be sorted according to the contents of a given field in either ascending or descending order. You can navigate to a specific record by its record number or step forward or backward in the found set by using the record navigation icons in the bottom of both views. You can, essentially, perform all the basic data operations that you can with FileMaker Pro.

WORKING WITH LIST VIEW

The List view in a FileMaker Mobile database is quite similar to the Table view in FileMaker Pro on your computer, as shown in Figure 26.3. Data is displayed in a columnar layout with field values in columns and records encompassing individual rows. No record may occupy more than one row, and the rows displayed represent the current found set.

Figure 26.3
Users can view multiple records and scroll left and right for multiple columns in List view.

26

Navigation in List view works consistently with Palm and Pocket PC applications and is somewhat different than you might expect within FileMaker Pro. The up/down triangle icons, located at the lower right of your screen, page up and down through sets of records. They do not change the currently active record, unless you scroll beyond the point at which your active record is visible. In those cases, FileMaker Mobile won't have an active record (Delete Record, for example, won't work) until you select one of the visible rows available or switch to Form view. You can also use the left/right triangles to scroll horizontally to see additional columns on your List view.

Clicking on a row will select the corresponding record and, if editing of field values in List view has been disabled, navigate to that record's Form view representation. If editing of field values is not disabled, clicking on a field in a specific row will allow editing of that field. The Form view navigation icon must then be used to switch to the selected record in Form view.

Also, in List view, you can sort the displayed found set by whatever column you choose, merely by clicking on the desired column header. Sorting may be toggled between ascending and descending order by successive clicks of the same column header.

Columns may be resized and reordered within List view in exactly the same manner as in FileMaker Pro. Resizing is accomplished by clicking on the right edge of the header for the column that you want to resize and dragging it to the desired width. Likewise, to reposition a column with respect to other columns, simply click and drag the column to the desired position.

WORKING WITH FORM VIEW

Form view on FileMaker Mobile 8 corresponds to a standard single-record layout in the FileMaker Pro client application running on your computer, as shown in Figure 26.4. Data for a single record is displayed with fields arranged vertically. Labels are either (by default) the names of the displayed fields or custom labels designated manually through the use of the FileMaker Mobile configuration application on your computer.

Figure 26.4
Form view allows users to view up to 50 fields for a given record.

In the configuration of a mobile database (which is covered in more detail later in the chapter), you can specify that a field should be associated with a value list and displayed as a pop-up menu, pop-up list, single check box, or notes field. Pop-up menus and pop-up lists work as pop-up menus and drop-down lists work in FileMaker Pro.

A single check box is your only check box option in FileMaker Mobile, allowing you to toggle a single value on and off. Multiple-value check boxes are not supported.

The notes field format is specific to FileMaker Mobile: It displays a small page icon that can be used to then show the complete contents of the field in a special viewing window. If the field allows data entry, the contents will be editable in the display window. This is, of course, an accommodation to the small screen size of handhelds.

FileMaker Mobile on your handheld also supports a calendar picker for date fields. There is also a time picker that allows time to be entered by minute, second, and so on.

FileMaker Mobile does not offer the radio button data display.

RECORD CONTROL FUNCTIONS

The Record Functions menu is accessed by clicking on the name of the selected database at the top of the screen. This menu, available in both List view and Form view, provides options for manipulation of the records in the mobile database. These are the options:

- New Record
- Delete Record
- Delete All Records
- Find Records
- Show All
- Go to Record
- Sort Records

These options will seem familiar to any FileMaker Pro user, but there are some important differences to keep in mind.

NEW RECORD   The New Record option adds, as you would expect, a new record to the database. It does not, however, act like the similar function in FileMaker Pro in that it will not perform any auto-enter functions such as serial number generation, date/time stamping, and other dynamic data entry or validations. Note that auto-enter and validation routines don't happen during synchronization either: It is likely that solutions of any complexity will require additional scripting to support such auto-population of data for records that have been added through a handheld device. One additional, important detail: The computer-based database does increment the next serial value within its auto-enter features, but doesn't actually set data into the respective fields in question. In other words, let's say you have a database with four records, with an auto-enter serial number field with the values 1, 2, 3, and 4, respectively. Then let's say that you add a record on your handheld device and

26

synchronize with the source database on your computer. There will be five records but the fifth record will have no number in the serial number field. If you then add another record on your computer, the serial number field for the next record will contain 6.

 To learn how to deal with the case of missing serial ID values, see "Missing Index Values" in the "Troubleshooting" section at the end of this chapter.

DELETE RECORD   Delete Record performs as you would expect, except it gives you the option of deleting the corresponding record on the computer-based version of the database as well. This feature should be used with care because deleting the record through this feature is as irrevocable a decision as deleting it in the main version of the database on your computer. It is also important to remember that your synchronization options may defeat this option, specifically when you choose to delete a record but not to delete that record in the original computer-based version of the database. In this case, if you have either Bi-directional or Download to Handheld Only synchronization specified, the next time you synchronize your handheld, the deleted record will be added back to your handheld.

DELETE ALL RECORDS   The Delete All Records option operates just as the Delete All Records option within FileMaker, and, consequently, there is the identical risk of unintentional data loss. And while we are on the subject of the risk of unintentional data loss, it is also very important to note that referential integrity rules are supported during synchronization. If you have deleted records on your handheld device (with the Delete Records on Your PC option selected) that have corresponding related records in the main computer-based solution, and those relationships are set for cascading delete, the record you deleted on the handheld will be deleted on the computer along with all of its dependent related records. Thus, with the Delete All Records option, it is possible to empty out multiple tables without necessarily intending to.

 If after synchronization you have missing records in both databases, see "Missing Records" in the "Troubleshooting" section at the end of this chapter.

PERFORMING FIND REQUESTS

FileMaker Mobile 8 does not offer users a Find mode in quite the same manner as FileMaker users are accustomed to. Rather, when you click the Find button at the bottom of each view (or choose the command from the Records menu), you will be presented with a Find Records dialog (as shown in Figure 26.5).

The dialog allows you to choose a field and enter criteria by which you want to search. Unlike with FileMaker Pro, you cannot enter multiple requests nor will the find process recognize operators like greater than, less than, and so on. After you perform a find request, you will (just as with FileMaker Pro) be left in the view from which you came.

The Show All option in the Record menu will add all records in the database to the found set. This will override any found set generated by a Find request but will not, unlike in FileMaker Pro, cause the last performed sort to be lost. When all records are being displayed, the "Found:" designator in the upper-right corner of the screen will read All and the most recent sort criteria will still be applied.

Figure 26.5
Users can change their found set by using the Find Records dialog.

Go to Record allows quick navigation to a specific record in the currently displayed found set by number. Thus, Go to Record with the option of 3 would show the third record in the current found set as last sorted. Because this ordinal designation is based on context, it is perhaps more likely that the first record or last record options would be more useful in day-to-day use.

SORTING RECORDSETS

The Sort Records command in the Record menu performs the function of ordering the records in your found set according to the contents of a (single) field that you specify. This ordering is, of course, based on the data type of the selected field and your designation of whether the sort should be in ascending or descending order. The same effect may be achieved in List view by clicking the field or column header. Subsequent clicks will toggle between ascending and descending sorts. You will notice that when a set is sorted by a specific field using either of the mentioned methods, that field's name will appear underlined in its List view column header. There is no "unsort" option as there is in FileMaker Pro, and note that Show All will preserve and reapply the last sort order chosen. Finally, note that sorting by number fields works only on the whole-number portion of your data. Decimal values will be ignored.

 For help with controlling the order in which records appear in your mobile database, see "Default Sort Order" in the "Troubleshooting" section at the end of this chapter.

EDIT FUNCTIONS

The Edit menu options are available only in Form view and present the user with standard GUI functions such as these:

- Undo
- Cut
- Copy
- Paste
- Select All

26
O

We assume that you are familiar with these functions, except to note certain specifics of their implementation in FileMaker Mobile 8.

The Undo option is limited in scope to the last field content change and will undo a change only while still in the field where the change was made. After you click to another field, the capability to undo changes in the original field using the Undo function is lost. As with FileMaker Pro, only one level of undo is available. There is, also, no concept of committing changes as there is in FileMaker Pro. A change is made as soon as a user begins typing.

Cut, Copy, and Paste will operate only on text and number fields, which must have editing of fields enabled. Just as in FileMaker Pro, number fields may contain text as well as numbers.

OPTIONS

The options presented in the Options menu pertain to display and functionality settings in the List and Form views on your handheld only:

- Font
- Form View Options—Accessible only from Form view
- List View Options—Accessible only from List view
- Field Options—Accessible only from List view
- Database Options
- About FileMaker Mobile 8
- Phone Lookup—Accessible only from Form view

Changes to font settings are local to your handheld and will remain in effect for the selected database; they are a change only for display purposes. Font choice here does not affect your data in any way.

FORM VIEW OPTIONS   The Form View Options allow you to determine whether field data is editable in Form view and whether field labels are left, center, or right justified. One important point to note is that because the Find Records dialog is independent of the view selected, any field may be searched by regardless of whether its contents are editable.

LIST VIEW OPTIONS   The List View Options allow you to determine whether field data is editable as well as whether columns are resizable, reorderable, locked (first column only), or sortable by clicking on the column header. Locking the first column ensures that the column is always present regardless of how far to the left a user scrolls. This is useful if that field contains a record identifier of some sort.

FIELD OPTIONS   Field Options allow you to choose an individual field and set its width, text alignment, and text color. The width is set in pixels, not characters. Character alignment may be set to left, center, or right alignment. Note that this option is available only in List view.

Database Options   Database Options include the following:

- **Include in Global Find (Palm OS only)**—Include in Global Find allows you to have the contents of your database indexed and included in the Palm OS global search function. This then means that outside FileMaker Mobile you can search for data that lies within one of your databases and, when results are returned by that search function, click directly into the database in question.

- **Backup at HotSync (Palm OS only)**—Backup at HotSync allows you to have your database backed up before the hotsync operation is performed. This gives you the option of returning your database to its presynchronization condition should something go awry during the synchronization or after the synchronization on the side of the computer-based version of your database. On Palm OS–based handhelds, these backups are placed in the `Palm Backup` directory and, on Windows, are appended with a `.pdb` extension.

- **Synchronize Database**—Synchronization of your database can be enabled or disabled from the Synchronize Database option. You can use this setting if you want to continue to use a database on your handheld device but for whatever reason do not want it to synchronize each time you dock with your computer.

- **Login**—FileMaker Mobile 8 databases on your handheld access your computer-based databases at synchronization time. This access is mediated by FileMaker Pro's native security controls for allowing or disallowing access to records and tables according to a user's privilege set. The Login option, under the Database Options menu item, allows you to define the account used to access the specific database from your handheld.

You may select from a database file's account (the account and password set to be tried via the File Options dialog within FileMaker Pro), the built-in FileMaker guest account, or an account that you specify. This an extremely important capability, especially when multiple handheld users are synchronizing to the same database hosted on FileMaker Server or shared as multiuser through FileMaker Pro. It might, for instance, allow users to see only their own records in a shared contact management database.

This capability to synchronize through a specific user account also gives you the opportunity, in conjunction with scripts written for the purpose and linked to synchronization (discussed later in this chapter), to perform certain actions based on a user's identity. These can include filtering data sets, tagging records with a user's ID, or reestablishing serial ID values.

26

Synchronizing with a FileMaker Database

You will need to turn to your computer to prepare a mobile database to be synchronized with a desktop or server-based database.

CONFIGURING A FILE TO BE PUBLISHED

Assuming that you have available a file you want to publish to your handheld device (or devices), the process of publishing is simply a matter of configuration through the use of the FileMaker Mobile 8 application.

The first step in preparing a file for publishing is turning on the extended privilege for FileMaker Mobile within the security settings for the appropriate privilege sets. You can do this from within FileMaker Mobile or from within FileMaker Pro. This then will allow any account associated with that privilege set to synchronize with your database.

→ For more information on extended privileges, **see** "Extended Privileges," **p. 342**.

Important note: When you want to prepare a file for synchronization, you must have it on your local computer the first time you configure it. You cannot initially set a file for mobile access if it is hosted on another computer. FileMaker Mobile requires that an internal setting be established in a file; this process can happen only on a local computer. After this initial configuration is complete, you can subsequently change configuration settings while it is hosted elsewhere. Configure a file once locally with FileMaker Mobile and it will remain configurable from a networked copy of FileMaker Mobile from that point forward in perpetuity.

The main screen in FileMaker Mobile, shown in Figure 26.6, provides a listing of all the FileMaker Pro files that have been configured for handheld sharing and shows whether their sharing is currently enabled.

Figure 26.6
The FileMaker Mobile 8 desktop application allows for the configuration of the handheld publishing settings for FileMaker 7 or 8 files.

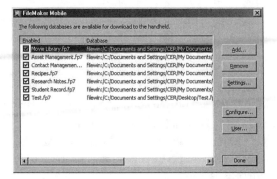

ADDING AND REMOVING FILES

Clicking the Add button prompts you to select the desired FileMaker Pro file and then places you in the Settings dialog. The selected file may be a local file or a database hosted by FileMaker Server, but again you will need to have a file on your local computer if this is the first time you are configuring it for FileMaker Mobile access. You can also, if you choose, remove files by clicking the Remove button. Note that this only removes files from the list; any settings contained within them remain.

PERMISSION SETTINGS

Clicking the Settings button will display the file settings options for the selected database (see Figure 26.7). Note that you must have [Full Access] privileges in order to configure a FileMaker database for mobile synchronization.

Figure 26.7
The Mobile Settings dialog in FileMaker Mobile 8 allows you to configure (or reconfigure) a single file for handheld access.

Within the Mobile Settings dialog, you have three settings to work with:

- Sharing
- Fields
- Synchronization

Sharing allows for the designation of which users, if any, are allowed to synch their handhelds to the selected database file. You can either choose to allow all users to synchronize with a given file, or choose to enable specific privilege sets to have access. In all cases, FileMaker Mobile will be enabling the [fmmobile] extended privilege within your FileMaker file.

From this dialog you can also shut off all access for users, regardless of other settings. This is normally used to temporarily disallow synchronization during upgrades, maintenance, and the like.

FIELD CONFIGURATION SETTINGS

The Specify Fields button of the Mobile Settings dialog allows you to specify which fields are to be published via FileMaker Mobile and to set their properties within the mobile database (see Figure 26.8).

26

Figure 26.8
The FileMaker Mobile 8 field options determine how field information will be displayed on your handheld device.

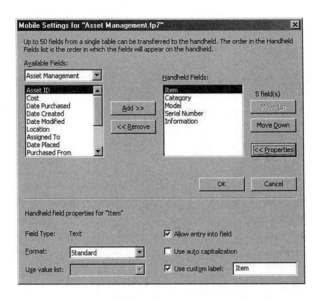

No more than 50 fields from a single table may be published as a FileMaker Mobile handheld published database. Only fields of data type Text, Number, Date, and Time are supported by FileMaker Mobile 8.

- **Available Fields**—Must all be from the same single table. If you try to change tables, the application will clear fields added from a prior table. The FileMaker Mobile 8 handheld version does not support related tables and operations.

- **Handheld Field Properties**—Specify how a field appears and its behavior in the mobile database. You can choose a value list to associate if you've selected a format that requires one. Note that value lists in FileMaker Mobile can only be derived from fixed custom values (as opposed to being dynamically generated from field values or related records). You can opt to disallow entry into fields, essentially making them read-only. You can also enable auto-capitalization as is the convention on handheld devices. Last, you can specify what field label to use.

It is important to keep in mind the limitations of FileMaker Mobile 8, especially that only one table and a maximum of 50 fields (of type Text, Number, Date, or Time) from that table can be published to a handheld per database file. This means that FileMaker Mobile 8 databases running on handheld devices are not relational. Methods for working around this limitation are covered in the section "FileMaker Extra: Publishing Related Data," later in this chapter.

SYNCHRONIZATION SETTINGS

The Synchronization button on the Mobile Settings dialog allows you to specify the rules by which FileMaker Mobile synchronizes data between two databases (see Figure 26.9). It is important to keep in mind that synchronization is a snapshot in time and that two data sets exist thereafter and will need to be reconciled at some future date. Also note that at the moment of synchronization, certain circumstances such as record locking can cause disparity between the computer/hosted data set and the handheld data set, so special attention must be paid to synchronization options.

Figure 26.9
The FileMaker Mobile 8 synchronization options determine what direction record data will flow between handheld and host/desktop.

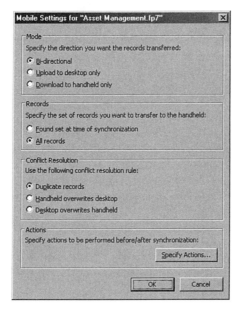

The Mode setting allows you to specify the direction in which records will be transferred at synchronization time. These options control what data you want copied where, and how to handle override logic:

- **Bi-directional**—Records are moved from handheld to computer and from computer to handheld. This is often useful when live data is to be edited or verified at some remote location and then reconciled. Inventory control systems might utilize this form of synchronization. In the case of the same record being edited on both a handheld and the source database, the timestamp for last modification is used to resolve the conflict.

- **Upload to Desktop Only**—Records move from handheld to computer only in a one-way transaction. In this case, the computer acts as a repository for changes made on the handheld, and the handheld data takes precedence over the desktop data. People using FileMaker Mobile 8 to manage data collection activities driven entirely from their handheld devices will often use this mode. At the end of each synchronization, the handheld version of the database will be empty (contain no records).

- **Download to Handheld Only**—Records move from computer to handheld only, and the desktop data will override the handheld as necessary. In this case, the handheld acts as a display tool for data that is maintained on the computer or hosted version of the database. Any records that have been added to the handheld and do not also exist in the source (desktop client or hosted) database will be deleted.

The Records option allows you to specify the set of records that are to be transferred to the handheld at the time of synchronization:

- **Found Set at Time of Synchronization**—It is important to note that the found set is not the same found set you may have present in FileMaker Pro. Instead, a script tied to the synchronization process must establish that found set. In other words, the found set referenced here must be created and is independent of the found set you, as the user, may be viewing at the time that the synchronization function is performed.

 For help with solving the problem of establishing a found set before synchronization, see "Found Sets and Sessions" in the "Troubleshooting" section at the end of this chapter.

- **All Records**—All records in the given table will be synchronized.

The Conflict Resolution setting designates what rule will be used to resolve conflicts that may occur in certain synchronization scenarios. The term *conflict* here is used to denote a record that has been modified both on the computer (or hosted) version and on the handheld version of the database. Of course, mode settings may override these settings when one database automatically takes precedence over another. The following are the choices available when reconciling conflicts in synchronization:

- **Duplicate Records**—Both versions of the record will be written to both of the designated databases. This will cause two similar versions of the same record to exist and will require that the user delete or modify the extraneous record.

- **Handheld Overwrites Desktop (or Server)**—The handheld's version of a conflicting record will be saved, and the computer's version deleted. Note that this operation creates a new record and deletes the conflicting record.

- **Desktop (or Server) Overwrites Handheld**—The computer's version of a conflicting record will be saved, and the handheld's version deleted.

The conditions for conflict resolution are based on the time and date of the last change made to a specific record. For example, let's say that you chose the Download to Handheld mode of synchronization, and then selected the Desktop Overwrites Handheld method of conflict resolution. In the case that a record is marked as having been changed on both sides, the desktop record would overwrite the record that was changed on the handheld.

The Actions setting allows you to specify a script to run before synchronization occurs and another after it is finished. It is through these means that you can perform tasks such as establishing a specific found set for synchronization or reconciling the lack of auto-entered serial IDs.

→ For help with scripting **see** Chapter 9, "Getting Started with Scripting," **p. 247**.

 To learn how to deal with the case of missing serial ID values, see "Missing Index Values" in the "Troubleshooting" section at the end of this chapter.

CONFIGURE

Clicking Configure in FileMaker Mobile 8 prompts you for the selection of a FileMaker Pro file and allows you to access its FileMaker Mobile settings in one step. It will not automatically add the file to the list of handheld published files. The Add button must be used for that. Use the Configure setting if you want to configure a file but then don't intend to use your current computer for synchronization.

USERS

Clicking the User button in FileMaker Mobile 8 displays the list of registered users and their Handheld License Keys applied on the specific copy of FileMaker Mobile 8 installed on the computer with which you're working. Multiple handhelds may be used with a single install of FileMaker Mobile 8, but each must have its own user code and license key.

Each handheld device is tied to one of the licenses used with FileMaker Mobile 8. In this scenario it is possible for an organization to have people typically out of the office synchronize with a single workstation shared among others and set with their key.

TROUBLESHOOTING

FOUND SETS AND SESSIONS

When I perform a find in my database and then synchronize my handheld, all records show up on my handheld instead of just the found set that I wanted.

This is because the synchronization process occurs in its own session and does not necessarily have the same found set as the one you see in your open copy of the database. The resolution is to explicitly define the desired found set in a script that is configured, in the FileMaker Mobile 8 administration panel, to run at synchronization time. This will ensure that the found set that is loaded into your handheld is what you expect it to be.

You could write a one-line script with a find request for records set as yours, or perhaps with a specific status, and so on. FileMaker Mobile will run the script, establish the found set you need, and synchronize just those records.

If you'd like to be able to synchronize the found set you have showing on your own computer, you'd need to write a routine for flagging your fields in a particular way, and then searching for that flag in the script tied to synchronization.

MISSING INDEX VALUES

When I add new records to my handheld, they don't seem to have ID numbers. These usually fill in automatically when I add a new record on my computer. Then when I perform a synchronization, the IDs are missing in my FileMaker Pro database as well.

Auto-enter functions are not performed when records are added to a master FileMaker database via handheld synchronization. Your best option is to populate these numbers manually with a script that is configured to run after synchronization. Here's a script that will do this:

```
Perform Find [ Specified Find Requests: Find Records; Criteria: fixme::id: "=" ]
      [ Restore ]
```

```
Replace Field Contents
        [ fixme::id; Replace with serial numbers: Entry option values ]
        [ No dialog; Update Entry Options ]
Exit Script [ ]
```

MISSING RECORDS

Help! I deleted unnecessary records from my handheld and then synched, but now those records are missing on the master database on the server.

It is very important to remember that FileMaker Mobile 8 on your handheld will give you the option of deleting records from your source or desktop/hosted database. It is also important to keep in mind that cascading deletes based on relationships are also performed as a result of deletions performed on your handheld. It is highly advisable to make backups of synchronized data often using FileMaker Server's backup routines or manually, in the case of single-user files.

DEFAULT SORT ORDER

How can I have the records that I synch to my handheld sorted in a specific order?

Records are transferred to your handheld at synchronization time in the order in which they exist in the synchronization session. Thus, let's say you want your data automatically sorted by last name and then by first name when it reaches your handheld. Simply have your pre-synch script perform that sort for you.

Keep in mind, however, that there is no unsort function on your handheld version of FileMaker Mobile 8, so if you choose to sort your data, it will remain sorted in that order by default.

FILEMAKER EXTRA: PUBLISHING RELATED DATA

FileMaker Mobile 8 does not support FileMaker Pro's relational data model in the publication of databases to handheld devices. As has been discussed before, it will publish only a single table from any given database file and can publish no more than 50 fields from that single table. This, although a hindrance, should not lead you to believe that FileMaker Mobile 8 cannot be used to manage related data; it just requires a little ingenuity and the willingness to think creatively about data presentation and management.

Let's begin with a simple and very common relational structure: a table of parent records (companies for this exercise) and a table of related children (employees). Designate a field, _kp_CompanyID in the Company table and _kf_CompanyID in the Employee table, to define the relationship. As it is, this simple database would not be publishable through FileMaker Mobile.

On a trivial level, you could consider putting the Companies and Employees databases in different physical files; this would, nominally, allow both tables to be published to your handheld simultaneously, but it would not link them to each other and would therefore not be very useful.

The other possible solutions require that you consider how the data is likely to be used in a mobile environment. Although Company is clearly the parent data structure, everyday practice may indicate that more often the focus for users is the Employee table. In this case, you might be more likely to need to contact a person at a company than the company itself. Let's say that this is true enough in this test case; you then would need a solution to the problem of displaying a list of employees with related information from the Company table—say, for example, the name of their company. It is worth noting that when looked at from this perspective, the data contains only one-to-one correspondences between the data elements in the two tables. (There will be only a single company for any given person/employee.)

At this point, given these assumptions, the solution is close at hand. You need merely to find a way to get the company data from the Company table, through the relationship and into a field in the Employee table, without using calculation fields (remember that calculation fields are not supported in FileMaker Mobile 8). A text field must serve as the repository for this information within the Employee table. You will need to write a script that will copy data from the Company table to the Employee table before synchronization (or you can set an auto-enter by calculation formula to pull data from the Company table and retrigger this calculation via a script). The script you might write would likely loop through your found set and push data into the Employee table (using the Set Field script step).

26

## CHAPTER 27

DOCUMENTING YOUR FILEMAKER SOLUTIONS

In this chapter

WHY IS DOCUMENTATION IMPORTANT?

There are two general types of software documentation: *user instructions* and *system documentation*. User instructions generally assist people who need to use or administer an application. System documentation is a resource for developers who need to make functional changes to a system. This chapter focuses on techniques for creating system documentation for FileMaker-based projects and covers a wide range of ways in which a developer can make a solution easier and more systematic to understand. Documentation for us goes far beyond an external document explaining various functions of your system: Elements of documentation are interwoven throughout one's database from commenting to naming conventions.

Creating high-quality documentation is an important yet often neglected activity in the software development process. It can be tempting to think that FileMaker is in some regard self-documenting. The natural language support it provides in naming fields, tables, scripts, and so on goes a long way toward making a system comprehensible. Also, people often choose FileMaker as a rapid application development tool because they're in a hurry to deploy a system and don't have time to budget for documentation. And finally, FileMaker systems often evolve organically. They get constantly added to and tweaked, and at no point can someone sit down, declare a system done, and produce documentation.

Nonetheless, it's important to balance the temptation to just get started and the need for speedy development, with the need to create a readable, maintainable system that will still be comprehensible after the original developers have moved on.

The most important step in documenting a system lies in developing a consistent naming convention and in making liberal use of comments. This "document as you go" approach is extremely economical and actually assists in the development process itself, by requiring that developers stop and think through how a routine or process should work before starting to build it.

Good documentation starts at the beginning of a project. It's a rare developer who can go back through a system and add comments at the end of a project.

DEVELOPING NAMING CONVENTIONS

To have a well-documented system, it is extremely important to create meaningful names for elements such as fields, table occurrences, layouts, scripts, and custom functions. Each developer has personal ideas about what constitutes a meaningful name. Some developers like to embed metadata into names, such as zr_Created_Date.d (in which the .d suffix indicates that the field is a date field). Others prefer a simpler approach, with names like CreationDate.

Each project may have unique requirements for naming conventions because of factors such as the complexity of the project, the number of developers, the developer turnover rate, or perhaps the need to interface with external systems. In general, the more complex your project, or the greater the number of developers involved (either at one time or across time), the more essential a consistent naming convention is. A good naming scheme can significantly lessen the amount of time it takes to bring a new developer up to speed on the system. The particular style used is less important than consistency throughout each project. Define your standards at the beginning of a project and stick with them.

USING COMMENTS EFFECTIVELY

Most programming and development environments give you some way to add comments to a system. Comments are descriptive information that you, the developer, supply throughout the system to clarify the meaning and usage of programming constructs. When commenting your work, try to keep two goals in mind: explaining why something exists or does something, and describing what the expectations around it are. Answer the questions "What goes in?" "What comes out?" and "What's its purpose?"

ADDING COMMENTS FOR FIELDS

The Define Database dialog allows developers to add comments to fields. Each comment can be up to 30,000 characters in length. The selected field's comment is displayed under the field name. View all comments by clicking the Options/Comments column header at the top of the field list. Field comments are included in the Database Design Report (covered later in this chapter) and are also accessible via the Get (FieldComment) function. Figure 27.1 shows an example of field comments.

Figure 27.1
Field comments can be displayed in the Fields tab of the Define Database dialog.

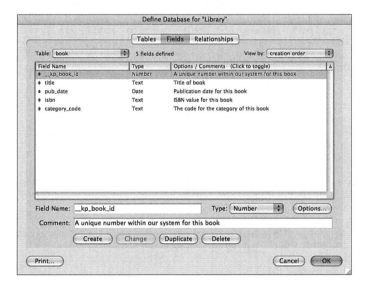

COMMENTING WITHIN FORMULAS

Formulas are defined in various places, including calculation fields, field validation, and some script steps such as If, Set Field, Set Variable, and Replace Field Contents. C-style and C++–style comments are both supported within calculation formulas. C-style comments begin with the characters /* and end with the */ characters. C-style comments can span multiple lines and can be nested within other comments. C++–style comments begin with // and continue through the end of the line. Here are a couple of examples:

```
/* concatenate author's name in the form last, first
    example:  Smith, John    */

name_last &

Case(WordCount(name_first) and WordCount(name_last);
", ")  //don't include comma if either field is empty

& name_first
```

SCRIPTS

The Comment script step can be added anywhere within a script. Up to 30,000 characters may be included in the dialog box. Within ScriptMaker, the Comment script step appears in bold text, preceded by a # character. When a script is printed, the Comment script step is in italic.

Here's a real-world example of a script that runs the first time a user opens the database. It represents what we'd consider good commenting:

```
OnOpen
# purpose: Default script that runs on first opening the file
#      (set via the File Options dialog)
# dependencies: security privileges; tests for full access
# NOTE: This database currently doesn't restrict access to the status area
#      or toolbars; however, if you wish it to, modify the lock down section
#      below.
# history: scl 2004sep22; slove2005jun22 added whosIN logging;
#      slove 2005jun28 added session handlers
#
# Create new session (every person logged in should have their
#      own session record in the session table)
Perform Script [ "CreateNew_SessionRecord" ]
#
# Restore Globals (loads default settings)
Perform Script [ "__Restore_Globals" ]
#
# Set WhosIn (record the account name of the person
#      logging in on the Admin layout)
Perform Script [ "__Add_WhosIn" ]
#
# Error Handling (uses custom function to toggle debug mode in scripts on/off)
If [ fnDebugMode ( DEVH__Home~tog::LoggedIn_Account_gt ) ≠ 1 ]
Allow User Abort [ Off ]
Set Error Capture [ On ]
End If
#
# test for Full Access privileges
If [ Get ( PrivilegeSetName ) = "[Full Access]" ]
Perform Script [ "Unlock_for_development" ]
Else
#
# NOTE: this system is currently OPEN
# to lock it down, simply change the settings below
Allow Toolbars [ On ]
Show/Hide Status Area
```

```
[ Show ]
End If
#
# Set initial window position
Perform Script [ "__Default_Window" ]
#
# Make sure the logged-in person has a corresponding People record
Perform Script [ "Check_RelatedPersonRecord" ]
#
#
# Open dev tools if full access (opens a layout exclusively used by developers)
If [ Get ( PrivilegeSetName ) = "[Full Access]" ]
Perform Script [ "Show_Developer_ToolsPalette" ]
End If
#
```

ADDING DESCRIPTIONS IN THE DEFINE ACCOUNTS & PRIVILEGES DIALOG

Accounts, privilege sets, and extended privileges can each have associated descriptions. Enter a description when defining these items in the Define Accounts & Privileges dialog box. Up to 30,000 characters may be included for each. The descriptions appear in their respective lists and are also included in the Database Design Report.

Figure 27.2 shows a real-world example.

Figure 27.2
Be certain to add descriptions to privilege sets; this information is helpful within this dialog and in the Database Design Report.

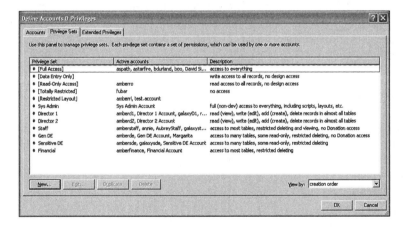

DOCUMENTING THE RELATIONSHIPS GRAPH

NEW One of the many new features of FileMaker 8 is the capability to add comment notes to the Relationships Graph. To do so, click the button with an A on it and drag a rectangle on the Relationships Graph. Refer to the example provided in Figure 27.3.

The Relationships Graph is one of the most difficult elements of a solution to document; in a moderately complex database, we've found it common to have literally hundreds of table occurrences in use.

27

Figure 27.3
Comment notes in FileMaker 8 make effectively documenting the Relationships Graph possible.

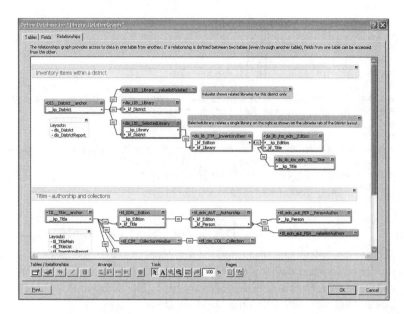

Soliant Consulting, the authors' custom development service firm, has developed a specific methodology called "The Anchor Method" for working with the Relationships Graph. There are two other general approaches in the FileMaker community as well. Regardless of which you prefer, we strongly urge you to adopt a systematic way to organize and name your table occurrences and to liberally use comment notes.

Using the Database Design Report

Beyond documenting your solution within its structure and code, FileMaker Pro 8 Advanced includes a Database Design Report (DDR) feature that is quite useful and may very well stand as the centerpiece for your system documentation. The report includes an overview of the system, along with detailed information about your database schema, including tables, fields, relationships, layouts, value lists, scripts, accounts, privilege sets, extended privileges, and custom functions. The report can be created as an integrated set of linked HTML documents or as a set of XML files.

> **TIP**
>
> Using XSLT, you can transform the XML output of the DDR into a Microsoft Word document that your constituents may find easier to digest and more commonly associated with what they think of as documentation.

Creating a DDR

Creating a Database Design Report is a simple task. But first, you must have FileMaker Pro 8 Advanced and you must open all the files that you want to include in the report. The files must be opened with an account that has full access privileges. After the files have been opened, choose Tools, Database Design Report to display the dialog box shown in Figure 27.4.

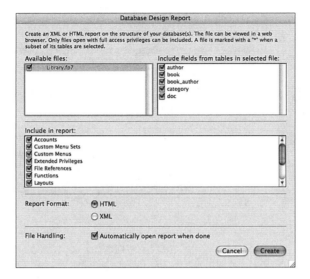

Figure 27.4
FileMaker's Database Design Report can document many aspects of your databases.

By default, all tables in all available files are included in the report. You can uncheck files or tables you do not want to include. You can also specify the types of information to include for each file. Choose either HTML or XML for the report format. Finally, click the Create button and specify the location to which to save the report files.

If you're not sure whether the HTML or XML version of the DDR is more useful to you, think of it this way: The HTML version produces a set of linked web pages that you can open and navigate immediately in a browser. The XML output is more appropriate if you need the data in a raw form and plan to manipulate it in some way before viewing or presenting it. One type of manipulation might consist of writing one or more XSLT stylesheets to transform the DDR XML data into a form suitable for importing into a FileMaker database.

WORKING WITH THE DDR IN HTML

The HTML version of the DDR includes a `Summary.html` document along with three additional HTML documents (`<filename>_ReportFrame.html`, `<filename>_TOCFrame.html`, and `<filename>.html`) for each of the FileMaker files in your solution. These three files all work together to create a frame-based view of database information for each database file. A `Styles.css` file is also created. This file includes formatting information used by all the HTML documents. To view the report, open the `Summary.html` file in any frames-capable web browser. See Figure 27.5 for an example of the Report Overview. Each of the solution's files is listed, along with counts of elements within those files. Click on a filename or any of the element counts to view details. All the details for a particular file are included on one (possibly lengthy) page. Use the navigation frame at the left side of the window to quickly move to the section you are interested in. You might also use your browser's Find feature to locate a particular element within the report.

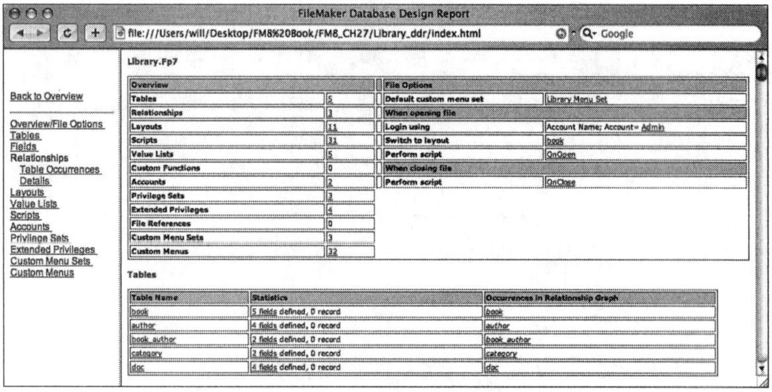

Figure 27.5
FileMaker Pro 8
Advanced can pro-
duce a Database
Design Report in an
HTML format.

TIP

> If you want to distribute the HTML-based DDR, one way is, of course, to host the files on a web server and distribute the URL (making sure that you give it only to people who should be allowed to see the internals of your database!). If you feel that hosting the files on the Web is insecure, or web hosting is impractical for other reasons, you can distrib-ute the HTML files as a group. If you do this, be sure to keep all the files together, in the same relative positions and with the same filenames they had when they were first gen-erated.

The DDR includes many hyperlinks that make it easy to navigate the report. For instance, the Fields section lists every layout, relationship, script, and value list that uses each field. Each of the listed items is a link that displays the element.

USING THE XML VERSION

When you choose to generate the DDR as XML, you'll get a file called Summary.xml, and an additional file called <filename>.xml for each database file you choose to analyze. The XML version of the DDR includes all the information in the HTML version, as well as many more details. (In particular, you get a great deal more information about the position and styling of layout objects.) Although the XML DDR can be viewed in any text editor, you will likely prefer to use a program that understands XML (for example, an XML-aware web browser such as Internet Explorer or Mozilla, or an XML editor such as Oxygen or XMLSpy). You may also want to use an XSL style sheet to format or transform the raw XML. Figure 27.6 shows an overview of an XML DDR viewed with most of the entities col-lapsed. The XML DDR contains an extensive amount of data broken down into 10 sections: BaseTableCatalog, RelationshipGraph, LayoutCatalog, ValueListCatalog, ScriptCatalog, AccountCatalog, PrivilegesCatalog, ExtendedPrivilegeCatalog, CustomFunctionCatalog, and Options. Each of these sections contains information about one area of the database. The XML element names in each section are relatively self-explanatory.

Figure 27.6
FileMaker Developer can produce a Database Design Report in an XML format.

USING THIRD-PARTY DOCUMENTATION TOOLS

In recent years, several programs have emerged to help fill the need for documenting FileMaker systems. These tools offer features for quickly identifying missing or unknown elements, tracking dependencies, reporting differences between two solutions, script tracing, and more. Various tools extract information from FileMaker systems in different ways. They may use the Database Design Report, use Apple Events, or even read data directly from the FileMaker files.

Each of the tools has strengths and weaknesses. For example, there can be substantial differences in the time required to extract data from solutions. The amount of information detail and the features included for using that information vary considerably from tool to tool as well. Having one or more of these tools can be very helpful for debugging and documenting systems. Check these publishers' web pages for the latest details on their tools for FileMaker 8:

Inspector by Beezwax—http://www.beezwax.net/inspector/

Brushfire by Chaparral Software—http://www.chapsoft.com

MetadataMagic by New Millennium—http://www.nmci.com

Analyzer by Waves in Motion—http://www.wmotion.com

You'll be well repaid by looking at each of these tools and becoming familiar with their capabilities. Each has useful features.

27

PUTTING THE FINISHING TOUCHES ON YOUR DOCUMENTATION

In addition to the items described previously in this chapter, several other kinds of documentation may be useful to include in your system documentation package. Many of these items can be derived from the work that was done in the project's initial analysis and design phase. These documents can be printed or kept as electronic documents, such as PDF files.

The documentation elements we recommend collecting for a database project are listed here:

- **Data Model**—A complete data model is essential for understanding how the database structure has been designed. An entity-relationship diagram (ERD) is one of the most popular data models. We recommend creating a layout within your database where a current ERD may be viewed. You can draw the ERD using FileMaker's layout tools, or copy an image in from applications like Visio or OmniGraffle.

→ For additional discussion of creating and using an ERD, **see** Chapter 5, "Relational Database Design," **p. 129**.

- **Documenting the Relationships Graph**—All the facts found on the Relationships Graph can be derived from the DDR report. However, the visual representation of the Relationships Graph provides an additional means for developers to gain insight into the system. The Relationships Graph can be printed or saved as a PDF file.

- **User Interface Diagrams**—For a complex system or a system with many subsystems, the overall navigation and use of the system should be documented. Depending on the scope and complexity of the system, it may be appropriate to include flowcharts, storyboards, or other diagrams to indicate how users interact with the system and access its features.

- **System Flowchart**—The system flowchart should document the overall structure of the entire system. It should show how the various parts of the system interconnect and relate to each other. The system flowchart should also show manual processes and external systems or agents that the FileMaker system depends on.

- **Process Descriptions**—Complex processes should be deconstructed and documented thoroughly with written descriptions. Decision trees, charts, and tables can provide additional details.

- **Screens and Reports**—A complete set of documentation often includes copies of all screens and reports used in the system. In some cases it may be helpful to produce two sets: one created with sample data in Browse mode and another created in Layout mode with field names.

- **Test Data**—Representative test data that shows both typical and extreme values can be a great asset in your documentation. Test data is especially helpful to those who are not familiar with the system. The test data can help eliminate assumptions about expected data and prevent misunderstandings between clients and developers.

Final Thoughts on Documentation

This chapter has covered various methods for documenting FileMaker systems. The specifics of the documentation standards you adopt may vary with every project. Ideally, system documentation should contain enough information for another developer to completely re-create the system, using the documentation you've created as his or her only information source. Clearly, maintaining complete and up-to-date documentation is a time-consuming task. Remember that many systems you create will exist longer than expected or perhaps be passed on to other developers. We encourage you to adopt, to the degree pragmatism allows, some of or all the ideas presented here. The result can mean higher quality work and a system that serves its constituents beyond just its initial release.

FileMaker Extra: Soliant Development Standards

For this final section of the book, we've opted to provide for your consideration the standards our own custom development service firm, Soliant Consulting, uses. We do not want to be guilty of thinking that our coding standards are the only ones available, and if the struggle we had internally to arrive at a single standard is any indication, we're very cognizant that other approaches are entirely valid and effective. The important point in all of this is to adopt a standard—*any* standard. On the other hand, we felt that a chapter on documentation and standards would be incomplete without presenting at least one concrete set.

Please know these standards are presented largely in their day-to-day undigested form without a great deal of exposition or details on the rationale behind the choices we and our organization made.

If you are interested in learning more about FileMaker standards, or in delving further into an excellent exploration behind why some of these decisions have been adopted, we strongly recommend you read the document that FileMaker Inc. itself has published on the topic (available free as a PDF download). To get to the FileMaker Development Conventions, go to the following site:

http://www.filemaker.com/products/upgrade/techbriefs.html

The authors of this book participated in the development of the FDC tech brief and believe that it serves as a comprehensive guide to standards in FileMaker.

Furthermore, in these standards we present the "Anchor Method" of managing the Relationships Graph in FileMaker. Roger Jacques, the initial creator of this approach (and a senior manager at Soliant), published an article, "Managing the FileMaker Pro 7 Relationship Graph," explaining the thinking behind the method in the September 2005 issue of *FileMaker Advisor Magazine*. An electronic version of that article is available, along with archives of all the magazine's articles, as a subscription service on the FileMaker Advisor website:

http://www.filemakeradvisor.com

We recommend that you include a copy of whatever standards you've used with a given solution so that a new developer to the project can review them if you are unavailable for whatever reason.

These conventions are compliant with version 1.0 of the FDC standards published November 1, 2005.

REQUIRED CONVENTIONS

All conventions in this section are required in order for a file or files to adhere to the Soliant coding and development standards.

NAMING CONVENTIONS

FILES

- Filenames may use only the characters A–Z, a–z, 0–9, and _ (underscore) and must begin with a letter. Spaces are not allowed, but InterCaps can be used to distinguish words.

- Files from one solution need to have a common prefix so that they sort together, even if there is only one file. For example:

    cbi_IndigoMain.fp7, cbi_Agents.fp7, and so on

TABLES

- Table names may use only the characters A–Z, a–z, 0–9, and _ (underscore) and must begin with a letter.

- Prefix developer tables with "z_"—for example, "z_Globals," "z_Resource," and so on.

- Always sort tables by name.

- Tables should always be named for the descriptive entity in question. In other words, for example, use "Invoice" instead of "Table3."

- Singular or plural naming convention is optional, but must remain consistent throughout the application—for example, Employees and Departments, or Employee and Department.

FIELDS

- Field names may use only the characters A–Z, a–z, 0–9, and _ (underscore) and must begin with a letter (with the exception of keys; see the subsection "Key Fields").

- Developer fields (except keys): Always prefix with "z_" and only "z_". No other prefixing. Use an optional suffix for more detail if you want (see the "Recommended Conventions" section later in this document). Spaces are not allowed in developer fields, but InterCaps can be used to distinguish words on object names. For example:

    z_FlagInvoicePaid

    z_TempError_gn (note the global denoted in the optional suffix)

- Always sort fields by name.

KEY FIELDS

- All fields used in relationships must be identified as keys with a "_k*_" prefix. For example:

  _kf_contact_n (contact foreign key)

- For primary keys we use two underscores to ensure that the field sorts to the top of the list. For example:

  __kp_contact_n (contact primary key)

- Only keys used in primary data relationships should be considered foreign keys. For the rest, use the following:

  _ka_SelectedContactName_t (alternate key)

  _kc_contactOrg_ct (compound key)

  _km_contact_t (multiline key)

  _kg_contact_gt (global key)

- The prefix "_k*_" means that keys will sort to the top of an alphabetized list of fields.

- Only kp and kf are mandatory designations, the rest are optional.

HOUSEKEEPING FIELDS

- All tables must have the following four housekeeping fields:

  z_recCreateAccountName

  z_recCreateTimestamp

  z_recModifyAccountName

  z_recModifyTimestamp

"TEMP" FIELDS RULE

- Any field that contains the word "temp" in it makes no assumptions about its contents except within a single script routine (that may also comprise nested scripts). At the end of a script, a temp field can be considered empty or over-writable.

- Note that FileMaker 8 introduced script variables. It is often no longer necessary to use temp fields for the purpose of storing variables; we have left the rule in the standards for those systems still in place using older versions of FileMaker.

LAYOUTS

- Layout names may use only the characters A–Z, a–z, 0–9, and _ (underscore) and must begin with a letter.

- Layout names need to make use of a prefix to indicate the "Anchor table occurrence (TO)" to which they are attached. (See the later section "Table Occurrence Naming" to understand what an "Anchor TO" is.) For example:

  ```
  EMP_EmployeeList

  COM_CompanyPopUp
  ```

- Layouts from the same Anchor TO should be grouped together in layout order.
- Any developer layouts should be prefixed with a z_.

SCRIPT NAMES

- Script names may be divided into functional groups. If so, the standards make no prescription as to what those groups should look like. (Sorting scripts might constitute one functional group, navigation scripts another.)
- If functional groups are not used, scripts must be ordered alphabetically.

VERSION CONTROL

- Version control for client deliverables should be managed via an enclosing folder name, not via changes to the filenames.
- No specific folder naming scheme is mandated. It could be alpha/beta/final, or it could be a simple timestamp.
- All compressed archive filenames should be formatted in the timestamp method. Time indication is optional as military time, or AM/PM for morning or afternoon.
- Version control applies to archived files, not individual FileMaker files or their surrounding folders. You need to apply the timestamp convention only when you compress/archive the project folder. For example:

```
AcmeCRM_2005_03_15.zip

Indigo_2005_03_16_PM.sit

ApricotEBP_2005_03_17_1500.tgz
```

SCRIPTING COMMENTS

We encourage liberal script comments, but these are the minimum requirements:

- All scripts will include three headers that identify the purpose, dependencies/variables, and edit history of a script. Each developer who edits a script will insert an ID line similar to this:

  Purpose: Navigate to Contacts Layout

  Dependencies: (examples: layout name for context, script parameters, script variables, or plug-in requirements)

  History: scl 2004 jan 01 (helpful to put the day last for quick editing)

- End each script with an Exit Script script step. This allows the logic of the script to conclude while leaving Script Debugger open. It also serves to explicitly demonstrate an end to the routine.

SCRIPT PARAMETERS

- All script parameters should be identified in the script comments as dependencies.
- The script parameter delimiter for multiple parameters should remain consistent throughout the application.
- Any delimiter other than a hard return can be used.

SCRIPT RESULTS

- If the script returns a result, the nature and meaning of the result should be documented.

SCRIPT VARIABLES

- Any global variables used should be listed as a dependency with expected initial state and resultant state at the end of the script.
- Optionally describe local variables as well.

RELATIONSHIPS GRAPH

- We have opted to standardize on the "Anchor Method" style for our systems. These are the primary reasons for this:
  - To help when selecting layout objects from a list dialog of table occurrences
  - To make the Relationships Graph itself more manageable/comprehensible by other developers
  - To make a meaningful naming convention possible
- In this scheme, those TOs linked together form a Table Occurrence Group (TOG) with one Anchor TO at the leftmost position.
- A TOG must be a complete island; there may never be a relationship line between any two TOGs.
- All other TOs in the group exist for the purpose of feeding related data to the Anchor TO.
- All user layouts should be associated only with an Anchor TO. Developer layouts used in scripts for establishing context, populating sample data, and so on may be based on any TO. Any layout that a user sees must be based on an Anchor TO.
- TOGs and TOs are read, and meaningful, from left to right. Even though the FileMaker Relationships Graph is bidirectional, the TOs are arranged hierarchically for clarity. The naming convention mentioned in the text that follows creates a similar hierarchical effect in pop-up dialogs.

27

- Some source tables may have multiple TOGs where they serve as an anchor. The decision to create a new TOG is based on functional requirements. Some examples follow:

  - Data needs to be fed to a set of list/detail screens.

  - An Anchor table is used in two functionally different ways, and each requires its own TOG.

  - A UI screen requires a source table; a TOG is based on a developer table.

Figure 27.7 shows a typical TOG.

Figure 27.7
An example of a typical TOG, with the Anchor TO leftmost on the graph.

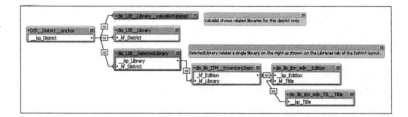

Figure 27.8 shows the same information that's included in the list of TO names used in a number of dialogs within FileMaker. Note that they order themselves hierarchically just as they appear on the Relationships Graph.

Figure 27.8
In dialogs that list TO names, this naming convention maps to the same organization that exists on the Relationships Graph.

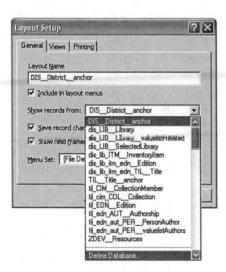

TABLE OCCURRENCE NAMING

The name of a TO describes the chain of source tables between the anchor and the TO itself, with optional attribute indicators. The attribute indicators can be functional names, names of keys, or any other means of clarifying the purpose of the TO. The ability to read a chain of TOs in both the graph and the various pop-ups and dialogs lends clarity. By reading the name of a single TO, one should be able to grasp where on the Relationships Graph it sits.

These are the rules that govern TO naming:

- All TOGs start with an anchor. An anchor is named in the following fashion:

  `DIS__District__tog` (or anchor)
- The first occurrence of an abbreviation is capped—for example, `DIS`.
- The double underscore makes the anchor sort to the top of all lists.
- The corresponding source table name is title case—for example, `District`.
- The `__tog` attribute indicates that this TO is the anchor for a TOG. You can optionally use `__anchor` if you'd like.
- Subsequent TOs start with the TOG name, but in lowercase:

  `dis_LIB__Library__valuelist`
- The leftmost TO name is the anchor; the TO above is part of the `DIS` TOG.
- The source table is indicated by the capped abbreviation `LIB`. All lowercase TOs are connected, and the single capped TO is the associated source table.
- The second element of the name, following two underscores, is the familiar name of the source table entity: `Library`.
- The optional attribute is the functional description: `__valuelist`.
- After an abbreviation for a source table has been established, it must remain consistent throughout the graph.
- Some developers use the optional suffix to list the keys used in establishing relationships to table occurrences. The `InventoryItem` table occurrence in Figure 27.7 might also be named:

  `dis_lib_ITM__InventoryItem__kf_Library`
- Abbreviations are used to save space: FileMaker Pro on Windows truncates TO names in several dialogs. Three character abbreviations are typical, but the length of the abbreviation is at the discretion of the developer. The only hard and fast requirement is that names are legible on Windows.

RECOMMENDED CONVENTIONS

The conventions in this section are not mandated, but they provide some standard ways of doing certain things, if you choose to do them.

CODING PRACTICES

- Calculation Dialog Comments:
  - Insert comments in the first line of a calc that are readable in ScriptMaker and Field Definitions windows:

    ```
    If [// this condition is true //]

    Set Field [// describe set value //]
    ```

27

- Liberally add comments to complex scripts and calculations. Use whitespace for legibility.
- Use the Let() function where you would have more than one or two nested functions.
- Reuse of Code:
    - Modular coding of scripts and use of subscripts.
    - Script parameters for reusable scripts.
    - In cases in which an array is used in a script parameter, write custom functions for parsing data into and out of the array.

NAMING CONVENTIONS

GENERAL PRACTICES Keep your names as short as reasonably possible. Some dialogs are still width-restricted in FileMaker on Windows.

FIELDS We use InterCaps for multiple words. Underscores are meant to differentiate between elements of a field (or table) name; however, user fields make an exception to that rule, where effort should be made to support ease of reading for end users.

- Use grouping of names to organize fields:

    Address_City

    Address_Street1

    Address_Street2

    Name_First

    Name_Full_c

    Name_Last

- Optional suffixes for all developer fields:
    - First character (or characters in combination) as special field:

        g (global)

        s (summary)

        r (repeating)

        c (calculation)

    - Second (or last) character as data type:

        n (number)

        t (text)

        d (date)

        i (time)

        m (timestamp)

        r (container)

Examples of developer fields that follow these conventions look like this:

- z_MainLogo_gr (global container)
- z_SortPreference_gt (global text)
- z_ColumnSortIcons_grr (global repeating text)
- z_recCreateModDisplay_ct (calc text)

Script Names   Scripts may be subdivided into functional groups and separated by a header. Additionally, insert a single hyphen to appear as a separator. For example:

```
-
------------ FILE MANAGEMENT
OnOpen
OnClose
Relogin for testing
-
------------ ADMIN ACCOUNT FUNCTIONS
Create New Account
Delete Account
```

Spaces are acceptable in script names. Keep in mind that on Windows, some dialogs open only to approximately 40–50 characters.

INDEX

SYMBOLS

& (ampersand) operators, 223

* (asterisk) wildcards, 641

$$layoutName variable, creating back buttons, 366

$$navHistory variable, creating back buttons, 366

= (equal sign), Import field mapping indicator

+ (plus sign) operators, 223

- (hyphens), layout names, 99

- scripts, 272

+ (plus sign) operators, 223

A

abbreviations, decoding, 396

Abs functions, 236

absolute paths, file references, 548

abstraction (scripts), 255-256

access logs, IWP, 642

access privileges
matrixes, 547
user accounts, troubleshooting, 350

Access via FileMaker Mobile extended privilege, 343

Access via FileMaker Network extended privilege, 343

Access via Instant Web Publishing extended privilege, 342

Access via ODBC/JDBC extended privilege, 343

Access via XML Web Publishing extended privilege, 343

Access via XSLT Web Publishing extended privilege, 343

Accounts & Privileges dialog, 645, 845

Accounts tab (Define Accounts & Privileges dialog), 331-332

ACID tests, 311-312

Actions option (Synchronization button), 836

Active Directory servers, 797-799, 816

Add Account script steps, 350

Add Fields to Portal dialog (Portal tool), 175

Add File button (Edit File Reference dialog), 203

Add Table Occurrence button (Relationships Graphs), 193, 205

addrecord.xsl stylesheets, 741

Admin accounts
access, removing via Developer Utilities (FileMaker Developer), 768
passwords, troubleshooting, 349
user-level internal security, 332

Administration Console, troubleshooting, 747-748

Advanced Web Publishing Options dialog (IWP Database Homepage), 641

aesthetics (report design), 280

aggregate functions, 239-240

agile development (software development), XP, 503

Align command (Arrange menu), 114

All Modifiable setting (Edit Privileges dialog), 338

All No Access setting (Edit Privileges dialog), 338

All View Only setting (Edit Privileges dialog), 338

Allow Creation of Records in This Table via This Relationship check box (Edit Relationship dialog), 169

Allow Creation of Records in This Table via This Relationship option, 476-478

Allow Deletion of Portal Records option (Portal Setup dialog), 475

Allow Exporting dialog (Edit Privileges dialog), 341

Allow Field to Be Entered in Browse Mode check box (Field Behavior option), 172

Allow Printing dialog (Edit Privileges dialog), 341

Allow User Abort scripts, 257, 651

Allow User to Modify Their Own Password option (Edit Privileges dialog), 341

Allow User to Override Data Validation Warnings option (Edit Privileges dialog), 341

Allow User to Override During Data Entry check box (Validation tab), 163

alpha conversion files, 546

Also Display Values from Second Field check box (Use Values from First Field option), 175

Also Reduce the Size of the Enclosing Part option (Set Sliding/Printing dialog), 116

Alternate Background Fill option (Part Definition dialog), 106

Always During Data Entry option (Validation dialog), 86

Always Lock Layout tools option (Layout mode), 107

graphics
IWP layout design restrictions, 653
layouts, adding to, 107

groups
data, exporting, 604-606
layout objects, 113
privilege sets, converting to, 552-553
scripts, 252

gSelectedRowID field, selection portal rows, 485, 488

[GT] operators, portals, 472

GTRR scripts. *See* Go to Related Record scripts

[Guest] accounts, user-level internal security, 332

H

handheld devices, deploying solutions to, 761

hard drives, FileMaker Server requirements, 783

headers/footers (columns), 103
IWP layout design restrictions, 655
sortable headers, 282-286
user interfaces, 387

hiding
layout elements in user interfaces, 383-384, 388
layouts, 101
report elements prior to printing, 278
scripts, 251-252
status area (IWP), application flow, 659-660
windows (multi-window interfaces), 372

highlighting portal rows
selection portal rows, 485-486
troubleshooting, 499

HighlightRow fields, selection portal rows, 485, 488

home pages (IWP), building, 662

horizontal dividers (reports), 280-282

horizontal portals, 480

house icon (IWP status area), 643

housekeeping fields, naming conventions, 853

HTML (Hypertext Markup Language)
DDR, 847-848
search result stylesheets, building, 721-723

HTML Table format (exporting data), 601

HTTP Web services, 684

hyphens (-), layout names, 99

Hypotenuse functions, 426

I

identifiers (WPE), 709

identity functions (plug-ins), 807-808

If - Else If script steps, 315

If script steps, 264

image files, importing, 580-582

Import Action (Import Field Mapping dialog), 569, 575

Import Field Mapping dialog, 569-575

Import option (container fields), 46

importing. *See also* exporting
Amazon.com XML data to FileMaker, 691-694
batch files, 578-582
digital pictures, 582-583
duplicating found sets, 592
Excel data, 576
Excel files, 577
EXIF data, 583
FileMaker Pro, 61
flat files, 568-582
found sets, 593
layouts, 96
multiple image files, 580-582
multiple text files, 579-580
ODBC data sources, 588-589
scripted imports, 590-591
scripts, 251
table records, 529
troubleshooting, 591-592
XML data to FileMaker, 684
FMPXMLRESULT grammar, 683, 686-689
troubleshooting, 695
XML stylesheets, 685-686
XSL stylesheets, 687-689

Include in Global Find option (FileMaker Mobile), 831

incomplete scripts, troubleshooting, 270

indexing
fields, 88-90, 228
FileMaker 8, 92
portals, 473
rules, solution conversion, 559

Indexing option (Storage Options dialog), 228

Indicate Web Compatibility check box (ScriptMaker), 650

InitializeGlobals scripts, 272

initiating scripts, 269

Insert menu (FileMaker Pro), 64
Layout mode, 107
Merge Field command, 122

Insert option (container fields), 46

INSERT statements, synchronizing records, 623

Insert, From Index command (FileMaker Pro), 64

Instant Web Publishing. *See* IWP (Instant Web Publishing)

Instant Web Publishing setup screen, 640, 646

Int functions, 235-236

integrity (data), troubleshooting, 62

interactive call stacks, 521

interfaces (user), 354
building, 357
Design element architectures, designing, 358
navigating, automatically accessing specific panes, 366-367
navigating, controlling Tab Control objects, 366-367
navigating, navigation palette layouts, 368
navigating, navigation portals, 367
navigating, pop-up menus/Go buttons, 367
navigating, tabbed navigation, 360-366
custom menus, 373
components of, 374
editing, 377-378
FileMaker control of, 374
managing, 375-376
menu items, editing, 378-379
menu sets, 375-376, 380-381